D1519676

*A Bibliography of
Nineteenth-Century
American
Piano Music*

Music Reference Collection

Series Adviser: Donald L. Hixon

Music for Oboe, Oboe D'Amore, and English Horn: A Bibliography of Materials at the Library of Congress
Compiled by Virginia Snodgrass Gifford

A Bibliography of Nineteenth-Century American Piano Music

With Location Sources and Composer Biography-Index

John Gillespie and Anna Gillespie

Music Reference Collection, Number 2

Greenwood Press
Westport, Connecticut • London, England

Library of Congress Cataloging in Publication Data

Gillespie, John, 1921-
   A Bibliography of Nineteenth-century American piano music.

   (Music reference collection, ISSN 0736-7740   ;
no. 2)
   Includes index.
   1.   Piano music—United States—19th century—Bibliography.   I. Title.   II. Series.
ML128.P3G54   1984   016.7864'05'0973   84-8993
ISBN 0-313-24097-3 (lib. bdg.)

Library of Congress Catalog Card Number: 84-8993
ISBN: 0-313-24097-3
ISSN: 0736-7740

First published in 1984

Greenwood Press
A division of Congressional Information Service, Inc.
88 Post Road West, Westport, Connecticut 06881

Printed in the United States of America

10   9   8   7   6   5   4   3   2   1

Contents

Preface

This bibliography is the outgrowth of research begun for an earlier publication[1] on nineteenth-century American piano music. The more libraries we investigated the more impressed we were by the enormous repertoire of piano music produced in the United States during the nineteenth century, and the more frustrated because most of the music was so difficult to find. Our objective has been to prepare a select, practical catalog of available, published music, not a complete bibliography of all nineteenth-century American piano music.

Nineteenth-century Americans depended on music for a large part of their home and public entertainment. Making music on the parlor piano, playing in an ensemble, singing with a choral group, going to musical events, all comprised an integral part of both social and cultural life. It seems fair to assume that in this congenial atmosphere a great deal of music would have been composed, and after three years of research at more than fifty libraries throughout the United States, we know that the nineteenth-century piano works alone number in the thousands.

If we were amazed at the quantity, we were overwhelmed by the wide differences in quality. This mountain of piano compositions ranges from excellent to fair to mediocre to awful. Pieces in the last two categories were easily eliminated unless, for some reason, a particular work was unique or had historical significance. Making selections from the first two categories was not so easy, and it was, inevitably, a subjective process.

This, then, is a select bibliography of nineteenth-century American piano music dating from its emergence during the closing years of the eighteenth century through its mature development, and

1. **Nineteenth-Century American Piano Music.** Selected and Introduced by John Gillespie. New York: Dover Publications, 1978.

extending into the first several decades of the twentieth century. It includes a brief biography for each composer except for a few for whom information is lacking.

By modern standards much of this music is strictly conservative, but remember that when it was written conservatism was the rule rather than the exception. The contemporary public enjoyed this music and bought hundreds of thousands of copies. Remember also that the United States was not alone in its musical conservatism. In Spain, for example, Granados and Albéniz were writing flamboyant, romantic music during the early twentieth century. In fact, during the late nineteenth century and early part of the twentieth century there were comparatively few of the so-called progressive composers like Bartōk, Schoenberg, and Stravinsky.

Both serious music and salon music are included in the bibliography, for each repertoire represents an important factor in America's musical, social, and cultural history. Most of us understand what "serious" or "art" music is, but what about "salon" music? Can it be defined? In an interesting article Hoyle Carpenter attempts, if not to define, at least to describe what is generally considered to be salon music:

> Salon music is, above all else, elegant. It is polite, well-mannered, graceful. It is never vulgar or uncouth. It sometimes expresses lofty sentiments, as in "The Maiden's Prayer," but it is never profound. It may imitate nature or it may take the form of refined dance music. Perhaps the most typical of all is the set of variations on some well-known song or operatic air.
> While this music makes but slight demands on the performer in the way of musical insight, the technical demands are often quite considerable. [2]

After playing through more than three thousand nineteenth-century American piano pieces, we are compelled to add that the borderline between serious music and salon music can at times be so slight as to be imperceptible. Many composers wrote successfully in both areas.

We used a set of general guidelines as a basis for selecting (1) the composers, (2) the individual works, and (3) the libraries that should be included.

We selected composers who, in our opinion, wrote the most characteristic examples of the music of the period. On the grounds that our interest lies principally in the nineteenth century, we

2. Hoyle Carpenter, "Salon Music in the Mid-Nineteenth Century." In **A Quarterly Journal of Studies in Civil War History** 4, no.3 (September 1958): 291.

decided, perhaps arbitrarily, to include composers who, although born in the eighteenth century, had active careers extending into the early nineteenth century and to exclude composers born after 1880. As a result of this cutoff date, composers included are generally classified as Classic or Romantic, although a few--Ernest Bloch, Carl Ruggles and Charles Ives, for example--employed more contemporary techniques.

It required another arbitrary decision to determine which composers could be considered "American" other than those born in the United States. There were many factors to consider. This was a period in American history when musicians were arriving daily in America--some to stay, some to visit--and American composers were going abroad to study. We decided that to qualify as "American" during this early part of America's history an emigrant composer would have had to spend ten or more years living in the United States and, more important, would have made significant contributions to the musical life of America while in residence. We felt that it would not be correct to include only those composers who became American citizens, for some of the composers represented here--British composer Richard Hoffman, for example--spent their entire adult lives in America yet never renounced their native citizenship. We have also included composers like Blair Fairchild, Arthur Bird, Otis Bardwell Boise, and Templeton Strong, all born in America but who, for one reason or another, lived most of their mature, productive years abroad.

We chose compositions representative of each composer's best efforts, whether sentimental salon music, dances, variations, sonatas, and so forth. Each composition had to be available. Since most of this music is out of print, we selected from works on file at one or more libraries and available via Xerox or microfilm copy. This bibliography therefore includes only works that are readily available to the public, works that may be copied, if desired, and taken home for study or pleasure. We have played through every composition listed, and own a Xerox or microfilm copy of almost all of them. Again, it is a personal, subjective bibliography.

No attempt was made to include all of any one composer's piano music, although in a few instances that may occur. Significant examples from a composer's repertoire may be included, even though such works were written in England or Europe. In many instances it is difficult, if not impossible, to determine which compositions are "American" products. That is, was the composer in European residence when he wrote the composition; or did he write it before emigrating to America and publish it later; or did he write it while living in the United States and send it to Europe to be published? For some composers it seemed unwise to cut the productive period into segments, so we have, for example, included some of Philip Anthony Corri's compositions written in England and some composed in America under his new name Arthur Clifton.

Of the more than fifty libraries investigated, we selected those having either a substantial collection of general nineteenth-century American piano music or a unique collection of an individual composer's works. For example, Coe College in Cedar Rapids, Iowa, has a good representative collection of the works of John Mokrejs, a former student, and the University of Kansas at Lawrence owns an extensive collection of the works of Carl Preyer, a onetime faculty member. In keeping with our decision that the works had to be available, some of the chosen libraries were later omitted as sources, one or two with significant holdings in American music, because the collections are restricted to the point where they are not available to an average student or researcher, or copying the music is either not allowed or limited to only a few copies a day.

If any work in the bibliography, particularly a fairly well-known composition, cannot be found at a certain library where one might expect to find it, that does not necessarily mean that the library does not own the work. It means that the piece was not available when we visited the library. It may have been misshelved or temporarily lost. We checked many of the libraries more than once and sometimes discovered that a work missing one time turned up the next.

Keep in mind that many libraries have not cataloged their nineteenth-century American piano music. There are, of course, well-preserved, cataloged collections, but more often the music is stored in boxes in library basements or other storerooms, not cataloged though frequently filed alphabetically by composer.

Tracking copyrights, publishers, and original publication dates of nineteenth-century American piano music would be a complete research project in itself. It is a confusing situation because frequently one composition will have two or three different publishers and two or three copyright dates. Further confusion arises because sometimes the title and opus number on the cover are not the same as those on the inside title page. The editions listed are those we have actually found at one or more of our library sources.

We learned that titles are often deceiving and that one should not be put off from trying out the music because of a poor title. Many compositions, especially those from the mid-nineteenth century, have sentimental, exaggerated titles, but the music is attractive and often delightful.

Using the Bibliography

The selected compositions have been divided into the five traditional categories for piano music: Music for Solo Piano; Music for Piano, One Hand; Music for Piano Duet (piano, 4 hands); Music for Two Pianos; Music for Piano and Orchestra. In each category composers and works are listed alphabetically. The format is as follows:

Line A has the title of the composition. Since this is a bibliography of piano music only, we have omitted from the title such expressions as "pour le piano," "for the pianoforte," and so forth, except when the term is necessary for correct understanding of the title. When one work includes several compositions under a general title, for example **Three Compositions, Op.28**, the work is listed alphabetically under the general title **when** a complete set is available. That is, if all three compositions of Opus 28 are available, they are identified under **Three Compositions, Op.28** with a cross-reference to the individual titles. However, if we only located, say, two of the compositions in Opus 28, they are listed according to individual titles.

Line B contains the abbreviated name of the publisher (see Appendix A), date of publication, and number of pages. For works published before 1826, the reader is referred to the following sources for further information:

1. Oscar G. Sonneck and William T. Upton. **A Bibliography of Early Secular American Music**. 1945. Reprint with a Preface by Irving Lowens. New York: Da Capo Press, 1964. Abbreviated to **SU** in bibliography.

2. Richard J. Wolfe. **Secular Music in America 1801-1825: A Bibliography**. 3 vols. New York: New York Public Library, 1964. Abbreviated to **W** in bibliography.

Line C lists the library or libraries where that composition may be found, with catalog numbers in parentheses. In general we have used the Library of Congress Union Catalog abbreviations for library names (see Appendix B). When a composition appears in an anthology or modern reprint, the abbreviation for the anthology or reprint (see Appendix C) follows the listing of library sources.

Line D gives individual titles within a suite, the several short compositions that comprise a larger work, and so forth, when applicable.

Line E appears only when a composition merits comment because of outstanding quality, a unique characteristic, historical value, or its degree of difficulty. Otherwise the work may be considered a good, medium-difficult example of the composer's art. Following are two sample entries:

Sample Entry 1
  CARR, BENJAMIN
    A Divertisement on the Favorite Air of the Plow-Boy
      Carr-J, ca.1818, 8p. (W.II:797)
      DLC(M1.A1C Case), also in CMM-M, No.49
      A pleasant work based on a song from Wm. Shield's **The Farmer**

Line A: The title is **A Divertisement on the Favorite Air**, etc.
Line B: It was published by J. Carr of Baltimore around 1818 and
         is eight pages in length. Further information may be
         found in Wolfe, Volume II, page 797.
Line C: DLC indicates that there is a copy at the Library of
         Congress. The catalog number is M1.A1C Case. CMM-M,
         No.49 indicates that this piece appears as No.49 in the
         modern reprint of Carr's **Musical Miscellany**.
Line D: No information necessary.
Line E: Further information and comment.

Sample Entry 2
  KELLEY, EDGAR STILLMAN
    Three Compositions, Op.2
      Schirmer, 1891, 3v. (9,5,11p.)
      CtY(Mc11A1K287, 2 only), CU(M25K4 1891, 3 only), DLC(M25.K),
      ICN(VM22K29t), IU(Joseffy), MBH(McAt4), NcU(M786.4K29c2),
      NNLc(JNG 74-209), OCl(M776.4 5264, 3 only), WM(786.4K29h,
      3 only), also in NC-G(2,3 only)
    1. **The Flower-seekers**; 2. **Confluentia**; 3. **The Headless
    Horseman**
    Three superb character pieces.
Line A: The general title is **Three Compositions, Op.2**.
Line B: It was published by G. Schirmer in 1891. There are three
         pieces in the collection, 9, 5, and 11 pages respectively.
Line C: The complete collection of three pieces is found in six
         libraries. Yale has only No.2, Berkeley, Cleveland, and
         Wisconsin have No.3 only. Numbers 2 and 3 also appear in
         a modern anthology **Nineteenth Century American Piano
         Music.**
Line D: The titles of the individual compositions are listed here.
Line E: Their quality warrants comment.

    Chapter VI supplies a biography-index of composers whose works
comprise this bibliography.   At the end of each biography
cross-references indicate the appropriate bibliographical chapter
(I, II, III, IV, V). For example, Otis Bardwell Boise wrote no
works for piano alone, so the reader would be referred only to
Chapter V (Works for Piano and Orchestra).

                                                JOHN GILLESPIE
                                                ANNA GILLESPIE

Acknowledgments

We offer our sincere thanks to the following librarians and researchers who helped to make this bibliography possible. Their advice, cooperation, and expertise are greatly appreciated.

Mildred Abraham, Richard Adkins, Mary Lou Allen, Gillian Anderson, Ronald Axsom, Rebeccah Ball, Sharon Bennett, Barbara Benson, Marie Bergbüchler, Carol Bierly, Evan Bonds, Elmer Booze, Sarah Boslaugh, Susan Bower, Patricia Brennan, Lois Brown, Neil Bunker, Kathryn Burnett, Warren Call, Victor Cardell, Robin Carlaw, J. Bunker Clark, Rosemary Cullen, William Dane, Peggy Daub, Carolyn Davis, Glenn Devitt, Don Draganski, John Drusedow, Peggy Dusch, John Emerson, Ernest Ferrata, Rachel Frew, Helen Furmanik, Jean Geil, Robert Giddings, Timothy Gmeiner, Diana Haskell, Thomas Heck, Timothy Hellner, Antonia Houston, Richard Jackson, Cecilia Jessum, Frederick Kent, David Knauss, Marion Korda, Betty Krause, Marion La Rochelle, Alfred E. Lemmon, Isabella Leland, Carol Lipinsky, Judi Lopez del Moral, Margaret Lospinuso, Leonore Mack, Sybil McShane, Richard Matthews, Robert Nardini, Lawrence Naukam, Pauline Norton, Geraldine Ostrove, Natalie Palme, Cynthia Peters, Edwin Quist, Neil Ratliff, Don Roberts, Margaret Sax, Janet Schroeder, Linda Seckelson-Simpson, Charles Sens, Wayne Shirley, Martin Silver, Greg Smith, Carol Tatian, John Toms, Kathryn Uthe, Philip Vandermeer, David Warrington, Mary Ann Weber, Ann and Charles Wilhite, Marilyn Wilkins, Janet Yarbrough, Philip Youngholm.

*A Bibliography of
Nineteenth-Century
American
Piano Music*

I
Music for Solo Piano

ALDEN, JOHN CARVER (1852–1935)

At Twilight (Romance)
    Ditson, 1903, 5p.
    DLC(M25.A)
Bagatelle in G Major
    Ditson, 1911, 7p.
    DLC(M25.A), MoSW(U), RPB(U)
Canzonetta
    Thompson, 1916, 3p.
    DLC(M25.A)
Chit Chat (Characteristic Dance)
    Wood, 1904, 7p.
    DLC(M30.A), NRU-E(U)
Evening Song
    Ditson, 1914, 5p.
    OCl(SM776.4)
Mazurka-Caprice
    Thompson, 1910, 11p.
    DLC(M25.A)
Le Rayon (Morceau de Concert)
    Ditson, 1904, 7p.
    DLC(M25.A)
Satellite (Polka-Caprice)
    Kunkel, 1881, 11p.
    DLC(M25.A), PP(U)
Souvenir de Vienne (Viennese Waltz)
    Wood, 1903, 9p.
    DLC(M32.A), NRU-E(U)
Valse Allemande (No.3 of Three Musical Thoughts)
    Ditson-CH, 1886, 7p.
    CtHT(U)

AMBROSE, PAUL (1868-1941)

Elaine (Valse lente), **Op.22, No.1**
    Schmidt, 1903, 7p.
    DLC(M32.A), MoSW(U)
    Rhythmically interesting and melodious.
Impromptu, Op.15, No.1
    Schroeder, 1900, 10p.
    DLC(M25.A)
Love Song, Op.44
    Presser, 1922, 5p.
    DLC(M25.A), NRU-E(U), OU(U)
    Left hand has a prominent melodic role.
March Caprice, Op.15, No.3
    Schroeder, 1900, 8p.
    DLC(M25.A)
    Lively octave study.
Whispering Winds, Op.9, No.1
    Schroeder, 1897, 7p.
    DLC(M25.A)

ANONYMOUS

Away with Melancholy
    Carr-J, n.d., 4p. [W.II:604]
    NNLc(AM1-I), NcD(RBR MusicB10,no.52), also in CMM-M,no.47
    Simple theme with six variations and coda.
Brilliant Variations on the Popular Melody "Wild Ashe Deer"
    Lee, 1854, 5p.
    NNLc(AM1-I), ViU(McR.92.06)
    Composer described as "A Lady of Va."
The Celebrated One Finger'd Sliding Waltz
    HewittMR, ca.1808, 2p. [W.II:653]
    DLC(M1.A1C), ICN(Case 8A 2626), NcD(RBR MusicB11,no.59),
      NcU(EAMC,no.66)
    Also called **The Much Admired Sliding Waltz.**
Italian Air (Arranged as a Rondo)
    Carr-J, n.d., 2p. [W.I:440]
    NNLc(AM1-I), also in CMM-M,no.40
The Italian Rondo
    Willig, n.d., 2p.
    Same as **Italian Air**
March. Composed and dedicated to the United States Marine Corps
    Willig, ca.1815, 2p. [W.II:619]
    ICN(Case8A 1932), NcD(M780.821 R245Bv.1-2), RPB(U), also in
      A-C(I)
    Composer described as "A Lady of Charleston, S.C."
      Attributed to Eliza Crawley Murden. (ca.1783-1847)
The Neapolitan Waltz
    Carr-J, n.d., 4p.
    NNLc(AM1-I), also in CMM-M,no.44
    Waltz with four "busy" variations plus coda.

"Oft in a Stilly Night" with Variations
    Willig, 1827, 5p.
    ICN(Case sm oM1.A13,no.2344), NBu(U), NNLc(AM1-I), NcD(RBR
       MusicB2,no.51), ViU(McR.48.17)
    Composer described simply as "A Lady."
United States Marine March (see **March**)
Yankee Doodle (An original American Air arranged with
    Variations)
    CarrMR, ca.1822, 4p. [W.III:983]
    ICN(Case8A 2789), NNLc(AM1-I), NcD(RBR MusicB91,no.14),
       NcU(EAMC,no.22), PP(K:1), also in C-MH
    Theme with eight variations. Probably the first of many
       such "arrangements."

AYRES, FREDERIC (1876-1926)

Fugue, Op.9, No.1 (see **Two Fugues, Op.9**)
Fugue, Op.9, No.2 (see **Two Fugues, Op.9**)
Fugue, Op.12, No.1 (from **Three Compositions for Piano**)
    Wa-Wan, 1910, 9p.
    DLC(M25.A), NRU-E(M25A985f), also in WW-L(V:149)
    Unusual theme. Fugue interrupted with homophonic sections.
Two Fugues, Op.9
    Stahl, 1910, 2v.(9,7p.)
    DLC(M25.A), MoSW(U)
    No.1. Rhythmically unusual subject; No.2. Contrapuntal,
       with harmonic and homophonic sections. Inspired by
       American Indian music.
Moonlight (An Intermezzo), **Op.12, No.2** (from **Three Compositions
    for Piano**)
    Schirmer, 1917, 7p.
    CtY(U), DLC(M25.A), MoSW(U), NRU-E(M25A985m)
    A difficult, atmospheric composition.
The Open Road (A Brilliant Intermezzo), **Op.11**
    Schirmer, 1916, 14p.
    DLC(M25.A), MoS(786.4), NNLc(JNG 74-448), NRU-E(M25A985o)
    Interesting harmonies. Some American Indian atmosphere.

BAERMANN, CARL (1839-1913)

Three Compositions
    Boston, 1914, 3v.(5,19,11p.)
    DLC(M25.B), MB-N(Piano)
    1. **Idyl** ("Louisa in her Garden"); 2. **Polonaise pathétique**;
       3. **Valse-Romance**
Etüden, Op.4
    André-J, 1877, 2v. in 1(77p.)
    NNLc(°MYD), NcU(M25.B37op.4), PP(U)
    Twelve magnificent, difficult studies.
Idyl (see **Three Compositions**)
Polonaise pathétique (see **Three Compositions**)

Valse-Romance (see **Three Compositions**)

BARBOUR, FLORENCE NEWELL (1866-1946)

Agitato (No.2 of **Six Melodic Etudes**)
    Schmidt, 1913, 5p.
    NRU-E(U)
At Chamonix (Mountain Suite)
    Schmidt, 1929, 6v.(5,7,7,5,7,7p.)
    DLC(M24.B212A5), NRU-E(M24B239a), OCL(SM776.415)
      1. **Morning Hymn** (Sunrise on Mount Blanc); 2. **Clouds like
      Dream Castles**; 3. **In the Wake of the Storm**; 4. **Spring
      approaches the Valley**; 5. **Moonlight's Haunting Spell**;
      6. **A Joyous Festival**
Bravura (No.6 of **Six Melodic Etudes**)
    Schmidt, 1913, 5p.
    NRU-E(U), OCL(SM776.47)
Humoresque (No.4 of **Six Melodic Etudes**)
    Schmidt, 1913, 5p.
    OCL(SM776.47)
    A delightful study for clear, exact touch.
The Light of Spring (No.1 of **Forest Sketches**)
    Schmidt, 1912, 7p.
    OCL(SM776.4)
The Lure of Summer Days (Reverie. No.4 of **Forest Sketches**)
    Schmidt, 1912, 7p.
    NRU-E(U)
    One of Barbour's finest lyrical compositions.
Prelude (No.1 of **Six Melodic Etudes**)
    Schmidt, 1913, 5p.
    NRU-E(U)
Revel of the Wood Nymphs (Scherzo. No.3 of **Forest Sketches**)
    Schmidt, 1912, 7p.
    NRU-E(U)
To my Piano (Reverie)
    Schmidt, 1913, 5p.
    NRU-E(U)
Valse Arabesque
    Schmidt, 1911, 7p.
    RPB(U)
Valse Impromptu
    Schmidt, 1912, 11p.
    NRU-E(U)
Venice (Suite)
    Schmidt, 1913, 26p.
    DLC(M24.B212V3), OCL(SM776.415)
      1. **Springtime in Venice**; 2. **Italian Dance**; 3. **Meditation
      in San Marco**; 4. **Song of the Gondolier**; 5. **Venetian
      Carnival** (On the Grand Canal)
A White Violet (No.2 of **Forest Sketches**)
    Schmidt, 1912, 5p.
    NRU-E(U)

BARTLETT, HOMER NEWTON (1845-1920)

Adieu (Melody-Caprice), **Op.19**
   Schirmer, 1875, 1903, 9p.
   DLC(M25.B), NcU(M786.4B289a)
   An unusual rondo with an old-fashioned refrain.
Aeolian Murmurings (Concert Study), **Op.123**
   Ditson, 1893, 11p.
   ICN(VM22B28p)
   Scintillating and difficult, with much right-hand
      virtuosity.
Amicitia (Friendship. Grand Concert Waltz), **Op.8**
   Pond, 1875, 15p.
   DLC(M32.B, M25.B)
L'Aurore (Etude mélodieuse), **Op.57**
   Schirmer, 1883, 7p.
   DLC(M25.B)
Ballade in D Flat, Op.119
   Ditson, 1893, 11p.
   CtHT(U), ICN(VM22B28p)
Second Ballade, Op.207
   Ditson, 1906, 10p.
   CtY(Mc11A1B282), DLC(M25.B), NcU(M786.43B289b2), PP(U),
      RPB(U)
Third Ballade (Founded on Japanese Themes), **Op.274**
   Ditson, 1919, 13p.
   DLC(M25.B), NRU-E(U)
   Some use of the pentatonic scale. Quotes the Japanese
      national anthem.
Benten (Caprice de Concert), **Op.127**
   Ditson, 1893, 13p.
   DLC(M25.B), ICN(VM22B28p), PP(U)
   Unusual and difficult.
Berceuse, Op.82
   Schirmer, 1887, 1907, 11p.
   CtY(Mc11A1B282), DLC(M25.B), MiU-C(U), MoSW(U),
      NcU(M786.4B289b), WM(786.4B28b)
The Brook, Op.233, No.2 (see **Two Concert Studies, Op.233**)
Capriccio in E Minor, Op.189, No.3
   Ditson, 1899, 9p.
   DLC(M25.B), ICN(VM22B28p)
Caprice Español, Op.115
   Ditson, 1896, 13p.
   DLC(M25.B), NcU(M786.4B289c), PP(U)
Caprice-Humoresque, Op.227
   Ditson, 1911, 7p.
   DLC(M25.B), NRU-E(U)
Two Compositions on Japanese Themes, Op.221
   Schirmer, 1908, 2v.(5,9p.)
   CtY(Mc11A1B282), DLC(M25.B), NNLc(JNN 75-6), NRU-E
      (U, 1 only)
      1. **Japanese Revery**; 2. **Japanese Romance** (Good use of
        pentatonic scale. Some feeling of impressionism.)

Two Concert Studies, Op.233
 Schirmer, 1911, 2v.(9,7p.)
 CtY(Mc11A1B282, 2 only), MoSW(U, 2 only), NRU-E(U, 2 only),
   OCl(SM776.47), PP(U, 2 only)
 1. **Etude de Concert** (Study in Double-Notes); 2. **The Brook**
Concert Study, Op.123 (see **Aeolian Murmurings, Op.123**)
Le Crépuscule (Twilight. Etude mélodieuse), **Op.30**
 Pond, 1878, 7p.
 DLC(M25.B), MiU-C(U)
"El Dorado" (Second Grande Polka de Concert), **Op.14**
 Pond, 1876, 1904, 15p.
 DLC(M31.B), PP(U)
 Equal in quality to Bartlett's **Polka, Op.1.**
Dondon-Bushi (Melody founded on a Japanese theme), **Op.246**
 Schirmer, 1918, 6p.
 DLC(M25.B)
Dragon Flies, Op.193, No.2 (see **Rural Scenes, Op.193**)
Etude de Concert, Op.233, No.1 (see **Two Concert Studies,
   Op.233**)
Etude mélodieuse No.3 (see **Le Ruisselet, Op.67**)
Etude mélodieuse No.4 (see **La Grace, Op.68**)
Etude mélodieuse No.5 (see **Le Rêve, Op.77**)
Gavotte Concertante (In Canon-form), **Op.245**
 Schirmer, 1913, 9p.
 CtY(Mc11A1B282), MoSW(U), NRU-E(U), PP(U)
 Effective composition in contrapuntal style.
La Grace (Etude mélodieuse No.4), **Op.68**
 Pond, 1885, 7p.
 DLC(M25.B), NcU(MF786.47B289g)
Grande Gavotte, Op.45
 Schirmer, 1882, 9p.
 NNLc(Music-Am[Sheet]75-279)
Grande Polka de Concert, Op.1
 Pond, 1867; Bartlett, 1895; Schirmer, 1906, 11p.
 CtHT(U), CtY(Mc11A1B282), DLC(M31.B), LN(U), MoS(786.44),
   MoSW(U), NNLc(°MYD-Amer), NRU-E(M31B289), NcU(M786.44
   B289g), OC(U), OCl(SM776.45), PP(U), ViU(U:2), also in
   NC-G
 "perhaps the most deservedly popular and successful of any
   Opus I by an American composer."
Grande Valse brillante, Op.159
 Schirmer, 1897, 9p.
 CtY(Mc11A1B282), NRU-E(U), WM(786.4B28g)
Harlequin (Albumleaf), **Op.107, No.2**
 Schirmer, 1891, 5p.
 CtY(Mc11A1B282), DLC(M25.B), MoS(786.4), WM(786.4B28h)
Japanese Revery, Op.221, No.1 (see **Two Compositions on
   Japanese Themes, Op.221**)
Japanese Romance, Op.221, No.2 (see **Two Compositions on
   Japanese Themes, Op.221**)
The Kranbach Nocturne, Op.217
 Kranich, 1905, 11p.
 DLC(M25.B)

Winner of a contest sponsored by Kranich and Bach for the
most meritorious piano composition developed from the
theme introduced in the musical romance entitled **The
Kranbach Nocturne** by Joseph Gray Kitchell.

Nocturne, Op.216
Ditson, 1905, 9p.
CtY(Mc11A1B282), DLC(M25.B), PP(U)

The Placid Lake, Op.193, No.1 (see **Rural Scenes, Op.193**)

Prelude in C Minor (The Approaching Storm)**, Op.230**
Schirmer, 1911, 5p.
CtY(Mc11A1B282), DLC(M25.B), MoSW(U), NRU-E(M25B289p),
WM(786.4B28p)

The Ramble (Morceau caractéristique)**, Op.75**
Schirmer, 1886, 7p.
CtY(Mc11A1B282), DLC(M25.B)

Le Rêve (Etude mélodieuse No.5)**, Op.77**
Pond, 1904, 11p., revised ed.
DLC(M25.B), PP(U)

Rêverie poétique, Op.156
Schirmer, 1897, 5p.
MoSW(U)

Romance No.4 (see **Solitude**)

Le Ruisselet (Etude mélodieuse No.3)**, Op.67**
Schirmer, 1886, 5p.
DLC(MT241.B11), MoSW(U), ViU(McR.163.14)

Rural Scenes, Op.193
Schirmer, 1901, 5v.(6,9,3,5,5p.)
DLC(M25.B), MoS(786.43), MoSW(U, 1,3,4,5 only), PP(U, 4
only), RPB(U, 1 only)
1. **The Placid Lake**; 2. **Dragon-Flies** (A Concert Study);
3. **The Wayside Flower**; 4. **The Woodland-Path**;
5. **Twilight Murmurings**
Attractive collection of nature tone-pictures.

Scherzo in D, Op.171
Church, 1900, 9p.
DLC(M25.B), NRU-E(U)

Solitude (Reverie. Romance No.4)
Pond, 1871, 9p.
PP(U)

Twilight Murmurings, Op.193, No.5 (see **Rural Scenes, Op.193**)

The Wayside Flower, Op.193, No.3 (see **Rural Scenes, Op.193**)

The Woodland-Path, Op.193, No.4 (see **Rural Scenes, Op.193**)

BASSFORD, WILLIAM KIPP (1839-1902)

Bagatelle, Op.102
Pond, 1885, 7p.
DLC(M25.B)

Barcarolle, Op.107, No.1 (from **3 Pièces caractéristiques,
Op.107**)
Schmidt, 1896, 7p.
DLC(M25.B), MoSW(U)

Etude de Concert, Op.32
    Firth-T, 1867, 7p.
    DLC(M25.B)
Etude-Impromptu, Op.19
    Hall-W, 1865, 7p.
    DLC(M25.B)
The Jealous Stream, Op.45
    Ditson-CH, 1867, 13p.
    DLC(M25.B)
Lamentation (To the memory of L. M. Gottschalk)
    HallS, 1870, 7p.
    CtHT(U), DLC(M25.B)
    Solemn work. Makes reference to Gottschalk's Last Hope.
Mazurka Caprice (Impromptu), Op.92
    Pond, 1886, 7p.
    DLC(M32.B)
La Mignonette (Valse élégante), Op.63
    Schuberth-E, 1874, 11p.
    DLC(M32.B)
Murmuring Rill (Mazurka Caprice), Op.24
    Firth-T, 1866, 7p.
    DLC(M32.B)
Polka brillante, Op.29
    Firth-T, 1866, 7p.
    CtHT(U), RPB(U)
Ricordanza (Valse), Op.93
    Pond, 1888, 7p.
    DLC(M32.B)
Tarantella (Etude), Op.10
    FirthS, 1864, 7p.
    DLC(M25.B)

BEACH, AMY MARCY CHENEY (1867-1944)

Ballad, Op.6
    Schmidt, 1894, 11p.
    CU(M25B4B25), DLC(M25.B), MoSW(U), PP(U)
Barcarolle, Op.28, No.1 (see Trois Morceaux caractéristiques,
    Op.28)
Cadenza to the first movement of the Third Concerto for the
    Pianoforte (C minor, Op.37) by Ludwig van Beethoven, Op.3
    Schmidt, 1888, 11p.
    IU(Joseffy), MB-N(Piano), NNLc(°MYD Cadenzas), OCl(M775.6.
    14343)
Two Compositions, Op.54
    Schmidt, 1903, 2v.(3,7p.)
    DCL(M25.B), ICN(sVM31B36g, 2 only), MoSW(U, 1 only), NRU-U
    (M30B365g, 2 only), PP(U), RPB(U), also in BC-G(1 only)
    1. Scottish Legend; 2. Gavotte fantastique
Three Compositions, Op.28 (see Trois Morceaux caractéristiques,
    Op.28)
Dancing Leaves, Op.102, No.2 (see Piano Compositions, Op.102)

Danse des Fleurs, Op.28, No.3 (see Trois Morceaux caracté-
  ristiques, Op.28)
Dreaming, Op.15, No.3 (see Four Sketches, Op.15)
Eskimos, Op.64
    Schmidt, 1907, 1943, 11p.
    DLC(M25.B), NRU-E(M25B365e)
    1. Arctic Night; 2. The Returning Hunter; 3. Exiles;
      4. With Dog-teams
    The composer states that "These pieces are founded on Folk
      Songs."
Fantasia Fugata, Op.87
    Presser, 1923, 10p.
    DLC(M25.B), IU(qM786.41B35f)
    The composer writes that for the opening motive she is "in-
      debted to 'Hamlet,' a large black Angora who had been
      placed on the keyboard with the hope that he might emu-
      late Scarlatti's cat and improvise a fugue theme."
Farewell, Summer, Op.102, No.1 (see Piano Compositions, Op.102)
Fire-Flies (Lucioles), Op.15, No.4 (see Four Sketches, Op.15)
From Grandmother's Garden, Op.97
    Presser, 1922, 5v.(5,3,5,7,5p.)
    DLC(M25.B), PP(U, 1,3 only)
    1. Morning Glories; 2. Heartsease; 3. Mignonette;
      4. Rosemary and Rue; 5. Honeysuckle
Gavotte fantastique, Op.54, No.2 (see Two Compositions, Op.54)
A Hermit Thrush at Eve, Op.92, No.1
    Schmidt, 1922, 7p.
    DLC(M25.B), Nh(U)
A Hermit Thrush at Morn, Op.92, No.2
    Schmidt, 1922, 9p.
    DLC(M25.B), Nh(U)
    The composer makes this notation: "These bird-calls are
      exact notations of hermit thrush songs, in the original
      keys but an octave lower, obtained at MacDowell Colony,
      Peterborough, N.H."
A Humming-Bird, Op.128, No.3 (see Three Pianoforte Pieces,
  Op.128)
Five Improvisations, Op.148
    ComposerP, 1938, 5v.(3,3,3,3,3p.)
    NRU-E(U, 3 only), PP(U)
In Autumn, Op.15, No.1 (see Four Sketches, Op.15)
Menuet Italien, Op.28, No.2 (see Trois Morceaux caractéri-
  stiques, Op.28)
Trois Morceaux caractéristiques, Op.28
    Schmidt, 1894, 3v.(5,7,7p.)
    DLC(M25.B), NRU-E(M32B365m, 2 only; U, 3 only), PP(U, 2
      only)
    1. Barcarolle; 2. Menuet Italien; 3. Danse des Fleurs
Phantoms, Op.15, No.2 (see Four Sketches, Op.15)
Piano Compositions, Op.102
    Ditson, 1924, 2v.(5,5p.)
    DLC(M25.B), NNLc(°MYD), PP(U, 1 only)
    1. Farewell, Summer; 2. Dancing Leaves

Three Pianoforte Pieces, Op.128
   Presser, 1932, 3v.(5,7,5p.)
   DLC(M25.B)
   1. **Scherzino** (A Peterborough Chipmunk); 2. **Young Birches;**
   3. **A Humming-bird**
Prelude and Fugue, Op.81
   Schirmer, 1918, 21p.
   DLC(M25.B), ICN(sVM25B36p), MoS(786.4), MoSW(U), NRU-E
   (M21R29A,v.2), PP(M786.4B35)
   Superbly dramatic and difficult work.
Les Rêves de Colombine (Suite française), **Op.65**
   Schmidt, 1907, 29p.
   Nh(U), NRU-E(M21R29A,v.1, 3 only), OCl(M776.415.1413)
   1. **La Fée de la Fontaine;** 2. **Le Prince gracieux;**
   3. **Valse amoureuse;** 4. **Sous les Etoiles;**
   5. **Danse d'Arlequin**
Scherzino, Op.128, No.1 (see **Three Piano Pieces, Op.128**)
Scottish Legend, Op.54, No.1 (see **Two Compositions, Op.54**)
Serenade (Richard Strauss. Transcription for the Pianoforte)
   Schmidt, 1902, 9p.
   Nh(U), ViU(U:2)
   A fine transcription of Strauss' song.
Four Sketches, Op.15
   Schmidt, 1892, 4v.(5,5,5,9p.)
   DLC(M25.B), MBH(P1W596.1), MoS(786.4), NNLc(Mus-Am[Sheet]
   74-443), NRU-E(M25B365p), PP(U, 1,2 only), WM(786.4B36c,
   1,3,4 only), also in NC-G(3,4 only)
   1. **In Autumn;** 2. **Phantoms;** 3. **Dreaming;** 4. **Fireflies**
Tyrolean Valse-Fantasie, Op.116
   Ditson, 1926, 16p.
   DLC(M25.B), MdBP(U), NRU-E(M32B365t), OCl(SM776.45)
Valse-Caprice, Op.4
   Schmidt, 1889, 11p.
   DLC(M32.B), PP(U)
   Good example of Mrs. Beach at her sparkling best.
Young Birches, Op.128, No.2 (see **Three Pianoforte Pieces,**
   Op.128)

BEACH, JOHN PARSONS (1877-1953)

A Garden Fancy
   Wa-Wan, 1907, 5p.
   DLC(M25.B), ICN(VM1W11v.6), MoS(786.4), NNLc(°MN Wa-Wan),
   NRU-E(M25B3655ga), also in WW-L(IV:153)
Intermezzo (in **Two Compositions for Pianoforte:** includes
   Mazurka by Shepherd)
   Wa-Wan, 1905, 7p.
   DLC(M1.W35v.4,no.30), ICN(VM1W11,v.4), NNLc(°MN Wa-Wan),
   NRU-E(M25B3655in), also in NC-G, WW-L(II:97)
   Interesting use of divided hands.
Monologue
   Wa-Wan, 1907, 4p.

DLC(M25.B), ICN(VM1W11v.6), NNLc(°MN Wa-Wan), NcU
   (M786.4B365m), NRU-E(M25B3655mo), PP(M786.4B352), also
   in WW-L(IV:9)
Strangely modern for the period, yet makes musical sense.
New Orleans Miniatures
   Wa-Wan, 1906, 19p.
   DLC(M1.W35v.5,no.36), ICN(VM1W11,v.5), LNT(L976.3[780]Z99),
      NNLc(°MN Wa-Wan), NRU-E(M24B3655ne), also in WW-L
      (II:203)
   1. Esplanade; 2. In an Ursuline Court; 3. Balcony Lyric;
      4. Place D'Orleans; 5. Masques; 6. Envoy
Valse lente
   Metro, 1899, 5p.
   DLC(M25.B)

BENEDICT, MILO (1866-1931)

Album Leaf III
   Petersilea, 1886, 3p.
   DLC(M25.B)
Pensée musicale
   Ross, 1884, 5p.
   DLC(M25.B), RPB(U)
Polonaise No.1, Op.2
   WhiteS, 1885, 9p.
   PP(U)

BERGE, WILLIAM (d.1883)

La Couronne (Mazurka de Salon), **Op.62**
   Ditson, 1859, 1887, 9p.
   CtY(Mc11A1B254.5), DLC(M1.A13.BCase), MiU-C(U), NBu(U),
      NNLc(AM2-I), PP(U)
Fort Sumpter Quick Step
   FirthP, 1861, 7p.
   CtHT(U), NNLc(AM2-I)
Last Rose of Summer (Grandes Variations de Concert), **Op.80**
   Pond, 1863, 1891, 17p.
   DLC(M27.B), NNLc(AM2-I)
La Promesse, Op.70
   FirthP, 1861, 1889, 11p.
   DLC(M25.B), NBu(U), NNLc(AM2-I)
Schottisch di bravura
   FirthP, 1856, 9p.
   CtY(Mc28Sch.67), DLC(M1.A13BCase), OC(U)

BETHUNE, THOMAS GREENE ["BLIND TOM"] (1849-1908)

The Battle of Manassas
   RootC, 1866, 11p.

InU(M1.S8), NNLc(AM2-I), OCl(SM776.4), also in EA-I, PM-H
Wildly descriptive, with copious footnotes.
Daylight (by Prof. W. F. Raymond, i.e. Blind Tom)
RootC, 1866, 5p.
DLC(M25.B), ICN(VM1497M67v.3), PP(U), ViU(°M1.S444,v.58,
no.17)
Strange, thick harmonies in six-four meter.
The Rainstorm, Op.6
Ditson, 1865, 1888, 11p.
DLC(M25.B)
Reve charmant (Nocturne)
Bethune, 1881, 10p.
DLC(M25.B)
Sewing Song (Imitation of the Sewing Machine)
Pond, 1888, 11p.
DLC(M25.B), PP(U)
Virginia Polka
Waters, n.d., 4p.
DLC(M31.B), InU(M1.S8)
Supposedly written when Bethune was ten years of age.
Water in the Moonlight
BrainardS, 1866, 5p.
DLC(M25.B), MiU-C(U)

BIRD, ARTHUR (1856-1923)

Albumblatt, Op.35, No.1
In HH-K(II:317)
Appassionato, Op.33, No.2 (see **Quatre Morceaux, Op.33**)
Berceuse, Op.21, No.3 (see **Trois Morceaux, Op.21**)
Capriccio (Humoreske), **Op.26, No.3** (see **Vier Klavier-
stücke, Op.26**)
Caprice, Op.20, No.6 (see **Sept Morceaux, Op.20**)
Etude, Op.31, No.3 (see **Trois Morceaux, Op.31**)
Fugue, Op.20, No.2 (see **Sept Morceaux, Op.20**)
Gavotte, Op.18, No.1 (see **Gavotte, Walzer und Menuett, Op.18**)
Gavotte, Op.21, No.2 (see **Trois Morceaux, Op.21**)
Gavotte, Op.26, No.1 (see **Vier Klavierstücke, Op.26**)
Gavotte, Op.46, No.3 (in **Quatre Morceaux, Op.46**)
Schirmer, 1910, 7p.
ViU(U:2)
Gavotte, Walzer und Menuett, Op.18
Hainauer, Schirmer, 1887, 3v.(7,7,7p.)
DLC(M25.B), MB-N(Vault M20B55,v.1), NcU(M786.45B618g)
1. Gavotte; 2. Walzer; 3. Menuett
Humoresque, Op.33, No.4 (see **Quatre Morceaux, Op.33**)
Intermezzo-Capriccio, Op.46, No.4 (in **Quatre Morceaux, Op.46**)
Schirmer, 1910, 7p.
DLC(M25.B), MoSW(U)
Vier Klavierstücke, Op.26
Hainauer, Schirmer, 1888, 4v.(7,9,7,11p.)
DLC(M25.B), MB-N(Vault M20B55,v.2)

1. Gavotte; 2. Valse Impromptu; 3. Capriccio;
  4. Tarantella
Mazurka, Op.31, No.2 (see Trois Morceaux, Op.31)
Mélodie, Op.20, No.7 (see Sept Morceaux, Op.20)
Menuet, Op.31, No.1 (see Trois Morceaux, Op.31)
Menuett, Op.18, No.3 (see Gavotte, Walzer und Menuett, Op.18)
Trois Morceaux, Op.21
    Hainauer, Schirmer, 1887, 3v.(9,7,7p.)
    DLC(M25.B, 1,2 only), IU(Joseffy), MB-N(Vault M20B55,v.2),
    NcU(M786.4B618m21, 3 only)
    1. Valse; 2. Gavotte; 3. Berceuse
Trois Morceaux, Op.31
    Schmidt, 1892, 3v.(7,7,7p.)
    DLC(M25.B), MoSW(U, 3 only), NcU(M786.4B618m31)
    1. Menuet; 2. Mazurka; 3. Etude
Quatre Morceaux, Op.33
    Schmidt, 1891, 4v.(7,9,7,7p.)
    CU(M32B5, 3 only), DLC(M25.B), MB-N(Vault M3.1B55), PP(U,
    2 only)
    1. Scherzando; 2. Appassionato; 3. Valse noble;
    4. Humoresque
Sept Morceaux, Op.20
    Hainauer, 1887, 7v.(7,7,5,9,6,11,7p.)
    MB-N(Vault M20B55), MoSW(U, 6 only), NcU(M786.4B618m20,
    1,3,4,5,6,7 only)
    1. Valse noble; 2. Fugue; 3. Réverie; 4. Scène
    humoresque; 5. Scène orientale; 6. Caprice;
    7. Mélodie
Vier Novelletten, Op.29
    Hainauer, Schirmer, 1890, 4v.(7,7,7,10p.)
    DLC(M25.B), MB-N(Vault M20B55,v.2)
    1. Allegro risoluto; 2. Allegretto; 3. Moderato;
    4. Allegretto
Rêverie, Op.20, No.3 (see Sept Morceaux, Op.20)
Scène humoresque, Op.20, No.4 (see Sept Morceaux, Op.20)
Scène orientale, Op.20, No.5 (see Sept Morceaux, Op.20)
Scherzando, Op.33, No.1 (see Quatre Morceaux, Op.33)
Scherzando, Op.35, No.2
    In HH-K(II:319)
Eight Sketches, Op.15 (see Acht Skizzen, Op.15)
Acht Skizzen, Op.15
    Hainauer, Schirmer, 1887, 8v.(5,5,5,7,5,9,3,5p.)
    DLC(M25.B), MB-N(Vault M20B55,v.1), NcU(M786.4B618s.15.1)
    An excellent collection of eight short, idiomatic pieces.
Tarantella, Op.26, No.4 (see Vier Klavierstücke, Op.26)
Thème varié, Op.27
    Hainauer, Schirmer, 1889, 15p.
    DLC(M27.B), MB-N(Vault M20B55,v.2)
Valse, Op.21, No.1 (see Trois Morceaux, Op.21)
Valse Impromptu, Op.26, No.2 (see Vier Klavierstücke, Op.26)
Valse noble, Op.20, No.1 (see Sept Morceaux, Op.20)
Valse noble, Op.33, No.3 (see Quatre Morceaux, Op.33)
Walzer, Op.18, No.2 (see Gavotte, Walzer und Menuett, Op.18)

BLAKE, CHARLES DUPEE (1846-1903)

Clayton's Grand March, Op.100
    White-S, 1877, 9p.
    CtY(Mc27A1), OC(U), PP(U), RPB(U), ViU(McR.37.18)
    A hit in its day, but rather pale by contemporary standards.
Come to the Feast (Second Grand Galop de Concert)
    WhiteSP, 1872, 7p.
    RPB(U)
    Amusingly presumptuous.   Sounds like circus music.
Dancing on the Meadow (Polka Rondo brillante)
    White-S, 1878, 7p.
    CtY(Mc28P7), RPB(U)
Golden Clouds (Morceau brillant), **Op.166**
    WhiteS, 1878, 8p.
    DLC(M25.B)
Marguerite (Fantasie)
    Sheard, n.d., 5p.
    RPB(U)
The Ocean Pearl (Nocturne)
    White-S, 1878, 1906, 7p.
    DLC(M25.B), RPB(U)
The Old Oaken Bucket (Transcription de Concert)
    WhiteS, 1880, 9p.
    RPB(U)
The Shepherd Boy's Farewell to his Flocks (Summer Idyl)
    WhiteS, 1879, 1907, 7p.
    DLC(M25.B)
The Shepherd's Evening Song (Morceau brillant), **Op.26**
    WhiteS, 1874, 7p.
    RPB(U)
Trembling Dew Drops (Summer Idyl)
    North, 1876, 7p.
    RPB(U)

BLIND TOM [see **THOMAS GREENE BETHUNE**]

BLOCH, ERNEST (1880-1959)

Ex-voto
    Broude, 1964, 3p.
    DLC(M25.B), NNLc(°MYDbox), NcU(M25B595e9), OCl(CM776.4
      B62E), PP(U)
    Composed around 1914.   Solemn and elegant.
In the Night (A Love-Poem)
    Schirmer, 1923, 7p.
    CU(M25B556I5), DLC(M25.B), ICN(sVM25B6495i), IU(qM786.41
      B62i), MoS(786.4), NNLc(°MYD), NRU-E(M25B651in),
      OCl(SM776.4), PP(M786.4B62511), WM(786.4B65i)
Nirvana (Poem)
    Schirmer, 1924, 7p.

CU(M25B556N5), DLC(M25.B), IU(MO 41230), NNLc(°MYD),
   NRU-E(M25B651ni), OCL(SM776.4), PP(M786.4B6251)

Poems of the Sea (A Cycle of Three Pieces)
   Schirmer, 1923, 23p.
   CU(M24B57P6), CtY(M24B651P7+), DLC(M24.B64P5), ICN(sVM24
      B65p), IU(qM786.41B62p), LNT(786B62p), MB-N(M25B56P6),
      MoS(786.4), NNLc(°°MYD+box), NRU-E(M25B651p), NcD
      (M786.41B651P), NcU(M24.B61p6), OCL(M776.4.164), PP
      (M786.4B62513), WM(786.4B65p), also in FPP(2 only)
   1. Waves; 2. Chanty; 3. At Sea
   Three tone poems representing Bloch at his best.

Five Sketches in Sepia
   Schirmer, 1924, 11p.
   CU(M24B57S5 1924), CtY(M25B651S6+), DLC(M25.B), ICN
      (sVM22B65f), IU(qM786.41B62f), MoS(786.4), NNLc(°MYD
      +box), NRU-E(M25B651s), NcD(M786.41B651F), OCL(M776.4.
      1638)
   1. Prélude; 2. Fumées sur la Ville; 3. Lucioles;
    4. Incertitude; 5. Epilogue
   Essays in free rhythm, irregular meters, new harmonies.

Sonata
   Carisch, 1936, 1957, 26p.
   DLC(M23.B634S5), IU(qM786.41B62s), NcU(M786.41B651s),
      OCL(M776.41.166), WM(786.4B65s)
   A large, serious three-movement work in an advanced musical
    idiom.

Visions et Prophéties (Visions and Prophecies)
   Schirmer, 1936, 1940, 13p.
   CU(M22B56V5 1940), DLC(M25.B), ICN(sVM24B65v), NNLc(°MYD),
      NRU-E(M25B651v), NcU(M786.4B651v), OCL(M776.4.1642),
      PP(M786.4B625)
   1. Moderato; 2. Poco lento; 3. Moderato—Poco più
   animato—Poco più calmo; 4. Adagio, piacevole;
   5. Poco agitato

BLODGETT, BENJAMIN COLMAN (1838-1925)

Andante and Capriccietto, Op.15
   Clarke, 1872, 7p.
   MNS(VZP-B62a)

Etude caractéristique, Op.10
   Tolman, 1865, 5p.
   DLC(M25.B), MiU-C(U)

Galop de Bravoure sur un thème du Farlow
   Russell, 1869, 9p.
   CtHT(U)
   The composer of the theme was probably Wm. G. Farlow, Har-
    vard Professor of Botany and enthusiastic music lover.

Valse brillante, Op.21
   Rottenbach, 1884, 9p.
   MNS(VZP-B62v)

BLUMENSCHEIN, WILLIAM LEONARD (1849-1916)

Allegretto and Barcarolle, Op.95
    Schmidt, 1901, 9p.
    ODa(786.4B658M)
Arlequinade (Impromptu), **Op.32**
    Schmidt, 1889, 9p.
    DLC(M25.B)
Barcarolle, Op.31
    Church, 1891, 7p.
    DLC(M25.B)
Impromptu, Op.22
    Church, 1893, 13p.
    DLC(M25.B), ICN(VM25B65i)
June Rose (Mazurka), **Op.54**
    In HH-K(IV:941)
Noche de Amor (Night of Love), **Op.124**
    Boston, 1907, 11p.
    DLC(M25.B), MoSW(U)
Nocturne
    Schirmer, 1877, 5p.
    DLC(M25.B)
Polonaise in C-sharp Minor, Op.127
    Ditson, 1908, 9p.
    DLC(M25.B)
    A truly superior work of this type.
Polonaise brillante, Op.123
    Boston, 1907, 13p.
    DLC(M25.B), MoSW(U), PP(U)
Polonaise Philomene, Op.107
    Presser, 1901, 7p.
    DLC(M25.B)
Scherzo, Op.30
    Church, 1891, 13p.
    ODa(786.4B658M)
Two Studies, Op.48
    Church, 1893, 2v.(7,7p.)
    ODa(786.4B658M)
    1. The Brooklet; 2. Toccata
Tarantelle brillante, Op.135
    Ditson, 1910, 9p.
    ODa(786.4B658M)

BOEKELMAN, BERNARDUS (1838-1930)

Abschied (Romanze), **Op.11**
    SchuberthJr, 1892, 5p.
    DLC(M25.B)
A Cheval (Morceau caractéristique), **Op.6**
    Schmidt, 1889, 7p.
    CtHT(U)
    An excellent work, inscribed "To Fair Farmington."

Ballabile, Op.3
    Schuberth-E, 1888, 11p.
    DLC(M25.B), IU(Joseffy), PP(U)
    The title refers to a "classic" dance in ballet.
Polonaise de Concert, Op.4
    Schuberth-E, 1887, 13p.
    IU(Joseffy), PP(U)
Yearning (Sehnsucht), **Op.8**
    Schuberth-F, 1895, 1907(2nd revised ed.), 5p.
    DLC(M25.B), IU(Joseffy)

BOLLINGER, SAMUEL (1872-1941)

Barcarola, Op.5, No.2
    Breitkopf, 1903, 5p.
    MoSHi(U)
Chopinesques, Op.4
    Schirmer, 1908, 3v.(9,5,9p.)
    DLC(M25.B), MoS(786.4, 1,3 only), MoSW(U, 2,3 only), NNLc
      (°MYDbox, 2 only), PP(U, 1,3 only)
    1. **Prélude** ("At Sea"); 2. **Nocturne;** 3. **Impromptu**
Dance Caprice, Op.7, No.1
    Breitkopf, 1903, 11p.
    MoSHi(U)
Danse humoristique, Op.7, No.2
    Breitkopf, 1903, 11p.
    DLC(M32.B), MoS(786.4), MoSW(U)
Danse mélancolique
    Mills-FA, 1901, 4p.
    MoSHi(U)
Elegy, Op.15, No.1
    Shattinger, 1913, 11p.
    DLC(M25.B), MoSW(U)
Humoreske, Op.5, No.3
    Breitkopf, 1903, 9p.
    MoSHi(U)
Idyl, Op.5, No.1
    Breitkopf, 1903, 5p.
    MoSHi(U)
Impromptu, Op.4, No.3 (see **Chopinesques, Op.4**)
In Memory of Chopin
    Bollinger, 1940, 5p.
    MoSHi(U)
    A dignified, sincere musical tribute.
Mazurka, Op.1, No.2
    Grude, 1896, 11p.
    MoSHi(U)
Nocturne, Op.4, No.2 (see **Chopinesques, Op.4**)
Prélude, Op.4, No.1 (see **Chopinesques, Op.4**)
Romanzo-Lamentoso, Op.1, No.3
    Grude, 1896, 15p.
    DLC(M25.B)

Tone-Poem, Op.8, No.2
    Schirmer, 1908, 5p.
    DLC(M25.B), MoS(786.4), MoSHi(U), MoSW(U)

BOROWSKI, FELIX (1872-1956)

Danse Hongroise
    Laudy, 1894, 7p.
    ICN(VM22B73p)
Grande Sonate Russe
    Laudy, Stevens, 1896, 27p.
    ICN(sVM23B73s), NNLc(Drexel°°MYDp.v.5,no.5), OCl
      (M776.41.175)
    A superb four-movement sonata in the grand manner.
Impromptu (en Forme d'une Valse)
    Cocks, Schuberth-E, 1897, 7p.
    DLC(M25.B)
Intermezzo Caprice
    Presser, 1918, 7p.
    DLC(M25.B)
Mazurka (No.2)
    Schirmer, 1897, 6p.
    CU(M32B6), NRU-E(U), OCl(SM776.45)
Nocturne
    Presser, 1907, 6p.
    DLC(M25.B), InU(M1.S8)
Nocturne lyrique
    ComposerMC, 1921, 9p.
    DLC(M25.B), NNLc(°MYDbox)
Sept Préludes
    Laudy, 1901, 37p., also 7v.
    DLC(M25.B), ICN(VM22B73pr), MoSW(U, 3,4 only),
      PP(U, 1 only)
    Seven contrasting works of superior quality.
Valse romantique
    Laudy, 1896, 7p.
    MoSW(U)

BRANDEIS, FREDERICK (1835-1899)

Caprice brillante, Op.40
    Schuberth-E, 1875, 13p.
    DLC(M25.B)
"Es wär' so schön gewesen." Trost in Tönen (Melody), **Op.85, No.1**
    Breitkopf, 1893, 5p.
    DLC(M25.B)
    Brief bit of introspection, like an Album-Leaf.
Fantasie, Op.41
    Martens, 1876, 9p.
    IU(Joseffy)

Gavotte, Op.53
    Pond, 1879, 7p.
    IU(Joseffy), NRU-E(M31B817)
Humoresque, Op.68 (see **Polka Humoresque, Op.68**)
Impromptu, Op.69, No.2
    Pond, 1900, 3p.
    NcU(M786.4B817i)
Infatuation Galop, Op.22
    Pond, 1870, 9p.
    RPB(U)
    Great fun, but difficult to play.
Melodie, Op.57, No.2 (from **Sechs Clavierstücke, Op.57**)
    Spear, 1887, 5p.
    MiU-C(U)
Menuett, Op.57, No.3 (from **Sechs Clavierstücke, Op.57**)
    Spear, 1887, 5p.
    RPB(U)
Nocturne, Op.65, No.3 (from **Six Characteristic Pieces, Op.65**)
    Brentano, 1882, 11p.
    PP(U)
Polka de Concert, Op.50
    Saalfield, 1878, 1880, 11p.
    DLC(M31.B), IU(Joseffy), NRU-E(U), RPB(U)
Polka fantastique, Op.50 (see **Polka de Concert, Op.50**)
Polka Humoresque (Caprice), **Op.68**
    Newhall, 1883, Ditson, 1897, 9p.
    DLC(M25.B; M31.B), IU(Joseffy), MoSW(U), PP(U)
Praeludium, Op.57, No.4 (from **Sechs Clavierstücke, Op.57**)
    Spear, 1887, 5p.
    RPB(U)
Still Life, Op.85, No.2
    In BC-G
Tarantelle (Caprice), **Op.64**
    Prochàzka, 1884, 11p.
    OCl(M776.4.1868)
Toccata, Op.54
    Pond, 1880, 13p.
    DLC(M25.B), IU(Joseffy), PP(U)
    Was also published as Op.51.
Toreador Song from Bizet's Carmen (Transcription)
    Pond, 1884, 7p.
    DLC(M34.B), IU(Joseffy), OCl(M776.4.1868)
    Great fun (i.e.difficult fun) for the pianist.

BREMNER, JAMES (d.1780)

Lesson
    In FH-M [SU:226]
March
    In FH-M [SU:247]
Overture (arrangement of Earl of Kelly's Overture)
    In FH-M [SU:319]

Trumpet Air
    In FH-M, P-H [SU:438]

BRISTOW, GEORGE (1825-1898)

Andante et Polonaise, Op.18
    Schott, n.d., 15p.
    NNLc(°MYD)
La belle Amérique (Nocturne), **Op.4**
    Pearson, 1850, 9p.
    DLC(M1.A13BCase)
L'Etoile du Soir (Nocturne), **Op.7**
    Lee, 1884, 9p.
    DLC(M25.B)
Grand Waltz de Bravura, Op.6
    FirthH, 1845, 15p.
    NNLc(AM2-I), NRU-E(U)
Impromptu, Op.76
    Grand, 1883, 15p.
    DLC(M25.B)
Miss Lucy Long (with Variations for the Pianoforte)
    Christman, 1842, 9p.
    DLC(M27.B)
**Rory O'Moore: A Favorite Irish Air Arranged with Brilliant
    and Easy Variations**
    FirthH, 1842, 6p.
    DLC(M1.A13BCase), NNLc(AM2-I), NRU-E(6677.F.39), PP(U),
        RPB(U)
La Sérénade (Nocturne), **Op.8**
    Pearson, 1850, 9p.
    DLC(M25.B), NBu(°M1C65,v.54,no.55), NcU(M786.43B861s)
Souvenir de Mount Vernon: Grande Valse brillante, Op.29)
    Gordon, 1861, 1867, 11p.
    NNLc(AM2-I), PP(U), also in NC-G

BROCKWAY, HOWARD (1870-1951)

Andante tranquillo, Op.21, No.1 (see **Four Pieces, Op.21**)
At Twilight, Op.39, No.1 (see **Two Piano Pieces, Op.39**)
Ballade, Op.10
    Schlesinger, 1894, 11p.
    DLC(M25.B), WM(786.4B86)
Capriccio, Op.25, No.1 (see **Two Pieces for Piano, Op.25**)
Sechs Clavierstücke, Op.8
    Schlesinger, 1894, 15p.
    DLC(M25.B), IU(Joseffy), WM(786.4B86s)
    1. Albumblatt; 2. Canonisches Lied; 3. Scherzino;
       4. Elfenspiel; 5. Elfen-Ständchen; 6. Marsch
Evening Song, Op.26, No.4 (in **Suite of Small Pieces, Op.26**)
    Schirmer, 1901, 3p.
    RPB(U)

Humoresque, Op.26, No.5 (in Suite of Small Pieces, Op.26)
    Schirmer, 1901, 3p.
    CtY(U), DLC(M24.B875op26), MoS(786.4), NRU-E(M25B864s)
An Idyl of Murmuring Water, Op.39, No.2 (see Two Piano Pieces,
  Op.39)
Ein Märchen, Op.36, No.1 (from Moods, Op.36)
    Church, 1910, 5p.
    NNLc(Music-Am[Sheet]75-229), PP(U)
March, Op.25, No.2 (see Two Pieces for Piano, Op.25)
Nocturne, Op.14
    Schlesinger, 1893, 7p.
    DLC(M25.B), IU(Joseffy)
Phantasiestück, Op.17
    Schlesinger, 1897, 14p.
    DLC(M25.B), IU(Joseffy), NNLc(JNG 75-165)
Two Piano Pieces, Op.39
    Schirmer, 1911, 2v.(6,9p.)
    DLC(M25.B, 2 only), NRU-E(M21R29A,v.1), NcU(M786.43B864a),
      PP(U)
    1. At Twilight; 2. An Idyl of Murmuring Water
Two Pieces for Piano, Op.25
    Schirmer, 1900, 2v.(5,7p.)
    CU(M25B83, 2 only), DLC(M25.B, 1 only), IU(Joseffy),
      MoS(786.4), MoSW(U, 2 only), NNLc(°MYD), NRU-E
      (M25B864t), NcU(M786.4B864c, 1 only)
    1. Capriccio; 2. March
Four Pieces for Pianoforte, Op.21
    Schirmer, 1899, 4v.(3,7,7,7p.)
    MoS(786.4), MoSW(U, 3,4 only), NNLc(°MYD), NRU-E
      (M25B864f), NcU(M786.4B864p)
    1. Andante tranquillo; 2. Scherzino; 3. Romance;
      4. Valse Caprice
Romance, Op.21, No.3 (see Four Pieces, Op.21)
Scherzino, Op.21, No.2 (see Four Pieces, Op.21)
Valse Caprice, Op.21, No.4 (see Four Pieces, Op.21)
Variationen über ein eigenes Thema, Op.7
    Schlesinger, 1894, 9p.
    DLC(M27.B), MoSW(U)
    A small-scale but very effective variation set.

BROUNOFF, PLATON (1863-1924)

In the Russian Village (A Symphonic Suite)
    Modern, 1899, 59p.
    DLC(M24.B), OC(786.4fB87in)
    1. Festive Procession; 2. Flirtation; 3. Love;
      4. The Crippled Beggars; 5. An Old Legend;
      6. Passing of the Exiles; 7. Hunting Scene (Troyka);
      8. Departure of Recruits; 9. Chorus and Dance
Nocturne
    Luckhardt, 1900, 7p.
    DLC(M25.B)

BROWN, WILLIAM (fl.1780s)

Three Rondos for Piano Forte or Harpsichord
    The author, ca.1787, 6p. [SU:361]
    DLC(M1.A1BCase), NNLc(JPG 78-26), also in A-C(I: 3 only),
    C-MH(1 only), M-E(1 only)
    Historically interesting rondos in Classic style.

BRYANT, GILMORE WARD (1859-1946)

A Brookside Fantasia, Op.38
    The author, 1907, 7p.
    DLC(M25.B)
Song of the Brook, Op.10
    Ellis, 1889, 9p.
    DLC(M25.B)

BUCK, DUDLEY (1839-1909)

By the Brookside, Op.8, No.2 (see Midsummer Fancies, Op.8)
Echoes of the Ballroom, Op.19, No.3 (see Winter Pictures, Op.19)
Fantasia on the Prayer from "Der Freischütz," Op.5
    Gordon, 1857, 13p.
    CtHT(U)
Farewell, Op.4, No.3 (see Three Nocturnes, Op.4)
In the Woods, Op.8, No.1 (see Midsummer Fancies, Op.8)
Introduction and Rondo, Op.7
    Tolman, 1865, 11p.
    DLC(M25.B), NNLc(AM2-I), OCl(SM776.41), also in NC-G
Midsummer Fancies (3 Characteristic Pieces), Op.8
    Beer, 1866, 3v.(7,7,7p.)
    CtHT(U), DLC(M25.B), MoS(786.4), PP(U, 3 only)
    1. In the Woods; 2. By the Brookside; 3. On the Seashore
Three Nocturnes, Op.4
    Tolman, 1865, 3v.(5,5,7p.)
    CtY(Mc11A1B852), DLC(M25.B), InU(M1.S8, 2 only)
    1. Reverie; 2. Spring-Song; 3. Farewell
On the Seashore, Op.8, No.3 (see Midsummer Fancies, Op.8)
Reverie, Op.4, No.1 (see Three Nocturnes, Op.4)
Scherzo-Caprice, Op.14
    Beer, 1866, 1894, 13p.
    CtHT(U), DLC(M25.B), NNLc(AM2-I), OC(U)
Sleigh Bells, Op.19, No.2 (see Winter Pictures, Op.19)
Spring-Song, Op.4, No.2 (see Three Nocturnes, Op.4)
Winter Pictures (3 Characteristic Pieces), Op.19
    Beer, 1866, 3v.(7,7,9p.)
    CtHT(U, 1 only), DLC(M25.B), NNLc(AM2-I, 1 only), RPB(U,
    3 only)
    1. Woodland Scene; 2. Sleigh Bells; 3. Echoes of
      the Ballroom
Woodland Scene, Op.19, No.1 (see Winter Pictures, Op.19)

BURLEIGH, HENRY (HARRY) THACKER (1866-1949)

From the Southland (Piano Sketches)
    Maxwell, 1907, 1910, Presser, 1914, 30p.
    CtY(Mc11A1B924), DLC(M24.B96), NNLc(°MYD), OCl(M776.4.194),
    WM(786.4B96)
    1. **Through Moanin' Pines**; 2. **The Frolic**; 3. **In De
      Col' Moonlight**; 4. **A Jubilee**; 5. **On Bended Knee**;
      6. **A New Hidin'-Place**

BURMEISTER, RICHARD (1860-1944)

Ballade, Op.8
    Breitkopf, 1899, 13p.
    DLC(M25.B)
    A superb composition in every respect.
Cadenz zum ersten Satz von Chopin's F moll Concert (Op.21),
  Op.3
    Rohlfing, 1897, 7p.
    DLC(M25.B)
    A first-rate cadenza to Chopin's Concerto.
Capriccio, Op.5
    Rohlfing, 1897, 5p.
    DLC(M25.B), WM(786.4B962c)
Capriccio No.2, Op.10
    Breitkopf, 1899, 11p.
    DLC(M25.B)
Elegy (transcribed from "Wanderer's Nightsong"), Op.4b
    Rohlfing, 1897, 7p.
    DLC(M25.B), MoSW(U)
"Persian Song," Op.6b
    Rohlfing, 1897, 1901, 1905, 5p.
    DLC(M25.B), MoSW(U), NNLc(°MYD+box), PP(U), WM(786.4
      B962pR)
    1897 ed. has an octave finale, 1901 a simplified finale.
    1905 includes both versions.

BURR, WILLARD (1852-1915)

Concert Nocturne in C Minor, Op.11, No.2 (see **Three Noc-
  turnes, Op.11**)
Concert Nocturne in D-flat Major, Op.11, No.1 (see **Three
  Nocturnes, Op.11**)
Nocturne in E Minor, Op.11, No.3 (see **Three Nocturnes,
  Op.11**)
Three Nocturnes, Op.11
    Ditson, 1886, 3v.(9,7,7p.)
    DLC(M25.B, 1,3 only), PP(U, 2 only)
    1. **Concert Nocturne in D-flat Major**; 2. **Concert Nocturne
      in C Minor**; 3. **Nocturne in E Minor** (Am Abend, auf dem
      Brienzer See)

CAMP, JOHN SPENCER (1858-1946)

  Album Leaf, Op.2, No.3
     Truette, 1893, 5p.
     DLC(M25.C)
  Bolero (In Sevilla), **Op.2, No.2**
     Truette, 1893, 7p.
     DLC(M25.C)

CAMPBELL-TIPTON, LOUIS (1877-1921)

  Album of Ten Piano Compositions, Op.1
     Consolidated, 1904, 45p., also issued separately
     CtY(Mc11A1C158), DLC(M25.T·[Tipton]), WM(786.4C19a)
     1. **Moment Musical**; 2. **Menuet**; 3. **Unrest**;
       4. **Canzonetta**; 5. **A Memory**; 6. **Scherzetto**;
       7. **Reverie**; 8. **At her Lattice**; 9. **Serenade**;
       10. **Valse**
  At her Lattice, Op.1, No.8 (see **Album of Ten Piano Compo-
     sitions, Op.1**)
  Canzonetta, Op.1, No.4 (see **Album of Ten Piano Composi-
     tions, Op.1**)
  The Four Seasons (see **Suite, Op.29**)
  Legend No.1, Op.14
     Schirmer, 1908, 5p.
     DLC(M25.T), NRU-E(M21R29A,v.1)
  Legend No.2, Op.15
     Schirmer, 1908, 5p.
     DLC(M25.T), NRU-E(M21R29A,v.1)
  A Memory, Op.1, No.5 (see **Album of Ten Piano Compositions,
     Op.1**)
  Menuet, Op.1, No.2 (see **Album of Ten Piano Compositions,
     Op.1**)
  Moment Musical, Op.1, No.1 (see **Album of Ten Piano Compo-
     sitions, Op.1**)
  Reverie, Op.1, No.7 (see **Album of Ten Piano Compositions,
     Op.1**)
  Scherzetto, Op.1, No.6 (see **Album of Ten Piano Compositions,
     Op.1**)
  Serenade, Op.1, No.9 (see **Album of Ten Piano Compositions,
     Op.1**)
  Serenade No.II
     Schirmer, 1908, 7p.
     MoSW(U), NRU-E(M21R29A,v.1)
  Solitude (Meditation)
     Ditson, 1888, 7p.
     DLC(M25.T)
  Sonata Heroic
     Wa-Wan, 1904, Schirmer, 1904, 1912, 24p.
     CU(M23C26), ICN(VM1W11,v.3), IU(Joseffy), MB-N(Piano), MoS
       (786.41), NNLc(°MN Wa-Wan), NRU-E(M23C192sh), NcU(M786.41
       C192s), PP(U), ViU(Music M23.C35 1904), also in WW-L(I:123)

A basically romantic, flamboyant work in one movement.
Suite (The Four Seasons), **Op.29**
     Leuckart, 1911, 11p.
     DLC(M24.T47op29), NNLc(°°MYD+box)
     1. **Spring;** 2. **Summer;** 3. **Autumn;** 4. **Winter**
Unrest, Op.1, No.3 (see **Album of Ten Piano Compositions, Op.1**)
Valse, Op.1, No.10 (see **Album of Ten Piano Compositions, Op.1**)

CAPEN, CHARLES LEMUEL (1850-?)

Gavotte in F Minor
     Schmidt, 1880, 7p.
     PP(U)
Scherzo alla Polacca
     Miles, 1889, 7p.
     DLC(M25.C)

CARPENTER, JOHN ALDEN (1876-1951)

Danza
     Schirmer, 1947, 14p.
     CtY(M25C295D19+), DLC(M30.C), NNLc(°MYD), NRU-E(M30C295d),
        PP(786.4C226d), PPi(qM786.4C22dan)
Diversions (Five Pieces for Piano)
     Schirmer, 1923, 25p.
     CU(M22C32D5), DLC(M25.C), ICN(sVM25C29d), IU(qM786.41C22d),
        LNT(786C22d), MBH(P1C228.2), MoS(786.4), NNLc(°MYD),
        NcD(M786.41C295D), OCl(M776.4.2069), PP(M786.4C221),
        WM(786.4C29d)
     1. **Lento;** 2. **Allegretto;** 3. **Animato;** 4. **Moderato;**
        5. **Adagio**
Impromptu
     Schirmer, 1915, 7p.
     CU(M25C32I5), DLC(M25.C), ICN(sVM25C29t), MBH(P1C228),
        Mos(786.4), MoSW(U), NNLc(°MYD+box), NRU-E(M21R29A,v.1),
        also in FPP
Little Dancer
     Schirmer, 1918, 7p.
     DLC(M25.C), ICN(sVM25C29tw), IU(qM786.41C22L), MoS(786.4),
        NNLc(°MYDbox), NRU-E(M21R29A), RPB(U), WM(786.4C29)
Little Indian
     Schirmer, 1918, 6p.
     CU(M25C32L5), ICN(sVM25C29tw), IU(MO 41259), LNT(786C22L)
        MoS(786.4), MoSW(U), NNLc(°MYDbox), NRU-E(M25C295Li),
        RPB(U), WM(786.4C29)
Nocturne
     Stevens, 1898, 7p.
     CtY(Mc20C22n), DLC(M25.C), IU(qM786.41C22n), PP(U)
     An early work, elegant and romantic.
Polonaise américaine
     Schirmer, 1915, 7p.

CU(M32C27P6 1915), CtY(Mc2OC22p), DLC(M25.C), ICN(sVM25C29t),
LNT(786C22po), MBH(P1C228), MoS(786.44), MoSW(U), NNLc
('MYDbox), NRU-E(U), OCl(SM776.45), ViU(Music M32.C3P6
1915), WM(786.4C29p)

Tango américain
Schirmer, 1921, 9p.
CU(M31C32T27), DLc(M30.C), MoS(786.45), NNLc('MYDbox),
OCl(SM776.45), PP(U), WM(786.4C29t)

Twilight Reverie
Miles, 1894, 7p.
DLC(M25.C)

CARR, BENJAMIN (1768-1831)

Twelve Airs Arranged with Variations or as Rondos, Op.XVII
Carr, 1825, 28p.
DLC(M1.A13Case), NNLc(AM1-I)
1. Une petite Overture; 2. The Campbells are Coming;
3. Duett for Two Performers; 4. Little Bo Peep;
5. La Serenade; 6. The Carolinian Waltz; 7. The
Sultan Saladin; 8. The Spanish Hymn; 9. Thema Con
Variazione; 10. Di Tanti Palpiti (arranged as a Duett);
11. Drink to me only with thine Eyes; 12. The Genoa
Ground

The Copenhagen Waltz (arranged with Variations)
Carr-J, n.d., 5p. [W.I:155]
PP(K:2), also in CMM-M,no.37

Di Tanti Palpiti or Hail to the Happy Day (arranged as a
Rondo)
Carr, ca.1823, 5p. [W.II:758]
DLC(M1.A1C Case), PP(K:5), also in CMM-M,no.75
A Cavatina from Rossini's **Tancredi.**

Three Divertimentos
CarrS, 1800, 3p. [SU:111, W.I:155]
In CMJ(1.1:34)

A Divertisement on the Favorite Air of the Plow-Boy
Carr-J, ca.1818, 8p. [W.II:797]
DLC(M1.A1C Case), also in CMM-M,no.49
Based on a song from William Shield's **The Farmer.**

Fantasia with Gramachree (also known as **Variations on
Gramachree Molly**)
Lucas-F, 1806, 7p.
ICN(Case8A 840), NNLc('MYDbox), PP(U), also in NC-G
The tune is identical to that sung to "The Harp that once
thru Tara's Halls."

The Federal Overture
Carr-B, 1794, 7p. [SU:139]; Musical, 1957, 7p. (ed. Lowens)
CU(M35C3CaseX), CtY(Nc50C23L952), DLC(ML410.C3287L7folio),
ICN(fV29.1484), IU(qM786.41C23fY1 Sp.Coll.), LNT
(L780.92C311fZl), NNLc('MYD-Amer), NRU-E(ML410C311L9),
NcU(F780.81C311fzl), OCl(q775.5.207), PP(U)
The only known original copy of this fine work is at NNLc.

Six Imitations of English, Scotch, Irish, Welch, Spanish and German Airs
    CarrS, n.d., 3p. [SU:385]
    In CMJ(1.1:38)
The Maid of Lodi
    CarrMS, ca.1812, 2p. [W.I:158]
    DLC(M1.A1C Case), PP(K:5A), RPB(U), also in A-C(I)
    Variations on a song by William Shield.
The much admired Mantua Waltz
    Willig-G, 1825, 5p. [W.I:158]
    DLC(M1.A13C Case), NNLc(Am.1-I), OC(HAS:°R-Mus), PP(K:2)
Musette de Nina
    Carr-T, ca.1819, 2p. [W.I:160]
    ICN(Case8A 1379), NNLc(AM1-I), PP(U), also in CMM-M,no.55
Paddy Carey (Arranged as a Rondo)
    Carr-J, ca.1816, 8p. [W.I:161]
    DLC(M1.A13C Case), ICN(Case8A 1376), MdBP(U), NNLc(AM1-I),
      PP(K:2), also in CMM-M,no.35
The Pianoforte Waltz
    Carr, ca.1824, 2p. [W.I:161]
    DLC(M1.A1C Case), PP(K:5), also in CMM-M,no.83
The Plow Boy as a Divertisement (see **A Divertisement on the Favorite Air of the Plow-Boy**)
Preludes, Op.13
    Carr-T, ca.1820, 12p. [W.I:162]
    DLC(M1.A1C Case), ICN(Case8A 1382), NNLc(AM1-I), PP(U),
      also in CMM-M,no.65
    Interesting early technical studies.
Six Progressive Sonatinas for the Pianoforte, Op.IX
    Carr-J, ca.1812, 16p. [W.I:164]
    DLC(M1.A1C), ICN(Case8A 1364), NNLc(AM1-I), PP(U), also
      in CMM-M,no.2
Rondo (in E-flat Major)
    CarrS, n.d., 2p. [W.I:163]
    NNLc(AM1-I), also in CMJ(2.5:21)
    "Performed at the Philadelphia Harmonick Society"
Rondo (in G Minor)
    CarrS, n.d., 2p. [W.I:162]
    In CMJ(1.3:13)
Rondo from the Overture to the opera of "The Archers" or Mountaineers of Switzerland
    Carr-J, ca.1813, 3p. [W.I:162]
    DLC(M21.H78P7), M1.A1C), MoS(786.4), PP(U, K:2), also in
      CMM-M,no.7
The Siege of Tripoli, An Historical Naval Sonata
    CarrS, ca.1804, 11p.; Blake, ca.1815, 9p. [W.I:163]
    DLC(M1.A1C Case), MBH(Safe 92), NNLc(AM1-I), PP(K:2), also
      in A-C(I)
    Typical battle piece, ending with "Yankee Doodle."
Six Sonatas (see Frances Linley, **A New Assistant for the Piano-forte or Harpsichord**) [SU:289]
Variations on the beautiful Scotch Air of Gramachree Molly (see **Fantasia with Gramachree**)

When the Hollow Drum (Arranged as a Rondo)
   Carr, n.d., 4p. [W.I:27]
   PP(K:5), also in CMM-M,no.85
   Based on a song by Samuel Arnold.

CARRENO, TERESA (1853-1917)

Gottschalk Waltz
   Ditson, 1863, 7p.
   InU(M1.S8), NNLc(AM2-I)
   Supposedly written when Carreño was ten years of age.
Intermezzo-Scherzoso, Op.34
   Schuberth-E, 1879, 7p.
   CtY(Mc11A1C232), DLC(M25.C)
March Triomphale, Op.8
   Ditson, 1873, 7p.
   RPB(U)
Polonaise, Op.35
   Ditson-CH, 1873, 9p.
   PP(U)
Sailing in the Twilight
   Ditson, 1875, 9p.
   MiU-C(U)
Spring-Time (Valse de Salon), **Op.26**
   Schuberth-E, 1879, 11p.
   DLC(M32.C), MoSW(U), NRU-E(U), PP(U)

CHADWICK, GEORGE WHITEFIELD (1854-1931)

Two Caprices
   Schmidt, 1882, 1888, 2v.(5,7p.)
   DLC(M25.C), MBH(P1W596.1), MB-N(M3.3C5C3), MoS(786.4),
      NNLc(Music-Am[Sheet]77-321, II only), NRU-E(M25C
      432c.2, II only), PP(U), RPB(U, II only), also in
      BC-G(II only), NC-G(II only)
   1. Caprice I; 2. Caprice II
Six Characteristic Pieces, Op.7
   Schmidt, 1882, 6v.(3,3,7,5,3,5p.)
   CU(M25C453op7:3, 3 only), DLC(M25.C, 1,2,3,5,6 only), IU
      (qM786.41C345c, 1 only), MBH(P1W596.1, 3 only), MB-N
      (M33C5op7), MoS(786.4), NNLc(°MYD+box, 3 only), NRU-E
      (M25C432pc.2, 2 only; C432pc.6, 6 only), PP(U, 1,3,4 only),
      also in NC-G(3 only)
   1.Congratulations; 2. Please Do; 3. Scherzino;
      4. Reminiscence of Chopin; 5. Irish Melody; 6. Etude
Congratulations, Op.7, No.1 (see **Six Characteristic Pieces,
   Op.7**)
Etude, Op.7, No.6 (see **Six Characteristic Pieces, Op.7**)
The Frogs (see **Five Pieces for the Piano**)
The Gloaming (see **Five Pieces for the Piano**)
In the Canoe (see **Five Pieces for the Piano**)

Irish Melody, Op.7, No.5 (see Six Characteristic Pieces, Op.7)
Five Pieces for the Piano
    Schirmer, 1905, 38p., also 5v.(8,7,9,5,8p.)
    DLC(M25.C), MB-N(M3.3C5P55), MoSw(U, 2,4 only), NRU-E
    (M25C432p.3, 3 only), NcU(M786.48C432p), PP(U, 1,3,5
    only)
    1. Prelude; 2. In the Canoe; 3. The Rill; 4. The
    Gloaming; 5. The Frogs
    Five effective, skillful miniatures.
Please Do, Op.7, No.2 (see Six Characteristic Pieces, Op.7)
Prelude (see Five Pieces for the Piano)
Reminiscence of Chopin, Op.7, No.4 (see Six Characteristic
   Pieces, Op.7)
The Rill (see Five Pieces for the Piano)
Scherzino, Op.7, No.3 (see Six Characteristic Pieces, Op.7)
Drei Walzer für das Pianoforte (Three Waltzes)
    Schmidt, 1890, 3v.(7,5,5p.)
    DLC(M32.C), MB-N(M3.3C5W25), NRU-E(M32C432w)

CHALLONER, ROBERT (fl.1870s)

From Youth to Age Waltzes
    Newhall, 1878, 11p.
    OC(Langstroth,v.27,p.153)
Home Sweet Home (Transcription)
    Ditson, n.d., 11p.
    PP(U)
The Old Folks at Home (Grande Paraphrase de Concert)
    Ditson, 1874, 1902, 13p.
    DLC(M25.C), PP(U [Foster]), RPB(U)

CHAPMAN, WILLIAM ROGERS (1855-1935)

Love Echoes (Idylle), Op.6
    Cady, 1876, 7p.
    DLC(M25.C)
    Interesting rhythmic treatment.
Murmuring Streamlet (Reverie)
    Harris, 1875, 7p.
    DLC(M25.C)

CHELIUS, HERMAN (1848-1941)

Angelic Vision
    Thompson, 1903, 9p.
    MeB(U)
Love Dreams
    Thompson, 1907, 7p.
    RPB(U)

Twilight
  Ross, 1891, White-S, 1903, 9p.
  PP(U)
  Interesting variation treatment. Difficult.

CLAASSEN, ARTHUR (1859-1920)

  Glückliche Stunde, Op.37, No.4 (see Four Piano Pieces, Op.37)
  Mazurka, Op.39, No.2 (see Two Pieces, Op.39)
  Novellette, Op.37, No.2 (see Four Piano Pieces, Op.37)
  Four Piano Pieces, Op.37
    Schirmer, 1899, 4v.(7,7,7,5p.)
    DLC(M25.C), MoSW(U, 1,4 only), PP(U, 3,4 only)
    1. Romance; 2. Novellette; 3. Valse lente;
       4. Glückliche Stunde (Blessed Hour)
  Two Pieces, Op.39
    Siegel, 1900, 5p.
    DLC(M25.C)
    1. Serenade; 2. Mazurka
  Romance, Op.37, No.1 (see Four Piano Pieces, Op.37)
  Serenade, Op.39, No.1 (see Two Pieces, Op.39)
  Valse lente, Op.37, No.3 (see Four Piano Pieces, Op.37)

CLARKE, WILLIAM HORATIO (1840-1913)

  The Chimes of St. James
    Nordheimer, 1884, 9p.
    DLC(M25.C)
    Salon fantasy on a church-bell theme.
  Silver Star Polka
    RussellT, 1860, 5p.
    RPB(U)
  A Storm on the Lake (Barcarolle)
    Nordheimer, 1884, 12p.
    DLC(M25.C)
    Old-fashioned storm piece with running commentary.

CLIFTON, ARTHUR [P. A. CORRI] (1784-1832)

  Blue Eye'd Mary with Variations
    CarrMS, ca.1820, 4p.
    NcD(RBR MusicB144,no.4)
  The Bonnie Boat (With easy Variations)
    Cole, n.d., 3p.
    CtY(Mc11A1C612), DLC(M1.A13C Case [Corri]), PP(U),
      ViU(McR.117.02)
  Divertimento alla Montanara (Corri)
    Weygand, n.d., 11p.
    DLC(M25.C Case), ICN(Case8A 724)
    Introduction, march and rondo.

La Galantina. Divertissement (Corri)
    Nolting, n.d., 11p.
    ICN(Case8A 725)
Green Grow the Rushes O! (Corri)
    Chappell, n.d., 8 p.
    ScCC(SMS-52 Acquisition 71.52.2)
LaFayette's Welcome to the United States in 1824 (A Grand
  March and Quick Step)
    Willig-G, 1824, 4p. [W.I:195]
    DLC(M1.A13C), ICN(Case8A 2405), NNLc(°MYDbox), InU(M1.S8),
      ViU(°M1.S444,v.89,no.21)
    Also existed for military band. The very ornate title
    reads:"Composed At the Request of the Committee of
    Arrangement for the City of Baltimore and Dedicated
    With Profound Veneration to That Distinguished Friend
    of America."
National Divertimento (In Which are Introduced "Hail Columbia"
  with a new Trio, and "Yankee Doodle" with Variations)
    Blake, ca.1821, 4p. [W.I:197]
    ICN(Case8A 2407)
Nos Galan or New Year's Night (Corri)
    n.p., n.d., 9p.
    ScCC(SMS86 Acquisition 71.52.3A)
An Original Air with Variations for the Pianoforte
    The author, 1821, 4p.
    DLC(M4.A2C63 in "A Collection of Music composed by A.
      Clifton"), also in A-C(II)
    One of Clifton's very finest compositions.
The Wilderness Sylph. Divertissement for the Piano Forte
  (Corri)
    Mitchell, n.d., 9p.
    NNLc(Microfilm°ZB-119), PP(U)
    Interesting classic-style work in three sections:
      1. **Andante Grazioso;** 2. **Intermezzo;** 3. **Marcia**
      Promenade

CLOUGH-LEITER, HENRY (1874-1956)

Pensive Melody
    In AC

COERNE, LOUIS ADOLPHE (1870-1922)

Canzonetta, Op.17, No.1
    Miles, 1894, 3p.
    DLC(M25.C)
Creative Art (Four Sketches), **Op.74**
    Summy, 1915, 11p.
    CtNLC(11C651C868), DLC(M25.C), MBH(P1C65), NNLc(°MYD),
      NRU-E(M25C672c)
    1. **Illusion;** 2. **Disillusion;** 3. **Vision;** 4. **Fulfilment**

Five Flower Impromptus, Op.115
    Schirmer, 1918, 5v.(5,3,3,3,3p.)
    MoS(786.4), NRU-E(U, 1 only)
    1. Silver Thistle; 2. Amaranth; 3. Magnolia;
    4. Violet; 5. Peony
Four-Leaved Clovers, Op.144, No.4
    Summy, 1920, 5p.
    DLC(M25.C)
Scherzo d'Amore, Op.99, No.1
    Boston, 1917, 9p.
    DLC(M25.C)
    A difficult and artfully conceived composition.
Drei Stücke für Klavier, Op.54
    Siegel, 1901, 11p.
    DLC(M25.C)
    1. Frühling im Walde; 2. Sehnsucht; 3. In Gedanken

COLE, ROSSETTER GLEASON (1866-1952)

Three Compositions, Op.3
    Schmidt, 1895, 3v.(3,3,5p.)
    DLC(M25.C), ICN(VM22C68p)
    1. Preludium; 2. Intermezzo; 3. Meditation
Intermezzo, Op.3, No.2 (see Three Compositions, Op.3)
Legend (A Concert Piece), **Op.31**
    Schirmer, 1916, 11p.
    DLC(M25.C), ICN(sVM25C68L), MoS(786.4), NNLc(°MYD),
    WM(786.4C68)
Meditation, Op.3, No.3 (see Three Compositions, Op.3)
Novelette, Op.1, No.1 (see Two Novelettes, Op.1)
Novelette, Op.1, No.2 (see Two Novelettes, Op.1)
Two Novelettes, Op.1
    Summy, 1894, 2v.(7,5p.)
    DLC(M25.C), ICN(VM22C68p)
    Obviously inspired by the music of Mendelssohn.
Preludium, Op.3, No.1 (see Three Compositions, Op.3)

COMBS, GILBERT RAYNOLDS (1863-1934)

Autumn, Op.29
    Combs, 1910, 5p.
    DLC(M25.C)
Chanson d'Amour, Op.27
    Combs, 1910, 5p.
    DLC(M25.C), PP(U)
Clotho, Op.15
    Combs, 1908, 5p.
    DLC(M25.C)
Nocturne, Op.6
    Church, 1906, 5p.
    DLC(M25.C)

CONRATH, LOUIS (1868-1927)

Air de Ballet
    Shattinger, 1936, 7p. (revised edition)
    DLC(M25.C), MoSW(U)
Barcarolle
    Kunkel, 1895, 9p.
    DLC(M25.C)
La Cascade (Impromptu)
    Kunkel, 1905, 9p.
    DLC(M25.C), MoSW(U)
Mazeppa (Caprice de Concert)
    Kunkel, 1893, 8p.
    DLC(M25.C), MoSW(U)
Nocturne (At Eve)
    Kunkel, 1891, 7p.
    DLC(M25.C), MoSW(U)
Papillons
    Kunkel, 1906, 11p.
    DLC(M25.C)

CONVERSE, FREDERICK SHEPHERD (1871-1940)

Three Easy Piano Pieces
    Fourwinds, 1937, 3v.(6,5,5p.)
    CtY(M25C766E1+), LNT(M25.C66E2), MB-N(M3.3C66E2), ViU
      (Music MT247.C75F6)
    1. **Air de Ballet**; 2. **Folk Song**: 3. **Minuet**
"From the Hills" (Pastels for Pianoforte)
    Birchard, 1925, 36p.
    DLC(M25.C), MB-N(M3.3C66F8), NRU-E(M25C766f)
    1. **Campfires**; 2. **Lake Solitude**; 3. **Shadows**;
      4. **The Dancers**
Prelude
    New England, 1936, 8p.
    CtY(M25C766P9), DLC(M25.C), ICN(8A 2545), IU(MO 27618),
      LNT(M25.C66P6), MB-N(ArchivesMT4B7N39 1936 C66), NNLc
      (°MYD+), NRU-E(M25C766P9), PP(M86.4C769p), ViU(Music
      M25C55 1936)
Scarecrow Sketches
    Ditson, 1924, 32p.
    DLC(M1527.C27S4), MB-N(M3.3C66S32), MoS(786.4), NNLc(°MSP),
      OCl(M776.49.235), PPi(qM786.4C76)
    1. **The Awakening of Scarecrow**; 2. **Witch Dance**;
      3. **Elégie**; 4. **Old Nick**; 5. **Tragedy**; 6. **Romance**
    Six excerpts from the Photo-Music-Drama "Puritan Passions."
      Based on Percy Mackaye's stage play "The Scarecrow."
Sonata for Piano
    New England, 1937, 28p.
    DLC(M23.C76.S6), IU(MO 27619), LNT(M23.C66no.1), MB-N(M3.3
      C66S666no.1), NNLc(°MYD+), ViU(Music M23C645no.1)
    Large-scale work in three movements.

Suite, Op.2
Schirmer, 1899, 27p.
DLC(M24.C744op2), ICN(VM24C76s), MBH(P1C768), MB-N(M3.3
C66op2), MoS(786.4)
1. Prelude; 2. Scherzando; 3. Quasi Fantasia;
4. Finale

COOKE, JAMES FRANCIS (1875-1960)

Black Swans at Fontainebleau (from Palaces in France)
Presser, 1934, 5p.
CtY(Mc11A1C772), NRU-E(M25C772p), PP(U)
Italian Lakes (Suite for the Pianoforte)
Presser, 1928, 37p.
CtY(Mc11A1C772), DLC(M24.C75I52), NRU-E(U, 1,5 only),
PP(U, 786.4C775i), PPi(qM786.4C77i)
1. Beautiful Isle; 2. Shadows on Lake Como;
3. Jasmine and Nightingales; 4. An Old Palace;
5. Fire Dance
Sea Gardens
Presser, 1925, 5p.
DLC(M25.C), RPB(U)

CORRI, ANTHONY PHILIP [see ARTHUR CLIFTON]

COVERLEY, ROBERT (1863-1944)

Ten Ballads
White-S, 1898, 31p.
DLC(M25.C), NcU(M25.C68B3), OCl(M776.4 2595)
Impromptu
White-S, 1897, 7p.
DLC(M25.C), NRU-E(U)
Impromptu No.2
Schmidt, 1902, 7p.
DLC(M25.C)

CROSS, MICHAEL HURLEY (1833-1897)

Fantaisie sur un Air Tyrolien
Fiot, 1849, 8p.
NcD(RBR Music old W.C.L. M780.88A512PA)
An appealing, unusual type of composition.
Nocturne
Lee, 1872, 7p.
DLC(M25.C), PP(U)
Rêverie
Boner, 1870, 7p.
DLC(M25.C)

DE KOVEN, REGINALD (1859-1920)

Andante classique, Op.93
   Millet, 1894, 6p.
   DLC(M25.D), also in HH-K(I:57)
Barcarolle, Op.371, No.3 (see Four Pieces for Piano, Op.371)
Three Compositions for Piano, Op.379
   Church, 1916, 3v.(5,7,7p.)
   DLC(M25.D), IU(qM786.41D369c), MoS(786.4), NNLc(°MYD)
   1. Monotone; 2. Romance; 3. Humoreske
Etude, Op.371, No.4 (see Four Pieces for Piano, Op.371)
Humoreske, Op.379, No.3 (see Three Compositions for Piano,
   Op.379)
In Minor Mode (Ten Preludes for the Piano), Op.165
   Church, 1901, 33p.
   CU(M25D47op165 1901), DLC(M25.D), NcU(M786.4D328i)
Magnolia Blossoms (Waltzes)
   Schirmer, 1893, 11p.
   CtY(U)
Moment Musical, Op.371, No.1 (see Four Pieces for Piano,
   Op.371)
Monotone, Op.379, No.1 (see Three Compositions for Piano,
   Op.379)
Nocturne, Op.371, No.2 (see Four Pieces for Piano, Op.371)
Four Pieces for Piano, Op.371
   Church, 1915, 4v.(7,9,7,9p.)
   DLC(M25.D), IU(qM786.41D369p), NNLc(°MYD+box, 1,2,4 only)
   1. Moment Musical; 2. Nocturne; 3. Barcarolle;
      4. Etude
Romance, Op.379, No.2 (see Three Compositions for Piano,
   Op.379)

DENNEE, CHARLES (1863-1946)

Album Leaf, Op.10, No.3 (see Trois Morceaux, Op.10)
Concert Etude, Op.40
   Schmidt, 1916, 11p.
   CtY(U), MB-N(U)
Danse orientale, Op.8, No.3 (see Suite moderne, Op.8)
Esprit du Soir (Serenade), Op.35
   Schmidt, 1910, 7p.
   NRU-E(U)
4 Etudes in Form of Pieces for the Pianoforte, Op.42
   Schmidt, 1924, 4v.(9,7,7,9p.)
   DLC(M25.D), MB-N(M3.3D46op42)
   1. Impromptu-Toccata; 2. Octave Waltz;
      3. Waltz-Etude; 4. Scherzo-Caprice
5 Etudes for the Cultivation of Style, Op.26
   Schmidt, 1896, 23p., also issued separately
   CtY(Mc11A1D418), DLC(M215.D, 2 only), ICN(VMT241D39f),
      MB-N(U)
   Excellent works for both study and performance.

       1. Toccata; 2. Le Papillon; 3. Impromptu;
          4. Caprice; 5. Tarantelle
Finale, Op.8, No.5 (see Suite moderne, Op.8)
Gavotte, Op.10, No.2 (see Trois Morceaux, Op.10)
Impromptu-Toccata, Op.42, No.1 (see Four Etudes, Op.42)
Trois Morceaux, Op.10
     Schmidt, 1885, 3v.(5,5,5p.)
     DLC(M25.D), NRU-E(U, 3 only), NcU(M786.4D398m)
     1. Serenade; 2. Gavotte; 3. Album Leaf
Novelette, Op.8, No.2 (see Suite moderne, Op.8)
Octave Waltz, Op.42, No.3 (see Four Etudes, Op.42)
Polonaise in A Flat, Op.39, No.2
     Schmidt, 1913, 7p.
     DLC(M25.D)
Prélude, Op.8, No.1 (see Suite moderne, Op.8)
Printemps en Foret (Impromptu), Op.34
     Schmidt, 1909, 11p.
     DLC(M25.D)
Romanza, Op.8, No.4 (see Suite moderne, Op.8)
Scherzo-Caprice, Op.42, No.4 (see Four Etudes, Op.42)
Serenade, Op.10, No.1 (see Trois Morceaux, Op.10)
Suite moderne, Op.8
     Schmidt, 1885, 5v.(7,5,5,3,6p.)
     DLC(M24.D32op8), MoSW(U, 1 only), NcU(M786.48D398s)
     1. Prélude; 2. Novelette; 3. Danse orientale;
          4. Romanza; 5. Finale (Etude caractéristique)
Waltz-Etude, Op.42, No.3 (see 4 Etudes, Op.42)

DEWEY, FERDINAND (1853-1900)

Forest Voices
     Stevens, 1891, 11p.
     DLC(M25.D)
The Night has a Thousand Eyes (Nocturne No.2)
     Stevens, 1888, 7p.
     DLC(M25.D)
     Both a song and a piano piece. Words by Bourdillon.
Undine (Nocturne in G Flat)
     Russell, 1883, Presser, 1903, 5p.
     DLC(M25.D), MoSW(U), WM(786.4D51)

DOENHOFF, ALBERT VON (1880-1940)

Arabesque
     Schirmer, 1914, 7p.
     DLC(M25.D)
Etude No.1 (see Three Modern Piano Etudes)
Etude No.2 (see Three Modern Piano Etudes)
Etude No.3 (see Three Modern Piano Etudes)
Three Modern Piano Etudes for the Virtuoso
     Schirmer, 1915, 3v.(7,7,9p.)

DLC(MT241.D63), IU(Joseffy), NNLc(°MYDbox)
Very difficult, superb studies.

DRESEL, OTTO (1826-1890)

"Autumn Song" (see Six Two-Part Songs)
"Greeting" (see Six Two-Part Songs)
"I Would that my Love" (see Six Two-Part Songs)
Vier Klavierstücke, Op.5
    Breitkopf, Ditson, 188_?, 11p.
    DLC(M25.D)
    1. Schlummerlied; 2. Praeludium; 3. Phantasiestück;
       4. Scherzino
"The Maybells and the Flowers" (see Six Two-Part Songs)
"O wert Thou in the cold Blast" (see Six Two-Part Songs)
"The Passage Bird's Farewell" (see Six Two-Part Songs)
Six Two-Part Songs composed by Mendelssohn (Arranged for the
  Piano)
    Richardson, 1854, 6v.(5,3,5,5,3,5p.)
    RPB(U)
    1. "I would that my Love"; 2. "The Passage Bird's
       Farewell"; 3. "Greeting"; 4. "Autumn Song";
       5. "O wert Thou in the cold Blast"; 6. "The Maybells
       and the Flowers"
An unusual idea successfully achieved.

DULCKEN, FERDINAND (1837-1901)

12 Concert Studies (Paraphrases) on Themes from the Works of
  Felix Mendelssohn-Bartholdy, Op.175
    Schmidt, 1887, 2v.(23,23p.)
    DLC(MT241.D88), IU(Joseffy, II only), NNLc(°MYD)
    Twelve excellent, difficult studies.
Etude en double Notes, Op.117
    Schuberth-E, 1877, 7p.
    IU(Joseffy)
Humoresque
    Schuberth-E, 1878, 9p.
    DLC(M25.D)
    Based on the theme "Over the fence is out."
Impromptu-Caprice
    Schuberth-E, 1882, 7p.
    DLC(M25.D)
Minuetto serioso
    Schuberth-E, 1876, 6p.
    MdBP(U)
Near the Brook (Thème varié)
    Schuberth-E, 1876, 12p.
    DLC(M27.D)
La Nuit de Mai (Idylle-Etude), Op.108
    Ditson-CH, 1877, 9p.

  DLC(M25.D)
Pizzicati-Variante (from Léo. Delibes' ballet "Sylvia"),
  Op.152
  Prochàzka, 1884, 11p.
  IU(Joseffy)
  A superb transcription, but very difficult.
Spring-Study, Op.184
  Church, 1892, 5p.
  IU(Joseffy)

DVORSKY, MICHEL [see **JOSEF HOFMANN**]

EICHHEIM, HENRY (1870-1942)

  Oriental Impressions
  Curwen, 1928, 29p.
  DLC(M25.E), ICN(sVM22E3350), NRU-E(M25E34o)
  1. **Japanese Sketch**; 2. **Japanese Nocturne**; 3. **Korean
  Sketch**; 4. **Nocturnal Impressions of Peking**; 5. **Chinese
  Sketch**
  Also exists in an orchestral version.

EMERY, STEPHEN ALBERT (1841-1891)

  Crystal Spring (Tremolo)
  RussellT, 1860, 6p.
  DeWHi(U)
  Good study in repeated notes.
  "Dream of Home" (Arranged as a Fantasie), **Op.7**
  Firth-T, 1866, 13p.
  RPB(U)
  Based on a song by Giorgio Stigelli.
  Impromptu, Op.18, No.5
  Russell, 1868, 5p.
  RPB(U)
  Menuet, Op.17, No.2 (see **Deux Morceaux brillants, Op.17**)
  Deux Morceaux brillants, Op.17
  Schmidt, 1868, 2v.(5,5p.)
  CtY(Mc11A1Em36, 1 only), DLC(M25.E, 1 only), RPB(U,
  2 only)
  1. **Polonaise**; 2. **Menuet**
  Polonaise, Op.17, No.1 (see **Deux Morceaux brillants, Op.17**)
  Erste Sonatella, Op.9
  Tolman, 1866, 9p.
  DLC(M23.E53op9), NcU(MF786.41E53s1)
  Zweite Sonatella, Op.11
  Tolman, 1867, 13p.
  DLC(M23.E53op11), NcU(MF786.41E53s2
  Sonatina, Op.29, No.1 (see **Two Sonatinas, Op.29**)
  Sonatina, Op.29, No.2 (see **Two Sonatinas, Op.29**)

Two Sonatinas, Op.29
 Schmidt, 1872, 2v.(11,9p.)
 RPB(U)
Up and Away (Scherzo), Op.34
 Schmidt, 1877, 9p.
 DLC(M25.E), NcU(MF786.4E53u)

EPSTEIN, ABRAHAM ISAAC (1858-1929)

 Melodie d'Amour (Rêverie)
  Kunkel, 1909, 9p.
  DLC(M25.E)
 Sunbeams on the Water
  Kunkel, 1888, 8p.
  DLC(M25.E)

EPSTEIN, MARCUS ISAAC (1855-1947)

 Polka-Caprice
  Kunkel, 1875, 13p.
  DLC(M25.E)
 Polonaise (Morceau de Concert), Op.33
  Kunkel, 1904, 11p.
  DLC(M25.E), MoSW(U)

FAIRCHILD, BLAIR (1877-1933)

 A Bel-Ebat (Trois Pièces pour Piano)
  Durand, 1925, 23p.
  DLC(M25.F), NRU-E(M25F16a), RPB(U)
  1. L'Aube à Bel-Ebat (Dawn at Bel-Ebat); 2. Mîdi sous
   les Ormes (Noon under the Elms); 3. Etincelles dans
   la Nuit (Starlight)
  Very impressionistic, very attractive, very difficult.
 Cinq Chants nègres (Five Negro Songs)
  Durand, 1927, 10p.
  DLC(M25.F), NNLc(°MYD+box)
 Coins de Jardin (Esquisses pour Piano), Op.18
  Durdilly, 1910, 2v.(3,4p.)
  CU(M25F22op18), DLC(M25.F)
  1. Lilacs; 2. Gardénias
 Curios (At the Antiquary Shop)
  Schott, 1926, 28p.
  DLC(M25.F), NNLc(°MYD)
  1. Le Médaillon avec une Mèche blonde (The Locket with
   the blond Lock of Hair); 2. Rayons de Soleil sur un
   vieux Lustre de Venise (Sunbeams on an old Venetian
   Candlestick); 3. Une petite Miniature (A little
   Miniature); 4. Petits Souliers de brocatelle (Little
   brocade Slippers); 5. Le Billet-doux trouvé dans le

Tiroir secret (The Love Letter found in the secret Drawer); 6. **L'Eventail** (The Fan); 7. **La vieille Harpe** (The old Harp); 8. **Paysage sur un vieux Saxe** (Landscape on an old Dresden Porcelain); 9. **Le vieux Saint en Bois sculpté** (The old Saint sculpted in Wood); 10. **Réflections du vieux Chat de L'Antiquaire** (Reflections of the Shopkeeper's old Cat)

En Voyage
    Durand, 1923, 56p.
    CU(M24F22E5), DLC(M25.F), MB-N(M3.3F15E6), MoS(786.4),
    MoSW(U)
    1. **Le Bateau** (The Boat); 2. **En Mer** (On the Ocean);
    3. **Le Train** (The Train); 4. **Soir d'Eté aux Environs de Chicago** (Summer Evening near Chicago); 5. **Près d'un Lac dans le Wisconsin** (Near a Lake in Wisconsin); 6. **Dans les Bois à Pointe-au-Pic** (In the Woods at Pointe-au-Pic); 7. **Paysage d'Eté au Canada** (Summer Landscape in Canada); 8. **Toccata**

Eté à Fontainebleau (Summer at Fontainebleau. Impressions)
    Schott, 1925, 30p.
    DLC(M25.F), NNLc(°MYD)
    1. **Moustiques** (Mosquitos); 2. **La petite Porte du Parc raconte une Histoire indiscrète** (The Park's side Entrance tells an indiscreet Story); 3. **Le jeune Satyre danse au Claire de Lune** (The young Satyr dances in the Moonlight); 4. **Berceuse des petits Crapauds** (Cradle song of the little Toads); 5. **A Minuit dans L'Allée du Roi** (Midnight on the King's Path); 6. **Par un Sentier mystérieux** (By a mysterious Path); 7. **Nénuphars sur un Lac oublié** (Water-lilies on a forgotten Lake); 8. **Reflets de Soleil sur une vieille Statue** (Reflections of the Sun on an old Statue); 9. **Les premiers Papillons jaunes** (The first yellow Butterflies)

From a Balcony
    Schott, 1927, 4v.(11,6,3,7p.)
    DLC(M25.F), NNLc(°MYD)
    1. **Wind in the Cypresses**; 2. **The Harbour at Dusk**;
    3. **The unseen Singer**; 4. **The Village Fair**

Gardénias, Op.18, No.2 (see **Coins de Jardin, Op.18**)
The Harbour at Dusk (see **From a Balcony**)
Lilacs, Op.18, No.1 (see **Coins de Jardin, Op.18**)
Romanesque (see **IV Romanesques**)
IIe Romanesque (see **IV Romanesques**)
IIIe Romanesque (see **IV Romanesques**)
IVe Romanesque (see **IV Romanesques**)
IV Romanesques
    Durand, 1928-29, 4v.(12,13,11,12p.)
    DLC(M25.F), NNLc(°°MYD+box, I only)
Some Indian Songs and Dances
    Schott, 1926, 14p.
    OC(784.751fF16)
    Twelve very short, stylized settings.
The Unseen Singer (see **From a Balcony**)

The Village Fair (see **From a Balcony**)
Wind in the Cypresses (see **From a Balcony**)

FAIRLAMB, JAMES REMINGTON (1838-1908)

Impromptu, Op.27
    Pond, 1865, 11p.
    DLC(M25.F), NNLc(°MYD+box)
Mazurka de Salon, Op.21
    Fries, 1864, 7p.
    DLC(M25.F)

FALK, LOUIS (1848-1925)

General Grant Polka
    Higgins, 1865, 5p.
    IU(q784.3Sh37,v.1,no.1)
Sonate (C moll), **Op.7**
    Falk, 1867, 17p.
    DLC(M23.F2op7)
    Serious, four-movement work.

FARWELL, ARTHUR (1872-1952)

American Indian Melodies, Op.11
    Wa-Wan, 1901, 27p.; Schirmer, 1914, 29p.
    CU(M1669F37), ICN(sVM22F24), IU(qM786.413F25a), MoS
    (786.48), NNLc(°MH Wa-Wan), NRU-E(M1669F247am),
    NcD(M786.41F247A), OCl(M770.9731.337), WM(786.4
    F24A), also in FA-H, WW-L(III:21)
    1. **Approach of the Thunder God;** 2. **The Old Man's
    Love Song;** 3. **Song of the Deathless Voice;**
    4. **Ichibuzzhi;** 5. **The Mother's Vow;** 6. **Inke-
    tunga's Thunder Song;** 7. **Song of the Ghost Dance;**
    8. **Song to the Spirit;** 9. **Song of the Leader**
    The collection is prefaced by a superb introductory essay.
Dawn, Op.12 (A Fantasy for Piano on Two Indian Themes)
    Wa-Wan, 1902, 7p.
    CtY(RareM2W111+v.1,no.4b), DLC(M25.F), ICN(VM1W11,v.1),
    LNT(786F25da), MBH(P1F257), MoS(786.4), NNLc(°MN
    Wa-Wan), NRU-E(M25F247da), RPB(U), WM(786.4F24DA),
    also in BC-G, WW-L(III:84)
The Domain of Hurakon, Op.15
    Wa-Wan, 1902, 17p.
    DLC(M25.F), ICN(sVM25F24d), IU(Joseffy), LNT(786F25d),
    NNLc(°MN Wa-Wan), NRU-E(M25F247do), PP(M786.4F25), WM
    (786.4F24D), also in WW-L(III:177)
    Based on three Indian melodies.
Flame-Voiced Night, Op.45, No.2
    Fischer, 1923, 17p.

DLC(M25.F), MoS(786.4), MoSW(U)
From Mesa and Plain (Indian, Cowboy and Negro Sketches),
   Op.20
   Wa-Wan, 1905, 5v.(5,5,2,1,5p.), also 10p.
   DLC(M1669F, 1 only; M25.F, 3 only), ICN(VM1W11,v.4), LNT
      (786F25n, 1 only; 786F25pa, 2 only; 786F25pra, 3 only),
      MoS(786.4,), NRU-E(M30F247pa, 1 only; M25F247pa, 2
      only; M25F247pr, 3 only), WM(786.4F24N, 1 only), also in
      WW-L(IV:57)
   1. **Navajo War Dance**; 2. **Pawnee Horses** (After an Omaha
      song); 3. **Prairie Miniature** (on cowboy themes); 4. **Wa-Wan
      Choral**; 5. **Plantation Melody**
Ichibuzzhi, Op.13
   Wa-Wan, 1902, 6p.
   CtY(RareM2W111+v.1,no.6), ICN(VM1W11,v.1), LNT(786F25ic),
      MBH(P1F257), NNLc(°MN Wa-Wan), NRU-E(M25F247i), PP(U,
      M786.4F25112), also in WW-L(III:117)
   Based on the Indian melody Farwell also harmonized in
      Op.11.
Impressions of the Wa-Wan Ceremony of the Omahas, Op.21
   Wa-Wan, 1906, 19p.
   DLC(M25.F), ICN(VM1W11,v.5), LNT(786F25i), MoS(786.4),
      NNLc(°MN Wa-Wan), NcD(M786.41F247I), PP(U), also in
      NC-G, WW-L(II:241)
   1. **Receiving the Messenger**; 2. **Nearing the Village**;
      3. **Song of the Approach**; 4. **Laying down the Pipes**;
      5. **Raising the Pipes**; 6. **Invocation**; 7. **Song of
      Peace**; 8. **Choral**
Navajo War Dance, Op.20, No.1 (see **From Mesa and Plain, Op.20**)
Navajo War Dance No.2, Op.29 (ed. John Kirkpatrick)
   Music, 1947, 8p.
   CtY(M31F247N3+no.2), DLC(M31.F), IU(qM786.41F25n2), LNT
      (786F25n2), NNLc(°MYD), NRU-E(M30F247N.2), NcU(M786.4
      F247n), RPB(U)
Owasco Memories, Op.8
   Wa-Wan, 1907, 13p.
   CtY(H Mc10,v.4), DLC(M24.F254op8), ICN(VM1W11,v.6), LNT
      (786F25o), MoS(786.4), NNLc(°MN Wa-Wan), NRU-E(M24
      F247o), also in WW-L(IV:167)
   1. **Spring Moods**; 2. **By Moonlight**; 3. **By Quiet Waters**;
      4. **Waltz**; 5. **Autumn comes**
   A miniature suite, complete with coda.
Pawnee Horses (see **From Mesa and Plain, Op.20**)
Plantation Melody (see **From Mesa and Plain, Op.20**)
Plantation Plaint, Op.78, No.2
   Schirmer, 1944, 5p.
   CtY(U), DLC(M25.F), IU(MO 41152), LNT(786F25pl), NRU-E
      (M25F247pl)
   An attractive blend of spiritual and blues.
Prairie Miniature (see **From Mesa and Plain, Op.20**)
Sourwood Mountain, Op.78, No.3
   In FPP
Symbolistic Study No.1, Op.16 (see **Toward the Dream, Op.16**)

Tone Pictures, after Pastels in Prose, Op.7
     The composer, 1895, 42p.
     DLC(M25.F), MB-N(Piano), NNLc(JNF 74-117), NRU-E(M25F247t)
     1. Roses and Lilies (Theodore de Banville); 2. The
        Sages' Dance (Judith Gautier); 3. The Stranger
        (Charles Baudelaire); 4. Indifference to the Lures
        of Spring (Gautier); 5. The Red Flower (Gautier);
        6. Anywhere out of the World (Baudelaire); 7. Eve-
        ning on the Water (Louis Bertrand); 8. A Poet gazes
        on the Moon (Gautier); 9. The Round Under the Bell
        (Bertrand)
     Original, intriguing musical interpretations of poetry.
Toward the Dream, Op.16 (Symbolistic Study No.1)
     Wa-Wan, 1904, 8p.
     ICN(VM1W11,v.3), LNT(786F25Sym), MoS(786.4), NNLc(°MN
        Wa-Wan), NRU-E(M25F247s.1), WM(786.4F24T), also in
        WW-L(I:175)
Treasured Deeps, Op.45, No.1
     Fischer, 1923, 7p.
     MoS(786.4)
Vale of Enitharmon, Op.91
     The composer, 1935, 11p.
     DLC(M25.F), NNLc(JNG 74-432)
Wa-Wan Choral (see **From Mesa and Plain, Op.20**)

FERRATA, GIUSEPPE (1865-1928)

Album Leaves, Op.11
     Fischer-J, 1903, 4v.(5,7,5,5p.)
     DLC(M25.F), LNT(786F41a), MoSW(U, 1,2 only), OCl(SM
        776.45, 2 only)
     1. Gavotte; 2. Menuet; 3. Le Sourire de Pierrette (Polka);
        4. Tarantelle
     Skillfully achieved, eminently pianistic miniatures.
At Sobieski's Court (see **Three Poetic Dance Impressions, Op.34**)
Brunette dansante, Op.30, No.1 (see **Trio of Original
     Dances, Op.30**)
Four Compositions for the Pianoforte, Op.13
     Fischer-J, 1903, 4v.(3,5,5,5p.)
     DLC(M31.F, 4 only), LNT(786F41m, 1,2,3 only; 786F41pe,
        4 only), MoSW(U, 3,4 only), NRU-E(U, 3 only), RPB(U,
        3 only)
     1. Melodie; 2. Menuetto; 3. Intermezzo; 4. Petit Trianon
        Gavotte
Four Compositions for the Pianoforte, Op.14
     Fischer-J, 1903, 4v.(5,5,5,7p.)
     DLC(M25.F), LNT(786F41se), MoS(786.4), MoSW(U, 1 only)
     1. Serenade triste; 2. Momento grazioso; 3. Petite Valse;
        4. Gavotte
Elfin Revel, Op.34, No.3 (see **Three Poetic Dance Impres-
     sions, Op.34**)
Gavotte, Op.11, No.1 (see **Album Leaves, Op.11**)

Gavotte, Op.14, No.4 (see Four Compositions, Op.14)
Gavotte, Op.30, No.3 (see Trio of Original Dances, Op.30)
Intermezzo, Op.13, No.3 (see Four Compositions, Op.13)
Love Song, Op.7, No.4
    Fischer-J, 1905, 3p.
    DLC(M39.F), LNT(786F41L), MoSW(U)
    A most impressive bit of romanticism.
Mazurian Round, Op.34, No.2 (see Three Poetic Dance Impres-
    sions, Op.34)
Melodie, Op.4, No.1 (see Piano Compositions, Op.4)
Melodie, Op.13, No.1 (see Four Compositions, Op.13)
Menuet, Op.11, No.2 (see Album Leaves, Op.11)
Menuetto, Op.13, No.2 (see Four Compositions, Op.13)
Minuet, Op.30, No.2 (see Trio of Original Dances, Op.30)
Minuet, Op.4, No.2 (see Piano Compositions, Op.4)
Momento grazioso, Op.14, no.2 (see Four Compositions,
    Op.14)
A Night on the Island of Amalasunta (Nocturne), Op.9, No.2b
    Fischer-J, 1914, 7p.
    DLC(M25.F), MoS(786.4), MoSW(U), NNLc(°MYDbox), PP(U)
    Transcribed for piano by Richard Lange.
Petite Fleur, Op.24, No.1
    Schirmer, 1910, 7p.
    LNT(786F41c), MoSW(U), PP(U)
Petite Valse, Op.14, No.3 (see Four Compositions, Op.14)
Petit Trianon Gavotte, Op.13, No.4 (see Four Compositions,
    Op.13)
Piano Compositions by Chevalier Giuseppe Ferrata, Op.4
    Church, 1901, 4v.(5,5,5,5p.)
    DLC(M25.F, 1,3,4 only), LNT(786F41p), MoS(786.4, 4 only)
    1. Melodie; 2. Minuetto; 3. Romance; 4. Sull' Organetto
Three Poetic Dance Impressions, Op.34
    Hinds, 1915, 3v.(5,7,8p.)
    DLC(M30.F), LNT(786F41d), PP(U, 1,2 only)
    1. At Sobieski's Court; 2. Mazurian Round; 3. Elfin
    Revel
Polonaise, Op.32
    Hinds, 1914, 12p.
    LNT(786F41po), MoS(786.4)
    Serious, impressive, difficult composition.
Romance, Op.4, No.3 (see Piano Compositions, Op.4)
Romance sans Paroles, Op.25, No.1
    Schirmer, 1910, 7p.
    LNT(786F41c)
Serenade triste, Op.14, No.1 (see Four Compositions, Op.14)
Serenata romanesca
    Bryant, 1918, 5p.
    DLC(M25.F), LNT(786.F41ser)
Le Sourire de Pierrette, Op.11, No.3 (see Album Leaves, Op.11)
Two Studies on Chopin's Valse, Op.64
    Fischer-J, 1902, 13p.
    CtY(Mc11A1F413), LNT(786F41po)
    Very imaginative and very difficult.

Sull' Organetto, Op.4, No.4 (see Piano Compositions, Op.4)
Tarantella, Op.11, No.4 (see Album Leaves, Op.11)
Toccata chromatique
    ArtPS, 1913, 18p.
    CtY(Mc11A1F413), LNT(786F41po), PP(U), WM(786.4F37)
    Large-scale, difficult concert work.
Four Tone Pictures, Op.33
    Hinds, 1914, 4v.(5,3,5,10p.)
    DLC(M25.F), LNT(786F41t), MoS(786.4), PP(U, 1,2,3 only)
Trio of Original Dances, Op.30
    Hinds, 1914, 3v.(5,3,5p.)
    DLC(M30.F), LNT(786F41tr), MoS(786.4)
    1. Brunette dansante; 2. Minuet; 3. Gavotte
Valse de Concert, Op.25, No.2
    Schirmer, 1910, 12p.
    LNT(786F41c)

FIQUE, CARL (1867-1930)

Album Leaf
    Chandler, 1910, 5p.
    DLC(M25.F), IU(Joseffy)
Elegy, Op.6, No.1 (see Elegy and Scherzo, Op.6)
Elegy and Scherzo, Op.6
    Schuberth-E, 1891, 2v.(5,9p.)
    DLC(M25.F)
    1. Elegy; 2. Scherzo
Humoresque, Op.4, No.2
    Church, 1890, 5p.
    DLC(M25.F)
Impromptu, Op.4, No.4
    Church, 1890, 7p.
    DLC(M25.F)
The Mill-Brook (Summer Sketches No.3)
    Schuberth-E, 1890, 5p.
    CtY(Mc11A1F514)
Old Castle Ruin (Summer Sketches No.4)
    Schuberth-E, 1890, 5p.
    CtY(Mc11A1F514)
Scherzo, Op.6, No.2 (see Elegy and Scherzo, Op.6)
Sérénade bohème, Op.25, No.1
    Schuberth-E, 1895, 6p.
    CtY(Mc11A1F514), DLC(M25.F)
Variations on a Theme from J.S. Bach's "Christmas Oratorio,"
  Op.7
    Schuberth-E, 1891, 9p.
    DLC(M27.F)
    Imaginative and effective variations on "Prepare thyself,
     Zion."

FLORIO, CARYL [see WILLIAM J. ROBJOHN]

FOERSTER, ADOLPH MARTIN (1854-1927)

Andante, Op.3
    Root, 1875, 7p.
    DLC(M25.F), NcU(MF786.4F654a)
    Attractive composition à la Schubert.
Two Concert Etudes, Op.37
    Summy, 1893, 2v.(7,5p.)
    DLC(M25.F), NNLc(°MYD+box)
    1. **Exultation**; 2. **Lamentation**
Eros (Melody), **Op.27, No.1**
    Presser, 1890, 7p.
    DLC(M25.F), NNLc(°MYD+box)
Exultation, Op.37, No.1 (see **Two Concert Etudes, Op.37**)
Homage to Mozart, Op.84, No.2
    Presser, 1919, 3p.
    DLC(M25.F), NNLc(°MYD+box)
Lamentation, Op.37, No.2 (see **Two Concert Etudes, Op.37**)
On the Sea
    Millet, 1894, 4p.
    DLC(M25.F), also in HH-K(II:421)
Sonnet, Op.13
    Pond, 1884, 5p.
    DLC(M25.F), IU(Joseffy), NcU(MF786.4F654s)
Suite in F Major, Op.46
    Kleber, 1898, 15p.
    DLC(M24.F), NNLc(°MYD+box), PP(U)
    1. **Prelude**; 2. **Waltz**; 3. **Intermezzo**; 4. **Finale** (Homage
      to Brahms)

FOOTE, ARTHUR WILLIAM (1853-1937)

Five Bagatelles, Op.34
    Schmidt, 1898, 5v.(5,5,5,7,5p.)
    CU(M25F6, 3 only; M22F66, 4 only), DLC(M25.F), MBH
      (P1F738, 3,4,5 only), MoS(786, 1,2,4 only), MoSW(U, 2
      only), NNLc(Music-Am[Sheet]75-698, 1 only; 75-697, 3 only;
      75-244, 4 only), NRU-E(M25F688Pie, 1 only; M25F688Pi,
      2 only; MT225F688wi, 3 only), PP(U, 3 only), RPB(U,
      1 only), also in HH-K(1,2 only)
    1. **Pierrot**; 2. **Pierrette**; 3. **Without Haste, With-
    out Rest** (Etude mignonne); 4. **Idyl**; 5. **Valse peu
    dansante**
Capriccio, Op.15, No.3 (see **Suite in D Minor, Op.15**)
Caprice, Op.27, No.5 (see **Nine Etudes, Op.27**)
Caprice, Op.27, No.9 (see **Nine Etudes, Op.27**)
Dusk, Op.73, No.2 (see **Five Silhouettes, Op.73**)
Eclogue, Op.8, No.2
    Schmidt, 1886, 5p.
    DLC(M25.F), MBH(°MC F738,v.1), MoS(786.4), NRU-E(M25F688e)
Etude Arabesque, Op.42, No.2
    Schmidt, 1899, 7p.

DLC(M25.F), MoSW(U), NRU-E(M22F68), PP(U)
Nine Etudes for Musical and Technical Development, Op.27
    Schmidt, 1892, 30p., also 9v.
    CU(M22F662op27 1892), MBH(P1F738, 5,9 only), MB-N(M3.3
        F66op27 1892a), MoSW(U), NNLc(°MYD), NRU-E(MT225F688),
        PP(U), ViU(Music MT225.F66op27 1892), WM(786.48F68)
    A useful, interesting and valuable set of studies.
Exaltation, Op.62, No.2
    Schmidt, 1907, 7p.
    DLC(M25.F), MoS(786), NNLc(JNG 74-428), NRU-E(M22F68),
        PP(U), RPB(U), WM(786.4F68e)
La Fileuse, Op.20, No.1 (see **Cinq Morceaux, Op.20**)
Flying Cloud, Op.73, No.4 (see **Five Silhouettes, Op.73**)
Gavotte, Op.3, No.2 (see **Trois Morceaux, Op.3**)
Gavotte in C Minor (No.II), Op.8, No.1
    Schmidt, 1886, 5p.
    MoS(786.4), NRU-E(M31F688g.2)
Idyl, Op.34, No.4 (see **Five Bagatelles, Op.34**)
Impromptu, Op.3, No.1 (see **Trois Morceaux, Op.3**)
An Irish Folk-Song (Transcription)
    Schmidt, 1894, 5p.
    DLC(M25.F), NRU-E(M38.5F688i)
    Attractive keyboard version of Foote's own song.
A Little Etude
    Schmidt, 1901, 3p.
    CtY(U), DLC(M25.F), NRU-E(M25F688et), PP(U)
A May Song, Op.60, No.2
    Schmidt, 1907, 7p.
    CU(M22F66), DLC(M25.F), MoS(786), MoSW(U), NRU-E(M25
        F688m)
Mazurka, Op.3, No.3 (see **Trois Morceaux, Op.3**)
Trois Morceaux, Op.3
    Schmidt, 1882, 3v.(7,5,5p.)
    DLC(M25.F), MBH(°McF738,v.1), MB-N(M3.3F66M67, 1,2 only),
        NRU-E(M25F688i, 1 only; M25F688m, 3 only), WM(786.4F68i,
        1 only)
    1. Impromptu; 2. Gavotte; 3. Mazurka
Nocturne, Op.6, No.2 (see **Cinq Pièces, Op.6**)
Oriental Dance, Op.73, No.5 (see **Five Silhouettes, Op.73**)
Petite Valse, Op.6, No.4 (see **Cinq Pièces, Op.6**)
Cinq Pièces, Op.6
    Schmidt, 1885, 5v.(4,9,3,3,9p.)
    DLC(M25.F), MBH(P1B12), MoS(786.4), NcU(MF786.44F688p.p,
        5 only), NRU-E(M32F688p, 5 only), PP(U, 4 only), RPB
        (U, 4 only)
    1. Prélude; 2. Nocturne; 3. Sarabande; 4. Petite
        Valse (l.h. alone); 5. Polonaise
Pierrette, Op.34, No.2 (see **Five Bagatelles, Op.34**)
Pierrot, Op.34, No.1 (see **Five Bagatelles, Op.34**)
Five Poems after Omar Khayyam, Op.41
    Schmidt, 1899, 25p.
    CU(M24F66op41), DLc(M25.F), IU(q786.41F73p), MBH(P1C65),
        MB-N(M3.3F66op41), NNLc(°MYD+box), NRU-E(M25F688po),

NcU(M786.48F688p), OCl(M776.415.3671), PP(M786.4F731),
RPB(U), ViU(°M25.F66F5op41 1899), WM(786.4F68)
One of Foote's very finest keyboard works.
Polonaise, Op.6, No.5 (see **Cinq Pièces, Op.6**)
Prelude, Op.73, No.1 (see **Five Silhouettes, Op.73**)
Prelude and Fugue, Op.15, Nos.1 and 2 (see **Suite in D Minor,
Op.15**)
Prelude and Nocturne, Op.6, Nos.1 and 2 (see **Cinq Pièces, Op.6**)
**Twenty Preludes for the Pianoforte in the form of Short
Technical Studies, Op.52**
Schmidt, 1903, 27p.
CU(M22F662op52 1903), CtY(M25F688+op52), MB-N(M25F7
op52), NRU-E(MT225F688p), PP(786.4F739p)
Revery, Op.60, No.1
Schmidt, 1907, 5p.
DLC(M25.F), MoS(786), NRU-E(M22F68), PP(U)
Romance, Op.15, No.3 (see **Suite in D Minor, Op.15**)
Sarabande, Op.6, No.3 (see **Cinq Pièces, Op.6**)
Scherzino, Op.42, No.1
Schmidt, 1899, 7p.
DLC(M25.F), NRU-E(M25F688sc), PP(U), WM(786.4F68sc)
Serenade, Op.18, No.1
BrainardS, 1887, 9p.
DLC(M25.F), MBH(°McF738,v.1), MB-N(M3.3F66op18no.1)
Serenade in F, Op.45
Schmidt, 1900, 15p.
DLC(M25.F), MBH(P1C65), MB-N(M25F7op45), NRU-E
(M25F688se), OCl(M776.4.3647), PP(M786.4F7311)
1. Invention; 2. Air; 3. A Dance; 4. Finale
Five Silhouettes, Op.73
Schmidt, 1913, 5v.(5,5,5,5,5p.)
CU(M22F66, 2 only), DLC(M25.F), MBH(°McF738,v.2),
MB-N(M3.3F66op73, 1 only), NRU-E(M25F688d, 2 only;
M32F688v, 3 only), PP(M786.4F73111), RPB(U, 4 only),
WM(786.4F68f, 2,4 only)
1. Prelude; 2. Dusk; 3. Valse triste; 4. Flying Cloud;
5. Oriental Dance
Suite in D Minor, Op.15
Schmidt, 1887, 20p.
DLC(M24.F71op15), IU(qM786.41F73sd), MBH(P1F738), MB-N
(M3.3F66op15), MoS(786.4), MoSW(U), NRU-E(M24F688s),
OCl(M776.415.3672), PP(U), also in NC-G
1. Prelude; 2. Fugue; 3. Romance; 4. Capriccio
Zweite Suite in C Moll, Op.30
Schmidt, 1894, 19p.
CU(M22F66), DLC(M24.F), MBH(P1F738), MB-N(M3.3F66op30),
MoS(786.4), MoSW(U), NRU-E(M24F68), also in PM-H(1 only)
1. Appassionato; 2. Romance; 3. Toccata
A superb, very difficult suite.
Toccatina, Op.45, No.4
Schmidt, 1900, 1907, 5p.
DLC(M25.F), NRU-E(M25F688t), PP(U)
Appears in the last movt. of **Serenade, Op.45** (rev.1914).

Valse peu dansante, Op.34, No.5 (see Five Bagatelles, Op.34)
Valse triste, Op.73, No.3 (see Five Silhouettes, Op.73)
Without Haste, Without Rest, Op.34, No.3 (see Five Bagatelles,
  Op.34)

FOSTER, STEPHEN COLLINS (1826-1864)

Holiday Schottisch
    FirthP, 1853, 5p.
    ICN(VM3F751H73), NNLc(AM2-I), also in BC-G, FHR
Santa Anna's Retreat from Buena Vista
    PetersWC, 1843, 5p.
    CU(M3F6CaseB°°), PP(U), also in FHR
Soirée Polka
    PetersWC, 1850, 2p.
    CU(M3F6CaseB°°), ICN(VM3F751S68), PP(U), also in AB-D, FHR
The Tioga Waltz
    n.p., n.d., 2p.
    CU(M3F6CaseB°°), DLC(M3.3.F7T76Case), NNLc(AM2-I), also
      in FHR
    Originally "composed and arranged for four flutes, by
      Stephen C. Foster, at the age of thirteen years. Per-
      formed at the College Commencement, Athens, Pa., 1839,
      by himself and three other students."
The Village Bells Polka
    Benteen, 1850, 5p.
    NNLc(°MYDbox), PP(U), ScCC(SMB23.22), NNLc(AM2-I), also
      in FHR

FRADEL, CHARLES (1821-1886)

Le Carousel (Rondo Burlesque)
    Balmer, 1861, 7p.
    DLC(M25.F), MiU-C(U)
Faust Quadrille (from Gounod's opera)
    HallS, 1864, 7p.
    NNLc(°MN, AM2-I), RPB(U)
    Genuine musical fun.
Première Grande Polonaise, Op.230
    HallS, 1860, 7p.
    IU(Joseffy), NNLc(AM2-I), NRU-E(U)
    A first-rate pianistic work in the grand manner.
Grand Valse sur "Le Pardon de Plöermel" (No.2 of Reflets
  harmonieux)
    Hidley, 1860, 7p.
    MiU-C(U), ViU(°M1.S444,v.12,no.22)
    Rather straightforward potpourri of airs from Meyberbeer's
      opera (also called Dinorah).
La mia Letizia (Cavatine variée), Op.173
    Breusing, 1869, 7p.
    CtHT(U)

The Cavatina is from Act II of Verdi's **I Lombardi alla Prima Crociata.** An interesting composition for those who know the opera.
Scherzino
Schirmer, 1876, 9p.
RPB(U)
Sonatine, Op.505, No.1
Grand, 1884, 5p.
DLC(M23.F799op505), NcU(M786.41F799s505.1)
Part of the "Course of Classics" of the Grand Conservatory of Music.
Sonatine (Serio-comic), **Op.511, No.1** (see **Six Sonatines, Op.511**)
Sonatine (Lieder), **Op.511, No.2** (see **Six Sonatines, Op.511**)
Sonatine (La Chasse), **Op.511, No.3** (see **Six Sonatines, Op.511**)
Sonatine (Au Bal. Semi-Burlesque), **Op.511, No.4** (see **Six Sonatines, Op.511**)
Sonatine (Adagio simplice), **Op.511, No.5** (see **Six Sonatines, Op.511**)
Sonatine (Eroica), **Op.511, No.6** (see **Six Sonatines, Op.511**)
Six Sonatines, Op.511
Grand, 1887, 6v.(7,6,7,7,5,7p.)
DLC(M23.F799op511), MiU-C(U, 2 only), NcU(M786.41F799s511), ViU(°M1.S444,v.106,no.11, 2 only)
Rather easy, brief but effective sonatinas.

FREER, ELEANOR EVEREST (1864-1942)

Lyric Studies, Op.3
Kaun, 1904, 27p.
DLC(MT225.F85), IU(Joseffy)
Nine very attractive works of varying difficulty.
Modern Dances, Op.31
Kaun, 1926, 12p.
DLC(M25.F), NRU-E(M1508F856Cd)
Four conservative dance pieces.
Scherzetto, Op.41, No.1
MusicL, 1935, 3p.
DLC(M25.F)

FRIML, RUDOLPH (1879-1972)

Aubade, Op.25
Schirmer, 1907, 7p.
MoSW(U), NRU-E(M22F91)
Impressive work in a lyrically romantic vein.
Bohemian Dance (Polka), **Op.29**
Schirmer, 1907, 5p.
MB-N(Piano), MoSW(U), NRU-E(M22F91), OCl(SM776.45)
Good example of an authentically ethnic Polka.

Concert Waltz, Op.12
　　Schirmer, 1905, 13p.
　　CtHT(U), DLC(M32.F), InU(M1.S8), MB-N(Piano), MoSw(U),
　　　　NRU-E(M22F91), PP(U), RPB(U), WM(786.4F91)
Crépuscule (Twilight)**, Op.36, No.2** (in 3 **Morceaux,**
　Op.36)
　　Schmidt, 1908, 5p.
　　CtY(Mc11A1F916), DLC(M25.F), NRU-E(U), OCl(SM776.4),
　　　　PP(U), RPB(U)
Drifting, Op.67
　　Schirmer, 1912, 11p.
　　CtY(Mc11A1F916), DLC(M25.F), MoSW(U), NNLc(°MYD), NRU-E
　　　　(M22F91), OCl(SM776.4), PP(U), RPB(U), WM(786.4F91d)
Etude in F, Op.44
　　Schirmer, 1908, 5p.
　　MB-N(Piano), NRU-E(U)
Etude fantastique, Op.61
　　Schmidt, 1910, 7p.
　　RPB(U)
Grand Concert Mazurka, Op.40
　　Schirmer, 1908, 9p.
　　MoS(786.44), OC(786.4fF91g)
Herald of Spring, Op.76
　　Schmidt, 1912, 11p.
　　CtY(Mc11A1F916), DLC(M25.F), PP(U)
　　Good study for crossing of hands.
Po-Ling and Ming-Toy: A Chinese Suite
　　Boston, 1924, 29p.
　　CtY(Mc11A1F916), MoS(786.4)
Réveil du Printemps, Op.32
　　Schmidt, 1907, 7p.
　　OCl(SM776.4), RPB(U)
Russian Romance, Op.30
　　Schirmer, 1907, 3p.
　　CtY(Mc11A1F916), NCU-E(M22F91), OCl(SM776.4), PP(U),
　　　　WM(786.4F91ru)
The Spirit of the Woods (Improvisation)
　　Schirmer, 1905, 11p.
　　DLC(M25.F), ViU(U:2)
Staccato Caprice, Op.39
　　Schirmer, 1908, 7p.
　　DLC(M25.F), NRU-E(U), PP(U), RPB(U)
　　Excellent, challenging etude.
Staccato Etude, Op.37
　　Schirmer, 1908, 5p.
　　DLC(M25.F), OCl(SM776.47), RPB(U)
Valse poétique, Op.13
　　Schirmer, 1905, 9p.
　　DLC(M32.F), OCl(SM776.45), PP(U), RPB(U)
Waltz, Op.60, No.5 (from Bohemian Suite, Op.60)
　　Schirmer, 1910, 7p.
　　CtY(Mc11A1F916), DLC(M24.F91op60), OCl(M776.415.3752)
　　　　WM(786.4F91bo)

GALLICO, PAOLO (1868-1955)

Chanson intime, Op.15, No.3
    Harms, 1910, 5p.
    DLC(M25.G)
Concert Paraphrase über Künstler Leben (Walzer von Johann
  Strauss)
    Cranz, 1909, 15p.
    DLC(M25.G)
    Impressive but difficult keyboard paraphrase.
Gavotte and Musette
    Schirmer, 1898, 5p.
    DLC(M31.G), MoSw(U), PP(U)
Mazurka-Caprice
    Schirmer, 1898, 9p.
    MoS(786.4), PP(U)
Suite mignonne
    Schirmer, 1900, 11p.
    DLC(M24.G), MoS(786.4)
    1. **Menuet**; 2. **Sarabande**; 3. **Bourrée**
Valse de Salon
    Schirmer, 1900, 11p.
    DLC(M32.G), IU(Joseffy), MoSW(U)

GANZ, RUDOLPH (1877-1972)

Adagietto, Op.29, No.1 (see **Two Concert Pieces, Op.29**)
After Midnight, Op.27, No.1 (from **Four Compositions, Op.27**)
    Fischer, 1919, 15p.
    CtY(Mc11A1G159op27no1), MoS(786.4), NRU-E(M25G211a),
      RPB(U), WM(786.4G211a)
    Difficult concert piece. An elegant witches' dance.
Bauerntanz, Op.24, No.3 (see **Vier Klavierstücke, Op.24**)
Cadenzas to the first and second movements of Haydn's
  Concerto in D Major
    Schirmer, 1945, 53p.(pp.23-25, 33-35)
    CU(M1011H38H.18:11 1945)
Cadenzas to the first and third movements of Beethoven's
  Piano Concerto in C Major, Op.15
    ComposerMC, 1921, 15p.
    ICRo(ML96.4G25box1), MoS(786.4), NNLc(°MYD Cadenzas)
3 Compositions pour Piano, Op.10
    Schmidt, 1909, 3v.(7,7,7p.)
    CtY(Mc11A1G159op10), DLC(M25.G), MoS(786.4), NRU-E
      (M25G211f, 3 only)
    1. **Marche fantastique**; 2. **Mélodie en sol**; 3. **Fileuse**
      pensive
Two Concert Pieces, Op.29
    ComposerMC, 1920-1922, 2v.(10,8p.)
    DLC(M25.G), MoS(786.4), NNLc(°MYD+box), WM(786.4G211s,
      2 only)
    1. **Adagietto**; 2. **Scherzino**

Etude-Caprice, Op.14, No.4 (see Vier Klavierstücke, Op.14)
Felsenweg, Op.24, No.4 (see Vier Klavierstücke, Op.24)
Fileuse pensive, Op.10, No.3 (see 3 Compositions, Op.10)
Heldengrab, Op.23, No.1 (see Vier Klavierstücke, Op.23)
Im Mai, Op.23, No.3 (see Vier Klavierstücke, Op.23)
Intermezzo, Op.23, No.2 (see Vier Klavierstücke, Op.23)
Vier Klavierstücke, Op.14
    Ries, 1911, 4v.(6,9,7,11p.)
    CtY(Mc11A1G159op14, 1,3,4 only), DLC(M25.G), MoS(786.4)
    1. Wellenspiel; 2. Menuett; 3. Melodie; 4. Etude-
    Caprice
Vier Klavierstücke, Op.23
    Ries. 1912. 4v.(5,7,7,10p.)
    CtY(Mc11A1G159op23, 1,4 only), DLC(M25.G), ICRo(ML96.4
    G25box1), MoSw(U, 3 only)
    1. Heldengrab; 2. Intermezzo; 3. Im Mai; 4. Tanz
Vier Klavierstücke, Op.24
    Rozsavölgyi, 1912, 4v.(5,5,5,5p.)
    DLC(M25.G), MoS(786.4), MoSW(U, 3 only)
    1. Sarabande; 2. Sérénade; 3. Bauerntanz; 4. Felsenweg
Marche fantastique, Op.10, No.1 (see 3 Compositions, Op.10)
Melodie, Op.14, No.3 (see Vier Klavierstücke, Op.14)
Mélodie en sol, Op.10, No.2 (see 3 Compositions, Op.10)
Menuett, Op.14, No.2 (see Vier Klavierstücke, Op.14)
Sarabande, Op.24, No.1 (see Vier Klavierstücke, Op.24)
Scherzino, Op.29, No.2 (see Two Concert Pieces, Op.29)
Sérénade, Op.24, No.2 (see Vier Klavierstücke, Op.24)
Symphonic Variations on a Theme by Brahms, Op.21
    ComposerMC, 1921, 49p.
    CU(M27G36op21), DLC(M27.G), ICRo(M27G35op21), IU(MO 41366),
    MoS(786.4), NNLc('MYD), WM(786.4G211)
    Huge concert work based on Brahms' song "Der Schmied."
Tanz, Op.23, No.4 (see Vier Klavierstücke, Op.23)
Wellenspiel, Op.14, No.1 (see Vier Klavierstücke, Op.14)

GEBHARD, HEINRICH (1878-1963)

Five Compositions for the Piano
    Boston, 1912, 5v.(7,11,9,15,9p.)
    CtY(U, 1,2,5 only), DLC(M25.G), MoSw(U, 1,2,3,4 only),
    NcU(MF786.45G283g, 5 only), PP(U, 1,3,5 only), RPB
    (U, 5 only), WM(786.48G29 4 only)
    1. Intermezzo; 2. Etude mélodique; 3. Impromptu;
    4. Etude-Cascades; 5. Gavotte
    Highly interesting collection rhythmically, harmonically
    and technically.
Three Concert Pieces for the Pianoforte
    Schirmer-EC, 1928, 3v.(11,9,15p.)
    DLC(M25.G), MBH(P1G26.1), MB-N(Piano)
    1. Voices of the Valley; 2. Moon Children; 3. Surf Riders
    Three imaginative, very difficult pieces.
Etude-Cascades (see Five Compositions)

Etude mélodique (see Five Compositions)
Gavotte (see Five Compositions)
Impromptu (see Five Compositions)
Intermezzo (see Five Compositions)
Love Poem
    Bach, 1918, 5p.
    DLC(Hopekirk Coll.,box 8)
Moon Children (see Three Concert Pieces)
Romance élégiaque (No.2 of Trois Morceaux)
    Boston, 1915, 7p.
    DLC(Hopekirk Coll.,box 8)
Surf Riders (see Three Concert Pieces)
Voices of the Valley (see Three Concert Pieces)

GEIBEL, ADAM (1855-1933)

Autumn Leaflet (Polka-Impromptu)
    Shaw, 1882, 7p.
    RPB(U)
Gavotte Allemande
    Meyer-L, 1876, 5p.
    CtY(Mc11A1G275), RPB(U)
In the Rose Garden
    Ditson, 1902, 7p.
    NRU-E(U)
Nocturne in E Flat
    Presser, 1909, 7p.
    MoS(786.4)
The Storm at Sea (Descriptive Fantasy)
    Shaw, 1884, 11p.
    DLC(M25.G), MoSW(U), NRU-E(U), RPB(U)
    The "ultimate" storm piece!

GILBERT, HENRY FRANKLIN BELKNAP (1868-1928)

The Island of the Fay (after Poe)
    Wa-Wan, 1904, 12p.
    CU(M25G5217CaseX), ICN(VM1.W11,v.3), NNLc(°MN Wa-Wan),
      NRU-E(M25G464i), NcU(M786.43G464i), WM(786.4G46i),
      also in WW-L(I:207)
    The composer quotes a long passage from Poe's short story
      of the same title.
Mazurka and Scherzo (in Three Pianoforte Compositions)
    Wa-Wan, 1902, 13p.
    NNLc(°MN Wa-Wan), NRU-E(M32G464Ma), NcU(MF786.44G464m)
      ViU(U:3), also in WW-L(III:143)
Negro Dances
    Gray-HW, 1914, 24p.
    IU(MO 41150), MBH(P1G37), MB-N(U), NNLc(°MYD-Amer),
      NRU-E(M30G474ne)
    Five diverse, attractive dances.

Negro Episode, Op.2, No.2 (from **Three Pianoforte Compositions**)
Wa-Wan, 1902, 3p.
CtY(RareM2W111+v.1,no.6), ICN(sVM25G46n), MoS(786.4),
NNLc(°MN Wa-Wan), NRU-E(M25G464t.2), NcU(M786.4G464n)
WM(786.4G46n), also in WW-L(III:114)
A Rag Bag (Six American Pieces), **Op.19**
Presser, 1927, 18p.
DLC(M25.G), NNLc(°MYD), NRU-E(M25G464r), PP(U), PPi
(qM25.G54R3x)
An impressive collection in a contemporary idiom.
Scherzo (from **Three Pianoforte Compositions**)
Wa-Wan, 1902, 7p.
NRU-E(M25G464sc), ViU(U:3), also in WW-L(III:148)
Usually coupled with the **Mazurka.**
Two Verlaine Moods
Wa-Wan, 1903, 11p.
NNLc(°MN Wa-Wan), NRU-E(M25G464ve), WM(786.4G46t),
also in WW-L(I:88)
Essays in musical impressionism.

GILFERT, CHARLES (ca.1787-1829)

"Ah! What is the Bosom's Commotion," with Six Variations
Appel, 1813, 9p.; Geib, 1821, 8p. [W.II:465]
CtY(Mc11A1G394), DLC(M1.A1GCase), also in A-C(I)
Variations on an attractive song by Michael Kelly.
The Favorite Serenading Waltz
Siegling, ca.1819-1825, 2p. [W.I:311]
ICN(Case8A 1860), RPB(U) ScCC(SMB12.22), ViU(McR.74.06)
Actually two tiny waltzes.
Miss Lettine's Favorite Dance
Siegling, 1823, 4p. [W.I:308]
ScCC(SMB12.21)
Nina, with Six Variations
Gilfert, ca.1813, 7p. [W.I:308]
DLC(M1.A1G), ICN(Case8A2458), NcD(RBR MusicB.85,no.25),
ScCC(SMS130-154)
"Wilt Thou Say Farewell Love" (A Favorite Canzonet by Thomas
Moore) **with Six Variations**
Gilfert, n.d., 8p.
PP(U [Moore])

GLEASON, FREDERICK GRANT (1848-1903)

Barcarola, Op.2
ChandlerFS, 1875, 7p.
ICN(sVM25G544b)
Incorrect opus number. Should be Op.3.
Canzonetta, Op.19, No.1
In HH-K(VI:1461)
Transcription from **Three Pieces for Orchestra, Op.19.**

Four Compositions, Op.8
    Chicago, 1879, 4v. in 3(3,3,3p.)
    ICN(sVM25G544c)
    1. **Hunting Song;** 2. **Romanze;** 3. **Hunting Song;** 4. **Allegro**
    Interesting pieces for young pianists.

GODOWSKY, LEOPOLD (1870–1938)

Arabesque, Op.16, No.2
    Schmidt, 1899, 11p.
    DLC(M25.G), IU(Joseffy), NRU-E(U)
Barcarolle-Valse, Op.16, No.4
    Schmidt, 1899, 15p.
    DLC(M25.G), IU(Joseffy), NNLc(°MYD), NRU-E(U)
Cadenza to W. A. Mozart's Concerto in A Major (K.488)
    Fischer, 1927, 11p.
    CU(M1010.5M686K488G6), NNLc(°MYD)
Capriccio, Op.15, No.3
    Schmidt, 1899, 9p.
    DLC(M25.G), IU(Joseffy)
Capriccio (Patetico)
    Schirmer, 1931, 7p.
    DLC(M25.G), NNLc(°MYD), PP(M25G589c)
    There is also a version for left hand alone.
Concert Study, Op.11, No.1 (from **Three Concert Studies, Op.11**)
    Schirmer, 1899, 9p.
    DLC(M25.G), MoS(786.4) NNLc(°MYD)
    Subtitled "grottesco."
Concert Study, Op.11, No.3 (from **Three Concert Studies, Op.11**)
    Schirmer, 1899, 9p.
    DLC(M25.G), IU(Joseffy)
Le Cygne (Camille Saint-Saens. Concert Transcription)
    Fischer, 1927, 9p.
    PP(U [Saint-Saens])
Ein Dämmerungsbild, Op.14, No.1
    Schirmer, 1899, 7p.
    DLC(M25.G), IU(Joseffy)
Etude macabre
    Schirmer, 1930, 9p.
    DLC(M25.G), NNLc(°MYDbox), NRU-E(M25G587e)
    There is also a version for left hand alone.
Fledermaus (Johann Strauss. Concert Paraphrase)
    Cranz, 1912, 16p.
    DLC(M34.S), NNLc(°°MYD), NcU(M786.4G589f)
    Extremely difficult, but immensely successful.
Frédéric Chopin. Etude, Op.10, No.1 (Arranged for the Left Hand)
    Schirmer, 1899, 7p.
    DLC(M26.G), NNLc(°MYD+box)
    Actually for two hands, with Chopin's parts reversed.

Frédéric Chopin. Etude, Op.25, No.6 (Arranged for the left
  Hand)
    Kleber, 1894, 7p.
    CU(fMT226C5), MoS(786.47), NNLc(°MYD)
    Actually for two hands, with Chopin's parts reversed.
Humoresque
    Fischer, 1918, 9p.
    DLC(M25.G)
Java Suite
    Fischer, 1925, 12 pieces in 4 v.
    DLC(M24.G586P4), PP(U, v.III only)
    For the mature pianist. Unique sound re-creation.
Mélodie méditative, Op.15, No.1
    Schmidt, 1899, 3p.
    DLC(M25.G), IU(Joseffy)
Paraphrase de Concert. Chopin Valse, Op.18
    Schmidt, 1899, 11p.
    IU(Joseffy), NRU-E(U)
    Highly imaginative (and difficult) concept.
Passacaglia (variations, cadenza, and fugue)
    Fischer, 1928, 42p.
    DLC(M25.G), NNLc(°MYD+), NRU-E(M27G589p), OC(M6.4qG58p)
    "Based upon the first eight measures of Schubert's
      Unfinished Symphony." A very grand, very difficult
      concert work.
Scherzino, Op.14, No.4
    Schirmer, 1899, 10p.
    IU(Joseffy)
Sonate in E Moll
    Schlesinger, 1911, 58p.
    DLC(M23.G59), MoSW(U), NNLc(°MYD), PP(M786.41G54),
      ViU(Music M23.G63 1911)
    Five extended movements. The finale includes a fugue
      on BACH.
Toccata (Perpetual Motion), **Op.13**
    Schmidt, 1899, 11p.
    CU(M25G645), DLC(M25.G), MoS(786.4), NRU-E(U)
    An extremely difficult virtuoso composition.
Triakontameron (Thirty Moods and Scenes in Triple Measure)
    Schirmer, 1920, 6v.
    CU(M22G62T7, 4,5 only), DLC(M25.G), LNT(786G543t), MoS
      (786.4 2,5 only), MoS(U, 1,3 only) NNLc(°MYD), OCl
      (M776.4.4253), PP(U, 1,2,3,4,6 only), WM(786.4G48tr,
      2,3,4 only), also in FPP(1 only)
Valse-Idylle, Op.14, No.3
    Schirmer, 1899, 7p.
    IU(Joseffy)
Walzermasken (24 Tonfantasien im Dreivierteltakt für Klavier)
    Schlesinger, 1912, 4v.(85p.)
    CU(M32G64W3), CtY(Mc11A1G547), DLC(M32.G), ICN(VM24G58w),
      NNLc(°MNp.v.21), NRU-E(M32G589w), PP(U, v.3 only),
      WM(786.4G58wa v.1 only)
    Exhaustive exploration of triple meter.

GOETSCHIUS, PERCY (1853-1943)

Two Mazurkas, Op.19
      Schirmer, 1908, 2v.(5,5p.)
      DLC(M32.G), MoSW(U)
      1. Mazurka in A Minor; 2. Mazurka in A Major
Revery, Op.14
      Schirmer, 1908, 7p.
      DLC(M25.G)
Sonata in B, Op.15
      Schirmer, 1908, 43p.
      DLC(M23.G6op15), MBH(P1F257), NNLc(°MYD)
      Large-scale work in three movements.

GOLDBECK, ROBERT (1839-1908)

Abendglocken
      Kunkel, 1879, 7p.
      ViU(McR.165.30)
Aquarelles, Op.18b
      Schuberth, 1857, 12v.(7,9,7,7,5,3,7,7,8,7,7,7p.)
      DLC(M25.G)
Ashes of Roses (Valse élégante)
      Kunkel, 1880, 7p.
      CtY(U), DLC(M32.G)
Auld Lang Syne (Grand Morceau de Concert)
      RootC, 1867, 11p.
      ICN(sVM27G61a), RPB(U), ViU(°M1.S444,v.168,no.7)
Caprice caractéristique, Op.51
      Schuberth-J, 1864, 11p.
      DLC(M25.G)
Caprice de Concert (d'après une Polka de Schulhoff)
      RootC, 1867, 11p.
      DLC(M25.G)
La Complainte, Op.33
      Schirmer, 1882, 7p.
      CtY(U)
Cradle Song
      Schirmer, 1879, 5p.
      DLC(M25.G), IU(Joseffy), MoSW(U)
Désir de Retour
      Schirmer, 1879, 7p.
      DLC(M25.G), MoSW(U)
Dreaming by the Brook
      Kunkel, 1881, 11p.
      CtHT(U), DLC(M25.G), IU(Joseffy), MoSW(U)
Dreams of Home Sweet Home (Concert Paraphrase)
      Kunkel, 1879, 13p.
      DLC(M25.G)
Faust (Caprice)
      The composer, 1864, 25p.
      DLC(M25.G), RPB(U)

Fleur de Bal (Redowa)
    FirthP, 1858, 7p.
    CtHT(U)
La Melodia d'Amore (Romanza)
    Kunkel, 1879, 9p.
    DLC(M25.G), IU(Joseffy), MoSW(U)
Mélodie et Canon (Amitié à St. Louis)
    Schirmer, 1879, 7p.
    DLC(M25.G), PP(U)
Minerva (Grande Polonaise de Concert)
    Schirmer, 1879, 17p.
    DLC(M30.G), IU(Joseffy), MoSW(U), PP(U)
Nocturne-Romance
    Ditson-CH, 1886, 7p.
    CtHT(U)
Petite Etude
    Schirmer, 1879, 3p.
    DLC(M25.G), IU(Joseffy)
Reverie Nocturne
    Kunkel, 1909, 7p.
    DLC(M25.G), MoSW(U)
Rosenasche (see **Ashes of Roses**)
Traumgewebe (Dream Visions)
    BrainardS, 1870, 9p.
    DLC(M25.G)
Il Trovatore (Fantaisie dramatique), **Op.23**
    Ditson, n.d., 13p.
    RPB(U)
Weeping Rock (Souvenir)
    Schirmer, 1879, 5p.
    DLC(M25.G), IU(Joseffy), PP(U)

GOLDMARK, RUBIN (1872-1936)

Deepening Shadows, Op.7, No.6 (see **Twilight Fantasies, Op.7**)
The First Anemone (see **Prairie Idylls**)
Forest Solitude, Op.7, No.4 (see **Twilight Fantasies, Op.7**)
From the Old Mission (see **Prairie Idylls**)
In the Forest, Op.12
    Ditson, 1908, 4v.(7,3,5,7p.)
    DLC(M25.G), IU(Joseffy), NRU-E(M21R29A,v.1, 2,3 only),
       PP(U, 1 only), RPB(U, 1,4 only)
    1. Titania's Waltz; 2. Weeping Willows; 3. In the Rushes;
       4. Soughing Pines
In Prairie-Dog Town (see **Prairie Idylls**)
In the Rushes, Op.12, No.3 (see **In the Forest, Op.12**)
The Meadow Lark (see **Prairie Idylls**)
Prairie Idylls (A Suite of Four Pieces)
    Schirmer, 1915, 4v.(5,7,3,7p.)
    DLC(M24.G62I5), MoS(786.4), MoSW(U), RPB(U, 2,3 only)
    1. The First Anemone; 2. The Meadow Lark; 3. From the
       Old Mission; 4. In Prairie-Dog Town (Humoreske)

Restless, Ceaseless, Op.7, No.3 (see Twilight Fantasies, Op.7)
Sorrowful Thought, Op.7, No.2 (see Twilight Fantasies, Op.7)
Soughing Pines, Op.12, No.4 (see In the Forest, Op.12)
Titania's Waltz, Op.12, No.1 (see In the Forest, Op.12)
Twilight, Op.7, No.1 (see Twilight Fantasies, Op.7)
Twilight Fantasies, Op.7
    Ditson, 1904, 6v.(5,3,7,5,5,3p.)
    DLC(M25.G), IU(Joseffy), OCl(SM776.4, 6 only), PP(U,
    3 only), RPB(U, 4 only)
    1. Twilight; 2. Sorrowful Thought; 3. Restless,
    Ceaseless; 4. Forest Solitude; 5. Yearning;
    6. Deepening Shadows
Weeping Willows, Op.12, No.2 (see In the Forest, Op.12)
Yearning, Op.7, No.5 (see Twilight Fantasies, Op.7)

GOTTSCHALK, LOUIS MOREAU [SEVEN OCTAVES] (1829-1869)

Amour chevaleresque (see Love and Chivalry)
Apothéose. Grande Marche Solennelle, Op.29
    Halls, 1858, 25p.
    CtY(Mc11A1G716), LNH(U), NNLc(AM2-I), NRU-E(M22G68,v.1),
    NcU(M786.44G687a), PP(U), also in GP-L(I:9)
Ardennes Mazurka (Souvenir des Ardennes)
    Halls, 1860, 11p.
    CtY(Mc11A1G716), LNH(U), NNLc(AM2-I), NRU-E(M22B68,v.1),
    NcU(M786.44G687so), also in GP-L(I:33)
Sixième Ballade, Op.85
    Schott, n.d., 11p.
    CtY(Mc11A1G716), LNH(U), MoS(786.4), NNLc(AM2-I), NRU-E
    (M22G68,v.1), NcU(M786.43G687b6), also in GP-J,
    GP-L(I:43)
Septième Ballade, Op.87
    Schott, n.d., 11p.
    CtY(Mc11A1G716), LNH(U), NNLc(AM2-I), NRU-E(M22G68,v.1),
    NcU(M786.43G687b7), PP(U), also in GP-L(I:55)
Huitième Ballade, Op.90
    Schott, n.d., 19p.
    CtY(Mc11A1G716), LNH(U), NNLc(AM2-I), NRU-E(M22G68,v.1),
    NcU(M786.43G687b8), PP(U), also in GP-L(I:67)
Deux Ballades, Op.4 (see Ossian, Op.4)
Bamboula (Danse de Nègres), **Op.2**
    Halls, ca.185_?, 17p.
    CU(M31G674op2CaseX), CtHT(U), CtY(Mc11A1G716), ICN
    (Case8A 794), InU(M1.S8) LNH(U), LNT(L976.3[780]Z99),
    MoSW(M25G716B), NNLc(AM2-I), NRU-E(M22G68,v.1), OCl
    (SM776.42), PP(U), ScCC(SMB58.10), ViU(°M1.S444,v.28,
    no.5; McR.34.05), also in GP-B, GP-J, GP-L(I:87)
Le Bananier (Chanson nègre), **Op.5**
    Schott, Halls, n.d., 5p.
    CtHT(U), CtY(Mc11A1G716), DLC(M25.G), ICN(Case8A 1098),
    IU(Joseffy), InU(M1.S8), LNH(U), LNT(L976.3[780]Z99),
    NNLc(AM2-I), NRU-E(M22G68,v.2), PP(U), RPB(U), ViU

(°M1.S444,v.28,no.6), WM(786.4G68ba), also in GP-B, GP-J,
GP-L(I:103)
The Banjo (An American Sketch), **Op.15**
HallS, 1855, 15p.
CU(M25G674op15CaseX), CtHT(U), CtY(Mc11A1G716), DLC(M25.G),
ICN(sVM25G687b), IU(Joseffy), InU(M1.S8), LNH(U), LNT
(L976.3[780]Z99), NNLc(AM2-I), NRU-E(M22G68,v.2), PP(U),
ViU(°M1.S444,v.149,no.1; McR.79.44), WM(786.4G68b), also
in GP-B, GP-J, GP-L(I:109), NC-G
Deuxième Banjo
Ditson, 1873, 23p.
DLC(M25.G), LNH(U), also in GP-L(I:123)
Bataille (Etude de Concert), **Op.64**
HallS, Schott, 1870, 19p.
CtY(Mc11A1G716), DLC(M25.G), LNH(U), MoS(786.4), NNLc
(JNG 73-215; AM2-I), NRU-E(M22G68,v.2), NcU(M786.47
G687b), PP(U), also in GP-L(I:145)
Battle Cry of Freedom (Grand Caprice de Concert), **Op.55**
RootC, 1865, 21p.
CtY(Mc11A1G716), DLC(M25.G), InU(M1.S8), NNLc(AM2-I),
NRU-E(M22G68,v.4), also in GP-L(I:159)
Also published as **Le Cri de Délivrance.**
Berceuse, Op.47
HallS, Ditson, 1862, 9p.
CU(M25G674op47CaseX), CtHT(U), CtY(Mc11A1G716), DLC(M25.G),
IU(Joseffy), InU(M1.S8), LNH(U), NBu(U), NNLc(JNG 73-216;
AM2-I), NRU-E(M22G68,v.2), PP(U), RPB(U), ViU(°M1.S444,
v.28,no.7), WM(786.4G68be), also in GP-B, GP-J, GP-L
(I:179), NC-G
La Brise (The Breeze. Valse de Concert)
Cady, 1878, 9p.
NNLc(AM2-I), PP(U), also in GP-L(I:187)
Caprice elégiaque, Op.56
Schott, n.d., 9p.
CtY(Mc11A1G716), LNH(U), NNLc(AM2-I), NRU-E(M22G68,v.3),
NcU(M786.4G687c), also in GP-L(I:197)
Caprice-Polka, Op.79
Ditson, 1873, 14p.
LNH(U), NNLc(AM2-I), NRU-E(M22G68,v.3), NcU(M786.44G687c),
also in GP-L(I:207)
Le Carnaval de Venise (Grand Caprice et Variations), **Op.89**
Schott, n.d., 27p.
CtY(Mc11A1G716), NNLc(AM2-I), NRU-E(M22G68,v.3), NcU
(M786.48G687c), PP(U), also in GP-L(I:221)
Célèbre (Grande) Tarantelle, Op.67
Ditson, Schott, 1874, 27p.; Ricordi, 1960, 20p.
CU(M31G674op67 1960), CtY(Mc11A1G716), LNH(U), NNLc
(AM2-I), PP(U), also in GP-L(III:14)
Also exists as **Grande Tarantelle** for (1) piano duet,
(2) two pianos and (3) piano and orchestra.
Chant de Guerre, Op.78
Ditson, 1873, 15p.
LNH(U), NNLc(AM2-I), NRU-E(M22G68,v.3), NcU(M786.43G687ch.g),

   also in GP-L(I:249)
Le Chant du Martyr, Op.64
   Ditson, 1864, 9p.
   CtY(Mc11A1G716), DLC(M25.G), LNH(U), NNLc(JNG 73-218;
   AM2-I), NRU-E(M22G68,v.3), NcU(M786.43G687ch.m), also
   in GP-L(I:263)
Chant du Soldat (Grand Caprice de Concert), **Op.23**
   HallS, 1857, 21p.
   CU(M25G674op23CaseX), CtY(Mc11A1G716), DLC(M25.G), LNH
   (U), NNLc(AM2-I), NRU-E(M22G68,v.3), NcU(M786.43G687ch.s),
   PP(U), also in GP-L(II:1)
La Chasse du Jeune Henri, Op.10
   Schott, n.d., 19p.
   CtY(Mc11A1G716), LNH(U), NNLc(AM2-I), NRU-E(M22G68,v.3),
   NcU(M786.43G687cha), PP(U), also in GP-L(II:21)
La Chute des Feuilles (Nocturne), **Op.42**
   HallS, 1860, 19p.
   CtY(Mc11A1G716), DLC(M25.G), LNH(U), MoS(786.4), NNLc
   (AM2-I), NRU-E(M22G68,v.3), NcU(M786.43E77c), PP(U),
   also in GP-L(II:41)
El Cocoyé (Grand Caprice cubain de Bravura), **Op.80**
   Ditson, 1873, 27p.
   CtY(Mc11A1G716), DLC(M25.G), LNH(U), NNLc(AM2-I), NRU-E
   (M22G68,v.4), NcU(M786.4G687co), also in GP-L(II:53]
Colliers d'Or (Deux Mazurkas), **Op.6**
   Schott, n.d., 2v.(5,4p.)
   LNH(U), NNLc(AM2-I), NRU-E(M22G68,v.4), NcU(M786.44
   G687co), also in GP-L(II:85)
La Colombe (The Dove. Petite Polka), **Op.49**
   HallS, 1864, 13p.
   LNH(U), NNLc(AM2-I), NRU-E(M22G68,v.4), NcU(M786.44
   G687col), ViU(McR.54.33), also in GP-L(II:93)
Columbia (Caprice américain), **Op.34**
   Pond, 1860, 13p.; Escudier, n.d., 16p.
   CtY(Mc11A1G716), DLC(M25.G), LNH(U), NNLc(AM2-I),
   NRU-E(M22G68,v.4), NcU(M786.4G687col), PP(U),
   also in GP-L(II:105)
Le Cri de Délivrance, Op.55 (see **Battle Cry of Freedom,
Op.55**)
Danse des Sylphes, Op.86
   Schott, n.d., 23p.
   CtY(Mc11A1G716), NNLc(AM2-I), NRU-E(M22G68,v.4), NcU
   (M786.43G687ds), also in GP-L(II:128)
Danse Ossianique, Op.12
   Gould, n.d., 9p.
   CtHT(U), CtY(Mc11A1G716), DLC(M25.G), InU(M1.S8), LNH(U),
   LNT(L976.3[780]Z99), MoS(786.4), NNLc(JNG 73-220; AM2-I),
   NRU-E(M22G68,v.4), NcU(M786.43G687d), PP(U), RPB(U), WM
   (786.4G68d), also in GP-L(II:119)
Danza, Op.33
   Scharfenberg, Pond, ca.1857, 11p.
   LNH(U), NNLc(JNG 73-221; AM2-I), NRU-E(M22G68,v.4), NcU
   M786.45G687d), also in GP-J, GP-L(II:151)

Dernier Amour (Etude de Concert), **Op.63**
    Schott, Ditson, 1870, 13p.
    DLC(M25.G), IU(Joseffy), LNH(U), LNT(L976.3[780]Z99),
      NNLc(JNG 73-222; AM2-I), NRU-E(M22G68,v.5), NcU
      (M786.47G687d), also in GP-L(II:163)
Dernière Espérance, Op.16 (see **The Last Hope, Op.16**)
The Dying Poet
    Ditson, 1864, 7p.
    CtY(Mc11A1G716), DLC(M25.G), InU(M2.S8), LN(U), LNH(U),
      LNT(L976.3[780]Z99), NNLc(AM2-I), NRU-E(M22G68,v.5),
      NcD(RBR Music 608), NcU(M786.43G687dy), OCl(SM776.4),
      PP(U), RPB(U), ViU(U:2), WM(786.4G68dp), also in GP-J,
      GP-L(II:181)
    Some editions bear Gottschalk's pseudonym "Seven
    Octaves." One of the composer's most famous lyrical
    compositions.
The Dying Swan (Romance poétique), **Op.100**
    Kunkel, 1870, 7p.
    LNT(L976.3[780]Z99), MoS(786.4), NNLc(AM2-I), NRU-E
      (M22G68,v.5), NcU(M786.43G687dys), also in BC-G,
      GP-L(II:189)
L'Etincelle, Op.20 (see **La Scintilla, Op.20**)
Fairy Land (Schottische de Concert)
    Ditson, 1891, 9p.
    NNLc(AM2-I), NRU-E(M22G68,v.5), NcU(M786.45G687f),
      RPB(U), also in GP-L(II:195)
    Composer listed as "Seven Octaves."
Fantôme de Bonheur, Op.36 (see **Illusions perdues, Op.36**)
La Favorita (Donizetti. Grande Fantaisie), **Op.68**
    Ditson, 1871, 23p.
    CtY(Mc11A1G716), NNLc(AM2-I), NRU-E(M22G68,v.5), NcU
      (M786.4G687fa), also in GP-L(II:203)
Les Follets (see **Forest Glade Polka, Op.25**)
Forest Glade Polka, Op.25
    Gould, 1853, Ditson, 1882, 9p.
    InU(M1.S8), LN(U), LNH(U), MoS(786.4), NNLc(JNG 73-223;
      AM2-I), NRU-E(M22G68,v.5), NcU(M786.44G687f), PP(U),
      also in GP-L(II:229)
Forget Me Not (Ne m'oubliez pas. Mazurka Caprice)
    Kunkel, 1870, 9p.
    DLC(M25.G), NNLc(AM2-I), NRU-E(M22G68,v.5), NcU
      (M786.44G687ne), also in GP-L(II:237)
La Gallina (Danse cubaine), **Op.53**
    HallS, 1869, 7p.
    IU(Joseffy), LNT(L976.3[780]Z99), NNLc(AM2-I), NRU-E
      (M22G68,v.5), NcU(M786.45G687g), ViU(°M1.S444,v.139,
      no.6), also in GP-L(II:245)
    A novel, intriguing type of "hen" piece.
La Gitanelle (Caprice caractéristique), **Op.35**
    HallS, Schott, 1860, 7p.
    CU(M25G674op35CaseX), CtY(Mc11A1G716), DLC(M25.G),
      LNH(U), NNLc(AM2-I), NRU-E(M22G68,v.6), NcU(M786.4
      G687g), also in GP-L(II:267)

God Save the Queen (Morceau de Concert), **Op.41**
  HallS, 1860, 11p.
  CtY(Mc11A1G716), DLC(M25.G), LNH(U), NNLc(AM2-I), NRU-E
  (M22G68v.6), NcU(M786.4G687go), PP(U), also in GP-L
  (II:275)
**Grande Fantaisie triomphale sur l'Hymne nationale brésilien,
  Op.69**
  Schott, n.d., 20p.
  LNH(U), NNLc(AM2-I), NRU-E(M22G68,v.5), NcU(M786.42G687g),
  also in GP-L(II:287)
Grande Tarantelle, Op.67 (see **Célèbre Tarantelle, Op.67**)
Grand Scherzo, Op.57
  HallS, 1870, 13p.
  CtY(Mc11A1G716), DLC(M25.G), NNLc(AM2-I), NRU-E(M22G68,
  v.6), NcU(M786.4G687gr), also in GP-J, GP-L(III:1)
The Hen, Op.53 (see **La Gallina, Op.53**)
Hercule (Grande Etude de Concert), **Op.88**
  Schott, n.d., 12p.
  CtY(Mc11A1G716), NNLc(AM2-I), NRU-E(M22G68,v.6), NcU
  (M786.47G687h), PP(U), also in GP-L(III:123)
Home, Sweet Home, Op.51
  HallS, 1864, 11p.; Schirmer, 1907, 9p.
  CtY(Mc11A1G716), DLC(M25.G), LNH(U), MoS(786.4), NNLc
  (AM2-I), NRU-E(M22G68,v.6), NcU(M786.4G687h), PP(U),
  ViU(°M1.S444,v.133,no.2), also in GP-L(III:135)
  One of the better settings of this old favorite.
Hurrah (Galop de Concert)
  Ditson, 1863, 1891, 9p.
  NNLc(AM2-I), NRU-E(M22G68,v.6), RPB(U), ViU(°M1.S444,
  v.106,no.1), also in GP-L(III:145)
  Composer's name listed as "Seven Octaves."
Illusions perdues (Caprice), **Op.36**
  HallS, 1864, 9p.
  CtY(Mc11A1G716), DLC(M25.G), InU(M1.S8), LNH(U), MoS
  (786.4), NNLc(AM2-I), NRU-E(M22G68,v.7), NcU(M786.4
  G687f), OCl(SM776.4), PP(U), also in GP-L(III:175)
  Also titled **Fantôme de Bonheur.**
Impromptu, Op.54
  HallS, 1869, 13p.
  CtY(Mc11A1G716), DLC(M25.G), InU(M1.S8), LNH(U), NNLc
  (AM2-I), NRU-E(M22G68,v.7), NcU(M786.4G687i), also
  in GP-L(III:183)
Jerusalem (Grande Fantaisie triomphale), **Op.13**
  HallS, 1855, 19p.
  CtY(Mc11A1G716), DLC(M25.G), LNH(U), NNLc(AM2-I),
  NRU-E(M22G68,v.7), NcU(M786.42G687j), also in
  GP-L(III:195)
  A paraphrase of Verdi's **I Lombardi.** Also exists
  in a superb version for two pianos.
Jeunesse (Mazurka brillante), **Op.70**
  HallS, 1860, 7p.
  InU(M1.S8), LNH(U), NNLc(AM2-I), NRU-E(M22G68,v.7),
  NcU(M786.44G687j), also in GP-L(III:215)

La Jota aragonesa (Caprice espagnol), **Op.14**
    HallS, 1855, 7p.
    CU(M25G674J6 1855CaseX), CtHT(U), DLC(M25.G), LNH(U),
      LNT(976.3[780]Z99), NNLc(AM2-I), NRU-E(M22G68,v.7),
      NcU(M786.45G687j), PP(U), also in GP-L(III:223)
    "Tiré de la grande symphonie à 10 pianos, **El Sitio
    de Zaragoza**."
The Last Hope (Religious Meditation), **Op.16**
    FirthP, 1854, 9p.; HallS, 1856, 11p.
    CU(M25G674op16CaseX), CtHT(U), CtY(Mc11A1G716), DLC
      (M25.G), InU(M1.S8), IU(M25G68op16H2 Spec.Coll.),
      LN(U), LNH(U), LNT(L976.3[780]Z99), MoS(786.4),
      NNLc(AM2-I), NRU-E(M22G68,v.7), OCl(SM776.8), PP(U),
      RPB(U), ViU(°M1.S444,v.146,no.17; McR.37.21), WM
      (786.4G68LCe), also in GP-B, GP-J, GP-L(III:241)
    Also titled **Dernière Espérance** and **Ultima esperanza**.
    Probably Gottschalk's most famous composition.
Love and Chivalry (Amour chevaleresque. Caprice élégant en
  Forme de Schottische)
    Ditson, 1863, 9p.
    LNT(Civil War, La.Coll.), NNLc(AM2-I), NRU-E(M22G68, v.7),
      NcU(M786.45G687a), RPB(U), ViU(McR.51.15), also in
      GP-L(I:1)
    Some editions give the composer as "Seven Octaves."
The Maiden's Blush (see **Le Sourire d'une jeune Fille**)
Le Mancenillier (La Sérénade), **Op.11**
    HallS, 1857), 7p.
    CU(M25G675S4CaseX), CtHT(U), CtY(Mc11A1G716), DLC(M25.G),
      ICN(sVM25G687rl), InU(M1.S8), LNH(U), LNT(L976.3[780]
      Z99), MoS(786.4), NBu(U), NNLc(AM2-I), NRU-E(M22G68,
      v.8), NcU(M786.43G687m), PP(U), RPB(U), ViU(°M1.S444,
      v.80,no.23), also in GP-J, GP-L(V:261)
    Also published as **La Sérénade**. No.1 in a collection,
    Rayons et Ombres.
Manchega (Etude de Concert), **Op.38**
    HallS, 1860, 13p.
    LNH(U), NNLc(AM2-I), NRU-E(M22G68,v.8), NcU(M786.47G687m),
      also in GP-J, GP-L(III:273)
Marche de Nuit, Op.17
    HallS, 1856, 13p.
    CU(M28G558op17CaseX), CtHT(U), CtY(Mc11A1G716), InU
      (M1.S8), LNH(U), LNT(L976.3[780]Z99), NBu(U), NNLc
      (JNG 73-228; AM2-I), NRU-E(M22G68,v.8), PP(U), RPB(U),
      ViU(°M1.S444,v.28,no.8; McR.55.08), WM(786.4G68mM),
      also in GP-L(III:283)
Marche funèbre, Op.61
    HallS, 1870, 9p.
    CtY(Mc11A1G716), DLC(M25.G), LNH(U), NNLc(AM2-I), NRU-E
      (M22G68,v.8), also in GP-L(IV:1)
Marguerite (Grande Valse brillante)
    Ditson, 1873, 9p.
    NNLc(AM2-I), NRU-E(M22G68,v.8), NcU(M786.45G687m),
      also in GP-L(IV:11)

Mazurka rustique, Op.81
    Ditson, 1873, 9p.
    LNH(U), NNLc(AM2-I), NRU-E(M22G68,v.8), NcU(M786.44
        G687ma), also in GP-L(IV:21)
La Mélancolie (Etude caractéristique d'après Godefroid)
    Schott, n.d., 9p.
    LNH(U), LNT(L976.3[780]Z99), NNLc(AM2-I), NRU-E(M22G68,
        v.8), NcU(M786.47G581m), also in GP-L(IV:29)
Minuit à Seville, Op.30
    Schott, n.d., 11p.; HallS, 1858, 16p.
    LNH(U), NNLc(AM2-I), NRU-E(M22G68,v.8), NcU(M786.43
        G687mi), also in GP-J, GP-L(IV:39)
Miserere du Trovatore (Paraphrase de Concert), **Op.52**
    HallS, 1864, 13p.
    CU(M34G667op52CaseX), CtY(Mc11A1G716), InU(M1.S8), LNH
        (U), LNT(Civil War La.Coll.), NNLc(AM2-I), NRU-E(M22
        G68,v.8), OCl(SM776.49), PP(U), also in GP-L(IV:53)
La Moissoneuse (Mazurka caractéristique), **Op.8**
    Schott, n.d., 9p.
    DLC(M25.G), NNLc(AM2-I), NRU-E(M22G68,v.9), NcU(M786.44
        G687mo), also in GP-L(IV:67)
Morte! (She is dead. Lamentation), **Op.60**
    HallS, 1869, 9p.; Schott, 1870, 7p.
    CU(M25G675M6 1880CaseX), CtHT(U), CtY(Mc11A1G716), DLC
        (M25.G), InU(M1.S8), LNH(U), MoS(786.4), NNLc(JNG 73-
        229; AM2-I), NRU-E(M22G68,v.9), NcU(M786.43G687mo), PP
        (U), RPB(U), ViU(McR.165.33), also in GP-J, GP-L(IV:73)
Murmures éoliens, Op.46
    Schott, 1862, 17p.; HallS, 1862, 19p.
    CU(M25G674op46 1862Case), CtHT(U), CtY(Mc11A1G716), IU
        (Joseffy), LNH(U), MoS(786.4), NNLc(JNN 73-2; AM2-I),
        NRU-E(M22G68,v.9), NcU(M786.4G687m), OCl(SM776.43),
        PP(U),RPB(U), also in GP-L(IV:81)
La Naiade, Op.27 (see **The Water Sprite, Op.27**)
Ne m'oubliez pas (see **Forget Me Not**)
Nuit des Tropiques
    Schott, n.d., 13p.
    LNH(U), NNLc(AM2-I), NRU-E(M22G68,v.9), also in GP-L(IV:99)
    Andante movement from **Symphonie romantique** transcribed
        for piano.
Ojos criollos (Danse cubaine), **Op.37**
    HallS, 1864, 7p.
    CU(M3OG674op37 1864CaseX), CtY(Mc11A1G716), InU(M1.S8),
        LNH(U), LNT(L976.3[780]Z99), NNLc(AM2-I), NRU-E(M22
        G68,v.9), NcU(M786.45G687o), ViU(°M1.S444,v.139,no.5),
        also in GP-J, GP-L(IV:153)
O, Ma Charmante, épargnez-moi (Caprice), **Op.44**
    HallS, 1862, 7p.
    CtY(Mc11A1G716), DLC(M25.G), LNH(U), NNLc(JNG 73-230;
        AM2-I), NRU-E(M22G68,v.8), NcU(M786.4G687o), PP(U),
        also in GP-J, GP-L(IV:113)
Orfa (Grande Polka], **Op.71**
    Ditson, 1864, 1892, 6p.

InU(M1.S8), LNH(U), LNT(L976.3[780]Z99), NNLc(AM2-I),
NRU-E(M22G68,v.9), NcU(M786.44G687o), RPB(U), also
in GP-L(IV:171)
Composer listed as "Seven Octaves."
Ossian (Deux Ballades), **Op.4**
BrainardS, n.d., 7p.; Himan, 187_?, 5p.
CtY(Mc11A1G716), LNH(U), LNT(L976.3[780]Z99), NNLc
(AM2-I), NRU-E(M22G68,v.9), NcU(M786.43G687o),
PP(U), also in GP-L(IV:177)
Pasquinade (Caprice), **Op.59**
HallS, 1870, 11p.; Schott, 1871, 9p.
CU(M25G674op59 1871), CtY(Mc11A1G716), DLC(M25.G), IU
(Joseffy), InU(M1.S8), LN(U), LNH(U), LNT(L976.3
[780]Z99), MoS(786.4), NNLc(AM2-I), NRU-E(M22G68,v.10),
OCL(SM776.42), PP(U), RPB(U), ViU(°M1.S444,v.28,no.9;
McR.158.14), WM(786.4G68pJ), also in GP-B, GP-J,
GP-L(IV:183)
Pastorella e Cavalliere (Caprice), **Op.32**
Ditson, 1860, 13p.; HallS, 1862, 17p.
CU(M25G674op32CaseX), CtHT(U), DLC(M25.G), IU(Joseffy),
InU(M1.S8), LNH(U), NNLc(AM2-I), NRU-E(M22G68,v.10),
NcU(M786.4G687p), PP(U), RPB(U), also in GP-L(IV:193)
Pensée poétique, **Op.62**
HallS, 1870, 7p.
CU(M25G674P4 1870CaseX), DLC(M25.G), MoS(786.4), NNLc
(AM2-I), NRU-E(M22G68,v.10), NcU(M786.43G687p),
PP(U), also in GP-L(IV:209)
Pensive (Polka-Redowa), **Op.68**
Ditson, 1864, 8p.
LNH(U), NNLc(AM2-I), NRU-E(M22G68,v.10), NcU(M786.44
G687p), RPB(U), also in GP-L(IV:217)
Polka de Salon, **Op.1**
Lafont, n.d., 7p.
LNT(L976.3[780]Z99), NNLc(AM2-I), NcU(M786.44G687po),
also in GP-L(IV:223)
Polonia (Grande Caprice de Concert), **Op.35**
HallS, 1861, 23p., 1889, 21p.
LNH(U), NNLc(AM2-I), NRU-E(M22G68,v.10), NcU(M786.4
G687po), also in GP-L(IV:231)
Printemps d'Amour (Mazurka. Caprice de Concert), **Op.40**
HallS, 1860, 15p.
CU(M32G673P7 1860CaseX), CtHT(U), CtY(Mc11A1G716), IU
(Joseffy), InU(M1.S8), LNH(U), NBu(U), NNLc(AM2-I),
NRU-E(M22G68,v.10), NcU(M786.44G687pr), PP(U), WM
(786.4G68pr), also in GP-L(IV:253)
Radieuse (Grande Valse de Concert), **Op.72**
Ditson, 1865, 20p.
LNT(L976.3[780]Z99), NNLc(Am2-I), NRU-E(U), OCL(SM
776.45), ViU(McR.54.32), also in GP-L(IV:267)
Arranged for two hands by Henry Maylath.
Rayons d'Azur (Polka de Salon), **Op.77**
Ditson, 1873, 10p.
LNH(U), NNLc(AM2-I), NRU-E(M22G68,v.20), also in GP-L(V:1)

Reflets du Passé, Op.28
   Ditson, 1858, 11p.
   CtY(Mc11A1G716), DLC(M25.G), LNH(U), NNLc(AM2-I), NRU-E
   (M22G68,v.11), NcU(M786.43G687r), OCl(SM776.4), also in
   GP-L(V:11)
Ricordati (Yearning. Nocturne), **Op.26**
   HallS, 1857, Ditson, 1887, 9p.
   CU(M25G674op26CaseX), CtY(Mc11A1G716), DLC(M25.G), ICN
   (VM1M36), IU(Joseffy), LNH(U), MoS(786.4), NNLc(JNG
   73-232; AM2-I), NRU-E(M22G68,v.11), PP(U), RPB(U),
   ViU(°M1.S444,v.28,no.10), also in GP-B, GP-L(V:43)
   No.2 in the collection **Rayons et Ombres.**
La Savane (Ballade créole), **Op.3**
   Gould, 185_?, 9p.
   CtY(Mc11A1G716), DLC(M25.G), ICN(sVM25G687s), InU
   (M1.S8), LNH(U), MoS(786.4), NNLc(AM2-I), NRU-E
   (M22G68,v.11), NcD(RBR MusicB.147,no.23), NcU(VMF
   786.4G687a), PP(U), also in GP-J, GP-L(V:51)
Scherzo romantique, Op.73
   Ditson, 1873, 14p.
   LNH(U), NNLc(AM2-I), NRU-E(M22G68,v.11), also in GP-L
   (V:61)
La Scintilla (Mazurka sentimentale), **Op.20(21)**
   FirthP, 1854, 9p.
   CtY(Mc11A1G716), ICN(VM1M36), InU(M1.S8), LN(U), LNH
   (U), LNT(L976.3[780]Z99), MoS(786.4), NNLc(JNG 73-233;
   AM2-I), NRU-E(M22G68,v.5), NcU(M786.44G687e), OCl
   (SM776.45), PP(U), ViU(McR.119.01), also in GP-L(V:75)
   Also published as **L'Etincelle** and **The Spark.** The
   opus number varies with the publisher.
La Sérénade, Op.11 (see **Le Mancenillier, Op.11**)
Ses Yeux (Polka de Concert), **Op.66**
   Schott, n.d., 14p.
   NNLc(AM2-I), NRU-E(M22G68,v.11), also in GP-J, GP-L
   (V:83)
   Arranged for two hands by L. Napoleon.
Solitude, Op.65
   HallS, 1871, 9p.
   CtY(Mc11A1G716), DLC(M25.G), IU(Joseffy), InU(M1.S8),
   LNH(U), MoS(786.4), NNLc(AM2-I), NRU-E(M22G68,v.11),
   NcU(M786.4G687so), PP(U), RPB(U), ScCC(SMS72-85),
   ViU(Music M25.G68S6 1871), also in GP-L(V:127)
Le Songe d'une Nuit d'Eté, Op.9
   Schott, n.d., 5p.
   CtY(Mc11A1G716), LNH(U), NNLc(AM2-I), NcU(M786.4
   G687ca), also in GP-L(V:135)
   Paraphrase of the Ambroise Thomas opera.
Sospiro (Valse poétique), **Op.24**
   HallS, 1857, 11p.
   LNH(U), NNLc(AM2-I), NRU-E(M22G68,v.11), NcU(M786.45
   G687so), also in GP-L(V:141)
Sourire d'une jeune Fille (Grande Valse de Concert)
   Schott, n.d., 8p.

NNLc(AM2-I), NRU-E(M22G68,v.8), NcU(M786.45G687s),
  RPB(U), also in GP-L(V:153)
Also titled **The Maiden's Blush.**
Souvenirs d'Andalousie (Caprice de Concert), **Op.22**
  Halls, 1855, 11p.
  CtY(Mc11A1G716), ICN(Piano pre-1870), LNH(U), LNT(L976.3
    [780]Z99), NNLc(AM2-I), NRU-E(M22G68,v.12), NcU(M786.4
    G387s.a), also in GP-J, GP-L(V:211)
Souvenir de Cuba (Mazurka), **Op.75**
  Ditson, 1873, 9p.
  LNH(U), NNLc(AM2-I), NRU-E(M22G68,v.12), also in GP-L
    (V:161)
Souvenirs de La Havane, Op.39
  Halls, 1860, 15p.
  CtY(Mc11A1G716), DLC(M25.G), LNH(U), NNLc(AM2-I), NRU-E
    M22G68,v.12), NcU(M786.4G687s.h.), also in GP-J,
    GP-L(V:169)
Souvenir de Lima (Mazurka), **Op.74**
  Ditson, 1873, 13p.
  CU(M32G673S6 1860CaseX), DLC(M25.G), LNH(U), NNLc
    (AM2-I), NRU-E(M22G68,v.12), also in GP-L(V:185)
Souvenir de Porto Rico (Marche des Gibaros), **Op.31**
  Schott, 1859, 11p.; Music, 1947, 12p.(ed. J. Kirkpatrick)
  CU(M28G558op31 1947), CtY(Mc11A1G716), LNH(U), MoSW(Music
    M28G716S), NNLc(AM2-I), NRU-E(M22G68,v.12), NcU(M786.4
    G687s[1947]), also in GP-J, GP-L(V:199)
The Spark, Op.20 (see **La Scintilla, Op.20**)
Suis-moi! (Caprice), **Op.45**
  Halls, 1862, 11p.
  LNH(U), LNT(Civil War La.Coll.), NNLc(AM2-I), NRU-E(M22
    G68,v.12), OCl(M776.4.42538), RPB(U), also in GP-J,
    GP-L(V:223)
Tournament Galop
  Waters, Ditson, 1854, 13p.
  CtY(Mc11A1G716), MoS(786.4), NNLc(AM2-I), NcU(M786.45G687t),
    also in GP-J, GP-L(V:235)
Tremolo (Grande Etude de Concert), **Op.58**
  Ditson, 1871, 15p.
  CU(M22G63), CtY(Mc11A1G716), DLC(M25.G), IU(Joseffy),
    MoS(786.4), NNLc(JNG 73-234; AM2-I), NRU-E(M22G68,
    v.13), NcU(M786.47G687t), PP(U), RPB(U), also in
    GP-L(V:249)
L'Union (Paraphrase de Concert sur les Airs nationaux),
  Op.48
  Halls, 1863, 19p.
  CU(M34G667op48CaseX), CtY(Mc11A1G716), IU(Joseffy), LNH
    (U), MoS(786.4), NNLc(JNG 73-235; AM2-I), NRU-E(M22
    G68,v.13), PP(U), also in GP-B, GP-J, GP-L(V:265),
    NC-G
Valse poétique, Op.24 (see **Sospiro, Op.24**)
Variations de Concert sur l'Hymne portugais, Op.91
  Schott, n.d., 21p.

CtY(Mc11A1G716), NNLc(AM2-I), NRU-E(M22G68,v.6), NcU
   (M786.48G687v), also in GP-L(III:153)
The Water Sprite (Polka de Salon), **Op.27**
   Ditson, 1853, 11p.
   CtY(Mc11A1G716), LNH(U), MoS(786.4), NNLc(AM2-I), NRU-E
   (M22G68,v.13), NcU(786.44G687n), OCl(SM776.45), PP(U),
   RPB(U), ViU(°M1.A13N.G68W3 1857), also in GP-L(V:291)
   Also titled **La Naiade**

GROBE, CHARLES (ca.1817-1879)

Affectionate Remembrance (Brilliant Variations on "The
   Dearest Spot of Earth to Me is Home"), **Op.860**
   Ditson, 1857, 9p.
   CtY(Mc26A7G), DLC(M27.G), InU(M1.S8), PP(U), RPB(U),
   ViU(°M1.S444,v.133,no.18; McR.68.27)
L'Amitié (Variations brillantes sur un Thème de l'Opéra
   La Fille du Régiment), **Op.21**
   Willig, 1844, 7p.
   RPB(U)
Les Amoureux (Variations brillantes sur le Thème favori
   "Love Not"), **Op.47**
   Lee, 1846, 7p.
   CtY(Mc11A1G891), PP(U), RPB(U), ScCC(SMB41.44), ViU
   (°M1.S444,v.71,no.12; McR.100.08)
Amusement des Amateurs (Variations brillantes sur un
   Thème favori de M. Keller "The Ravel Polka"), **Op.111**
   Lee, Mayo, 1847, 11p.
   CtHT(U), InU(M1.S8), NRU-E(U), ScCC(SMB53.8), ViU
   (°M1.S444,v.71,no.14; McR.49.07)
   One of Grobe's very attractive works.
"The Angels are Waiting for Me" (Transcription), **Op.1825**
   Lee, 1867, 7p.
   CtY(Mc11A1G891), DLC(M27.G)
Anvil Chorus, Op.910 (see **Sounds from the Catskills**)
The Battle of Buena Vista, Op.101
   Willig, 1847, 13p.
   CtY(Mc11A1G891), ICN(Case sm oM1.A13,no.2468), LN(U), LNH
   (U), NBu(°M1C65,v.32,no.29), NNLc(Drexel 5535; AM2-I),
   NcU(EAMC,no.4), ViU(°M1.S444,v.72,no.1)
   Blow by blow musical description of the famous battle.
The Battle of Palo Alto and Resaca de la Palma, Op.72
   Benteen, 1846, 9p.
   CtY(Mc11A1G891), NBu(°M1C65,v.32,no.28), ViU(McR.129.25)
   Another "battle" with interpolated text.
"Believe Me if all Those Endearing Young Charms" (see **My
   Lodging is On the Cold Ground, Op.1022**)
Les Bords d'Ohio (Variations brillantes sur le Thème
   favori de S. C. Foster, "My Old Kentucky Home"), **Op.385**
   FirthP, 1853, 8p.
   CtY(Mc26A7), MiU-C(U), NRU-E(U), PP(U, [Foster]), RPB
   (U), ScCC(SMB23.16), ViU(McR.80.20), also in BC-G

Les Bords du Delaware (Variations brillantes sur un Motif allemand), **Op.137**
    Walker, 1849, 11p.
    CtHT(U), CtY(Mc26Grobe), DLC(M27.G), ICN(Piano pre-1870),
        InU(M1.S8), NNLc(AM2-I), NRU-E(U), NcD(RBR MusicB2,
        no.34), PP(U), RPB(U), ScCC(SMB58.20)

Les Bords du Mississippi (Variations brillantes sur le Thème favori de M. Strakosch "Un Carnaval à Naples"), **Op.350**
    HallS, 1858, 10p.
    NcD(RBR MusicB2,no.11), RPB(U), ViU(McR.80.19)
    Vivacious Grobe. Compare with the original polka by
    Strakosch.

Bright Dreams of the Past ("Ever of Thee" with Brilliant Variations and Finale), **Op.1046**
    RussellT, 1858, 7p.
    CtY(Mc11A1G891), InU(M1.S8), NNLc(Am2-I), NcD(RBR MusicB15,
        no.23), NcU(EAMC,no.70), PP(U), RPB(U), ViU(McR.174.16)

Un Carnaval à Naples Polka (see **Les Bords du Mississippi, Op.350**)

"Charity" (with Variations), **Op.120**
    Lee, 1852, 7p.
    CtY(Mc11A1G891), DLC(M27.G), ICN(Piano pre-1870), InU
        (M1.S8), NBu(°M1C65,v.41,no.19), NNLc(AM2-I), NRU-E(U),
        NcD(RBR°music old M780.88A512PD), NcU(EAMC,no.6), PP(U),
        RPB(U), ViU(°M1.S444,v.130,no.14; McR.68.26)

"Come Ye Disconsolate" (with Variations), **Op.223**
    Lee, 1852, 7p.
    CtHT(U), CtY(Mc11A1G891), InU(M1.S8), NNLc(AM2-I), NcU
        (EAMC,no.22), PP(U), RPB(U), ViU(°M1.S444,v.161,no.6;
        McR.68.25)

Constant Love (Brilliant Variations on "Kathleen Mavourneen"), **Op.834**
    Bech, 1857, 9p.
    CtY(Mc11A1G891), InU(M1.S8), NcD(RBR Music fH887,no.43),
        ViU(°M1.S444,v.9,no.19)

The Continent is Ours (Brilliant Variations on "Yankee Doodle" and "Hail Columbia"), **Op.956**
    Lee, 1857, 1858, 9p.
    DLC(M1.A13G Case), ICN(VM1F91,no.375), NBu(U), ViU
        (McR.84.24)
    Only "Yankee Doodle" appears under this opus number.
    See "Hail Columbia," which is **Op.962.**

Cornucopia of Pleasure (Brilliant Variations on Maretzek's celebrated "Rondo Finale" sung by Madame Laborde in **Linda di Chamounix**), **Op.141**
    Walker, 1850, 11p.
    MiU-C(U), PPi(qr786.4P53594), RPB(U)
    Ranks among Grobe's very best compositions.

"The Dearest Spot of Earth to me is Home" (see **Affectionate Remembrance, Op.860**)

"Dixie's Land" (with Brilliant Variations), **Op.1250**
    FirthP, 1860, 9p.
    DLC(M27.G), InU(M1.S8), LNH(U), MiU-C(U), NNLc(AM2-I),

NcD(RBR°music old780.88A512PE), RPB(U), ViU(McR.
125.12), WM(786.4G87di)

Enchanting Dreams (Brilliant Variations on **Gertrude's
Dream Waltz**), **Op.425**
　　Ditson, 1854, 9p.
　　RPB(U), ScCC(SMB23.28)
　　Variations on a waltz formerly attributed to Beethoven.

"Ever of Thee" (see **Bright Dreams of the Past, Op.1046**)

Fisher's Hornpipe (with Brilliant Variations), **Op.592**
　　HallS, 1855, 7p.
　　CtY(Mc11A1G891), DLC(M27.G), InU(M1.S8), NRU-E(U), ViU
　　　(°M1.S444,v.107,no.7)

Les Fleurs du Plaisir (Variations brillantes sur un Thème
suisse), **Op.109**
　　Willig, 1847, 11p.
　　CtY(Mc26Grobe)

"Flow Gently, Sweet Afton" (see **Heures de Loisir, Op.73**)

"From Greenland's Icy Mountains" (with Variations), **Op.307**
　　Lee, 1852, 7p.
　　CtHT(U), CtY(Mc11A1G891), DLC(M27.G), NNLc(AM2-I), PP(U),
　　　RPB(U), ViU(°M1.S444,v.71,no.9)

"Gentle Nettie Moore" (or "The Little White Cottage,"
with Brilliant Variations), **Op.1094**
　　Ditson, 1859, 9p.
　　LN(U), RPB(U)
　　Original song by G. S. Pike (1857).

Gertrude's Dream Waltz (see **Enchanting Dreams, Op.425**)

"Hail Columbia, Happy Land!" (with Brilliant Variations),
Op.962
　　Lee, 1858, 9p.
　　DLC(M1.A13G Case), ICN(VM1F91,no.375), NNLc(AM2-I),
　　　ViU(McR.171.17)

Heures de Loisir (Variations sur le Chant favori "Flow
Gently, Sweet Afton"), **Op.73**
　　Willig, 1846, 7p.
　　CtHT(U), ICN(Case sm oM1.A13,no.2275), NNLc(AM2-I),
　　　RPB(U), ScCC(SMB53.6), ViU(McR.73.14)

"Home, Sweet Home" (with Variations), **Op.207**
　　Lee, 1851, 7p.
　　CtY(Mc11A1G891), NNLc(AM2-I), NcU(Vault FolioM20.M8,
　　　no.22), PP(U), RPB(U), ViU(McR.94.21)

"Home, Sweet Home" (with Brilliant Variations), **Op.964**
　　Ditson, 1867, 9p.
　　CtHT(U), CtY(Mc26A7), DLC(M1.A13G Case), ICN(Piano pre-
　　　1870), MiU-C(U), NcD(RBR°music oldM780.88A512PE),
　　　RPB(U), ViU(°M1.S444,v.9, no.6)

Hopeless, not Heartless (Brilliant Variations on "No One
to Love"), **Op.1375**
　　Lee, 1861, 9p.
　　CtY(Mc11A1G891), DLC(M25.G), InU(M1.S8), MiU-C(U), NNLc
　　　(AM2-I), NRU-E(7518.F.37), PP(U), RPB(U), ViU(°M1.S444,
　　　v.9,no.8)
　　Attractive variations on a song by Edward Walker.

Les Ideales (Variations amusantes sur la Polka favorite de Jenny Lind), **Op.114**
    Lee, 1848, 11p.
    InU(M1.S8), NNLc(AM2-I), NcD(RBR musicB.34,no.4), RPB(U),
      ScCC(SMB53.7), ViU(°M1.S444,v.123,no.25)
"Kathleen Mavourneen" (see **Constant Love, Op.834**)
Killarney (Fantasie), **Op.1980**
    Lee, 1874, 9p.
    CtY(Mc11A1G891), DLC(M25.G)
Linden Hall Polka, Op.1530
    Lee, n.d., 5p.
    NBu(U)
"The Little White Cottage" (see **"Gentle Nettie Moore,"** **Op.1094**)
"Lorena" (with Brilliant Variations), **Op.1515**
    Higgins, 1864, 9p.
    CtY(Mc26A7), DLC(M27.G), ICN(Case sm oM1.A13,no.3192),
      InU(M1.S8), NNLc(AM2-I), PP(U), RP(U), WM(786.4G87L)
      The original is a beautiful sentimental song by J. P.
      Webster.
"Love Not" (see **Les Amoureux, Op.47**)
"Mary of Argyle" (with Variations), **Op.211**
    Lee, 1852, 7p.
    CtY(Mc11A1G891), DLC(M27.G), InU(M1.S8), NNLc(AM2-I),
      NRU-E(U), PP(U), RPB(U), ViU(°M1.S444,v.46,no.51)
"Mary of Argyle" (with Brilliant Variations), **Op.1001**
    Ditson, 1858, 9p.
    CtY(Mc11A1G891), ViU(°M1.S444,v.107,no.25)
"My Lodging is on the Cold Ground" (or "Believe me if all those, etc.," with Brilliant Variations), **Op.1022**
    Ditson, 1858, 9p.
    NNLc(AM2-I), RPB(U)
"My Old Kentucky Home" (see **Les Bords d'Ohio, Op.385**)
"No One to Love" (see **Hopeless, not Heartless, Op.1375**)
"Oh Boys, Carry Me Long" (the beautiful Plantation Melody by Stephen C. Foster, arranged with Variations), **Op.301**
    FirthP, 1853, 7p.
    CtY(Mc11A1G891), NcU(Vault FolioM20.M8,no.23), RPB(U)
"Old Dog Tray" (with Brilliant Variations)
    Pond, 1855, 9p.
    CtY(Mc11A1G891), DLC(M27.G), ICN(Piano pre-1870), InU
      (M1.S8), RPB(U)
"Old Folks at Home" ("Swanee River," with Variations)
    Ditson, 1875, 9p.
    NRU-E(U), RPB(U), ViU(°M1.S444,v.76,no.10)
"Old Rosin the Beau" (with Variations), **Op.724**
    Ditson, 1858, 5p.
    CtY(Mc26A7), DLC(M27.G)
"Old Uncle Ned" (with Variations), **Op.126**
    Lee, 1849, 5p.
    CtY(Mc11A1G891), NcU(EAMC,no.52), ViU(°M1.S444,v.103,
      no.15)
Pestal (see **"Yes!, The Die is Cast," Op.219**)

Pleyel's German Hymn (with Variations), **Op.430**
Lee, 1854, 7p.
CtY(Mc11A1G891), InU(M1.S8), NBu(°M1C65,v.31,no.44),
NNLc(AM2-I), NRU-E(U), NcD(RBR°music oldM780.88A512PE),
PP(U), RPB(U), ViU(°M1.S444,v.161,no.2)
"Poland is Not Yet Lost" (Varié), **Op.105**
Benteen, 1847, 7p.
NNLc(AM2-I), ScCC(SMB53.11), ViU(McR.7.18)
Prayer from "Il Moise in Egitto" (with Variations), **Op.445**
Lee, 1854, 7p.
CtY(Mc11A1G891)
Rossini's famous opera "prayer" with one variation.
Prayer from "Tancredi" (with Variations), **Op.446**
Lee, 1854, 7p.
NcD(RBR musicB74,no.16)
Ravel Polka (see **Amusement des Amateurs, Op.111**)
"Robin Adair" (with Brilliant Variations), **Op.1789**
Lee, 1866, 9p.
ViU(U:3)
Salut à Boston (Variations brillantes sur le Chant favori
"When other Friends are round Thee"), **Op.112**
Benteen, Mayo, 1848, 9p.
MiU-C(U), RPB(U), ScCC(SMB23.18), ViU(°M1.S444,v.86,
no.38)
"Shells of Ocean" (see **Variations brillantes, etc., Op.384**)
Soldier's Joy (with Brilliant Variations), **Op.569**
Halls, 1855, 7p.
CtY(Mc11A1G891), NRU-E(U)
Great fun with an old fiddle tune.
Sounds from the Catskills (Brilliant Variations on the
"Anvil Chorus" from **Il Trovatore**), **Op.910**
Ditson, 1857, 9p.
ViU(U:3)
The Stars and Stripes Forever (Brilliant Variations on
"The Star-Spangled Banner"), **Op.490**
Miller, 1854, 9p.
DLC(M1.A13G Case), ICN(Piano pre-1870), MiU-C(U), NBu
(U), NNLc(AM2-I), NRU-E(M1667G873s), NcU(EAMC,no.96),
PP(U), RPB(U)
An amusing example of the "patriotic" Grobe. He even
works in "Yankee Doodle" at the end.
"The Star-Spangled Banner" (see **The Stars and Stripes
Forever, Op.490**)
"Strike the Cymbal" (with Variations), **Op.353**
Lee, 1853, 7p.
CtY(Mc11A1G891), InU(M1.S8), NNLc(AM2-I), NRU-E(U),
PP(U), RPB(U)
Based on a song (with chorus) by Vincenzo Pucitta.
"Tis the Last Rose of Summer" (with Brilliant Variations),
Op.723
Lee, 1856, 7p.
CtY(Mc11A1G891), DLC(M27.G), NRU-E(U), ScCC(SMB23.19),
ViU(°M1.S444,v.3,no.3)

Tumultous Joy! (Brilliant Variations on Wallerstein's **Storm
  Polka),** **Op.656**
> Ditson, 1856, 9p.
> InU(M1.S8), NcD(RBR musicB34,no.3), ScCC(SMB23.20)
United States Grand Waltz, Op.43
> Lee, 1845, 5p.
> DLC(M1.A12 I11), InU(M1.S8), NNLc(AM2-I), NcU(EAMC,no.42),
>   PP(U), ViU(°M1.S444,v.145,no.11), also in NC-G
> One of the comparatively few compositions by Grobe not
>   based one someone else's theme.
**Variations brillantes sur le Thème favori "Shells of Ocean,"
  Op.384**
> Ditson, 1853, 9p.
> CtHT(U), CtY(Mc11A1G891), DLC(M27.G), ICN(Piano pre-1870),
>   InU(M1.S8), MiU-C(U), NNLc(AM2-I), NRU-E(U), NcD(RBR
>   MusicB34,no.2), NcU(EAMC,no.80), PP(U), RPB(U), ScCC
>   (SMB23.21), ViU(°M1.S444,v.107,no.27)
> The original song is by J. W. Cherry.
Virginia Rose Bud (with Variations), **Op.129**
> Lee, 1849, 7p.
> CtY(Mc11A1G891), InU(M1.S8)
"When other Friends are round Thee" (see **Salut à Boston, Op.112)**
"The Wild Ashe Deer" (with Variations), **Op.851**
> Lee, 1857, 5p.
> NcD(RBR Music873)
> Theme, two variations and finale. See a similar treat-
>   ment by "A Lady of Va." (**ANONYMOUS).**
"Wings of a Dove" (with Variations), **Op.22**
> Lee, 1855, 6p.
> CtHT(U), InU(M1.S8), NNLc(°MYD+box), NcU(EAMC,no.6), PP(U),
>   RPB(U), ViU(McR.92.17)
"Yankee Doodle" (see **The Continent is Ours, Op.956)**
"Yes! The Die is Cast" (**Pestal,** Chant favori varié), **Op.219**
> Willig, 1851, 9p.
> CtHT(U), CtY(Mc11A1G891), DLC(M1.A13G Case), InU(M1.S8),
>   ICN(Case sm oM1.A13,no.2627), MiU-C(U), NRU-E(U),
>   OCL(SM776.48), PP(U), ViU(°M1.S444,v.46, no.35;
>   McR.46.13)

GRUNN, HOMER (1880-1944)

Desert Suite, Op.7 (Five Tone Pictures)
> Fox, 1913, 25p.
> CtY(Mc11A1G926), DLC(M24.G89op7), PP(U)
> 1. **At Sunrise;** 2. **Cholla Dance;** 3. **The Mesa;** 4. **Mirage;**
>   5. **Oasis**
'Tis Raining (A Study)
> Ditson, 1929, 5p.
> OCL(SM776.47)
Zuni Impressions (Indian Suite), **Op.27**
> Boston, 1917, 15p.
> CtY(U), DLC(M24.G89op27), MoS(786.4), NRU-E(U, 4 only)

1. The Flute-god; 2. The Rainbow Spring; 3. A
Mysterious Story; 4. Kor'kokshi Dance

HACKH, OTTO (1851-1917)

Carmen de Bizet (Fantasie dramatique), **Op.22**
    Grand, 1884, 15p.
    DLC(M39.B [Bizet]), IU(Joseffy)
    Very grand (and entertaining) paraphrase.
Fenella (Polka de Concert), **Op.21**
    Grand, 1884, 11p.
    DLC(M31.H), IU(Joseffy)
Les Feux-follets (Deuxième Etude de Concert), **Op.134**
    Cranz, 1897, 9p.
    DLC(M25.H)
    Superb concert piece.
Idylle, Op.11
    Grand, 1881, 7p.
    DLC(M25.H), IU(Joseffy), MiU-C(U)
Mazurka-Caprice, Op.14
    Grand, 1882, 13p.
    CtY(Mc11A1H115), DLC(M32.H), IU(Joseffy), MiU-C(U),
      PP(U)
La Naiade, Op.151, No.3 (from **Trois Scènes de Ballet, Op.151**)
    Schirmer, 1895, 7p.
    RPB(U)
Nocturne, Op.12
    Grand, 1882, 7p.
    DLC(M25.H), IU(Joseffy)
Polonaise de la Cour, Op.60
    Schuberth-E, 1893, 7p.
    MoSW(U)
Spinnerlied (Spinning Song), **Op.50**
    Church, 1890, 9p.
    IU(Joseffy)

HADLEY, HENRY KIMBALL (1871-1937)

Album-blatt, Op.35, No.6
    Schmidt, 1904, 7p.
    CtY(Mc11A1H117)
Dance of the Satyrs
    Mills, 1940, 5p.
    RPB(U)
    Alternating triple and quintuple meters.
Intermezzo, Op.16 (from **Ballet Suite No.3**)
    Church, 1898, 7p.
    RPB(U)
Six Tone Pictures, Op.14
    Ditson, 1898, 23p.
    MoS(786.4), NNLc(°MYD), NRU-E(M25H13t)

1. Fascination; 2. Fate(canon); 3. Fidelity;
4. Folly; 5. Fury; 6. Festivity

HANCE, JAMES F. (fl.1815-1835)

The Admired Hungarian Air (with Variations)
Dubois, 1818-1820, 6p. [W.I:336]
ICN(Case8A 1057), NNLc(AM1-I), RPB(U)
First Grand Fantasie (containing The German Hymn and
Copenhagen Waltz with Variations)
DuboisS, n.d., 12p.
ICN(Case sm oM1.A13,no.1205)
Second Grand Fantasie (Introduction and Brilliant Variations
to the Russian Dance)
DuboisS, n.d., 9p.
CtHT(U), DLC(M1.A13H), NBu(°M1C66,v.38,no.12), NNLc
(AM1-I), NRU-E(U), RPB(U), ViU(°M1.S444,v.132,no.24),
also in A-C(II)
The Opera Waltz (The Motives from Il Barbiere)
DuboisS, n.d., 3p.
DLC(M1.A13H Case), NNLc(AM1-I), ViU(°M1.S444,v.75,no.5)
"Will You come to the Bower?" (Favourite Air with Variations),
Op.15
DuboisS, 183_?, 7p. [W.II:590]
CtHT(U), CtY(Mc11A1H190), DLC(M1.A13H Case), ICN(Case sm
oM1.A13,no.1247), InU(M1.S8), NNLc(AM1-I), NRU-E(6671.
F29), PP(U), RPB(U)
Arranged from a song by Thomas Moore.

HECKSCHER, CELESTE DE LONGPRE (1860-1928)

Impromptu, Op.6
Boner, 1896, 5p.
NNLc(°MYDbox), NcU(M786.4H458i), RPB(U)
An Old French Dance
Gray-HW, 1912, 8p.
PP(U)
Valse bohème, Op.10
Boner, 1896, 5p.
PP(U)

HEILMAN, WILLIAM CLIFFORD (1877-1946)

April Green (see Four Pieces)
Arabesque
Harvard Musical Review, Feb.1913, 4p.
PWm(M786.4)
Two Compositions, Op.6
Schirmer, 1907, 2v.(5,13p.)
DLC(M25.H), MBH(P1F257), MoSW(U), PP(U), PWm(M786.4

H36313, 1 only; M786.4H36317, 2 only)
1. Intermezzo in E-flat Minor; 2. Scherzo in G Minor
Dusting the Keys (Humoresque)
Schirmer, 1928, 5p.
PWm(M780.8Heilman)
Amusing use of the interval of the second.
Fountains (Four Waltzes)
Schirmer, 1924, 19p.
PWm(M786.4H36312)
Intermezzo in E-flat Minor, Op.6, No.1 (see **Two Compositions, Op.6**)
Minuet
Boston, 1899, 7p.
PWm(M786.4H36314)
An Old Garden (see **Four Pieces**)
Four Pieces for the Pianoforte
Boston, 1920, 4v.(9,7,5,9p.)
PWm(M780.8Heilman)
1. The Prism in the Sun; 2. Winter Boughs; 3. An Old
Garden; 4. April Green
The Prism in the Sun (see **Four Pieces**)
Scherzo in G Minor, Op.6, No.2 (see **Two Compositions, Op.6**)
Winter Boughs (see **Four Pieces**)

HEINRICH, ANTHONY PHILIP (1781-1861)

Adieu to America
n.p., n.d., 11p.
NRU-E(Vault M1.A13H469 Presentation Copy)
1. Introduzione (The Sadness of Contemplation); 2. **The
Adieu** (Salutations); 3. **Farewell Invocation** (The
Blessing); 4. **Hope of Reunion**
Amaranth (see **The Princess Victoria's Waltz Rondo**)
La buona Mattina (Sonata)
BaconH, 1820, pp.25-39 [Wolfe.I:362]
NcU(M786.41H469b), also in NC-G
Excerpted from **The Dawning of Music in Kentucky.**
Caprice dansante concertante (Le Minuet du Grand-père et
La Valse des grands Enfants di Bravura)
The author, 1853, 9p.
DLC(M1.A13.H), NRU-E(Vault M1.A13H469), NcU(M786.45H469c)
**The Dawning of Music in Kentucky or The Pleasures of Harmony
in the Solitudes of Nature**
BaconH, 1820, 147p. [Wolfe.I:362] ; DaCapo, 1972
DLC(M1.A13H42Case), ICN(5A 7468), IU(M2.3U5E2v.10 Ref.),
NcU(M1.A13H45 1972), NNLc(JMN 76-20), NRU-E(M1.A13
H469 1820a), PP(780.81H364d)
The Debarkation March
In A-C(II)
The Devil's Grand Tarantella (La Promenade du Diable)
Bradlee, 183_?, 15p.
PP(U)

Il Divertimento di Londra (The Grand Argyll March and Har-
  monic Waltz)
    Bradlee, 183_?, 10p.
    NcU(M786.4H469dL), PP(U)
A Divertimento for the Pianoforte
    BaconH, 1820, 5p. [W.I:363]
    NcU(M786.4H469d)
Divertimento Leggiadro (Petit Preludio to his Musical Adven-
  tures)
    The author, 1849, 11p.
    DLC(M1.A13H), InU(M1.S8)
    "A Companion Piece to The Valentine."
An Elegiac Impromptu (Fantasia dolorosa)
    Christman, 1840, 5p.
    DLC(M25.H), NcU(MF786.42H469e)
Fantasia dolorosa (see An Elegiac Impromptu)
The First Labour of Hercules (Un Pezzo di gran Bravura à la
  Valse austraico)
    Wetherbee, 183_?, 15p.
    NNLc(°MYDbox), NcU(M786.4H469f), PP(U)
The Hickory or Last Ideas in America ("The Musical Week,"
  Day 1)
    Johanning, 1835, 14p.
    NNLc(°MYD)
    A potpourri of national airs.
Impromptu (First Number of Friday in "The Musical Week."
  The Sensitive Plant)
    Johanning, 1835, 5p.
    NNLc(°MYD), NcU(M786.4H469i)
Indian Fanfares
    Christman, 1841, 9p.
    NNLc(AM1-I), PP(U)
    1. The Camanche Revel; 2. The Sioux Galliarde; 3. The
      Manitou Air Dance
    Heinrich notes that "These Fanfares will serve as Quick
      Steps for Military Bands."
Ischl or Union of Spirits (Toccata Grande. No.2 in Legends
  of the Wild Wood)
    n.p., n.d., 19p.
    NRU-E(Vault M1.A13H469 Presentation Copy)
The Laurel and the Cypress (Petit Impromptu)
    Holt, 1847, 2p.
    InU(M1.S8), NNLc(AM2-I)
    A touching tribute to Mendelssohn.
The Maiden's Dirge
    In BC-G
Ouissahicon (No.3 in Legends of the Wild Wood)
    n.p., n.d., 9p.
    NRU-E(Vault M1.A13H469 Presentation Copy)
The Princess Victoria's Waltz Rondo (The Amaranth.
  "Musical Week," day 4)
    Johanning, n.d., 5p.
    DLC(M25.H)

The Return from School (Images of Musical Thought, No.3)
    Christman, 1842, 7p.
    DLC(M1.A12I6Case), MeB(U)
The Rübezahl Dance on the Schneekoppe (or **Wild Waltz of the
  Giant Mountain**; Followed by a Coda: **The Demon**)
    Bradlee, n.d., 15p.
    PP(U)
The Sensitive Plant (see **Impromptu**)
Song without Words
    In PM-H
Toccatina Capriciosa
    In A-C(II)
The Valentine (Scherzo)
    The composer, 1849, 8p.
    DLC(M25.H)
The Yankee Welcome to Boz (Two Waltzes)
    Christman, 1842, 6p.
    RPB(U)
    1. The Rose of Albion; 2. The Cosmopolitan Waltz
    Boz, i.e. Charles Dickens.

HELLER, ROBERT [see **WILLIAM HENRY PALMER**]

HENNINGES, REINHOLD E. (ca.1836-1913)

Album Leaves (Two Songs without Words)
    BrainardS, 1870, 5p.
    MiU-C(U)
Barcarolle
    BrainardS, 1879, 5p.
    DLC(M25.H), OCl(M776.4H393p)
The Cavaliers (Polonaise militaire)
    BrainardS, 1888, 8p.
    OCl(M776.4.4657)
Forest Winds (Impromptu)
    BrainardS, 1867, 5p.
    MiU-C(U)
Prince Carnaval (Polonaise brillante)
    BrainardS, 1872, 9p.
    OCl(M776.4H393p)

HERBERT, VICTOR (1859-1924)

Al Fresco (Intermezzo)
    Witmark, 1904, 7p.
    CU(M25H485), DLC(M25.H), NRU-E(M25H537a), PP(U)
    Originally published under the pseudonym Frank Roland.
La Coquette (see **Six Piano Pieces**)
Fleurette (Valse lente)
    Witmark, 1903, 4p.

CtY(U), DLC(M32.H), InU(M1.S8), NRU-E(M25H537f), ViU(U:3)
Ghazel (see **Six Piano Pieces**)
The Mountain Brook (see **Six Piano Pieces**)
On the Promenade (see **Six Piano Pieces**)
Pañuelo (from **Four Dances from the opera "Natoma"**)
    Schirmer, 1911, 7p.
    ViU(U:2)
Six Piano Pieces
    Witmark, 1900, 29p., also issued separately
    CU(M22H467 1900), DLC(M25.H), MoSW(U), NBu(U, 1 only),
      NNLc(°MYD), NcU(M786.4H53a), PP(U), RPB(U, 5 only),
      ViU(U:3, 1,2 only), also in NC-G(4,6 only)
    1. **Yesterthoughts**; 2. **Punchinello**; 3. **Ghazel**; 4. **La Coquette**; 5. **On the Promenade**; 6. **The Mountain Brook**
Punchinello (see **Six Piano Pieces**)
La Serenata
    In AC
Yesterthoughts (see **Six Piano Pieces**)

HESSELBERG, EDOUARD G. [D'ESSENELLI] (1870-1935)

Russian Rhapsody
    Presser, 1927, 15p.
    DLC(M25.H), IU(qM786.41H464r), PP(U)
A Russian Suite
    BrainardS, 1902, 46p.
    DLC(M24.H)
    1. **Daybreak**; 2. **The Fisherman's Song**; 3. **With the Pigeons**; 4. **Twilight**; 5. **Midnight Revel** (Mazurka); 6. **Midnight Revel** (Polonaise)

HEWITT, GEORGE WASHINGTON (1811-1893)

Introduction and Variations on Sir H. R. Bishop's favorite song "I'm Saddest When I Sing"
    Fiot, 1847, 10p.
    ViU(°M1.S444,v.46,no.34)
Rêverie d'Amour (Morceau brillant)
    Bech, 1856, 11p.
    DLC(M1.A13H Case)
"Rock'd in the Cradle of the Deep" (see **Un Souvenir de l'Océan**)
Un Souvenir de l'Océan (Musical Illustration of J. P. Knight's beautiful song "Rock'd in the Cradle of the Deep"), **Op.54**
    Ditson, 1859, 11p.
    DLC(M27.K [Knight])
Une Voix des Ondes (A Voice from the Waves. Pensée romantique)
    Ditson, 1852, 7p.
    CtHT(U), DLC(M25.H), ICN(Piano pre-1870), InU(M1.S8),
      NBu(U), NRU-E(U), NcU(EAMC,no.80), RPB(U), ViU(°M1.S444,v.134,no.35

HEWITT, JAMES (1770-1827)

The Battle of Trenton (A Favorite Historical Military Sonata)
    Blake, 1812-1814, 14p. [W.I:372]
    DLC(M1.A1H Case), NBu(U), NNLc(JPG 78-53,no.2; AM1-I),
    PP(U), RPB(U), also in M-E, HC-W
The 4th of July (A Grand Military Sonata)
    HewittMR, 1801, 14p. [W.I:373]
    DLC(M1.A1H Case), CtY(RareSC Mc1OH234v.2), NNLc(AM1-I),
    PP(U)
The Hag in a Corner (A Favorite Irish Air)
    Hewitt, 1810, 3p. [W.I:375]
    ICN(Case8A1583)
"Mark My Alford" (A Favorite Air with Variations)
    HewittMR, 1808, 5p. [W.I:377]
    DLC(M1.A1H), ICN(Case8A1721), InU(M1.S8), NNLc(AM1-I),
    PP(U), RPB(U), ScCC(SMB2.46), also in C-MH, HC-W, NC-G
    The theme is identical to the French folk song "Ah, vous
    dirais-je maman."
The New Federal Overture
    CarrB, ca.1797, 8p. [SU:140]
    DLC(M1.A1H Case), NNLc(AM1-I), also in A-C(I)
A Sonata for the Piano Forte ("The Plough Boy" with Variations)
    HewittMR, 1809, 6p. [W.I:381]
    DLC(M1.A1H Case), ICN(Case8A15), NBu(U), NNLc(AM1-I),
    PP(U), RPB(U), also in HC-W
Three Sonatas for the Pianoforte, Op.5
    CarrMR, 1795-1796, 17p. [SU:395]
    DLC(M1.A1H Case), ICN(Case8A118), also in A-C(I: III only),
    HC-W(I only)
Yankee Doodle (with Variations)
    HewittMR, 1807-1810, 5p. [W.I:383]
    CtHT(U), DLC(M1.A1H Case), ICN(Case8A952), NNLc(AM1-I),
    ViU(McR.66.61), also in A-C(I), BC-G

HILL, EDWARD BURLINGAME (1872-1960)

At the Grave of a Hero
    Wa-Wan, 1903, 5p.
    DLC(M1.W35), ICN(VM1W11,v.2), NNLc(°MH Wa-Wan,v.2), NRU-E
    (M25H6448at), also in WW-L(I:49)
Country Idyls, Op.10
    Schirmer, 1903, 15p.
    DLC(M25.H), MBH(P1H55)
    1. A Spring Morning; 2. A Starlit Night; 3. An Autumn
    Hunting-Song; 4. An August Lullaby; 5. In a Garden
    by Moonlight; 6. A Summer Evening
From a Mountain Top, Op.8, No.3 (see Three Poetical Sketches,
    Op.8)
A Mid Summer Lullaby, Op.8, No.2 (see Three Poetical Sketches,
    Op.8)
Moonlight, Op.8, No.1 (see Three Poetical Sketches, Op.8)

Three Poetical Sketches, Op.8
Breitkopf, 1902, 3v.(3,5,5p.)
DLC(M25.H)
1. **Moonlight**; 2. **A Mid-Summer Lullaby**; 3. **From a Mountain Top**
Four Sketches after Stephen Crane, Op.7
Breitkopf, 1900, 4v.(3,2,3,3p.)
CtY(McAt4), DLC(M25.H), MoS(786.4), also in NC-G
Trois Valses ("Extraits de l'Opus 28")
Paris: Editions de la Nouvelle Revue française, 1922, 8p.
CU(ML5R415,Apr.1922°CaseX), CtY(La1OR32b,v.3), LNT(780.5
R454Suppl.1921-22), MB-N(U)

HOFFMAN, EDWARD (1836-?)

Ange des Fleurs (Nocturne)
Pond, 1866, 11p.
NBu(U)
La Belle du Soir (Grande Valse de Concert)
Cottier, 1869, 9p.
MiU-C(U)
Birds of Spring (A Woodland Sketch)
Cory, 1864, 9p.
NcU(Vault FolioM20.M8,no.11)
Grand Fantasia on the Popular Theme "The Mocking Bird"
(Grand Paraphrase de Concert)
Lee, 1864, 15p.
CtHT(U), CtY(Mc26A7), IU(q786.41H675mSp.Coll.), InU
(M1.S8) LN(U), LNT(L976.3[780]Z99), MiU-C(U), NRU-E(U),
NcD(RBR MusicB80,no.13), NcU(M786.42H699g), OCl(SM776.48),
RPB(U), ViU(°M1.S444,v.76,no.18; McR.54.03)
Hoffman's "claim to fame" begins with "Auld Lang Syne."
Grand Fantasia: "The Whippoorwill" (Grand Paraphrase de Concert)
Stech, 1869, 13p.
DLC(M25.H)
The Harp on the Tree (Romance)
Ditson, 1866, 11p.
RPB(U), ViU(McR.51.03)
The Hoffman Polka
Ditson, 1878, 13p.
RPB(U)
Love vs. Flirtation (Romance)
Pond, 1866, 11p.
RPB(U)
"The Mocking Bird" (see **Grand Fantasia on, etc.**)
The Night Dew (Mazurka)
Sawyer, 1867, 9p.
ViU(U:3)
"Oh! Whisper What Thou Feelest" (Fantasia de Salon)
Ditson, 1865, 9p.
RPB(U)

Actually a theme with three variations.
Pinafore (Caprice de Concert)
    Ditson, 1879, 15p.
    RPB(U)
    Artful Gilbert and Sullivan potpourri.
Polka de Concert
    Ditson, 1882, 11p.
    RPB(U)
Reign of Roses (Polka de Salon)
    Tremaine, 1868, 9p.
    RPB(U)
Romanza
    Ditson-CH, 1879, 7p.
    MiU-C(U)
"The Whippoorwill" (see **Grand Fantasia**)
Withering Flowers (Morceau élégant)
    Pond, 1867, 11p.
    RPB(U)
    Free variations on a sentimental theme.

HOFFMAN, RICHARD (1831-1909)

Barcarolle
    Schirmer, 1876, 13p.
    DLC(M25.H)
Beyond (Reverie), **Op.86**
    Pond, 1885, 7p.
    RPB(U)
"By the Sad Sea Waves" (Reverie)
    Halls, 1864, 11p.
    CtY(Mc11A1H675), DLC(M25.H), InU(M1.S8), NBu(U), NNLc
      (°MYD+box), NcU(EAMC,no.2), RPB(U)
    Transcription of a ballad by J. Benedict.
Caprice de Concert (sur les Motifs de **Favorita, Huguenots**
    et **Traviata**
    Beer, 1860, 13p.
    DLC(M25.H), MoSW(U), NNLc(°MYDp.v.2), PP(U), RPB(U)
    An elegant, difficult Victorian potpourri.
Third Caprice de Concert (see **Crispino e la Comare**)
Fourth Caprice de Concert (on Themes from **Mignon** by
    Ambroise Thomas)
    Pond, 1874, 17p.
    RPB(U)
Chi-Ci Pipi Nini (Cuban Dance)
    Ditson, 1872, 9p.
    DLC(M25.H), MoSW(U), NNLc(°MYD+box), NRU-E(U), PP(U),
      RPB(U), ViU(McR.159.45), also in BC-G
Crispino e la Comare (3me **Caprice de Concert**)
    Schirmer, 1866, 16p.
    Cty(Mc11A1H675), DLC(M25.H), ViU(°M1.S444,v.22,no.15)
    Bravura piece based on an opera (1850) by Federico and
      Luigi Ricci.

Dinorah (Caprice de Concert on Themes from Meyerbeer's opera)
  Pond, 1863, 17p.
  DLc(M25.H), NRU-E(U), RPB(U)
Dixiana (Caprice on the Popular Negro Minstrel's Melody
 "Dixie's Land")
  Ditson, 1861, 7p.
  DLC(M25.H), PP(U), RPB(U), also in NC-G
La Gazelle (Andante élégant)
  Schott, 1858, 6p.
  CtY(Mc11A1H675), DLC(M25.H), ICN(Piano pre-1870), InU
   (M1.S8), MoS(U), NBu(U), NNLc(°MYD+box), NcU(M786.4
   H711g), PP(U), RPB(U), ViU(°M1.S444,v.94,no.8; McR.
   146.30)
Les Huguenots (Grand Duo dramatique)
  Beer, n.d., 17p.
  CtY(Mc11A1H675)
  Transcription from Meyerbeer's opera.
Impromptu
  HallS, 1867, 9p.
  DLC(M25.H), NNLc(°MYD+box), NcU(MF786.4H711i)
In Memoriam L. M. G.
  Pond, 1870, 7p.
  DLC(M25.H), PP(U), also in PM-H
  A moving musical tribute to Gottschalk.
Memory (Ballad)
  Pond, 1864, 9p.
  CtY(Mc11A1H675), DLC(M25.H), NBu(U), NRU-E(U)
Meyerbeer et Donizetti (Fantaisie de Salon)
  Schirmer, 1868, 9p.
  CtY(Mc11A1H675), PP(U)
Mignon (see **Fourth Caprice de Concert**)
Polka de Concert
  Breusing, 1859, 10p.
  MiU-C(U), NRU-E(U), PP(U), RPB(U)
Rigoletto (Fantaisie Caprice)
  Beer, 1864, 15p.
  DLC(M34.V [Verdi]), ViU(McR.125.11)
  Potpourri of airs from Verdi's opera.
Robin Adair (Improvisation)
  Schirmer, 1870, 13p.
  NRU-E(U)
Scherzo di Bravura, Op.101
  Pond, 1890, 15p.
  CtY(Mc11A1H675), DLC(M25.H), NRU-E(U), PP(U)
Solitude (Pensée fugitive)
  Pond, 1863, 9p.
  CtHT(U), CtY(Mc11A1H675), DLC(M25.H), InU(M1.S8),
   NRU-E(U), NcU(Vault FolioM20.M8,no.10), PP(U), RPB(U)
Sonate bouffe
  Schirmer, 1869, 15p.
  PP(U)
  The Lancers, "Three Blind Mice" and "Pop goes the Weasel"
  are used as thematic material.

Souvenir de Trovatore (de Verdi)
HallS, 1856, 11p.
CtHT(U), CtY(Mc11A1H675), DLC(M25.H), MiU-C(U), MoS
(786.4), NBu(U), NNLc(°MYDp.v.2), NRU-E(Vault M25H711s),
NcU(EAMC,no.92), RPB(U), ViU(°M1.S444,v.106,no.23)
Spinning Song, Op.100
Pond, 1889, 13p.
CtY(Mc11A1H675), DLC(M25.H), PP(U)
Tarantelle
Pond, 1872, 14p.
CtY(Mc11A1H675), RPB(U)
Ten Minutes with Mozart (Transcription from **Don Giovanni**)
FirthP, 1862, 11p.
RPB(U)
Also includes "Non più andrai"?

HOFMANN, JOSEF CASIMIR [MICHEL DVORSKY] (1876-1957)

Charakterskizzen, Op.40
Zimmermann, 1908, 37p.
DLC(M24.H695), MoS(786.4), NNLc(°MYD), NRU-E(Vault M22
H71c), PP(786.4H673)
1. **Vision**; 2. **Jadis**; 3. **Nenien**; 4. **Kaleidoskop**
Difficult, musicianly concert pieces.
The Devil's Mill
WillisW, 1887, 7p.
DLC(M25.H), NRU-E(Vault M22H71c), PP(U), RPB(U)
Supposedly composed when Hofmann was eight years old.
Durch die Wolken, Op.18
Hainauer, 1893, 10p.
NNLc(°°MYDp.v.1,no.13), PP(U)
Trois Impressions (Dvorsky)
Schirmer, 1915, 3v.(7,7,9p.)
CU(M20C6v.1, 2 only), CtY(U, 3 only), DLC(M25.H), MoS
(786.4)< NNLc(°°MYD), NRU-E(M25H7132i), OCl(SM776.4,
3 only)
1. **Penguine**; 2. **L'Orient et l'Occident**; 3. **Le Sanctuaire**
Intermezzo, Op.34
Schuberth-E, n.d., 5p.
CtY(Mc10v.4), IU(Joseffy), PP(U)
Novelette, Op.27
Zimmermann, 1897, 7p.
NNLc(°MYD)
Novelette, Op.28
Zimmermann, 1897, 7p.
NNLc(°MYD)
Old and New (Valse de Concert)
WillisW, 1888, 7p.
RPB(U)
Composed when Hofmann was around twelve years of age.
L'Orient et l'Occident (see **Trois Impressions**)
Penguine (see **Trois Impressions**)

Romanze
    Century, n.d., 5p.
    RPB(U)
Le Sanctuaire (see **Trois Impressions**)
Valse Caprice, Op.53
    Schirmer, 1902, 7p.
    CtY(Mc11A1H676), DLC(M32.H), IU(MaLq786.4H677v), NNLc
      (°°MYD+box), NRU-E(M22H71c), PP(U)
Valse in A Flat
    Ditson, 1887, 7p.
    CtHT(U), CtY(Mc11A1H676), ICN(8A1099)
World's Kinder Tanz
    New YorkW, 1888, 2p.
    RPB(U)
    "Written for the New York World (newspaper) by Master
      Joseph Hofmann."

HOHNSTOCK, ADELE (d.1856)

Celebrated Concert Polka
    Reed, n.d., Schuberth, 1849, 5p.
    DLC(M1.A13H Case), PP(U)
Le Diamant (Polka brillante), Op.7
    André, 1854, 9p.
    PP(U), ViU(McR.29.14)
La Gracieuse (Polka de Salon)
    André, 1855, 7p.
    NcU(EAMC,no.15)
Hohnstock Concert Polka with Variations, Op.1
    Fiot, 1849, 13p.
    NNLc(AM2-I), NcD(RBR MusicB4,no.3), PP(U), ViU(McR.
      49.02)
    The "celebrated" concert polka supplied with intro-
      duction and three variations.
Sentimental Polka
    Walker, 1855, 9p.
    NcU(EAMC,no.15), PP(U)

HOLDEN, T. L. (fl.ca.1810-1820)

The Copenhagen Waltz (with Variations)
    Dubois, 1817-1818, 3p. [W.I:391]
    DLC(M1.A13H), NcU(EAMC,no.57), PP(U), also in A-C(I)

HOLST, EDUARD (ca.1843-1899)

Acacia (Companion Piece to **Narcissus**)
    Ditson, 1895, 5p.
    CtHT(U)
    A "tribute" to Ethelbert Nevin's famous **Narcissus**.

Dance of the Demon (Grand Galop de Concert)
    Rohlfing, 1888, 9p.
    CtY(Mc11A1H74), DLC(M25.H), InU(M1.S8), LN(U), MoSw(U),
        OCL(SM776.45), PP(U), RPB(U)
The Dying Shepherd (Fantasie descriptive)
    Witmark, 1896, 4p.
    CtY(Mc11A1H74), DLC(M25.H), InU(M1.S8)
Grande Polonaise brillante
    Rohlfing, 1902, 10p.
    DLC(M25.H)
The June-bugs Dance (Polka Rondo)
    Remick, 1888, 7p.
    InU(M1.S8), PP(U)
Pattering Rain (Morceau de Salon)
    Harms, 1894, 7p.
    CtY(Mc11A1H74)
Revel of the Witches (Morceau fantasque)
    Steffen, 1888, 9p.
    RPB(U)
Whispering Leaves (Mazurka-Caprice)
    Rohlfing, 1888, 9p.
    NRU-E(U)

HOMMANN, CHARLES (fl.early 19th c.)

Three Fugues for the Pianoforte
    FiotM, 183_?, 11p.
    DLC(M1.A13H Case), NcU(Microfilm 55-M580)
    Interesting, well-constructed works.
Rondo
    Blake, n.d., 11p.
    DLC(M1.A13H Case), NcU(M786.41H768r)
    Historically interesting.

HOPEKIRK, HELEN (1856-1945)

Cronan (see Iona Memories)
Gavotte
    Schirmer, 1885, 5p.
    DLC(M31.H)
In the Ruins (see Iona Memories)
Iona Memories
    Schirmer, 1909, 4v.(11,5,7,5p.)
    DLC(M25.H, 2,3,4 only), PP(U, 1,2,3 only)
    1. **Wandering**; 2. **Cronan** (A Hushing Song); 3. **In the
        Ruins**; 4. **A Twilight Tale**
Romance
    Prochàzka, 1885, 5p.
    DLC(M25.H)
Serenade
    Boosey, 1895, 8p.

        DLC(M25.H)
Serenata (Suite)
    Boston, 1920, 20p.
    DLC(M24.H816), NNLc(°MYD), PP(M786.4H771)
    1. Maestoso; 2. Minuet; 3. Sarabande; 4. Arioso;
       5. Rigaudon
Sundown
    Schirmer, 1909, 7p.
    MoSW(U), NRU-E(M25H791s), PP(U)
A Twilight Tale (see Iona Memories)
Wandering (see Iona Memories)

HOPKINS, CHARLES JEROME (1836-1898)

"Cicily" (Valse de Concert), Op.23
    Ditson, 1867, 15p.
    DLC(M25.H)
    Very grand with much romantic sweep.
Dash-Away Galop
    Gordon, 1865, 9p.
    MiU-C(U), NRU-E(U)
Home Sweet Home (Varié), Op.4
    Halls, 1858, 7p.
    PP(U), ViU(McR.174.29)
A Midnight Barcarolle, Op.12
    Pond, 1893, 9p.
    DLC(M25.H), ICN(Piano pre-1870), NRU-E(U)
Serenade de "Don Pasquale" (de Donizetti), Op.22
    Ditson, 1867, 15p.
    DLC(M34.H)
    Attractive variation treatment.
Snow-Nymph (Polka-Caprice), Op.24
    Ditson, 1867, 13p.
    DLC(M25.H)
The Wind Demon (Rhapsodie caractéristique), Op.11
    Ditson, 1865, 11p.
    IU(Joseffy), NNLc(°MYD Amer)
    Bombastic, flamboyant fun-to-play salon piece.

HUGO, JOHN ADAM (1873-1945)

Albumblatt, Op.6, No.1 (see Fünf Klavierstücke, Op.6)
Andante Cantabile, Op.5, No.1
    Hasey, 1897, 5p.
    DLC(M25.H)
Caractéristique, Op.6, No.5 (see Fünf Klavierstücke, Op.6)
Fünf Klavierstücke, Op.6
    Fontana, 1902, 5v.(5,5,3,5,7p.)
    DLC(M25.H)
    1. Albumblatt; 2. Polonaise; 3. Ein Traum; 4. Lied
       ohne Worte; 5. Caractéristique

Lied ohne Worte, Op.6, No.4 (see Fünf Klavierstücke, Op.6)
Polonaise, Op.6, No.2 (see Fünf Klavierstücke, Op.6)
Romanze, Op.5, No.3
    Hasey, 1897, 5p.
    DLC(M25.H)
Ein Traum, Op.6, No.3 (see Fünf Klavierstücke, Op.6)

HUPFELD, CHARLES F. (ca.1788-1864)

A Favorite Waltz with Variations
    Bacon, ca.1820, 7p. [W.I:435]
    DLC(M1.A1H Case), PP(U; K:4), also in A-C(II)
Thema original with Variations
    Blake, ca.1822, 9p. [W.I:433]
    PP(K:32)
    An extremely fine work by this early composer.

HUSS, HENRY HOLDEN (1862-1953)

Albumblatt (see Drei Bagatellen)
Album-Leaf, Op.23, No.5 (see Six Pieces, Op.23)
Drei Bagatellen
    Schmidt, 1889, 3v.(5,5,5p.)
    DLC(M25.H), IU(Joseffy, I only), MoS(786.4, II only),
      OCl(SM776.4, III only), PP(U, I only)
    I. Etude mélodique; II. Albumblatt; III. Pastorale
Ballade
    Schirmer, 1885, 11p.
    DLC(M25.H)
Etude mélodique (see Drei Bagatellen)
Etude romantique, Op.23, No.1 (see Six Pieces, Op.23)
Gavotte, Op.20, No.3 (see Three Pieces, Op.20)
Gavotte capricieuse, Op.18, No.2 (see Menuet et Gavotte
  capricieuse, Op.18)
Impromptu, Op.23, NO.4 (see Six Pieces, Op.23)
Intermezzo in B Flat, Op.23, No.2 (see Six Pieces, Op.23)
Intermezzo in G, Op.23, No.3 (see Six Pieces, Op.23)
Menuet et Gavotte capricieuse, Op.18
    Schirmer, 1901, 2v.(7,5p.)
    CtY(H963, 1only), DLC(M31.H, 2 only), IU(Joseffy), MoS
      (786.4, 1 only), MoSW(U, 2 only), NRU-E(U, 1 only),
      NcU(M786.45H972m, H972g), RPB(U, 2 only)
    1. Menuet; 2. Gavotte capricieuse
Nocturne, Op.20, No.2 (see Three Pieces, Op.20)
La Nuit (Poem), Op.21
    Schirmer, 1904, 5p.
    CtY(U), DLC(M25.H), ICN(Case8A 1695,no.18), MoSW(U),
      NRU-E(M21M67,v.2), PP(U), RPB(U)
    Imaginative use of chromaticism.
On the Lake, Op.26, No.2 (Etude. From Three Pieces, Op.26)
    Schirmer, 1917, 11p.

LN(U), NRU-E(U)
Pastorale (see **Drei Bagatellen**)
Three Pieces for Pianoforte, Op.20
    Schirmer, 1904, 3v.(9,5,5p.)
    CtY(U, 2 only), DLC(M25.H), MoS(786.43, 2 only), NcU
      (M786.4H972p), RPB(U, 1,2 only)
    1. **Valse**; 2. **Nocturne**; 3. **Gavotte**
Six Pieces for the Pianoforte, Op.23
    Schirmer, 1912, 6v.(11,3,1,9,3,15p.)
    CtY(U, 1 only), DLC(M25.H), MoS(786.4, 1 only), MoSW
      (U, 2,4 only), RPB(U, 5 only)
    1. **Etude romantique**; 2. **Intermezzo in B Flat**
      (Brahmsianer); 3. **Intermezzo in G** (Brahmsianer);
      4. **Impromptu**; 5. **Album-Leaf**; 6. **Polonaise**
      brillante
Polonaise brillante, Op.23, No.6 (see **Six Pieces, Op.23**)
Prelude Appassionata
    Schmidt, 1891, 7p.
    DLC(M25.H), IU(Joseffy)
Prélude en Rébémol, Op.17, No.1 (see **Quatre Préludes,
    Op.17**)
Prélude en Ré Majeur, Op.17, No.2 (see **Quatre Préludes,
    Op.17**)
Prélude en Mi Majeur, Op.17, No.3 (see **Quatre Préludes,
    Op.17**)
Prélude en Labémol Majeur, Op.17, No.4 (see **Quatre
    Préludes, Op.17**)
Quatre Préludes en Forme d'Etudes, Op.17
    Schirmer, 1901, 4v.(7,5,5,7p.)
    CtY(U, 2,3 only), DLC(M25.H), IU(Joseffy), MoS(786.4),
      MoSW(U, 1,2,4 only), NNLc(°MYD+box), NRU-E(M21R29Av.2,
      3 only), NcU(M786.4H972pr), PP(U, 2,3 only), RPB(U,
      3 only), WM(786.4H967)
    1. **Prélude en Rébémol**; 2. **Prélude en Ré Majeur**;
      3. **Prélude en Mi Majeur**; 4. **Prélude en Labémol Majeur**
    No.3, for right hand alone, is particularly valuable.
The Rivulet (Etude)
    Schmidt, 1891, 5p.
    DLC(M25.H), IU(Joseffy)
    Cover page reads **Prelude Appassionata. The Rivulet (Etude)**.
    Fine right-hand study piece.
Valse, Op.20, No.1 (see **Three Pieces, Op.20**)

HUTCHESON, ERNEST (1871-1951)

Album Leaf, Op.12, No.3 (see **Three Piano Pieces, Op.12**)
Andante tranquillo, Op.10, No.1 (see **Four Pieces, Op.10**)
Capriccio, Op.10, No.2 (see **Four Pieces, Op.10**)
Humoresque, Op.12, No.2 (see **Three Piano Pieces, Op.12**)
Idyl, Op.12, No.1 (see **Three Piano Pieces, Op.12**)
Three Piano Pieces, Op.12
    ComposerMC, 1922, 1923, 3v.(6,14, 3p.)

CtY(Mc11A1H970, 1 only), DLC(M25.H), PP(U, 1 only), WM
(786.4H97i, 1 only)
1. Idyll; 2. Humoresque; 3. Album Leaf
Four Pieces for Piano, Op.10
Schirmer, 1904, 4v.(5,10,5,15p.)
DLC(M25.H), IU(Joseffy, 1,2,3 only), MB-N(Piano, 1,3
only), MoS(786.4), MoSW(U, 3,4 only), NNLc(°MYD-Amer),
OC(786.4fH973, 1,2,4 only), OCl(SM776.4, 1 only) PP(U,
1,2,4 only)
1. Andante tranquillo; 2. Capriccio; 3. Sarabande;
4. Scherzo
Prelude (F-sharp Minor), **Op.11, No.1** (from **Two Pieces for
Piano, Op.11**)
ComposerMC, 1921, 7p.
DLC(M25.H), LN(U)
Ride of the Valkyries (R. Wagner. Transcription)
Presser, 1920, 18p.
CtY(Mc11A1H970), OCl(CM776.49W125WA7)
A superb, very difficult transcription.
Sarabande, Op.10, No.3 (see **Four Pieces, Op.10**)
Scherzo, Op.10, No.4 (see **Four Pieces, Op.10**)
Suite, Op.1
Ries, 1895, 30p.
DLC(M24.H)
1. Preludio; 2. Scherzino; 3. Fuge; 4. Menuetto;
5. Toccata

HYLLESTED, AUGUST (1858-1946)

Album Leaf
Prochàzka, 1886, 5p.
DLC(M25.H)
Andante con espressione, Op.16, No.1 (see **Suite de Ballet,
Op.16**)
Impromptu No.1
BrainardS, 1891, 7p.
DLC(M25.H)
Mazurka, Op.16, No.4 (see **Suite de Ballet, Op.16**)
Polka, Op.16, No.2 (see **Suite de Ballet, Op.16**)
Romantique Suite (or Sketches from the Time of Margaret
Queen of Denmark, Sweden and Norway 1353-1412)
BrainardS, 1891, 6v.(6,10,8,14,6,14p.)
DLC(M24.H)
1. The Troubadour; 2. Hunting Scene; 3. In the Rose
Garden; 4. The Jester; 5. Serenade;
6. Before the Tournament
Suite de Ballet, Op.16
Church, 1893, 4v.(7,9,13,9p.)
DLC(M24.H)
1. Andante con espressione; 2. Polka; 3. Valse;
4. Mazurka
Valse, Op.16, No.3 (see **Suite de Ballet, Op.16**)

IUCHO, WILHELM (fl.ca.1830-1860)

The Arkansas Traveler (A Western Refrain with Introduction
   and Easy Variations)
      FirthP, 1851, 5p.
      CtY(Mc11A1Iu2), DLC(M1.A13.I Case), InU(M1.S8), NNLc(AM2-I),
      RPB(U), ViU(°M1.A13N A753 1851), also in AB-D
Beauties of Elise e Claudio, Op.15 (Composed by Mercadente.
   Selected and Arranged as a Divertimento)
      HewittC, n.d., 7p.
      RPB(U)
Beauties of Masaniello, Op.7 (Composed by Auber. Selected
   and Arranged as a Divertimento)
      HallS, 1850, 7p.
      NcD(RBR MusicB89,no.3)
Echoes from I Puritani (Donizetti)
      FirthP, 1852, 7p.
      NcD(RBR MusicB38,no.1)
Introduction and Variations on the Favorite Italian Air
   "Buonanotte"
      FirthH, 1831, 7p.
      CtY(Mc11A1Iu2), NNLc(AM2-I), RPB(U)
Introduction and Variations on the Favorite Scotch Ballad
   "Oft in the Stilly Night"
      DuboisB, n.d., 14p.
      DLC(M1.A13.I Case), NNLc(AM2-I), RPB(U), ViU(McR.68.14),
      WM(786.4I92o)
      See another setting by "A Lady" (ANONYMOUS).
Larmes de Nuit (Nocturne)
      Pond, 1860, 10p.
      DLC(M25.I), NNLc(AM2-I), ViU(McR.29.02)
The Last Rose of Summer (with Variations), **Op.114**
      Waters, 1854, 11p.
      CtHT(U), NcU(EAMC,no.18), RPB(U)
"Oft in the Stilly Night" (see **Introduction and Var.**)
Recollections of Oberon (Weber. Fantasie de Salon)
      FirthP, 1854, 7p.
      DeWHi(U), RPB(U)
Sonata in C
      Hewitt, 1831, 9p.
      PPi(qr786.4P53)
Sourire du Matin (Reverie), **Op.133**
      FirthP, 1861, 11p.
      DLC(M25.I), InU(M1.S8), RPB(U)
Souvenirs of Kentucky (Grand Fantasie), **Op.108**
      HallS, 1854, 15p.
      CtY(Mc11A1Iu2), DLC(M25.I)
      A sometimes difficult potpourri of various tunes
      with variations.
"Take this Lute"
      Sarles, 1852, 7p.
      CtHT(U), CtY(Mc11A1Iu2)
      Transcription of a song by Julius Benedict.

IVES, CHARLES (1874-1954)

The Anti-Abolitionist Riots in the 1830s and 1840s
Mercury, 1949, 4p.
CU(M25I83 1949), CtY(M25I95A6+), DLC(M25.I), ICN(sVM25
I95a), IU(qM786.41Iv3a), LNT(M25.I8A5), MBN(M25I9S7,
no.9 1949), NNLc(°MYD-Amer.box), NcU(M786.4I95a), OCl
(M776.4.50632), PP(786.4Iv3a), ViU(Music M25.I93A5)
Also called **Study, Piano, no.9.** Written 1908-1909.
Invention
Hinshaw, 1975, 2p.
NcD(M786.4I95I62 1975), NcU(M25.I93I5), also in PM-H
Modern edition of a much earlier work (1896?)
Piano Works by Charles Ives, Henry Cowell, Carl Ruggles
New Music, Oct., 1947, pp.8-12 (20th anniversary edition)
CU(N4v.21 CaseX), DLC(M1.N55,v.21,no.1 Case), ICN(VM1N53,
v.21,no.1), IU(M1.N48,v.21,no.1), LNT(786.1A P57),
MoS(786.4.P52), NNLc(°MN N511,v.21,no.1), OCl(q770.5
N466,v.21,no.1), PP(786.4P573w), ViU(Music M1.N55,v.21,
no.1)
1. **22** (pp.8-9); 2. **Three Protests** (pp.10-12)
First Sonata for Piano
Peer, 1954, 50p.
CU(M23I9), CtY(M23.5I95+no.1), DLC(M23.I92no.1), ICN
(sVM23I95s1), IU(qM786.41Iv3s1), LNT(786I95soP),
MBN(M23I9no.1), MoS(786.41), NNLc(Mus.Res.Amer-°MYD),
NcD(M786.41I955no.1), NcU(M23I92no.1), NRU-E(M23
I952.1), OCl(M776.41.5071), PP(786.41Iv3s1), ViU
(Music M23I92no.1 1954)
Written 1902-1909.
Second Pianoforte Sonata "Concord, Mass., 1840-60"
Arrow, 1947, 68p.
CU(M23I92 1947), CtY(M23.5I95+no.2), DLC(M23.I92no.2),
ICN(VM23I95s2), IU(qM786.41Iv3s2Spec.Coll.), LNT
(786I95soP2), MBH(P.2Iv3), MBN(M23I9no.2 1947),
MoS(786.41), NNLc(°MYD-Amer), NRU-E(M23I952.2A),
NcD(M786.4I955no.2), NcU(M23I92no.2 1947),
OCl(M776.41.5074), PP(786.41Iv3s2a), ViU(Music M23
I92no.2 1947)
1. **Emerson;** 2. **Hawthorne;** 3. **The Alcotts;** 4. **Thoreau**
Ives' "classic" sonata was originally published in 1920.
Some South-Paw Pitching (ed. Henry Cowell)
Mercury, 1949, 5p.
CtY(M25I95S9+no.21), DLC(M25.I), ICN(sVM25I95s), IU
M25I94no.21K5), MBN(M25I9S7no.21 1949), NNLc(°MYD-
Amer.box), NRU-E(M25I95S9), NcD(M786.41I95So),
NcU(M25I93no.21), OCl(M776.4.50636), PP(786.4Iv3s),
ViU(Music M25I93S8no.21 1975)
Also called **Study, Piano, No.21.**
Study No.22
Merion, 1973, 3p.
CtY(M25I95S9+no.22), DLC(M25.I), IU(M25I94S7no.22),
MBN(M25I9S7no.22 1973), NRU-E(M25I95S92no.22 1973),

NcU(M25.I93no.22), ViU(Music M25I93S8no.22)
Three Page Sonata (ed. Henry Cowell)
   Mercury, 1949, 11p.
   CU(M23I95), CtY(M23.5I95+), DLC(M23.I92T5), ICN(sVM23
      I95s), IU(M23I94T53), LNT(786I95s), MBN(M23I9T5), MoS
      (M786.41.I9t), NNLc(°MYD-Amer; JNG 76-154), NRU-E(M23
      I952), NcD(M786.41I95T), NcU(M25.I92T5), OCl(M776.41.
      508), PP(M786.41Iv3), ViU(Music M23I92T4 1975)
Waltz-rondo (ed. J. Kirkpatrick and J. Cox)
   Associated, 1978, 15p.
   MBN(U), NcU(M32.I93W3), ViU(Music M25I93W3)

JOHNS, CLAYTON (1857-1932)

Canzone (see **Four Pieces for the Pianoforte**)
En Route (Etude)
   Boston, 1902, 7p.
   DLC(M25.J), IU(Joseffy), PP(U), RPB(U)
   Study in lightness. Unusual rhythmic interest.
Impromptu Capriccietto
   Schmidt, 1886, 7p.
   DLC(M25.J)
Introduction and Fugue in E Minor, Op.24
   Church, 1889, 7p.
   DLC(M25.J), ICN(VM25J65i), MoS(786.4), NNLc(°MYD+box),
      NRU-E(M21R29Av.2), NcU(M786.4J65in)
   Short introduction and well-constructed fugue.
Mazurka
   In HH-K(I:109)
Two Mazurkas in G
   Russell, 1880, 2v.(7,7p.)
   DLC(M32.J), NNLc(°MYD+box), NcU(M786.44J65m)
Four Pieces for the Pianoforte
   SchirmerJr, 1893, 4v.(10,6,5,4p.)
   CtY(Mc11A1J62, 1 only), DLC(M25.J, 2,3,4 only), MoSW
      (U, 3 only), NRU-E(M21R29Av.1), NcU(M786.43J65c,
      3 only), PP(U, 2,3 only), RPB(U, 2,3 only)
   1. **Valse**; 2. **Romance**; 3. **Canzone**; 4. **Promenade**
Promenade (see **Four Pieces for the Pianoforte**)
Romance (see **Four Pieces for the Pianoforte**)
Valse (see **Four Pieces for the Pianoforte**)

JOHNS, PAUL EMILE (ca.1798-1860)

Album Louisianais (Hommage aux Dames de la Nouvelle
   Orléans)
   Pleyel, ca.1819
   LNH(U), NNLc(°MP U.S.)
   1. **Valse** (pp.25-29); 2. **Polonaise héroique** (pp.30-35)
Polonaise héroique (see **Album Louisianais**)
Valse (see **Album Louisianais**)

JOHNSON, GUSTAVUS (1856-ca.1932)

Dance of the Goblins, Op.30, No.6 (see **Suite populaire, Op.30**)

Danse andalouse, Op.24 ("Spain." Characteristic Dance)
    Schmitt, 1902, 7p.
    NRU-E(U)

In Joyful Vein, Op.30, No.3 (see **Suite populaire, Op.30**)

Intrata, Op.30, No.1 (see **Suite populaire, Op.30**)

Nocturne, Op.16
    Schmidt, 1889, 9p.
    DLC(M25.J)

On the Lagoon, Op.30, No.5 (see **Suite populaire, Op.30**)

Romanza, Op.30, No.4 (see **Suite populaire, Op.30**)

Suite populaire, Op.30
    Schmitt, 1905, 6v.(5,7,3,3,9,5p.)
    DLC(M24.J)
    1. **Intrata** (Marcia fantastica); 2. **With Spirit and Abandon** (Valse Caprice); 3. **In Joyful Vein** (Allegretto scherzando); 4. **Romanza** (Andante Appassionata); 5. **On the Lagoon** (Barcarole); 6. **Dance of the Goblins** (Gavotte grotesque)

Second Tarantelle, Op.8
    Schmidt, 1889, 7p.
    NRU-E(U)

With Spirit and Abandon, Op.30, No.2 (see **Suite populaire, Op.30**)

JONAS, ALBERTO (1868-1943)

A una Niña (Romance)
    Schirmer, 1892, 7p.
    DLC(M25.J)

Capriccio, Op.19, No.2 (see **In Memoriam D. Scarlatti, Op.19**)

Capricho
    Schirmer, 1893, 7p.
    CU(M25J64), DLC(M25.J), NRU-E(U)
    Impressive dance in a Spanish idiom.

Chant du Soir (Evening Song), **Op.21, No.5**
    Fischer, 1932, 7p.
    NRU-E(U)

Concert Mazurka, Op.15
    Schirmer, 1900, 9p.
    DLC(M32.J), MBN(Piano), MoSW(U)

Fantasiestücke, Op.10
    Schirmer, 1899, 19p.
    MoS(789.4), MoSW(U)
    1. **Wintertage im Norden** (Winter-days in the North); 2. **Trübe Stunden** (Clouded Hours); 3. **San Souci**; 4. **Einsame Hütten** (Lonely Huts); 5. **Le Moulin de chez nous** (Our old Windmill); 6. **Dämmerungslied** (Twilight Song)

In Memoriam Domenico Scarlatti, Op.19
    Fischer, 1919, 2v.(5,5p.)
    DLC(M25.J)
    1. Pastorale; 2. Capriccio
Marche militaire, Op.21, No.6 (Concert transcription of
  Schubert's Op.51, No.3)
    Fischer, 1932, 15p.
    DLC(M34.S [Schubert])
Pastorale, Op.7, No.1
    Summy, 1896, 5p.
    IU(Joseffy)
Toccata, Op.14
    Schirmer, 1900, 7p.
    CU(M25J645), DLC(M25.J), MBN(Piano), MoSW(U), NRU-E(M21M67
      v.3), OCL(SM776.4)
Valse in C-sharp Minor, Op.8
    Ditson, 1899, 7p.
    NRU-E(U)

JOSEFFY, RAFAEL (1852-1915)

Aquarelle
    Schirmer, 1882, 5p.
    DLC(M25.J), IU(Joseffy), NNLc(°MYDbox), NRU-E(M22J83),
      PP(U)
Arabesque (from Two Sketches for Piano)
    Schirmer, 1909, 5p.
    IU(Joseffy), NRU-E(M22J83)
Aria di Pergolese ("Nina")
    Schuberth-E, 1879, Schirmer, 1882, 5p.
    CtY(McA1J77), DLC(M25.J)
    Sensitive, musicianly transcription.
Arietta di Balletto by Ch. W. Gluck (Paraphrase from
  Alceste)
    Schuberth-E, 1881, 1909, 9p.
    CtHT(U), DLC(M34.J), IU(Joseffy), MoS(786.4), NRU-E(U)
At the Spring (An der Quelle)
    Pond, 1884, 11p.
    CU(M25J685), CtHT(U), CtY(Mc11A1J77), DLC(M25.J), IU
      (Joseffy), NNLc(°MYD+box), NRU-E(M22J83), PP(U),
      WM(786.4J83a)
Barcarolle
    Schuberth-E, 1879, 6p.
    DLC(M25.J), IU(MO 48077)
Cadence to Mozart's Concerto in A Major (K.488)
    Schirmer, 1882, 9p.
    DLC(M25.J)
Chanson d'Amour
    Schirmer, 1888, 5p.
    DLC(M25.J), NRU-E(M22J83)
Columbia! (by P. S. Gilmore. Paraphrase)
    Schuberth-E, 1880, 16p.

IU(Joseffy)
Concert Study on Chopin's Waltz in D Flat (Op.64)
  Schuberth-E, 1879, 7p.
  DLC(M25.J), NNLc(°MYDbox)
Csàrdàs (Danse hongroise)
  Schirmer, 1887, 7p.
  CU(M2OC6v3), CtY(Mc11A1J77), DLC(M25.J), IU(Joseffy),
    NNLc(°MYD+box), NRU-E(M22J83), PP(U)
Csàrdàs No.2
  Schirmer, 1909, 9p.
  DLC(M25.J), IU(Joseffy), NNLc(°MYD), NRU-E(M22J83)
Etude No.1 (from **Zwei Etüden**)
  Cranz, 1880, 9p.
  NNLc(°MYD), PP(U)
Etude in A Flat
  Schirmer, 1887, 7p.
  CtHT(U), IU(Joseffy), MBN(Piano), MoS(786.4), MoSW(U),
    NNLc(°MYDbox), NRU-E(M22J83), PP(U)
Idylle, Op.25
  Schirmer, Schott, n.d., 5p.
  IU(Joseffy), NRU-E(M22J83)
Impromptu
  Schirmer, 1887, 7p.
  DLC(M25.J), MoSW(U), NRU-E(M22J83)
Second Melody
  Schirmer, 1882, 5p.
  CtY(Mc11A1J77), NRU-E(M22J83)
Minuet of Boccherini (Transcription)
  Schuberth-E, 1879, Schirmer, 1884, 7p.
  InU(M1.S8), NNLc(°MYDp.v.59,no.10), NRU-E(M22J83), ViU
    (°M1.S444,v.106,no.6)
Die Mühle (The Mill), **Op.23**
  André, n.d., 9p.; Schuberth-E, 1879, 8p.
  CtY(Mc11A1J77), IU(Joseffy), MoS(786.4), MoSW(U), NRU-E
    (M25J832m), OCl(CM776.4J7733MI), PP(U), RPB(U), WM
    (786.4J83m)
"Nina" of Pergolese (see **Aria di Pergolese**)
Pizzicati from "Sylvia" Ballet by Delibes (Concert
  Transcription)
  Schirmer, 1882, 11p.
  CU(M2OC6v.3), IU(Joseffy), NNLc(°MYDbox)
Polka noble
  Schuberth-E, Ditson, 1879, 9p.
  DLC(M25.J), NNLc(°MYD+box), PP(U), WM(786.4J83p)
Polka noble II
  Ebner, n.d., 9p.
  IU(Joseffy)
Romance sans Paroles
  Schirmer, 1887, 7p.
  CtY(Mc10v.4), DLC(M25.J), IU(MO 48086), NRU-E(M22J83)
Souvenir d'Amérique (Valses)
  Schirmer, 1881, 17p.
  DLC(M32.J), IU(MO 48083), MoS(786.45), NRU-E(M22J83), PP(U)

Spinnlied (Spinning Song)
    Schirmer, 1882, 9p.
    CtY(Mc11A1J77), DLC(M25.J), IU(Joseffy), MoSW(U), NNLc
       (°MYDbox), NRU-E(M22J83), OCl(M776.4.5177)
    One of the better "spinning" songs.
Spring Song
    Schirmer, 1913, 5p.
    DLC(M25.J), IU(Joseffy), MoSW(U), NRU-E(M22J83)
Tanz Arabeske
    Schuberth-E, 1879, 15p.
    IU(Joseffy)
    A very difficult but rewarding composition.
Valse Caprice, Op.22
    André, n.d., 9p.
    IU(MO 48081)
Valse-Impromptu
    Schuberth-E, 1889, 11p.
    CtY(U), DLC(M32.J), IU(MO 48063), NNLc(°MYD+box)
Wiegenlied (Cradle-Song)
    Schirmer, 1909, 5p.
    CtY(Mc11A1J77), DLC(M25.J), IU(Joseffy), NRU-E(M22J83),
       PP(U), WM(786.4J83w)

KAUN, HUGO (1863-1932)

Arabeske, Op.2, No.1
    Kaun, 1905, 7p. (revised ed.)
    DLC(M25.K)
Ballade, Op.93, No.1 (from Fünf Klavierstücke, Op.93)
    Zimmermann, 1913, 7p.
    DLC(M25.K), WM(786.4K21f)
Barcarolle, Op.42, No.4 (see Vier Stücke, Op.42)
Berceuse, Op.93, No.4 (from Fünf Klavierstücke, Op.93)
    Zimmermann, 1913, 5p.
    DLC(M25.K), WM(786.4K21f)
Humoreske, Op.56, No.1 (see Drei Stücke, Op.56)
In Springtime (Im Frühling), Op.7, No.3
    Kaun, 1905, 5p.
    DLC(M25.K), MoSW(U)
Melodie-Etude, Op.42, No.2 (see Vier Stücke, Op.42)
Menuett, Op.7, No.1
    Kaun, 1905, 7p.
    DLC(M25.K)
Menuett, Op.30, No.2 (Eisenach: BACH. From Im Thüringerland,
    Op.30)
    Challier, 1904, 6p.
    NNLc(JMG 76-600), WM(786.4K21i)
    Artful minuet based on BACH.
Menuett, Op.42, No.3 (see Vier Stücke, Op.42)
Mümmelmann, Op.111
    Zimmermann, 1919, 27p.
    DLC(M25.K), WM(A Ref.786.4K21m)

1. **Auerhahn Balze** (Oktaven-Etude); 2. **Mümmelmann**
   (Fuge); 3. **Einsam im Walde;** 4. **Fuchsjagd;**
   5. **Nebelgestalten**
Nocturno, Op.56, No.3 (see **Drei Stücke, Op.56**)
Octaven-Etude, Op.34, No.4 (from **Vier Stücke, Op.34**)
   Stahl, 1901, 5p.
   CU(fMT229K3), DLC(M25.K)
Pierrot und Columbine (Vier Episoden für Pianoforte), **Op.71**
   Challier, 1907, 30p.
   DLC(M24.K21op.71), MoS(786.4), NNLc('MYD), WM(786.4K21pi)
   1. **Begegnung;** 2. **Werbung** (Serenata); 3. **Liebesfrühling**
      (Duett); 4. **Zwist und Versöhnung**
Praeludien, Op.118
   André, 1925, 3v.(18,19,17p.)
   DLC(M25.K), WM(786.4K21p)
   Sixteen effective, imaginative preludes.
Präludium, Op.56, No.2 (see **Drei Stücke, Op.56**)
Quelle im Walde, Op.93, No.3 (from **Fünf Klavierstücke, Op.93**)
   Zimmermann, 1913, 7p.
   DLC(M25.K), OCl(M776.4.5257), WM(786.4K21f)
Sonate (A dur), **Op.2**
   SchroederN, Rohlfing, 1888, 27p.
   DLC(M23.K215op.2), OCl(M776.41.528), WM(786.4K21s)
   Large-scale, four-movement work.
Drei Stücke, Op.56
   Kahnt, 1904, 3v.(11,7,5p.)
   CU(M25K374), DLC(M25.K)
   1. **Humoreske;** 2. **Präludium;** 3. **Nocturno**
Vier Stücke, Op.42
   Rohlfing, 1895, 4v.(7,5,7,5p.)
   DLC(M25.K), IU(Joseffy), PP(U, 2,3,4 only)
   1. **Valse élégante;** 2. **Melodie-Etude;** 3. **Menuett;**
      4. **Barcarole** (Etude)
Valse élégante, Op.42, No.1 (see **Vier Stücke, Op.42**)
Variationen über ein Originalthema, Op.1
   Kaun, 1906, 15p.
   DLC(M27.K)
Waldesgespräche (Voices of the Woods), **Op.78**
   Vieweg, 1908, 4v.(3,5,5,7p.)
   CU(M24K38, 2,3,4 only), DLC(M25.K), MoSW(U, 1 only),
   NNLc('MYD+box), WM(786.4K21w)
Walzer, Op.93, No.2 (from **Fünf Klavierstücke, Op.93**)
   Zimmermann, 1913, 7p.
   DLC(M25.K), WM(786.4K21f)

KELLER, WALTER (1873-1940)

Canon in A Flat, Op.8, No.1
   Gilbert, 1915, 7p.
   DLC(M25.K), PP(U)
Prelude and Fugue in F, Op.10
   Gilbert, 1919, 17p.

DLC(M214.K26P6), IU(MaLq.786.4K28p), MBH(P.3B12.5), NNLc
(°MYD+box)
The Fugue can be played simultaneously with the Prelude as
a work for two pianos.

KELLEY, EDGAR STILLMAN (1857-1944)

Ballet Episode
    Ditson, 1897, 7p.
    DLC(M25.K), OCl(SM776.45), WM(786.4K29)
Three Compositions, Op.2
    Schirmer, 1891, 3v.(9,5,11p.)
    CU(M25K4 1891, 3 only), CtY(Mc11A1K287, 2 only), DLC
    (M25.K), ICN(VM22K29t), IU(Joseffy), MBH(McAt4), NNLc
    (JNG 74-209), OCl(M776.4.5264, 3 only), WM(786.4K29h,
    3 only), also in NC-G (2,3 only)
    1. The Flower-seekers; 2. Confluentia; 3. The Headless
       Horseman
Confluentia, Op.2, No.2 (see **Three Compositions, Op.2**)
The Flower-seekers, Op.2, No.1 (see **Three Compositions, Op.2**)
The Headless Horseman, Op.2, No.3 (see **Three Compositions, Op.2**)
"The Lady picking Mulberries" (Transcription)
    Ditson, 1888, 5p.
    OC(786.4fK29L)
    Pleasant transcription of Kelley's own song.
Lyric Opera Sketches, Op.13
    Millet, 1894, 6p.
    DLC(M25.K), also in HH-K(IV:889)
    1. For a Gavotte Movement; 2. For a Waltz Chorus
Polonaise, Op.35
    ArtPS, 1916, 13p.
    OC(786.4fK29p)
Sky Line, Op.34, No.1
    ComposerP, 1916, 1943, 6p.
    NcU(M25.K4S5), PP(U)
    "Evokes a nocturnal mood." (The composer).

KLAUSER, KARL [Editor] (1823-1905)

Half Hours with the Best Composers
    Millet, 1894-1895, 5v.
    DLC(M20.H22), ICN(6A 1509), IU(q786.4K66h), MBH(SL Cl.Sh.
    M1H169), MdBP(M20.K63), NNLc(7°MN), OCl(M776.408.541)
    The best 19th-century anthology containing American
     piano music. See also Appendix C.

KLEIN, BRUNO OSCAR (1858-1911)

Alla Tarantella, Op.50, No.4 (see **Italian Suite, Op.50**)
Canzonetta, Op.50, No.2 (see **Italian Suite, Op.50**)

Capriccio, Op.41
    Schmidt, 1890, 13p.
    DLC(M25.K), IU(Joseffy), PP(U)
Cuban Dance, Op.75, No.3 (from Five Piano Pieces, Op.75)
    Schuberth-E, 1901, 5p.
    CtY(Mc11A1K67)
Elegia, Op.25, No.4 (see Suite, Op.25)
Elfenmärchen (Concertstück), Op.18
    Hofmeister, Schirmer, 1888, 23p.
    DLC(M25.K), IU(Joseffy)
Gavotte, Op.25, No.5 (see Suite, Op.25)
Gretchen am Spinnrad, Op.21
    Kunkel, 1882, 9p.
    DLC(M25.K), PP(U)
    Good example of a "spinning" song.
Impromptu, Op.52, No.1 (see Seven Piano Pieces, Op.52)
Italian Suite, Op.50
    Schirmer, 1895, 4v.(7,5,7,11p.)
    CU(M24K6 1,3,4 only), DLC(M24.K 1,3,4 only), IU(Joseffy),
    MoS(786.4)
    1. Preludio; 2. Canzonetta; 3. Minuetto; 4. Alla
    Tarantella
Minuetto, Op.25, No.3 (see Suite, Op.25)
Minuetto, Op.50, No.3 (see Italian Suite, Op.50.)
Momento grazioso, Op.52, No.2 (see Seven Piano Pieces, Op.52)
Deux Morceaux, Op.39
    Schirmer, 1888, 2v.(8,9p.)
    CU(M32K554op.39:2, 2 only), DLC(M25.K, 1 only), IU(Joseffy),
    PP(U, 1 only)
    1. Romance; 2. Valse noble
A Northern Idyll, Op.52, No.6 (see Seven Piano Pieces, Op.52)
Notturno (Wiegenlied), Op.14, No.2
    Schirmer, 1881, 7p.
    CtY(Mc11A1K67), DLC(M25.K)
Deuxième Pensée poétique, Op.54, No.1 (from A Book of New
  Piano Music, Op.54)
    Schirmer, 1896, 7p.
    IU(Joseffy)
Troisième Pensée poétique, Op.54, No.5 (from A Book of New
  Piano Music, Op.54)
    Schirmer, 1896, 7p.
    IU(Joseffy)
Seven Piano Pieces, Op.52
    Schuberth-E, 1895, 7v.(5,5,3,7,7,6,7p.)
    DLC(M25.K, 2,4,5,6,7only), IU(Joseffy)
    1. Impromptu; 2. Momento grazioso; 3. Remembrance;
    4. The Swallows; 5. Valse mélancolique; 6. A Northern
    Idyl; 7. A Spanish Intermezzo
Preludio, Op.25, No.1 (see Suite, Op.25)
Preludio, Op.50, No.1 (see Italian Suite, Op.50)
Remembrance, Op.52, No.3 (see Seven Piano Pieces, Op.52)
Romance, Op.39, No.1 (see Deux Morceaux, Op.39)
Sérénade américaine, Op.54, No.8 (from A Book of New Piano

Music, Op.54)
   Schirmer, 1896, 7p.
   IU(Joseffy)
A Spanish Intermezzo, Op.52, No.7 (see Seven Piano Pieces,
   Op.52)
Suite, Op.25
   Schirmer, 1886, 35p., also issued separately
   DLC(M24.K), IU(Joseffy), NNLc(°MYD), NRU-E(M24K645), OCl
      (M776.45.5345), PP(U, 3,5 only)
   1. Preludio; 2. Thema con Variazioni; 3. Minuetto;
      4. Elegia; 5. Gavotte
The Swallows, Op.52, No.4 (see Seven Piano Pieces, Op.52)
Tempo di Polka, Op.54, No.6 (from A Book of New Piano Music,
   Op.54)
   Schirmer, 1896, 7p.
   IU(Joseffy)
Thema con Variazioni, Op.25, No.2 (see Suite, Op.25)
Zweite Valse Caprice, Op.16
   Schirmer, 1881, 11p.
   DLC(M32.K)
Valse fantastique, Op.54, No.7 (from A Book of New Piano
   Music, Op.54)
   Schirmer, 1896, 9p.
   IU(Joseffy)
Valse—Impromptu, Op.32, No.2
   Schirmer, 1885, 9p.
   CtY(Mc11A1J67)
Valse mélancolique, Op.52, No.5 (see Seven Piano Pieces, Op.52)
Valse noble, Op.39, No.2 (see Deux Morceaux, Op.39)

KOELLING, ADOLPH (1840-?)

Barcarolle (see Six Characteristic Pieces)
Six Characteristic Pieces
   Chicago, 1885, 6v.(5,7,9,7,5,7p.)
   DLC(M25.K, 1,3 only), IU(Joseffy)
   1. Barcarolle; 2. Gavotte; 3. Galop Caprice; 4. Valse
      Caprice (Impromptu); 5. Serenata; 6. 2ième Valse
      gracieuse
   Consistently interesting, musicianly collection.
Fantasiestück, Op.23
   Grand, 1882, 13p.
   DLC(M25.K)
   Early use of dissonance.
Galop Caprice (see Six Characteristic Pieces)
Gavotte (see Six Characteristic Pieces)
Impromptu, Op.10
   Schuberth-E, 1878, 8p.
   CtY(Mc11A1K83), DLC(M25.K)
Serenata (see Six Characteristic Pieces)
Valse Caprice (see Six Characteristic Pieces)
2ième Valse gracieuse (see Six Characteristic Pieces)

KOELLING, CARL (1831-ca.1914)

Bird of the Forest, Op.142
   Presser, 1894, 9p.
   PP(U)
Caprice de Concert, Op.305
   Ditson, 1886, 11p.
   DLC(M25.K), PP(U)
La Chasse au Lion (Galop brillant), **Op.55**
   Schirmer, 1906, 11p.
   NRU-E(U), ViU(McR.132.14)
   A flamboyant, fun salon piece.
La Chasse infernale (Grand Galop brillant), **Op.23**
   Century, 1908, 7p.
   CtHT(U), NRU-E(U)
Die Erzählung in der Spinnstube (Spinning-room Story), **Op.115**
   Cranz, n.d., 9p.
   ViU(U:3)
Flora Mazurka, Op.307
   Schuberth-E, 1889, 7p.
   CtY(Mc11A1K831)
The Fountain, Op.378, No.5
   Presser, 1907, 6p.
   WM(786.4K77fo)
Grande Valse brillante, Op.21
   Cranz, n.d., 11p.
   ICN(VM22K77o), IU(Joseffy)
Grand Galop, Op.23 (see **La Chasse infernale,** Op.23)
Hungary (Rapsodie mignonne), **Op.410**
   Presser, 1907, 7p.
   DLC(M25.K), InU(M1.S8), LN(U), MoSW(U), NRU-E(U), OCl
      (SM776.4)
Der Lerche Morgensang (The Lark's Morning Song), **Op.169**
   Schirmer, 1906, 7p.
   CtY(Mc11A1K831), DLC(M25.K), NRU-E(U), PP(U)
La Naiade (Etude d'Agilité), **Op.27**
   Cranz, n.d., 9p.
   ICN(VM22K77o), IU(Joseffy)
   Attractive "mermaid" piece.
Sunbeam (Nocturne), **Op.373, No.3**
   Summy, 1905, 7p.
   CtY(Mc11A1K831), DLC(M25.K)
Wohin? (Nocturno), **Op.209**
   Forberg, n.d., 9p.
   DLC(M25.K), IU(Joseffy)

KREIDER, NOBLE (1874-1959)

Ballade, Op.3
   Wa-Wan, 1906, 10p.
   ICN(VM1W11v.5), NNLc(°MN Wa-Wan), NRU-E(M25K92ba), also
      in WW-L(II:279)

Loosely based on Indian themes.
Impromptu, Op.5
    Wa-Wan, 1907, 8p.
    DLC(M25.K), ICN(VM1W11v.6), LNT(786K87st), NNLc(°MN Wa-Wan),
      NRU-E(M25K92im), also in WW-L(IV:19)
Three Moods, Op.9
    Schirmer, 1913, 3v.(5,5,11p.)
    DLc(M25.K), LNT(786K87m), MoS(786.4), MoSW(U, 2 only)
    1. "surge on surge..."; 2. The Valley of White Poppies;
      3. "Sword-storms, giddy with slaughter.."
    Difficult, unusual and dissonant.
Nocturne, Op.4, No.2
    Wa-Wan, 1907, 7p.
    DLC(M25.K), ICN(VM1W11v.6), LNT(786K87n), MoS(786.4),
      NNLc(°MN Wa-Wan), NRU-E(M25K92no), also in WW-L(IV:99)
Prelude in D Flat, Op.8
    Boston, 1911, 7p.
    LNT(786K87st), PP(U)
    Unusual chord spacing.
Six Preludes, Op.7
    Wa-Wan, 1910, 13p.
    DLC(M25.K), LNT(786K87pr), MB-N(Vault M25K73op.7), also in
      WW-L(V:161)
**Preludes Nos.2, 3 and 5 (from Six Preludes for Pianoforte,
  Op.7)**
    Wa-Wan, 1908, 3v.
    ICN(VM1W11v.7), NNLc(°MN Wa-Wan), NRU-E(M25K92p), also in
      WW-L(V:85)
Study, Op.6, No.1
    Wa-Wan, 1908, 6p.
    DLC(M1.W35 Wa-Wan), also in WW-L(V:99)
Study, Op.6, No.2
    Wa-Wan, 1908, 6p.
    DLC(M1.W35 Wa-Wan), LNT(786K87st), also in WW-L(V:105)

KROEGER, ERNEST RICHARD (1862-1934)

American Character Sketches, Op.53
    Thiebes, 1902, 10v.(3,3,5,5,3,5,5,5,5,5)
    DLC(M25.K), MoS(786.4, 1,2,4,6,8,9,10 only), NcU(M786.48
      K93a)
    1. The Gamin; 2. Prairie Sadness; 3. Song of the
      Mountaineer; 4. The Lonely Ranchman; 5. Unca's
      Death Song; 6. The Aged Negro; 7. An Indian Lament;
      8. Mountain Dance; 9. Indian Air with Variations;
      10. Voodoo Night Scene
Arabian Song, Op.31, No.2
    Millet, 1894, 3p.
    DLC(M25.K), also in HH-K(III:685)
Birds of the Forest, Op.20, No.7
    Kunkel, 1888, 6p.
    PP(U)

Complaint, Op.68, No.2 (from **For the Piano, Op.68**)
    Ditson, 1909, 3p.
    OCL(SM776.4), RPB(U)
Zwölf Concert-Etüden, Op.30
    Breitkopf, 1894, 2v.(29,31p.)
    ICN(VMT241K93z), MoS(786.47), OCL(M776.47.54), PP(U,
    v.1 only)
    1. Castor und Pollux; 2. Illusion; 3. Im Grünen;
    4. Mouvement perpétuel; 5. Heldengesang; 6. Liebes-
    botschaft; 7. Capriccio; 8. Hymnus; 9. Sehnsucht;
    10. Unruhe; 11. Romanze; 12. Sturm
    Superlative collection of challenging etudes.
Dance of the Dryads, Op.63, No.6 (see **Six Pièces, Op.63**)
Declaration (Melody), **Op.31, No.1**
    Millet, 1894, 4p.
    DLC(M25.K), also in HH-K(III:681)
Dream of the Woods, Op.63, No.1 (see **Six Pièces, Op.63**)
Egeria, Op.35
    Kunkel, 1897, 11p.
    DLC(M25.K), MoSW(U)
    "Fountain" music.
Elegy (In Memoriam Franz Liszt), **Op.13**
    Kunkel, 1887, 7p.
    ICN(8A 1736)
Elfenreigen (Charakter-Etude), **Op.17**
    Kunkel, 1887, 10p.
    ICN(VMT241K93e), IU(Joseffy), MoS(786.4), PP(U)
Hindu Song, Op.64, No.4 (from **Oriental Pictures, Op.64**)
    Willis, 1906, 5p.
    DLC(M25.K), NcU(M786.43K930.h)
Drei mythologische Scenen, Op.46
    Breitkopf, 1901, 3v.(9,15,13p.)
    DLC(M25.K), ICN(VM22K93d), MoS(786.4), MoSW(U, 1 only),
    NcU(M786.4K93m.a, 2 only)
    1. Arion; 2. An den Ufern des Lethe; 3. Ixion
Nocturne, Op.63, No.4 (see **Six Pièces, Op.63**)
Pensée fugitive, Op.63, No.5 (see **Six Pièces, Op.63**)
Six Pièces, Op.63
    Willis, 1905, 6v.(5,7,5,5,7,5p.)
    DLC(M25.K), NcU(M786.4K93p)
    1. Rêve des Bois; 2. Romanze; 3. Valsette; 4. Nocturne;
    5. Pensée fugitive; 6. Danse des Dryades
Präludium und Fuge, Op.41
    Breitkopf, 1899, 13p.
    DLC(M25.K), ICN(VM25K93p), MoS(786.4)
The Rivulet, Op.3
    Kunkel, 1884, 13p.
    DLC(M25.K), MoSW(U), PP(U), WM(786.4K93ri)
Romanze, Op.63, No.2 (see **Six Pièces, Op.63**)
Scherzo, Op.45
    Breitkopf, 1901, 11p.
    DLC(M25.K), ICN(VM22K93q), MoS(786.4), MoSW(U), NcU(M786.4
    K93s), WM(786.4K93s)

Sonate (in D-flat Major), **Op.40**
    Breitkopf, 1899, 45p.
    DLC(M23.K93op.40), ICN(VM23K93q), MoS(786.41), MoSW(U),
        NcU(M786.41K93s)
    Large-scale work in three movements.
Stimmungen, Op.60
    Breitkopf, 1904, 2v.(23,28p.)
    MoS(786.4)
    Fine collection of twenty character pieces.
Suite in F moll, Op.33
    Breitkopf, 1896, 33p.
    DLC(M24.K), ICN(VM24K93s), MoS(786.4), OCl(M776.415.5465)
    1. Präludium; 2. Intermezzo; 3. Scherzo; 4. Canon;
        5. Finale
Valsette, Op.63, No.3 (see Six Pièces, Op.63)
16 Variationen über ein elegisches Thema, Op.54
    Breitkopf, 1894, 1903, 21p.
    MoS(786.4), NcU(M786.48K93v.)

KÜRSTEINER, JEAN PAUL (1864-1943)

Second Nocturne
    Schirmer, 1910, 6p.
    DLC(M25.K), NRU-E(M21M67v.3)
Third Nocturne in A Flat
    Kürsteiner, 1911, 9p.
    DLC(M25.K)

KUNKEL, CHARLES [JEAN PAUL, CLAUDE MELNOTTE] (1840-1923)

Alpine Storm (A Summer Idyl), **Op.105**
    Kunkel, 1902, 11p.
    DLC(M25.K), MoS(786.4), MoSW(U), NRU-E(U)
Ernani (Verdi. Grand Concert Paraphrase)
    Kunkel, 1918, 11p.
    DLC(M34.V [Verdi])
Faust (de Gounod. Morceau de Concert)
    Pond, 1864, 21p.
    DLC(M34.K)
Hiawatha (An Indian Legend)
    Kunkel, 1897, 7p.
    DLC(M25.K)
"Home Sweet Home" (Concert Paraphrase)
    Kunkel, 1907, 11p.
    DLC(M27.P [Paul])
Les Huguenots (Meyerbeer. Fantasia)
    Kunkel, 1880, 9p.
    MoSW(U [Kunkel's Album No.7])
    Published under the pseudonym Jean Paul.
"Last Rose of Summer" (Concert Paraphrase)
    Kunkel, 1907, 11p.

DLC(M27.P [Paul])
"Massa's in the Cold, Cold Ground" (S. C. Foster. Concert
Paraphrase)
Kunkel, 1905, 17p.
DLC(M27.F [Foster])
"Borrows" an idea here and there from Gottschalk.
"The Mocking Bird" (Paraphrase de Concert)
Kunkel, 1911, 13p.
DLC(M25.K)
A Morning in the Woods (Idylle)
Peters-JL, 1864, 14p.
DLC(M25.K), NBu(U), IU(MaLxq784.3Sh37v.3,no.12), ViU
(°M1.S444,v.58,no.11), WM(786.4K98m)
"My Old Kentucky Home" (S. C. Foster. Grand Concert Para-
phrase)
Kunkel, 1905, 17p.
DLC(M27.F [Foster]), MoSW(U)
"Old Folks at Home" (S. C. Foster. Concert Paraphrase)
Kunkel, 1894, 13p.
DLC(M27.K), ICN(8A 3255), MiU-C(U)
Spinnlied (Caprice-Etude)
Peters-AC, 1861, 11p.
DLC(M25.K), PP(U)
"Thou Art ever Nigh" (Romance after Batiste and Ravina)
Kunkel, 1868, 9p.
DLC(M25.K), MoS(786.4 [Kunkel's Album No.10])
Il Trovatore (Verdi. Second Paraphrase de Concert), **Op.22**
Church, 1863, 13p.
CtHT(U)
Vive la République (Paraphrase de Concert)
Kunkel, 1870, 15p.; 1897, 18p.
DLC(M27.K), MoS(786.4 [Kunkel's Album No.10])
For the 1897 revised edition (DLC), Kunkel "borrows", al-
most note for note, five pages from Gottschalk's **L'Union**.

KUNKEL, JACOB (1846-1882)

The Flirt (Polka caractéristique)
Dobmeyer, 1867, 8p.
CtHT(U)
German's Triumphal March
Kunkel, 1870, 13p.
DLC(M25.K), ICN(Piano pre-1870), MiU-C(U), NBu(U), NNLc
(°MYD+box), NRU-E(U), NcU(EAMC,no.24), OCl(SM776.44),
ViU(°M1.S444,v.98,no.22)
Mountain Spring (Caprice descriptive)
Dobmeyer, 1867, 13p.
CtHT(U), DLC(M25.K), ViU(McR.113.23), PP(U)
Sparkling, virtuosic "water" music.
My Idol (Reverie poétique)
Dobmeyer, 1868, 8p.
DLC(M25.K)

On the Beautiful Blue Danube (Concert Paraphrase)
     Kunkel, 1876, 21p.
     DLC(M32.S [Strauss]), IU(Joseffy)
Sunshower (Caprice descriptif)
     Kunkel, 1870, 7p.
     DLC(M25.K), MoS(786.4 [Kunkel's Album No.12])
The Zephyr and the Brook (Tone Poem)
     Kunkel, 1881, 9p.
     DLC(M25.K)

LA FORGE, FRANK (1879-1953)

Gavotte and Musette
     Schirmer, 1912, 7p.
     DLC(M25.L), NRU-E(M21R29Av.1)
Improvisation
     Schirmer, 1912, 5p.
     DLC(M25.L), NRU-E(M21R29Av.2)
Romance
     Schirmer, 1911, 1939, 5p.
     DLC(M25.L), IU(M25L3R6), LN(U), MoSW(U), OCl(SM776.4),
        PP(786.4L134r), RPB(U), WM(786.4L16r)
Valse de Concert
     Schirmer, 1912, 13p.
     MoS(786.4), PP(M786.4L13), WM(786.4L16v)

LA HACHE, THEODORE VON (ca.1822-1869)

Armide (Polka de Concert)
     Werlein, 1854, 7p.
     DLC(M22.L), LNT(L976.3[780]Z99)
Le Carnaval de Venise (Variations de Salon), Op.114
     FirthP, 1854, 9p.
     DLC(M22.L), LNT(L976.3[780]Z99)
Elégie (à la Mémoire de Mme. G. T. Beauregard)
     The composer, 1864, 7p.
     DLC(M25.L), LN(U), LNT(Civil War, La.Coll.)
Fantasia and Variations on the Ethiopian Air "The Rose of
   Alabama," Op.2
     Fiot, 1846, 11p.
     LNT(L976.3[780]Z99), PP(U), RPB(U)
Freedom's Tear (Reverie)
     Werlein, 1861, 7p.
     NcD(RBR MusicCr.3469)
     Delightful keyboard aria à la Bellini.
Grand Polka militaire, Op.119
     Werlein, 1859, 5p.
     LN(U)
Improvisation on Foley Hall's beautiful Melody "Ever of
   Thee," Op.306
     Snow, 1859, 11p.

RPB(U)
Attractive variations on a sentimental song.
Improvisation on the "Bonnie Blue Flag," Op.537
Blackmar, 1864, 9p.
LN(U), LNH(U), LNT(Civil War, La.Coll.), NNLc(AM2-I)
Improvisation on the Favorite Melody "Her Bright Smile Haunts me still," Op.503
Blackmar, 1862, 7p.
LN(U), LNH(U), NcD(RBR MusicCr.3573)
New Pic Nic Polka, Op.211
Blackmar, 1858, 7p.
LN(R786.4L18c v.2), NNLc(AM2-I)
Includes a part for cornet solo!
Picnic Polka, Op.102
Ditson, 1854, 1883, 7p.
LN(R786.44L18pi), NNLc(AM2-I), NcD(M780.8m987m)
One of his early "hits." Includes bird-call imitations.
La première Flèche de Cupidon (Première Polka de Salon), **Op.142**
n.p., n.d., 7p.
LN(R786.4L18a)

LAMBERT, ALEXANDER (1862-1929)

Canzonetta
Schirmer, 1887, 7p.
DLC(M25.L), OCL(M776.4.553), PP(U), WM(786.4L22)
Etude in G, Op.4, No.2
Schirmer, 1888, 5p.
DLC(M25.L), MoSW(U), PP(U)
Good study in right-hand figurations.

LANE, EASTWOOD (1879-1951)

Adirondack Sketches (A Suite)
Fischer-J, 1922, 22p.
CtY(Mc11A1L241), DLC(M24.L255A3), LNT(M24.L3A), MoS(786.4), OCL(M776.415.556)
1. The Old Guide's Story; 2. The Legend of Lonesome Lake; 3. Down Stream; 4. The Land of the Loon; 5. A Dirge for Jo Indian; 6. Lumber-Jack Dance
Five American Dances
Fischer-J, 1919, 24p., also issued separately
CtY(Mc11A1L241), IU(M30L25A43), LNT(M30.L3F), MoS(786.4), OCL(M776.45.555), WM(786.4L26c, 1 only)
1. The Crap-Shooters; 2. Around the Hall; 3. A Gringo Tango; 4. North of Boston; 5. Powwow
A sincere attempt at Americana.
The Blue-Robed Mandarins (from **"Mongoliana"**)
Fischer-J, 1922, 4p.
ViU(U:2)

Here are Ladies (Five Piano Pieces)
 Fischer-J, 1944, 17p.
 OCL(M776.4.55614)
  1. Serenade for Madame Chiang Kai-shek; 2. Grandmother's
   Sunday School Days; 3. Lines for Ann Rutledge; 4. Her
   Mother was Irish; 5. Shropshire Lass
Persimmon Pucker
 Fischer-J, 1926, 7p.
 NNLc(°MYD+box), RPB(U)
 Swingy, with jazz overtones.
Sea Burial (from "Eastern Seas")
 Fischer-J, 1925, 7p.
 OCL(SM776.4)

LANG, MARGARET RUTHVEN (1867-1972)

Méditation, Op.26
 Schmidt, 1897, 5p.
 DLC(M25.L), MoS(786.4), NRU-E(U), PP(U)
Petit Roman en six Chapitres, Op.18
 Schmidt, 1894, 6v.(31p.)
 MB-N(M24L280p.18)
  1. Le Chevalier (Tempo di gavotta); 2. Madame la
   Princesse (Andantino); 3. Bal chez Mme. la Princesse
   (Tempo di ballo); 4. Monsieur le Prince (Andante con
   moto); 5. L'Epée de M. le Prince (Allegro con fuoco);
   6. La Mort du Chevalier (Andante)
Revery, Op.31
 Church, 1899, 7p.
 DLC(M25.L), ICN(VM22L27c), MoS(786.4), RPB(U)
Rhapsody in E Minor, Op.21
 Schmidt, 1895, 9p.
 DLC(M25.L), MBH(P.1W596.1), NRU-E(U)
A Spring Idyl, Op.33
 Church, 1899, 5p.
 ICN(VM22L27c), OC(786.4fL271s)
Starlight
 Millet, 1894, 5p.
 DLC(M25.L), also in HH-K(II:478)
Twilight
 Millet, 1894, 6p.
 DLC(M25.L), also in HH-K(II:473)

LAVALLEE, CALIXA (1842-1891)

Le Fleur de Mai Polka
 Cluett, 1859, 7p.
 ICN(Piano pre-1870), NBu(U), RPB(U)
L'Oiseau-Mouche (Humming Bird. Bluette de Salon), **Op.11**
 HallS, n.d., 7p.
 DLC(M25.L)

Le Papillon (The Butterfly. Etude de Concert), **Op.18**
Schmidt, 1884, 9p.
CU(fMT241L3), DLC(M25.L), MoS(786.47), MoSW(U), NNLc
(°MYD+box), NRU-E(U), NcD(RBR MusicB12,no.6), OCl
(SM776.47), PP(U), RPB(U)
Souvenir de Tolède (Mazurka de Salon), **Op.17**
Schmidt, 1884, 11p.
PP(U)

LEVY, HENIOT (1879-1946)

Canzonetta (see **Vier Klavierstücke**)
Chant sans Paroles (see **Vier Klavierstücke**)
Vier Klavierstücke
Pantheon, 1907, 4v.(5,5,5,5p.)
DLC(M25.L)
1. Canzonetta; 2. Chant sans Paroles; 3. Scherzino;
4. Romanze
Zehn Konzert-Etüden (Ten Concert Studies)
Breitkopf, 1923, 10v.(7,7,9,9,11,5,7,7,9,13p.)
ICN(Case sm oM4.L58no.13, nos.2-10 only), NNLc(°MYD)
Menuet
Fischer, 1917, 9p.
DLC(M25.L), PP(U)
Menuet in E Flat, Op.9, No.2 (from **Two Compositions, Op.9**)
Schirmer, 1908, 7p.
MoSW(U), PP(U)
Poème de Mai
Fischer, 1917, 7p.
DLC(M25.L), PP(U)
Romanze (see **Vier Klavierstücke**)
Scherzino (see **Vier Klavierstücke**)
Variationen über ein Original-Thema
Breitkopf, 1923, 19p.
DLC(M27.L), NNLc(°MYD)

LEWING, ADELE (1866-1943)

Romance, Op.17
Ditson, 1898, 5p.
DLC(M25.L)
Song without Words, Op.16
Ditson, 1898, 5p.
DLC(M25.L)

LIEBLING, EMIL (1851-1914)

Album Blatt, Op.18
Chicago, 1881, 5p.
DLC(M25.L), NRU-E(M21R29), PP(U), WM(786.4L71a)

Canzonetta, Op.26
    Church, 1895, 5p.
    DLC(M25.L), MoS(786.4), NRU-E(U), RPB(U)
Concert Polonaise, Op.41
    Schirmer, 1907, 11p.
    DLC(M25.L), ICN(VM22L71c), IEN(M25.L635C6), MoS(786.4), WM
      (786.4L71)
Feu-Follet (Will-o'-the-Wisp. Scherzo), **Op.17**
    Chicago, 1881, 7p.
    CtY(Mc11A1L622), DLC(M25.L), IU(Joseffy), MoS(786.4), WM
      (786.4L71f)
Florence (Grande Valse de Concert), **Op.12**
    Chicago, 1880, 11p.; Schirmer, 1908, 15p.
    DLC(M32.L), IU(Joseffy), MdBP(U), MoSW(U), NRU-E(M21R29)
      PP(U), WM(786.4L71fl)
Gavotte moderne, Op.11
    Schmidt, 1889, 7p.
    DLC(M31.L), IU(Joseffy), MoSW(U)
Manuela (Air de Ballet), **Op.29**
    Church, 1896, 7p.
    DLC(M25.L), MoSW(U), OC(786.4fL71), OCl(M776.4.5702)
Mazurka de Concert, Op.30
    Church, 1896, 11p.
    DLC(M25.L), IU(Joseffy), OCl(M776.4.5702)
Second Menuet, Op.35
    Schirmer, 1899, 7p.
    DLC(M32.L), MoS(786.4), WM(786.4L71)
Menuetto scherzoso (in E Minor), **Op.28**
    Church, 1895, 9p.
    IU(Joseffy)
Le Météore (Grand Galop brillant), **Op.10**
    Chicago, 1879, 9p.
    DLC(M31.L), IU(Joseffy), MoSW(U), NRU-E(U)
Momento appassionato, Op.24
    Millet, 1894, 3p.
    DLC(M25.L), NRU-E(M25L716m), also in HH-K(II:265)
Momento scherzando, Op.25
    Millet, 1894, 6p.
    DLC(M25.L), also in HH-K(II:268)
Première Romance de Concert (poétique), **Op.20**
    BrainardS, 1891, 6p.
    ICN(VM22L71d), IU(Joseffy), MoS(786.4)
Deuxième Romance de Concert (dramatique), **Op.21**
    BrainardS, 1891, 7p.
    DLC(M25.L), ICN(VM22L71d), PP(U)
Scherzo, Op.40
    Schirmer, 1907, 7p.
    LN(U), MdBP(U), MoS(786.4), PP(U)
Serenade, Op.34, No.1
    Schirmer, 1899, 7p.
    DLC(M25.L), MoSW(U)
Spring Song, Op.33
    Church, 1896, 5p.

CtY(Mc11A1L622), IU(Joseffy), MoS(786.4), MoSW(U),
NRU-E(U), PP(U)

LIEBLING, GEORG (1865-1946)

Impromptu on Black Keys, Op.60
Schmidt, 1925, 7p.
DLC(M25.L), MoSW(U), NNLc(°MYDbox), NRU-E(U)
An extremely difficult work.
Octaven-Etude, Op.8
Schlesinger, 1894, 7p.
CU(fMT229L5), IU(Joseffy), MoSW(U)
Tarantella, Op.25
Augener, 1898, 13p.
DLC(M25.L)
Tema con Variazioni, Op.23
Ascherberg, 1900, 10p.
DLC(M27.L)
Toccata de Concert, Op.41
Novello, 1899, 9p.
MoS(786.4)
Twilight, Op.24, No.5
Ascherberg, 1901, 5p.
DLC(M25.L)

LINLEY, FRANCIS [Editor] (ca.1770-1800)

A New Assistant for the Piano-forte or Harpsichord
Carr-J, 1796, 32p. [SU:289]
MBH(P.1H49), NNLc(°MKDM+Mus.Res.), NcU(M786.41L757S)
Contains six sonatas by B. Carr. No.VI is in A-C(I).

LOOMIS, HARVEY WORTHINGTON (1865-1930)

Harlequin, Op.56, No.4
Witmark, 1900, 9p.
DLC(M25.L), LNT(786L87c)
Hungarian Rhapsody, Op.53, No.2
Ditson, 1900, 13p.
DLC(M25.L)
Intermezzo from "The Tragedy of Death," Op.72
Wa-Wan, 1902, 10p.
NNLc(°MN Wa-Wan), NRU-E(M25L863ti), also in WW-L(III:73)
Lyrics of the Red Man, Op.76
Wa-Wan, 1903-1904, 2v. in 1
CU(M24L662L8), ICN(VM1W11V2), LNT(786L87L), MB-N(Piano),
MoS(786.4), NNLc(°MN Wa-Wan), NRU-E(M1669L863ly), PP(U),
also in AB-D(v.2 only), NC-G(v.1 only), WW-L(I:21;
II:245)
A superb collection founded on Indian melodies.

Star Rays (in **Three Pianoforte Compositions**)
    Wa-Wan, 1902, 3p.
    ICN(VM1W11v.1), NNLc(°MN Wa-Wan), NRU-E(M25L863st), NcU
      (MF786.44G464m), ViU(U:3), also in WW-L(III:153)

LYNES, FRANK (1858-1913)

The Approach of Spring, Op.9, No.1
    Schmidt, 1888, 5p.
    NRU-E(U)
In the Swing, Op.9, No.2
    Schmidt, 1888, 7p.
    CtY(Mc11A1L988)
Nocturne in A, Op.37, No.1
    Schmidt, 1902, 7p.
    DLC(M25.L)
Rain of Pearls (Octave Study), **Op.48**
    Schmidt, 1907, 7p.
    CtY(Mc11A1L988), PP(U)
Revery, Op.44
    Schmidt, 1904, 5p.
    DLC(M25.L)
Scherzino, Op.9, No.4
    Schmidt, 1888, 7p.
    NRU-E(U)
Valse brillante, Op.16, No.1
    Schmidt, 1890, 7p.
    NRU-E(U)
Whispering Zephyrs, Op.29, No.2
    Schmidt, 1900, 7p.
    NRU-E(U)

MAAS, LOUIS (1852-1889)

Erinnerung an Norwegen (Sechs kleinere Phantasiebilder),
    Op.13
    Breitkopf, n.d., 29p.
    DLC(M24.M), IU(Joseffy), MoSW(U, 6 only)
    1. **Norsk Bondedans;** 2. **Paa Saeteren;** 3. **Paa Bandaks-
      vandet;** 4. **Baekken i Dalen;** 5. **Aftensang;**
      6. **Folkedans**
    Impressive tone pictures inspired by Norway.
Drei Impromptus, Op.5
    Breitkopf, n.d., 21p.
    IU(qM786.41M112i)
Reverie du Soir, Op.20
    Schirmer, 1882, 7p.
    DLC(M25.M), PP(U)
Valse allemande, Op.21
    Schirmer, 1882, 7p.
    NNLc(°MYD), NcU(M786.45M111v), OCl(SM776.45)

MACDOWELL, EDWARD [EDGAR THORN] (1860-1908)

Der Adler (The Eagle), **Op.32, No.1** (see **Vier kleine Poesien, Op.32**)
Air and Rigaudon, Op.49
Breitkopf, 1894, 2v.(3,5p.)
IU(q.786.4M14r, 2 only), MdBP(U), MoS(786.4, 2 only), MoSW
(U, 2 only), NNLc(°MYD-Amer.box), NRU-E(M22M13r,v.6), PP
(U, 2 only), RPB(U, 2 only), WM(786.4M13r, 2 only), also
in HH-K(IV:837)
1. Air; 2. Rigaudon
Alla Tarantella, Op.39, No.2 (see **Twelve Etudes, Op.39**)
Amourette, Op.1
Schmidt, 1899, 5p.
DLC(M3.3.M141op.1), MBH(P.1M14.6), MoS(786.4), MoSW(U),
NNLc(°MYD+box op.1), NRU-E(U), RPB(U)
Published under MacDowell's pseudonym Edgar Thorn.
Arabesque, Op.39, No.4 (see **Twelve Etudes, Op.39**)
Aus verklungenen Märchen, Op.4 (see **Forgotten Fairy Tales, Op.4**)
Barcarolle, Op.18, No.1 (see **Zwei Stücke, Op.18**)
Bluette, Op.46, No.8 (see **Zwölf Virtuosen-Etüden, Op.46**)
Burleske, Op.46, No.7 (see **Zwölf Virtuosen-Etüden, Op.46**)
Deux Chansons gracieuses (Edgar Thorn)
Schott, 1899, 13p.
MoS(786.4), NNLc(°MYD-Amer)
Czardas, Op.24, No.4 (see **Vier Stücke, Op.24**)
Dance of the Dryads, Op.19, No.4 (see **Forest Idyls, Op.19**)
Dance of the Gnomes, Op.39, No.6 (see **Twelve Etudes, Op.39**)
The Eagle, Op.32, No.1 (see **Vier kleinen Poesien, Op.32**)
Elfin Dance, Op.46, No.5 (see **Zwölf Virtuosen-Etüden, Op.46**)
Etude de Concert, Op.36
Schmidt, 1889, 11p.
CU(fMT241M144op.36), CtY(Mc20M14a,v.3), DLC(M25.M), ICN
(sVMT241M13e), IU(qM786.41M14e1917), LNT(786M14p), MoS
(786.47), MoSW(U), NNLc(°MYD+box op.36), NRU-E(M22M13v.3),
OCl(SM776.47), PP(U), RPB(U), ViU(McR.173.28), WM(786.48
M138et)
Zwölf Etüden zur Ausbildung der Technik und des Vortrags, Op.39
(see **Twelve Etudes, Op.39**)
Twelve Etudes for the Development of Technique and Style, Op.39
Schmidt, 1890, 1918, 37p., also issued separately
CU(M22M212op.39), CtHT(U, 8 only), CtY(Mc11A1M148), DLC
(M25.M), ICN(VMT225M13t), IU(M25.M14op.39), InU(M1.S8),
LNT(M25.M33E7, 12 only), MB-N(P.1M14.2), MoS(786.47),
MoSW(U), NNLc(°MYDop.39), NRU-E(M22M13v.3), OCl(M776.47.
603), PP(M786.4M14115), RPB(U), ViU(°MT225M33op39 1890),
WM(786.48M138)
1. Hunting Song; 2. Alla Tarantella; 3. Romance;
4. Arabesque; 5. In the Forest; 6. Dance of the Gnomes;
7. Idyll; 8. Shadow Dance; 9. Intermezzo; 10. Melody;
11. Scherzino; 12. Hungarian
An outstanding, eminently useful collection.

Six Fancies, Op.7 (Edgar Thorn)
  Schmidt, 1899, 15p.
  CU(M22M212op.7), DLC(M25.M), MoS(786.4), NNLc(°MYD+box op.7),
    NRU-E(M22M13r v.6), NcU(M25.M25F3), PP(M786.4M14191),
    ViU(U:3), WM(786.4M13si)
  1. A Tin Soldier's Love; 2. To a Humming Bird; 3. Summer
    Song; 4. Across Fields; 5. Bluette; 6. An Elfin Round
Zwei Fantasiestücke zum Concertgebrauch, Op.17
  Hainauer, 1898, 2v.(7,11p.)
  CU(M25M15op.17:2, 2 only), CtHT(U, 2 only), CtY(Mc20M14a
    v.1), DLC(M25.M), ICN(sVM32M13w), IU(qM786.41M14h, 2
    only), InU(M1.S8, 2 only), MBH(P.1F738, 2 only), MB-N
    (Piano, 1 only), MoSW(U), NNLc(°MYD+box), NRU-E(M22M13
    v.1, 2 only), NcU(MF786.4M138f.w, 2 only), PP(U), RPB(U,
    2 only), ViU(McR.157.52, 2 only), WM(786.4M13zw), also
    in NC-G(2 only)
  1. Erzählung (A Tale); 2. Hexentanz (Witches' Dance)
  Two excellent, contrasting character pieces.
Fireside Tales, Op.61
  Schmidt, 1902, 21p.
  CU(M24M14op.61), CtY(Mc20M14+op.61), DLC(M3.3.M14op61Case),
    ICN(VM22M13f), InU(M1.S8), LNT(786M14p), MBH(P.1M14), MoSW
    (M24M148F), NNLc(°MYDop.61), NRU-E(M3.3M138op.61), NcU(M24.
    M14op.61), OCl(M776.415.60241), PP(M786.4fM14), ViU(Music
    M25M138F5 1902), WM(786.4M13fi), also in MP-H
  1. An Old Love Story; 2. Of Br'er Rabbit; 3. From a German
    Forest; 4. Of Salamanders; 5. A Haunted House; 6. By
    Smouldering Embers
  A superb collection containing some of MacDowell's best work.
Forest Idyls (Wald-Idyllen), Op.19
  Kahnt, 1884, 1912, 18p.; also 4v.(3,9,3,7p.)
  CU(M22M212op.19 1912), CtHT(U, 3 only), CtY(Mc20M14a,v.2),
    DLC(M25.M), ICN(sVM22M13), LNT(786M14p), MBH(P.1F738, 4
    only), MoS(786.4), MoSW(U, 1,3,4 only), NNLc(°MYD-Amer.box),
    NRU-E(M22M13v.2), PP(U, 3,4 only), WM(786.4M13wa)
  1. Forest Stillness (Waldesstille); 2. Play of the Nymphs
    (Spiel der Nymphen); 3. Reverie (Träumerei); 4. Dance
    of the Dryads (Driadentanz)
Forest Stillness, Op.19, No.1 (see Forest Idyls, Op.19)
Forgotten Fairy Tales, Op.4 (Edgar Thorn)
  Schmidt, 1899, 11p.
  CU(M22M212op.4), DLC(M25.M), ICN(VM22M13fo), MBH(P.1M14.2),
    NNLc(°MYD+box op.4), NRU-E(M22M13r v.6), NcU(M25.M25F6),
    PP(U), RPB(U), ViU(Music M25M138F6 1899)
  1. Sung outside the Prince's Door; 2. Of a Tailor and a
    Bear; 3. Beauty in the Rose Garden; 4. From Dwarf-Land
Sechs Gedichte nach Heinrich Heine, Op.31 (see Six Poems, Op.31)
Hexentanz, Op.17, No.2 (see Zwei Fantasiestücke, Op.17)
Humoreske, Op.18, No.2 (see Zwei Stücke, Op.18)
Hungarian, Op.39, No.12 (see Twelve Etudes, Op.39)
Hunting Song, Op.39, No.1 (see Twelve Etudes, Op.39)
Idyll, Op.39, No.7 (see Twelve Etudes, Op.39)
Idyllen, Op.28 (see Six Idyls after Goethe, Op.28)

Six Idyls after Goethe, Op.28
   Schirmer, 1887, 1898, Hainauer, 1898, 19p.
   CU(M22M212op.28 1898), CtY(Mc2OM14a,v.2), DLC(M25.M), ICN
   (sVM22M13i), IU(qM786.41M14i), InU(M1.S8), LN(U), MBH
   (P.1M14), MoSW(U), NNLc(°MYDop.28), NRU-E(M22M13v.2),
   OCl(M776.4.6033), PP(M786.4fM1414), RPB(U), WM(786.4M13i)
Impromptu, Op.46, No.11 (see **Zwölf Virtuosen-Etüden, Op.46**)
Improvisation, Op.46, No.4 (see **Zwölf Virtuosen-Etüden, Op.46**)
In Lilting Rhythm, Op.2 (Edgar Thorn)
   Schmidt, 1899, 2v. in 1(13p.)
   CU(M25M15op.2), DLC(M25.M), NNLc(°MYD+box op.2), PP(U), ViU
   (McR.173.24)
   Two charming pieces in waltz style.
Intermezzo, Op.10, No.4 (see **Erste Moderne Suite, Op.10**)
Intermezzo, Op.39, No.9 (see **Twelve Etudes, Op.39**)
In the Forest, Op.39, No.5 (see **Twelve Etudes, Op.39**)
Vier kleine Poesien, Op.32 (Four Little Poems, Op.32)
   Breitkopf, 1894, 1906, 9p., also issued separately
   CU(M22M212op.32 1906), CtY(Mc11A1M148), DLC(M25.M), ICN
   (sVM22M13fp), IU(Joseffy), InU(M1.S8), MBH(P.1F738),
   MB-N(Piano), MoS(786.4), MoSW(U), NNLc(°MYD+box op.32),
   NRU-E(M22M13v.3), NcU(M786.4M138L.w 4 only), OCl(M776.4.
   6024), PP(M786.4M14123), RPB(U), WM(786.4M13f)
   1. The Eagle; 2. The Brook; 3. Moonshine; 4. Winter
Sechs kleine Stücke nach Skizzen von J. S. Bach (see **Six Little
   Pieces after Sketches of J. S. Bach**)
Six Little Pieces after Sketches of J. S. Bach
   Schmidt, 1890, 1918, 13p.
   CU(M38B18 1918), CtY(Mc2OM14s), DLC(M25.M), ICN(VMT244M13Si),
   NNLc(°MYD-Amer), NRU-E(M22M13v.3), ViU(Music M25M139S58
   1918)
   1. Courante; 2. Menuet; 3. Gigue; 4. Menuet;
   5. Menuet; 6. Marche
Marionettes, Op.38
   Hainauer, 1888, 13p.; Schmidt, 1901, 16p.
   CU(M24M14op.38, 1901), CtY(M25M138+op.38), DLC(M3.3.M14op.38
   1901Case), IU(qM786.41M14m), LN(U), LNT(786M14p), MBH(P.1
   M14), MB-N(Piano), MoS(786.4), MoSW(U), NNLc(°MYDop.38),
   NRU-E(M3.3M138op.38), NcU(M786.48M138m), PP(786.4M142m),
   ViU(Music M24M14op.38), WM(786.4M13m)
   1. Prologue; 2. Soubrette; 3. Lover; 4. Witch;
   5. Clown; 6. Villain; 7. Sweetheart; 8. Epilogue
Märzwind (March Wind), Op.46, No.10 (see **Zwölf Virtuosen-
   Etüden, Op.46**)
Melody, Op.39, No.10 (see **Twelve Etudes, Op.39**)
Erste moderne Suite, Op.10
   Breitkopf, 1891, 1906, 33p.
   CU(M24M14op.10), CtY(Mc2OM14a v.1), DLC(M24.M14op.10 1906),
   IU(Joseffy), LNT(786M14p), MBH(P.1M14.1), MoSW(U), NNLc
   (°MYDop.10), NRU-E(M22M13v.1), OCl(M776.415.6033), PP(U),
   WM(786.4M13Su)
   1. Praeludium; 2. Presto; 3. Andantino ed Allegretto;
   4. Intermezzo; 5. Rhapsodie; Fugue

Zweite moderne Suite, Op.14
>   Schirmer, 1883, 27p.
>   CU(M24M14op.14), CtY(Mc20M14a v.1), DLC(M24.M14op.14 1883),
>   LNT(786M14p), NNLc(°MYD-Amer), NRU-E(M22M13v.1), PP(M786.4
>   M14119), WM(786.4M13Su)
>   1. Praeludium; 2. Fugato; 3. Rhapsodie; 4. Scherzino;
>   5. Marsch; 6. Phantasie-Tanz

Moto perpetuo, Op.46, No.2 (see **Zwölf Virtuosen-Etüden, Op.46**)

New England Idyls, Op.62
>   Schmidt, 1902, 34p.
>   CU(M24M14op.62), CtY(M25M138+op.62), DLC(M3.3.M14op.62Case),
>   ICN(VM22M13n), IU(qM786.41M14nSpec.Coll.), InU(M1.S8), MBH
>   (P.1M14), MB-N(P.1M14.5), MoS(786.4), MoSW(M25M148N2), NNLc
>   (°MYDop.62), NRU-E(M3.3M138op.62), NcU(M25.M25op.62), OCL
>   (M776.4.6026), PP(M786.4fM1413), WM(786.4M13n), also in MP-H
>   1. An Old Garden; 2. Mid-summer; 3. Mid-winter; 4. With
>   Sweet Lavender; 5. In deep Woods; 6. Indian Idyl; 7. To
>   an old White Pine; 8. From Puritan Days; 9. From a log
>   Cabin; 10. The Joy of Autumn
>   Superb examples of the composer's skill with short pieces.

Novelette, Op.46, No.1 (see **Zwölf Virtuosen-Etüden, Op.46**)

Les Orientales, Op.37
>   Schmidt, 1889, 9p., also issued separately
>   CU(M25M15op.37 1917), CtY(Mc20M14a v.3), DLC(M25.M), ICN
>   (sVM22M13o), IU(MaLq.786.4M14O), InU(M1.S8), LNT(786M14p),
>   MoSW(U, 1,3 only), NNLc(°MYDop.37), NRU-E(M22M13v.3), PP
>   (U, 1,2,3 only), RPB(U, 1 only), WM(786.4M13o)
>   1. Clair de Lune; 2. Dans le Hamac; 3. Danse andalouse

Play of the Nymphs, Op.19, No.2 (see **Forest Idyls, Op.19**)

Six Poems after Heinrich Heine, Op.31
>   Hainauer, 1887, Schmidt, 1901, 23p., also issued separately
>   CU(M22M212op.31 1887,1901), CtY(Mc20M14a,v.3), DLC(M25.M),
>   IU(qM786.41M14g Spec.Coll.), InU(M1.S8, 2,6 only), LNT(786
>   M14p), MBH(P.1M14), MB-N(P.1M14), MoS(786.4, 2 only), MoSW(U,
>   4,6 only), NNLc(°MYDop.31), NRU-E(M22M13v.3), NcU(MF786.4
>   M138g), OCL(M776.4.6036), PP(U, 2 only), RPB(U, 2 only),
>   ViU(U:2), WM(786.4M13g)
>   1. From a Fisherman's Hut; 2. Scotch Poem; 3. From Long
>   Ago; 4. The Post Waggon; 5. The Shepherd Boy; 6. The
>   Monologue

Polonaise, Op.46, No.12 (see **Zwölf Virtuosen-Etüden, Op.46**)

Prélude et Fugue, Op.13
>   Fritzsch, 1883, 7p.
>   CtY(Mc20M14a v.1), DLC(M25.M), IU(Joseffy), MBH(P.1F738),
>   NNLc(°MYD-Amer.box), NRU-E(M22M13v.1), WM(786.4M13p)
>   One of MacDowell's rare--and successful--ventures into poly-
>   phonic writing.

Revery (Träumerei), Op.19, No.3 (see **Forest Idyls, Op.19**)

Rigaudon, Op.49, No.2 (see **Air and Rigaudon, Op.49**)

Romance, Op.39, No.3 (see **Twelve Etudes, Op.39**)

Scherzino, Op.39, No.11 (see **Twelve Etudes, Op.39**)

Scotch Poem, Op.31, No.2 (see **Six Poems after Heinrich Heine,
Op.31**)

Sea Pieces, Op.55
   Schmidt, 1899, 38p.
   CU(M24M14op.55 1899), CtY(Mc20M14+op.55), DLC(M24.M14op.55
      1910), ICN(VM25M13s), IU(qM786.41M14se), InU(M1.S8), LNT
      (786M14p), MBH(P.1M14), MB-N(HaleColl.786.4 M14), Mos(786.4),
      MoSW(U), NNLc(°MYDop.55), NRU-E(M24M138op.55 1899), NcU
      (M786.4M138s1899), OCL(M776.415.603), PP(786.4M142S), RPB
      (U), ViU(Music M25M138S4 1898), WM(786.4M13), also in BC-G
      (3,4 only), MP-H
   1. To the Sea; 2. From a Wandering Iceberg; 3. A.D.1620;
      4. Starlight; 5. Song; 6. From the Depths;
      7. Nautilus; 8. In Mid-Ocean
Serenata, Op.16
   Jung, 1895, 5p.
   CtY(Mc20M14a v.1), DLC(M25.M), IU(Joseffy), MBH(P.1F738),
      MoSW(U), NNLc(°MYD+box op.16), NRU-E(M22M13v.1), PP(U),
      ViU(McR.168.04), WM(786.4M13se), also in NC-G
Shadow Dance, Op.39, No.8 (see **Twelve Etudes, Op.39**)
Shattentanz ((Shadow Dance), Op.39, No.8 (see **Twelve Etudes,
   Op.39)**
Sonata No.1 (Tragica), Op.45
   Breitkopf, 1893, 29p.; Schirmer, 1922, 41p.
   CU(M23M14op.45 1893), CtY(Mc11A1M148), DLC(M23.M14op.45),
      ICN(sVM23M13S1), IU(qM786.41M14s1), LN(U), LNT(786M14p),
      MBH(P1.M14.1), MB-N(Piano), MoS(786.41), MoSW(U), NNLc
      (°MYDop.45), NRU-E(M22M13v.4), NcU(M786.41M138s1), OCL
      (M776.41.6031), PP(M786.41M1411), ViU(Music M23M132 op.45),
      WM(786.4M13s1B)
   Four-movement sonata.
Sonata No.2 (Eroica), Op.50
   Breitkopf, 1895, 1917, Kalmus, n.d., 37p.
   CU(M23M14op.50 1895), CtY(Mc11A1M148), DLC(M23.M14op.50),
      ICN(VM23M13s2), IU(qM786.41M14s2), LNT(786M14p), MBH(P.1
      M14.1), MoS(786.41), MoSW(M23M148No.2), NNLc(°MYDop.50),
      NRU-E(M22M13v.4), NcU(M786.41M138s2), OCL(M776.41.604),
      PP(M786.41M14111), ViU(Music M23M132 1895), WM(786.4M13
      s2)
   Four-movement sonata.
Sonata No.3 (Norse), Op.57
   Schmidt, 1900, Kalmus, n.d., 28p.
   CU(M23M14op.57 1900), CtY(Mc20M14a v.4), DLC(M23.M14op.57),
      ICN(VM23M13s3), IU(qM786.41M14s3), LNT(786M14p), MBH(P.1
      B732.3), MoSW(U), NNLc(°°MYDp.v.4,no.4op.57), NRU-E(M22
      M13v.4), NcU(M786.41M138s3), PP(786.41M148s3), WM(786.4
      M13s3)
   Three-movement sonata.
Sonata No.4 (Keltic), Op.59
   Schmidt, 1900, Kalmus, n.d., 31p.
   CU(M23M14op.59 1901), CtY(Mc20M14a v.4), DLC(M23.M14op.59),
      ICN(VM23M13s4), IU(M23M33op.59), LNT(786M14p), MBH(P1.
      B732.3), MoS(786.4), MoSW(U), NNLc(°MYDop.57), NRU-E(M22
      M13v.4), NcU(M786.41M138s4), OCL(M776.41.606), PP(786.41
      M148s4), WM(786.4M13s4)

Three-movement sonata.
Spiel der Nymphen (Play of the Nymphs), Op.19, No.2 (see
  Forest Idyls, Op.19)
Zwei Stücke, Op.18
    Schirmer, 1884, Schmidt, 1894, Hainauer, 1898, 2v.(7,7p.)
    CtY(Mc20M14a v.2), DLC(M3.3.M14op.18 1894), IU(Joseffy, 2
      only), MoSW(U, 2 only), NNLc(JNN75-4), NRU-E(M22M13v.2),
      NcU(MF786.4M138b), PP(U, 1 only), WM(786.4M13z)
    1. Barcarolle; 2. Humoreske
Vier Stücke, Op.24
    Hainauer, 1898, 19p.
    CtY(Mc20M14a v.2), DLC(M25.M), IU(qM786.41M14stuW, 3 only;
      Joseffy, 1,4 only), MBH(P.1M14.3), MoSW(U, 4 only), NNLc
      (°MYDop.24), NRU-E(M25M138Stv), NcU(MF786.4M138co24), OCl
      (M776.4.6028), PP(U, 3,4 only), WM(786.4M13v)
    1. Humoreske; 2. Marsch; 3. Wiegenlied; 4. Czardas
A Tale (Erzählung), Op.17, No.1 (see Zwei Fantasiestücke,
  Op.17)
To a Wild Rose, Op.51, No.1 (see Woodland Sketches, Op.51)
Träumerei, Op.46, No.9 (see Zwölf Virtuosen-Etüden, Op.46)
Valse triste, Op.46, No.6 (see Zwölf Virtuosen-Etüden, Op.46)
Zwölf Virtuosen-Etüden, Op.46
    Breitkopf, 1894, 47p., also issued separately (12v.)
    CU(fMT241M144op.46), CtY(Mc20M14a v.4), DLC(M3.3.M14op.46A),
      ICN(VMT225M13v), IU(M22M138), LNT(M25M33v.5), MBH(P.1M14.1),
      MB-N(Piano), MoS(786.4, 4,10 only), MoSW(M25M148V), NNLc
      (°MYDop.46), NcU(M786.4M138e6), OCl(M776.47.6037), PP(M786.4
      M14116), RPB(U, 6,8 only), WM(786.48M138e)
    1. Novellette; 2. Moto perpetuo; 3. Wilde Jagd; 4. Impro-
      visation; 5. Elfentanz; 6. Valse triste; 7. Burleske;
      8. Bluette; 9. Träumerei; 10. Märzwind; 11. Impromtu;
      12. Polonaise
    Equally fine as study pieces and concert works.
Waldesstille (Forest Stillness), Op.19, No.1 (see Forest
  Idyls, Op.19)
Wald Idyllen, Op.19 (see Forest Idyls, Op.19)
Wild Chase (Wilde Jagd), Op.46, No.3 (see Zwölf Virtuosen-
  Etüden, Op.46)
Witches' Dance (Hexentanz), Op.17, No.2 (see Zwei Fantasie-
  stücke, Op.17)
Woodland Sketches, Op.51
    Schmidt, 1899, 28p.
    CU(M24M14op.51CaseX), CtY(Mc11A1M148), DLC(M24.M14op.51 1910),
      ICN(8A72), IU(qM786.41M14w), InU(M1.S8), LN(U), LNT(786M14p),
      MBH(P.1M14), MB-N(Piano), MoS(786.4), MoSW(M24M148W 1899),
      NNLc(°MYDop.51), NRU-E(M25M138w), NcU(M24.M14op.51 1899),
      OCl(M776.415.60412), PP(786.4M142w3), RPB(U), ViU(Music
      M24M14op.51J8 1896), also in AB-D(1 only), EA-I(1 only),
      MP-H
    1. To a Wild Rose; 2. Will o' the Wisp; 3. At an old
      Trysting Place; 4. In Autumn; 5. From an Indian Lodge;
      6. To a Waterlily; 7. From Uncle Remus; 8. A Deserted
      Farm; 9. By a Meadow Brook; 10. Told at Sunset

MACFADYEN, ALEXANDER (1879-1936)

At Twilight, Op.25, No.2 (see **Three Mood-Pictures, Op.25**)
Concert Etude, Op.10
    Kaun, 1907, 9p.
    DLC(M25.M), WM(786.48M139)
Country Dance
    Church, 1913, 7p.
    Cty(Mc11A1M162), DCL(M30.M), NRU-E(U), RPB(U), WM(786.4
    M14c)
Etude-Caprice, Op.22, No.1 (from **Three Etudes, Op.22**)
    Schirmer, 1920, 7p.
    PP(U)
Etude harmonieuse, Op.22, No.3 (from **Three Etudes, Op.22**)
    Schirmer, 1920, 9p.
    PP(U)
Etude héroïque
    Ditson, 1927, 7p.
    DLC(M25.M), OU(U)
Improvisation, Op.25, No.3 (see **Three Mood-Pictures, Op.25**)
Three Mood-Pictures, Op.25
    Schirmer, 1920, 3v.(5,5,5p.)
    DLC(M25.M), WM(786.4M14)
    1. **Nocturne**; 2. **At Twilight**; 3. **Improvisation**
Nocturne, Op.20, No.1
    Church, 1917, 7p.
    DLC(M25.M), MoS(786.4), WM(786.4M14)
Nocturne, Op.25, No.1 (see **Three Mood-Pictures, Op.25**)
Paraphrase on "St. Patrick's Day in the Morning"
    Badger, 1927, 7p.
    WM(786.4M14sa)
Reverie
    Kaun, 1916, 3p.
    DLC(M25.M), WM(786.4M14re)
Rolling Stones (Morceau brillant)
    Schirmer, 1923, 7p.
    NRU-E(U)
Romance and Scherzo, Op.11
    Kaun, 1907, 2v.(5,7p.)
    WM(786.4M14ro, 786.4M14sc)
    1. **Romance**; 2. **Scherzo**
Sonata, Op.21
    Schirmer, 1921, 39p.
    DLC(M23.M19op.21), MoS(786.41), MoSW(U), NNLc(°MYD),
    WM(786.4M14so)

MANNEY, CHARLES FONTEYN (1872-1951)

Ballade romantique
    Ditson, 1912, 9p.
    DLC(M25.M), MoSW(U)

Coquetterie, Op.14, No.3 (from **Three Pieces for Piano, Op.14**)
   Ditson, 1905, 7p.
   RPB(U)
Dialogue d'Amour, Op.25, No.2 (from **Piano Pieces, Op.25**)
   Ditson, 1917, 5p.
   RPB(U)
Roving, Op.25, No.4 (from **Piano Pieces, Op.25**)
   Ditson, 1917, 7p.
   DLC(M25.M), MoSW(U)
Song at Sunrise (Petite Rhapsodie)
   Ditson, 1909, 7p.
   RPB(U)
Yearnings (Sehnsucht)
   Ditson, 1892, 5p.
   DLC(M25.M), MoSW(U)

MARETZEK, MAX (1821-1897)

German Polka
   Walker, 1849, 7p.
   CtY(Mc28P7), ICN(Piano pre-1870), RPB(U)
Invitation à La Polka
   Walker, 1849. 9p.
   CtY(Mc28P7), NNLc(AM2-I), NcD(RBR MusicB9,no.23), RPB(U)
The Tip Top Polka
   Walker, 1850, 11p.
   CtY(Mc28P7), NBu(°M1C66,v.38,no.2), NNLc(AM2-I), NRU-E(U),
      NcU(EAMC,no.38), PP(U), RPB(U)

MARSTON, GEORGE W. (1840-1901)

Adagietto (No.3 of **Three Compositions for the Piano**)
   Schmidt, 1889, 5p.
   RPB(U)
Album Leaf (No.2 of **Three Compositions for the Piano**)
   Schmidt, 1889, 5p.
   RPB(U)
Impromptu Caprice
   Schmidt, 1886, 7p.
   DLC(M25.M)
Reverie
   Schmidt, 1895, 5p.
   MeP(U)
Romanza
   Schmidt, 1878, 3p.
   MeP(U)
Serenade (Nocturne)
   Ditson, 1867, 7p.
   DLC(M25.M)
Suite in A Minor
   Russell, 1874, 7p.

PP(U)
1. Sarabande; 2. Gigue; 3. Alternative; 4. Gavotte
Cinq Tyroliennes
n.p., 1872, 7p.
MeP(U)

MASON, DANIEL GREGORY (1873-1953)

Ballade in E Flat, Op.16, No.2
Ditson, 1920, 11p.
IU(MO 41146)
Birthday Waltzes, Op.1
Schirmer-EC, 1923, 16p.
DLC(M32.M), ViU(°M22M3 1923)
Composed in 1894. There are nine brief waltzes and an
Epilogue ("Many happy returns") which contains references
to previous waltzes.
Color Contrasts (Study for Touch)
Leeds, 1949, 4p.
CU(M21U7), LNT(M21.U52L2)
From an album U.S.A. Compositions for Piano by Contempo-
rarary American Composers.
Country Pictures (Ländliche Bilder), Op.9
Breitkopf, 1914, 2v.(19,17p.), Associated reprint, 1942
CU(M24M38c 1942), DLC(M25.M), IU(qM786.41M38c), MBH(P.1M38),
NNLc(°MYD-Amer, book II only), NRU-E(M25M398c), PP(U),
ViU(°M22M28op.9, 1914; Music M25M27op.9 1942)
1. Cloud Pageant; 2. Chimney Swallows; 3. At Sunset;
4. The Whippoorwill; 5. The Quiet Hour; 6. Night Wind
Elegy (in free variation form), Op.2
Metzler, 1902, 20p.
DLC(M25.M), ICN(8A 576)
Composed in 1899. Fine theme with nine variations.
Impromptu, Op.3, No.2
Church, 1908, 7p.
CtY(U), DLC(M25.M), MoS(786.4)
Impromptu, Op.16, No.1
Ditson, 1917, 9p.
DLC(M25.M), NNLc(°MYD), PP(U)
Ländliche Bilder, Op.9 (see Country Pictures, Op.9)
Three Preludes, Op.33
Marks, 1943, 8p.
OC(786.4fM398)
Composed between 1920 and 1924. The first is a mildly dis-
sonant improvisation, the second a solemn waltz.
Romance, Op.3, No.1
Church, 1908, 7p.
DLC(M25.M), MoSW(U)
Three Silhouettes, Op.21
Schirmer, 1923, 3v.(5,5,9p.)
DLC(M25.M), MoS(786.4), NNLc(°MYD+box), ViU(Music M25M27
op.21)

Variations on "Yankee Doodle" in the Styles of various
   Composers, Op.6
      Breitkopf, 1912, 13p.
      CU(M27M35op.6), DLC(M27.M), MoS(786.48), NNLc(°MYD+box),
         PP(U), WM(786.4M38)
      Seven skillful, amusing variations.

MASON, WILLIAM (1829-1908)

   "Ah! vous dirais-je maman" (Caprice grotesque), Op.22
      Pond, 1864, 9p.
      CtY(U), DLC(M25.M), PP(U), RPB(U)
   Two Album Leaves, Op.45
      Schirmer, 1895, 5p.
      IU(Joseffy), LNT(786M382a), MoS(786.4)
   Amitié pour Amitié, Op.4
      Richardson, 1854, 7p.
      CtY(U), DLC(M25.M), MBH(P.1B12c.2), MoSW(U), NBu(U), NNLc
         (°MYDbox), PP(U), RPB(U)
   Amourette, Op.48
      Schirmer, 1896, 11p.
      DLC(M25.M), MoSW(U), NNLc(°MYD+box)
   Première Ballade, Op.12
      Pond, 1863, 9p.
      NcU(M786.43M421ba), RPB(U)
   Barcarole et Ballade, Op.15
      Pond, 1864, 15p.
      NNLc(AM2-I), NcD(RBR Music766), NcU(M786.43M421ba)
      Title page reads Ballade et Barcarole, Op.13.
   Berceuse, Op.34
      Pond, 1871, 1896, 11p.
      DLC(M25.M), MoSW(U), NRU-E(U), PP(U), ViU(°M1.S444,v.33,
         no.26)
   Capriccio fantastico, Op.50
      Schirmer, 1897, 11p.
      DLC(M25.M), MB-N(U), MoS(786.4), NNLc(°MYD), PP(U)
   Two Caprices, Op.31
      Pond, 1869, Koppitz, 1870, 2v.(7,7p.)
      DLC(M25.M), also in NC-G(2 only)
      1. Scherzo; 2. Novelette
   Concert Galop, Op.11
      Pond, 1862, 15p.
      CtHT(U), DLC(M25.M), InU(M1.S8), NRU-E(U), RPB(U)
   Danse antique, Op.38
      In PM-H
   Dance Caprice, Op.36
      Schuberth-E, 1882, 7p.
      DLC(M25.M), IU(Joseffy), PP(U)
   Danse rustique (à la gigue), Op.16
      Pond, 1860, 10p.
      CtHT(U), DLC(M25.M), InU(M1.S8), MoS(786.45), NBu(U), NNLc
         (°MYD+box), NRU-E(M31M412r), PP(U), RPB(U)

L'Espiègle (Polka-Caprice)
Ashdown, n.d., 7p.
RPB(U)
Etude de Concert, Op.9
Hall, 1856, 9p.
MBH(P.1B12c.2), NcU(M786.47M421e)
Gavotte in D Major (from the Sixth Sonate for Violoncello by
Johann Sebastian Bach. Transcription)
Schirmer, 1874, 7p.
CtY(U), NNLc(°MYD+box), NRU-E(M38B118S9S.1012G1 1874),
RPB(U)
Deux Humoresques de Bal, Op.23
Schuberth-J, 1866, 2v.(9,9p.)
CtHT(U), RPB(U, 2 only)
1. **Polka Caprice**; 2. **Mazurka Caprice**
Improvisation, Op.51
Schirmer, 1900, 9p.
CU(M25M335op.51), CtY(Mc11A1M38), DLC(M25.M), IU(Joseffy),
LNT(786M382i), MoSW(U), NNLc(Music-Am[Sheet]74-482),
PP(U)
Beautiful example of Mason's best writing.
Lullaby, Op.10
FirthP, 1857, 5p.
CtHT(U), DLC(M25.M), NBu(U), NNLc(°MYD+box), RPB(U),
also in AB-D
Mazurka brillante, Op.49
Schirmer, 1897, 13p.
NNLc(°MYD), NcU(M786.44M421m), PP(U)
Mazurka-Caprice, Op.23, No.2 (see **Deux Humoresques de Bal,
Op.23**)
Melody, Op.40
Schuberth-E, 1882, 7p.
DLC(M25.M), IU(Joseffy), NRU-E(U), PP(U)
Monody, Op.13
Pond, 1865, 7p.
CtY(U), DLC(M25.M), MoSW(U), NNLc(°MYDbox), PP(U)
Novelette, Op.31, No.2 (see **Two Caprices, Op.31**)
A Pastoral Novellette
In HH-K(V:1253)
Two Pianoforte Pieces, Op.46
Presser, 1895, 2v.(7,3p.)
IU(Joseffy), NNLc(AM2-I, 2 only)
1. **Toccatina**; 2. **Prelude in F**
Polka-Caprice, Op.23, No.1 (see **Deux Humoresques de Bal,
Op.23**)
Polka gracieuse, Op.14
RootC, 1861, 11p.
ICN(Case sm oM1.A13vo.2746), NNLc(AM2-I), RPB(U)
An artful example of superb polka writing.
Prelude in F, Op.46, No.2 (see **Two Pianoforte Pieces, Op.46**)
Prelude (in Scherzo Form)**, Op.30**
Koppitz, 1870, 7p.
DLC(M25.M), MBH(P.1B12C.2), NRU-E(U), PP(U)

Prélude mélodique, Op.47
    Schirmer, 1895, 7p.
    NNLc(°MYD+box), PP(U), WM(786.4M39p)
    A gratifying piece to play.
Reverie (Au Matin), Op.19, No.1 (from **Deux Reveries, Op.19**)
    FirthP, 1860, 9p.
    NRU-E(U)
Reverie poétique, Op.24
    Schirmer, 1885, 9p.
    DLC(M25.M), MBH(P.1B12C.2), MoS(786.4), PP(U)
Romance-Etude, Op.32
    Pond, 1871, 9p.
    DLC(M25.M), NNLc(°MYD+box), NRU-E(MT241M412r), PP(U)
Romance-Idyl, Op.42
    Schuberth-E, 1882, 7p.
    IU(Joseffy), PP(U)
Deux Romances sans Paroles, Op.1
    Reed, 1845, 2v.(5,5p.)
    MBH(P.1B12c.2), OCl(SM776.43, 2 only), PP(U), RPB(U,
      2 only), ViU(°M1.S444,v.151,no.8, 2 only)
    No.1 is especially beautiful.
Scherzo, Op.31, No.1 (see **Two Caprices, Op.31**)
Scherzo, Op.41
    Schuberth-E, 1882, 10p.
    IU(Joseffy)
Silver Spring, Op.6
    FirthP, 1856, 15p.
    CU(M25M335op.6CaseX), CtY(Mc11A1M38), DLC(M25.M), IU
      (qM786.41M381s 1885), InU(M1.S8), NBu(U), NNLc(°MYDbox),
      NRU-E(M25M412s), OCl(M776.4.60855), PP(U), RPB(U), ViU
      (°M1.A13N.M384S5 1856), WM(786.4M39spo), alsoin NC-G
    One of Mason's very finest compositions. It may be classed
      as a difficult salon piece, but it should also be consid-
      ered a challenging concert work.
Spring Dawn (Mazurka-Caprice), **Op.20**
    Breusing, 1861, 7p.
    CtHT(U), DLC(M25.M), MoSW(U), DLC(°MYD+box 1861), NRU-E
      (M32M412sp 1889), OCl(SM776.45), PP(U), ViU(McR.118.14),
      WM(786.4M39sp)
    An effective and impressive example of this type of work.
Toccata, Op.37
    Schuberth-E, 1882, 7p.
    DLC(M25.M), IU(Joseffy), PP(U), RPB(U)
    A fine octave study.
Toccatina, Op.46, No.1 (see **Two Pianoforte Pieces, Op.46**)
Valse de Bravoure, Op.5
    Richardson, n.d., 17p.
    NRU-E(U)
    A difficult, well-written concert waltz. Incorrectly
      printed as Op.15.
Valse-Impromptu, Op.28
    Pond, 1869, 10p.
    MBH(P.1B12C.2), PP(U), RPB(U)

MAYLATH, HEINRICH [HENRY] (1827-1883)

Caprice brillant, Op.38
    Mollenhauer, 1871, 9p.
    DLC(M25.M), PP(U)
Feu Follet (Morceau caractéristique), **Op.112**
    Spear, 1881, 7p.
    DLC(M25.M)
    Good study in triplets.
Illustration élégante to Rode's Celebrated Air
    Mollenhauer, 1871, 13p.
    DLC(M27.M), MiU-C(U)
    Introduction, theme, variation and polacca finale. The
      theme, from Rode's **Air varié, Op.10, No.2,** was origi-
      nally for violin accompanied by strings or piano.
"Silver Threads among the Gold" (Transcription)
    Harris, 1874, 9p.
    RPB(U)
    H. P. Danks' well-known theme with variation and Rondo à
    la Polacca.

MEINEKE [MEINECKE], CHRISTOPHER [CHARLES] (ca.1782-1850)

"Araby's Daughter" from Lalla Rookh (with Variations)
    Klemm, 1826, 10p.
    CtY(Mc26A7), DLC(M1.A13M Case), ICN(Case sm oM1.A13,
      no.1865), InU(M1.S8), NcU(EAMC,no.48), PP(U)
    Same melody as "The Old Oaken Bucket," written by George
      Kialmark. **Lalla Rookh** was a series of tales in verse
      connected together by a story in prose by Thomas Moore.
"Brignal Banks" (A Favorite Scotch Air with Variations)
    WilligJr, 1827, 9p.
    DeWHi(U), NNLc(AM1-I), NcD(RBR MusicB10,no.6), PP(U;
      K:32), ViU(°M1.S444,v.75,no.9)
"Come rest in this Bosom" ("Fleuve du Tage" with Variations)
    Cole, 1822, 5p. [W.II:705]
    DLC(M1.A13M Case), ICN(Case8A 1249), NNLc(AM1-I), NcU(EAMC,
      no.48), PP(U), ViU(°M1.S444,v.156,no.37; McR.9.27)
    Original music by J.-J. Benoit Pollet, words by Thomas Moore.
Divertimento (in which are introduced the favorite Airs of
    "Pipe de Tabac," "Di Tanti Palpiti," and the "Drunken Sailor"
    or "Columbus")
    Willig, 1825, 11p. [W.II:560]
    PP(K:32), NNLc(AM1-I), RPB(U), also in A-C(II)
The Favorite Swiss Air with Variations
    WilligJr, n.d., 11p.
    DLC(M1.A13M Case), RPB(U)
"Kinlock of Kinlock" (A favorite Scotch Air, with Variations)
    Cole, 1825, 12p. [W.II:562]
    ICN(Case8A 2579), MB-N(VaultM1.A18v.1,no.24), NBu(U),
      NNLc(AM1-I), NcD(RBR MusicB126,no.19), PP(U)
    The popular theme is supplied with nine creative variations.

"Look out upon the Stars my Love" (A Celebrated Air with
   Variations)
      Cole, 1824, Willig, n.d., 8p. [W.II:562]
      DLC(M1.A13M Case), InU(M1.S8), NNLc(AM1-I), NcU(EAMC,no.49)
"Malbrouk" (A Celebrated French Air with Variations)
      Cole, ca.1828, 4p.
      DLC(M1.A13M Case), InU(M1.S8), NcU(EAMC,no.1)
      Popular theme ("We won't go Home until Morning") with six
         delightful, sparkling variations.
"Non più andrai" (A favourite Air from Mozart's opera **The
   Marriage of Figaro** with Variations)
      Klemm, 1828, 7p.
      DLC(M1.A13M Case)
Railroad March. For the Fourth of July
      WilligJr, 1828, 3p.
      DLC(M1.A13M), ICN(Case sm oM1.A13,no.2636), NNLc(VWIP+),
         NcU(EAMC,no.1), PP(U), ViU(McR.167.01)
"They're a' noddin" (A favourite Scotch Air with Variations)
      Cole, ca.1824, 8p. [W.II:565]
      ICN(Case8A 2071)
      One of Meineke's best works in variation form.
**Variations of Gilfert's Favorite Air "I left Thee Where I found
   Thee Love"**
      Klemm, 1828, 13p.
      IU(Joseffy), PP(U)
Variations to the Favorite Air "Au Clair de la Lune"
      WilligJr, 1827, 7p.
      RPB(U), also in A-C(II)

MELNOTTE, CLAUDE [see **CHARLES KUNKEL**]

MERZ, KARL (1836-1890)

   Bitter Tears (Two Nocturnes)
      Brainard, 1865, 7p.
      DLC(M25.M), MiU-C(U), NNLc(AM2-I), PP(U)
   Deliciosa or Leonore Polka
      Ditson, n.d., 5p.
      CtHT(U), CtY(Mc11A1M559), ICN(Piano pre-1870), LNT(976.3
         [780]Z99p), NNLc(AM2-I), NRU-E(U), NcD(RBR°music old
         M780.88A512cs), NcU(M786.44M577d), PP(U), RPB(U), ViU
         (McR.84.02)
   "Her bright Smile Haunts me Still" (Brilliant Transcription)
      Brainard, 1864, 7p.
      MiU-C(U), NBu(U)
   L'Inquiétude (1st Allegro from **Sonate, Op.50**)
      Russell, 1864, 11p.
      DLC(M23.M52op.50), NcU(M786.41M577s50.aI)
   Romping Polka (Halcyon Days, No.3)
      Ditson, 1857, 7p.
      CtY(Mc11A1M559)

METZ, JULIUS (fl.1819-1857)

Cronstadt Polka
Cook, 1856, 5p.
CtY(Mc11A1M568)
Eclipse Polka
Vanderbeek, 1853, 7p.
RPB(U)
"The Merry Mountain Horn" (Composed by H. R. Bishop. Arranged as a Rondo)
Hewitt, 1831, 11p.
RPB(U)
"Soffri Amore" (Cavatina from Rossini's opera **L'Italiana in Algerie** Arranged as a Divertimento)
Mesier, n.d., 7p.
ICN(Case sm oM1.A13,v.1141)
A Spanish Air with Variations
DuboisS, n.d., 3p.
CtY(Mc26A7), DLC(M1.A1M), PP(U)
Spanish Waltz with Variations
Geib, 1820, 7p. [W.II:570]
DLC(M1.A1M Case), ICN(Case8A 2017)

MILDENBERG, ALBERT (1878-1918)

Arabian Night (Romance)
Schirmer, 1905, 5p.
DLC(M25.M), IU(Joseffy), RPB(U)
Astarte (Intermezzo)
Schirmer, 1904, 7p.
RPB(U)
Nonchalance
LuckhardtB, 1906, 5p.
CtY(Mc11A1M592), DLC(M25.M)

MILLER, W. B. (fl.1860s)

"The Girl I Left behind Me" (with Variations)
Whittemore, 1866, 5p.
ICN(Piano pre-1870), IU(°q.784.3sh37v.13,no.52), InU
(M1.S8), RPB(U), ViU(°M1.S444,v.88,no.42)

MILLS, SEBASTIAN BACH (1838-1898)

Barcarolle No.2, Op.28
Pond, 1875, 11p.
DLC(M25.M), NcU(M786.4M657b2)
Barcarolle venetienne, Op.12
Pond, 1865, 15p.
DLC(M25.M), PP(U), RPB(U)

La Cambrienne (Fantaisie élégante), **Op.9**
    Jones, 1850, 13p.
    NRU-E(U)
Cradle Song, Op.34
    Pond, 1887, 11p.
    CtY(Mc11A1M628), DLC(M25.M), IU(Joseffy)
    Good example of Mills's expertise in lyricism.
Etude de Concert, Op.15, No.1 (see **2 Etudes de Concert, Op.15**)
Etude de Concert, Op.15, No.2 (see **2 Etudes de Concert, Op.15**)
2 Etudes de Concert, Op.15
    Schmidt, 1882, 2v.(7,9p.)
    DLC(MT241.M65), IU(Joseffy), MoSW(U, 2 only)
Fairy Fingers (Etude-Caprice), **Op.24**
    Pond, 1868, 9p.
    RPB(U), ViU(McR.137.39)
    A superb right-hand study.
Fantaisie dramatique sur Faust (de Gounod), **Op.17**
    Schuberth-J, 1864, 23p.
    RPB(U)
Fascination (Mazurka-Impromptu), **Op.30**
    Pond, 1880, 9p.
    NcU(M786.44M657f)
"Hail Columbia" (Paraphrase de Concert), **Op.8**
    Pond, 1876, 15p.
    DLC(M27.M)
Improvista on Two Welsh Melodies, Op.37
    Pond, 1888, 11p.
    DLC(M27.M)
    Uses parts of his earlier **Welsh Air.**
Méditation au Soir (Evening Thoughts), **Op.32**
    Pond, 1882, 12p.
    DLC(M25.M), NNLc(°MYD+box), PP(U)
Murmuring Fountain (Caprice), **Op.22**
    Pond, 1866, 11p.
    CtHT(U), DLC(M25.M), NBu(U), RPB(U)
"Old Folks at Home" (Concert-Transcription), **Op.36**
    Schroeder, 1887, 11p.
    PP(U)
Polka Caprice, Op.18
    Schirmer, 1865, 9p.
    ViU(McR.170.25)
Recollections of Home (Caprice populaire), **Op.23**
    Pond, 1868, 14p.
    DLC(M25.M), InU(M1.S8), LN(U), MiU-C(U), NRU-E(U), RPB(U),
      ViU(°M1.S444,v.140,no.9), WM(786.4M65r)
Recollections of Scotland (Fantasie), **Op.41**
    Schroeder, 1891, 15p.
    DLC(M25.M), NNLc(AM2-I), PP(U)
    A difficult caprice on Scottish airs, including "Auld
      Lang Syne" and "The Campbells are Coming."
Romance, Op.45
    Pond, 1895, 7p.
    DLC(M25.M), PP(U)

Saltarello, Op.26
    Pond, 1871, 9p.
    RPB(U)
Tarantelle, Op.13
    Pond, 1863, 13p.
    CU(M31.M5 1891), CtHT(U), CtY(Mc11A1M628), DLC(M30.M), IU
        (MaLq786.4M62t), InU(M1.S8), MiU-C(U), NNLc(°MYDbox), NcU
        (MF786.45M657t), NRU-E(U), PP(U), RPB(U), ViU(°M1.S444,
        v.139,no.2), WM(786.4M65)
    One of the most popular tarantellas of the 19th century.
2nd Tarantelle, Op.20
    Pond, 1865, 15p.
    CtHT(U), NRU-E(U), RPB(U)
Welsh Air with Brilliant Variations
    Pond, 1860, 9p.
    NRU-E(U), RPB(U)
    Attractive variations on "Ar Hyd y Nos."

MOKREJS, JOHN (1875-1968)

Arabesque, Op.9, No.4
    Summy, 1909, 9p.
    NRU-E(U)
Boutade, Op.57, No.2
    Odowan, 1935, 7p.
    DLC(M25.M), IaCrC(M25M87B6)
Dance of ye Witch of Salem Town (Valcik II), Op.14
    Odowan, 1909, 7p.
    DLC(M30.M), IaCrC(M25M87D34), NNLc(°MNp.v.42)
Intermezzo, Op.9, No.3 (from Four Concert Pieces, Op.9)
    Summy, 1911, 7p.
    DLC(M25.M)
Military Nocturne (The Camp Bugle)
    Odowan, 1902, 5p.
    IaCrC(M25M87M5)
    Most unusual nocturne, based on "Taps."
Out of the West, Op.57, No.1
    Odowan, 1906, 6p.
    DLC(M25.M), NNLc(°MYD), NRU-E(U), OC(786.4fM71o),
Prelude, Op.9, No.1 (from Four Concert Pieces, Op.9)
    Summy, 1910, 7p.
    DLC(M25.M)
Valcik in C Major, Op.46
    Summy, 1928, 9p.
    IaCrC(M25M87V3), NRU-E(U)
Valcik in C Minor, Op.41, No.2 (from Two Compositions for
  Pianoforte, Op.41)
    Church, 1926, 11p.
    CtY(Mc11A1M729), DLC(M25.M), IU(qM786.41M72c)
Valcik in D Flat
    Odowan, 1903, 5p.
    DLC(M32.M), IaCrC(M25M87V34), NNLc(°MYD), RPB(U)

Valcik in D Flat (Revised and enlarged edition of 1903
  Valcik)
    Odowan, 1959, 5p.
    DLC(M32.M), IaCrC(M25M87V33), MoS(786.4), NRU-E(U), also
      in P-S

MOLLER, JOHN CHRISTOPHER (1755-1803)

The Chase (Composed by Moler)
    Graupner, ca.1811, 3p. [W.II:575]
    DLC(M1.A1M), ICN(Case8A 454), NBu(U), NNLc(AM1-I)
Favorite. La Chasse (see **The Chase**)
Meddley (with the most favorite Airs and Variations)
    Willig, ca.1796, 6p. [SU:257]
    DLC(M1.A1M Case), ICN(Case8A 169), NNLc(AM1-I), NRU-E (Vault
      M1.A1B691), also in A-C(I)
Rondo (In Third No. in Moller and Capron's **Monthly Numbers**)
    Moller, 1793, 3p. [SU:359]
    DLC(M1.A1M), NNLc(AM1-I), also in A-C(I)
Sinfonia (In First No. in Moller and Capron's **Monthly Numbers**)
    Moller, 1793, 4p. [SU:384]
    DLC(M1.A1M Case), MoS(786.4), also in P-H
Sonata VIII
    In C-MH

MORAN, PETER K. (d.1831)

"The Bonny Boat" (Scotch Air with Variations)
    DuboisS, 1826, 5p.
    CtY(Mc26A7), DLC(M1.A13M Case), NBu(°M1.C65,v.1,no.40),
      NNLc(AM1-I), NcU(EAMC,no.9), ViU(McR.45.02)
"The Carrier Pigeon" (Composed by Moran and Arranged as a
  Rondo)
    Jackson, 1825, Riley, n.d., 8p. [W.II:593]
    NNLc(AM1-I), ScCC(SMB26.2)
"Come Buy my Cherries" (Sir J. Stevenson's Celebrated Air
  Arranged as a Rondo)
    Dubois, 1819, 6p. [W.II:849]
    NNLc(AM1-I), ScCC(SMB28.12)
A Fantasia
    In A-C(II)
A Favorite Swiss Waltz with Variations
    Dubois, ca.1817-1818, 5p. [W.II:599]
    CtY(Mc11A1M793), DLC(M1.A13M Case), ICN(Case8A 1517), NBu
      (°M1.C65,v.1,no.24), NNLc(AM1-I), NRU-E(530275v.1), NcD
      (RBR MusicB154,no.20), PP(U), RPB(U), ViU(McR.11.15)
"Kinlock of Kinlock" (with Variations)
    Bradlee, 183_?, 3p.
    CtY(Mc11A1M793), DLC(M1.A13M Case), ICN(Case sm oM1.A13,
      no.461), InU(M1.S8), NBu(°M1.C65,v.19,no.5), NRU-E(U),
      PP(U), ViU(°M1.S444,v.71,no.24; McR.101.35)

"The Knight Errant" (A Celebrated French Romance Arranged with
Variations)
> Dubois, ca.1821, 9p. [W.II:426]
> DLC(M1.A1M Case), InU(M1.S8), NNLc(AM1-I)
> Original song by Hortensia, Queen of Holland.

"Mi pizzica mi stimola," Thema from Masaniello (Arranged as a
Rondo)
> Blake, 1829, 7p.
> DLC(M1.A13M Case), ICN(Case sm oM1.A13,no.2132), RPB(U)
> Attractive variations on a melody from Auber's opera
> **Masaniello.**

Moran's favourite Variations to the Suabian Air
> Willig, ca.1817-1819, 5p. [W.II:596]
> CtY(RareM20J94+v.2,no.18), DLC(M1.A1M Case), ICN(Case 8A
> 1749), NNLc(AM1-I), NRU-E(811173), NcD(RBR MusicB85,no.28),
> NcU(EAMC,no.57), PP(U), RPB(U), Also in A-C(II)
> The Suabian Air is "Ach, du lieber Augustin."

"Robin Adair" (A Favorite Irish Melody with Introduction and
Variations)
> Dubois, 1819, 9p. [W.II:597]
> InU(M1.S8), NBu(U), NcD(RBR MusicB144,no.6)
> One of Moran's most interesting sets of variations.

Stanz Waltz with Variations
> Dubois, ca.1817-1818, 5p. [W.II:598]
> CtY(Mc28W1), DLC(M1.A1M Case), ICN(Case8A 2593), NRU-E
> (8018.F.9), PP(U), RPB(U), ViU(°M1.S444,v.164,no.42)

Suabian Air (see **Moran's favourite Variations,** etc.)

The Swiss Waltz with Variations
> Bradlee, 182_?, 5p. [W.II:599]
> CtY(RareM21V299+no.27), DLC(M1.A13M), ICN(Case sm oM1.
> A13,no.487), MB-N(VaultM1A18v.1,no.12), NcD(RBR Music
> B85,no.27)
> Different edition, but same music as **A Favorite Swiss
> Waltz.**

Variations sur L'Air "Fleuve du Tage" ("Come rest in this
Bosom")
> Jackson, ca.1823-1826), 8p. [W.II:705]
> ICN(Case8A 2645), InU(M1.S8)

A Venetian Air, Arranged with Variations
> Dubois, 1819, 6p. [W.II:599]
> CtY(Mc26A7), DLC(M1.A13M Case), NRU-E(7190719), RPB(U)

MURDEN, ELIZA CRAWLEY (see **ANONYMOUS: United States Marine
March**)

NEVIN, ARTHUR FINLEY (1871-1943)

As the Moon Rose (see **From Edgeworth Hills**)
The Fire Fly (see **From Edgeworth Hills**)
From Edgeworth Hills (Suite)
> Church, 1903, 4v.(5,4,3,7p.)

CtY(Mc11A1N417, 3,4 only), DLC(M24.N), MoS(786.4),
   MoSW(U, 3 only), NNLc(°MYD), NRU-E(M24N526f)
1. **Panorama**; 2. **Sylphs**; 3. **As the Moon Rose**; 4. **Fire Fly**
Panorama (see **From Edgeworth Hills**)
Southern Sketches (Free Fantasies)
   Church, 1923, 19p.
   MoS(786.4)
1. **Neath the Magnolias**; 2. **Sun Glaze on the River**;
   3. **Twilight** (From the Lowlands); 4. **"Jus' Strummin'"**
   (From the Lowlands); 5. **Sunset on the Mississippi**
Sylphs (see **From Edgeworth Hills**)

NEVIN, ETHELBERT (1862-1901)

Alba, Op.25, No.1 (see **Un Giorno in Venezia, Op.25**)
Arlecchino, Op.21, No.1 (see **Maggio in Toscana, Op.21**)
Barcarolle, Op.13, No.5 (see **Water Scenes, Op.13**)
Barchetta, Op.21, No.3 (see **Maggio in Toscana, Op.21**)
Buona Notte, Op.25, No.4 (see **Un Giorno in Venezia, Op.25**)
Canzone Amorosa, Op.25, No.3 (see **Un Giorno in Venezia, Op.25**)
Dragon Fly, Op.13, No.1 (see **Water Scenes, op.13**)
En Passant, Op.30
   Church, 1899, 29p.
   DLC(M3.3.N5op.30), InU(M1.S8), Mos(786.4), MoSW(U), NNLc
   (°MYD), NRU-E(M22N52v.3), OCl(M776.4.6784)
1. **A Fontainebleau**; 2. **In Dreamland**; 3. **Napoli**; 4. **At Home**
Egyptian Love Song
   Schirmer, 1908, 5p.
   DLC(M25.N), MoSW(U), NRU-E(M22N52v.3)
Etude in Form of a Romance, Op.18, No.1 (see **Two Etudes, Op.18**)
Etude in Form of a Scherzo, Op.18, No.2 (see **Two Etudes, Op.18**)
Two Etudes, Op.18
   Boston, 1892, 2v.(11,13p.)
   DLC(M25.N), MBH(P.1W596.1), MB-N(Piano, 1 only), MoSW(U),
   NNLc(°MYD-Amer), NRU-E(M22N52v.3), PP(U), RPB(U, 2 only),
   ViU(McR.127.41 and 127.42), also in NC-G
1. **Etude in Form of a Romance**; 2. **Etude in Form of a Scherzo**
A striking departure from Nevin's basic salon-music style.
Un Giorno in Venezia (A Day in Venice), **Op.25**
   Church, 1898, 20p., also issued separately
   CU(M2ON48), CtY(Mc2ON41+op.25), DLC(M24.N5op.25), ICN
   (VM22N52d), IU(qM786.41N41d), InU(M1.S8), MoS(786.4),
   MoSW(U), NNLc(°MYD), NRU-E(M22N52v.2), NcD(M786.43N526
   G499 1898), OCl(M776.415.683), PP(M786.4N4116), ViU
   (Music M25N526G5 1898), WM(786.4N52g), also in BC-G
   (1 only)
1. **Alba**; 2. **Gondolieri**; 3. **Canzone Amorosa**; 4. **Buona Notte**
Gondolieri, Op.25, No.2 (see **Un Giorno in Venezia, Op.25**)

La Guitare (Pierrot et Pierrette)
    Boston, 1896, 5p.
    CtY(Mc11A1N418), DLC(M25.N), MB-N(Piano), MoSW(U), NNLc
    (JNG 76-510,no.4), NRU-E(M22N52v.3), PP(U)
In Arcady (Four Pastoral Scenes), **Op.16**
    Boston, 1892, 30p., also issued separately
    CU(M2ON48), CtY(M24N526+op.16), DLC(M25.N), IU(qM786.41
    N41i), InU(M1.S8), LN(U, 2 only), MB-N(Piano), MoS
    (786.4), MoSW(U), NNLc(°MYD+box), NRU-E(M22N52v.1),
    OCL(M776.43.677), PP(M786.4fN41), ViU(Music M25N526I5
    1892), WM(786.4N52i)
    1. **A Shepherd's Tale**; 2. **Shepherds All and Maidens Fair**;
       3. **Lullabye**; 4. **Tournament** (à la Polonaise)
Intermezzo, Op.7, No.3 (see **Four Piano Compositions, Op.7**)
Lullabye, Op.16, No.3 (see **In Arcady, Op.16**)
Maggio in Toscana (May in Tuscany), **Op.21**
    Boston, 1895, 31p., also issued separately
    CU(M2ON48), CtY(Mc2ON41+op.21), DLC(M24.N5op.21), LN(U,
    3,5 only), MB-N(Piano), MoS(786.4), MoSW(U), NNLc(°MYD),
    NRU-E(M22N52v.2), OCL(M776.43.678), PP(M786.4N4114),
    RPB(U, 1 only), WM(786.4N52m)
    1. **Arlecchino**; 2. **Notturno** (In Boccacio's Villa);
       3. **Barchetta**; 4. **Misericordia** (At Midnight on the Lung'
       Arno); 5. **Il Rusignuolo**; 6. **La Pastorella** (Montepiano)
Melodies (Arranged from Original Songs)
    Boston, 1888, 23p.
    CU(M2ON48), CtY(Mc4ON41m), DLC(M38.5.N), InU(M1.S8), MoSW
    (U), NNLc(°MYD+), NRU-E(M22N52v.2), OCL(M776.49.676)
    PP(U)
    1. **One Spring Morning**; 2. **At Twilight**; 3. **Tell Me**;
       4. **The Rosary**; 5. **Time Enough**; 6. **The Merry, Merry
       Lark**; 7. **Oh, That We Two were Maying**
    Attractive keyboard settings of seven popular Nevin songs.
Misericordia, Op.21, No.4 (see **Maggio in Toscana, Op.21**)
Napoli, Op.30, No.3 (see **En Passant, Op.30**)
Narcissus, Op.13, No.4 (see **Water Scenes, Op.13**)
Notturno, Op.21, No.2 (see **Maggio in Toscana, Op.21**)
O'er Hill and Dale
    Church, 1902, 22p.
    CtY(U), DLC(M25.N), MoS(786.4), MoSW(U), NNLc(°MYD+box),
    OCL(M776.415.6836), WM(786.4N52o)
    1. **It was a Lover and his Lass**; 2. **The Thrush**; 3. **Love
       is astraying, ever since Maying**; 4. **The Lark is on
       the Wing**
Ophelia, Op.13, No.2 (see **Water Scenes, Op.13**)
La Pastorella, Op.21, No.6 (see **Maggio in Toscana, Op.21**)
Four Piano Compositions, Op.7
    Boston, 1890, 23p., also issued separately
    CU(M2ON48), CtY(Mc11A1N418, 1,2,3 only), DLC(M25.N), InU
    (M1.S8), MBH(P.1W596.1), MB-N(Piano, 2,3 only), MoS
    (786.4, 3 only), MoSW(U), NNLc(JNG 76-510,no.1), NRU-E
    (M22N52v.1), PP(U, 2,3 only), RPB(U, 1 only), ViU(McR.
    158.04, 1 only), also in AC(1 only)

1. Valser gentile; 2. Slumber Song; 3. Intermezzo;
   4. Song of the Brook
Pierrot et Pierrette (see La Guitare)
Il Rusignuolo, Op.21, No.5 (see Maggio in Toscana, Op.21)
Shepherds All and Maidens Fair, Op.16, No.2 (see In Arcady,
   Op.16)
A Shepherd's Tale, Op.16, No.1 (see In Arcady, Op.16)
Sketchbook (A Group of Songs and Piano Pieces), Op.2
   Boston, 1888, 31p.
   CU(M20N48), CtY(Mc20N41+op.2), DLC(M1.621.N), InU(M1.S8),
   MBH(VP.1B72), MoS(784), MoSW(U), NNLc(°MP [U.S.]), NRU-E
   (M22N52v.1), OCl(M774.3.677), PP(U, 1,3 only), ViU(Music
   M1620N4S5 1888), WM(784.8N52sk)
   1. Gavotte; 3. Love Song; 5. Berceuse; 7. Serenata;
      9. Valse Rhapsodie
Slumber Song, Op.7, No.2 (see Four Piano Compositions, Op.7)
Song of the Brook, Op.7, No.4 (see Four Piano Compositions, Op.7)
Tempo di Valse, Op.2, No.2 (Posthumous [1884])
   Schirmer, 1906, 5p.
   DLC(M32.N), MoSW(U), NRU-E(M22N52,v.3)
Tournament, Op.16, No.4 (see In Arcady, Op.16)
Valzer gentile, Op.7, No.1 (see Four Piano Compositions, Op.7)
Water Nymph, Op.13, No.3 (see Water Scenes, Op.13)
Water Scenes, Op.13
   Boston, 1891, 27p., also issued separately
   CU(M24N48), CtY(Mc20N41+op.13), DLC(M25.N), IU(qM786.41
   N41w Spec.Coll.), LN(U, 4 only), MBH(P.1C65), MB-N
   (P.1N41), MoS(786.4, 4 only), MoSW(U, 4 only), NNLc
   (°MYD), NRU-E(M22N52v.1), OCl(M776.415.684), PP(M786.4
   N4111), RPB(U), ViU(Music M25.N526W3 1891), WM(786.4
   N52W), also in AB-D(4 only)
   1. Dragon Fly; 2. Ophelia; 3. Water Nymph; 4. Narcissus;
      5. Barcarolle

NEWMAN, MR. (fl.1800-1810)

Three Sonatas for the Piano Forte or Harpsichord, Op.1
   HewittMR, ca.1807-1810, 12p. [W.II:635]
   InU(M1.S8), NBu(U), NNLc(AM1-I), also in A-C(I:III only),
   C-MH(I only)
Short, three-movement sonatas reminiscent of Haydn.

NICHOLL, HORACE WADHAM (1848-1922)

Twelve Concert Preludes and Fugues, Op.31, Book I
   Schirmer, 1916, 6v.(15,13,19,19,21,17p.)
   CtY(Mc11A1N514op.31[v.1]), DLC(M25.N 3,5 only), NNLc(°MYD)
   1. E Major (Cantilena and Fugue); 2. D Major (Alla Corale
      and Fugue); 3. A Minor (Quasi Capriccio and Fugue);
      4. F Major (Quasi Overtura and Fugue); 5. D-flat
      Major (Quasi Intermezzo and Fugue); 6. E Minor

(Quasi Barcarola and Fugue)
Very difficult. Valuable for concentrated study of fugue.
Nocturne
    Kunkel, 1879, 7p.
    DLC(M25.N), IU(Joseffy), NNLc(°MYD+box), PPi(qr786.4P535
    994)
Prelude and Fugue in E Major, Op.31, No.1 (see **Twelve Concert
Preludes and Fugues, Op.31**)
Prelude and Fugue in D Major, Op.31, No.2 (see **Twelve Concert
Preludes and Fugues, Op.31**)
Prelude and Fugue in A Minor, Op.31, No.3 (see **Twelve Concert
Preludes and Fugues, Op.31**)
Prelude and Fugue in F Major, Op.31, No.4 (see **Twelve Concert
Preludes and Fugues, Op.31**)
Prelude and Fugue in D-flat Major, Op.31, No.5 (see **Twelve
Concert Preludes and Fugues, Op.31**)
Prelude and Fugue in E Minor, Op.31, No.6 (see **Twelve Concert
Preludes and Fugues, Op.31**)
Sentiments poétiques, Op.21
    Schuberth-E, 1888, 2v. in 1(15,18p.)
    DLC(M25.N), NNLc(°MYD)
    1. Questionings; 2. Regrets; 3. Despair; 4. Retro-
    spection; 5. Remembrance; 6. Moods; 7. Purity;
    8. Passionateness; 9. Devotion; 10. Misgivings;
    11. Melancholy; 12. Thoughtfulness

OLDBERG, ARNE (1874-1962)

Arabesque, Op.31
    Summy, 1913,13p.
    DLC(M25.O), IE(S786.4 Ol195), IEN(RareCaseM22.053), IU
    (qM786.41 Ol1a)
Canzonetta, Op.30, No.2
    Summy, 1915, 9p.
    DLC(M25.O), IE(S786.4 Ol198), IEN(RareCaseM22.053), MoSW(U)
    Attractive work with some tricky, difficult passages.
Capriccio, Op.13, No.3 (see **Trois Morceaux, Op.13**)
Chanson triste, Op.13, No.2 (see **Trois Morceaux, Op.13**)
La Coquette, Op.14
    Summy, 1902, 7p.
    DLC(M25.O), IE(S786.4 Ol19), IEN(RareCaseM25.052C6)
Erinnerung, Op.6
    Summy, 1896, 7p.
    DLC(M25.O), IEN(RareCaseM25.052E7)
Fantaisie, Op.3
    Summy, 1896, 15p.
    DLC(M25.O), IEN(RareCaseM25.052F31)
Fantasia et Fuga, C Moll (J. S. Bach), **Op.12** (Transcription)
    Summy, 1907, 11p.
    IEN(RareCaseM22.053)
    A fine transcription of Bach's great organ work.
Fantasia fugata, Op.2

Summy, 1896, 9 p.
DLC(M25.0), IEN(RareCaseM22.053)
Clever mélange of old and new.
Improvisation, Op.32
Schirmer, 1913, 9p.
DLC(M25.0), IE(S786.4 0l196), IEN(M25.052I5op.32), NNLc
(°MYD), NRU-E(U)
A Legend, Op.26
Wa-Wan, 1907, 14p.
DLC(M25.0), ICN(VM1W11v.6), MoS(786.4), NNLc(°MN Wa-Wan),
NRU-E(M25 044le), PP(U), also in WW-L(IV:129)
Three Miniatures, Op.27
Wa-Wan, 1907-1908, 3v.
DLC(M25.0), ICN(VM1W11v.6-7), IEN(RareM25.052M52 and M54,
1,2 only), MoS(786.4, 3 only), NNLc(°MN Wa-Wan), NRU-E
(M25 044m.2), also in WW-L(IV:203; V:94; IV:191)
1. Badinage; 2. Intermezzo; 3. Carillon
Trois Morceaux, Op.13
Summy, 1902, 3v.(5,3,5p.)
DLC(M25.0), IE(S786.4 0l16, 1 only; 0l18, 3 only). IEN
(RareCaseM22.053)
1. Scherzino; 2. Chanson triste; 3. Capriccio
Praeludium, Op.5, No.1
Summy, 1906, 5p.
DLC(M25.0), IE(S786.4 0l13no.1), .IEN(M25.052P72op.5no.1),
MoSW(U), PP(U), WM(786.4 044p)
Praeludium, Op.5, No.2
Summy, 1898, 5p.
ICN(sVM25 044op.5,no.2), IE(S786.4 0l13no.2), IEN(Rare Case
M22.053)
Praeludium et Toccata, Op.1
Summy, 1896, 11p.
DLC(M25.0), IEN(RareCaseM25.052P7)
Prélude à la russe, Op.33
Schirmer, 1913, 9p.
DLC(M25.0), IE(S786.4 0l197), IEN(RareCaseM25.052I5op.32),
NNLc(°MYD), OCL(SM776.4)
Scherzino, Op.13, No.1 (see **Trois Morceaux, op.13**)
Sonata, Op.28
Summy, 1909, 39p.
IEN(RareCaseM22.053), MBH(P.1C65)
Impressive three-movement, very difficult work.
Theme and Variations, Op.25
Summy, 1907, 18p.
DLC(M27.0), IE(S786.4 0l1t), IEN(RareCaseM22.053), PP(U)

OREM, PRESTON WARE (1865-1938)

American Indian Rhapsody (On themes recorded and suggested
by Thurlow Lieurance)
Presser, 1918, 15p.
CtY(Mc11A10r3), DLC(M25.0), IU(qM786.410r1a), MoS(786.4),

NNLc(°MYD), NRU-E(M25C124I19)
Dramatic, flamboyant fantasy on Indian melodies.
Sonata in F Minor
    North, 1885, 7p.
    DLC(M23.066), NcU(M786.41 066s)

ORTH, JOHN (1850-1932)

Four Compositions, Op.8
    Schirmer, 1899, 4v.(7,7,7,7p.)
    DLC(M25.0), MoS(786.4), MoSW(U), PP(U, 1 only)
    1. Menuet-Fantaisie; 2. Seconde Danse caractèristique;
      3. Seconde Polonaise; 4. Staccato brillant
Danse caractéristique, Op.2, No.5
    Schmidt, 1886, 1906, 7p.
    NRU-E(U)
Seconde Danse caractéristique, Op.8, No.2 (see **Four Compositions, Op.8**)
En Route, Op.14, No.3 (see **Trois Pièces, Op.14**)
Etude brillante (in A Flat), **Op.10, No.3**
    Ditson, 1899, 7p.
    DLC(M25.0)
Fantaisie-Impromptu, Op.12, No.1
    Schirmer, 1903, 11p.
    DLC(M25.0), MoSW(U), NRU-E(U)
Méditation, Op.14, No.2 (see **Trois Pièces, Op.14**)
Menuet-Fantaisie, Op.8, No.1 (see **Four Compositions, Op.8**)
Morceau chromatique, Op.11, No.1 (from **Trois Morceaux, Op.11**)
    Ditson, 1902, 13p.
    RPB(U)
Nocturne, Op.6, No.1
    Schmidt, 1890, 7p.
    CtY(U), DLC(M25.0)
Trois Pièces, Op.14
    Schirmer, 1904, 3v.(7,5,7p.)
    DLC(M25.0), MoSW(U, 1 only), RPB(U, 1 only), WM(786.4
      077e, 3 only)
    1. Première Tarantelle; 2. Méditation; 3. En Route
Polonaise in A
    Schmidt, 1886, 9p.
    NRU-E(U)
Seconde Polonaise, Op.8, No.3 (see **Four Compositions, Op.8**)
Romance
    Schmidt, 1887, 5p.
    DLC(M25.0), MoSW(U)
Romanza appassionata, Op.7, No.1
    Ditson, 1897, 5p.
    DLC(M25.0), PP(U)
Rushing Waters, Op.18, No.1
    Boston, 1918, 6p.
    MTO(Vault 01.J)
Staccato brillant, Op.8, No.4 (see **Four Compositions, Op.8**)

Staccato de Concert, Op.15
   Schirmer, 1905, 7p.
   DLC(M25.0), MoSW(U)
Première Tarantelle, Op.14, No.1 (see **Trois Pièces, Op.14**)
Wild Horseman, Op.20, No.1
   Boston, 1924, 5p.
   MTO(Vault 01.J)

O'SULLIVAN, PATRICK (1871-1947)

Etude (No.III in **Sept Morceaux**)
   Stahl, 1901, 5p.
   DLC(M25.0)
   Good example of O'Sullivan's chromatic style.
30 Irish Melodies
   Stahl, Schirmer, 1905, 33p.
   KyLoU(U)
   No.30 is a theme with four attractive variations.
Nocturne (No.VIII in **Dix Morceaux**)
   Stahl, 1902, 11p.
   DLC(M25.0)
Prélude (No.VI in **Dix Morceaux**)
   Stahl, 1902, 4p.
   DLC(M25.0)
Prélude (No.VII in **Dix Morceaux**)
   Stahl, 1902, 3p.
   DLC(M25.0)
   Compelling lyricism, like a Chopin nocturne.

OTTERSTROM, THORWALD (1868-1942)

24 Fugen für Klavier
   Friis, 1909, 4v. in 1(150p.)
   DLC(M25.0), ICN(VM22 089f), MoS(786.4), NNLc(°MYD),
     OCl(M776.4.7084), PP(U, 3,4 only)
   Very difficult concert fugues. Superb for technique.
Konzert-Etüden
   Hansen, 1907, 6v.(14,7,9,7,7,9p.)
   NjP(MT241.091q[SVL]), PP(U)
   1. **Des Dur** (Passagen); 2. **A Dur** (Terzen); 3. **Fis moll**
     (Passagen); 4. **G moll** (Sexten); 5. **E Dur** (Oktaven);
     6. **E moll** (Verschiedene Doppelgriffe)
   Difficult, demanding and rewarding.
24 Präludien für Klavier
   Friis, 1904, 4v.(24,18,32,17p.)
   DLC(M25.0,v.1 only), ICN(VM22 089f), IU(Joseffy), WM(786.4
     089)
   Very difficult, musicianly compositions.
The Spinning Wheel
   Thiebes, 1900, 11p.
   DLC(M25.0), MoSW(U)

PAINE, JOHN KNOWLES (1839-1906)

Birthday Impromptu, Op.41, No.2 (see Three Piano Pieces, Op.41)
Four Characteristic Pieces, Op.25
    Russell, 1876, 23p., also issued separately
    DLC(M25.P), MB-N(M3.3P2op.25), also in PP-S
    1. Dance; 2. Romance; 3. Impromptu; 4. Rondo giocoso
Vier Charakterstücke, Op.11
    Forberg, n.d., 17p.
    DLC(M25.P Case), also in PP-S
A Christmas Gift, Op.7
    Russell, 1864, 7p.
    DLC(M25.P), also in PM-H, PP-S
Columbus March and Hymn (Arranged for piano solo by Arthur
    Foote)
    Ditson, 1892, 19p.
    DLC(M35.P), MB-N(M3.3P2C63), NBu(U)
Fuga giocosa, Op.41, No.3 (see Three Piano Pieces, Op.41)
A Funeral March In Memory of President Lincoln, Op.9
    Beer, 1865, 6p.
    DLC(M20.C59P), also in PP-S
In the Country (Sketches for the Piano), **Op.26**
    Russell, 1876, 10v.(5,5,7,3,5,5,5,5,5,7p.)
    DLC(M25.P), MB-N(M3.3P2op.26), NNLc(°MYD-Amer), NcU(M786.43
    P145i), also in PP-S
    1. Woodnotes; 2. Wayside Flowers; 3. Under the Lindens;
    4. The Shepherd's Lament; 5. Village Dance; 6. Rainy
    Day; 7. The Mill; 8. Gypsies; 9. Farewell; 10. Wel-
    come Home
    Delightful miniature sketches bearing Paine's unique charm.
Nocturne, Op.45
    Schmidt, 1889, 7p.
    DLC(M25.P), MB-N(M3.3P2op.45), NcU(M786.43P145n), also in
    PP-S
    A superb nocturne.
Three Piano Pieces, Op.41
    Schmidt, 1884, 3v.(7,3,5p.)
    CtY(Mc11A1P161, 2 only), DLC(M25.P), IU(MO 14987, 3 only),
    MBH(P.1W596.1), MB-N(M3.3P2op.41, 3 only), NRU-E(M25
    P145f, 3 only), NcU(M786.43P145p41, 1,2 only), ViU(McR.
    173.35, 3 only), also in NC-G(2,3 only), PP-S
    1. Spring Idyl; 2. Birthday Impromptu; 3. Fuga giocosa
Romance, Op.12
    Koppitz, 1869, 7p.
    DLC(M25.P), MBH(P.1B12), MB-N(M3.3P2op.12), NNLc(AM2-I),
    NcU(M786.4P145r12), RPB(U), also in PP-S
    Strangely moving, much use of lower register.
Romance, Op.39
    Ditson, 1883, 7p.
    DLC(M25.P), MBH(P.1W596.1), NcU(M786.4P145r39), also in
    PP-S
Spring Idyl, Op.41, No.1 (see Three Piano Pieces, Op.41)

PALMER, COURTLANDT (1872–1951)

Nocturne
    Schirmer, 1911, 8p.
    DLC(M25.P), NNLc(°MNZ-Amer.rev.ed.), WM(786.4P16)
Prélude
    Schirmer, 1911, 7p.
    DLC(M25.P), NNLc(°MNZ-Amer.rev.ed.), PP(U)
Sonate für Klavier
    Hug, ca.1934, 19p.
    CtY(Mc11A1P182), DLC(M23.P154S6), MB-N(Hale Coll.78.
      64P18)

PALMER, WILLIAM HENRY [ROBERT HELLER] (1830–1878)

Caprice sentimentale, Op.11
    Dodworth, 1858, 11p.
    DLC(ML410.H46C6), NcU(MF786.43H477c), NNLc(°MYD)
    Also published in **Melody Magic.**
Coronella, Op.14, No.3 (from **Trois Mazurkas, Op.14**)
    Dodworth, 1862, 7p.
    NRU-E(U)
Etude de Bravoura, Op.10
    Dodworth, 1858, 12p.
    NcU(MF786.47H4765e)
    Fine study, also published in **Melody Magic.**
Fuchsia, Op.14, No.1 (from **Trois Mazurkas, Op.14**)
    Dodworth, 1862, 9p.
    NBu(U)
Josephine Mazurka (No.1 in **Twilight Musings**)
    Dodworth, 1855, 6p.
    ICN(Piano pre-1870), MiU-C(U), NBu(U), NNLc(Drexel 5538),
        PP(U), RPB(U)
Laughing Water (Morceau de Salon)
    Dodworth, 1863, 9p.
    DLC(M25.H [Heller]), MiU-C(U)
Melody Magic
    Clapham, 1932, 84p.
    NNLc(°MYD)
    A book compiled by Harry L. Clapham. Contains a biography
      of Palmer (stage name Robert Heller), a magician, mimic
      and musician. Included are three of Palmer's compositions:
      Etude de Bravoura; Caprice sentimentale; Souvenir d'Hiver.
Souvenir d'Hiver (Valse brillante), **Op.15**
    Lee, 1857, 17p.
    NcU(MF786.45H477s), PP(U)
    Also published in **Melody Magic.**
Way-Side Flowers (Pleasing Fantasia on the "Drinking Song"
  in **Lucrezia Borgia**)
    Gould, 1854, 7p.
    PP(U)
    An effective, tasteful keyboard paraphrase.

PARKER, HORATIO WILLIAM (1863-1919)

Ballad, Op.25, No.2 (see Six Lyrics, Op.25)
Barcarolle, Op.25, No.5 (see Six Lyrics, Op.25)
Caprice, Op.9, No.4 (see Cinq Morceaux, Op.9)
Capricietto
    Millet, 1895, 5p.
    CtY(Ma33EP4), DLC(M25.P), NcU(M25.P37C3), also in HH-K
        (V:1097)
Conte sérieux, Op.49, No.1 (see Trois Morceaux, Op.49)
Dialogue
    Millet, 1895, 5p.
    DLC(M25.P), also in HH-K(V:1102)
Elégie, Op.9, No.1 (see Cinq Morceaux, Op.9)
Etude mélodieuse, Op.19, No.3 (see Four Sketches, Op.19)
Fairy Tale, Op.25, No.4 (see Six Lyrics, Op.25)
Gavotte, Op.9, No.5 (see Cinq Morceaux, Op.9)
Impromptu, Op.9, No.3 (see Cinq Morceaux, Op.9)
Six Lyrics for the Piano without Octaves, Op.25
    Schirmer, 1891, 6v.(7,7,5,7,7,7p.)
    DLC(M1380.P), CtY(Ma33Aop.25), MoS(786.4), MoSW(U, 6 only)
    1. Reverie; 2. Ballad; 3. Rondino; 4. Fairy Tale;
        5. Barcarolle; 6. Novelette
    Actually Op.23. Incorrectly published.
Trois Morceaux caractéristiques, Op.49
    Church, 1899, 3v.(7,5,7p.)
    CtY(Mc11A1P22), DLC(M25.P), ICN(VM22P23t), MoS(786.4, 1
        only), NNLc(°MYD+box), NRU-E(M21R29A, 3 only), PP(U, 2,3
        only), also in NC-G(1,2 only)
    1. Conte sérieux; 2. La Sauterelle; 3. Valse gracile
    Parker at his very best.
Cinq Morceaux caractéristiques, Op.9
    Schmidt, 1886, 5v.(5,7,5,7,5p.)
    CtY(Mc11A1P22), DLC(M25.P), NcU(M786.48P239m)
    1. Elégie; 2. Scherzo; 3. Impromptu; 4. Caprice;
        5. Gavotte
Nocturne, Op.19, No.4 (see Four Sketches, Op.19)
Novelette, Op.25, No.6 (see Six Lyrics, Op.25)
Reverie, Op.25, No.1 (see Six Lyrics, Op.25)
Romanza, Op.19, No.1 (see Four Sketches, Op.19)
Rondino, Op.25, No.3 (see Six Lyrics, Op.25)
La Sauterelle, Op.49, No.2 (see Trois Morceaux, Op.49)
Scherzino, Op.19, No.2 (see Four Sketches, Op.19)
Scherzo, Op.9, No.2 (see Cinq Morceaux, Op.9)
Four Sketches, Op.19
    Schmidt, 1890, 4v.(5,5,5,5p.)
    CtY(Ma33Aop.19, 2,3 only), DLC(M25.P), InU(M1.S8), MB-N
        (Piano, 2 only), MoS(786.4, 2,3 only), NNLc(°MYD+box,
        4 only), NcU(M786.4P239s)
    1. Romanza; 2. Scherzino; 3. Etude mélodieuse;
        4. Nocturne
    Brief, unpretentious and artful quartet of pieces.
Valse gracile, Op.49, No.3 (see Trois Morceaux, Op.49)

PARKER, JAMES CUTLER DUNN (1828-1916)

Polonaise brillante, Op.2
    BrainardS, 1857, 11p.
    PP(U)

PARSONS, ALBERT ROSS (1847-1933)

Air from the Suite in D for Orchestra by Johann Sebastian Bach
    (Transcription)
    Schirmer, 1886, 5p.
    PP(U)
Rataplan (Concert Caprice on a Theme by Arthur Sullivan)
    Schirmer, 1882, 9p.
    DLC(M25.P)
    Based on the Bouncer's song from Cox and Box.

PARSONS, EDWARD A. (1849-1929)

Caprice sur le Chant populaire "Home Sweet Home"
    Pond, 1885, 13p.
    DLC(M27.P)
Crispino (Fantasie de Concert)
    Gordon, 1871, 15p.
    DLC(M25.P)
"Home Sweet Home" (see Caprice sur le Chant....)
Legend of the Fountain
    Pond, 1887, 11p.
    CtY(U), DLC(M25.P)
"Old Folks at Home" ("Suwanee River," Paraphrase élégante)
    Ditson, 1890, 13p.
    DLC(M27.P), RPB(U)

PATTISON, JOHN NELSON (1840-1905)

Bagatelle ("We Won't Go Home Till Morning")
    Pond, 1866, 7p.
    DLC(M25.P), NNLc(AM2-I)
Grand Fantasie on Themes from the Opera of "The Doctor of
    Alcantara" by Jules Eichberg
    Pond, 1868, 23p.
    ViU(°M1.S444,v.22,no.14)
Le Lever du Soleil (Sunrise. Mazurka-Caprice)
    Ditson, 1864, 7p.
    CtHT(U), CtY(Mc11A1P278), DLC(M25.P), IU(MaLq784.3Sh37,v.11,
        no.38), InU(M1.S8), MiU-C(U), NBu(°M1.C66v.41,no.19),
        NNLc(AM2-I), NRU-E(U), RPB(U), ViU(°M1.S444,v.94,no.14;
        McR.57.20)
Midnight (Redowa fantastique)
    Pond, 1865, 9p.

ICN(Piano pre-1870), NBu(U), RPB(U)
The Promenade (Rhapsody No.1), **Op.63**
Pond, 1876, 9p.
DLC(M25.P)
The Robin and the Cricket (Mazurka caractéristique)
Ditson, 1867, 7p.
RPB(U)
Attractive salon piece in dialogue style.
Soirée et Bal (Introduction et Grande Polka de Concert)
Ditson, 1868, 17p.
RPB(U)
Twilight (Mazurka-Caprice)
Pond, 1862, 7p.
MiU-C(U)
Valse Etude
The composer, 1884, 7p.
CtY(Mc11A1P278)

PAUL, JEAN [see **CHARLES KUNKEL**]

PEASE, ALFRED HUMPHRIES (1838-1882)

Delta Kappa Epsilon Grand March
ChurchJr, 1861, 6p.
CtHT(U), CtY(Mc11A1P321), ICN(VM1N71v.4), LN(U), NNLc(AM2-I),
OCl(SM776.44), PP(U), RPB(U), ViU(°M1.650P437D4 1861), WM
(786.4P36d)
Fantaisie comique
Lyon, 1898, 9p.
DLC(M25.P)
La Périchole (Offenbach. Fantaisie élégante)
Cottier, 1871, 11p.
NBu(U)
Polonaise (from **Mignon.** Transcription de Concert)
Pond, 1875, 19p.
DLC(M34.T [Thomas]), NRU-E(U)
Fine concert paraphrase.
Sans Souci (Galop Caprice)
Cottier, 1869, 9p.
NBu(U)
Souvenir de Berlin (Fantaisie)
FirthP, 1861, 11p.
DLC(M25.P)

PENFIELD, SMITH NEWELL (1837-1920)

Gavotte in Canon Form
Church, 1901, 5p.
DLC(M31.P), MoSW(U)
An unusual treatment of the traditional dance form.

Poem of Life (Four Characteristic Pieces in the Form of a
    Sonata), **Op.10**
    RootC, n.d., 4v.(11,7,7,11p.)
    DLC(M23.P46op.10), NcU(M786.41P398p)
    1. **The Stream of Time;** 2. **The Cascade of Pleasure;**
        3. **The Vale of Romance;** 4. **Parnassus**
Souvenir de Paris (Rondino), **Op.11**
    RootC, 1869, 5p.
    RPB(U)

PERABO, JOHANN ERNST (1845-1920)

Etude, Op.9, No.1 (see **Drei Studien, Op.9**)
Etude, Op.9, No.2 (see **Drei Studien, Op.9**)
Etude, Op.9, No.3 (see **Drei Studien, Op.9**)
Moment Musical, Op.1
    Ditson, 1872, 7p.
    DLC(M22.P47C6)
Pensée fugitive, Op.6
    Russell, 1873, 5p.
    DLC(M25.P)
Pensées, Op.11
    Augener, n.d., 15p.
    NcU(MF786.4P426p)
    A curious volume containing an attractive piano composition,
        then a vocal setting of the Soliloquy from Shakespeare's
        Hamlet, followed by a keyboard postlude.
Prelude, Op.3
    Russell, 1873, 10p.
    DLC(M25.P), MBH(P.1B91)
Scherzo, Op.2
    Russell, 1873, 11p.
    DLC(M25.P)
    A fine example of expert scherzo writing.
Drei Studien, Op.9
    Kistner, n.d., 3v.(5,11,7p.)
    DLC(M25.P), IU(Joseffy, 2,3 only)
    Three interesting and useful etudes.

PERRY, EDWARD BAXTER (1855-1924)

Autumn Reverie (from **Characteristic Studies**)
    Presser, 1895, 7p.
    CtY(Mc11A1P429)
Ballade (Last Island)
    Presser, 1896, 23p.
    DLC(M25.P)
Die Lorelei (Fantasy)
    Thompson, 1888, 13p.
    DLC(M25.P), IU(MO 14994Spec.Coll.), MoSW(U), NNLc(°MYDp.v.59,
        no.15), NcU(M786.42P458L), PP(U)

Memories (A Romance)
    Presser, 1920, 9p.
    NRU-E(U)
Nocturne, Op.6
    Zumsteeg, Ditson, 1878, 7p.
    NcU(M786.43P462n)
Reverie, Op.4
    Zumsteeg, Ditson, 1878, 5p.
    NcU(M786.43P462r)
Romance caractéristique, Op.10, No.2
    Schmidt, 1886, 5p.
    MoSW(U), OCl(SM776.4)
Why?, Op.9, No.1
    Schmidt, 1879, 3p.
    DLC(M25.P)

PIRANI, EUGENIO (1852-1939)

Belsazar (Ballade), **Op.65**
    Schlesinger, 1904, 14p.
    DLC(M25.P), IU(Joseffy), NNLc(°MYD+box)
Concert-Etudes (From his High School of Piano-Playing), **Op.88**
    Schirmer, 1908, 15v.(67p.), also issued separately
    CU(fMT241P5, 1,13 only), DLC(M25.P, 13 only), IU(Joseffy,
        13 only), NNLc(°MYD+box, 13 only), NRU-E(U, 14 only),
        OC(M6.4qP667), OCl(M776.3.7339)
    1. Firefly; 2. Organ-Tones; 3. Spinning-Wheel; 4. Song
    without Words; 5. Warbling Birds; 6. Raindrops; 7. Valse
    de Concert; 8. Danse des Gnomes; 9. Harp-Chords; 10. Valse
    Languissante; 11. Light Cavalry; 12. Fairy Revelry;
    13. Scherzo; 14. Fughetta; 15. Harmonies du Soir
    Fifteen technical studies of high musical qualities.
Fantasia on a Popular Italian Song "Funiculi-Funicula"
    Fischer, 1909, 9p.
    DLC(M25.P), MoS(786.4), NNLc(°MYD+box), PP(U)
Gavotte, Op.25, No.1
    Schuberth-E, 1888, 7p.
    DLC(M25.P), PP(U)
Im Walde (Ballade), **Op.47a**
    Schlesinger, 1904, 17p.
    DLC(M25.P), IU(Joseffy), MoS(786.4), NNLc(°MYD+box)

PLATT, RICHARD (1877- ?)

Chanson in F
    Ditson, 1910, 5p.
    DLC(M25.P)
Nocturne in G Minor
    Ditson, 1913, 7p.
    DLC(M25.P)
    A charming study in impressionism.

Suite in G moll, Op.2
    Challier, 1897, 26p.
    DLC(M24.P)
    1. Vorspiel; 2. Romanze; 3. Scherzo; 4. Rondo-Finale
Valse Impromptu in G
    Ditson, 1910, 11p.
    CtY(Mc11A1P697), DLC(M32.P)

PRATT, SILAS GAMALIEL (1846-1916)

The Carousal (Paraphrase on the Song "We won't go Home until
    Morning")
    Lyon, 1867, 10p.
    DLC(M25.P; M27.P), RPB(U)
    An amusing composition--fun to play and fun to hear.
Fantaisie-Caprice, Op.24
    Root, 1877, 9p.
    IU(Joseffy)
Fantaisie Impromptu, Op.28
    Root, 1877, 11p.
    IU(Joseffy)
"Lena" (with Brilliant Variations)
    Lyon, 1866, 11p.
    DLC(M27.P), ICN(Case sm oM1.A13no.3302), IU(MaLxq784.3Sh37,
        v.37,no.33)
    Difficult variations on a sentimental song.
Nocturne Impromptu, Op.36
    BrainardS, 1879, 7p.
    DLC(M25.P), IU(Joseffy)

PREYER, CARL ADOLPH (1863-1947)

The Brook Nymphs (Humoresque), Op.50
    White-S, 1917, 9p.
    KU(Univ.Archives), NRU-E(U)
    Scherzo from unpublished Sonata, Op.50.
Canzonetta, Op.40, No.2
    Schirmer, 1901, 5p.
    DLC(M25.P), MoSW(U)
Concert Etude (Aspiration)
    Schuberth-E, 1938, 5p.
    KU(Univ.Archives)
Danse fantastique, Op.8
    Kunkel, 1888, 6p.
    KU(Univ.Archives)
Dialogue without Words, Op.36, No.1
    Ditson, 1900, 5p.
    DLC(M25.P), IU(MO 42233), KU(Univ.Archives), MoSW(U)
Etude in F-sharp Minor (Combat)
    Schuberth-E, 1946, 7p.
    KU(folioM25.P74.E7 F-sharp min.)

Festal Polonaise, Op.14
    Kunkel, 1887, 9p.
    KU(Univ.Archives)
Hudson River Sketches
    Schuberth-E, 1946, 1948, 2v.(7,9p.)
    KU(68-4966, 1 only; Univ.Archives, 2 only)
    1. Palisades; 2. Spuyten Duyvil Toccato
Improvisation
    Schuberth-E, 1938, 5p.
    KU(Univ.Archives)
Palisades (see Hudson River Sketches)
Scherzo, Op.48
    Breitkopf, 1907, 15p.
    CU(M25.P74), DLC(M25.P)
Sonate No.1, Op.33
    Breitkopf, 1899, 25p.
    DLC(M23.P89op.33), KU(Univ.Archives)
    Serious four-movement sonata.
Sonata No.4
    Fischer, 1949, 43p.
    CtY(Mc11A1P929), DLC(M23.P89no.4), IU(qM786.41P92s4), KU
        (786.4154P929s no.4 1949), LNT(786P924s), NNLc(°MYD)
        NcU(M786.41P944s4), PP(786.41P92)
    Written in 1939, the sonata won 1st prize in a contest
        judged by A. Copland, H. Barlow and C. Haubiel. A
        large, difficult, rewarding work in four movements.
Spuyten Duyvil Toccato (see Hudson River Sketches)
Toccata, Op.36, No.2
    Ditson, 1900, 9p.
    DLC(M25.P), KU(Univ.Archives), NRU-E(U)
Theme with Variations (from unpublished Sonatina, 1944)
    Schuberth-E, 1949, 7p.
    KU(folioM27.P73S6)
    A substantial work composed in 1929.
Variationen über ein eigenes Thema, Op.32
    Breitkopf, 1897, 15p.
    DLC(M27.P), KU(Univ.Archives)
    Theme and eleven difficult variations.

RALSTON, FRANCES [FANNY] MARION (1875-1952)

Caprice (see Three Characteristic Pieces)
Three Characteristic Pieces
    Summy, 1918, 11p.
    DLC(M25.R), RPB(U)
    1. Moment musical; 2. Interlude; 3. Caprice
Interlude (see Three Characteristic Pieces)
Moment musical (see Three Characteristic Pieces)
Pastorale
    Thiebes, 1899, 5p.
    DLC(M25.R)
    A prize-winning lyrical piece with much charm.

Romanza, Op.1
    Balmer, 1888, 7p.
    DLC(M25.R), LN(U)
Sonata in E
    Summy, 1921, 28p.
    DLC(M23.R175), MoSW(U)
    Substantial four-movement work.
Song without Words, Op.10, No.1
    Balmer, 1905, 6p.
    DLC(M25.R)
Theme and Variations
    Summy, 1919, 17p.
    DLC(M27.R), MoSW(U)
    Rather ordinary theme with superb, stylish variations.
Valse Impromptu
    Balmer, 1890, 7p.
    LN(U)

REINAGLE, ALEXANDER (1756-1809)

La Chasse
    CarrMR, 1794, 2p. [SU:59]
    CtY(RareM1619C697+no.46), DLC(M1.A1R Case), also in BC-G
    "A New Lesson for the Piano Forte Composed in an easy
        familiar Style."
A Selection of the most Favorite Scots Tunes (with Variations
    for the Pianoforte or Harpsichord)
    The author, 1787, 28p. [SU:375]
    DLC(M1.A1R), PP(U, photostat), also in RS-HM
Sonatas
    In C-MH(I only), M-E(I only, 1st movt.), P-H(II only), RP-H
    These sonatas rank with the finest productions of the period.

RITTER, FREDERIC LOUIS (1834-1891)

Acht Clavierstücke, Op.5
    Schott, 1870, 2v.(9,9p.)
    DLC(M25.R), NNLc(Drexel 3497.13), NcU(MF786.4R614c)
    1. Capriccietto; 2. Im Frühling; 3. Herbstlied; 4. Zur
        Weinlese; 5. Allegretto scherzando; 6. Fantasiestück;
        7. Im Winter; 8. Allegro molto vivace
Préambule und Scherzo, Op.2
    Schuberth-J, 1866, 14p.
    DLC(M25.R), NcU(M786.4R614p), PP(U)
Suite, Op.16
    Martens, 1882, 6v.(5,5,5,7,7,7p.)
    DLC(M24.R), NcU(M786.48R614s)
    1. Fantasia; 2. Menuetto; 3. Promenade; 4. Valse;
        5. Marche sentimentale; 6. Jig
Voices of the Night, Op.12
    Schuberth-E, 1878, 14p.

DLC(M25.R)
Three compositions of contrasting mood and style.

RIVE-KING, JULIE (1854-1937)

Ballade et Polonaise de Concert (Transcription of Vieuxtemps,
Op.38)
Kunkel, 1879, 15p.
DLC(M25.K), WM(786.4R62p)
Bubbling Spring
Kunkel, 1879, 11p.
DLC(M25.K), MoSW(U), NNLc(°MYD+box), NRU-E(U), RPB(U), WM
(786.4R62b)
Superb example of sparkling salon music. Borrows freely
from Chopin in the middle section.
Carmen (Bizet. Paraphrase de Concert)
Kunkel, 1879, 17p.
NRU-E(U), OCl(M776.4R523p)
Gems of Scotland (Caprice de Concert)
Kunkel, 1878, 17p.
DLC(M25.K), MoSW(U), NRU-E(U), PP(U)
Geschichten aus dem Wiener Wald (Paraphrase de Concert)
Kunkel, 1881, 19p.
DLC(M25.K), ICN(VM35R62g), IU(Joseffy), OCl(M776.4R523p)
Difficult potpourri of Strauss waltzes.
Impromptu
Schirmer, 1879, 9p.
DLC(M25.K), IU(Joseffy)
Impromptu Mazurka
Russell, 1879, 10p.
DLC(M25.K), IU(Joseffy)
Mazurka des Graces (Caprice)
Kunkel, 1879, 11p.
OCl(M776.4R523p)
On Blooming Meadows (Concert Waltz)
Kunkel, 1878, 13p.
DLC(M32.K), IU(Joseffy), MoSW(U), NNLc(°MYD+box), NRU-E(U),
OCl(M776.4R523p), PP(U), WM(786.4R62p)
Polonaise héroique
Kunkel, 1879, 11p.
DLC(M30.K), IU(Joseffy), NNLc(°MYD), NcU(M786.44R621p),
OCl(M776.4R523p)
Wiener Bonbons (Valse de Johann Strauss, Op.307. Paraphrase
de Concert)
Kunkel, 1878, 17p.
DLC(M32.S), IU(Joseffy), NRU-E(U), OCl(M776.4R523p),
WM(786.4R62p)

ROBJOHN, WILLIAM JAMES [CARYL FLORIO] (1843-1920)

Fountain in the Sunlight (Idylle)

RootC, 1866, 7p.
   MiU-C(U)
Mazurka (No.1 in **Deux Morceaux de Salon**)
   Fischer, 1913, 7p.
   NNLc(°MYD+box), NcU(MF786.4R666d), PP(U)
   Published under the pseudonym of Caryl Florio.
Soft Breezes in the Solemn Night (Nocturne)
   RootC, 1866, 7p.
   MiU-C(U), NNLc(AM2-I), RPB(U)
Sonata No.1 in A
   Whitney, 1865, 17p.
   NcA(U), PP(U)
   Youthful, conservative four-movement work.
Sonata No.2 in B Flat
   Whitney, 1866, 21p.
   DLC(M23.R66), NcU(M786.41R666s2)

ROBYN, ALFRED GEORGE (1860-1935)

Album Leaf, Op.38, No.1 (see **Four Impromptus, Op.38**)
Aubade (Moment musical), **Op.39**
   Balmer, 1889, 7p.
   DLC(M25.R), LN(U), OCl(SM776.4)
Four Characteristic Pieces, Op.37
   The composer, 1882, 13p.
   NRU-E(U)
   1. **Barcarolle;** 2. **Intermezzo;** 3. **Berceuse;**
      4. **Improvisata**
   Attractive set of four, short contrasting pieces.
L'Espérance (Reverie), **Op.146**
   The composer, 1882, 9p.
   DLC(M25.R)
Gavotte, Op.38, No.3 (see **Four Impromptus, Op.38**)
Four Impromptus, Op.38
   Balmer, 1887, 13p., also issued separately
   CtY(Mc11A1R579), DLC(M25.R), OCl(M776.42.7863), PP(U)
   1. **Album Leaf;** 2. **Romance;** 3. **Gavotte;** 4. **Mazurka**
L'Innocence, Op.68
   The composer, 1882, 9p.
   DLC(M25.R)
Manzanillo
   Feist, 1909, 5p.
   CtY(Mc28A1), MoSW(U), OCl(SM776.4), PP(U), RPB(U), ViU
      (McR.110.05), WM(786.4R66m)
Mazurka, Op.38, No.4 (see **Four Impromptus, Op.38**)
Méditation poétique (Morceau de Concert)
   Balmer, 1881, 9p.
   RPB(U)
Mélodie célèste (Nocturne)
   Balmer, 1880, 7p.
   DLC(M25.R), MoS(786.4)

Romance, Op.38, No.2 (see Four Impromptus, Op.38)
Le Ruisseau (The Rivulet. Caprice brillante)
    Balmer, 1887, 9p., revised ed.
    Same composition as L'Innocence (see above)

ROGERS, CLARA KATHLEEN (1844-1931)

Romanza, Op.31
    Millet, 1894, 8p.
    DLC(M25.R), also in HH-K(V:1201)
Scherzo, Op.32
    Millet, 1894, 4p.
    DLC(M25.R), PP(U), also in HH-K(V:1209)

ROGERS, JAMES HOTCHKISS (1857-1940)

Air de Ballet, Op.24, No.1
    Ditson, 1904, 5p.
    DLC(M25.R), NcU(M786.4R727a)
Autrefois (Petite Suite dans le Style ancien)
    Schirmer, 1903, 5v.in 1(3,3,3,3,3p.)
    DLC(M24.R), NcU(M786.48R727a), RPB(U, 2 only)
    1. Allemande; 2. Courante; 3. Air varié; 4. Menuet;
       5. Gigue
Etude mélodique
    Schirmer, 1909, 5p.
    DLC(M25.R), NRU-E(U), PPi(qM786.4R61), RPB(U)
Prelude-Arabesque
    Church, 1900, 7p.
    DLC(M25.R), IU(qM786.41R63p), also in P-S
Tarantelle (No.4 of Suite mignonne)
    Church, 1901, 5p.
    CU(M31R6), DLC(M24.R)
Toccatina, Op.38, No.2 (from Two Piano Pieces, Op.38)
    Pond, 1901, 5p.
    DLC(M25.R), NcU(M786.4R727p)
    Sparkling, impressive little virtuoso piece.

RUGGLES, CARL (1876-1971)

Evocation No.4 (Chant for Piano)
    New Music, 1945(v.18,no.2), 4p.
    CtY(Ref.M2N532+v.18no.2), ICN(VM1N53v.18no.2), IU(M1N48
       v.18no.2 Ref.), NNLc(°MN N511v.18no.2), NcU(Music
       Vault M780.5N532v.18no.2), OCl(q.770.5N466v.18no.2), WM
       (R786.4R932E4)
Evocations: 3 Chants for Piano
    New Music, 1943(v.16,no.3), 11p.
    CtY(Ref.M2N532+v.16no.3), ICN(VM1N53v.16no.3), IU(M1N48
       v.16no.3 Ref.), NNLc(°MN N511v.16no.3), WM(786.4R932E)

Evocations: 4 Chants for Piano
    American, 1943, 1956, 9p.
    CtY(M25R932E9+), LNT(M25R84E8), MB-N(M25R85E8 1956), NNLc
    (°MYD-Amer.box), NcU(M786.43R932e), OCl(M776.4.7973)
    1. Largo(1937); 2. Andante con fantasia(1941); 3. Moderato
    appassionato(1943:first printed as No.4); 4. Adagio soste-
    nuto(1940:first printed as No.3)
Organum
    New Music, 1947(v.21,no.1), pp.4-7
    CtY(M2N532+v.21no.1), ICN(VM1N53v.21no.1), IU(MI N48,v.21
    no.1), LNT(786.1A P57), MoS(786.4P52), NNLc(°MN N511v.21
    no.1), NcU(VaultM780.5N532v.21no.1)
    In **Piano Works by Ives, Cowell, Ruggles** (See Appendix C).

RYBNER [RUBNER], PETER MARTIN CORNELIUS (1853-1929)

Ewig Dein, Op.7, No.2 (from **Albumblätter, Op.7**)
    Kahnt, n.d., 3p.
    MoSW(U)
Frühlingsweben, Op.13, No.1 (see **Zwei Idyllen, Op.13**)
Zwei Idyllen, Op.13
    Schott, n.d., 2v.(6,5p.)
    DLC(M25.R)
    1. Frühlingsweben; 2. Waldesruf
Die Meistersinger von Nürnberg von Richard Wagner (Concert-
    Paraphrase)
    Schott, n.d., 19p.
    DLC(M34.R)
Valse magique sur le nom de Basch, Op.10
    Hansen, n.d., 7p.
    NNLc(MYD+box)
Waldesruf, Op.13, No.2 (see **Zwei Idyllen, Op.13**)

RYDER, THOMAS PHILANDER (1836-1887)

Chanson des Alpes (Fantaisie), **Op.51**
    WhiteSP, 1870, 11p.
    DLC(M25.R), MoSW(U), NNLc(AM2-I), NRU-E(U), ViU(McR.138.36)
Danse des Demons (Tarantelle de Concert), **Op.78**
    White-S, 1875, 13p.
    ViU(°M1.S444,v.39,no.42)
Golden Harvest (Rondo Caprice), **Op.76**
    WhiteS, 1874, 7p.
    RPB(U)
    Good example of one of Ryder's better salon pieces.
"Home Sweet Home" (Fantaisie de Salon), **Op.53**
    WhiteSP, 1871, 7p.
    RPB(U)
Woodland Belle Schottische, Op.92
    WhiteS, 1877, 5p.
    CtY(Mc28Sch.67)

SAAR, LOUIS VICTOR FRANZ (1868-1937)

Ballade, Op.18, No.1 (see Two Ballades, Op.18)
Ballade, Op.18, No.2 (see Two Ballades, Op.18)
Two Ballades, Op.18
    Schirmer, 1897, 2v.(9,9p.)
    DLC(M25.S), IU(Joseffy), MoS(786.4, 1 only), MoSW(U, 2 only)
    1. Ballade in D Minor; 2. Ballade in F Major
Capriccio, Op.53, No.3 (see Three Piano Compositions, Op.53)
Elegie, Op.53, No.2 (see Three Piano Compositions, Op.53)
Etude-Badinage, Op.89, No.3
    WillisM, 1921, 5p.
    DLC(M25.S), NRU-E(U), WM(786.4S11i9c)
Etude-Burlesque, Op.98, No.2
    Ditson, 1921, 5p.
    DLC(M25.S), MoSW(U)
Gavotte moderne, Op.24, No.2
    Schirmer, 1898, 7p.
    DLC(M25.S), MdBP(U), MoS(786.4)
Intermezzo, Op.23, No.1
    Schmidt, 1898, 5p.
    DLC(M25.S), MoSW(U)
Three Piano Compositions, Op.53
    Church, 1906, 3v.(5,5,7p.)
    CtY(Mc11A1Sa12 3v.), DLC(M25.S), MoSW(U), OCl(M776.4.8007)
    1. Romanza; 2. Elegie; 3. Capriccio
Poem, Op.99, No.1 (from Two Melodious Studies, Op.99)
    Summy, 1921, 7p.
    DLC(M25.S), MoSW(U)
Romanza, Op.53, No.1 (see Three Piano Compositions, Op.53)
Sérénade, Op.24, No.3
    Schirmer, 1898, 9p.
    DLC(M25.S), MoSW(U)
Valse noble, Op.24, No.1
    Schirmer, 1898, 5p.
    DLC(M25.S), MdBP(U), MoS(786.4), PP(U)
Variations and Fugue in G, Op.29
    Ditson, 1899, 23p.
    DLC(M27.S), IU(Joseffy)
    Twelve variations plus a four-voice fugue.

SALMON, ALVAH GLOVER (1868-1917)

Capriccietto, Op.26, No.3 (from Trois Morceaux, Op.26)
    Thompson, 1900, 5p.
    RPB(U)
Chanson triste, Op.23, No.2 (from Quatre Morceaux, Op.23)
    Thompson, 1900, 5p.
    RPB(U)
Danse caractéristique, Op.10
    Thompson, 1900, 7p.
    RPB(U)

Humoresque, Op.12, No.5 (from **Album Leaves, Op.12**)
    Thompson, 1899, 3p.
    RPB(U)
Intermezzo, Op.23, No.3 (from **Quatre Morceaux, Op.23**)
    Thompson, 1900, 5p.
    MoS(786.4), RPB(U)
Legende, Op.42, No.1 (from **Charakterstücke, Op.42**)
    Ditson, 1902, 9p.
    RPB(U)
Moment musical, Op.23, No.1 (from **Quatre Morceaux, Op.23**)
    Thompson, 1900, 5p.
    RPB(U)
Romance, Op.8, No.1 (from **Salonstücke, Op.8**)
    Ditson, 1900, 5p.
    DLC(M25.S), MoS(786.4), RPB(U)
    An outstandingly beautiful composition.
Scherzo, Op.30
    Thompson, 1900, 9p.
    DLC(M25.S)
Tarantelle fantastique, Op.14
    Thompson, 1900, 11p.
    RPB(U)

SCHEHLMANN, LOUIS (1854-1903)

At the Brook (Moment musical in A Flat)
    Presser, 1899, 4p.
    DLC(M25.S)
Capriccietto, Op.29, No.1
    Ditson, 1890, 5p.
    DLC(M25.S)
Consolation
    Ellis, 1900, 3p.
    ViU(U:2)
Gondolier's Song
    Ellis, 1900, 5p.
    ViU(U:2)
Idylle, Op.32, No.1
    Church, 1890, 7p.
    DLC(M25.S)
Sirenengesang (Siren's Song), **Op.28, No.2**
    Church, 1889, 7p.
    DLC(M25.S)

SCHELLING, ERNEST (1876-1939)

Au Chateau de Wiligrad
    Schirmer, 1904, 7p.
    DLC(M25.S), MdBP(U), MoS(786.4)
Fatalisme (from **Six Compositions pour le Piano**)
    Schirmer, 1904, 6p.

DLC(M25.S), MdBP(U), MoS(786.4), NcD(M786.41S322F)
Attractively lugubrious, much use of low register.
Gavotte (from **Six Compositions pour le Piano**)
Schirmer, 1904, 8p.
DLC(M25.S), IU(Joseffy), MdBP(U), MoS(786.4)
Nocturne (Ragusa)
Fischer, 1926, 11p.
DLC(M25.S), ICN(Case8A 1695no.34), IU(MO 57708), MoSW(U),
NNLc(°MYD), NRU-E(M25.S32n), WM(786.4S322n)
Unusual, with effective use of glissando.
Romance (from **Six Compositions pour le Piano**)
Schirmer, 1904, 4p.
DLC(M25.S), IU(Joseffy), MoS(786.4), MoSW(U)
Thème et Variations
Schirmer, 1904, 32p.
DLC(M27.S), ICN(Case8A 1695no.32), IU(Joseffy), MB-N(U),
MoS(786.4), MoSW(U), NNLc(°°MYD), PP(M786.4Sch2)
Fifteen very difficult, superb variations.
Valse gracieuse (from **Six Compositions pour le Piano**)
Schirmer, 1904, 11p.
IU(Joseffy), MoSW(U)

SCHLESINGER, SEBASTIAN BENSON (1837-1917)

Album-Blatt
Prüfer, 1883, 5p.
MBH(P.1B91)
Etude in C Minor, Op.11
Prüfer, 1884, 5p.
DLC(M25.S), IU(Joseffy), MBH(P.1B91)
Hungarian Fantasy (Mazurka Caprice)
Presser, 1902, 7p.
OCl(SM776.4), ViU(U:2)
Nocturne, Op.13
Prüfer, 1885, 9p.
DLC(M25.S), MBH(P.1B91)
Novelette
Prüfer, 1884, 7p.
MBH(P.1B91)

SCHOENEFELD, HENRY (1857-1936)

Etude, Op.6, No.2
Schuberth-E, 1880, 9p.
DLC(M25.S)
Good study for scalar technique.
Impromptu, Op.6, No.1
Schuberth-E, 1880, 5p.
DLC(M25.S)
Valse élégante, Op.16
In HH-K(IV:993)

SEEBOECK, WILLIAM CHARLES ERNEST (1859-1907)

Butterfly
    Church, 1900, 5p.
    DLC(M25.S), MoS(786.4), OC(786.4fS45b)
By the Spring, Op.41
    Rohlfing, 1889, 11p.
    DLC(M25.S), PP(U)
Le Dauphin
    In AC
Gavotte à L'Antique (Portrait de "Putzi")
    In HH-K(III:525)
Minuet à L'Antico
    Church, 1895, 5p.
    CtY(Mc11A1Se32), MoS(786.4), MoSW(U), NRU-E(U), RPB(U), WM
        (786.4S45m)
Four Piano Pieces
    Chicago, 1884, 4v.(5,3,5,7p.)
    ICN(sVM22S45f)
    1. Gavotte and Musette; 2. Chaconne; 3. Impromptu;
        4. Scherzo
Portrait N.D.S. (Natalie)
    Millet, 1894, 5p.
    DLC(M25.S), also in HH-K(III:530)
Portrait No.2 A.T.M. (from Campscenes 1889), Op.42, No.2
    Rohlfing, 1891, 5p.
    DLC(M25.S), MoSW(U)
Serenata Napolitana
    Church, 1897, 7p.
    CtY(Mc11A1Se32), DLC(M25.S)

SEVEN OCTAVES [see LOUIS MOREAU GOTTSCHALK]

SHAW, OLIVER (1779-1848)

Bangor March
    Bradlee, n.d., 3p.
    CtHT(U), CtY(Mc27A1), DLC(M1.A13S Case), ICN(VM1F91no.206),
        NBu(°M1.C65v.33,no.23), NcU(EAMC,no.7)
The Clinton Waltzes
    Oakes, 1845, 8p.
    CtY(Mc28W1)
Metacom's Grand March
    Bradlee, 1840, 3p.
    CtY(Mc27A1), DLC(M1.A12I4), ICN(Case sm oM1.A13no.683), PP(U)
Welcome The Nation's Guest (A Military Divertimento for the
    Pianoforte, Composed and Respectfully Dedicated to General
    Lafayette, on his visit to Providence)
    The author, 1824, 6p. [W.II:795]
    DLC(M1.A13S Case), ICN(Case8A 2705), NBu(°M1C65v.2,no.1),
        NNLc(AM1-I), PP(U [Lafayette file]), also in A-C(II)

SHEPHERD, ARTHUR (1880-1958)

Autumn Fields
    Fischer, 1936, 5p. (included in the collection **Masters
    of Our Day**)
    CU(M1380S454A3), IU(qM786.3Sh4a), NNLc(°MYDbox)
    Mostly two-part flowing counterpoint.
Capriccio II
    Ricordi, 1954, 12p.
    CtY(Mc20Sh48c no.2), DLC(M25.S), NNLc(JNG 74-336), NcU
    (M786.4S548c2), OCl(M776.42.825), PP(786.4Sh48C)
    Very difficult concert work.
Eclogue
    Presser, 1956, 5p.
    NNLc(°MYDbox), NcU(M786.4S548e), PP(786.4Sh48e), WM(786.4
    S548e)
Exotic Dance
    Oxford, 1930, 7p.
    DLC(M25.S), IU(qM786.41Sh4e), NRU-E(M30S548e), NcD(M786.41
    s548E), OCl(M776.45.8333)
Gigue fantasque
    Presser, 1956, 11p.
    NNLc(°MYD), NcU(M786.45S548g), PP(786.4Sh48g), WM(786.4
    S548g)
In Modo ostinato
    Presser, 1956, 5p.
    NNLc(°MYD), NcU(M786.4S548i)
Lento amabile
    Presser, 1956, 5p.
    NNLc(°MYDbox), NcU(M786.4S548L)
    Free use of dissonance.
Mazurka, Op.2, No.1
    Wa-Wan, 1905, 9p.
    ICN(VM1W11v.4), LNT(786Sh4m), NNLc(°MN Wa-Wan), NRU-E
    (M32S548Ma), also in NC-G, WW-L(II:87)
    An impressive and effective concert mazurka.
Prelude, Op.2, No.2
    Wa-Wan, 1906, 3p.
    DLC(M25.S), LNT(786Sh4m), NNLc(°MN Wa-Wan), NRU-E(M25
    S548pr), also in WW-L(II:173)
Sonata, Op.4
    Boston, 1911, 54p.
    DLC(M23.S54op.4), NNLc(JNG 74-79), NRU-E(M23S548)
    Serious three-movement sonata.
Second Sonata
    Oxford, 1930, 27p.
    DLC(M23.S542), IU(qM786.41Sh4s2), NcU(M786.41S548s2),
    OCl(M776.41.8335), WM(786.4S548s2)
Theme and Variations, Op.1
    Wa-Wan, 1905, 16p.
    ICN(VM1W11v.4), MoS(786.4), NNLc(°MN Wa-Wan), NRU-E
    (M27S548), also in WW-L(II:127)
    Very fine example of Shepherd's skill in variation.

SHERWOOD, EDGAR HARMON (1845-1919)

Broken Dreams (Morceau élégant)
    Gibbons, 1878, 7p.
    DLC(M25.S), NRU-E(U)
Crimson Lake (Caprice brillant)
    Ditson, 1879, 9p.
    DLC(M25.S), NRU-E(U)
The Dreamer (Marche poétique)
    Pond, 1872, 7p.
    CtY(Mc11A1Sh58)
Fantasie ("Lucia")
    Mackie, 1881, 11p.
    DLC(M34.D [Donizetti])
Faun Dance
    Shaw-JP, 1871, 7p.
    NBu(U)
Footsteps in the Snow (Paraphrase de Concert)
    Mackie, 1878, 9p.
    DLC(M25.S), NBu(U), NRU-E(U)
Grand Menuet in A Flat
    Gibbons, 1885, 9p.
    CtY(Mc11A1Sh58), DLC(M25.S), MoSW(U), PP(U), RPB(U),
        WM(786.4S55g)
Grand Polka de Concert
    WillisM, 1910, 9p.
    NRU-E(U)
Manzanita (Mazurka Caprice)
    Pond, 1875, 9p.
    NRU-E(U)
La Marchesa (Morceau caractéristique)
    Pond, 1874, 9p.
    DLC(M25.S), OU(U)
    Good example of Sherwood's best writing style.
La Missouri Mazurka (Morceau caractéristique)
    Gibbons, 1877, 7p.
    NBu(U)
The Nun and the Fountain (Fantaisie illustrative)
    Pond, 1875, 13p.
    DLC(M25.S), NRU-E(U)
Polaria (Polka de Concert)
    Pond, 1875, 9p.
    DLC(M31.S), NRU-E(U), OU(U)
Polonaise (in B Flat)
    Gibbons, 1879, 7p.
    PP(U)

SHERWOOD, WILLIAM HALL (1854-1911)

Allegro patetico, Op.12
    Prochàzka, 1885, 7p.
    DLC(M25.S), MoSW(U), WM(786.4S553)

Autumn, Op.15
    Ditson, 1899, 7p.
    ICN(sVM25S544c), NRU-E(U), OCl(SM776.4), RPB(U), ViU(McR.
    156.29)
Capriccio, Op.4
    Breitkopf, n.d., 11p.
    DLC(M25.S)
Exhilaration, Op.14, No.3
    Church, 1890, 7p.
    DLC(M25.S), OCl(M776.4.83772), PPi(qr786.4P535995), RPB(U)
Greetings, Op.5, No.3 (see Suite, Op.5)
Idylle, Op.5, No.2 (see Suite, Op.5)
Mazurka, Op.6, No.1 (see Two Mazurkas, Op.6)
Mazurka, Op.6, No.2 (see Two Mazurkas, Op.6)
Two Mazurkas, Op.6
    Schirmer, 1883, 2v.(7,7p.)
    DLC(M32.S), IU(Joseffy), MoSW(U), OCl(M776.4-83772, 1 only),
    ViU(McR.156.27, 1 only)
    1. **Mazurka in C Minor**; 2. **Mazurka in A Minor**
Medea, Op.13
    Church, 1890, 19p.
    PPi(qr786.4P535995), ViU(McR.156.28)
    Fine dramatic tone poem. Prefaced with analysis and
    annotations by A. J. Goodrich.
Novelette, Op.5, No.5 (see Suite, Op.5)
Prelude, Op.5, No.1 (see Suite, Op.5)
Regrets, Op.5, No.4 (see Suite, Op.5)
Romanza appassionata, Op.8
    Schirmer, 1883, 9p.
    DLC(M25.S), IU(Joseffy), MoSW(U), OCl(776.4.83772), ViU
    (McR.156.22)
Scherzo in E Major, Op.7
    Schirmer, 1883, 9p.
    DLC(M25.S), MoSW(U)
Scherzo-Caprice (with Intermezzo quasi Romanza), Op.9
    Schirmer, 1883, 15p.
    IU(Joseffy), MoSW(U), ViU(McR.156.23)
Suite, Op.5
    Schirmer, 1883, 5v.(7,3,5,5,7p.)
    DLC(M25.S), IU(Joseffy), MoSW(U, 1,2,4,5 only), OCl(M776.4.
    83772, 4 only), RPB(U, 2,5 only), ViU(McR.156.26; 156.31;
    156.30; 156.24; 156.25), also in PM-H(1 only)
    1. **Prelude**; 2. **Idylle**; 3. **Greetings**; 4. **Regrets**;
        5. **Novelette**

SIEVEKING, MARTINUS (1867-1950)

L'Angelus (d'après Millet)
    Schirmer, 1897, 7p.
    CtY(Mc10v.4), DLC(M25.S), MoSW(U)
Berceuse
    Church, 1907, 5p.

CtY(Mc11A1Si16), DLC(M25.S), RPB(U)
Dream of the Flowers (Valse lente), **Op.10**
    Kunkel, 1897, 7p.
    RPB(U)
Souffrance
    Stahl, 1914, 5p.
    PP(U)
Variations et Fugue sur un Thème original
    Stahl, 1914, 30 p.
    DLC(M27.S)

SMITH, GERRIT (1859-1912)

A Colorado Summer (A Cycle of Ten Pieces), **Op.21**
    Church, 1900, 39p.
    DLC(M24.S), NNLc(°MYD-Amer)
    1. Artist's Brush; 2. At Moonlight; 3. In the Cañon;
       4. Alpine Rose; 5. On the Heights; 6. Mariposa Lily;
       7. By the Stream; 8. Columbine; 9. Arbutus; 10. Cloud
       Shadows
    This collection may have an incorrect opus no.(See below).
Gavotte, Op.21, No.2
    In HH-K(V:1357)
Romance, Op.21, No.1
    Millet, 1895, 4p.
    DLC(M25.S), also in HH-K(V:1362)

SMITH, WILSON GEORGE (1855-1929)

Arach'ne Spinning, Op.78
    Schmidt, 1899, 7p.
    WM(786.4S663a)
Autumn Sketches, Op.103
    Fox, 1912, 22p.
    DLC(M24.S68op.103), NNLc(°MYD), MoSW(U), NRU-E(M24S66)
    1. In Autumn; 2. The Chase; 3. Wayside Flowers; 4. Autumn
      Enchantment; 5. By the Mill-Stream; 6. Autumn
      Memories
Barcarolle (Souvenir de Petosky), **Op.74, No.2**
    Hatch, 1897, 5p.
    NRU-E(U)
Concert Polonaise, Op.37
    BrainardS, 1887, 11p.
    DLC(M32.S), PPi(qr786.4P535994)
Etudes-Arabesques On an Original Theme, Op.75
    Presser, 1898, 31p.
    ICN(VMT243S66e), OCl(M776.3.85)
    Theme with twenty-one creative variations.
Gavotte, Op.25, No.1
    WhiteS, 1885, 7p.
    CtY(Mc11A1Sm68), DLC(M25.S), NcU(MF786.45S663g)

Hommage à Schumann, Op.57, No.1 (from **Romantic Studies, Op.57**)
  Presser, 1894, 5p.
  MoSW(U)
  Tasteful reproduction of Schumann's style.
In a Flower Garden, Op.105, No.2 (from **Five Nature Sketches, Op.105**)
  Fox, 1912, 5p.
  CtY(Mc11A1Sm68)
Pensée d'Amour (Romance), **Op.27**
  WhiteS, 1886, 5p.
  DLC(M25.S), PPi(qr786.4P535994)
Prelude Agitato, Op.107
  Schmidt, 1914, 7p.
  NRU-E(U), OCl(SM776.4)
  Stylish and difficult technical study.
Romanza appassionata, Op.95, No.1
  Schirmer, 1908, 7p.
  DLC(M25.S), MoS(786.4 [filed under **Summer Sketches, Op.100**]),
    RPB(U)
Sans Souci (Caprice joyeux), **Op.97, No.1**
  Schirmer, 1906, 5p.
  DLC(M25.S), MoSW(U)
Scherzo valsant, Op.95
  Schirmer, 1905, 7p.
  NRU-E(U), NcU(M786.4S664s)
Sonnet d'Amour, Op.59, No.2
  In AC
Supplication, Op.16 (Transcription from Robt. Franz)
  Ashmall, 1888, 5p.
  PPi(qr786.4P535994)
Third Tarantelle, Op.84, No.4
  Ditson, 1901, 7p.
  NcU(M786.45S664t3)
Thematic Octave Studies (In the Form of Variations on an
  Original Theme), **Op.68**
  Church, 1896, 29p.
  ICN(VMT229S66t), IU(qM786.3Sm68t 1902), LN(U), NNLc(°MYD),
    NRU-E(MT229S664t), OCl(M776.33.837), ViU(Music MT225S66
    1902)
  Twenty-five excellent variation etudes.

SONNECK, OSCAR GEORGE THEODORE (1873-1928)

Ballade, Op.11, No.1 (see **Drei Concertstücke, Op.11**)
Capriccio, Op.11, No.2 (see **Drei Concertstücke, Op.11**)
Drei Concertstücke, Op.11
  Firnberg, 1900, 21p.
  DLC(M3.3.S7op.11 Case), NNLc(°MYD)
  1. Ballade; 2. Capriccio; 3. Interludio-Scherzoso
  Very interesting musically, very difficult technically.
Interludio-Scherzoso, Op.11, No.3 (see **Drei Concertstücke,
  Op.11**)

SPANUTH, AUGUST (1857-1920)

Barcarole
    Breitkopf, 1898, 5p.
    DLC(M25.S)
Nocturne
    Rohlfing, 1889, 7p.
    DLC(M25.S)

SPROSS, CHARLES GILBERT (1874-1961)

Barcarolle
    Church, 1915, 11p.
    DLC(M25.S), MoS(786.4)
Improvisation in D Flat
    Church, 1927, 5p.
    NPA(780S)
Polonaise brillante
    Church, 1915, 13p.
    DLC(M25.S)
Prelude in B Minor
    Church, 1929, 7p.
    NPA(780S)
Three Rural Sketches
    Church, 1934, 3v.(5,5,5p.)
    NPA(780S)
    1. Country Dance; 2. Swaying Willows; 3. Time of Lilacs
Scherzo fantastique
    Church, 1924, 13p.
    NPA(780S)

STERNBERG, CONSTANTIN (1852-1924)

L'Agitation (Caprice)**, Op.74**
    Schuberth-E, 1897, 11p.
    DLC(M25.S), IU(Joseffy)
    Excellent study in lightness and dexterity.
Allegro brioso e drammatico, Op.106, No.1 (see **Three Preludes, Op.106**)
Allegro leggiero, Op.106, No.3 (see **Three Preludes, Op.106**)
Barcarolle, Op.22, No.9 (from **Al Fresco, Op.22**)
    Schuberth-E, 1883, 9p.
    ViU(McR.115.46)
Caprice, Op.20, No.1 (see **Drei Clavierstücke, Op.20**)
Drei Clavierstücke, Op.20
    Hainauer, 1897, 3v.(11,7,5p.)
    IU(Joseffy), NNLc(°MYD+box, 3 only)
    1. Caprice; 2. Gavotte; 3. Etude
Concert Polonaise, Op.38
    Prochàzka, 1886, 9p.
    DLC(M32.S), WM(786.4S83c)

Danse phrygienne (d'après Saint-Saens)
     Schirmer, 1882, 7p.
     DLC(M30.S), IU(Joseffy)
     Good transcription from **Samson and Delilah.**
Etude, Op.20, No.3 (see **Drei Clavierstücke, Op.20**)
Etude de Concert, Op.88
     Schuberth-E, 1902, 7p.
     DLC(M25.S), MoSW(U)
Seconde Etude de Concert, Op.94
     Schuberth-E, 1904, 7p.
     DLC(M25.S), PP(U)
     Includes a variant by Josef Hofmann.
Troisième Etude de Concert, Op.103
     Schirmer, 1911, 15p.
     DLC(M25.S), MB-N(Piano), MoSW(U), NNLc(°MYD+box), NRU-E(U)
Gavotte, Op.20, No.2 (see **Drei Clavierstücke, Op.20**)
Historiette musicale, Op.50, No.2
     Rohlfing, 1888, 7p.
     DLC(M25.S), PP(U)
Humoresque, Op.26
     Schirmer, 1883, 9p.
     DLC(M25.S), MoSW(U)
Impromptu, Op.83
     Schuberth-E, 1901, 11p.
     DLC(M25.S), MoSW(U)
Minuet of Ye Olden Tyme
     ArtPS, 1919, 5p.
     ViU(U:2)
Deux Morceaux, Op.68
     In HH-K(III:733)
     1. Le Tourbillon; 2. Songe d'Amour
Poetico, Op.106, No.2 (see **Three Preludes, Op.106**)
Prélude agité et Bourrée variée
     Peters-CF, 1905, 8p.
     DLC(M25.S), PP(U)
Three Preludes, Op.106
     Schirmer, 1913, 3v.(5,5,5p.)
     MoS(786.4)
     1. **Allegro brioso e drammatico**; 2. **Poetico**; 3. **Allegro
        leggiero**
Songe d'Amour, Op.68, No.2 (see **Deux Morceaux, Op.68**)
The Spinning Top (Caprice), **Op.86**
     Summy, 1901, 7p.
     CtY(Mc11A1St46), DLC(M25.S), PP(U), WM(786.4S83b)
Le Tourbillon, Op.68, No.2 (see **Deux Morceaux, Op.68**)

STOCKHOFF, WALTER WILLIAM (1876-1968)

Canon in moto contrario
     Shattinger, 1953, 7p.
     DLC(M25.S), MoS(786.4), MoSw(U), OCl(SM776.4), WM(786.4
     S86c)

Fantasia
    Shattinger, 1952, 22p.
    DLC(M25.S), MoS(786.42), MoSW(U), OC(786.4fS864), OCl
      (M776.42.854), WM(786.4S86f)
In the Mountains (Seven Impressions), **Op.2**
    Breitkopf, 1914, 47p.
    CtY(Mc11A1St62), DLC(M25.S), LNT(786St6i), NNLc(°MYD)
    1. **In the Solitude of the Mountain Fastness;** 2. **With the**
      Trout; 3. **The Hermit;** 4. **Merriment by a Brook;** 5. **The**
      Indian; 6. **The Ranchman;** 7. **The Stage-coach**
Metamorphosen (Three Soliloquies)
    Breitkopf, 1924, 25p.
    DLC(M25.S)
Zwölf Quodlibets, Op.1
    Breitkopf, 1903, 29p.
    CU(M25S885op.1), CtY(Mc11A1St62), DLC(M25.S), MoS(786.4),
      MoSW(U), NNLc(°MYD), WM(786.4S86)
Sonata
    Breitkopf, 1916, 33p.
    CU(M23S757S6), DLC(M23.S86), IU(qM786.41St62s), MoS(786.4),
      MoSW(U), NNLc(°MYD), PP(U)
    Sectional sonata in one movement.

STOJOWSKI, SIGISMUND (1876-1946)

Amourette de Pierrot, Op.30, No.1 (see **Trois Esquisses, Op.30**)
Aspirations, Op.39
    Heugel, 1914, 28p., also issued separately
    DLC(M25.S), MoS(786.4), OC(786.4fS87)
    1. **Vers L'Azur** (Prélude); 2. **Vers La Tombe** (Elégie); 3. **Vers**
      Le Caprice (Intermède); 4. **Vers L'Amour** (Romance); 5. **Vers**
      La Joie (Rhapsodie)
    Very compelling romantic and post-romantic tone poems.
Aus Sturm und Stille, Op.29
    Peters-CF, 1928, 35p.
    MoS(786.4), NcU(M786.4S87c9)
    1. **Ballade;** 2. **Aufschwung;** 3. **Zwielicht;** 4. **Capriccio;**
      5. **Ständchen;** 6. **Valse-Impromptu**
Bruissements, Op.36, No.4 (see **Poème d'Eté, Op.36**)
Deux Caprices-Etudes, Op.2
    Stevens, 1892, 2v.(11,7p.)
    DLC(M25.S), IU(Joseffy, 1 only), MoS(786.4 1 only), PP(U,
      1 only), WM(786.48S87, 2 only)
    1. **La Fileuse;** 2. **Toccatina**
Chant d'Amour, Op.26, No.3
    Schirmer, 1908, 5p.
    CtY(Mc11A1St7), DLC(M25.S), MB-N(U), MoSW(U), NRU-E(U),
      NcU(M786.4S87c6c), PP(U)
Cosaque fantastique, Op.12, No.6 (from **Danses humoresques,**
    Op.12)
    Augener, 1894, 7p.
    CtY(Mc11A1St7), MoS(786.4)

Cracovienne, Op.12, No.4 (from Danses humoresques, Op.12)
     Stevens, 1894, 7p.
     DLC(M25.S), WM(786.4S87c)
Trois Esquisses, Op.30
     Schmidt, 1908, 3v.(5,5,7p.)
     CtY(U, 1 only), DLC(M25.S, 1 only), ICN(sVM25S873b, 3 only),
     NRU-E(M25S873e)
     1. Amourette de Pierrot; 2. Feuilles mortes; 3. Près du
     Ruisseau
Fantaisie, Op.38
     Heugel, 1912, 16p.
     DLC(M25.S)
     Grandiose, romantic and difficult.
Feuilles mortes, Op.30, No.2 (see Trois Esquisses, Op.30)
La Fileuse, Op.2, No.1 (see Deux Caprice-Etudes, Op.2)
Fleurettes, Op.36, No.3 (see Poème d'Eté, Op.36)
Mazurka brillante, Op.28, No.2 (see Two Mazurkas, Op.28)
Mazurka fantasque, Op.28, No.1 (see Two Mazurkas, Op.28)
Two Mazurkas, Op.28
     Schmidt, 1908, 2v.(7,11p.)
     NRU-E(M32S87)
     1. Mazurka fantasque; 2. Mazurka brillante
Poème d'Eté, Op.36
     Schirmer, 1910, 4v.(7,13,5,13p.)
     CtY(Mc11A1St7, 2 only), DLC(M25.S), MoS(786.4), MoSW(U,
     1 only), NNLc(°MYD+), NRU-E(M25S873po), PP(U, 2,3 only),
     WM(786.4S87b, 4 only)
     1. Reves; 2. Rayons et Reflets; 3. Fleurettes;
     4. Bruissements
Polnische Idyllen, Op.24
     Peters-CF, 1901, 23p.
     DLC(M25.S), MoS(786.4), MoSW(U), NcU(M786.4S87c4)
     1. Einsamkeit; 2. Auf zur Ernte!; 3. Dorfcoquette;
     4. Tanz-Vision; 5. Fest-Nachklänge
Près du Ruisseau, Op.30, No.3 (see Trois Esquisses, Op.30)
Rayons et Reflets, Op.36, No.2 (see Poème d'Eté, Op.36)
Rêves, Op.36, No.1 (see Poème d'Eté, Op.36)
Romantische Stücke, Op.25
     Peters-CF, 1902, 28p.
     DLC(M25.S), MoS(786.43), NNLc(°°MYD), NRU-E(M22S87)
     1. Geständniss; 2. En valsant; 3. Idylle; 4. Barcarolle;
     5. Frühlingserwachen
Sérénade, Op.8, No.3
     Stevens, 1892, 7p.
     DLC(M25.S), IU(Joseffy), NRU-E(M25S873s), OCl(M776.4.
     86472)
Vier Stücke, Op.26
     Peters-CF, 1903, 35p.
     DLC(M25.S), IU(qM786.41St6v), MoS(786.4), NNLc(°°MYD),
     NRU-E(M25S873St)
     1. Mélodie; 2. In tempo di Minuetto; 3. Chant d'Amour;
     4. Thème cracovien varié
Toccatina, Op.2, No.2 (see Deux Caprices-Etudes, Op.2)

Valse (Danse humoresque), **Op.12, No.2**
    Presser, 1893, 7p.
    CtY(Mc11A1St7), DLC(M30.S), MoS(786.4), MoSW(U), PP(U)
Variations et Fugue sur un Thème original, Op.42
    Heugel, 1923, 29p.
    DLC(M27.S)
    Very difficult. Theme is in seven-four meter.

STRAKOSCH, MAURICE (1825-1887)

Another Polka
    HallS, 1852, 7p.
    CtHT(U), CtY(Mc11A1St819), LNT(L976.3[780]Z99), NNLc
        (AM2-I)
The Banjo (Capriccio caractéristique)
    Pond, 1880, 9p.
    CtY(Mc11A1St82), NNLc(AM2-I), NRU-E(U), NcU(EAMC,no.65)
Caprice (Sur le Rondo Finale introduit dans **Linda de Chamounix**
    de Max Maretzek)
    Walker, 1849, 9p.
    PPi(qr786.4P53594)
    See Grobe's **Cornucopia of Pleasure** for a better setting.
Caprice russe, Op.38
    Schuberth-J, n.d., 11p.
    DLC(M25.S)
Un Carnaval à Naples (Polka)
    HallS, 1848, 5p.
    InU(M1.S8), MiU-C(U), NRU-E(7092.F.9v.11), NcD(RBR MusicB.2,
        no.19), NcU(EAMC,no.46), PP(U), ViU(°M1.S444,v.18,no.37)
    Great fun. See Grobe's **Bords du Mississippi** for variations
        on Strakosch's Polka.
Flirtation Polka (Burlesque musicale)
    Reed, 1849, 7p.
    CtHT(U), CtY(Mc28P7), ICN(Piano pre-1870), MiU-C(U), NBu
        (°M1.C65v.35,no.6), NNLc(AM2-I), NcD(RBR°music old W.C.L.
        M780.88A512PA), ScCC(SMB35.48), ViU(°M1.S444,v.94,no.12)
**Grand Fantasie dramatique sur des Motifs de "Lucia di Lammer-
    moor"**
    Reed, 1848, 19p.
    CtY(Mc11A1St82), LN(U), NNLc(AM2-I), NRU-E(U), ViU(McR.56.11)
The Magic Bell (Reverie)
    HallS, 1848, 10p.
    CtHT(U), CtY(Mc11A1St82), DLC(M25.S), ICN(Piano pre-1870),
        InU(M1.S8), MiU-C(U), NBu(U), NNLc(AM2-I), NRU-E(7092.F.
        15v.11), NcU(MF786.43S896r), PP(U), ViU(°M1.S444,v.152,
        no.10; McR.55.10), WM(786.4S889m)
    Much use of repeated notes. Fine salon piece.
The Magyar Polka (Morceau caractéristique)
    HallS, 1852, 9p.
    CtHT(U), CtY(Mc28P7)
La Mélancolie (Nocturne)
    HallS, 1850, 7p.

NBu(°M1.C65v.41,no.16), ViU(°M1.S444,v.133,no.7)
Mercedes (Caprice Polka)
     Hall, 1848, 7p.
     NNLc(AM2-I), NcD(RBR MusicB15,no.34), PP(U), ViU(°M1.S444,
          v.46,no.15)
Musical Rockets
     HallS, 1853, 15p.
     CtHT(U), DLC(M25.S), ICN(Piano pre-1870), InU(M1.S8), MoSW
          (U), NNLc(AM2-I), NRU-E(U), NcD(RBR MusicB15no.34), NcU
          (EAMC,no.98), PP(K:33), ViU(°M1.S444,v.152,no.1)
La Nayade (Etude fantastique)
     Walker, 1849, 9p.
     NNLc(°MYD+box), NRU-E(7092.F.5v.11), NcU(MF786.47S896n),
          PP(U)
Une Nuit dans les Tropiques (Rêverie sur un Motif du **Desert** de
     Félicien David)
     Oates, 1850, 7p.
     CtY(Mc11A1St81), DLC(M39.S), ICN(Piano pre-1870), NNLc(AM2-I),
          PP(U), ScCC(SMB54.9)
Reminiscenze dell'Opera "Lucrezia Borgia," Op.31
     HallS, n.d., 7p.
     CtY(Mc11A1St82), NRU-E(7092.F.16v.11)
Rêverie (see **The Magic Bell**)
Rosée du Matin (Etude poétique)
     Peters-WC, 1850, 11p.
     NNLc(°MYD+box)
Sea Serpent Polka
     Reed, n.d., 8p.
     CtY(Mc11A1St819), InU(M1.S8), LNT(L976.3[780]Z99), NNLc
          (AM2-I), NRU-E(7092.F.11v.11), PP(U), ViU(°M1.S444,v.77,
          no.13)
Sleighride Polka
     Breusing, 1850, 7p.
     IU(Joseffy), NNLc(AM2-I), ViU(McR.3.31)
Souvenir de l'Amérique (Amusement de Salon sur des Motivs
     éthiopiens)
     Peters-WC, 1849, 9p.
     CtY(Mc11A1St82), ScCC(SMB54.15)
     Amusing potpourri of Minstrel Show favorites.
Souvenir de Boston (Polka de Salon)
     Reed, 1848, 7p.
     NBu(°M1.C66v.38,no.5)
Souvenir de Palermo (Tarantella Siciliana)
     Reed, 1849, 9p.
     InU(M1.S8)
Souvenir du Lac de Como (Mélodie)
     HallS, 1848, 4p.
     NBu(°M1.C65v.52,no.22)
Tremolo (In Octaves)
     Chickering, 1849, 7p.
     CtHT(U), DLC(M25.S), ICN(8A 1646), NRU-E(U)
     Good study in technique.

STRONG, TEMPLETON (1856-1948)

Ballade, Op.22
   Kistner, 1905, 21p.
   DLC(M25.S)
   Written earlier than 1905.
Zweite Ballade, Op.34
   Henn, 1888, 11p.
   CtY(M25S924+op.34)
Fünf Charakterstücke, Op.6
   Kistner, n.d., 19p.
   CtY(Mc11A1St.88), DLC(M25.S)
   1. Pastorale; 2. Pastorale; 3. Ekloge; 4. Idylle;
      5. Pastorale
In the Forest, Op.36, No.2 (from **Four Poems, Op.36**)
   Breitkopf, 1896, 5p.
   DLC(M25.S), MoSW(U)
In Tirol (Neun Charakterstücke), **Op.7**
   Kistner, n.d., 45p.
   CtY(Mc11A1St88), DLC(M25.S)
   1. Gruss; 2. Was das Bächlein dem Mühlrad erzählt;
      3. Festlichkeit im Dorfe; 4. Ein trauriges kleines
      Mädchen; 5. Kleine Kinder im tiefen Walde; 6. Des
      Müllers Lied; 7. Scheiden und Leiden; 8. In der
      Dämmerung im Walde; 9. Abschied
A Midsummer Night's Dream, Op.36, No.4 (from **Four Poems, Op.36**)
   Schmidt, 1896, 11p.
   CtY(Mc11A1St88), DLC(M25.S), NRU-E(U), PP(U)
Petite Suite (Morceaux à deux Voix dans le Style du Passé)
   Henn, 1917, 11p.
   DLC(M24.S9P3)
   1. **Le Reveur** (Prelude); 2. **Un Don Juan** (Gavotte); 3. **Le
      Chevrier** (Pastorale); 4. **L'Inévitable Pédant** (Fugue)
   Excellent two-part writing.
Suite, Op.8
   Kistner, 1882, 39p.
   DLC(M24.S95op.8), NNLc(°MYD)
   1. **Praeludium;** 2. **Caprice;** 3. **Gigue;** 4. **Romanze;**
      5. **Polka fugale** (Ein Scherz); 6. **Fugue**

TAYLOR, RAYNER (ca.1747-1825)

The Bells
   In P-H
La Bretonne
   In A-C(II)
Divertimento II
   In A-C(I)
Fye: Nay Prithee John (A Favorite Old Catch with Variations)
   Longman, 1775, 8p.
   PP(U)
   A splendid example of Taylor's best variation writing.

March and Rondo
   CarrS, ca.1804, 1p. [W.II:900]
   In CMJ(2.5:14)
Martini's favorite Minuet with Variations
   Longman, 1775, 8p.
   DLC(M27.T Case), NNLc(°ZB-398no.2)
   Another fine variation set in Classic style.
Rondo for the Forte Piano
   CarrMR, ca.1794-1798, 3p. [SU:360]
   DLC(M1.A1T Case), IU(Film MO 70091), NNLc(AM1-I), also in
   C-MH

THIBAULT, CHARLES (d.ca.1853)

"Che faro senza Euridice" (Gluck. Arranged as a Rondo), **Op.14**
   DuboisS, 1826, 9p.
   DLC(M1.A13T), ICN(Case sm oM1.A13no.1188)
   Delightful fusion of rondo and variation treatment.
L'Espérance (A Fantasia with Variations on a French Theme),
  Op.8
   The author, ca.1824-1825, 12p. [W.II:906]
   ICN(Case8A 2750), NNLc(AM1-I), NcD(RBR MusicB157no.5)
Le Printemps (A Rondo with an Introduction), **Op.6**
   DuboisS, ca.1823, 11p. [W.II:907]
   NcD(RBR MusicB157no.6)
Rondo from the Chorus of Highlanders (La Dame blanche by
  Boieldieu), **Op.18**
   DuboisS, 1827, 6p.
   ICN(Case sm oM1.A13no.1195)
Russian Air (with an Introduction and Variations)
   Dubois, ca.1818-1820, 9p. [W.II:907]
   CtHT(U), ICN(Case8A 2879), NcD(RBR MusicB157no.13)
Le Souvenir (with Variations for the Harp or Pianoforte)
   DuboisS, 1823, 6p. [W.II:907]
   NNLc(AM1-I), ViRV(31.21.41)

THORN, EDGAR [see **EDWARD MACDOWELL**]

TROYER, CARLOS (1837-1920)

Ghost Dance of the Zuñis (from **Two Pianoforte Compositions**)
   Wa-Wan, 1904, 7p.
   CtY(RareM2W111+v.3,no.20), ICN(VM1W11v.3), NNLc(°MN Wa-Wan),
   NRU-E(M30T864gh), PP(U), also in NC-G, WW-L(I:183)
   Interesting essay in ethnic music.
Kiowa-Apache War Dance
   Wa-Wan, 1907, 11p.
   DLC(M25.T), ICN(VM1W11v.6), NNLc(°MN Wa-Wan), NRU-E(M30
   T864Ki), NcU(MF786.45T864k), WM(786.4T86k), also in WW-L
   (IV:78)

TURNER, ALFRED DUDLEY (1854-1888)

Berceuse
    Ditson, 1882, 11p.
    DLC(M25.T)
    Unusual. Uses the left-hand harmonic scheme from Chopin's
      Berceuse, Op.57 with a new right hand.
Etude de Concert, Op.16, No.1
    New England, 1883, 7p.
    DLC(M25.T)
    Effective study in five-four meter.
Humoresque (No.3 of **Six Concert Etudes**)
    New England, 1881, 13p.
    PP(U)
Mazurka serioso
    Prüfer, 1882, 7p.
    MiU-C(U)
2 Preludes and Fugues (in Octaves), **Op.22**
    BostonC, 1884, 13p.
    DLC(M25.T)
    Most unusual and imaginative--and difficult!
A Romance (Der Gruss)
    New England, 1882, 7p.
    MB-N(ArchivesMT4B7N39 1882 T87)

VENTH, CARL (1860-1938)

Frithjof und Ingeborg (Fünf Charakterstücke nach der Frithjof-
    Saga), **Op.69**
        Schuberth-FJr., 1891, 23p.
        DLC(M25.V), NNLc(°MYD)
        1. **Frithjof**; 2. **Ingeborg**; 3. **Frithjof's Traum**; 4. **Frith-**
            jof und Ingeborg vor Balder's Tempel; 5. **Frithjof's Rück-**
            kehr und Versöhnung
Sonata (Dionysus)
    The author, 1922, 24p.
    DLC(M23.V467D4)
    Substantial, serious work in one movement.

VOGRICH, MAX (1852-1916)

Anecdote (see **Drei Concert Programm-Stücke**)
At the Fountain (Transcription. Originally composed for violon-
    cello by Carl Davidoff)
        Schirmer, 1889, 11p.
        CU(M20C6v.3)
        Great study in right-hand repeated notes.
Cantique orientale
    Hofmeister, 1908, 7p.
    DLC(M25.V)
    Reprint of **Etude de Concert No.3**.

Drei Concert Programm-Stücke
Augener, n.d., 3v.(9,11,6p.)
DLC(M25.V)
1. **Was die Möven sagen** (What the Sea-gulls say); 2. **Freudiges Erwarten** (Joyful Awaiting); 3. **Anecdote**
Etudes de Concert
Schirmer, 1894, 6v.(11,7,7,7,5,13p.)
DLC(M25.V, 1-3,5,6 only), IU(Joseffy, 1-3,5,6 only), MoSW(U, 1-3,5,6 only), PP(U, 4 only)
Freudiges Erwarten (see **Drei Concert Programm-Stücke**)
Mazurka No.1 in F (from **Trois Mazurkas**)
Schirmer, 1890, 7p.
DLC(M32.V), IU(Joseffy), MoSW(U), WM(786.4V88v.1)
Mazurka No.3 in A (from **Trois Mazurkas**)
Schirmer, 1890, 7p.
DLC(M32.V), MoSW(U), WM(786.4V88v.3)
Nuit d'Alger (Fantaisie orientale)
Hofmeister, 1908, 11p.
DLC(M25.V)
Romancero
Schirmer, 1888, 19p.
DLC(M25.V), MoSW(U)
Sarabande et Fugue
Schirmer, 1890, 7p.
DLC(M25.V), IU(Joseffy), MoSW(U), WM(786.4V88s)
Staccato Caprice
Hofmeister, 1886, 10p.
CU(M25V635S7), CtY(U), DLC(M25.V), IU(Joseffy), MoS(786.4), MoSW(U), NRU-E(M21R29), NcD(M786.41V885S), OCl(SM776.4), WM(786.4V88t)
Brilliant and sparkling, with a key signature of six sharps.
Was die Möven sagen (see **Drei Concert Programm-Stücke**)

WARREN, GEORGE WILLIAM (1828-1902)

The Andes (Marche di Bravura)
Pond, 1863, 14p.
CtY(U), IU(MaLxq.784.3Sh37v.10,no.3), NBu(U), NNLc(°MYDbox), NRU-E(U), NcU(MF786.44W288a), PP(U), RPB(U), ViU(°M1.S444,v.106,no.28), also in NC-G
Supposedly inspired by a painting by Frederick Church.
Bobolink Polka
FirthS, 1856, 7p.
CtHT(U), CtY(Mc11A1W25), ICN(Piano pre-1870W), IU(MaLxq784.3Sh37v.10,no.2), NBu(°M1.C66v.23,no.47), NNLc(AM2-I), PP(U), RPB(U), ViU(°M1.S444,v.47,no.6)
Bombastes Furioso (Marcia pomposo)
Pond, 1868, 11p.
CtHT(U), LN(U), NNLc(AM2-I), RPB(U)
Caprice quasi Polonaise in F Major
Pond, 1865, 11p.
DLC(M30.W), InU(M1.S8), NNLc(°MYD), NcU(MF786.44W288c)

Cassie (Danse espagnole)
  Pond, 1865, 9p.
  CtY(Mc11A1W25), NNLc(AM2-I), NRU-E(U)
Ellsworth Requiem
  FirthP, 1861, 6p.
  CtY(Mc11A1W252), NNLc(AM2-I), PP(U), ViU(McR.4.02)
  Funeral march with lyrical middle section.
Española (Valse-Caprice)
  Pond, 1893, 9p.
  DLC(M32.W), NNLc(°MYDbox)
Shanghai Polka
  FirthP, 1854, 6p.
  CtHT(U), LN(U), NNLc(AM2-I)
The Song of the Brook (Pastorale)
  Pond, 1865, 9p.
  DLC(M25.W), InU(M1.S8), NNLc(AM2-I), NcD(RBR MusicW288S),
    RPB(U), ViU(°M1.S444,v.171,no.30; McR.24.43)
The Song of the Robin (Romance)
  Ditson, 1857, 7p.
  CtHT(U), CtY(Mc11A1W252), DLC(M25.W), ICN(Piano pre-1870W),
    NBu(U), NNLc(AM2-I), NcD(RBR Music824), PP(U), RPB(U),
    ViU(McR.153.40)
Tam O'Shanter
  Himan, 1897, 7p.
  CtHT(U), CtY(Mc11A1W252), DLC(M25.W), ICN(VM1F.91no.232),
    LN(U), LNT(L976.3[780]Z99), MoSW(U), NBu(U), NNLc(AM2-I),
    NRU-E(U), OCl(SM776.4), PP(U), RPB(U), ViU(°M1.S444,v.171,
    no.30; McR.54.01)
Under the Lindens (Idylle)
  Pond, 1874, 9p.
  CtY(Mc11A1W25), DLC(M25.W)

WARREN, SAMUEL PROWSE (1841-1915)

  Eventide, Op.25, No.1 (see **Three Pieces, Op.25**)
  Humoresque, Op.25, No.2 (see **Three Pieces, Op.25**)
  Impromptu, Op.25, No.3 (see **Three Pieces, Op.25**)
  Three Pieces, Op.25
    Schuberth-E, 1904, 3v.(3,10,5p.)
    DLC(M25.W), NNLc(°MYD+box, 2,3 only)
    1. **Eventide**; 2. **Humoresque**; 3. **Impromptu**
  Prelude and Fugue (in F Minor)
    Schirmer, 1901, 11p.
    DLC(M25.W)
    Serious concert piece with difficult fugue.

WEBER, HENRY [HEINRICH] (1812-1878)

  The Storm (An Imitation of Nature)
    Benson, 1855, 11p.
    CtY(Mc11A1W381), DLC(M25.W), ICN(Piano pre-1870W), InU(M1.

S8), NBu(U), NRU-E(U), NcD(RBR Music 758), NcU(EAMC,
no.35), OCl(SM776.43), PP(U), RPB(U), ViU(°M1.S444,v.58,
no.21)
Wildly popular in its day. Inspired by the Storm movement
of Beethoven's **"Pastoral" Symphony.**
Storm and Sunshine (Episode from the Mexican War)
McClure, 1860, 9p.
ViU(McR.99.25)

WELS, CHARLES (1825-1906)

Nocturne (Mignon), **Op.54**
Schuberth-J, 1865, 5p.
DLC(M25.W)
Une Nuit d'Eté (Nocturno), **Op.16**
FirthP, 1853, 9p.
DLC(M1.A13W Case)
Fifteen Preludes, Op.121
Rockar, 1891, 15p.
DLC(M25.W)
"Sleep Well, Sweet Angel!" (Transcription from F. Abt), **Op.72,
No.1**
Schirmer, 1866, 7p.
PP(U)
Solitude and Memory (Two Songs without Words)
FirthP, 1851, 11p.
CtY(Mc11A1W46)
Souvenir de la Grande Duchesse, Op.79
Ditson, 1868, 11p.
DLC(M25.W)
Musicianly Offenbach potpourri.
Spinning Wheel (Morceau caractéristique), **Op.86**
Ditson, 1869, 11p.
DLC(M25.W), PP(U)
"Spirto gentil" (La Favorita. Transcription and Variation),
Op.9
FirthS, 1852, 11p.
NcD(RBR MusicB38,no.10), RPB(U)
Elegant piano setting of an aria from Donizetti's opera.
Transcription et Variation sur "Di provenza il mar" (La
Traviata), Op.45
FirthP, 1857, 7p.
NcD(RBR MusicB149,no.13)

WHELPLEY, BENJAMIN (1864-1946)

Album Leaf, Op.2, No.1
Boston, 1898, 5p.
CtY(Mc11A1W573), DLC(M25.W), NRU-E(U), RPB(U), also in AC
Five Characteristic Pieces, Op.11
Boston, 1907, 19p.

DLC(M25.W), NRU-E(U, 1,3 only), NcU(M786.4W567b1), RPB(U)
    1. Spring Madrigal; 2. The Nightingale; 3. Song of the
    Fountain; 4. At Evening; 5. Dance by Moonlight
Evening Song, Op.3, No.1
    SchirmerJr, 1899, 7p.
    NRU-E(U), RPB(U)
In the Garden, Op.4, No.1
    Boston, 1901, 7p.
    NRU-E(U)
Serenade, Op.4, No.3
    Boston, 1901, 6p.
    NRU-E(U)
Under Bright Skies
    Boston, 1898, 8p.
    NRU-E(U)

WHITING, ARTHUR (1861-1936)

Album Leaf (see Bagatelles)
Bagatelle (in D-flat Major)
    Millet, 1895, 4p.
    DLC(M25.W), also in HH-K(V:1312)
Bagatelle (see Bagatelles)
Bagatelles
    Schirmer, 1895, 27p., also issued separately
    DLC(M25.W), IU(Joseffy), MBH(P.1W596), NNLc(°MYD), also in
    NC-G(2,3 only)
    1. Caprice; 2. Humoreske; 3. Bagatelle; 4. Scherzino;
    5. Idylle; 6. Albumleaf
Caprice (see Bagatelles)
Concert Etude, Op.5, No.1
    Schirmer, 1886, 8p.
    DLC(M25.W), MBH(P.1W596), NRU-E(M21R29Av.1), PP(U)
    Fine concert piece and octave study.
Le Cortège qui passe, Op.20, No.3 (see Cinq Morceaux, Op.20)
Etude mélodique, Op.20, No.2 (see Cinq Morceaux, Op.20)
La Fileuse, Op.20, No.1 (see Cinq Morceaux, Op.20)
Humoreske (see Bagatelles)
Idylle (see Bagatelles)
Cinq Morceaux, Op.20
    Schirmer, 1904, 5v.(5,5,5,5,7p.)
    CtY(Mc11A1W589, 1,4 only), DLC(M25.W), MoS(786.4), NNLc
    (°MYD+), NRU-E(M21R29Av.1), PP(U, 1,3 only)
    1. La Fileuse; 2. Etude mélodique; 3. Le Cortège qui
    passe; 4. Nocturne; 5. Polonaise
Nocturne, Op.20, No.4 (see Cinq Morceaux, Op.20)
Polonaise, Op.20, No.5 (see Cinq Morceaux, Op.20)
Quasi Sarabande, Op.5, No.2
    Schirmer, 1886, 5p.
    DLC(M25.W), MBH(P.1W596), NRU-E(M25W598Q), OCl(SM776.47)
    Different, unusual approach to the sarabande.
Scherzino (see Bagatelles)

Suite moderne, Op.15
   Schirmer, 1900, 41p.
   CtY(Mc20W58+op.15), DLC(M25.W), IU(Joseffy), LNT(786W58su),
   MBH(P.1D35.2), MoS(786.4), NRU-E(M21R29Av.2)
   1. Prélude; 2. Chansonnette; 3. Rhapsodie; 4. Danse;
      5. Intermède; 6. Romance; 7. Caprice; 8. Mélodie
      et Arabesque; 9. Finale

WHITING, GEORGE ELBRIDGE (1840-1923)

Legend for a Child
   Millet, 1895, 4p.
   DLC(M25.W), also in HH-K(V:1417)
Scherzino
   Millet, 1895, 9p.
   DLC(M25.W), also in HH-K(V:1409)

WHITNEY, SAMUEL BRENTON (1842-1914)

L'Elisir d'amore (Fantaisie élégante)
   Harris, 1867, 15p.
   DLC(M25.W), RPB(U)
Grand Fantasia Burletta (on the well-known A.B.C. Song), **Op.20**
   GordonS, 1867, 10p.
   MiU-C(U), NNLc(AM2-I)
The Spray of the Cascade (Caprice. Valse styrienne)
   Harris, 1867, 9p.
   MiU-C(U)
Tarantelle in A Flat, Op.23
   Russell, 1875, Ditson, 1898, 13p.
   RPB(U)

WILSON, GRENVILLE DEAN (1833-1897)

The Chapel in the Mountains
   Ditson, 1887, 7p.
   CtY(Mc11A1W69), DLC(M25.W), NRU-E(U), PP(U), RPB(U)
Crystal Chimes (Morceau de Salon), **Op.24**
   WhiteSP, 1870, 9p.
   RPB(U)
L'Etourdie (Caprice brillant), **Op.20**
   Koppitz, 1870, 11p.
   RPB(U)
A Gleam of Sunshine (Morceau de Salon), **Op.145**
   Shaw, 1882, 7p.
   MiU-C(U)
Moonlight on the Hudson (Morceau de Salon), **Op.60**
   Ditson, 1905, 11p.
   NRU-E(U), ViU(McR.134.28)
Phantom Dance (Morceau de Salon), **Op.92**

Ditson, 1877, 7p.
NcD(RBR MusicB17,no.18)
Queen of the Night (Romance), **Op.33**
White, 1872, 9p.
CtHT(U)
Silver Chimes (Morceau brillant), **Op.168**
Ditson, 1893, 9p.
NRU-E(U)
Tripping Thro' the Meadows (Polka Rondo), **Op.26**
White, 1871, 7p.
CtY(Mc28P7), DCL(M25.W), IU(MLqM786.41W693t Spec.Coll.),
    MoSW(U), NNLc(AM2-I), NcD(RBR MusicB80no.18a), PP(U),
    RPB(U)
Les Voix du Matin, Op.19
Prüfer, 1869, 5p.
RPB(U)

WOLFSOHN, CARL (1834-1907)

Adieu à Hohnstock (Pensée fugitive)
AndréG, 1860, 7p.
MiU-C(U)
Au Bord du Lac
Lee, 1868, 7p.
DLC(M25.W), MiU-C(U), PP(U)
Good study piece for chromatic passage work.
Berceuse (No.1 of **Trois Morceaux caractéristiques**)
Meyer, 1868, 7p.
MdBP(U)
Fantaisie-Caprice (sur un Thème original), **Op.10**
n.p., n.d., 19p.
PP(U), RPB(U)
Faust (de Gounod. Transcription de Concert)
AndréG, 1869, 17p.
RPB(U)
Polka Caprice
Walker, 1855, 9p.
MiU-C(U), NBu(°M1.C65v.44,no.18), NNLc(AM2-I), NcU(EAMC,
    no.15), ViU(McR.3.33)
Melodious and vivacious dance composition.
Redowa de Concert
Walker, 1855, 9p.
DLC(M20.C8no.24), ICN(Piano pre-1870W), NNLc(AM2-I), NcU
    (MF786.4W861r), PP(U), RPB(U)
One of the composer's very best salon pieces.

WOLLENHAUPT, HERMANN (1827-1863)

Air varié, Op.11
Hagen, 1860, 5p.
MeB(U)

Andante elégiaque, Op.45
  Breusing, 1858, 14p.
  PP(U), ViU(McR.145.20)
Andante et Etude, Op.7
  Beer, 1848, 7p.
  CtHT(U)
  1. Souvenir; 2. Salut
Le dernier Sourire (Scherzo brillante)**, Op.72**
  Pond, 1863, 15p.
  CtHT(U), CtY(Mc11A1W83), DCL(M25.W), IU(MaLq786.4W834l), InU
    (M1.S8), LN(U), MoS(786.4), MoSW(U), NNLc(AM2-I), NRU-E
    (U), NcU(MF786.4W864d), OCL(SM776.4), PP(U), RPB(U), ViU
    (°M1.S444,v.133,no.6; McR.57.11), WM(786.4W86d)
  Very fine scherzo, extremely popular in its day.
Galop di Bravura, Op.24
  Meyer, 1854, 11p.
  RPB(U), ViU(°M1.S444,v.98,no.21; McR.54.11)
La Gazelle Polka, Op.23, No.2
  Ditson, n.d., Fischer, 1904, 9p.
  DLC(M25.W), MoS(786.4), NNLc(AM2-I), NRU-E(U), OCL(SM776.45),
    PP(U), RPB(U), ViU(°M1.S444,v.98,no.20), WM(786.4W86ga)
Grand March de Concert, Op.19
  FirthP, 1853, 9p.
  CtHT(U), CtY(Mc11A1W83), DLC(M25.W), DeWHi(U), ICN(Piano
    pre-1870W), InU(M1.S8), LN(U), MiU-C(U), MoSW(U), NNLc
    (AM2-I), NRU-E(U), NcD(RBR MusicB149no.10), PP(U), RPB
    (U), ViU(°M1.S444,v.119,no.16; McR.79.49), WM(786.4W86g)
Grande Marche militaire, Op.31
  Kistner, n.d., 11p.
  CtY(Mc11A1W83), DLC(M22.W864), ICN(Piano pre-1870W), LN(U),
    MoS(786.4), NNLc(AM2-I), NRU-E(U), PP(U), RPB(U), ViU
    (McR.57.14)
Grande Valse brillante
  Hall, n.d., 11p.
  MdBP(U), RPB(U)
Hélène (Grande Valse brillante)**, Op.26**
  MeyerT, 1854, Ditson, n.d., 11p.
  CtHT(U), NBu(U), NNLc(AM2-I), NRU-E(U), PP(U), RPB(U)
Illustrations de l'Opera de G. Verdi "Il Trovatore," Op.46
  Schirmer, 1859, 19p.
  MiU-C(U), RPB(U)
Illustration sur "Le Brindisi" de l'Opera "Lucrezia Borgia,"
  Op.50
  FirthP, 1859, 11p.
  CtHT(U), NNLc(°MYD), NcU(EAMC,no.32), RPB(U)
Impromptu sur Kriegers-Lust, Op.9
  Bote, 1849, 5p.
  CtY(Mc11A1W83), PP(U), ViU(McR.78.31)
The Last Smile, Op.72, (see **Le dernier Sourire, Op.72**)
Mazeppa (Grand Galop de Concert)**, Op.43**
  Schirmer, 1858, 16p.
  NcU(EAMC,no.2), RPB(U), ViU(°M1.S444,v.139,no.4)
Cinq Morceaux caractéristiques en Forme d'Etudes, Op.22

Meyer, 1854, 19p.; Ditson, 1910, 23p., also issued separate-
ly
CtY(Mc11A1W83, 1 only), DLC(M25.W, 1 only), MoSW(U, 1 only),
   NNLc(AM2-I), NRU-E(U, 1 only), RPB(U), WM(786.4W86)
Excellent study pieces for technique.
Murmuring Zephyrs (Mazurka brillante), **Op.69**
Pond, 1863, 11p.
ICN(Piano pre-1870), IU(MaLxq784.3Sh37v.10,no.23)
Nocturne, Op.22
Spina, n.d., Century, 1913, 7p.
OCL(SM776.43), ViU(U:3)
Nocturne romantique, Op.15
Schirmer, 1857, 7p.
NNLc(AM2-I), ViU(°M1.S444,v.28,no.19), WM(786.4W86n)
**Paraphrase on the Spinning Song from R. Wagner's opera "Flying
Dutchman," Op.67**
Pond, 1863, 15p.
CtY(Mc11A1W83), DLC(M25.W), NRU-E(U)
Paraphrase sur des Airs de L'Opera "Traviata"
FirthP, 1859, 13p.
NNLc(°MYD), RPB(U), ScCC(SMS72-85)
2 Polkas de Salon, Op.14
Kahnt, Breusing, 185_?, 2v.(7,9p.)
CtY(Mc11A1W83, 2 only), ViU(U:3)
1. La Rose; 2. La Violette
La Rose, Op.14, No.1 (see **2 Polkas de Salon, Op.14**)
Le Ruisseau (Valse Etude), **Op.25**
Meyer, 1854, WhiteS, n.d., 7p.
CtHT(U), NNLc(AM2-I), NRU-E(U), NcD(RBR°music old786.4C697B),
   PP(U), RPB(U), ViU(°M1.S444,v.28,no.18; McR.54.10), WM
   (786.4W86r)
Understandably a great favorite in its day.
Scherzo brillant, Op.72
Another title for (see) **Le dernier Sourire, Op.72.**
Schottisch, Op.37, No.1
HallS, n.d., 7p.
ScCC(SMB7.12)
Souvenir de Niagara (Grand Divertissement de bravoure), **Op.34**
Ditson, n.d., 15p.
DLC(M25.W), MoS(786.4), NBu(U), NcU(EAMC,no.32), WM(786.4
   W86s)
Sparkling Diamonds (Mazurka fantastique), **Op.53**
Hagen, 1859, 13p.
MeB(U), RPB(U)
Superb, difficult morceau de salon.
The Sweetest Smile (Polka), **Op.49**
Schirmer, n.d., 10p.
NRU-E(U), RPB(U)
"Thou art a Lovely Flower" (Improvisation), **Op.30**
HallS, n.d., 5p.
CtY(Mc11A1W83)
The score includes the original song.

Valse styrienne, Op.27, No.2 (from **Mazurka et Valse styrienne, Op.27**)

>   MeyerT, 1854, 9p.
>   CtHT(U), CtY(Mc11A1W83), DLC(M25.W), ICN(Piano pre-1870W), IU(MaLq786.4W834v), LN(U), LNT(L976.3[780]Z99), MoSW(U), NRU-E(U), NcU(EAMC,no.32), OCl(SM776.45), ViU(°M1.S444, v.28,no.27; McR.132.22), WM(786.4W86v)

La Violette Polka, Op.14, No.2 (see **2 Polkas de Salon, Op.14**)

The Whispering Wind (Mazurka Caprice), **Op.38**

>   HallS, 1856, 15p.
>   CtHT(U), CtY(Mc11A1W83), DLC(M25.W), ICN(Piano pre-1870), InU(M1.S8), MoS(786.4), MoSW(U), NBu(U), NNLc(AM2-I), NRU-E(U), NcD(RBR MusicB149no.5), OCl(SM776.45), RPB(U), ViU(°M1.S444,v.94,no.5; McR.54.12), WM(786.4W86w)

II
Music for Piano, One Hand
(Left Hand alone, unless otherwise specified)

ALDEN, JOHN CARVER (1852-1935)

Gavotte
Wood, 1902, 7p.
DLC(M31.A), OCl(SM776.45), PP(U)
Good study for left-hand flexibility.

FOOTE, ARTHUR (1853-1937)

A Little Waltz, Op.6, No.4
Schmidt, 1885, 3p.
DLC(M25.F), MoS(786.4), NNLc(°MYD+box), NRU-E(M26F688W),
PP(U), RPB(U), WM(786.402F68)
See Section I: **Cinq Pièces, Op.6.** A delightful and
skillfully designed miniature waltz.
Three Pieces for the Left Hand Alone, Op.37
Schmidt, 1897, 11p., also issued separately
CU(M22F66, 3 only), DLC(M26.F), MBH(P.1F738), MB-N(M3.3
F66op.37 1897a), MoSW(U), NNLc(°MYD-Amer), NRU-E(M22
F68), PP(M786.4F73), RPB(U)
1. **Prélude-Etude**; 2. **Polka**; 3. **Romanze**
Very fine trio of well-structured compositions.
Polka, Op.37, No.2 (see **Three Pieces, Op.37**)
Prélude-Etude, Op.37, No.1 (see **Three Pieces, Op.37**)
Prélude-Etude (right hand alone)**, Op.37, No.1**
Schmidt, 1897, 6p.
DLC(M26.2F)
Arranged from **Three Pieces, Op.37.** Welcome item in a very
restricted repertoire.
Romanze, Op.37, No.3 (see **Three Pieces, Op.37**)

GANZ, RUDOLPH (1877-1972)

Two Capriccios, Op.26
　　Schirmer, 1917, 2v.(7,11p.)
　　CtY(Mc11A1G159b, 2 only), DLC(M26.G, 1 only; M26.2G, 2
　　　only), LN(U, 1 only), MoSW(U, 2 only), NNLc(°MYD),
　　　NRU-E(M21M67v.2), PP(M786.4G151), WM(786.402G21, 1 only)
　　1. For the left Hand alone; 2. For the right Hand alone

GODOWSKY, LEOPOLD (1870-1938)

Capriccio (see Concert Album)
Concert Album (Piano Compositions for the Left Hand Alone)
　　Schirmer, 1930, 27p., also issued separately
　　NNLc(°MYD), OCl(M776.401.433)
　　1. Méditation; 2. Impromptu; 3. Capriccio(Patetico);
　　　4. Intermezzo(Malinconico); 5. Elegy; 6. Etude macabre
Elegy (see Concert Album)
Etude macabre (see Concert Album)
Impromptu (see Concert Album)
Intermezzo (see Concert Album)
Méditation (see Concert Album)
Prelude and Fugue (B.A.C.H.)
　　Schirmer, 1930, 13p.
　　DLC(M26.G), NNLc(°MYDbox), PP(M786.4G54413)
　　Fugue subject based on BACH. Virtuoso composition.
Suite
　　Schirmer, 1930, 39p.
　　DLC(M26.G)
　　1. Allemande; 2. Gavotte; 3. Sarabande; 4. Bourrée;
　　　5. Sicilienne; 6. Menuet; 7. Gigue
　　Great tour de force for left hand.
Symphonic Metamorphoses (of the Schatz-Walzer Themes from **The
　Gypsy Baron** by Johann Strauss)
　　Fischer, 1941, 21p.
　　DLC(M26.G), NNLc(°MYD)
　　Ingenious virtuoso piece.

HOFFMAN, RICHARD (1831-1909)

Venetian Serenade
　　Presser, 1907, 3p.
　　PP(U)
　　Setting of "O Sole Mio."

HOFMANN, JOSEF (1876-1957)

Etude in C dur, Op.32
　　Schuberth-E, n.d., 7p.
　　IU(Joseffy)

HUSS, HENRY HOLDEN (1862-1953)

Prélude, Op.17, No.3 (Right Hand alone. From **Quatre Préludes en Forme d'Etudes, Op.17** [I])
Schirmer, 1901, 5p.
CtY(U), DLC(M25.H), IU(Joseffy), MoS(786.4), NNLc(°MYD+box), NRU-E(M21R29Av.2), NcU(M786.4H972pr), PP(U), RPB(U), WM (786.4H967)
A valuable asset to right-hand literature.

JOSEFFY, RAFAEL (1852-1915)

Gavotte in E Major (Transcription from the Six Sonata for Violin by J. S. Bach)
Schuberth-E, 1880, 7p.
CtY(U), DLC(M26.B), NNLc(°MYDp.v.59,no.22), NRU-E(M38B11GJ), WM(786.402B11g)

KUNKEL, CHARLES [JEAN PAUL, CLAUDE MELNOTTE] (1840-1923)

The Banjo (Caprice de Concert)
Kunkel, 1911, 11p.
DLC(M26.K)
Miserere from Verdi's "Il Trovatore" (Concert Paraphrase)
Kunkel, 1916, 11p.
DLC(M26.K)
Thoroughgoing work-out for the left hand.
Old Black Joe (S. C. Foster. Grand Concert Piece)
Kunkel, 1911, 13p.
DLC(M26.K)
Another left-hand tour de force.
Sextette from Donizetti's "Lucia di Lammermoor" (Grand Concert Paraphrase)
Kunkel, 1911, 11p.
DLC(M26.K)

ROBYN, ALFRED GEORGE (1860-1935)

"Annie Laurie" (Transcription)
Balmer, 1887, 5p.
DLC(M26.R), MoSW(U), WM(786.402R66)
Fine left-hand study piece.

SAAR, LOUIS VICTOR (1868-1937)

"Believe Me, If All Those Endearing Young Charms" (Irish Folk Song)
ArtPS, 1933, 3p.
MoSW(U)

SPROSS, CHARLES GILBERT (1874-1961)

Album Leaf
Church, 1913, 7p.
DLC(M26.S), NPA(U), PP(U)
Song Without Words
Church, 1913, 7p.
CtY(Mc11A1Sp86), DLC(M26.S), NPA(U), PP(U)

STRAKOSCH, MAURICE (1825-1887)

Prayer from the Opera of "Othello," Op.36
HallS, 1848, 5p.
CtY(Mc11A1St82), DLC(M26.S), LN(U), NNLc(°MYD+box), NRU-E
(M1508R835op; 7092.F7v.11)
Good study in arpeggiated left-hand chords.

III
Music for Piano Duet
(Piano, 4 Hands)

BARTLETT, HOMER NEWTON (1845-1920)

Grande Polka de Concert, Op.1
Schirmer, 1906, 19p.
DLC(M212.B), MoSW(U), NRU-E(M211B289P7 1906)
Arranged by the composer and equally as delightful as the
original solo version.
Kuma Saka (Founded on Japanese Themes)**, Op.218**
Schirmer, 1907, 7p.
DLC(M204.B), NNLc(°MYD-Amer)
Another example of Bartlett's fascination with oriental
music (See [I]).

BIRD, ARTHUR (1856-1923)

Amerikanische Weisen (Rondes américaines)**, Op.23**
Hainauer, Schirmer, 1887, 3v.(13,13,15p.)
MB-N(VaultM20B55v.3), NRU-E(M201B61)
Three delightful waltzes. First-class writing.
Introduction et Fugue, Op.16
Hainauer, Schirmer, 1887, 24p.
MB-N(VaultM20B55v.3), NRU-E(M204B61)
Superb arrangement of the original version (1886) for
orchestra and organ.

BOEKELMAN, BERNARDUS (1838-1930)

Polonaise de Concert, Op.4
Schuberth-E, 1889, 11p.
DLC(M216.B72)

CLIFTON, ARTHUR [P. A. CORRI] (1784-1832)

  Aglaia and Euphrosyne, A Serenade Duett [Corri]
      Weygand, 182_?, 15p.
      CtY(RareM200D854+no.10)

CLOUGH-LEITER, HENRY (1874-1956)

  Vier Novelletten, Op.52
      Boston, 1911, 31p., also issued separately
      InU(M1.S8, 1,2 only), RPB(U)
      1. **Im Blumengarten;** 2. **Elfenreigen;** 3. **Erzählung;** 4. **In
      der Spinnstube**

COERNE, LOUIS ADOLPHE (1870-1922)

  Hiawatha (Symphonic Poem), **Op.18**
      Miles, 1894, 4 parts in 1v.(79p.)
      CtNLC(15.2C651H52), DLC(M209.C67op.18), ICN(sVM209C67h),
      NNLc(°MYD)
      1. **His Birth and Childhood;** 2. **His Wooing;** 3. **The Wedding
      Feast;** 4. **Finale**
      Good arrangement from the orchestral score for study.

CONRATH, LOUIS (1868-1927)

  Tarantella
      Kunkel, 1891, 15p.
      DLC(M204.C), MoSW(U)

CONVERSE, FREDERICK SHEPHERD (1871-1940)

  Valzer poetici, Op.5
      Miles, 1896, 25p.
      CtY(M204C766+), ICN(8A 2546), IU(MO 27632), LNT(M204.C66V2),
      MB-N(M3.3C66op.5), NRU-E(M204C766V2op.5), PP(MCH.26Con.36)
      Six brief, graceful waltzes.

EPSTEIN, MARCUS ISAAC (1855-1947)

  Grand Operatic Fantasia, No.1
      Kunkel, 1876, 31p.
      DLC(M212.E)
  International Fantasie
      Kunkel, 1875, 33p.
      DLC(M212.E)
      Mélange of **Pique-Dame, Il Trovatore, Grande-Duchesse, Faust,
      Star-Spangled Banner, God Save the Queen, Yankee Doodle.**

FOOTE, ARTHUR (1853-1937)

Air, Op.21, No.1 (from **Three Duets, Op.21**)
    Schmidt, 1891, 5p.
    DLC(M209.F68op.21,no.1), MoS(786.4)
    Beautifully written in neo-Baroque style.
Zwölf kleine Stücke (12 Duets on Five Notes)
    Schmidt, 1891, 15p.
    CU(M1389F66K5), DLC(M209.F68), ICN(sVM201F68t), IU(qM786.49
    F73t), NRU-E(M1390F688)
    Easy, tuneful pieces for young performers.

FOSTER, STEPHEN COLLINS (1826-1864)

The Soiree Polka (Arranged for four hands)
    Peters-FC, 1850, 5p.
    CU(M3F6CaseB°°), ICN(VM3F751S68), also in FHR

GILBERT, HENRY FRANKLIN BELKNAP (1868-1928)

Three American Dances
    Boston, 1919, 23p.
    DLC(M204.G), MBH(P.2G37), NNLc(°MYD), NRU-E(M204G464am)
    1. Uncle Remus; 2. Delphine; 3. B'rer Rabbit
    Three stylish essays in Americana.

GODOWSKY, LEOPOLD (1870-1938)

Three Suites (from **Miniatures**)
    Fischer, 1918, 3v.(11,11,11p.)
    CU(M1389G62M5, 1 only), CtY(Mc11A1G547), DLC(M1389.G6M4),
    IU(qM786.49G54m), MoS(786.49), NNLc(°MYD), NRU-E(M201
    G589), OCl(M776.4.42524), WM(786.41G58, 1,3 only)

GOTTSCHALK, LOUIS MOREAU [SEVEN OCTAVES] (1829-1869)

Le Bananier (Chanson nègre), **Op.5**
    Schott, n.d., 9p.
    CU(M204G607CaseX), CtY(R Mc70G71), NRU-E(M212.G687B2)
La dernière Espérance (Méditation réligieuse), **Op.16**
    Schott, n.d., 11p.
    CtY(R Mc70G71)
La Gallina (Danse cubaine), **Op.53**
    Halls, 1865, 13p.
    CtY(R Mc70G71), DLC(M204.G), PP(U), ViU(McR.165.37), also
    in GP-L(II:253), PM-H
Oberon Overture (Weber)
    Ditson, 1901, 31p.
    DLC(M204.G), NNLc(AM2-I), NRU-E(M22G68v.9), NcU(M786.492
    W373o.o), also in GP-L(IV:121)

Ouverture de Guillaume Tell (Rossini. Grand Morceau de
  Concert)
    HallS, 1864, 19p.
    DLC(M212.G), IU(Joseffy), LNT(L976.3[780]Z99), NRU-E(M22
      G68v.13), NcU(M786.492R835g.o.), also in GP-L(III:73)
Ojos criollos (Caprice brillant), **Op.37**
    HallS, 1860, 11p.
    CU(M211G674op.37CaseX), CtY(R Mc7OG71), LNH(U), LNT(M204
      G604), MoS(786.49), NNLc(AM2-I), NRU-E(M204G687 03 1860),
      NcU(M786.492G687o), PP(U), WM(786.41G68o), also in GP-L
      (IV:159)
Radieuse (Grande Valse de Concert), **Op.72**
    Ditson, 1865, 20p.
    CtHT(U), CtY(R Mc7OG71), DLC(M212.G), LNH(U), MoS(786.49),
      NNLc(°MYD-Amer), NRU-E(M22G68v.10), NcU(MF786.492G687r),
      PP(U), WM(786.41G68), also in GP-L(IV:279)
"Réponds moi" (Danse cubaine)
    HallS, 1864, 13p.
    CtY(R Mc7OG71), DLC(M212.G), IU(xq784.3Sh37v.7,no.11),
      InU(M1.S8), NNLc(AM2-I), NRU-E(M22G68v.11), NcU(M786.45
      G687r), also in GP-L(V:29)
La Scintilla (The Spark. Mazurka sentimentale), **Op.21**
    Ditson, 1854, 11p.
    CtY(R Mc7OG71), LNH(U)
Ses Yeux (Her Eyes. Polka de Concert), **Op.66**
    Hall, 1875, 28p.
    CtHT(U), CtY(R Mc7OG71), also in GP-L(V:97)

HACKH, OTTO (1852-1917)

Menuet fantastique, Op.74
    Schuberth-E, 1895, 11p.
    NcD(RBR MusicB12,no.17)

HANCE, JAMES F. (fl.1815-1835)

"Finch' han dal vino," Aria from "Don Giovanni"
    DuboisS, 1827, 7p.
    NcD(RBR MusicB10,no.37), PP(U)
The Nightingale (A Military Air arranged as a Duett)
    Hewitt, ca.1825, Ditson, n.d., 15p. [W.I:222]
    CtHT(U), DLC(M1.A13H), NNLc(AM1-I)
    The original "air" is by J. B. Cramer.

HECKSCHER, CELESTE DE LONGPRE (1860-1928)

Dances of the Pyrenees (Arranged from the orchestral score)
    Gray, 1913, 43p.
    DLC(M209.H449), NNLc(°MYD)
    1. Seguidilla; 2. Intermezzo; 3. Pastorale; 4. Bolero

HEWITT, GEORGE WASHINGTON (1811-1893)

Invitation à la Danse (Quadrilles Composed and Arranged as
  Duetts)
    Lee, 1850, 11p.
    NNLc(AM2-I), NcD(RBR MusicB2,no.36)

HOLST, EDUARD (ca.1843-1899)

The June—Bugs Dance (Polka-Rondo)
    Remick, 1889, 9p.
    InU(M1.S8), NBu(U), WM(786.41H75)
Ilma (Grande Valse de Concert)
    Chicago, 1881, 15p.
    MoSW(U), PP(U)

KLEIN, BRUNO OSCAR (1858-1911)

Four American Dances, Op.80
    Schuberth-E, 1901, Second Series, vols.6-9
    DLC(M204.K, 8,9 only), MoSW(U)
    Orchestral pieces arranged by the composer.

KOELLING, CARL (1831-ca.1914)

La Chasse infernale (Grand Galop brillant)
    Ditson, 1870, 17p.
    IU(MaLxq784.3Sh37v.7,no.53)
    "arrangée à quatre mains par Charles Wels."

KUNKEL, CHARLES [CLAUDE MELNOTTE, JEAN PAUL] (1840-1923)

La Sonnambula (Bellini. Fantasia)
    Kunkel, n.d., 13p.
    MoSW(U, in **Kunkel's Album No.4**)
    Published under Kunkel's pseudonym Jean Paul.
Il Trovatore (Grand Fantasie), **Op.117**
    Kunkel, 1892, 17p.
    DLC(M212.V [Verdi])
    An enjoyable potpourri of airs from Verdi's opera published
      under Kunkel's pseudonym Claude Melnotte.

MACDOWELL, EDWARD [Edgar Thorn] (1860-1908)

Benedick (A Sketch for the Scherzo from the **Second Concerto**
  for Pianoforte)
    MacDowell, 1947, 15p.
    ICRo(ML96.5.M33B4), NNLc(°MNZ-Amer), PP(M786.49M141)

Photographed from the composer's manuscript.
Hamlet and Ophelia, Op.22
Schirmer, 191_?, 27p.
CtY(M209M138+op.22), DLC(M3.3.M14op.22B 1885), LNT(786.2
M14po), MoS(786.49), NRU-E(M209M13H)
Mondbilder (After H. C. Andersen's **Picture-book without Pic-
tures), Op.21**
Hainauer, Schirmer, 1886, 25p.
CU(M203M14op.21), CtY(M204M138+op.21), DLC(M3.3.M14op.21),
LNT(786.2M14m), MBH(P.2B23), MB-N(P.2M14), MoSW(M204
M148M), NNLc(°MYDop.21), NRU-E(M204M138M), NcU(M786.492
M138c1), OCl(M776.402.6136), WM(786.41M13m)
1. **Das Hindumädchen** (The Hindoo Maiden); 2. **Storch-
geschichte** (Story of the Stork); 3. **In Tyrol** (In the
Tyrol); 4. **Der Schwan** (The Swan); 5. **Bärenbesuch** (Visit
of the Bears)
Drei Poesien, Op.20
Hainauer, 1886, 19p.
CtY(M204M138+op.20), DLC(M3.3.M14op.20), LNT(786.2M14po),
MB-N(P2.M14.1), MoSW(Spec.M203M148P), NNLc(°MYD+box op.20),
NRU-E(M204M138P), NcU(M786.492M138c), PP(MCH.26MAC.4),
WM(786.41M13d)
1. **Nachts am Meere** (Night by the Sea); 2. **Erzählung aus der
Ritterzeit** (A Tale from Knightly Times); 3. **Ballade**
(Ballad)
Die Sarazenen und die schöne Alda (Zwei Fragmente nach dem
Rolandslied), **Op.30**
Breitkopf, 1891, 17p.
DLC(M3.3.M14op.30B), MBH(P.2M14.1), MoS(786.49), NNLc(°MYD-
Amer), NRU-E(M209M13H), PP(MCH.26MAC.5), WM(786.41M13)

MASON, WILLIAM (1829-1908)

Amitié pour Amitié, Op.4
BrainardS, 1868, 11p.
CtY(Mc70M38)
Arranged for piano duet by Karl Klauser.

MERZ, KARL (1836-1890)

Welcome to the Hero (Grande Polonaise militaire)
Whittemore, 1865, 15p.
DLC(M212.M)

MORAN, PETER K. (d.1831)

"Ah Beauteous Maid if Thou'lt be Mine" (with Variations)
Jackson, n.d., 9p.
InU(M1.S8), NNLc(AM2-I)
Same composition as **"Fal Lal La"** (see below).

A Duett (In which are introduced **The Tyrolese Air** and
   Copenhagen Waltz)
      Dubois, 182_?, 7p. [W.II:594]
      CtY(Mc7OM793), DLC(M1.A13M Case), ICN(Case sm oM1.A13no.1498),
         InU(M1.S8), NNLc(AM1-I; AM2-I), NRU-E(U), RPB(U), ViU(°M1.
         S444,v.75,no.10; McR.17.54)
"Fal Lal La" (A Favorite Air)
      DuboisS, n.d., 9p.
      DLC(M1.A13M), ICN(Case sm oM1.A13no.1305), NNLc(AM1-I)
      Same composition as **"Ah Beauteous Maid"** (see above).
Popular Airs (among which is "Hail Columbia")
      DuboisS, ca.1825-1837, 11p.
      ICN(Case sm oM1.A13no.1423)

NEVIN, ETHELBERT (1862-1901)

   Country Dance, Op.6, No.2 (see **Three Dances, Op.6**)
   Three Dances, Op.6
      Boston, 1890, 3v.(8,11,10p.)
      CtHT(U, 2 only), CtY(Mc6ON41+op.6), DLC(M204.N, 2 only),
         InU(M1.S8), IU(qM786.49N417v, 1 only), MBH(P.2N41), MB-N
         (Piano, 2 only), MoS(786.49), MoSW(U), NNLc(°MYD-Amer),
         NRU-E(M204N52), PP(U, 1,2 only), WM(786.41N52t)
      1. **Valse Caprice**; 2. **Country Dance**; 3. **Mazurka**
   Mazurka, Op.6, No.3 (see **Three Dances, Op.6**)
   Valse Caprice, Op.6, No.1 (see **Three Dances, Op.6**)
   Valzer gentile, Op.7, No.1
      SchirmerJr, 1890, 7p.
      CtY(Mc11A1N418), DLC(M212.N), MoS(786.4), PP(U)

PAINE, JOHN KNOWLES (1839-1906)

   Prelude to the Scenes from "The Birds" of Aristophanes
      Boston, 1905, 21p.
      IU(qM786.49P166p)
      Skillful arrangement from the orchestral score.

WELS, CHARLES (1825-1906)

   Race for Life (Galop brillant), **Op.87**
      Ditson-CH, 1870, 15p.
      ViU(°M1.S444,v.31,no.9)

WOLLENHAUPT, HERMANN (1827-1863)

   Stories of Nocomis (Pictures of the West. 4 Morceaux caracté-
      ristiques), **Op.48**
      Schirmer, 1858, 29p.
      CtHT(U), NNLc(AM2-I), ViU(McR.145.23)

IV
Music for Two Pianos

BEACH, AMY MARCY CHENEY (1867-1944)

Suite for Two Pianos founded upon Old Irish Melodies, Op.104
Church, 1924, 4v.(28,23,25,34p.)
DLC(M214.B37S7), MBH(P.3B35), NRU-E(M214B36), PP(MFCh.25,
Bea.1), WM(786.42B36)
1. Prelude; 2. Old-Time Peasant-Dance; 3. The Ancient
Cabin; 4. Finale
Magnificent, very difficult concert work.
Variations on Balkan Themes, Op.60
Schmidt, 1942, 2v.in 1(20p.)
DLC(M215.B36op.60), MBH(P.3B35.2 2v.), NNLc(°MYD 1942),
NRU-E(M25B365v)
Difficult, rewarding variation set.

BLOCH, ERNEST (1880-1959)

Evocations
Schirmer, 1938, 41p.
CU(M215B55), MoS(786.491), OCL(M776.4022.1573)
1. Contemplation; 2. Houang-Ti God of War; 3. Renouveau
The composer's arrangement of his orchestral trilogy.

BOEKELMAN, BERNARDUS (1838-1930)

Marche d'Inauguration (2 pianos, 8 hands)
Schuberth-E, 1885, 22p.
CtY(R Mc97B62), DLC(M216.B72), PP(MFCh.25aBoe.1), ViU
(Music M216.B6 1885), WM(786.43B67m)
A welcome item in eight-hand repertoire.

Polonaise de Concert, Op.4 (2 pianos, 8 hands)
    Schuberth-E, 1889, 21p.
    CtY(R Mc97B62)
    Arrangement by H. W. Nicholl

BURMEISTER, RICHARD (1860-1944)

Organ Fantasia and Fugue in G Minor (Transcription from J. S.
    Bach)
    International, 1945, 23p.
    OC(R786.491fB1b, filed under Bach)
Etüden in Variationenform, Op.13 von Robert Schumann
    Luckhardt, 1889, 47p.
    MoSW(U)

CONRATH, LOUIS (1868-1927)

Intermezzo
    Kunkel, 1899, 11p.
    DLC(M214.C75 I5), MoSW(U)
Sarabande and Variations (Suite in form of Characteristic
    Pieces)
    Kunkel, 1897, 29p.
    DLC(M214.C75 S3)

GEBHARD, HEINRICH (1878-1963)

Waltz Suite
    Schirmer-EC, 1929, 26p.
    DLC(M215.G3W2), MBH(P.3B12.8), NRU-E(M214G293w), OCl(M776.
      4022.414)
    Seven sparkling, attractive waltzes.

GODOWSKY, LEOPOLD (1870-1938)

Contrapuntal Paraphrase on Weber's "Invitation to the Dance"
    Fischer, 1922, 3 parts in 1v.(74p.)
    CU(M215G618C6P), DLC(ML96.G56Case), NNLc(°MYD), PP(MFCh.25
      God.10 Box475)
    Also included is an optional accompaniment of a third piano.
      A mammoth, very difficult and overwhelming keyboard work.

GOTTSCHALK, LOUIS MOREAU [SEVEN OCTAVES] (1829-1869)

Jerusalem (Verdi's I Lombardi. Fantaisie triomphale), Op.84
    Hartmann, n.d., 26p.
    CtY(R Mc80G71)
    Terrific, virtuosic two-piano paraphrase.

GRUNN, HOMER (1880-1944)

Humoresque nègre
    Schirmer, 1934, 7p.
    DLC(M214.G88H9), OO(786.492.2nG926.H)

HESSELBERG, EDOUARD [D'ESSENELLI] (1870-1935)

Russian Rhapsody (Based on Traditional Folk Songs and Dances)
    Presser, 1930, 22p.
    DLC(M214.H56R6)

HILL, EDWARD BURLINGAME (1872-1960)

Jazz Study, Op.7, No.1
    Schirmer, 1924, 7p.
    DLC(M214.H625J3), IU(qM786.492H55j), LNT(M214.H55J3no.1),
      MBH(P.3B12.4), MB-N(U), MoSW(U), NcD(M786.493H645J),
      OCl(M776.4022.4712), PP(U), WM(786.42H645j)
Jazz Study No.2
    Schirmer, 1935, 7p.
    DLC(M214.H625J3), IU(qM786.492H55j), MB-N(U), NcD(M786.493
      H645J), WM(786.42H645j)
Jazz Study No.3
    Schirmer, 1935, 9p.
    DLC(M214.H625J3), IU(qM786.492H55j), MB-N(U), NcD(M786.493
      H645J), WM(786.42H645j)
Jazz Study No.4
    Schirmer, 1935, 11p.
    DLC(M214.H625J3), IU(qM786.492H55j), MB-N(U), NcD(M786.493
      H645J)

HOLST, EDUARD (ca.1843-1899)

Dance of the Demon (Grand Galop de Concert. 2 pianos, 8 hands)
    Rohlfing, 1888, 21p.
    DLC(M216.H680D3), MoS(786.493)
March of the Phantoms (Grand March de Concert. 2 pianos, 8
hands)
    Rohlfing, 1888, 20p.
    DLC(M216.H68M3), MoS(786.493)
The Sleigh Ride (Grand Galop de Concert. 4 hands or 8 hands)
    Rohlfing, 1890, 11p.
    CtY(R Mc98H74 [8h.]), DLC(M213.H75H3 [8h.]), MoS(786.493
      [4h.]), PP(U [4h.])

IVES, CHARLES (1874-1954)

Three Quarter-Tone Pieces

Peters-CF, 1968, 26p.
CU(M214 I94Q8), CtY(M215I95Q1+), DLC(M215.I), IU(M215 I94
Q8), LNT(M215.I), MB-N(M215 I95Q3), NNLc(°MYD-Amer),
NRU-E(M214 I95Q), NcU(M214.I9Q3), OCl(M776.4022.5083),
ViU(Music M215I95Q3 1968)
The two pianos are tuned one quarter-tone apart.

KAUN, HUGO (1863-1932)

Erste Suite, Op.92
  Zimmermann, 1913, 31p.
  DLC(M24.K21op.92), MoSW(U), PP(MFCh.25Kau.2box478), WM
  (786.42K21e)
  1. **Märkische Heide**; 2. **Abendstimmung**; 3. **Menuett**
Suite (im alten Styl), **Op.81**
  Heinrichshofen, 1917, 45p., also issued separately
  DLC(M214.K21op.81, 2 only), NNLc(°MYD), PP(MFCh.25Kau.1),
  WM(786.4K21pi, 2 only)
  1. **Praeludium**; 2. **Passacaglia**; 3. **Gavotte**; 4. **Gigue**
  Large-scale serious concert work.

KELLER, WALTER (1873-1940)

Prelude and Fugue in F, Op.10
  Gilbert, 1919, 7p.
  DLC(M214.K26P6), IU(MaLq786.4K28p), MBH(P.3B12.5), NNLc
  (°MYD+box)
  When played simultaneously, the Prelude and Fugue become
  a work for two pianos!

KUNKEL, CHARLES [JEAN PAUL, CLAUDE MELNOTTE] (1840-1923)

Grand Fantasie on Themes from Gounod's opera "Faust"
  Kunkel, 1898, 25p.
  DLC(M215.G7K7)

LEVY, HENIOT (1879-1946)

In the Fall
  Summy, 1935, 5p.
  DLC(M214.L55 I5)
Ping-Pong
  Summy, 1935, 5p.
  DLC(M214.L55 P4)

MACFADYEN, ALEXANDER (1879-1936)

Country Dance (2 pianos, 8 hands)

Church, 1922, 2 parts(9,9p.)
WM(786.43M14c)

MASON, DANIEL GREGORY (1873-1953)

Divertimento, Op.26a
    Fischer, 1927, 2v.(15,13p.)
    DLC(M214.M44op.26), MBH(P.3B12.4), MoSW(U)
    1. March; 2. Fugue
    Also available for wind quintet.
Scherzo, Op.22b
    Fischer, 1931, 27p.
    DLC(M214.M43op.22b), NNLc(°MYD-Amer)

PIRANI, EUGENIO (1852-1939)

Airs bohémiens, Op.35
    Schlesinger, n.d., 13p.
    LNT(786.3P66ai)
Etude de Concert, Op.51
    Schlesinger, 1893, 15p.
    DLC(M214.P66op.51), NNLc(°MYD+box)
Gavotte, Op.34
    Schlesinger, n.d., 7p.
    CtY(U), LNT(786.3P66g), MoS(786.491), WM(786.42P66)

PLATT, RICHARD (1877-d. ?)

Prelude and Pastorale
    Ditson, 1927, 2v.(11,12p.)
    DLC(M214.P716), MBH(P.3B12.9), NRU-E(M214P719pr; M214
        P719pa)

PREYER, CARL A. (1863-1947)

Thousand and One Nights (Joh. Strauss. Transcription)
    Marks, 1949, 24p.
    KU(M786.49.P92t)

SAAR, LOUIS VICTOR (1868-1937)

A Second Piano Part to the Fifteen Two-Part Inventions of
    J. S. Bach
    Schirmer, 1932, 39p.
    MBH(P.3B12.8), MB-N(786.48Sa), NcU(M786.494B11i2.1)
Suite (Arranged and adapted from Serenade No.7, K.250 [Haffner]
    by Mozart)
    Schirmer, 1927, 39p.

CU(M215M68K250 1927)
1. **Minuetto;** 2. **Romance;** 3. **Scherzo;** 4. **Rondo**
Arranged from movements 1-4 of Mozart's Serenade.

SEEBOECK, WILLIAM CHARLES ERNEST (1859-1907)

  Minuet à l'Antico (arranged by Victor Saar)
      Church, 1919, 9p.
      DLC(M215.S), MoSW(U), NRU-E(M215S451mS), OCl(M776.4022.
      8204

SPROSS, CHARLES GILBERT (1874-1961)

  Valse Caprice
      Church, 1914, 2v.(11,12p.)
      NPA(780S)

STRONG, TEMPLETON (1856-1948)

  An der Hexenhöhle, Op.29, No.3 (see **Drei Sinfonische Idyllen,**
      Op.29)
  An der Nixenquelle, Op.29, No.2 (see **Drei Sinfonische Idyllen,**
      Op.29)
  Trois Morceaux
      Henn, 1924, 11p.
      DLC(M214.S9M7)
      1. **Intrada;** 2. **Sarabande;** 3. **Babillage**
  Drei Sinfonische Idyllen, Op.29
      Jost, 1887, 3v.(11,21,41p.)
      DLC(M214.S9op.29), LNT(786.3St84pt.1, 2 only), MoSW(U, 3 only)
      1. **Unter den Tannen** (Elfenspiel); 2. **An der Nixenquelle;**
         3. **An der Hexenhöhle**
  Unter den Tannen, Op.29, No.1 (see **Drei Sinfonische Idyllen,**
      Op.29)

V
Music for Piano and Orchestra

BEACH, AMY MARCY CHENEY (1867-1944)

Concerto in C-sharp Minor, Op.45
   Breitkopf, Schmidt, 1900, 87p. (Arr. two pianos)
   CtY(H Mn32B35+op.45), DLC(M1011.B36op.45), ICN(6A 1517),
      MBH(P.3B35.1), MB-N(M1011B38no.1 1900), NNLc(JNG 73-300)
Concerto in C-sharp Minor, Op.45
   Breitkopf, 1900, 141p. (Score)
   PP(Fl.320p)

BLOCH, ERNEST (1880-1959)

Concerto Grosso (for String Orchestra with Piano Obbligato)
   SummyB, 1925, 48p.(Score)
   CU(M1110B66 1925), ICN(VM1040B62c), IU(M1110B49C6), NcD
      (M785.6B651C), NcU(M785.6B651c), OCl(M775.91.163),
      PP(Fl.1117s), WM(786.6B65co)
   1. Prelude; 2. Dirge; 3. Pastorale and Rustic Dances;
      4. Fugue
Concerto symphonique
   BooseyH, 1950, 110p. (Arr. two pianos)
   DLC(M1011.B63C6), IU(qM786.492B62cs), MoS(786.491), OCl
      (M776.4022.1572), WM(786.42B651c)
Concerto symphonique
   BooseyH, 1950, 249p. (Score)
   CU(M1010B547 1950), DLC(M1010B63C6), MB-N(Min.M1010B58C6),
      NcD(M785.61B651c), NcU(Min.M785.6B651c), OCl(M776.6.1665),
      WM(786.662B651c)
Scherzo fantasque
   Schirmer, 1950, 40p. (Arr. two pianos)
   DLC(M1011B63S3), MoS(786.491), NNLc(°MYD), WM(786.42B651s)

Scherzo fantasque
Schirmer, 1950, 74p. (Score)
CU(M1010B55 1950), DLC(M1010.B63S3 1950a), ICN(VM1010B65s),
IU(M1010B63S3 1950A), MoS(M785.8), NcD(M785.6B651S), NcU
(M786.494B651s), PP(FL.264p)

BOISE, OTIS BARDWELL (1844-1912)

Concerto in G moll
Hofmeister, 1889, 37p. (Arr. two pianos)
IU(Joseffy), NNLc(°MYD)
One of the first concertos written by a native-born American.
Peabody Conservatory has the manuscript orchestral score.

BOROWSKI, FELIX (1872-1956)

Concerto, Ré Mineur
ComposerMC, 1921, 74p. (Arr. two pianos)
DLC(M1011.B73), NNLc(°MYD), PP(U), WM(786.42B74c)

BURMEISTER, RICHARD (1860-1944)

Concert in D moll
Luckhardt, Schirmer, 1890, 67p. (Arr. two pianos)
DLC(M1011.B95), IU(Joseffy)

CARPENTER, JOHN ALDEN (1876-1951)

Concertino
Schirmer, 1920, 65p. (Arr. two pianos)
DLC(M1011.C26C5), IU(qM786.492C22c), MoS(786.491), NcD
(M785.61C295c), NcU(M786.494C429c), ViU(Music M1011
C36C6), WM(786.42C295c)
Concertino
Schirmer, 1920, 80p. (Score)
CU(M1010C25 1920), DLC(M1010.C28), LNT(786.3C22co)

CLIFTON, ARTHUR [P. A. CORRI] (1784-1832)

Concerto da Camera for the Piano Forte (with Accompaniments
for Two Violins, Flute, Viola and Violoncello) [Corri]
Chappell, 1812, 6 parts
PP(U)

CONRATH, LOUIS (1868-1927)

Concerto in B-flat Minor

Kunkel, 1894, 47p. (Arr. two pianos)
DLC(M1011.C75), NNLc(°MYD), OCl(M776.4022.2445)

CONVERSE, FREDERICK SHEPHERD (1871-1940)

Concertino
Birchard, 1940, 49p. (Arr. two pianos)
DLC(M1011.C76C6), MB-N(M3.3C66C6662)
Night and Day, Op.11
Boston, 1906, 61p. (Arr. two pianos)
DLC(M1011.C76op.11), MBH(P.3B35.1), NRU-E(M215C76)
Two unusual tone poems for piano and orchestra.
Night and Day, Op.11
Boston, 1906, 89p. (Score)
DLC(M1010.C76op.11), MBH(OS.3C768.1), NNLc(°MW-Amer)
  PP(Fl.337p)

GANZ, RUDOLPH (1877-1972)

Concerto in E-flat Major, Op.32
Fischer, 1945, 84p. (Arr. two pianos)
DLC(M1011.G22op.32), NNLc(°MYD), OCl(M776.4022.406)
An expertly-designed, inspired and difficult work.
Konzertstück, Op.4
Schmidt, 1902, 32p. (Arr. two pianos)
DLC(M1011.G22op.4)

GEBHARD, HEINRICH (1878-1963)

Divertissement (Piano and Chamber Orchestra)
SchirmerEC, 1932, 44p. (Arr. two pianos)
DLC(M1011.G314), NNLc(°MYD+), NRU-E(M215G29D)
A sparkling work eminently worth reviving.

GOTTSCHALK, LOUIS MOREAU [SEVEN OCTAVES] (1829-1869)

Grand Tarantelle, Op.67
BooseyH, 1963, 40p. (Arr. two pianos)
CU(M1011G673op.67), CtY(M1011G687+op.67), DLC(M1011.G665
  op.67), LNH(U), MoS(786.491)
Solo piano edited by Eugene List. One of the most delight-
  ful short works in the repertoire.
Grand Tarantelle, Op.67
BooseyH, 1964, 66p. (Score)
CU(M1010G673op.67), DLC(M1010.G756op.67), IU(qM786.492
  G716t), MoS(785.8), NNLc(°MW-Amer), NRU-E(M215G687g),
  PP(786.492G716t; Fl.283p)
Score reconstructed and orchestrated by Hershy Kay.

HADLEY, HENRY (1871-1937)

Concertino, Op.131
   Birchard, 1937, 40p. (Arr. two pianos)
   DLC(M1011.H12op.131), NNLc(°MYD+), NRU-E(M215H131c)

HUSS, HENRY HOLDEN (1862-1953)

Concerto in B, Op.10
   Schirmer, 1898, 66p. (Arr. two pianos)
   DLC(M1011.H97op.10 1898), IU(Joseffy), MBH(P.3C356.1),
    MB-N(M1011A2P5v.5), NNLc(°°MYD), NcD(M785.61H972C)
   Extremely difficult, lushly romantic composition.

HUTCHESON, ERNEST (1871-1951)

March (for Two Pianos and Orchestra of Strings)
   Fischer, 1928, 2v.(21,21p., piano scores and parts)
   NNLc(°MW-Amer), NRU-E(M1145H973m), PP(Fl.560p)
   A most unusual, original concept.

JOSEFFY, RAFAEL (1852-1915)

Mährchen (Scherzo fantastique)
   Prochàzka, 1884, 23p. (Arr. two pianos)
   OC(786.49fV91.1)

KAUN, HUGO (1863-1932)

Concert, B Dur, Op.19
   Rohlfing, 1889, 40p. (Arr. two pianos)
   DLC(M1011.K22op.19), PP(U)
Concert, Op.50
   Rahter, 1903, 59p. (Arr. two pianos)
   DLC(M1011.K22op.50), ICN(VM1011K21c), MBH(OS.2K16), MoSW
    (U), NNLc(°MW), PP(U)
Concert, Op.50
   Rahter, 1903, 125p. (Score)
   DLC(M1010.K26op.50), ICN(VM1010K21c), NRU-E(M1010.K213.1),
    PP(Fl.627p), WM(R786.42K21CF)

LIEBLING, GEORG (1865-1946)

Concerto eroico, Op.22
   Oppenheimer, 1900, 55p. (Arr. two pianos)
   DLC(M1011.L72op.22), NRU-E(M215D853)
   A popular and frequently performed concerto in its day.

LOEFFLER, CHARLES MARTIN (1861-1935)

A Pagan Poem, Op.14 (after Virgil)
  Schirmer, 1909, 63p. (Arr. two pianos by H. Gebhard)
  CtY(Mn32L82+op.14), DLC(M215.L83P3), NNLc(°MYD), NRU-E
    (M215L825p), PPi(qM786.4901 L76p.)
  A superb tone poem for orchestra with piano, English Horn
    and three offstage trumpets.
A Pagan Poem, Op.14 (after Virgil)
  Schirmer, 1909, 107p. (Score)
  PP(FL.1975)

MAAS, LOUIS (1852-1889)

Concert in C moll, Op.12
  Breitkopf, n.d., 71p. (Arr. two pianos)
  PP(MCH.25 MAA.15box481)
Concert in C moll, Op.12
  Breitkopf, 1887, 300p. (Score)
  PP(FL.480p)

MACDOWELL, EDWARD (1860-1908)

Concerto No.1 in A Minor, Op.15
  Breitkopf, 1910, 53p. (Arr. two pianos)
  CU(M37M22c.1), CtY(Mn32M14+op.15), DLC(M1011.M15op.15), IU
    (qM786.492M14c1), LNT(M1011.M3op.15), MBH(P.1M14.4), MB-N
    (M1011A2P5v.5), MoSW(M1011.M148no.1), NNLc(°MYDop.15),
    NRU-E(M215M138.1), OCl(M776.4022.6125), PP(U), WM(786.42
    M13)
Concerto No.1 in A Minor, Op.15
  Breitkopf, 1911, 116p. (Score)
  DLC(M1010.M13op.15), ICN(Case ms VM 1010M13c1), IU(M1010.
    M23op.15 B7), NNLc(°MW-Amer.op.15), NRU-E(M1010.M138.1),
    OCl(M776.6.6021), PP(FL.409p)
Concerto No.2 in D Minor, Op.23
  Breitkopf, 1890, 45p. (Arr. two pianos)
  CU(M1011M14c.2 1890, 1922), CtY(M1011M138+op.23S3), DLC(M1011.
    M15op.23), ICN(VM1011M13c2), IU(qM786.492M14c2), LN(U),
    LNT(M1011.M3op.23), MBH(P.3cM14), MB-N(M1011A2P5v.5),
    MoSW(M1011M148no.2), NNLc(°MYDop.23), NRU-E(M215M138.2),
    NcD(M785.61M138DPop.23), NcU(M786.4M138c2), OCl(M776.4022.
    613), PP(786.492M148c2), WM(786.42M13c)
  One of the great romantic concertos of all times. Compares
    admirably with any similar European works of this type.
Concerto No.2 in D Minor, Op.23
  Breitkopf, 1907, 98p. (Score)
  DLC(M1010.M13op.23), ICN(VM1010M13c2), MoS(785.6), MoSW
    (M1010M148no.2), NNLc(°MW-Amer.op.23), NcU(M785.6M138c2),
    NRU-E(M1010M138.2), OCl(M775.6.60221), PP(785.6M148c2;
    FL.365p)

MACFADYEN, ALEXANDER (1879-1936)

Concertstück, Op.19
    Badger, 1926, 54p. (Arr. two pianos)
    DLC(M1011.M17op.19), MoSW(U), WM(786.42M14c)

MASON, DANIEL GREGORY (1873-1953)

Prelude and Fugue, Op.20
    Fischer-J, 1933, 33p. (Arr. two pianos)
    CtY(Mn32M38+op.20), DLC(M1011.M417op.20), NNLc(°MYD),
      NRU-E(M215M398p), ViU(°M215M28op.20 1933), WM(786.42M39)
Prelude and Fugue, Op.20
    Fischer-J, 1933, 63p. (Score)
    DLC(M1010.M417op.20), IU(MaLq786.492M38p), NNLc(°MW-Amer.+),
      PP(FL.688p)

OLDBERG, ARNE (1874-1962)

Symphonic Concerto in G Minor, Op.17
    Wa-Wan, 1907, 73p. (Arr. two pianos)
    CU(M1011 065op.17CaseX), DLC(M1011.044op.17), IEN(M1011.
      054op.17), NNLc(°MYD), also in WW-L(V:1)
    A significant, mature work worthy of performance today.

PALMER, COURTLANDT (1872-1951)

Concerto
    Hug, 1941, 34p. (Arr. two pianos)
    DLC(M1011.P18C6), NNLc(°MYD)
Concerto
    Hug, 1941, 69p. (Score)
    DLC(M1010.P325C6), NNLc(°MW-Amer)

PIRANI, EUGENIO (1852-1939)

Fantasia (per 2 Pianoforte o per Pianoforte con Orchestra),
  Op.87
    Schlesinger, 1908, 23p. (Arr. two pianos)
    DLC(M1011.P65op.87), MoSW(U)
Scene veneziane, Op.44
    Schlesinger, n.d., 51p. (Score)
    DLC(M1010.P66op.44), LNT(786.3P66s), NNLc(°MW), PP(U;
      FL.571p)
    1. Gondolata; 2. In San Marco; 3. Ultima notte di
    carnevale
    Three very original descriptive scenes.

· **PREYER, CARL** (1863-1947)

Concertstück, Op.49
 Breitkopf, 1908, 39p. (Arr. two pianos)
 DLC(M214.P92C7), KU(Univ.Archives), NRU-E(M214P944)
 KU University Archives has the manuscript score orches-
  trated by Carl Busch of which the Philadelphia Free
  Library has a copy (Fl.713p).

RALSTON, FRANCES [FANNY] MARION (1875-1952)

Rhapsodie, Op.50
 Morrison, 1938, 40p. (Arr. two pianos)
 DLC(M1011.R19op.50)

SCHELLING, ERNEST (1876-1939)

Impressions from an Artist's Life (Symphonic Variations)
 Leuckart, 1925, 88p. (Arr. two pianos)
 NNLc(°°MYD)
Impressions from an Artist's Life (Symphonic Variations)
 Leuckart, 1925, 145p. (Score)
 MU(ScoreM1010S322I5), PP(Fl.528p)
Suite fantastique, Op.7
 Rahter, 1908, 68p. (Arr. two pianos)
 DLC(M1011.S33op.7), ICN(Case8A 1695no.33), MoSW(U), NRU-E
  (M215.S32), PP(U)
 1. Allegro marziale; 2. Scherzo; 3. Intermezzo;
  4. Virginia Reel
  Original addition to piano and orchestra literature.
Suite fantastique, Op.7
 Rahter, 1908, 99p. (Score)
 DLC(M1010.S32op.7), ICN(VM1010S32s), NRU-E(M1010S322S),
  PP(Fl.423p)

STOJOWSKI, SIGISMUND (1876-1946)

Concerto en Fa dièze, Op.3
 Lucas, Stevens, 1893, 79p. (Arr. two pianos)
 DLC(M1011.S87+op.3), ICN(VM1011S87c), IU(Joseffy), MBH
  (P.3P13), MB-N(M1011.S87op.3), MoSW(U), NNLc(°MYD)
Concerto en Fa dièze, Op.3
 Lucas, 1893, 102p. (Score)
 DLC(M1010.S87op.3), ICN(VM1010S87c), IU(Joseffy), NRU-E
  (M1010S873), PP(Fl.605p)
Prologue, Scherzo et Variations (2e Concerto), **Op.32**
 Heugel, 1914, 61p. (Arr. two pianos)
 DLC(M1011.S87op.32), ICN(VM1011S87c2), MB-N(M1011.S87
  op.32), NNLc(°MYD+)
Prologue, Scherzo et Variations, Op.32

  Heugel, 1923, 197p. (Score)
  DLC(M1010.S87op.32), PP(Fl.614p)
Rhapsodie symphonique, Op.23
  Peters-CF, 1907, 35p. (Arr. two pianos)
  MoSW(U), NNLc(°°MYD)
Rhapsodie symphonique, Op.23
  Peters-CF, 1907, 64p. (Score)
  DLC(M1010.S87op.23), NNLc(°°MW), NcU(M786.4S87c3)

VOGRICH, MAX (1852-1916)

  Grosses Concert in E moll
  Schirmer, 1888, 87p. (Arr. two pianos)
  DLC(M1011.V88), IU(Joseffy)

WHITING, ARTHUR (1861-1936)

  Fantasy, Op.11
  Schirmer, 1897, 43p. (Arr. two pianos)
  DLC(M1011.W59op.11), IU(Joseffy), MBH(P.3Sa2), MB-N
    (M3.3W53op.11A2), NNLc(°MYD+), NRU-E(M215W598)

VI
Composer Biography-Index

ALDEN, JOHN CARVER (b. Boston, MA, 17 September 1852; d. Cambridge, MA, 20 October 1935). Teacher, pianist, composer. He studied the piano with Carl Faelton at the New England Conservatory in Boston, and had further training at the Leipzig Conservatory under Oscar Paul and Benjamin Papperitz. In 1880 he was hired as Faelton's teaching associate at the New England Conservatory and by 1886 had become a permanent faculty member. He also taught at the Quincy Mansion School in Wollaston, MA (1897-98) and at Converse College, Spartanburg, SC, where he spent 19 years (1903-22), then retired and returned to New England. Alden's music is conservative, rhythmically and melodically interesting, consistently idiomatic. [I,II]

AMBROSE, PAUL (b. Hamilton, Ontario, Canada, 11 October 1868; d. Hamilton, 1 June 1941). Organist, teacher, composer. Born into a family of organists (father, grandfather, great-grandfather), he studied first with his father, composer Robert Steele Ambrose, at the Collegiate Institute in Ontario. In 1886 he moved to New York City, where he continued his studies with Albert Ross Parsons, Kate Chittenden, Samuel Prowse Warren, Bruno Oscar Klein and Dudley Buck, and immediately launched his long career as organist and choirmaster. He served four years at the Madison Avenue Methodist Episcopal Church (1886-90) and more than 25 years at St. James's Methodist Episcopal Church (1890-1917). In addition to his church work he taught music and lectured on music history at various institutions in the area, including the Westminster School, Simsbury, CT and the American Institute of Applied Music (formerly the Metropolitan Conservatory) in New York. From 1903 to 1934 he lived in Trenton, NJ. He taught piano at the State Normal School (1903-17), was organist-choirmaster at the First Presbyterian Church (1917-33) and attained a reputation as one of Trenton's leading musicians. Although he retired to his birthplace in January, 1934, he remained active, serving as guest organist at Christ Church Cathedral and as a member of the Canadian College of Organists. Ambrose was a conservative composer whose music presents an interesting challenge in technical and rhythmic matters. [I]

AYRES, FREDERIC (b. Binghamton, NY, 17 March 1876; d.   Colorado Springs, CO, 23 November 1926). Teacher, composer. His name was Frederic   Ayres   Johnson   but   he   used   "Frederic   Ayres" professionally. After graduating from Binghamton High School, he spent a year at Cornell University (1892-93) studying electrical engineering, had another two years of private study, then was hired by the Stow Manufacturing Company in Binghamton to design a line of small electric motors. Despite his success in inventing a system of motor speed control patented as "multispeed motors," he gave up engineering in 1897 when he found an opportunity to study musical composition, which he described as his "proper work." He studied with Edgar Stillman Kelley in New York (1897-1901) and Arthur Foote in Boston during the summer of 1899, then poor health interrupted his studies and caused him to move to Las Cruces, NM in 1901. The next year he tried the climate at Colorado Springs, where he regained his health and remained for the rest of his life, devoting his time to composing, teaching privately and writing. Ayres was an   original,   forward-looking   composer   who   admired   and   used contrapuntal techniques. [I]

BAERMANN, CARL (b. Munich, Germany, 9 July 1839; d.   Newton, MA, 17 January 1913). Teacher, pianist, composer. He came naturally to music at an early age, for he was born into a family of distinguished musicians: grandfather Heinrich Joseph was a celebrated clarinettist, great-uncle Carl a famous bassoonist and his father Carl was another well-known clarinettist. He studied with Franz Lachner and Peter Cornelius in Munich, and made his professional début at the age of 15. When he later studied with Liszt, he became a favorite pupil and the two formed a lasting friendship. Baermann established his own reputation as a concert pianist and was appointed a royal professor by King Ludwig of Bavaria. Having been granted a two-year leave of absence, he visited America in 1881, made a spectacular début in Boston, MA and decided to remain. For the next three decades he concertized (more performances with the Boston Symphony Orchestra than any other performer of the time) and taught, both privately and at the New England Conservatory. He was especially influential in improving the public taste, not only through his programs but through his many students (notably Amy Beach and Frederick L. Converse) who in turn imbued their pupils with his high standards. The Baermann Society (1908-13), formed by a group of prominent Bostonians to honor him for his contribution to American music and to foster his high ideals, is witness to the fine reputation he held in his own time. Baermann's music is noted for its superb craftsmanship and innate beauty. [I]

BARBOUR, FLORENCE NEWELL (b. Providence, RI, 4 August 1866; d. Providence, 24 July 1946). Pianist, poet, artist, composer. She was educated in the Providence public schools and studied music with her mother, an accomplished musician. In 1885 she became organist-choir director of the Fourth Baptist Church in Providence, and in 1891 moved to Rochester, NY, having married Dr. Clarence A. Barbour, pastor of the Lake Avenue Baptist Church in Rochester and later president of Colgate-Rochester Divinity School. After 38 years in Rochester, they returned to Providence when Dr. Barbour was appointed president of Brown University. Throughout her life Mrs. Barbour successfully managed several careers as wife, mother, composer and performer. She gave solo recitals, played with ensembles and orchestras and composed steadily, sometimes also writing the lyrics and designing and drawing the covers for her songs. Almost all of her large repertory was published by leading music firms. Mrs. Barbour's music is conservative, with interesting harmonies and a tendency to sentimental melody. [I]

BARTLETT, HOMER NEWTON (b. Olive, NY, 28 December 1845; d. Hoboken, NJ, 3 April 1920). Organist, teacher, composer. He was raised in Ellenville, NY, where his father owned a general store. A mostly self-taught prodigy, he played the violin in public at the age of eight, the piano at nine and was composing at ten. After graduating from the Ellenville Academy (1861), he studied with Emil Guyon, Alfred Pease, Sebastian Bach Mills, O. F. Jacobsen and Max Braun in New York, and unlike most American composers of that time he had all his musical education in the United States. During his long and distinguished career as teacher and organist in New York City, he took private pupils, was on the faculty of the Grand Conservatory of Music and was organist at the Old Spring Street Church, the Marble Collegiate Church and, for more than 30 years, at the Madison Avenue Baptist Church. Although his **Grande Polka de Concert, Op.1** (1867) was condescendingly described by Rupert Hughes as "outrageously popular," it stands as a brilliant example of the type of music demanded--and enjoyed--by mid-nineteenth century American society. From **Opus 1** he went on to write many important large-scale works and virtuoso piano pieces, and his music in general has been described as "distinctly sane, musical, interestingly harmonized, brilliant and always effective." [I,III]

BASSFORD, WILLIAM KIPP (b. New York, NY, 23 April 1839; d. Belleville, NJ, 22 December 1902). Organist, pianist, teacher, composer. As the son of an early New York piano manufacturer, he was familiar with music and musical celebrities from early childhood. He studied with Samuel P. Jackson and had "finishing lessons" with Louis Moreau Gottschalk. After touring the country for five years as concert pianist with various singers, he settled in New York as organist, composer and teacher. He was organist and music director at Dr. William Adams's church on Madison Avenue for 21 years, and later held organ positions at several churches in New Jersey, his last post being at Calvary Church, East Orange.

Contemporary reports describe him as a highly successful teacher. Bassford's best piano works, serious and well structured, could be considered salon music, due to a tendency to emphasize right-hand passages. [I]

BEACH, AMY MARCY CHENEY (b. Henniker, NH, 5 September 1867; d. New York, NY, 27 December 1944). Pianist, composer. Apparently a sensitive child with innate musical talent, remarkable memory and perfect pitch, she began music lessons at the age of six with her mother, a singer and pianist. After the family moved to Boston in 1875 she had piano lessons with Ernst Perabo and Carl Baermann, and on her own studied orchestral scores and theory texts. She was therefore self-taught in theory, except for one course with Junius W. Hill (winter, 1881-82). She made her début at the Boston Music Hall in 1883 and her first appearance with the Boston Symphony Orchestra in 1885, then that same year married Dr. Henry Harris Aubrey Beach, a prominent Boston surgeon 24 years her senior. She gave up concertizing after her marriage, but with the support of her husband, who gave her intelligent criticism and encouragement, she composed all during her married life, signing her works "Mrs. H. H. A. Beach." When Dr. Beach died in 1910, she made her first trip abroad and resumed her concert career, playing her own works in Hamburg, Leipzig, Berlin and other European cities (1911-14). In the meanwhile performances of her **Gaelic Symphony, Op.32** in Leipzig and Berlin strengthened her reputation as a composer. She returned to the United States and lived the rest of her life in New York City except when making concert tours or summering at either Cape Cod or the MacDowell Colony (1921-28, 1930-38) at Peterborough, NH. The foremost American woman composer of her day, she was also the first woman to write successfully in the larger forms. Her piano compositions reveal complex harmonies, altered chords, frequent modulations and some use of folk tunes. [I,IV,V]

BEACH, JOHN PARSONS (b. Gloversville, NY, 11 October 1877; d. Pasadena, CA, 6 November 1953). Pianist, teacher, composer. He studied music in Boston, MA with George Chadwick at the New England Conservatory, and privately with Clayton Johns and Charles M. Loeffler. After graduating from the Conservatory, he taught piano at the Northwestern Conservatory in Minneapolis, MN (1900-04), spent three years in New Orleans (1904-07) and then returned to Boston (1907-10). It was at this time that Arthur Farwell of the Wa-Wan Press gave him encouragement, helped him to find pupils and published 13 of his early compositions. In 1910 he began a seven-year stay in Europe during which time he studied with André Gédalge and Harold Bauer in Paris and fought on the Italian front during World War I. After the war he lived in New York City, then spent his last 18 years in Pasadena. In 1939 John Tasker Howard (**Our American Music**) placed Beach among "the modernists," along with Charles Ives and Carl Ruggles, and observed that he was "one of the first to branch into radical paths," but it is difficult now to find any radical characteristics in his piano music. [I]

BENEDICT, MILO ELLSWORTH (b. Cornwall, VT, 9 June 1866; d. Concord, NH, 17 December 1931). Teacher, composer. Considered a piano prodigy in his day, he was improvising at the age of four, by eight had composed several pieces, including a dirge on the death of a friend, and by nine was performing in public as "the boy pianist and musical wonder" of Vermont. From 1879 he was under the guidance of Carlyle Petersilea, head of the Petersilea Academy in Boston, MA, and while in Europe with Petersilea (1883-84) he spent three months at Weimar with Liszt. On returning to Boston, he continued his studies with Calixa Lavallée at the Academy and later became a teacher there. He was for many years a well-known piano teacher in Boston, and was also the Boston correspondent for the Chicago **Music News.** He moved to Concord, NH (city directories list him 1917-31), where he taught for a time at St. Paul's School and took private pupils up to the time of his death. His book **Musical People in Retrospect** (1931) contains recollections of celebrities he had known. Benedict's well-disciplined, elegant piano compositions show evidence of a substantial talent. [I]

BERGE, WILLIAM (b. Germany; d. New York, NY, March, 1883). Pianist, teacher, composer. He arrived in the United States around 1846, and lived mostly in New York. He became known as a pianist, and wrote many arrangements and transcriptions. His known piano works are strictly salon pieces. [I]

BETHUNE, THOMAS GREENE [known also as Thomas Greene Wiggins and popularly as "Blind Tom"] (b. Wiley Jones Plantation, Harris County, GA, 25 May 1849; d. Hoboken, NJ, 13 June 1908). Pianist, singer, composer. The year after his birth he was included as makeweight when his parents Charity and Mingo Wiggins, slaves on the Jones Plantation, were purchased at auction by General James N. Bethune, a lawyer from Columbus, GA. He had awesome handicaps, for he was born blind and as he developed he displayed strange behavior described variously as spinning, rocking or twitching, often with accompanying whoops, whines or weird cries. Although labeled an idiot, "Blind Tom" was more likely an **idiot savant** born with innate musical skills and a prodigiously retentive memory. Before he reached the age of four he could play the tunes he heard General Bethune's daughters play on the piano, at five he began to compose and at eight gave his first professional performance, an "exhibition" arranged by Bethune. From that time (1857) he toured and performed for about 35 seasons, always managed by guardians who in fact owned him, even after the emancipation of slaves, and reaped the profits of his skills. Before the Civil War he appeared only in the South; after the war his itinerary gradually expanded to include the whole United States and part of Canada; and in 1866 he caused a sensation in Europe, especially in England and Scotland. At a typical performance he played the piano and sang, often his own compositions; gave imitations of recitations (in Greek, Latin, German, French) or speeches (i.e., an American stump orator); did imitations of sounds (bagpipes, music box, rain, wind, water, storms, etc.); and finally played piano paraphrases of opera airs, usually a program's highlight because of Bethune's dazzling improvisations.   Sometimes he would astonish his audience with musical stunts, such as that described in the New York **Argus** (Jan., 1866): "With his right hand he plays 'Yankee Doodle' in B Flat. With his left hand he performs 'Fisher's Hornpipe' in C. At the same time he sings 'Tramp, Tramp' in another key--maintaining three distinct processes in that discord, and apparently without any effort whatever."   He added to his repertory by hearing other musicians play or sing.   For example, the composer William Henry Palmer gave him "lessons" by repeatedly playing such works as Thalberg's **Home, Sweet Home** and Mendelssohn's **Spring Song**; and a Major Macconico, owner of a baritone voice, sang "Rocked in the Cradle of the Deep" so that he might imitate the baritone and learn the song.   Because of his incredible memory he could play the piece or sing the song again anytime, even years later.   Although he was flamboyantly promoted, many testimonials exist as witness to his innate talent, notably that of Ignaz Moscheles on Sept. 11, 1866: "I happened to be present at a performance of his (Tom's) at Southsea, and ...began to test his abilities by extemporising a short rhythmical piece which he imitated to perfection...I went so far as to play him that part of my **Recollections of Ireland,** in which the three melodies are blended, and even that he imitated with most of its intricacies and changes...I next put my hands on the keys at random, and was surprised to hear him name every note of such flagrant discord...Tom's technical acquirements are very remarkable..."   The income generated by his unique talents went largely to a succession of owner-manager-guardians.   Shortly after his first exhibitions in 1857 he was leased out as a slave-musician to Perry Oliver, a tobacco planter from Savannah, GA. By 1862 he was back with Bethune, who after the Civil War became Tom's guardian-manager, described by Geneva Handy Southall, Bethune's biographer, as "legal re-enslavement."   From 1870 to 1884 he was managed by John G. Bethune, the General's son, who acquired legal guardianship on the grounds that Tom was **non compos mentis.**   After John Bethune's death in 1884, the General resumed control until John's widow (Eliza Bethune, later Eliza Lerche) acquired guardianship in 1887. She apparently exhibited him for some years, then kept him in seclusion at her home in Hoboken, NJ. When rumors of his death persisted, she allowed him to make a final appearance at the Circle Theater in New York in 1904. He was still in her custody when he died and was buried--as Thomas Wiggins--in the Evergreen Cemetery in Brooklyn, NY. Bethune wrote explicitly descriptive, flamboyant salon pieces for the piano.   [I]

BIRD, ARTHUR (b. Watertown, MA, 23 July 1856; d.   Berlin, Germany, 22 December 1923). Organist, pianist, writer, composer.   He had his first music lessons with his father and uncle, both noted singing teachers and also composers and compilers of hymn tunes.   During his teens he played the organ at various churches in the Boston area and was graduated from Watertown High School. In 1875 he took advanced music studies at the Berlin Hochschule under Carl Haupt,

Eduard Rohde and Albert Loeschhorn. When he returned to the United States (1877), he became the organist at St. Matthew's Church, Halifax, Nova Scotia and also taught at the Mount St. Vincent and the Young Ladies' academies there. In 1881 he returned to Berlin, where he studied with Heinrich Urban, and except for a brief return to the United States to conduct his second orchestral suite at the Milwaukee Musical Festival (July, 1886), he spent the rest of his life in and around Berlin. During 1885-86 he joined Liszt's ongoing circle of musical disciples at Weimar and had many of his compositions performed at Liszt's private gatherings. The first public concert of his works also took place in 1886 when the Berlin Philharmonic performed his symphony, overture and suite. Bird earned an excellent reputation in Germany, and most of his music was published there. Although he composed very little after 1895, he remained active in musical affairs. He was the Berlin correspondent for the Chicago journal **Musical Leader** and also wrote articles for **Etude, Musician** and other music periodicals. Bird's piano pieces show a large harmonic vocabulary and some rhythmic ingenuity. The music sounds fresh and spontaneous and is eminently well crafted. [I,III]

BLAKE, CHARLES DUPEE (b. Walpole, MA, 13 September 1846; d. Walpole, 23 November 1903). Organist, composer. He was one of the most prolific, successful and well-paid composers of his time. From about the age of nine he studied for five years with Handel Pond, a then well-known teacher, and later with John Knowles Paine and James Cutler Dunn Parker. Rather than compose serious compositions he preferred to write popular pieces having mass appeal, and it is estimated that he composed more than 5000 such works under as many as 11 different **noms de plume.** One of his most successful compositions, **Clayton's Grand March** sold more than 200,000 copies. He was a church organist from age 13, and held posts at several churches in the Boston area. When he moved to Providence, RI (1872) to work in the music store of the Cory Brothers, he became organist at the Church of the Mediator; however, because of the great demand for his compositions, he resigned as organist within a year to devote himself fully to composition. For most of his life he was affiliated with White, Smith and Co., the Boston firm that held an exclusive contract to publish all of his instrumental works. At its best Blake's piano music is melodious and facile, showing a tendency toward excess sentimentality. [I]

BLIND TOM [see **THOMAS GREENE BETHUNE**]

BLOCH, ERNEST (b. Geneva, Switzerland, 24 July 1880; d. Portland, OR, 15 July 1959). Teacher, composer. By the age of nine he had begun violin lessons with Albert Gos, a local teacher, and was writing pieces for his instrument. He later studied with Louis Rey and Emile Jaques-Dalcroze in Geneva (1894-96), with Eugène Ysaÿe and François Rasse in Brussels (1896-99), and with Ivan Knorr in Frankfort (1900-01). Then he spent nearly three years in Munich (1901-03) working independently except for some lessons with Ludwig Thuille, and another year in Paris, where he developed a close relationship with Debussy. When he returned to Geneva he married, went to work in his family's clock business and composed in his spare time. He conducted orchestral concerts at Neuchâtel and Lausanne (1909-10) and lectured on aesthetics at the Geneva Conservatory (1911-15). In 1916 he made his first visit to the United States as conductor for the Maud Allan dance company. Although the tour lasted only six weeks, he stayed in New York City, supporting himself by giving private lessons and also teaching at the David Mannes School of Music (1917-20) and the Julius Hartt School of Music in Hartford, CT (1919-20). He also conducted orchestral concerts of his own works, and acquired a reputation as a "Jewish" composer. He was the first director of the Cleveland Institute of Music (1920-25) but resigned because of resistance to changes he proposed in the curriculum; i.e., he wanted to eliminate examinations and textbooks and give students more direct musical experience. He was director of the San Francisco Conservatory (1925-30), and when he left there he was able to return to Europe, having been subsidized by sympathetic friends on the condition that he would devote himself to composition. He lived mostly in Switzerland (1930-38), where he composed and sometimes traveled to other cities to conduct his works with various orchestras, then because of anti-Semitic feeling in Europe and his desire to protect his American citizenship (1924), he returned to the United States in December, 1938. He lived at Lake Grove, OR (1939-41) and from 1941 to his death at Agate Beach, OR. In 1940 he was appointed a professor of music at the University of California at Berkeley, where he taught one semester a year until his retirement in 1952. In 1955 he was awarded a Mus.D. from Brandeis University and another from Reed College. During his lifetime Bloch witnessed the decline of 19th-century music and the development of 20th-century music. Like many 19th-century composers, he claimed the importance of melody in his works; like many 20th-century composers, he felt free to write in a variety of styles--neoromantic, neoclassic, expressionistic and others less sharply defined. Above all, he was an independent, creative composer who believed that music is an expression of the human spirit. [I,IV,V]

BLODGETT, BENJAMIN COLMAN (b. Boston, MA, 12 March 1838; d. Seattle, WA, 22 September 1925). Organist, pianist, teacher, composer. His piano studies with James Hooten and organ studies with W. R. Babcock must have begun early, for at the age of 12 he was organist at the Essex Street Congregational Church in Boston (1850-53) and at 15 organist at Eliot Church in Newton (1853-58). At the Leipzig Conservatory he studied with Ignaz Moscheles, Louis Plaidy, Ernst F. Richter and Moritz Hauptmann. When he returned to Boston, he became organist at the Park Street Church, taught privately and appeared in concerts. From 1865 to 1879 he taught piano, organ and harmony at the Maplewood Institute, Pittsfield, MA, then began his long association with Smith College at Northhampton, MA (1879-1903). Initially director of music and professor of piano, in 1900 he was appointed director of the newly established School of Music. During his years at Smith he became well known for his teaching and lecture-recitals, and he resigned only because the college voted to close its music and art schools. In 1904 Mrs. Leland Stanford, widow of Senator Stanford, selected him as organist for the Memorial Church she had built on the Stanford campus in memory of her husband. Blodgett's duties included playing a daily organ recital and, in 1905, directing the choir. In 1906 he took leave; by 1907 he had left the position. He retired from public life in 1914 and spent his last years in Seattle. Blodgett's old-fashioned piano compositions are filled with lyrical, romantic melodies that give his music a unique charm. [I]

BLUMENSCHEIN, WILLIAM LEONARD (b. Brensbach, Germany, 16 December 1849; d. Dayton OH, 27 March 1916). Choral conductor, organist, teacher, composer. The family moved to the United States in 1851 and settled in Pittsburgh, PA, where William was educated in the public schools and had singing and piano lessons with local teachers. He worked as a cashier in a large dry goods store until he had saved enough money for further music studies in Europe. He studied at the Leipzig Conservatory (1869-72) with Carl Reinecke, Ernst Wenzel, Oscar Paul, Benjamin Papperitz, Ernst F. Richter and Ferdinand David, then returned to Pittsburgh and taught piano and voice. In 1876 he became director of two Ohio choral groups: the Portsmouth Harmonic Society and the Ironton Choral Union (1876-78). In 1878 he moved to Dayton, OH and began a nearly 30-year term as director of the Dayton Philharmonic Society, and that same year became organist and choir director of the Third Street Presbyterian Church (1878-95). One of Ohio's most successful musicians, he was noted for his choral conducting and teaching. He conducted the Ohio Sängerfest in 1882 and 1884, the Indianapolis Lyra Society (1883-84), the Spring Orpheus Society (1885-87); and for five years (1891-96) conducted the chorus at the Cincinnati May Music Festival directed by Theodore Thomas. Blumenschein's best piano music uses forms--polonaise, barcarolle, mazurka--that rely on characteristic rhythmic patterns. [I]

BOEKELMAN, BERNARDUS (b. Utrecht, Holland, 9 June 1838; d. New York, NY, 2 August 1930). Pianist, teacher, composer. He had his first music studies with his father Anton J. Boekelman, an organist and choral director, and later studied at the Leipzig Conservatory (1857-60) with Ignaz Moscheles, Ernst F. Richter and Moritz Hauptmann. From 1862 to 1864 he was in Berlin working under Hans von Bülow, Friedrich Kiel and Carl Weitzmann, then sometime in 1864 emigrated to Mexico. In 1866 he settled in New York, where he spent his first season touring through the eastern part of the state as pianist with Carl Formes, the bass opera singer, and François

Jehin-Prume, the violinist. Boekelman established a reputation as pianist, teacher and editor in New York, and around 1867 founded the New York Trio Club (R. Richter, violin; Emil Schenck, cellist), which he directed as pianist until 1888. He was music director at Miss Porter's and Mrs. Dow's Young Ladies' School at Farmington, CT (1883-97), and from 1897 at Mrs. Dow's School at Briarcliff Manor, NY. His analytical editions of Bach's **Well-Tempered Clavier** and **Two-Part Inventions**--with the part-writing denoted in colors--were widely used in his lifetime. His piano compositions, written within a romantic framework, reveal an interesting variety of keyboard figurations. [I,III,IV]

BOISE, OTIS BARDWELL (b. Oberlin, OH, 13 August 1844; d. Baltimore, MD, 2 December 1912). Composer, teacher, writer. His family having moved to Cleveland, OH, he was educated in the public schools there, and at the age of 14 became organist at St. Paul's Church. In order to keep him out of the Civil War his father sent him to Europe for advanced musical studies. He was a pupil of Ignaz Moscheles, Ernst Wenzel, Moritz Hauptmann and Ernst F. Richter at the Leipzig Conservatory (1861-63) and of Theodore Kullak in Berlin (1864-65). When he returned to Cleveland he took private pupils and became organist at the Euclid Avenue Presbyterian Church (1865-70). From 1870 to 1876 he lived in New York City, where he taught at the New York Conservatory and was organist at the Fifth Avenue Presbyterian Church. In 1876 he moved to the south of France to recuperate from pneumonia, took his family with him and remained in Europe for two years. He made a nostalgic visit to Leipzig to visit old student haunts and renew acquaintance with those of his professors who were still living, and while there, Richter performed one of Boise's choral works at the St. Thomas Church. In the early summer of 1876 he took one of his new scores to Weimar, where Liszt graciously played it through, made suggestions and asked him to rework it and also write a four-hand arrangement that the two of them could play. Boise accomplished this assignment within two weeks, and for the rest of that summer and the next, as he finished each composition he took it to Weimar, where Liszt was "uniformly kind and helpful." The second summer he also attended Liszt's piano class. When he returned to the United States he settled in New York City (1878-88). For three years he was an organist and teacher, then gave up both his pupils and the organ position to go into business, hoping to save a faltering parasol-umbrella firm in which he had invested. When the business failed, he moved his family (now five daughters) to Europe, where they could live more economically. He spent more than a decade (1888-1901) in Berlin composing and teaching, and attained recognition as an outstanding theory teacher and excellent lecturer and writer. From 1901 until his death he taught theory and composition at the Peabody Conservatory, Baltimore, and was a music critic for the Baltimore **News**. He published **Harmony Made Practical** (1900) and **Music and Its Masters** (1902). In 1875 Boise's **Concerto in G Minor** received its first performance (Baltimore). Sidney Lanier remarked that "...it was the fulfillment of the best promise, well worth any encouragement of native talent, taste and advancement of American Art." [V]

BOLLINGER, SAMUEL (b. Fort Smith, AR, 22 September 1872; d. Fort Smith, 4 April 1941). Teacher, pianist, composer. He had his first music lessons with Emil Winkler, a former Leipzig Conservatory student then living in Fort Smith, and also studied with his father, an amateur musician. His further education was financed by a brother, owner of a thriving music store, with the understanding that when he returned to Fort Smith he would operate a small music school in connection with the music store. At the Leipzig Conservatory (1891-96) he studied with Carl Reinecke, Bruno Zwintscher and Gustav Schreck, and while in Leipzig he also taught at the Conservatory for a time and was organist at the American Church (1893-95). In 1894 he experienced the first attack of paralysis in his hands, a condition that would trouble him intermittently for the rest of his life. When he returned to Fort Smith he opened the music school, as promised, but being ill-suited to business, he managed it for only two years. From 1898 to 1906 he lived in San Francisco, CA. He opened a downtown studio and established a reputation as a fine teacher, then the tragic San Francisco earthquake in April, 1906 prompted him to move to Chicago, where he taught for one year and then moved to St. Louis. He taught at the Strassberger Conservatory (1907-15), at his own studio (1915-19) and in 1919 opened the Bollinger Piano School. He became one of the most sought-after piano teachers in St. Louis, and as a composer was recognized for his difficult, artistic music. Poor health forced him to close his school after a few years, but he continued to teach privately until 1928. That year his wife died, and since he was partially blind and an invalid, he returned to Fort Smith to be cared for by his family. Bollinger's disciplined piano works have been described as "excellent in workmanship, original in conception." [I]

BOROWSKI, FELIX (b. Burton-in-Kendal, Westmorland, England, 10 March 1872; d. Chicago IL, 6 September 1956). Teacher, critic, composer. He had piano and violin lessons with his father, a member of a distinguished Polish family removed to England during the Polish revolution of the 1860s, and also music lessons with his English mother, a pupil of William Sterndale Bennett. During his London school years he studied with Jacques Rosenthal, and later attended the Cologne Conservatory (1887-90), where he studied with Georg Joseph Japha, Ernst Heuser and Gustav Jensen. When he returned to London he continued his studies with Adolf Pollitzer. In 1890 he was engaged to teach violin at a girls' college in Aberdeen, Scotland, and when the school failed he returned to London and concentrated on composing. From 1897 he lived in Chicago, IL. He taught violin, composition and music history at the Chicago Musical College (1897-1925), and from 1916 was also president. In 1925 he joined the faculty of Northwestern University, first as a special lecturer in music history and later as professor of musicology (1937-42). In the meantime he composed, conducted and became a well-known critic and writer. He was Chicago correspondent for the **Musical Courier** (1905); critic for the Chicago **Evening Post** (1906-09) and Chicago **Record-Herald** (1909-18); and from 1917 until his death contributed articles and reviews to the **Christian Science Monitor**. In 1942 he became music editor of the new Chicago **Sun**. From 1908 he was for many years editor of the Chicago Symphony Orchestra program book. In addition, he built the music collection at the Newberry Library, a loving endeavor that began shortly after his arrival in Chicago and continued through his nearly 60 years' residence. Borowski's overtly romantic piano music owes much of its appeal to ethnic color and imaginative harmonies. [I,V]

BRANDEIS, FREDERICK (b. Vienna, Austria, 5 July 1835; d. New York, NY, 14 May 1899). Pianist, organist, teacher, composer. As a boy he studied at the Vienna Conservatory with Carl Czerny, Joseph Fischhof and Johann Rufinatscha, and when the family emigrated to New York City in 1849, having lost its fortune during the Austrian rebellion against Emperor Ferdinand, he continued his music studies with Wilhelm Meyerhofer. He made his début as a solo pianist in New York in 1851, then for several years toured with various concert companies, including that of William Vincent Wallace, sometimes as solo pianist and sometimes as conductor. After spending about a year in the West, he settled in New York, where he composed, gave private lessons and held several organ positions: St. John the Evangelist, from 1860 until it was destroyed by fire; St. James's Roman Catholic Church; the 44th Street Synagogue (1880-86); and St. Peter and St. Paul's Roman Catholic Church in Brooklyn (1886-99). His piano repertoire is striking in its variety of styles, textures and choice of musical forms. [I]

BREMNER, JAMES (d. Philadelphia, PA, September, 1780). Organist, conductor, concert organizer, composer. He was a relative of Robert Bremner, the Scotch music publisher, editor and composer. He settled in Philadelphia in 1763, opened a music school in December of that year and as concert promoter and organist soon proved to be a major influence in the musical life of the city. He organized some of Philadelphia's earliest public subscription concerts given to raise money for charitable causes. For example, the proceeds from his concert of February 21, 1764 went to the organ fund at St. Peter's Church; and the 30 pounds raised at a later concert (April 10, 1765) benefitted the Boys and Girls Charity School of the College of Philadelphia. The latter, a concert of solemn vocal and instrumental music directed by Bremner, was one of the first important concerts in America in which a chorus took a prominent part. He was organist at St. Peter's Church in 1763 and organist at Christ Church in 1767. He apparently left Christ Church within a year or two, then returned in 1774 and was organist there until his death. Highly regarded as a teacher, he was eulogized by Francis Hopkinson, his most important pupil, in a poem entitled "In Memory of Mr. James Bremner." Bremner's extant clavier works are pleasant, brief compositions in pre-Classic style. [I]

BRISTOW, GEORGE FREDERICK (b. Brooklyn, NY, 19 December 1825; d. New York, NY, 13 December 1898). Violinist, pianist, organist, conductor, teacher, composer. He had all his education and spent his entire life in or near New York City where his father, English composer-conductor William Richard Bristow, had brought the family about a year before he was born. He was, so to speak, a purely "American" product, and he became an ardent advocate of American music written by American composers. After early piano lessons with his father, he studied with Henry Christian Timm, George Macfarren and Ole Bull. When barely in his teens he was hired as a violinist with the Olympic Theater Orchestra, a six-man ensemble that performed in popular musical comedies. In 1843 he joined the roster of violinists in the New York Philharmonic Society Orchestra (founded 1842, but no record found of first-season performers) and, except for a few months during 1854 when he resigned because he felt the orchestra was ignoring music written by American composers, he remained a member until 1879. He sometimes played--and often led the violin section--in other orchestras, notably those that accompanied Jenny Lind (1850-51) and Marietta Alboni (1852), and Jullien's Orchestra (1853-54). A many-sided musician, he was also organist at several churches, director of the choir at St. George's Chapel (1854-60) and conductor of the New York Harmonic Society (1851-62) and the Mendelssohn Society (1867-71). Despite his many musical activities, from 1854 until his death he was a visiting teacher in the New York public schools, where he made an important contribution to music education in the city. Although with Anthony Philip Heinrich and William Henry Fry he attempted to establish an "American" musical style and often chose American topics for his works, Bristow's music remained European. The piano works, for example, reveal at times a particularly strong Schubert influence. [I]

BROCKWAY, HOWARD (b. Brooklyn, NY, 22 November 1870; d. New York, NY, 20 February 1951). Pianist, teacher, composer. As a child he was taken to concerts and given piano lessons and at 16 he composed a few small works; but he studied business when he attended the Polytechnic Institute of Brooklyn. At the age of 19 he went to work as a bookkeeper, lasted one week on the job, then determined to have a career in music. In New York he studied piano with H. O. C. Kortheuer, and in Berlin (1890-95) studied piano with Carl Heinrich Barth and composition with Otis B. Boise. A successful concert of his chamber and orchestral works given by the Berlin Philharmonic Orchestra (February 23, 1895) greatly enhanced his reputation as a composer. When he returned to the United States, he settled permanently in New York, except for a few years spent in Baltimore, MD teaching at the Peabody Conservatory (1903-09). In New York he composed, gave concerts and lecture-recitals, and taught at the

David Mannes Music School (later Mannes College of Music) and at the Institute of Musical Art (later Juilliard) from 1925 until 1940. In 1910 he was elected to the Institute of Arts and Letters, where his personal papers are now housed. In 1911 he toured extensively with Mary Garden. After 1911 he composed very little but published arrangements of Kentucky mountain folk songs that he had collected with Loraine Wyman (**Lonesome Tunes,** 1916; **Twenty Kentucky Mountain Songs,** 1920). Brockway's keyboard music shows notable harmonic and melodic originality. He is at his best in the short characteristic piece. [I]

BROUNOFF, PLATON (b. Elisabethgrad, Russia, 10 May 1863; d. New York, NY, 11 July 1924). Pianist, singer, teacher, composer. At the age of 16 he began three years of study at the Warsaw Conservatory with Gustav Roguski, Alexander Zarzycki and others and when he returned home he made a concert tour of neighboring cities. From 1883 until 1891 he lived in St. Petersburg. He continued his musical training at the Imperial Conservatory under Rimsky-Korsakoff, Nikolai Solovieff and Anton Rubinstein; sang in operas, gave piano recitals and composed many works that were published. In 1891 he went to the United States, stopping first with his brother at La Porte, IN--he gave his first American concert there--then spending ten months in New Haven, CT, and finally settling in New York City (1892). He was a multitalented musician. Besides composing, he lectured on Russian music and related topics for the New York Board of Education and the Modern Arts Forum; taught opera classes at the Institute of Musical Art (later Juilliard); and conducted the Modern Symphony Orchestra, Russian Choral Society and People's Male Chorus. His piano music is very old-fashioned and correct, entirely Russian in character. [I]

BROWN, WILLIAM (fl. 1780s). Flutist, concert manager, composer. He appeared in America during the early 1780s and for the remainder of the decade was an extremely active flutist and concert manager, mostly in Philadelphia. He was apparently energetic and ambitious, for despite the hardships of travel at the time he moved back and forth among the various eastern cities (New York, Philadelphia, Baltimore) and as far south as Charleston. As far as we know he gave his first American concert in New York in August, 1783, then not too long afterward left for Philadelphia, where he organized and performed in two subscription concerts in October, 1783. In February, 1784 he was in Baltimore giving a benefit concert for himself, for which he advertised that "his superior talents on the German flute gained much applause in Europe and this country." He seems to have left Baltimore for Charleston, then returned to Philadelphia, since an advertisement for a Philadelphia concert in July, 1784 describes him as "lately arrived from Charleston." In the fall of 1785 he was in New York, where he initiated the Subscription Concerts, giving one in October, 1785 and a second in March, 1786. Although they were successful, he discontinued the series and returned to Philadelphia, where for the next few years he performed frequently in benefit concerts, subscription concerts and especially the City Concerts (October, 1786-March, 1788), a series organized jointly and variously by Alexander Reinagle, Henri Capron, Alexander Juhan and Brown. Although contemporary sources depict him as hustling and abrasive--he quarreled publicly with Capron--Brown was evidently a competent performer and composer. It is a measure of his standing that, when he dedicated his **Three Rondos** (1787) to Francis Hopkinson, the distinguished poet-composer and patriot accepted the honor. The **Rondos** are written in a passable if not overly exciting pre-Classic style. Note: Where Brown came from or where he went after leaving Philadelphia is not known. Carl Engel proposed two possibilities in his article "Introducing Mr. Braun" (**Musical Quarterly,** Vol.XXX, No.1, Jan. 1944, p.63). Brown might have been one Wilhelm Braun, a flutist who lived in Cassel, Germany during 1770-80, then went to America but by 1806 had returned to Germany and was living at Hanau. Or was he a fifer who came to America with a Hessian regiment during the American Revolutionary War and then stayed and later adopted the English spelling of his name? [I]

BRYANT, GILMORE WARD (b. Bethel, VT, 8 August 1859; d. 1946). Pianist, teacher, composer. He studied in Boston and New York with Carlyle Petersilea and William H. Sherwood. From 1885 he taught at several southern schools, in 1889 was music director of the Wesleyan Female Institute at Staunton, VA. In 1898 he founded the Southern Conservatory at Durham, NC, and was still directing it in the 1920s. Bryant's keyboard compositions provide examples of pleasant salon music. [I]

BUCK, DUDLEY (b. Hartford, CT, 10 March 1839; d. West Orange, NJ, 6 October 1909). Organist, teacher, composer. Since his father, owner of a line of steamers, intended him for the shipping business, he had no formal music training until the age of 16, when he began piano study with William J. Babcock, a local teacher. That same year (1855) he entered Trinity College in Hartford. Three years later he went to the Leipzig Conservatory (1858-60), where his teachers included Ignaz Moscheles, Moritz Hauptmann, Ernst F. Richter, Louis Plaidy and Julius Rietz; then he went to Dresden (1860-61) to continue his studies with Rietz, who had moved there early in 1860, and with Johann Gottlob Schneider, the Dresden court organist. After a year in Paris (1861-62), most of it spent learning about organ construction at the government organ factory, he returned to Hartford. He took private pupils and was organist at the North Congregational Church until 1869, when he moved to Chicago, IL, having been appointed organist at St. James's Episcopal Church. While in Chicago he began the concert tours that established his reputation as an organist. Over a 15-year period he made organ tours, not only in large cities but small towns as well, playing classical music so delightfully that even audiences unfamiliar with it enjoyed it. When the devastating Chicago fire (October, 1871) destroyed his home, library, music and mementos, he moved within a week to Boston, MA. He became organist for the Music Hall Association and at St. Paul's Church, and also taught at the New England Conservatory. In 1875 Theodore Thomas engaged him as assistant conductor of the Central Park Garden Concerts in New York. After a brief period with Thomas he settled in Brooklyn, where for many years he was organist at Holy Trinity Church and director of the Apollo Club (1877-1902). In 1902 he also took charge of the music at Plymouth Church in Hartford, but the following year he resigned all his positions. In retirement he continued to compose and spent long periods in Europe. Buck ranks as one of America's finest sacred-music composers, better known for his organ music than his piano works. His piano compositions, however, reveal the same musical expertise in matters both technical and lyrical. [I]

BURLEIGH, HENRY [HARRY] THACKER (b. Erie, PA, 2 December 1866; d. Stamford, CT, 12 September 1949). Singer, arranger, composer. His intimate knowledge of black spirituals came from his maternal grandfather, who had been born a slave. After finishing Erie High School, he worked on the lake steamers out of Buffalo and sang in local churches, then won a scholarship at the National Conservatory in New York City, where he studied with Christian Fritsch, Rubin Goldmark, John White and Max Spicker (1892-96). He also played double bass and later timpani in the Conservatory orchestra, was orchestra librarian and sometimes taught singing and solfeggio. Dvořák, then director of the Conservatory, befriended him and enjoyed hearing him sing black spirituals and folk songs. An "indestructible baritone," he was the soloist at St. George's Episcopal Church on East 16th Street for 52 years (1894-1946) and at the Temple Emanu-El on East 65th Street for 25 years (1900-25). He also gave many song recitals in the United States and Europe. From 1911 to his death he was a music editor for his publisher G. Ricordi and Co. In 1917 he was awarded the Spingarn Medal given by the National Association for the Advancement of Colored People "for the highest achievement by an American citizen of African descent in the year 1916." He wrote about 100 artistic arrangements of black spirituals--"Deep River" is perhaps the most famous--and was the first composer to give serious treatment to this musical form. He also composed more than 200 songs. Burleigh's small piano repertoire sparkles with verve, imagination and rhythmic ingenuity. [I]

BURMEISTER, RICHARD (b. Hamburg, Germany, 7 December 1860; d. Berlin, Germany, 19 February 1944). Pianist, teacher, composer. He was a pupil and associate of Liszt at Weimar, Rome and Budapest (1880-83), then toured extensively through Europe. From 1885 until 1903 he lived in the United States. He was head of the piano department at the Peabody Conservatory in Baltimore, MD (1885-97), except for a leave in 1893 when he made a European concert tour; and director of the Scharwenka Conservatory in New York (1897-1903). After returning to Europe, he taught at the Dresden

Conservatory (1903-06) and at the Klindworth-Scharwenka Conservatory in Berlin (1907-25). Burmeister's romantic piano pieces are superbly crafted, with creative harmonies and artful modulations. [I,IV,V]

BURR, WILLARD (b. Ravenna, OH, 7 January 1852; d. Boston, MA, 8 May 1915). Teacher, composer. He was educated at Oberlin College in Oberlin, OH, where he received an A.B. in 1876, was graduated from the Conservatory in 1877 and received an A.M. in 1879. During 1879-80 he studied in Europe, mostly with Carl August Haupt in Berlin, and from 1885 until his death he had a career as teacher and composer in Boston. A champion of American music, he made an address at the MTNA meeting in Cleveland (1884) in which he recommended giving concerts of American works only or, at the least, concerts including some American works. In 1885 he presented to Congress a proposal for an international copyright law which would protect the rights of American composers. Burr's few piano pieces emphasize lyrical melodies over sparse accompaniments. [I]

CAMP, JOHN SPENCER (b. Middletown, CT, 30 January 1858; d. Hartford, CT, 1 February 1946). Organist, conductor, composer. He was graduated from Wesleyan University in Middletown (1878), and after postgraduate studies in law and Latin received an A.M. in 1881. As a composer he was completely American-trained, studying first in Connecticut with Edward A. Parsons and Harry Rowe Shelley (New Haven) and Dudley Buck (Hartford), then in New York City with Samuel Prowse Warren and Antonín Dvořák. He made his career in Hartford, where he was organist at the Park Congregational Church (1881-1906) and the Center Congregational Church (1906-18); conductor of the Hartford Philharmonic Orchestra (1902-11); and also gave organ recitals and lectures on music. A businessman as well as a musician, he was president and treasurer of Pratt and Cady, a heavy machinery firm (1898-1911), and treasurer and president of Austin Organ Company (1911-30). In 1929 he made a gift of $100,000 to Wesleyan University to endow the John Spencer Camp Chair of Music, the incumbent to be college organist and choir director. He received an honorary Mus.D. from Trinity College (1921) and another from Wesleyan (1933). Camp's unpretentious piano pieces are pleasant, light textured, not difficult. [I]

CAMPBELL-TIPTON, LOUIS (b. Chicago, IL, 21 November 1877; d. Paris, France, 1 May 1921). Teacher, composer. Like Arthur Bird and Templeton Strong, he was an expatriate American composer. He studied with various teachers in Chicago and Boston, then at the Leipzig Conservatory with Gustav Schreck and Carl Reinecke, among others (1896-99). He returned to Chicago and taught theory and composition at the Chicago Musical College (1901-04). From 1905 until his death he made his home in Paris, where he taught privately. His early keyboard pieces show his Germanic training;

CAPEN, CHARLES LEMUEL (b. Dedham, MA, 9 February 1850; d. ?). Little is known about him. The Boston city directories (1879-98) list him as a music teacher. He was also a member of the Harvard Musical Association and is known to have been on the faculty of the New England Conservatory of Music, where Benjamin Whelpley was one of his pupils. His keyboard repertoire consists mainly of appealing pieces in salon-music style. [I]

CARPENTER, JOHN ALDEN (b. Park Ridge, IL, 28 February 1876; d. Chicago, IL, 26 April 1951). Composer. Unlike most of his contemporaries, he had nearly all of his musical education in the United States. He studied first with his mother, a well-trained church singer, then with Amy Fay and W. C. E. Seeboeck in Chicago and with John Knowles Paine while at Harvard (1893-97). After graduating from Harvard he joined George B. Carpenter and Co., the family vessels supplies firm, and for nearly 40 years managed a dual career as businessman-composer. From 1909 until 1936 he was vice-president of the firm, but at the same time continued to compose and take additional training: some lessons (Rome, 1906) with Edward Elgar, whose music he greatly admired; and several gratifying years working with Bernhard Ziehn in Chicago (1908-12). During his lifetime his talents were both recognized and rewarded. He was made a member of the Legion of Honor (1921); given an honorary A.M. from Harvard (1922), two honorary doctorates in music (University of Wisconsin in 1933 and Northwestern University in 1941), and the Gold Medal of the National Institute of Arts and Letters, which was awarded only once every nine years. Carpenter successfully covered several stylistic periods in his piano music, from Romanticism through Impressionism to an attractive contemporary idiom. [I,V]

CARR, BENJAMIN (b. London, England, 12 September 1768; d. Philadelphia, PA, 24 May 1831). Publisher, editor, singer, organist, concert organizer, composer. He was a well-trained and remarkably versatile musician who for nearly four decades (1793-1831) greatly influenced the quality and direction of American music. He studied with some of England's finest church musicians, including Dr. Samuel Arnold and Charles Wesley, and learned about publishing and selling music in his father's London music shop. Early in 1793 he emigrated to America and apparently at once opened a music store in New York City, for in April of that year he advertised "'Freedom Triumphant,' a new song just published by B. Carr, 131 William Street" (the shop purchased by James Hewitt in 1797). By July he had settled in Philadelphia, where he opened B. Carr and Co., "a Musical Repository for the sale of music and musical instruments of all kinds." His father Joseph and brother Thomas having also emigrated to America, they most likely were his associates in the Philadelphia shop before opening another branch in Baltimore, MD in 1794. The Carrs thus established one of America's pioneer music-publishing houses. Besides selling musical instruments and other musical merchandise at his Musical

Repository, Benjamin imported, printed and sold music: favorite
tunes from English ballad operas; songs by popular English
composers and some by Haydn; piano sonatas, rondos and
divertissements by Haydn, Mozart, Hummel and others; songs by Carr
himself and Rayner Taylor; and American patriotic songs and
keyboard arrangements of those songs. "Yankee Doodle" (1794),
"Hail Columbia" (1798) and "The Star-Spangled Banner" (ca.1814) all
first appeared in print in Carr publications. In 1794 he began his
career as concert organizer, joining with Alexander Reinagle and
others in directing a series of "amateur and professional concerts"
in which he often appeared as a singer and sometimes as a piano
soloist. During his early years in Philadelphia he was also
involved in the theater, performing as a singer-actor and composing
works for stage performances. As organist he served for a time at
St. Joseph's Church and for many years at St. Augustine's Roman
Catholic Church (1801-31), where he improved both the choir and the
quality of the music. A prolific composer, he composed about 85
sacred works--Masses, motets, vespers, litanies, hymns, anthems,
voluntaries, etc.--and more than 270 secular works--mostly songs,
piano pieces and piano arrangements, and some operas, the most
successful being **The Archers of Switzerland,** of which little
survives. From 1800 he devoted much of his time to editing **The
Musical Journal for the Piano Forte,** published in Baltimore by his
father with works "selected and arranged by B. Carr of
Philadelphia." [The **Journal** was issued weekly for five years
(1800-04), usually a four-page number containing one or more
compositions (one week instrumental works, the next week vocal).]
Carr's keen business sense and musical instincts led him to select
a wide variety of music by the best composers of the day: marches,
waltzes, variations on popular tunes, sonatas and sonatinas. Eight
years after the **Journal** was discontinued he edited a new series
called **Carr's Musical Miscellany in Occasional Numbers,** not a
subscription offering but a series of individual issues of original
compositions composed or arranged expressly for the **Miscellany** and
published irregularly between 1812 and 1825. In 1825 the **Miscellany**
was divided into **Lyricks** (vocal) and **Le Clavecin** (instrumental).
Carr was also one of the founders of the Musical Fund Society
(1820). Highly respected and admired by his contemporaries, he is
known to later generations as the "father of Philadalphia music."
More than that, he must be recognized as a pioneer in promoting
American music and publishing the works of American composers. [I]

CARRENO, TERESA (b. Caracas, Venezuela, 22 December 1853; d. New
York, NY, 12 June 1917). Pianist, teacher, composer. Her
grandfather was the Venezuelan composer José Cayetano Carreño. Her
father Manuel Antonio Carreño was minister of finance and also an
excellent pianist who gave her early piano lessons. When political
upheaval forced the family to leave Venezuela (1862), they settled
in New York City. A musical prodigy, Teresa's first public piano
performance in November of that year was followed by spectacularly
successful concerts in New York and Boston, a tour through New
England and, in the Fall of 1863, a performance for President

Lincoln. Her playing attracted the attention of the noted pianist Louis M. Gottschalk, who gave her occasional lessons and greatly influenced her career; she often included his piano works on her early concert programs. By the time she reached her teens her family had moved to Paris, where she studied with Georges Amadée St. Claire Mathias and Emmanuel Bazin. She also studied singing and met Anton Rubinstein, who became her lifelong adviser. Her Paris début (May, 1866) marked the beginning of her long and remarkably successful career as a concert pianist. She toured Europe for several years, returned to America in the Fall of 1872 and the next year married the French violinist Emile Sauret. When the marriage dissolved within two years, she remained in the United States and had a brief career as a singer, making her formal début under the management of Max Strakosch in New York in February, 1876. That same year she married the baritone Giovanni Tagliapietra, and during this marriage she lived mostly in New York, where she gave young Edward MacDowell informal yet influential instruction. (Later on she was one of the first to play MacDowell's works on concert programs.) This marriage also faltered and in 1889 she moved to Berlin, where she resumed her concert career and established herself as one of the world's great pianists. For almost 30 years she lived in Berlin, continuing to perform and simultaneously acquiring an impressive reputation as a teacher, often with a waiting list of 50 or more students. In 1892 she married the composer-pianist Eugen d'Albert. During their brief and stormy time together they played two-piano concerts, and he changed her brilliant, headlong style to a more thoughtful, controlled interpretation. From 1902 until her death she was married to Arturo Tagliapietra, a younger brother of Giovanni. They lived in Berlin, and she continued her intense concert schedule almost until the crisis of World War I forced them to leave Germany. She made her final appearances in New York and Havana (March, 1917), and died a few months later. Carreño's piano music, both "serious" and salon, sparkles with vivacious rhythms and occasional Latin color. It is, of course, eminently pianistic. [I]

CHADWICK, GEORGE WHITEFIELD (b. Lowell, MA, 13 November 1854; d. Boston, MA, 4 April 1931). Organist, conductor, teacher, composer. His father was an amateur musician who taught a singing class and conducted a local orchestra. His brother Fitz Henry Chadwick, 14 years older and a church organist, gave him his first piano lessons. He attended high school, then joined his father's insurance business but continued with his music. He studied piano with Carlyle Petersilea, organ with Dudley Buck (1873) and Eugene Thayer (1874-75), and meanwhile also studied at the New England Conservatory, where his teachers included Stephen Emery and George Whiting. At the age of 21 he left the insurance business for a career in music. He taught for one year at Olivet College in Olivet, MI (1876), serving as a one-man music department, then in 1877 went to Leipzig to study privately with Salomon Jadassohn and later at the Leipzig Conservatory, where he made rapid progress as

a composer. He also worked under Joseph Rheinberger in Munich from
the Fall of 1879 until he returned to Boston in the Spring of 1880.
He composed, gave private lessons and for 17 years was organist at
various churches, including the South Congregational Church, Boston
(1883-93). From 1882 he taught at the New England Conservatory, and
from 1897 until his death was also director. He conducted the
large student orchestra at the Conservatory, often appeared as
guest conductor for major orchestras, and was director-conductor of
the Springfield (1889-99) and Worcester (1897-1901) festivals in
Massachusetts. To celebrate the fiftieth anniversary of his return
from Germany, festivals were held at the New England Conservatory
and at the Eastman School of Music at Rochester, NY. He was awarded
an A.M. from Yale (1897), an LL.D. from Tufts (1905) and the Gold
Medal of the National Institute of Arts and Letters (1928).
Chadwick's keyboard works show a tasteful blend of Romanticism and
technical deftness. He had a special knack for infusing a gentle
humor into his music. [I]

CHALLONER, ROBERT (fl. 1870s). Teacher, writer, composer. We have
little information about him. He is listed in the Louisville, KY
city directories (1874-79) as a music teacher, and published at
least three books: **Music Made Easy: the Rudiments of Music
Explained in a Concise and Novel Manner** (1879); **The First Twenty
Hours in Music: Lessons for a Beginner on the Piano or Parlor Organ**
(1880); and **The History of the Science and Art of Music: Its
Origin, Development and Progress** (1880). Challoner's flamboyant
salon pieces, featuring manifold octave passages and glittering
scale figurations, are diverting and challenging. [I]

CHAPMAN, WILLIAM ROGERS (b. Hanover, MA, 4 August 1855; d. Palm
Beach, FL, 27 March 1935). Conductor, organist, teacher, composer.
He was raised in Bethel, ME, and at the age of 14 went to the
Collegiate Dutch Reformed Church in New York to study theology.
Eye problems forced him to leave his studies, and for nearly 15
months he was blind. During this helpless period his mother played
and sang for him, indirectly diverting him from the ministry to a
career in music. He studied with Sebastian Bach Mills, William
Mason and George Bristow in New York City, and in 1871 obtained an
organ position at Mamaroneck, Long Island. After further studies
with Charles Fradel and Henry Stephen Cutler, he gave a series of
piano and organ concerts, including some of his own works on the
programs, and remained in New York, making a career as conductor,
organist and teacher. He taught in the New York city schools
(1876-87) and also took private pupils. He was organist at the
Presbyterian Church of the Covenant (1877-90) and at the Madison
Avenue Reformed Church (1891-1905). An outstanding choral
conductor, he organized and directed the Musurgia Society, a male
chorus (1884-92) and the Rubinstein Club, a women's group
(1884-1931). In 1888 he joined these two choruses, added some
voices and organized the Metropolitan Musical Society, which gave
concerts at the Metropolitan Opera House for many seasons. When he

resigned from the Musurgia Society in 1892, he formed the Apollo Club of New York, 50 male voices (1892-1905). In 1897 he inaugurated the yearly Maine Music Festivals at Bangor and Portland, and thereafter divided his time between New York and Maine. Chapman's skill in rhythmic design gives his salon pieces high levels of quality. [I]

CHELIUS, HERMAN P. (b. Bavaria, March, 1848; d. Dorchester, MA, 7 January 1941). Organist, pianist, teacher, composer. He emigrated to the United States when he was about 12, and at the age of 14 gave an organ recital at the Boston Music Hall. According to Boston city directories (1869-1925), he was an active organist and teacher in Boston for more than 50 years. He was organist at the Tremont Temple for about 12 years, taught for many years at the Boston Conservatory of Music, and as organist appeared on the lecture circuit with Mark Twain, Henry W. Longfellow and Ralph Waldo Emerson. A talented composer of difficult salon music, Chelius often achieved unusual treatment of standard musical forms. [I]

CLAASSEN, ARTHUR (b. Stargard, Prussia, 19 February 1859; d. San Francisco, CA, 16 March 1920). Conductor, composer. In 1875 he entered the music school at Weimar, where he studied with Carl Wilhelm Müller-Hartung, A. W. Gottschalk and B. Sulze. A devoted follower of Liszt, who found his youthful works interesting, he sometimes copied the Liszt style in his own compositions. Between 1880 and 1884 he conducted a theater orchestra at Göttingen and the Nowak Victoria Theater in Magdeburg. In 1884 he emigrated to the United States, having been recommended by Leopold Damrosch for the post of conductor of the Brooklyn Arion Society, a position he held for 25 years (1884-1909). From 1910 until 1919 he lived in San Antonio, TX, where he became conductor of the Beethoven Choral Society (male), organized the Mozart Society (female) and with them performed many choral works with the San Antonio Symphony. He also conducted many large festivals, including the 31st Texas State Music Festival. Claassen's piano music is, stylistically, mostly salon music with some "serious" overtones. [I]

CLARKE, WILLIAM HORATIO (b. Newton, MA, 8 March 1840; d. Reading, MA, 11 December 1913). Organist, teacher, organ builder, composer. His mother was a church singer, and his father played the ophicleide in the town band and also in a Newton church before the parish acquired an organ in 1852. At the age of seven he played the flageolet, and at nine was composing small church works. He had some formal organ lessons, then for about 15 years (1856-71) was organist at various churches in Dedham, Boston, Waltham and Woburn. He was supervisor of music for the Dayton, OH public schools (1872-74), then between 1874 and 1878 lived in Indianapolis, IN, where he established a large organ factory and became organist of the Roberts Park Church. He returned to Boston (1878-80), where he was organist at the Tremont Temple, gave organ recitals and wrote

and edited musical articles. In 1880 he moved to Toronto, Canada
to become organist at the Jarvis Street Baptist Church, playing an
organ that he had built some years earlier, but in 1884 he was
called back to Indianapolis to build a large organ for the Plymouth
Church, where he remained as organist and gave weekly Saturday
afternoon organ recitals. Around 1887 he returned to his hometown,
and about three years later built a music chapel with a large (4
manuals, 100 stops) organ at Clarigold Hall, his Reading estate.
He intended to open a school for organists there but abandoned his
plans because of illness, and in 1892 retired from all his
activities. Although paralyzed, he carried on his work as an organ
consultant by correspondence, and many of the instruments built
under his supervision are still being used in the United States and
Canada. He also continued to compose and lecture, having a
specially equipped van to transport him. Clarke wrote highly
descriptive salon music for the piano, old-fashioned but frequently
charming. [I]

CLIFTON, ARTHUR [PHILIP ANTHONY CORRI] (b. Edinburgh, Scotland,
1784; d. Baltimore, MD, 10 February 1832). Singer, teacher,
organist, composer. He was a son of Domenico Corri, the Italian
composer and music publisher who lived for many years in London and
Edinburgh, and before Philip was 30 he was a successful composer in
London. Besides having his works published, he was an original
founder of the London Philharmonic Society (1813) and had sung in
its first three concerts. At some point between 1813 and 1817 he
emigrated to America, and the facts of his life at this time--why
he moved and why he changed his name--are confusing. He apparently
left England because of marital problems (described by an
acquaintance as "his wife's defection"), went first to New York
City, then Philadelphia and ultimately settled in Baltimore. He
changed his name, remarried--records at St. Paul's Episcopal Church
in Baltimore reveal that he was baptized Arthur Clifton on December
31, 1817 and the next day married Alphonse Ringgold--and began a
new career as voice teacher, performer, organist and composer. As
early as 1819 he was organist at the First Presbyterian Church and
issued **An Original Collection of Psalm Tunes** "extracted from
ancient and modern composers, to which are added several tunes
composed especially for this work." In 1821 he visited London and
under his original name took part in a Philharmonic Society
concert. He returned to Baltimore, and according to the city
directories (1822-31) he was a professor of music until his death.
For many years he directed The Anacreontic Society, which met
weekly at his home, and he frequently appeared in concerts as a
singer or pianist. He composed many songs, duets and piano
compositions, and his opera **The Enterprise** (1822) offers an
uncommon example of American opera at that time. Clifton was an
excellent composer of substantial, Classic-style piano pieces,
outstanding in their clarity of texture and imaginative keyboard
patterns. Both his English and American works are noteworthy.
[I,III,V]

CLOUGH-LEIGHTER, HENRY (b. Washington, DC, 13 May 1874; d. Wollaston, MA, 15 September 1956). Organist, editor, composer. He began piano lessons with his mother at about the age of five, from nine to twelve was a soprano soloist at St. John's Church and at thirteen began organ studies with George Walter and composition with Edward Kimball. At 14 he played the organ at St. Michael's and All Angels Church, at 15 played at the Church of the Incarnation. Still in Washington, he was organist simultaneously at the Church of the Epiphany and the Jewish Synagogue (1892-98). He was organist at Grace Church (1898-99) and at Christ Church (1900-01) in Providence, RI, and from 1901 played for many years at the First Congregational Church in Milton, MA. During the 1900-01 academic year he was music supervisor for the Westerly, RI schools and also taught theory at the Howe School of Music in Boston, MA. From 1901 he was a music editor in Boston, with the Oliver Ditson Co. (1901-08); the Boston Music Co. (1908-21); and, as editor in chief, with E. C. Schirmer (1921-56). His small piano repertoire is romantically appealing, particularly the pieces for piano duet. [I,III]

COERNE, LOUIS ADOLPHE (b. Newark, NJ, 27 February 1870; d. Boston, MA, 11 September 1922). Conductor, organist, teacher, composer. He began violin lessons in Stuttgart, Germany, where his family lived for a time, and was graduated from the Boston Latin School in 1888. He studied with John Knowles Paine at Harvard (1888-90), and at the same time had violin lessons with Franz Kneisel, then concertmaster of the Boston Symphony Orchestra. At the Munich Conservatory (1890-93) he studied with Joseph Rheinberger (until Rheinberger's death in 1901) and with Ludwig Abel. When he returned to Boston he spent a year as organist at different churches, and in 1894 conducted his symphonic poem **Hiawatha** with the Boston Symphony Orchestra. From 1894 until 1897 he lived in Buffalo, NY, where he was director of the Liedertafel and organist of the Church of the Messiah; and from 1897 to 1899 was in Columbus, OH, where he was director of the Arion Club and the Männerchor and also organist of Trinity Church. During an interval in Germany (1899-1902) he composed, published, did some teaching and also completed and edited Rheinberger's unfinished **Mass in A Minor.** He was in charge of music for the Harvard summer session in 1903, and was associate professor at Smith College in Northampton, MA for the academic year 1903-04. He then worked in New York and at Harvard doing research for his thesis "The Evolution of Modern Orchestration," for which he received (1905) the first Ph.D. in music given at Harvard and also the first at any American university. He lived again in Germany (1905-07), where his opera **Zenobia** was produced in Bremen in 1905, then held a music position in Troy, NY (1907-09). He was music director at Olivet College in Michigan (1909-10), receiving an honorary Mus.D. there the last year; professor at the University of Wisconsin at Madison (1910-15), where he also played the organ at the First Congregational Church and directed the Männerchor; and from 1915 until his death he was head of music at the Connecticut College for Women in New London, CT. Coerne's competent piano music, structured with care, shows a frequent use of impressionist techniques. [I,III]

COLE, ROSSETTER GLEASON (b. Clyde, MI, 5 February 1866; d. Lake Bluff, IL, 18 May 1952). Teacher, composer. He studied music with Calvin B. Cady at the University of Michigan at Ann Arbor, and following graduation (1888) taught English and Latin in high schools in Ann Arbor and Aurora, IL. From 1890 to 1892 he had advanced studies under Max Bruch in Berlin, then returned to the United States. He taught at Ripon College in Ripon, WI (1892-94); at Grinnell College in Grinnell, IA (1894-1901); then from 1902--except for two years when he taught at the University of Wisconsin at Madison (1907-09)--he lived in Chicago. He composed, took private pupils and for many years was Dean of the Cosmopolitan School of Music. From 1908 until 1939 he was in charge of music at the summer sessions at Columbia University in New York City. He was awarded an honorary A.M. from the University of Michigan (1913) and an honorary Mus.D. from Grinnell College (1937). Cole's piano music is lightly textured, with an occasional Germanic nod to Mendelssohn. [I]

COMBS, GILBERT RAYNOLDS (b. Philadelphia, PA, 5 January 1863; d. Mt. Airy, PA, 14 June 1934). Organist, teacher, composer. After initial music lessons with his father, also an organist and composer, he was trained at the Philadelphia Musical Institute and in New York and Europe. At the age of 22 he founded the Broad Street Conservatory (now Combs College of Music) in Philadelphia, a flourishing school--between 1885 and 1932 more than 64,000 students were enrolled--which he directed until his death. He was also organist at several city churches, notably the Immanuel Presbyterian Church (12 years) and the Tenth Presbyterian Church (6 years). He published **The Science of Piano-Playing** and **Introductory Steps to the Science of Piano-Playing.** Combs's typical--and best--piano works are character pieces similar to those of Edward MacDowell. [I]

CONRATH, LOUIS (b. Sedalia, MO, 30 July 1868; d. St. Louis, MO, 24 February 1927). Teacher, pianist, composer. He studied at the Leipzig Conservatory (1884-88) with Carl Reinecke, Oscar Paul and Salomon Jadassohn, then returned to Missouri and settled in St. Louis, where he spent the rest of his life as teacher and composer. He taught at the Beethoven Conservatory; at Ehling and Conrath College, founded jointly with Victor Ehling in 1894; and from about 1914 until his death, at the Strassberger Conservatory. At one time Conrath and Charles Kunkel, another St. Louis composer-pianist, began a revival of two-piano music, giving a series of concerts at which they played nearly all the two-piano compositions written by the great masters. Conrath composed a great deal of piano music and wrote successfully in both fields, "serious" music and salon music. Many pieces, particularly those written in a romantically flamboyant grand manner, are worthy of any performer's repertoire. [I,III,IV,V]

CONVERSE, FREDERICK SHEPHERD (b. Newton, MA, 5 January 1871; d. Westwood, MA, 8 June 1940). Teacher, composer. At the age of ten he began piano lessons with a local teacher, later studied with Junius W. Hill of Wellesley College and while at Harvard (1889-93) with John Knowles Paine. To please his father he made an attempt at a business career but after a few unhappy months returned to music. He resumed his musical studies in Boston, working with Carl Baermann in piano and George Chadwick in composition, then went to the Munich Conservatory (1896-98), where his most important teacher was Joseph Rheinberger. When he returned to Boston he began teaching, and about 1900 purchased a large estate in Westwood, where he lived a vigorous country life managing a farm and raising a family. At the same time he kept up an active musical life in Boston. He taught at the New England Conservatory from 1900 to 1902 and at Harvard from 1903 until 1906, when he took leave in order to study the condition of opera at major European opera centers. Having decided to devote all his time to composition, he resigned from Harvard in 1907 and stayed abroad for another two years. When he returned to Boston his career flourished, and his opera **The Pipe of Desire** (1905) was produced at the Metropolitan Opera House in New York City in 1910, a landmark event in that it was the first American opera to be performed there. Although these were some of his most fruitful years as a composer, he was energetically involved in the city's musical affairs, helping to organize the Boston Opera Company and serving as vice-president (1908-14). In 1920 he returned to the faculty of the New England Conservatory and from 1931 until his retirement in 1938 was also Dean of the faculty. His music was well received in his lifetime, and many of his works were performed by major orchestras. He was awarded the David Bispham Medal from the American Opera Society of Chicago (1926), an honorary Mus.D. from Boston University (1933) and was elected a member of the American Academy of Arts and Letters (1937). Converse was a progressive composer whose piano compositions, artfully designed, intrigue the listener with their admixture of mild dissonance and rhythmic ingenuity. [I,III,V]

COOKE, JAMES FRANCIS (b. Bay City, MI, 14 November 1875; d. Philadelphia, PA, 3 March 1960). Editor, writer, teacher, composer. He was educated at the Brooklyn Boys' High School and studied music in New York with Raymond Woodman and Walter Hall. After further training with Max Meyer-Olbersleben and Hermann Ritter at the Würzburg Conservatory, he returned to Brooklyn and began his long, active and diverse career. He taught, lectured and gave recitals, and was also an organist and choral conductor. Between 1901 and 1905 he published the results of his extensive investigations of the methods used at European conservatories. He was the editor of **Etude** (1907-49), president of the Theodore Presser Co. (1925-36), and head of the Presser Foundation

(1918-56). Brilliant and creative, he was awarded 15 honorary degrees, and in 1930 made a Chevalier of the French Legion of Honor for "his services in art, education and public affairs." He wrote several plays and hundreds of magazine and newspaper articles, and made countless speeches on music. Cooke's piano music is uncomplicated, melodious, not too difficult and openly romantic. [I]

CORRI, PHILIP ANTHONY [see **ARTHUR CLIFTON**]

COVERLEY, ROBERT (b. Oporto, Portugal, 6 September 1863; d. Oporto, 19 September 1944). Composer. His musical talent showed at a very early age, but because his parents refused to let him have music lessons he was self-taught until the age of 14. He had his first formal instruction from a graduate of the Paris Conservatory, and continued his studies with Thomas Henry Weist-Hill and Joseph Ludwig in London, where he became well known for his light music. He visited America in 1883, settled in New York City the following year and quickly attained a reputation for his effective marches and patriotic songs, especially **The Passing Regiment,** a military march for band. Like the marches, Coverley's piano music is, for the most part, spirited and melodious. [I]

CROSS, MICHAEL HURLEY (b. Philadelphia, PA, 13 April 1833; d. Philadelphia, 26 September 1897). Organist, conductor, teacher, composer. He was born, educated and spent his entire career in Philadelphia. He studied piano and organ with his father Benjamin Cross, one of Philadelphia's pioneer musicians; violin with Charles Hommann and Charles Hupfeld; composition and theory with Leopold Meignen; and violoncello with Leopold Engelke. From the age of 15 he was a church organist, known especially for his insistence on conducting the choir and his habit of improvising at the organ. He served many churches, including St. Patrick's, St. John's, First Baptist, St. Peter and St. Paul's (1862-80) and Holy Trinity (1880-97). He also conducted the Orpheus Club, a male group (1872-97); the Euridice Chorus, a women's chorus (1886-97); and the mixed Cecilian Chorus. He was an outstanding teacher and a talented, cultured man; like his father, he improved music in Philadelphia. His piano music, written throughout his long career, is refined, disciplined and highly enjoyable for performer and listener. [I]

DE KOVEN, [HENRY LOUIS] REGINALD (b. Middletown, CT, 3 April 1859; d. Chicago, IL, 16 January 1920). Critic, composer. After the family moved to England in 1872, his father prepared him for Oxford. He had a year of piano study with Wilhelm Speidel in Stuttgart before taking a degree in history at St. John's College, Oxford (1879), and after graduation had another year at Stuttgart during which he studied piano with Siegmund Lebert and theory with

Dionys Pruckner. Following further composition studies with Johann Christian Hauff in Frankfort and singing lessons with Luigi Vannucini in Florence, Italy, he returned to the United States in 1882 and went to work in a bank. Two years later he married and joined his father-in-law's dry goods firm in Chicago, but he was a discontented businessman and continued to compose whenever possible. Encouraged to try a career in music when his comic opera **The Begum** had a successful production in Philadelphia in 1887, the next year he went to Vienna to study light opera with F. F. Richard Genée. He worked another year for his father-in-law and at the same time was music critic for the Chicago **Evening Post** (1889-90), then the striking response to his romantic opera **Robin Hood** produced in Chicago in 1890--it had more than 3000 successful performances--finally convinced him to give up business for a career as a composer. He studied opera with Léo Delibes in Paris for a brief time before Delibes's death in 1891, then settled in New York as music critic for the New York **World** (1891-97) and **Harper's Weekly** (1895-97). From 1897 to 1905 he lived in Washington, DC, where he was music critic for the New York **Journal** (1898-1900) and in 1902 founded--and for three seasons directed--the Washington Philharmonic Orchestra. He was again living in New York during 1905-13 and returned to his post as music critic for the **World** (1907-12); he lived in Europe during 1913-16; and spent the last years of his life in New York as music critic for the New York **Herald.** De Koven was one of the most prolific, successful and well-known American composers of light opera, and his song "O Promise Me" from **Robin Hood** has been a favorite solo at generations of American weddings. In his stage works and piano pieces he has been described as "master of a style singularly perspicuous and attractive, marked by decided melodies which flow in an easy, graceful manner." [I]

DENNEE, CHARLES FREDERICK (b. Oswego, NY, 1 September 1863; d. Brookline, MA, 29 April 1946). Pianist, teacher, composer. Apart from some studies with Hans von Bülow during Bülow's visit to America in 1889-90, he was a wholly American-trained composer. From the age of seven he studied piano with Frank Schilling, a local teacher, and on Schilling's recommendation was sent in 1879 to the New England Conservatory in Boston, MA, where his teachers included Alfred Dudley Turner and Stephen Emery. About a year later his father's business failed, so to support himself he gave music lessons and in 1881 was hired to play for Boston dancing classes. After graduation (1883) he was appointed to teach piano at the Conservatory, and he taught there for more than 62 years. Meanwhile until 1897, when he crushed his hand in a carriage accident, he also maintained a heavy concert schedule, giving more than a thousand concerts or lecture-recitals in the United States and Canada. Although he eventually regained some use of his hand, he stopped concertizing and concentrated on teaching and composing. He published a selection of essays titled **Musical Journeys** (1938) and was editor of a new edition of the **Century Library of Music** and also of several volumes of **Music and**

Musicians. Dennée's piano music was praised and performed during the composer's lifetime. One critic wrote that "he is fertile in ideas for subjects, and extraordinarily quick to discover means of motivating these ideas attractively." [I]

DEWEY, FERDINAND (b. East Brookfield, VT, ca.1853; d. Beverly, MA, 14 May 1900). Composer. The Boston city directories from 1885 through 1895 list him as a music teacher, and according to his obituary notice he was a prominent figure in Boston music circles. His descriptive, colorful salon music is pleasant, melodious, not difficult. [I]

DOENHOFF, ALBERT VON (b. Louisville, KY, 16 March 1880; d. New York, NY, 3 October 1940). Pianist, teacher, composer. The son of Hélène von Doenhoff, an opera singer and teacher, he had a fine musical background and was given a thorough musical education. As a child he had lessons at the Cincinnati College of Music, then studied in New York with Alexander Lambert at the New York College of Music (1891-95), with Xaver Scharwenka (1895-98), and with Rafael Joseffy at the National Conservatory (1899-1905). His teaching career began in 1897 and continued until his death, and following his piano début in New York in 1905, he was also an active concert pianist. Between 1910 and 1915 he made more than one hundred appearances with various orchestras in New York. Doenhoff's best piano music, most of it very difficult, is challenging for the performer, but eminently worth the effort. [I]

DRESEL, OTTO (b. Geisenheim, Germany, 20 December 1826; d. Beverly, MA, 26 July 1890). Pianist, writer, composer. He was a pupil of Moritz Hauptmann at Leipzig, and also had the friendship and guidance of Ferdinand Hiller and Mendelssohn. In 1848 he visited New York City, where he played in a series of concerts (1849) and was the pianist in Theodore Eisfeld's chamber-music concerts in 1851. He returned briefly to Germany, then settled in Boston, MA in 1852, and until his retirement in 1868 he was Boston's outstanding pianist. A cultivated musician, he broadened and improved the taste of the city's concert-going public. He played fine German classical music on his programs; was the first to successfully introduce the songs of his close friend Robert Franz to America; gave chamber-music concerts like those presented by Eisfeld in New York; and expounded his views in articles published in Dwight's **Journal of Music.** For many years the Bach Club met weekly at his home during the winter to sing Bach and Handel. Dresel's piano transcriptions are equal to the best of his nineteenth-century contemporaries. [I]

DULCKEN, FERDINAND QUENTIN (b. London, England, 1 June 1837; d. Astoria, NY, 10 December 1901). Pianist, teacher. He was the son of Louise David Dulcken (a pianist who gave lessons to Queen

Victoria) and nephew of the violinist Ferdinand David. He studied at the Leipzig Conservatory with Ignaz Moscheles, Moritz Hauptmann, Niels Gade and Carl Becker, and later worked under Ferdinand Hiller in Cologne. He taught at the Warsaw Conservatory and at Moscow and St. Petersburg, then lived in Paris for several years. Meanwhile he made extensive tours through Europe with Henri Wieniawski, Henri Vieuxtemps, Apolinary de Kontski and others; and when he emigrated to America (1876) he continued to make tours with prominent artists, including Eduard Reményi, Marie Rôze, Rafael Joseffy. He spent the rest of his life in New York as teacher and composer. Dulcken's keyboard music is well crafted with interesting and original melodic and rhythmic features. [I]

DVORSKY, MICHEL [see **JOSEF HOFMANN**]

EICHHEIM, HENRY (b. Chicago, IL, 3 January 1870; d. Montecito, CA, 22 August 1942). Violinist, conductor, composer. He had early music lessons with his father Meinhard Eichheim, a cellist in the Theodore Thomas Orchestra, and also studied at the Chicago Musical College, where his teachers included Simon Jacobsohn, Leopold Lichtenberg and Carl Becker. After graduating in 1888 he spent one year as a violinist with the Thomas Orchestra, then for 22 years played violin in the Boston Symphony Orchestra (1890-1912). While in Massachusetts he also conducted the symphony orchestra at Winchester for four years. From 1912 he focused his creative energy on composition, and sometimes gave solo recitals. During four extensive tours (1915, 1919, 1922, 1928) of the Far East--Japan, China, Korea, Burma, etc.--he made voluminous notes on oriental music and authentic oriental instruments, some of which he later included in his own scores. He frequently lectured on oriental music, and was one of the first to attempt to perform and interpret it for American audiences. His music, once widely performed and acclaimed, is not heard today; his large collection of oriental instruments is housed at the University of California at Santa Barbara. Eichheim's piano music might be characterized as a type of oriental impressionism. [I]

EMERY, STEPHEN ALBERT (b. Paris, ME, 4 October 1841; d. Boston, MA, 15 April 1891). Teacher, writer, composer. When poor health forced him to leave Colby College at Waterville, ME after his freshman year (1859), he pursued his interest in music and had his first lessons with Henry S. Edwards of Portland, ME. In 1862 he entered the Leipzig Conservatory, where his teachers included Louis Plaidy, Benjamin Papperitz, Ernst F. Richter and Moritz Hauptmann, then for a brief time studied piano with Fritz Spindler in Dresden. He returned to Portland in 1864, taught privately there for two years, then spent the rest of his life in Boston, MA. One of the original faculty of the New England Conservatory, he taught harmony, theory and composition there from 1867 until his death. He was an assistant editor of the Boston **Musical Herald,** and wrote the well-known **Elements of Harmony** (1880). Emery wrote both salon and "serious" music. It is, for the most part, technically difficult, stylish and appealing. [I]

EPSTEIN, ABRAHAM ISAAC (b. Mobile, AL, 18 January 1858; d. St. Louis, MO, 8 April 1929). Pianist, organist, teacher, composer. One of three brothers who all became well-known pianists, he studied with Hermann Lawitsky, Léon Prévost and Samuel Prowse Warren. When he was about 15 his family moved to Kalamazoo, MI, where he became organist at both the Jewish Temple and the Presbyterian Church, then from 1878 until his death he lived in St. Louis, MO. During his long and distinguished career there he taught at the Beethoven Conservatory of Music for fifty years (1878-1929) and was organist at both the Shaare Emeth Temple and St. John's Methodist Episcopal Church for 45 years (1879-1924). An exceptional accompanist, he played for most of the prominent artists appearing in St. Louis, and with his brother Marcus became famous for two-piano recitals. Epstein wrote primarily light, "pretty" salon music for the piano. [I]

EPSTEIN, MARCUS ISAAC (b. Mobile, AL, 7 June 1855; d. St. Louis, MO, 2 May 1947). Pianist, teacher, composer. He was one of three brothers who all became well-known pianists. He studied at the Leipzig Conservatory (1871-74) with Carl Reinecke, Salomon Jadassohn and Ernst F. Richter, then like his brother Abraham settled in St. Louis, MO. He taught at the Beethoven Conservatory from 1879 until his retirement in the 1930s, and with his brother became famous for two-piano recitals. His keyboard repertoire, some of it quite difficult, concentrates on dance types like the polka and polonaise. [I,III]

FAIRCHILD, BLAIR (b. Belmont, MA, 23 June 1877; d. Paris, France, 23 April 1933). Composer. While at Harvard he studied music with John Knowles Paine and Walter Spalding, and after graduating in 1899 studied piano with Giuseppe Buonamici in Italy. He served in the United States foreign service (1901-03) in Constantinople and Teheran before deciding on a career in music. In 1903 he settled in Paris and, except for sporadic visits to New York, remained there until his death, an expatriate composer considered American by Europeans and European by Americans. He had several years of study with Charles M. Widor and J. B. Ganaye, became a successful teacher and composer, and was the first American-born composer to have a work performed in a French government-subsidized theater (**Dame Libellule** at the Opéra Comique, 1921). During World War I he represented the American Friends of Musicians in France, and for this relief work was awarded membership in the French Legion of Honor. Fairchild's piano music, most of it very difficult, is variously conservative and impressionistic, but frequently shows a convincingly contemporary approach. [I]

FAIRLAMB, JAMES REMINGTON (b. Philadelphia, PA, 23 January 1838; d. Ingleside, NY, 16 April 1908). Organist, composer. He had early lessons with his mother and with Charles Boyer, organist of St. Stephen's Church, and all through his teen years played the organ at different Philadelphia churches, including the Tabernacle Baptist and the Clinton St. Presbyterian. From 1858 until 1865 he lived in Europe. He studied piano with Antoine Marmontel in Paris and composition with Teodulo Mabellini in Florence, then in 1861 President Lincoln appointed him as American consul in Zurich, Switzerland, a post he held until 1865. When he returned to the United States he located temporarily in Washington, DC, where he was organist at the church of the Epiphany and also formed an amateur opera company that produced his grand opera **Valérie** (in 1869 he produced a reduced version in Philadelphia under the title **Treasured Tokens**). From 1870 he was organist at a succession of churches in Washington, DC, Philadelphia, New York City and in Jersey City and Elizabeth, NJ. He was one of the founders of the American Guild of Organists (1896). Fairlamb's few piano works which, according to one writer, have "spontaneity and charm," are classed as salon music. [I]

FALK, LOUIS (b. Unter Ostern, near Darmstadt, Germany, 11 December 1848; d. Chicago, IL, 1925). Organist, teacher composer. When he was about two his family emigrated to America, lived about four years in Pittsburgh, PA and then moved to Rochester, NY. He began piano lessons at the age of eight and by eleven was organist at the North Street Baptist Church, Rochester. During 1860-65 his family lived in Chicago, IL, where he attended St. Paul's Evangelical Church School and continued with his music studies. At the age of 13 he began earning extra money by playing the violin in a small orchestra at McVicker's Theater. Late in 1865 he left for Germany, where he worked for two years under Wilhelm Volckmar at Homberg and another two years at the Leipzig Conservatory studying with Ignaz Moscheles, Benjamin Papperitz, Ernst F. Richter, Moritz Hauptmann, Carl Reinecke and Ferdinand David. When he returned to Chicago in 1869 he joined the faculty of the Chicago Musical College, an association that lasted for nearly 50 years, and began an equally durable career as organist. He was at the Unity Church from 1869 until the building burned in 1871; at the Union Park Congregational Church (1871-98); at the Oak Park Congregational Church (1898-1908); and at the New Church in Kenwood from 1908 until about 1923. At the same time he was organist at the Jewish synagogue on Saturdays, first at the Sinai Temple, later for 11 years at the Zion Temple. He also gave organ recitals, and was a pioneer organ recitalist in the Midwest. Being primarily an organist, Falk wrote little piano music. [I]

FARWELL, ARTHUR (b. St. Paul, MN, 23 April 1872; d. New York, NY, 20 January 1952). Editor, critic, composer. Since his father owned a wholesale hardware firm in St. Paul, he grew up "chiefly amongst tools and electricity." Nevertheless, he began violin lessons at the age of nine, and was initially inspired to become a composer during a summer vacation in the White Mountains just before entering college when he and three other amateurs (four-hand piano, cello and violin) attempted to play Schubert's Unfinished Symphony. That joyful experience and the later delight of hearing the Boston Symphony Orchestra convinced him that he wanted to be a composer. He later claimed that he stayed with electrical engineering at the Massachusetts Institute of Technology in Boston only because he could attend the BSO concerts every week through the season. After graduating in 1893, he studied with George Chadwick and Homer Norris in Boston (1894-97), with Engelbert Humperdinck and Hans Pfitzner in Germany (1897-99) and with Alexandre Guilmant in Paris (1899). He lectured on music history at Cornell University in Ithaca, NY (1899-1901) and then, discouraged because he was unable to find a publisher for his **American Indian Melodies** and aware that other American composers were also finding it difficult to get their unconventional works published, he founded the Wa-Wan Press at Newton Center, MA. Named for an Omaha Indian ceremony celebrating "peace, fellowship and song," its purpose was to publish recognizably "American" music, especially works based on any folk music to be found on American soil (Indian, Negro, cowboy, Spanish, etc.). Altogether the Wa-Wan Press (1901-11) offered its subscribers several hundred compositions (vocal and instrumental) by 37 composers issued in beautifully designed and printed editions, often with an introduction by Farwell. To meet the Press's deficits he made lecture tours and wrote articles. After he moved to New York in 1909 to join the editorial staff of **Musical America**, it became increasingly difficult to manage the Press by long distance, and in 1912 he sold most of the Wa-Wan catalog (Carlos Troyer and Henry F. B. Gilbert works excepted) to G. Schirmer, New York. While serving as supervisor of municipal concerts in New York (1910-13), he became intensely interested in, and an ardent supporter of, community music, and with William Chauncy Langdon developed the idea of the community pageant: a drama having a city or town as its hero and the history of that community as its plot, with special emphasis on the historical "spirit" of the place. He organized pageants, masques and open-air concerts, and often composed the music and conducted at the events. He was also director of the Music School Settlement in New York (1915-18). When World War I interrupted these activities, he moved to California. He was acting head of the music department at the University of California at Berkeley (1918-19); he organized and conducted the Santa Barbara Community Chorus (1919-21); and he was the first recipient of the composer's fellowship at the Pasadena Music and Art Association (1921-25). Between 1927 and 1939 he taught theory and music history at Michigan State College in East Lansing, where he also, beginning in April, 1936, printed his music on his own lithographic handpress. He was an important and influential writer on music (chief critic of **Musical America** [1909-14], co-editor of **The Art of Music,** Vol.IV, and author of more than a hundred articles besides the introductions and essays he wrote for the Wa-Wan Press) and he made a strong and persistent plea for the musical expression of America's diverse cultures. His fascinating repertoire of "American" piano music and the means used to achieve it can be explained in Farwell's own words: "I am working for beauty and individuality, to learn the secrets of art - what it is that makes for the magical quality of the artistic,- working open-mindedly in any direction that presents itself as having possibilities - anxious to strike out paths for American advance - much more ready to invite my soul up in the High Sierras and record what arrives, than to hang around Carnegie Hall to find out what Honegger or Hindemith are doing." [I]

FERRATA, GIUSEPPE (b. Gradoli, Italy, 1 January 1865; d. New Orleans, LA, 28 March 1928). Pianist, teacher, composer. At the age of seven he played the clarinet in the town band, and before he was ten had become assistant conductor. He also studied piano with a local teacher, and at 14 won a scholarship at the Liceo Musicale of the Royal Academy of St. Cecilia in Rome, where he studied piano with Giovanni Sgambati and composition with Eugenio Terziani. He was 16 and still at the Academy when an uncle arranged an audition for him with Liszt, who accepted him as a pupil and worked with him for three winters in Rome. At graduation (1885) Liszt handed out the awards, and Ferrata received a first prize in piano, a first in composition and the grand prix awarded by the government. He lived mostly in Rome composing, teaching and performing until 1892 when he moved to the United States, and almost immediately embarked upon a new career as composer, teacher and pianist. He taught at Mount St. Mary's College, Emmitsburg, MA (1892-93); Greenville Female College, Greenville, SC (1894-1900); Brenau Conservatory, Gainsville, GA (1900-02); Beaver College, Beaver, PA (1902-07); and from 1908 until his death at Newcomb College of Tulane University, where he was the first director of the music department. He was highly regarded as a teacher, his music was played by major orchestras around the world and he was the recipient of many awards: knighted by the King of Portugal (1887), knighted by the King of Italy (1904) and made a Knight Commander of the Order of the Crown of Italy (1914). Ferrata excelled in the epigrammatic piano piece and wrote many delightful works in this genre. [I]

FIQUE, CARL (b. St. Magnus, near Bremen, Germany, 17 April 1867; d. Brooklyn, NY, 7 December 1930). Organist, teacher, conductor, composer. His family emigrated to America when he was about four, and settled in Hoboken, NJ. He attended the Hoboken Academy, had his first piano lessons with his uncle Frederick Bechtel, director of the Adelphi Conservatory in Brooklyn, and later studied at the Leipzig Conservatory with Carl Reinecke and Salomon Jadassohn. From 1887 he made his home in Brooklyn. He taught organ, piano and theory; was organist-choirmaster at the Zion Lutheran Church (1887-1928); directed the United Singers of Brooklyn (1904-21); and also organized and directed the Fiqué Choral Society and the Cosmopolitan Opera Players. A successful lecturer, between 1897 and 1915 he gave many lecture-recitals at the Brooklyn Academy of Music under the auspices of the Brooklyn Institute of Arts and Sciences.

Since he died alone while practising on a Saturday night at the Zion Lutheran Church, it is not precisely known whether he died late Saturday or early Sunday, December 7. Fiqué's Germanic background and education influenced his piano music, in matters of harmonic and contrapuntal texture, technical expertise and ethnic color. [I]

FLORIO, CARYL [see **WILLIAM JAMES ROBJOHN**]

FOERSTER, ADOLPH MARTIN (b. Pittsburgh, PA, 2 February 1854; d. Pittsburgh, 10 August 1927). Teacher, composer. His mother was an amateur pianist and his father a well-known portrait painter. After early lessons with his mother and Jean Manns in Pittsburgh, he attended the Leipzig Conservatory (1872-75), where he was a pupil of Ernst F. Richter, Benjamin Papperitz, Leo Grill, Adolph Schimon and Ernst F. Wenzel. He then taught for one year at the Fort Wayne (Indiana) Conservatory (1875-76) before returning to Pittsburgh, where he was active for 50 years and became one of the city's most prominent musicians. He taught voice and piano, conducted the Symphonic Society (1879-90) and Musical Union (1883-90), and in 1890 retired in order to have more time for composing. Emil Liebling wrote of his music: "The piano pieces of Mr. Adolph Foerster are melodious, exceedingly well written, thoroughly practical and should figure extensively in the every day curriculum of every teacher." [I]

FOOTE, ARTHUR WILLIAM (b. Salem, MA, 5 March 1853; d. Boston, MA, 8 April 1937). Teacher, pianist, organist, composer. Although his father, editor and part owner of the Salem **Gazette,** was apparently not musical, he allowed his children to have music lessons. Arthur was about 12 when he began piano studies with Fanny Paine, a pupil of Benjamin J. Lang, and when he was 14 he played for Lang, who recommended that he enroll in Stephen Emery's harmony class at the New England Conservatory in Boston. While at Harvard (1870-74) he studied with John Knowles Paine, and in his last two years led the Glee Club. The summer following graduation he took piano and organ lessons with Lang, and with Lang's encouragement returned that autumn to Harvard for another year with Paine. In 1875 he received an A.M. from Harvard, the first master's degree in music given in the United States, and that same year opened a teaching studio in Boston. He was exceptional for his time in that, apart from a few lessons in Paris with Stephen Heller studying Heller's own works (summer, 1883), he was wholly American trained. He made his piano début in 1876, from 1883 made eight solo appearances with the Boston Symphony Orchestra, gave occasional organ and piano recitals and appeared in chamber-music concerts (1880-95), but his chief interests were teaching and composing. One of Boston's outstanding piano teachers for more than 60 years, he also composed steadily, and almost everything he wrote was published in Boston by Arthur P. Schmidt, a faithful champion of American composers. He was organist at the Church of the Disciples (1876-78) and at the First Unitarian Church (1878-1910). In 1911 he served as acting chairman of the music department and guest lecturer for the summer session at the University of California at Berkeley, and from 1921 until his death taught at the New England Conservatory in Boston, giving ten lectures yearly on piano playing and piano teaching. He was elected to the National Institute of Arts and Letters (1898) and the American Academy of Arts and Sciences (1913); he received an honorary Mus.D. from Trinity College, Hartford, CT in 1919 and one from Dartmouth College, Dartmouth, NH in 1925. Foote was a superb, sensitive musician whose richly imaginative yet disciplined piano compositions are finely crafted. He ranks among the very best American composers of piano music. [I,II,III]

FOSTER, STEPHEN COLLINS (b. Lawrenceville [now in Pittsburgh], PA, 4 July 1826; d. New York, NY, 13 January 1864). Composer. As a child he taught himself to play several instruments but his businessman father failed to nurture this obvious talent with music lessons. He may have had some instruction from Henry Kleber, a German living in Pittsburgh, but he was mostly a self-taught musician. He attended academies in the Pennsylvania towns of Athens and Towanda, and his first known musical composition **The Tioga Waltz** was, according to the printed music, "composed and arranged for four flutes by Stephen Collins Foster at the age of 13 years. Performed at the college commencement, Athens, Pennsylvania, 1839, by himself and three other students." He stayed just one week at Jefferson College in Canonsburg, PA, then lived at home--the family had moved to Allegheny, PA--until 1846, a worry to his parents because of what they thought were his "idle, dreaming ways" and "strange talent for music." He was, however, already beginning to write the songs that would make him famous, and while working as a bookkeeper for his brother Dunning Foster in Cincinnati, OH (1846-50) he continued to compose. He had a unique musical background, for he had grown up hearing the rich melodies sung by Negroes working along the Ohio River, the music of the minstrel shows and the homey songs of traveling troupes and "singing families." More significantly, he had no contact with the foreign influences dominating music all along the East Coast. The American public understood his songs, and by 1850 enough of them had been successfully published to enable him to return to Allegheny and support himself as a songwriter. That same year he married, and some of his finest songs were published during the early years of the marriage: "Camptown Races" (1850), "Old Folks at Home" (1851), "Massa's in de Cold, Cold Ground" (1852), and "My old Kentucky Home" (1853). By 1861 mounting marital problems and his poor business sense forced his wife and daughter to leave him, and he spent his last years alone in New York, ill and dissipated and sometimes so poor that he sold his songs for pitifully small sums. He died in the Bellevue Hospital charity ward, but since his death his songs have brought him worldwide fame and memorials. He was the first musician to be elected to the Hall of Fame for Great Americans and the first American composer whose works were issued in a complete edition (reproductions privately printed by the Josiah K. Lilly Foundation). Lilly also assembled a vast collection of Fosteriana and presented it to the Stephen Foster Memorial Association in Pittsburgh. Foster's piano music, not comparable to his songs, is basically charming, easy salon music. [I,III]

FRADEL, CHARLES (b. Vienna, Austria, 29 August 1821; d. Tremont, NY, 7 November 1886). Pianist, teacher, composer. He studied with Simon Sechter in Vienna, and from about 1850 to 1857 was active in Paris and London as concert pianist and teacher, often under the patronage of royal or aristocratic families. He taught Prince Richard Metternich in Paris, and at one time was court pianist for the Duke of Saxe-Weimar-Eisenach. Around 1857 he emigrated to America and settled in New York City, where he began his American career as teacher and performer. At "his first annual concert in America," given at Irving Hall on March 16, 1866, he was assisted by Theodore Thomas, Sebastian Bach Mills and Robert Goldbeck, and he played his own **Polonaise.** He taught piano at the Grand Conservatory of Music in New York during its first year (1875-76). Fradel's substantial keyboard repertoire includes numerous operatic settings (paraphrases, potpourris) plus some useful sonatinas and interesting concert pieces. [I]

FREER, ELEANOR EVEREST (b. Philadelphia, PA, 14 May 1864; d. Chicago, IL, 13 December 1942). Singer, composer. Her mother was an amateur singer and her father Cornelius Everest was an organist, music teacher and voice coach to opera singers, and their home was a lively social and musical center where many celebrities came to visit and perform. She had her first lessons with her father, and from 1883 to 1886 was enrolled at the Ecole Marchesi in Paris, where she studied voice with Mme. Mathilde Marchesi and diction with Benjamin Godard. In 1866 she returned to Philadelphia with a "certificate of professorship," the Marchesi diploma that allowed her to teach the Marchesi method in the United States, and was soon teaching 60 voice lessons a week. During 1889-91 she also taught at the National Conservatory of Music in New York. After her marriage in 1891 she and her husband, a doctor and later also a lawyer, lived in Leipzig, where they studied and took full advantage of the city's musical entertainments (1892-99). From 1899 they lived in Chicago, and she gave her time to her family and social life until 1902, when she began five years of theory studies with Bernhard Ziehn. She was a staunch advocate of American music, founded the American Opera Society of Chicago (1921) and founded and for five years directed the "Opera in Our Language" Foundation. Freer's piano music is conservative but melodically and rhythmically interesting and useful. [I]

FRIML, [CHARLES] RUDOLPH (b. Prague, Czechoslovakia, 7 December 1879; d. Hollywood, CA, 12 November 1972). Pianist, composer. His musical talent appeared early, and he began composing at the age of ten. When he was 14 his father, an amateur performer on the zither and accordion, sent him to the Prague Conservatory, where he studied piano with Joseph Jiránek and composition with Antonin Dvořák, and made friends with a fellow student, the violinist Jan Kubelik. After graduation (1896) he accompanied Kubelik on an extended concert tour through Europe. In 1901 they toured the United States; in 1904 he made his solo piano début at Carnegie Hall in New York City; in 1906 he joined Kubelik for a second American tour, and afterward settled in New York as a pianist and teacher. That same year he played his First Piano Concerto with the New York Philharmonic Orchestra under Walter Damrosch. He made concert tours throughout the country, and became well known for his skillful keyboard improvisations, then his concert career was interrupted by an unexpected commission to compose an operetta. When Victor Herbert, who had been commissioned to write an operetta for Emma Trentini, the Italian coloratura, quarreled with the star, Friml was invited to replace Herbert. **The Firefly** (1912), written for Trentini, made a spectacular success on Broadway, largely because of two hit songs "Giannina Mia" and "Sympathy," and he began a new career as a composer of operettas. Between 1912 and 1930 he had 20 operettas produced on Broadway, some--**Rose Marie** (1924), **The Vagabond King** (1925), **The Three Musketeers** (1928)--even more successful than **The Firefly.** The immensely popular songs from his operettas--"Rose Marie," "Only a Rose," "Song of the Vagabonds," "Some Day," the duet "The Indian Love Call"--attained international fame, and some are still heard today. When operettas were no longer popular, he moved to Hollywood, CA, where he adapted three of them for films: **Rose Marie** in 1928, 1936 and 1954; **The Vagabond King** in 1930 and 1958; and **The Firefly** in 1937. For the film version of **The Firefly** he wrote, in collaboration with Herbert Stothart, the astonishingly successful (he later called it an abortion) "The Donkey Serenade." Throughout his long life he remained active as a pianist, conductor and arranger. His music collection is now housed in the music library at the University of California, Los Angeles. Friml's piano catalog presents a successful fusion of salon and "serious" styles. It is, expectedly, eminently melodic, appealing and very idiomatic for the keyboard. [I]

GALLICO, PAOLO (b. Trieste, 13 May 1868; d. New York, NY, 6 July 1955). Pianist, teacher, composer. At the age of 11 he began music lessons with L. Cimoso in Trieste, and by the time he was 15 he was giving recitals. At the Vienna Conservatory (1883-86) he studied with Julius Epstein and Anton Bruckner, and after his début in Milan in 1888 made many successful tours throughout Europe. In 1892 he emigrated to the United States, settled in New York and made a career as concert pianist and teacher. With the violinist Alexander Saslavsky and the cellist Henry Bramsen, he formed the New York Trio. He was the father of Paul Gallico, the well-known journalist and writer. Gallico's skill in modulation and his talent in improvisation combine to give his piano compositions unusual continuity and impressive stature. [I]

GANZ, RUDOLPH (b. Zurich, Switzerland, 24 February 1877; d. Chicago, IL, 2 August 1972). Pianist, teacher, conductor, composer. He had cello lessons with Friedrich Hegar and piano lessons with Robert Freund in Zurich; had further piano studies with his great-uncle Carl Eschmann-Dumur in Lausanne, Switzerland (1893-96); spent about a year working with F. Blumer in Strasburg, Alsace; and in 1899 was in Berlin studying piano with Ferruccio Busoni and composition with Heinrich Urban. In December, 1899 he made his piano début with the Berlin Philharmonic Orchestra, and in 1900 settled in Chicago. He was head of the piano department of the Chicago Musical College (now affiliated with Roosevelt University) from 1900 until 1905, then for about 20 years maintained a heavy concert schedule, touring through Europe, Canada and America and establishing a reputation as one of the foremost pianists of his time. Remarkable for his large concerto repertoire and his support of contemporary music, he gave first performances of works by contemporary composers such as Ravel, Bartók, Dohnányi, Debussy, d'Indy and Loeffler. From 1921 to 1927 he was music director of the St. Louis Symphony Orchestra, then in 1927 returned to the Chicago Musical College where he was vice-president (1927-33), president (1933-54) and president emeritus from 1954. He also conducted the Young Peoples Concerts of the New York Philharmonic Society (1938-49). Highly respected as a teacher, he taught almost until his death at the age of 95. Ganz's piano compositions are in general quite difficult. Infused with German romanticism, enhanced with sensitive chromaticisms, they provide unusual and rewarding challenges for the mature pianist. [I,II,V]

GEBHARD, HEINRICH (b. Sobernheim, Germany, 25 July 1878; d. North Arlington, NJ, 5 May 1963). Pianist, teacher, composer. He was taken to the United States as a boy and lived in Boston, MA, where he attended Roxbury High School and studied piano with Clayton Johns. In Vienna (1896-99) he studied piano with Theodore Leschetizsky and composition with Richard Heuberger. After making his début with the Boston Symphony Orchestra in 1899, he was an active and highly successful pianist and teacher for more than 50 years. He made 35 appearances with the Boston Symphony Orchestra in the years 1901-33, and also performed with other leading American orchestras; he gave solo recitals, and played with chamber-music ensembles, especially the Kneisel Quartet. Recognized as the finest interpreter of Charles Martin Loeffler's **A Pagan Poem,** he played the piano part at the first performance in Boston, later performed it 36 times in major American cities, and also arranged the work for two pianos. In 1955 he retired to North Arlington. His book **The Art of Pedaling** (1963) was published posthumously with an introduction by Leonard Bernstein, one of his pupils. Gebhard's serious approach to piano composition produced outstanding works, some of them extremely difficult, but always rewarding. Stylistically they reflect his interest in and involvement with impressionist music. [I,IV,V]

GEIBEL, ADAM (b. Neuenheim, Germany, 15 September 1855; d. Germantown, PA, 3 August 1933). Organist, teacher, publisher, composer. When nine days old he lost his sight because of a toxic eyewash, so when his family emigrated to Philadelphia he was educated at the Pennsylvania Institute for Instruction of the Blind (1864-74). He studied piano, organ, violin and composition with David Duffle Wood at the Institute, was graduated in 1872, then returned for two years of postgraduate work which he paid for by working as an assistant teacher. He was a regular member of the Institute faculty (1884-1901); from 1885 was organist at the John B. Stetson Mission; and from 1908 conductor of the Stetson Chorus. He was assistant organist to Dr. Wood at the Baptist Temple (1891-96), and also organist at several other churches in the area. In 1897 he founded the music publishing firm of Geibel and Lehman, and in 1906 became president of the Adam Geibel Publishing Co. He was awarded a Mus.D. from Temple University (1911). As a composer Geibel is best remembered for his lullaby "Kentucky Babe." His best piano compositions are sentimental salon pieces. [I]

GILBERT, HENRY FRANKLIN BELKNAP (b. Somerville, MA, 26 September 1868; d. Cambridge, MA, 19 May 1928). Composer. He may have had some musical training with his father, a bank clerk and also a singer, church organist and composer of hymns, but he taught himself how to play wind instruments. After graduating from Reading High School, he went to Boston for his musical education. He studied with George Whiting and George Henry Howard at the New England Conservatory (1886-87), had violin lessons with Emil Mollenhauer, and from 1889 to 1892 studied composition with Edward MacDowell, being the first pupil MacDowell accepted when he returned to America after years in Europe. He earned money playing in small orchestras in theaters, resort hotels and dance halls, but eventually resented this commercial hack music and decided to keep his music separate from his livelihood. He worked in an uncle's printing company and later for several music publishers, then in 1893 went to the World Columbian Exposition in Chicago, IL to pursue his interest in folk and ethnic music. He found work as a bread-and-pie cutter in a restaurant, and spent his free time roaming the fair grounds and making notes on Oriental and Slavic folk music. The following year a small inheritance made it possible for him to travel in England and France, where he spent most of his time reading French literature and collecting scores for Josiah D. Whitney, the Harvard science professor whose library became the core of the Harvard music library. Later that year in Cambridge, MA he and Whitney organized a series of chamber-music concerts illustrating Slavic themes found in modern East European music. Over the next six years he held a variety of jobs--real estate agent, factory worker, silkworm grower--working only enough to provide the essentials and only as much as his frail health, caused by a congenital heart defect, would permit. In 1901, having heard of the striking success of Gustave Charpentier's **Louise**, a popular opera epitomizing the folk spirit of Paris, he took a cattle boat to Europe in order to hear it, an experience that emboldened him to give all his time to composition. He returned home determined to compose music that would reflect the spirit of the American people and be wholly free of German and French influences. Despite poverty and poor health, he tramped around the country listening to the music of ordinary people and making notes on the melodies he heard in the fields, streets and music halls; along the rivers and even over department-store music counters. He used American materials, especially Negro and Indian themes, in his compositions, and was the first to use Negro spirituals and ragtime elements in concert orchestral works. His **Comedy Overture on Negro Themes** brought him his first noticeable success when it was performed (April, 1911) by the Boston Symphony Orchestra and enthusiastically received by both audience and critics. Many of his early works were published (Wa-Wan Press) by Arthur Farwell, another zealous defender of American music. Gilbert was a department editor for **The Art of Music** (1916) and a contributor to the **Musical Quarterly,** the **New Music Review** and other periodicals. In 1917-18 he lectured on "humor in music" at Harvard and Columbia. Gilbert's early works show a pleasant blend of romanticism and impressionism, later works are more contemporary. His ethnic or "American" compositions are successful in their attempted authenticity. [I,III]

GILFERT, CHARLES H. (b. Germany, ca.1787; d. New York, NY, 30 July 1829). Pianist, theater manager, music publisher, composer. The earliest notice we have of him is found on the program of a benefit concert given in New York on February 27, 1800, where he is listed as "C. H. Gilfert lately from Europe," and according to an advertisement in the New York **Evening Post,** he was still living in New York and giving piano lessons as late as November 5, 1812. Meanwhile he had apparently been dividing his time between New York and Charleston, SC, and between 1813 and 1825 Charleston was his base of operations. A versatile and energetic musician, he owned a "musical establishment" at 40 Broad Street, Charleston (ca.1813-17); was a member of the Philharmonic Society Orchestra and composed several works for that body; and was manager of two theaters: the Charleston Theater from 1817 to 1825, and "the Theater" in Richmond, VA from 1819 to 1823. His wife--late in 1815 he married Agnes Holman, an accomplished actress--played leading roles in both companies and assisted him as manager. In December 1817 he took over the Charleston Theater; managed it for eight seasons, some of them extremely successful (President Monroe attended in April, 1819; Lafayette was present in March, 1825); and during slow seasons usually took his company to Savannah, GA, where they had a highly enthusiastic following. In the meantime when his father-in-law Joseph Holman, who had planned a theater in Richmond, died before completing his plans, Gilfert took over the project and managed the Richmond Theater--called simply "the Theater"--from its opening on June 11, 1819 until October 7, 1823 when it failed because too many free tickets had been distributed to the stockholders. Near the end of the 1825 season he left Charleston to become manager of the theater in Albany, NY, and from early 1826 until his death managed the Bowery Theater in New York City. W. Stanley Hoole (**The Ante-Bellum Charleston Theater,** University of Alabama Press, 1946) felt that "Gilfert's ability as a manager and musician in Charleston cannot be too highly commended. For years he kept the drama on a high and respectable plane and brought leading American actors to the small, isolated Southern city." Throughout his busy career Gilfert also composed and arranged music, including three ballad operas, about 25 songs and an equal number of solo piano pieces, mostly dances and sets of variations. He excelled in composing piano variations, characterized by a variety of keyboard figurations, imaginative melodic transformations and interesting left-hand passages. [I]

GLEASON, FREDERICK GRANT (b. Middletown, CT, 17 December 1848; d. Chicago, IL, 6 December 1903). Organist, teacher, composer. Although his parents were musical and his talent showed at an early age, his father wanted him to become a minister. He was already 16 when he began serious music studies with Dudley Buck at Hartford, but thereafter had ten years of thorough musical training. In 1869 he studied at the Leipzig Conservatory with Ignaz Moscheles, Ernst F. Richter, Louis Plaidy and Johann Christian Lobe, and after Moscheles died (March 10, 1870) he moved to Berlin and continued his studies with Oscar Raif, Carl F. Weitzmann, Albert Loeschhorn and Carl August Haupt. Except for a visit home to Hartford (1872) and some time studying with Oscar Beringer in London that same year, he remained in Berlin until 1875. When he returned to the United States, he became organist of the Asylum Hill Congregational Church, Hartford, and in 1876 organist of the First Congregational Church, New Britain, CT. From 1877 until his death he lived in Chicago, having been appointed teacher of piano, organ, composition and orchestration at the Hershey School of Music. He was director of the Chicago Auditorium concerts (1900-03), editor of the **Musical Bulletin** (from 1871), editor of the **Music Review** (from 1891), and music critic for the **Chicago Tribune** (1884-89). He was the first president of the Manuscript Society of Chicago (1896-98), an early organization for the encouragement and protection of American composers, and again president at the time of his death. Gleason's small piano collection is tuneful, useful for young pianists. [I]

GODOWSKY, LEOPOLD (b. Soshly, near Wilno, Poland [now Vilnius, Lithuanian S.S.R.], 13 February 1870; d. New York, NY, 21 November 1938). Pianist, teacher, composer. He showed a remarkable talent from age three, and after a strikingly successful first public recital when he was nine, he was taken on a tour through Poland and Germany. He studied at the Berlin Hochschule für Musik (1881-84) under Ernst Rudorff and Woldemar Bargiel, then during 1884-86 appeared in America with the singers Clara Louise Kellogg and Emma Thursby and toured Canada with the violinist Ovide Musin. He returned to Europe and lived in Paris (1887-90), where he became the protégé and pupil of Saint-Saëns and a favorite performer in the Paris salons. He gave a command performance for the celebration of Queen Victoria's golden jubilee in 1887, and played frequently in both Paris and London. From 1890 until 1900 he lived mostly in America, the first five years in New York. He toured the country (1890-91), became an American citizen (1891) and conducted a class for piano teachers at the Broad Street Conservatory, Philadelphia, PA (1894). From 1895 to 1900 he was head of the piano department at the Chicago Conservatory of Music in Illinois. Besides teaching, composing and making tours, he devoted much time to piano practice, and when in 1900 he was engaged for a Berlin concert it was so successful he was immediately signed for five more appearances. He lived in Berlin until 1909, establishing a reputation as a masterful teacher and attaining fame as one of the most celebrated pianists of his day. In 1909 he moved to Vienna to become director of the master school of piano-playing at the Akademie der Tonkunst. He toured the United States during 1912-1914, then because of World War I again made his home in America. After the war he resumed his peripatetic life, expanding his concert tours--Europe, China, Japan, Java, the Philippines, Hawaii, South America, Mexico, Canada, the USA--and giving master classes in the West and on the Pacific Coast. His concert career ended abruptly in 1930 when he suffered a stroke in a studio while recording the Chopin Nocturnes, but he continued to compose. Godowsky wrote a great quantity of fascinating piano music: elaborate paraphrases, transcriptions, studies in rhythm, concerto cadenzas, left-hand pieces, exotic tone poems. He delighted in presenting the pianist with complex contrapuntal textures and intricate technical problems. [I,II,III,IV]

GOETSCHIUS, PERCY (b. Paterson, NJ, 30 August 1853; d. Manchester, NH, 29 October 1943). Teacher, theorist, writer, composer. Although he had some preliminary music lessons, he studied engineering with his father until he was 20, then went to Germany and lived there for 17 years. He studied at the Stuttgart Conservatory (1873-76) with Sigmund Lebert, Dionys Pruckner, Immanuel Faiszt and Arpad Doppler, and after graduation remained as a teacher. He taught harmony, composition and music history (1876-90) and in 1885 earned the rank of Royal Württemburg Professor. He also wrote music reviews for German periodicals and published his first book **The Material Used in Musical Composition** (1882), intended primarily for his English-speaking pupils. On his return to the United States he taught piano, theory and music history at Syracuse University in Syracuse, NY (1890-92), and received an honorary doctorate there in 1892. That same year he moved to Boston, MA, where he taught at the New England Conservatory (1892-96), opened a private studio (1896-1905) and was organist at the First Parish Church in Brookline (1897-1905). In 1905 he became head of the theory and composition department at the newly organized Institute of Musical Art (now a part of Juillard) in New York City, where for the next 20 years he had a pronounced effect on music education in the United States. After retiring to Manchester (1925) he continued to write and publish. His books on theory were at one time widely used. Goetschius, the supreme theorist, the elegant contrapuntist and revered teacher of others, composed music that is notable for its lyricism, its textural consistency and its compact structural designs. [I]

GOLDBECK, ROBERT (b. Potsdam, Prussia [now East Germany], 19 April 1839; d. St. Louis, MO, 16 May 1908). Pianist, teacher composer. He had early music lessons with his uncle Louis Köhler, a well-known composer and teacher, and subsequently became the protégé of the German naturalist Alexander von Humboldt, who sent him to Brunswick to study with Henry Litolff (1853-57). In Paris (1857-60) letters of introduction from his patron gave him access to the best social and musical circles, where he played many recitals and met distinguished musical and literary celebrities. He made his London début in 1860, and the following year emigrated to the United States and began a nearly 50-year roving career as teacher, performer, composer and publisher. He lived in New York (1861-67), composing, teaching and performing; spent about a year and a half in Boston, MA assisting Eben Tourjée in establishing the New England Conservatory; lived in Chicago, IL (1868-73), where he taught at the Chicago Conservatory and published **Goldbeck's Monthly Journal of Music** (1873); then settled in St. Louis for about ten years. He conducted the Harmonic Society, taught at the Beethoven Conservatory, founded the St. Louis College of Music (1880) and published another journal: **Goldbeck's Musical Instructor** (1882-83), later titled **Goldbeck's Musical Art** (1883-85). In the Fall of 1885 he moved back to New York and may have remained there five or six years teaching and giving recitals, but it is also possible that, when his uncle Louis Köhler died in 1866 and left him the conservatory at Königsberg, he went abroad for a time to take charge of it. He was back in St. Louis during 1892-94, in Chicago (1894-99), in London (1899-1902) and finally again in St. Louis, where he was head of Strassberger's Conservatory from 1902 until his death. Goldbeck was a versatile and seemingly tireless musician as well as a prolific composer of melodious and competently designed salon music. [I]

GOLDMARK, RUBIN (b. New York, NY, 15 August 1872; d. New York, NY, 6 March 1936). Teacher, pianist, composer. He was a nephew of the Hungarian composer Carl Goldmark. At the age of seven he began piano lessons with Alfred Livonius in New York, and later attended the Vienna Conservatory (1889-91), where he studied piano with Anton Door and composition with Robert Fuchs. When he returned to New York he studied piano with Rafael Joseffy and composition with Dvořák at the National Conservatory (1891-93), and at the same time taught piano and theory there. Having moved (1894) to Colorado because of health problems, he taught at the Colorado College Conservatory in Colorado Springs (1895-1901), but when his health improved he returned to New York (1902). He taught piano and theory privately, was head of the composition department at the Juilliard School of Music (1924-36) and gave several hundred lecture-recitals in the United States and Canada. In 1900 Colorado College awarded

him an honorary M.A. Goldmark often looked to nature for
inspiration in his piano compositions. A true Americanist, he
developed his themes freely and spontaneously, thereby creating
imaginative and often ingenious character pieces. [I]

GOTTSCHALK, LOUIS MOREAU (b. New Orleans, LA, 8 May 1829; d.
Tijuca, Brazil, 18 December 1869). Pianist, composer. The son of
an English-Jewish father and a French-Creole mother, he grew up
admidst the rich musical mixture permeating the old quarter of New
Orleans: the traditional songs and dances of the Creoles and the
pulsating rhythms of the Blacks and Latins. Musically precocious,
he began lessons at the age of five with François Letellier,
organist of the St. Louis Cathedral, and by the age of seven was
proficient enough to substitute for Letellier at the cathedral
organ. He was barely thirteen when his parents, acting on
Letellier's advice, sent him to Paris (May 17, 1842) for further
training. He studied piano with Charles Hallé and Camille Stamaty
and composition with Pierre Maleden, then in April, 1845 gave a
recital at the Salle Pleyel at which Chopin, present in the highly
enthusiastic audience, prophesied that he would become "the king of
pianists." He studied, composed and performed, often playing his
own compositions, and within a few years had become the darling of
Paris, dazzling his audiences with his virtuoso playing and
delighting them with his exotic "Creole" pieces. He made his
professional début at the Salle Pleyel in April, 1849, toured
Switzerland and France in the summer of 1850, then spent an
immensely successful year in Spain. He won the patronage of
Isabella II, and his concerts caused a sensation, especially when
he played the new works composed expressly for the Spanish tour.
After nearly 11 years abroad, he returned to America in early 1853
and in February gave a recital in New York, but his great European
reputation had not reached America, and success came slowly. In
October his father's death, hastened perhaps by financial failures,
changed his life abruptly. Affluent all his life, he now found
himself responsible for the care of his mother and six younger
siblings, a problem he solved by making more tours, giving more
concerts on each tour and deliberately composing the kind of
compositions he knew the American public would buy. For three
hectic years he toured throughout the United States, except for
making a long visit to Cuba (1854-55) and occasional appearances in
Canada, then fled to Havana to recuperate (Feb., 1857). Details are
lacking, but he seems to have spent the next five years wandering
through the West Indies and into parts of South America, sometimes
resting and enjoying life, sometimes giving concerts "wherever I
found a piano." By February, 1862 he was back in New York for the
beginning of a killing concert schedule which he was to maintain
for more than three years and during which he traveled an estimated
95,000 miles and played about 1100 recitals. He ended the tour in
California in September, 1865, left for South America that same
month, and never returned home. He gave a concert in Panama in
October and then, so far as is known, spent his last four years
traveling and concertizing in Peru, Chile, Uruguay and finally

Brazil. He arrived in Rio de Janeiro in May, 1869, gave concerts in June and July, then began organizing "monster concerts" involving hundreds of performers. Despite recurring attacks of fever and prostrating heat, he kept up a heavy schedule of rehearsing and performing until November 24, when he collapsed while playing his composition **Morte!**. Removed to the higher, cooler suburb of Tijuca, he died there on December 18; in 1870 his remains were reburied in Greenwood Cemetery, Brooklyn, NY. Gottschalk was the first American composer to write true nationalist music and the first American pianist to achieve international fame. Except for some songs, a few orchestral pieces and possibly three operas, Gottschalk wrote--and wrote well--for his own instrument. The more than one hundred solo piano works include early Afro-American pieces, West Indian dances, patriotic variations, virtuoso pieces in the European tradition, dances and descriptive pieces. Their highly eclectic, composite style is the natural result of his cosmopolitan existence. [I,III,IV,V]

GROBE, CHARLES (b. Saxe-Weimar, Germany, ca.1817; d. Stroudsburg, PA, 20 October 1879). Pianist, teacher, composer. The son of a Lutheran minister, he emigrated to the United States in 1839. He was a professor of music at the Wesleyan Female Collegiate Institute in Wilmington, DE from 1840 to about 1862, and after leaving the Institute continued to live in Wilmington for another eight years. Newspaper notices and the Wilmington city directories--he is last listed in 1870-71--indicate that he gave private music lessons and operated a music store. They also reveal that he was an active and highly respected member of the community. Leaving Wilmington in 1870, he went to Pennington, NJ, where he was appointed "principal of music" at the Pennington Seminary (1870-1874). His last teaching position was at the Centenary Collegiate Institute in Hackettstown, NJ (1874-79). If opus numbers can be depended upon, Grobe produced a staggering amount of piano music--almost 2000 compositions. Because of his prolificacy, a matter of awe and praise in his day, he has been called a piano-piece factory, but a great many of his works were published and the public obviously bought them and played them. Beyond that, his wide-ranging repertoire provides us with an index to the traditional and favorite tunes sung and played in mid-19th-century America and makes an important commentary on the social and cultural tastes of the era. Within the scope of his fertile imagination and ingenuity, Grobe provided something for almost everyone. Perhaps half of his piano repertoire consists of variations on a given theme--someone else's theme--and his titles usually explain that he has embellished the theme "with brilliant variations." A typical Grobe composition begins with a simple introduction. Then the theme appears, followed by one to three variations and a finale. Throughout the piece, the emphasis is on melody and accompaniment. Note: Documented information about Grobe's life and career is sparse. Research by Ann L. Wilhite of Midland Lutheran College, Freemont, Nebraska has disclosed the latest information, included above. [I]

GRUNN, [JOHN] HOMER (b. West Salem, WI, 5 May 1880; d. Los Angeles, CA, 7 June 1944). Pianist, teacher, composer. In 1896 he began four years of piano study with Emil Liebling in Chicago, meanwhile studying theory with Adolph Brune, then went to Germany, where he had additional piano training under Ernst Jedlicza at the Stern Conservatory in Berlin. From 1903 to 1907 he taught piano at the Chicago Musical College; and from 1907 to 1910 he was director of the piano department at the Arizona School of Music in Phoenix, where he pursued his interest in the chants and dances of the Southwest Indians. In 1910 he settled permanently in Los Angeles. He taught privately, was a member (piano) of the Brahms Quintet Chamber Music Organization and gave concerts in the West and Midwest. Grunn's best piano pieces are those inspired by contact with the West and his study of American Indian chants. [I,IV]

HACKH, OTTO [CHRISTOPH] (b. Stuttgart, Germany, 30 September 1851; d. Brooklyn, NY, 22 September 1917). Pianist, teacher, composer. He studied at the Stuttgart Conservatory with Dionys Pruckner, Wilhelm Speidel and Max Seifriz, and from 1872 was also an assistant teacher under Speidel. He made piano concert tours for several seasons, chiefly in Germany, Switzerland and London, then in 1880 went to New York City. He was head of the piano department at The Grand Conservatory of New York (1880-89), then taught privately for two years. After spending several years in Europe (1891-95), he resumed his private teaching in New York and Brooklyn. Hackh composed a varied collection of piano pieces: operatic transcriptions, delightful (and difficult) salon pieces and some excellent serious works (études, polonaises, character pieces). [I,III]

HADLEY, HENRY [KIMBALL] (b. Somerville, MA, 20 December 1871; d. New York, NY, 6 September 1937). Conductor, composer. His grandfather and father taught music in the Somerville public schools. He had early music lessons with his father; at the age of 16 became organist of the First Congregational Church, where his mother sang in the choir; and later studied with Stephen Emery and George Chadwick at the New England Conservatory in Boston. During the 1893-94 season he toured the United States as conductor of the Laura Schirmer-Mapleson Opera Company, then studied counterpoint with Eusebius Mandyczewski in Vienna (1894-95). He was director of music at St. Paul's Episcopal Church in Garden City, NY from 1895 until 1904, when he resigned in order to have more time for composing and conducting. Meanwhile his Second Symphony had received the Paderewski Prize in 1901. He spent five years in Europe (1904-09) conducting extensively, the last year at the Stadttheater of Mainz, where he produced his one-act opera **Safie.** After returning to the United States, he was conductor of the Seattle Symphony Orchestra (1909-11), first conductor of the San Francisco Symphony Orchestra (1911-15), and associate conductor of the New York Philharmonic Orchestra (1920-27). An advocate of American music, he formed the Manhattan Symphony Orchestra (1929) with the intention of including works by American composers on every program. He was one of the most prominent and successful conductor-composers of his day, frequently appearing as guest conductor in America and Europe and also conducting in Japan and Argentina. In 1924 he conducted the Worcester (MA) Festival; in 1934 was the first conductor of the Berkshire Symphonic Festival at Stockbridge, MA (now the Berkshire Festival, Lenox); in 1935 conducted the Chicago Symphony Orchestra at the Century of Progress Exposition celebrating Chicago's one hundredth anniversary. He was the founder and first president of the Association for American Composers and Conductors (1933), which after his death endowed the Henry Hadley Memorial Library, a collection of compositions by American composers now housed at the New York Public Library. He was a member of the National Institute of Arts and Letters and the American Academy of Arts and Letters, was awarded the Order of Merit by the French government and given an honorary Mus.D. from Tufts University (1925). A prolific composer, he received many awards and prizes for his compositions, now rarely heard. Hadley wrote principally short pieces for piano, epigrammatic works enhanced with inventive rhythms and distinctively styled. [I,V]

HANCE, JAMES F. (fl.New York, NY, 1815-1835). Teacher, composer. Little is known about this composer. His piano works included in the Bibliography were published (undated) by William Dubois or Dubois and Stodard in New York. According to Wolfe, the New York **Evening Post** (Sept.1, 1827) announced the publication of his **New System of Musical Education.** New York City directories of the mid 1820s list him as a "professor of music"; however, the last known listing (1833) suggests that he gave up his musical career and became a carpenter. Hance wrote light, tuneful piano music, mostly variations, that appealed to the general public. [I,III]

HECKSCHER, CELESTE DE LONGPRE, née Massey (b. Philadelphia, PA, 23 February 1860; d. Philadelphia, 18 February 1928). Pianist, composer. From early childhood she could improvise at the piano, and was only 10 when she began publishing her first songs. She studied composition with Henry Albert Lang, orchestration with Wassili Leps and piano with Zerndahl. Her symphonic suite **Dances of the Pyrenees** was performed by the Philadelphia Symphony Orchestra in February, 1911 and subsequently by other leading American orchestras; her opera **The Rose of Destiny** was produced at the Philadelphia Opera House in May, 1918. She was for many years president of the Philadelphia Operatic Society. Mrs. Heckscher wrote very few piano pieces, but each shows expert handling of musical materials and a feeling for the keyboard idiom. [I,III]

HEILMAN, WILLIAM CLIFFORD (b. Williamsport, PA, 27 September 1877; d. Williamsport, 20 December 1946). Teacher composer. After graduating from Harvard (1900) with honors in music, he continued his musical education in Europe (1900-04), studying with Joseph

Rheinberger in Munich and Charles M. Widor in Paris. On his return
to the United States, he was appointed an instructor in the Harvard
music department, became an assistant professor in 1910, a lecturer
in 1920 and retired in 1930. For a time he was organist at the
Church of the Epiphany in Winchester, MA. Interested in art as well
as music, during sabbatical leaves and other trips through Europe,
England and North Africa he made architectural drawings in crayon
and watercolor, and after retiring from teaching divided his time
between composing and drawing. He came from a well-to-do family of
furniture manufacturers, and was in turn a generous patron of the
Williamsport Library, contributing annually gifts of music or books
or funds for their purchase. Heilman's attractive, well-designed
piano music was considerably influenced by late German
romanticism. [I]

HEINRICH, ANTHONY PHILIP [ANTON PHILIPP] (b. Schönbüchel, Bohemia
[now in Czechoslovakia], 11 March 1781; d. New York, NY, 3 May
1861). Violinist, teacher, composer. The adopted son and heir of a
wealthy uncle, he became a successful and influential merchant.
When the Napoleonic wars threatened the Austrian economy, he took a
boatload of Bohemian wares to America (1810), hoping to make a new
start there, and settled in Philadelphia, PA. An amateur musician,
self-taught except for early violin and piano lessons, he became
director of music, without salary, at the Southwark Theater, then
the following year the Austrian financial crash left him
practically destitute. Although he married and had a daughter
(Antonia, born during a visit to Bohemia in 1813), his family life
was brief. Antonia, left with a relative in Bohemia, was separated
from him for 24 years, and his wife died shortly after they
returned to America. When a second business venture failed
(1816-17), he began to think seriously of a career in music. In
1817 he walked 300 miles across Pennsylvania to Pittsburgh, having
been offered a salaried position as director of music at the
Theater, but the company experienced financial difficulties and he
was soon out of work. He continued west, traveling 400 miles down
the Ohio River to Kentucky, and ended his journey at Lexington,
then Kentucky's largest town. He arrived around the end of
October, and immediately began to perform, conduct and teach. On
November 12 he presented a "grand concert of vocal and instrumental
music," most likely a benefit for himself, at which he directed the
orchestra-band and also played the violin and piano. He opened the
concert with the "full band" in a **SIMFONIA con MINUETTO** (probably
the First Symphony) by Beethoven, and although they may have played
only the first movement, as the record stands this was the first
known performance of a Beethoven symphony in America. In the spring
(1818) he retired to a log house in the woods near Bardstown, where
he practised long hours on his violin and, though he lacked formal
training in theory and composition, began to compose. More than
anything else this enthusiastic, romantic new American wanted to
write "American" music and be recognized as an "American" composer,
and he made a brave attempt at translating America--its history,
heroes, weather, landscapes, Indians, natural wonders, current

events--into musical sound.   About two years later he sent his collection--songs, piano pieces and violin pieces--to Bacon and Hart, music publishers in Philadelphia, where they were published in one volume **The Dawning of Music in Kentucky, or The Pleasures of Harmony in the Solitudes of Nature** (May, 1820). Much admired in its day, the collection is significant now because it is one of the earliest musical anthologies to appear in America. In a delightful "criticism" of his collection in the Boston **Euterpeiad** (April 13, 1822) Heinrich is called, for the first time, the "Beethoven of America," a phrase later often used to describe him.   He lived in Boston (1823-26) playing in concerts and giving lessons to raise money to go abroad to find Antonia, but when he finally sailed for Europe (Sept., 1826) a shipboard accident that damaged his violin and broke his finger prevented him from raising more money to go beyond England. He lived there (1826-31), supporting himself by playing violin in the Drury Lane and Vauxhall Gardens orchestras, teaching privately and composing.   Although he was desperately poor, these were stimulating years, for he heard Paganini play and met and dined with Mendelssohn. He returned to Boston (1831-33); was in London again (1833-35); and finally reached the Continent (1835), only to learn that Antonia had already gone to America. For some reason he remained in Europe for about two years.   He gave a highly acclaimed concert of his works at Graz in 1836, and that same year established an international reputation as a composer with an entry in Gustav Schilling's **Encyclopädie** (in 1839 he was also included in Fétis's **Biographie universelle**).   In the Fall of 1837 he returned to the United States, was finally reunited with his daughter and for the next twenty years lived mostly in New York teaching, performing and composing.   On his last visit to Europe (1857-59) he climaxed his career with three concerts at Prague in 1857, the last devoted exclusively to his orchestral works.   A contradictory figure, he was in a way amazingly successful and beloved, known affectionately as "Father Heinrich" or "Caro Padre"; yet he was also sometimes laughed at as "old Father Heinrich," and he died in poverty and neglect. Looking back, we must credit him with foresight.   In his enthusiasm for everything American and his interest in American Indian lore, he predicted the future.   Long after he was forgotten, a later generation of American musicians became aware of nationalism and struggled long and hard to accomplish what he had tried to do all by himself.   His piano music is flowery, complicated and repetitious--he reworked the same materials over and over--but it shows a fine sense of the dramatic and a fertile, free-flowing imagination. [I]

HELLER, ROBERT [see **WILLIAM HENRY PALMER**]

HENNINGES, REINHOLD (b. Halle, Germany, 20 March 1836; d. Cleveland, OH, 2 August 1913). Teacher, conductor, composer.   He emigrated to America around 1859, settled first in Mansfield, OH, and in 1867 moved permanently to Cleveland, where he became a leading conductor, teacher and composer. He conducted the Heights

Männerchor and the Orpheus Society; taught privately and at the Cleveland Institute of Music; and for a time was organist at the First Methodist Church. In 1888 he joined the music faculty of Shorter College, Rome, GA. Most of Henninges' piano works are conservative salon pieces with some Chopin influence. [I]

HERBERT, VICTOR (b. Dublin, Ireland, 1 February 1859; d. New York, NY, 26 May 1924). Cellist, conductor, composer. An infant when his father died, he was seven when his mother and stepfather, a German physician, moved to Stuttgart, Germany, where he began musical training. He later studied the cello with Bernhard Cossman at Baden-Baden and composition with Max Seifriz at the Stuttgart Conservatory. After a tour as soloist through Germany, France and Italy, he joined the court orchestra at Stuttgart (1883-86) and met his future wife, Therese Foerster, a soprano at the court opera. In the meantime he had already begun composing, and was soloist in his **Suite for Cello and Orchestra, Op.3** (1883) and in his **Cello Concerto, Op.8** (1885). Married in August, 1886, the Herberts arrived in New York in October, she to sing a starring role at the Metropolitan Opera House and he to play the cello in the opera orchestra. Once in New York, he extended his activities well beyond the opera house orchestra, performing with other orchestras and chamber ensembles, conducting and teaching. Around 1889 he was appointed to the faculty of the National Conservatory of Music. A competent conductor, he directed summer concerts, festivals and short tours, then in 1893 succeeded the late Patrick S. Gilmore as bandmaster of the nationally known 22nd Regiment Band of the New York National Guard, and made many successful tours with it. He conducted the Pittsburgh Symphony Orchestra (1898-1904); was one of a series of guest conductors with the New York Philharmonic Society (1905-06); and organized the Victor Herbert Orchestra, famous for its lyrical and sprightly music. Meanwhile in 1893 William MacDonald, manager of the Bostonians (a light opera troupe), commissioned him to write a light opera. Encouraged by the success of his score for **Prince Ananias** (1894), he wrote **The Wizard of the Nile** (1895), an even greater success, and thus began a long and immensely successful and profitable career as a composer of operettas. His attempts at serious opera--**Natoma** (1911), **Madeleine** (1914)--were unsuccessful, but the American public loved his beautiful operettas, especially **Babes in Toyland** (1903), **The Red Mill** (1906), **Naughty Marietta** (1910), **Sweethearts** (1913), **Eileen** (1917) and **Orange Blossoms** (1922). Herbert's fame rests on the operettas, but he was also a virtuoso cellist, an accomplished conductor and an articulate spokesman for the rights of the composer. His testimony had an important effect on the copyright law of 1909; in 1913 he was one of the founders of the American Society of Composers, Authors and Publishers. His small amount of piano music is, expectedly, melodious and rhythmically engaging. [I]

HESSELBERG, EDOUARD GREGORY [D'ESSENELLI] (b. Riga, Russia, 3 May 1870; d. Los Angeles, CA, 12 June 1935). Pianist, teacher, composer. His interest in music may have come from his maternal granduncle Charles Davidoff, a well-known cellist. After early music lessons with his mother, he attended the Conservatory of the Moscow Philharmonic Society (1888-92) and also studied privately with Anton Rubinstein. In 1892 he emigrated to the United States, and began a wide-ranging and busy career as a teacher, performer and composer, always giving concerts wherever he happened to be teaching. He was head of the piano department at the Ithaca Conservatory, Ithaca, NY (1895-96); taught at the School of Music, Denver University, Denver, CO (1896-1900); at Wesleyan College Conservatory, Macon, GA (1900-05); and was director of the School of Music at Belmont College in Nashville, TN (1905-1912). He then spent several years in Toronto, Canada (1912-18), where he was a senior professor and examiner at the Toronto, London and Hamilton conservatories, and also maintained a studio for private teaching. While there he wrote "A Review of Music in Canada" for the International Edition of **Modern Music and Musicians** (1913-14). When he returned to the United States, he taught at the Sherwood School in Chicago, IL (1919-22), then became co-director of the Gunn School there. In 1926 he began giving concerts featuring Russian music at the Orpheum and Keith theaters. After 1927 he made concert tours in Europe, and by 1932 had settled in New York with a private studio. He was the father of the American actor Melvyn Douglas. Hesselberg's old-fashioned piano pieces are amply spiced with Russian melodic phrases and rhythms. [I,IV]

HEWITT, GEORGE WASHINGTON (b. New York, NY, 22 February 1811; d. Burlington, NJ, 4 May 1893). Teacher, composer. He was the youngest son of James Hewitt and, like most members of that family, was trained in music. After an unsuccessful attempt at music publishing in Philadelphia, PA, around 1840 he settled in Burlington, where he was professor of music at St. Mary's Hall, a girls' boarding school, and organist at St. Mary's Episcopal Church. A prolific composer, his sparkling salon pieces were in great demand in his lifetime, and some of his songs became favorites during the Civil War. [I,III]

HEWITT, JAMES (b. Dartmoor, England, 4 June 1770; d. Boston, MA, 2 August 1827). Conductor, violinist, publisher, composer. Before he went to America he played in the orchestra at Astley's Amphitheater in London, and obviously was already a well-trained musician. Shortly after arriving in New York on the brig **Bristol** (Sept. 5, 1792), he and four fellow passengers--Jean Gehot, B. Bergmann, William Young and a Mr. Philipps--placed an advertisement in the New York **Daily Advertiser** announcing that they were professors of music, had just arrived and planned to give a concert in October. Their concert was postponed until January, 1793, and when it did take place only Hewitt, Bergmann and Philipps were on hand. From the time of his arrival in America until 1825, when he became

seriously ill with a severe facial cancer, this versatile musician
followed a steady schedule of musical activities, largely in New
York and Boston. During his years in New York (1792-1811), he was a
violinist in numerous concerts; organized other concerts; conducted
the orchestra of the Old American Company (1793); and for a time
also conducted the Park Street Theater orchestra. As early as 1793
he also began publishing music, and in 1797 purchased the New York
branch of Benjamin Carr's Musical Repository, where he published
music and sold both music and musical instruments. At the same
time he was a composer, writing songs, piano music, violin music,
and music for ballad operas. Meanwhile he had extended his
multiple activities to Boston, and from 1811 to 1816 lived there,
continuing his busy musical life and also serving for a time as
organist at Trinity Episcopal Church. In 1816 he returned to New
York, and between 1820 and 1825 traveled frequently between New
York, Boston, Charleston (SC) and Augusta (GA). In publishing or
performing works by composers like Handel, Haydn and Mozart, he
exerted a beneficial influence on early American public taste, an
influence that continued long after his death through the
activities of his six children, all cultured, well-trained
musicians. Hewitt's tasteful piano repertoire contains something
for everyone--sonatas, variations, dance music, and battle pieces.
[I]

HILL, EDWARD BURLINGAME (b. Cambridge, MA, 9 September 1872; d.
Francestown, NH, 9 July 1960). Teacher, composer. There was music
in his childhood because his father, an amateur musician and fine
lieder singer, brought his musical friends home, especially the
distinguished Boston music critic W. F. Apthorp, who often came to
the house to play the classics. Hill was educated at Browne and
Nichols preparatory school (1884-89) and at Harvard College, where
he enrolled in all John Knowles Paine's music courses and was
graduated (1894) with highest honors in music, having produced a
piano sonata and a paper on "Program Music." He continued his
musical studies with Benjamin J. Lang and Frederick Field Bullard
in Boston (1894-95), and with Arthur Whiting and Howard Parkhurst
in New York (1895-97), then spent the summer of 1898 working under
Charles Marie Widor in Paris. He taught piano and harmony in Boston
(1898-1908), was assistant music critic on the **Boston Transcript**
(1901-08) and published many articles in musical journals.
Meanwhile in 1902 he studied orchestration with George Chadwick.
From 1908 to 1940 he was a member of the Harvard faculty, upholding
a family tradition: his grandfather Thomas Hill was president of
Harvard (1862-68) and his father Henry B. Hill a professor of
chemistry there. Appointed an instructor in the music department
in 1908, he was promoted to assistant professor in 1918, associate
professor in 1926 and professor in 1928; he was also department
chairman (1928-35). In 1940 he retired to Francestown. An authority
and well-known lecturer on French music, he gave a course of Lowell
lectures entitled "The Growth of French Music" in January, 1920 and
published **Modern French Music** in 1924. He was a member of the
National Institute of Arts and Letters (1916) and the American

Academy of Arts and Sciences (1929), and as a composer was made a Chevalier of the Legion of Honor (1937). Hill's early piano music reflects his interest in French impressionism and there are hints here and there of a MacDowell influence. His later piano works were often inspired by jazz. [I,IV]

HOFFMAN, EDWARD (b. Manchester, England, 7 February 1836; d. ?). Pianist, composer. Little information has been found concerning him. Louis Moreau Gottschalk mentions him in **Notes of a Pianist:** "I have engaged Madame Variani, an American soprano, for a week. She is married to Edward Hoffman, a talented pianist and brother to Richard Hoffman." According to Jones's **Handbook of American Music and Musicians,** he "was the writer of many popular piano pieces which have had a wide circulation." Indeed, Hoffman's salon music was obviously meant for a popular following. [I]

HOFFMAN, RICHARD (b. Manchester, England, 24 May 1831; d. Mt. Kisco, NY, 17 August 1909). Pianist, teacher, composer. The son of Richard Hoffman-Andrews, an English composer-musician who played in the Gentlemen's Concerts in Manchester, he described himself as having been raised "steeped" in music. He studied with his father and had some lessons with Leopold de Meyer in London. Having been invited to live with an uncle in New York, he arrived there in 1847 and almost immediately made friends with Joseph Burke, the Irish violinist. He and Burke gave concerts together (in America he used his original family name of "Hoffman"; his grandfather, an actor, had added the "Andrews" to save his family embarrassment), and on November 27, 1847 he made his formal début with the New York Philharmonic Society. He toured with Burke through the East (1849-50), Midwest and parts of Canada (1850), and then the two friends accompanied Jenny Lind on her American tours (1850-52), Burke as conductor and violinist and Hoffman as piano accompanist and soloist. At the conclusion of the second Lind tour, he settled in New York as a pianist, teacher and composer, rarely making concert appearances outside of New York but frequently performing with the New York Philharmonic Society. His lasting association with the Society--he was an honorary member for more than forty years and made about twenty appearances with the orchestra (1847-1885)--culminated in 1892 when he was a soloist at one of three concerts commemorating the Society's 50th anniversary. During winter seasons in New York he also practiced long hours and took private pupils; during summers at Little Boar's Head, NH he composed, rested, played for his friends and for nearly 30 years was organist at St. Andrew's-by-the-Sea Church. His last public appearance as soloist was on December 1, 1897 in a testimonial concert organized by his friends and pupils in recognition of his début 50 years earlier and his half-century of music in New York City. A good friend of Louis M. Gottschalk, he sometimes played two-piano duets in concerts with him (1853, 1862). He was awarded an honorary Mus.D. at Hobart College, Geneva, NY (1893). His book **Some Musical Recollections of Fifty Years** was published (1910) posthumously with a biographical note by his wife. Of his six children one daughter married Dr. W. K. Draper and became the mother of Ruth Draper, the monologist, and his youngest daughter Malvina became an important sculptress. Hoffman composed about 100 piano salon pieces, including many operatic paraphrases or fantasies. He was a very talented composer, and his elegance and brilliance as a pianist are clearly evident in his piano compositions. [I,II]

HOFMANN, JOSEF CASIMIR [MICHEL DVORSKY] (b. Cracow, Poland, 20 January 1876; d. Los Angeles, CA, 16 February 1957). Pianist, composer. Both parents were professional musicians, his father being the conductor at the Cracow Theater and his mother a singer in the company. He studied music with his sister Wanda and with his father, and before he reached the age of six played in a public concert. The children made a tour of neighboring cities and towns, and before he was ten he had made a wide concert tour through Europe. After his American début—he was eleven—at the Metropolitan Opera House in New York City (November 29, 1887) brought him extravagant praise from public and critics alike, he began an intensive and extensive tour across the United States, playing more than 50 concerts in about ten weeks, until the Society for the Prevention of Cruelty to Children protested, claiming he was being exploited by his father. An anonymous benefactor, later found to be Alfred Corning Clark, offered the family $50,000 for his further education, with the stipulation that he would not appear on the concert stage until he was 18. His father accepted the offer and they returned to Germany, where he studied with Heinrich Urban in Berlin and from 1892 with Anton Rubinstein, who proved to be the greatest influence in his life. Twice weekly he went to Dresden from Berlin for his lessons, and later told his wife that he and Rubinstein worked mostly on interpretation. After a nearly seven years' hiatus, he played his first concert at Hamburg on March 14, 1894, performing Rubinstein's Concerto in D Minor, with Rubinstein conducting. For the next 40 years he toured on the concert circuit—Russia, Europe, America, Mexico, South America and England, returning again and again, especially to Russia and America. He usually summered in Switzerland and tried to take every third year off to rest. In 1905 he married Marie Eustis, a divorcée 11 years his senior, and in 1927 divorced her to marry Betty Short, a pupil 30 years his junior. In 1924 he became head of the piano department of the newly organized Curtis Institute of Music in Philadelphia, PA, and was director from 1927 to 1938. On November 28, 1937 he celebrated the 50th anniversary of his American début with a concert at the Metropolitan Opera House. Owner of more than 70 patents (shock absorbers, springs, etc.), after he moved to Los Angeles (1939) he spent much of his time working on improved piano actions and recording techniques. He composed more than a hundred works, often using the pseudonym Michel Dvorsky, and published **Piano Playing** (1908) and **Piano Questions Answered** (1909). He received an honorary Mus.D from the University of Pennsylvania (1933). A brilliant technician and elegant interpreter, he was lionized all over the world, and ranks among the great pianists of his or any age. Hofmann's piano works--he was composing at age eight and publishing at age eleven--range from scintillating salon waltzes to technically demanding concert pieces. They are uniformly romantic, appealing and eminently pianistic. [I,II]

HOHNSTOCK, ADELE [ADELAIDE] (b. Brunswick, Germany, ?; d. Philadelphia, PA, January 1856). Pianist, teacher, composer. The sister of Carl Hohnstock, a well-known piano and violin teacher in Philadelphia during the mid-nineteenth century, she is known to have appeared in concerts in Paris and Hamburg before emigrating to the United States with her brother (1848). She was recognized as an excellent pianist and teacher, and accompanied her brother on his concert tours. She resided with him until her death. Hohnstock's flamboyant, often difficult, polkas were extremely popular in their day. [I]

HOLDEN, T. L. (fl.ca.1810-20). According to Wolfe, he is an "unidentified" composer. Judging from the numerous editions, his **Copenhagen Waltz** with three salon-type variations was very popular in its day. [I]

HOLST, EDUARD (b. Copenhagen, Denmark, ca.1843; d. New York, NY, 4 February 1899). He arrived in New York around 1874, a seemingly versatile entertainer-musician who appeared as an actor, dancer, playwright, conductor and composer. He wrote band music, comedy music, a comic operetta (**Our Flats**, 1897), songs and piano music. The piano music is light and displays great melodic sensitivity. [I,III,IV]

HOMMANN (spelled variously **Homman, Hommans, Hommand**), **CHARLES** (fl. Philadelphia, PA, ca.1819-ca.1850). Organist, violinist, violist, teacher, composer. Very little documentation exists concerning his life, although recent research by Ronald B. Axsom in connection with his master's thesis **The Orchestral Music of Charles Hommann** (West Chester State College, West Chester, PA, 1982) substantiates the following facts. He was the son of John (Johann) C. Homman, a German immigrant musician active in Philadelphia from about 1797 until 1842. Charles Hommann was organist at St. James's Church (1819-29) and at one time organist at the Third Dutch Reformed Church (also known as Bethune's Church for its pastor George Washington Bethune). He is listed as a viola player on the program of the first concert (second performance) for the benefit of the Musical Fund Society (May 8, 1821). In the Philharmonic Society's 1835 composition contest he won the gold medal for his **Overture in D Major** and also second prize, possibly for his song "Oh Come to Me, Beloved One." An unsigned, handwritten entry (1896) found on the cover page of the cello part to Hommann's **String Quartet in D**

Minor states that Hommann was "an excellent violinist, pianist and organist" and that "he (Homann) gave me (the unknown writer) violin lessons for several years." On the margin of the cello part (now at the Free Library of Philadelphia, chamber-music collection) is typed "Gift of Francis T. Cross," who very likely was a descendant of Michael Hurley Cross, a later 19th-century Philadelphia musician who studied with Hommann. Hommann left Philadelphia around the mid-1850s, for according to **The Musical World** (June 16, 1855) he was living in Brooklyn, NY in 1855. Whether or not he returned to Philadelphia is not known, but he was apparently not there in 1864 to sign as one of the executors when the will of Charles F. Hupfeld was probated. Note: Hommann's sister Costantia married Hupfeld, a prominent violinist, conductor and publisher. Hommann and Hupfeld must have been close friends, for Hupfeld named him as coexecutor and willed him his viola. Hommann's structured piano pieces show a talent for design and a flair for contrapuntal devices. [I]

HOPEKIRK, HELEN (b. Edinburgh, Scotland, 20 May 1856; d. Cambridge, MA, 19 November 1945). Pianist, teacher, composer. Her father owned a music business. From about the age of nine she studied with Alexander MacKenzie and George Lichtenstein, then continued her training under Carl Reinecke, Salomon Jadassohn, Louis Maas and Ernst F. Richter at the Leipzig Conservatory (1876-78). She made her German début at a Gewandhaus concert in 1878 and her London début at the Crystal Palace in 1879, and for the next three seasons toured through England and Scotland, appearing with leading orchestras and giving many recitals. After her marriage (1882) to William A. Wilson, an Edinburgh businessman and music critic, she continued her concert career under his guidance. She made her American début with the Boston Symphony Orchestra in 1883, toured the country for three seasons and then moved to Vienna, Austria, where she studied piano with Theodore Leschetizky and composition with Karel Navrátil (1887-89). Back on the concert circuit, she performed in Europe, the United States and Great Britain (1889-92), returning each spring to Vienna. In the fall of 1892 she moved to Paris, where she studied composition with Richard Mandl, devoted her time largely to composing and also began to accept pupils. Five years later she settled in Boston, MA, having been invited by George Chadwick, newly appointed director of the New England Conservatory and a former fellow student at Leipzig, to join the Conservatory faculty. Preferring to teach privately, she resigned from the Conservatory (1901) and kept a studio at her home, first in Boston, later Brookline. An interest in folk song resulted in her edition of **Seventy Scottish Songs** (1905). Keenly interested in the music of contemporary French composers, she often included works by Fauré, Debussy, d'Indy and Franck on her programs. She made her last public appearance in a recital of her own compositions at Steinert Hall, Boston, in April 1939, at the age of eighty-two. Hopekirk's piano works are often Scottish in feeling. She admired and frequently used classic musical forms. [I]

HOPKINS, CHARLES JEROME (b. Burlington, VT, 4 April 1836; d. Athenia [now part of Clifton], NJ, 4 November 1898). Organist, teacher, promoter, composer. He may have had some musical instruction at home or at church--his father John Henry Hopkins was the first bishop of Vermont--but he was mostly self-taught in music. He played the organ at the age of 10, and over a 20-year period was organist at several churches in Burlington and New York. Preparing for a career in medicine, he attended the University of Vermont (1851-52) and the New York Medical College, but in 1856 he began teaching, composing and lecturing on music. An early and ardent supporter of American music and culture, he founded the American Music Association (1856) to promote works by American composers and gave lecture-recitals to inform the public about American music. In 1865 he began the Orpheon Free Schools--singing classes organized at various times and locations--which during a 20-year span enrolled about 30,000 pupils. He was the founder and editor of the **New York Philharmonic Journal** (1868-85). According to contemporary reports and descriptions, he was a dynamic, flamboyant personality. In 1889 he made a lecture-concert tour in England, representing himself as an ambassador of American culture and American music, but his aggressive tactics in trying to obtain subscribers to the concerts caused him a law suit. He composed several hundred works, including **Taffy and Old Munch,** a children's fairy tale written especially for children's voices; the operas **Samuel** and **Dumb Love;** choruses, songs, piano pieces. His published works include two collections of church music, an Orpheon Class-Book, piano pieces and others. He willed his manuscripts to Amy Fay, the American pianist. In its own fashion Hopkins's keyboard salon music, with its rolling arpeggios, hammered octave passages and glistening scale arabesques, is very flamboyant and very grand. [I]

HUGO, JOHN ADAM (b. Bridgeport, CT, 5 January 1873; d. Bridgeport, 29 December 1945). Teacher, pianist, composer. At the age of 15 he began an extended course of study at the Stuttgart Conservatory (1888-97), where he was a pupil of Wilhelm Speidel, Immanuel Faiszt, Arpad Doppler and Hermann Zumpe, then for about two years toured as a concert pianist in Germany, Italy and England. When he returned to the United States he taught piano at the Peabody Conservatory in Baltimore, MD (1898-1900), and for several years was director of music at a women's college there. About 1906 he returned to his hometown and opened a piano studio. His opera **The Temple Dancer** was first performed at the Metropolitan Opera House in New York City (1919) and later produced in Chicago and Honolulu. Hugo's piano pieces, with their earnest attention to structural and textural details, fall rather consistently into the "serious" category and are characteristically romantic. [I]

HUPFELD (spelled variously **Hupfield, Hupfeldt, Hupffield, Hopefield), CHARLES F.** (b. Germany, ca.1788; d. Philadelphia, PA, 15 July 1864). Violinist, conductor, composer. Precise information about him has yet to be uncovered, largely due to the confusion surrounding the Hupfeld family--a father and two brothers, all musicians active in Philadelphia within the first half of the 19th century. It is believed that he was Charles F. Hupfeld, Jr., son of Charles Frederick Hupfeld, a German who arrived in Philadelphia sometime around 1800. Charles Jr. appeared as a solo violinist, in chamber groups and as a conductor. He and his brother John, also a violinist, frequently played in chamber-music ensembles (ca.1816-20) that led to the establishment of the Musical Fund Society in 1820. One of the founders of the Society, he was also one of the conductors of the Society's first concert (April 24, 1821, repeated May 8, 1821) and later became principal conductor of the orchestra (1828-45). He was a close friend and brother-in-law of Charles Hommann, and gave music lessons to Michael Hurley Cross. Anthony Philip Heinrich's **Tema di Mozart and an Original Air, varied for the Violin,** found in **The Dawning of Music in Kentucky,** is dedicated to the Hupfeld brothers. Hupfeld's few piano compositions--mostly variation sets--are creative and pleasing. [I]

HUSS, HENRY HOLDEN (b. Newark, NJ, 21 June 1862; d. New York, NY, 17 September 1953). Pianist, teacher, composer. He was a descendant of Jan Hus, the Bohemian religious reformer and martyr. After initial lessons with his father George John Huss, an organist and teacher in the United States for more than 50 years, he studied with Otis B. Boise in New York (1879-82) and with Joseph Rheinberger and Joseph Giehrl at the Munich Conservatory (1882-85). From 1885 he made his home in New York, where he taught privately and also for a time at Thurston College. He made concert tours in the United States and Europe, often playing his own concerto with leading orchestras, and after his marriage (1904) gave joint recitals with his wife, concert soprano Hildegard Hoffman. Huss's finely written piano compositions were widely played in his lifetime and are well worth reviving. [I,II,V]

HUTCHESON, ERNEST (b. Melbourne, Australia, 20 July 1871; d. New York, NY, 9 February 1951). Pianist, teacher, composer. As a child he studied with the composer Max Vogrich and George William Torrance, an Irish composer-priest, both at that time living in Melbourne, and before he was seven he made a concert tour in Australia. At the Leipzig Conservatory (1885-90) he studied with Carl Reinecke, Salomon Jadassohn and Bruno Zwintscher, after graduation made a second Australian tour and then went to Weimar to study with Bernhard Stavenhagen, one of Liszt's last pupils. He concentrated on studying and teaching, making very few appearances until 1898, when he played his own concerto with the Berlin Philharmonic Orchestra and subsequently toured in Germany, Russia and England. From 1900 to 1912 he was head of the piano department at the Peabody Conservatory, Baltimore, MD but resigned in order to continue his concert career, and from then on he concertized steadily and successfully in both Europe and America. He built up an impressive repertoire, including more than 20 concertos, and in 1915 overwhelmed a New York audience by playing three concertos (Liszt's E-Flat, Tchaikovsky's B-Flat Minor and MacDowell's D Minor) on one program; in 1919 he repeated the feat, performing three Beethoven concertos in one evening. In 1911 he became head of the piano department at the Chautauqua summer school; in 1924 he joined the piano faculty at the Juilliard Graduate School, became dean in 1927 and later president (1937-45). In retirement he continued to take private pupils and occasionally taught at Juilliard. For several winters he appeared on nationwide radio, making about 50 Sunday broadcasts featuring piano concertos. He published **Elements of Piano Technique** (1907), a guide to Strauss's **Elektra** (1910), **The Literature of the Piano** (1948) and many articles. During his long career Hutcheson composed a wide variety of piano music, from romantic poems and character pieces with notable emotional appeal to 20th century sketches featuring free harmony, dissonance and linear counterpoint. [I,V]

HYLLESTED, AUGUST (b. Stockholm, Sweden, 17 June 1858; d. Blairmore, Scotland, 5 April 1946). Pianist, teacher, composer. His parents were Danish but he was born in Stockholm, where his father held the position of stadtmusicus. Having begun his musical training at an early age, he made a tour of Scandinavia when he was about 13, then in 1871 went to the Copenhagen Conservatory for additional music study with Johann Peter Hartmann, Lars Tofte, Carl Attrup and Niels W. Gade. He made another tour of Scandinavia (1875), this time with the Strakosch Company, performing sometimes as soloist and sometimes as assistant conductor, and when he returned to Copenhagen (1876) was appointed organist at the Cathedral. In 1879 he went to Germany. He studied with Theodore Kullak in Berlin; went to Weimar, played for Liszt and received a letter of recommendation; then returned to Berlin and studied with Friedrich Kiel. After a tour of the British Isles (1883-84), he went to the United States (1885). He played concerts in New York City with the Belgian violinist Ovide Musin, toured the eastern United States and Canada and then settled in Chicago, IL, where he was assistant director of the Chicago Musical College (1886-91) and director of the piano department of the Gottschalk Lyric School (1891-94). From about 1895 until his retirement in 1923 he lived a peripatetic existence: concert tours in Scandinavia and Europe until about 1897; in Chicago again until around 1903; lived in Glasgow, Scotland (1903-14); back in America (1916-19); in Scandinavia (1920-21); and finally retired to Blairmore in 1923. Hyllested's romantic salon pieces have a nostalgic charm. [I]

IUCHO, WILHELM (fl.New York, ca.1830-60). Teacher, composer. Although several of his piano compositions appear in the Bibliography, the only information we have about him to date is that he is listed in the New York city directory of 1833 as a "professor of music" living at 42 Great Jones Street. Iucho wrote many salon pieces for piano. He preferred the operatic potpourri and the theme with variations. [I]

IVES, CHARLES EDWARD (b. Danbury, CT, 20 October 1874; d.   New York, NY, 19 May 1954). Composer. Thirty years ago music critic Olin Downes called Ives "an American original." He was also a purely American product, for both his education and his musical training were, so to speak, wholly "made in America." He had an exceptionally close relationship with his father, an innovative musician and bandmaster who had "a reverence, a devotion and a talent for music which was unusual." It was his father, himself a musical experimenter, who trained him thoroughly in the essentials of music, made him aware of the countless musical sounds one could hear in everyday life and encouraged him to try his own musical experiments. At the age of 12 he was already composing and playing the drums in his father's band, and at 14 became a paid organist at the First Baptist Church in Danbury (1888-92). While attending the Hopkins Grammar School in New Haven, he played the organ at St. Thomas's Episcopal Church from May, 1893 until he entered Yale College in the fall of 1894. About a month later his father died, leaving him, as he later described it, in an "awful vacuum." During his Yale years (1894-98) he played the organ at the Centre Church on the Green, studied music with Dudley Buck and Harry Rowe Shelley and attended Horatio Parker's music courses. He was an indifferent student but his natural composing talent flourished, producing songs, marches, overtures, anthems, organ pieces, a quartet, a symphony. The year he graduated he was hired as a clerk by the Mutual Life Insurance Co. in New York City, where he worked by day, composed nights and weekends and still managed to keep up a convivial social life with his bachelor friends. He also, during the early years in New York, played the organ at the First Presbyterian Church in Bloomfield, NJ (1899) and at the Central Presbyterian Church in New York (1899-1902). From the time he joined Mutual he lived a double life, one part creative composer and one part successful businessman. Although heart problems bothered him as early as 1906, he maintained his way of life.   In 1907 he and his partner Julian Myrick opened their own Mutual agency, Ives and Co. (later Ives and Myrick), an immensely successful firm that over a 21-year span sold more than $450,000,000 of life insurance policies. After his marriage to Harmony Twitchell in 1908, his life was richly productive. The business prospered and he composed some of his most successful works, but it was a draining, exhausting existence. During World War I he added more burdens with Red Cross and Liberty Loans work, and in October, 1918 suffered a severe heart attack. Away from business for a year, he gradually reduced his work load and finally retired January 1, 1930. He never regained his health, never regained his creative spark. In his own words, he "couldn't seem to compose any more; nothing went well, nothing sounded right." He composed few original works but revised and renewed earlier compositions, and he lived to see some of his works getting public performances. In 1947 he was awarded the Pulitzer Prize for his **Third Symphony**. Ives's superb piano music--an intriguing mélange of the complex and the naive, a compelling fusion of the traditional with the contemporary--is truly "American." [I,IV]

JOHNS, CLAYTON (b. New Castle, DE, 24 November 1857; d. Boston, MA, 5 March 1932). Pianist, teacher, composer. His parents hoped that he would study for the law, he preferred music and they somehow compromised on architecture, so after graduating from Rugby Academy in Wilmington, DE, he studied architecture in the Philadelphia office of T. P. Chandler (1875-78). In January of 1879 he began a trial period of music study with W. F. Apthorp in Boston, and two months later, having been advised by Apthorp to continue, he took special studies with John Knowles Paine of Harvard (1879-81). After finishing with Paine, he had a year of piano study with William H. Sherwood in Boston, then further training in Berlin, studying piano with Friedrich Grabau and Oscar Raif and composition with Friedrich Kiel (1882-84). He returned to the United States in October, 1884, and settled in Boston as a teacher, pianist and composer. Although he disliked performing in public, he gave an annual recital for more than 20 years. He taught at the New England Conservatory (1912-28), and after retiring continued to take private pupils. He was known especially for his songs. He published **The Essentials of Pianoforte Playing** (1909), **From Bach to Chopin** (1911) and **Reminiscences of a Musician** (1929). Johns wrote durable, well-fashioned piano pieces which, with their felicitous mingling of harmony, rhythm and melody, reflect his sound musicianship. [I]

JOHNS, [PAUL] EMILE (b. Cracow, Poland, ca.1798; d. Paris, France, 10 August 1860). Pianist, music dealer, publisher, composer. When he arrived in New Orleans is not known, but he appeared there as a pianist in 1818, and New Orleans was his home for the rest of his life. He took part in the city's musical entertainments from about 1822, when he was listed in the city directory as a pianoforte teacher, until sometime in 1827. He usually appeared as an assisting artist but in February, 1824 he was featured in three concerts as either piano soloist or composer. That same month the French opera company in the city performed his one-act comic opera **The Military Stay, or The Double Trick.** His last public performance may have been at a benefit concert at which he "improvised a piece on the piano" (May 30, 1827). He seems to have given up concertizing about this time, perhaps because he felt neglected as a performer and composer or because he realized he could make more money in the music business. He was already a music dealer, for a year earlier (January, 1826) he had advertised new music from Paris for sale either at his home or at the shop of a friend. In December, 1830 he established E. Johns and Company, music sellers and stationers, which had agreements with the principal music vendors and editors in London, Paris and the principal cities of Germany. In Paris he dealt with Pleyel and Sons, the firm that published his **Album Louisianais: Hommage aux Dames de la Nouvelle Orléans** sometime between 1831 and 1834. This album contains his

only surviving compositions--six strophic songs and two piano
pieces (waltz, polonaise), each dedicated to a different New
Orleans belle of French ancestry. It is believed that during a
summer business trip to Paris (1832) Camille Pleyel introduced him,
a Polish exile in America, to Frédéric Chopin, a Polish exile in
France. Since Chopin dedicated his **Mazurkas, Opus 7** "to M. E.
Johns, of New Orleans," we can only assume that the two countrymen
had a congenial meeting. To meet competition, Johns gradually
added other merchandise to his business: furniture, art prints,
sewing supplies, saddles, and by 1837 he was printing and selling
books. In 1846 he sold the business to a Mr. T. Mayo, around 1852
Mayo sold it to Philip Werlein and today Werlein's is the largest
music store in New Orleans. After he sold the business, he became a
cotton dealer and wholesale merchant, and was also the Russian
consul in New Orleans (1848-60). He was on a visit to Europe in the
summer of 1860 when he died suddenly in Paris, where he is buried.
Johns's two extant pieces for piano are expectedly romantic and
charmingly tinged with Chopinisms. [I]

JOHNSON, GUSTAVUS (b. Hull, England, 2 November 1856; d.
ca.1932). Pianist, teacher, composer. He was raised in Sweden,
his father's native country, and studied music in Stockholm with
Johann Conrad Nordquist and Gustave Mankell. In September, 1875 he
emigrated to the United States, spent several months in Providence,
RI, about a year teaching in Minneapolis, MN, another few years in
Wisconsin and then returned to Minneapolis, where he was a teacher
and performer for more than 40 years. He taught at the Northwest
Conservatory, then in 1898 established the Johnson Piano School,
which became the Johnson School of Music, Oratory and Dramatic Art
(1900) and eventually the Minneapolis College of Music. Besides
teaching, he composed and gave numerous recitals in Minnesota,
Wisconsin, Iowa and Illinois. In the early 1920s he moved to the
East, possibly to Boston, MA to be with his daughter. It is not
known whether he continued in music. Johnson's piano catalog
contains some pleasant, romantic works. [I]

JONAS, ALBERTO (b. Madrid, Spain, 8 June 1868; d. Philadelphia,
PA, 9 November 1943). Teacher, pianist, composer. He studied at
the Madrid Conservatory and at the Brussels Conservatory (1886-90),
where he was a pupil of Arthur De Greef and François Gevaert, and
from September, 1890 worked for three months with Anton Rubinstein
at the St. Petersburg Conservatory. After making his début with the
Berlin Philharmonic Orchestra (1891), he embarked on a series of
concert tours in Europe, England, Central America, the United
States and Canada, in the meanwhile making his American début in
New York (1893). He then spent about ten years in the United
States, giving concerts and teaching piano at the School of Music
of the University of Michigan at Ann Arbor (1894-98) and at the
Michigan Conservatory in Detroit (1898-1904), where he was also
director. During 1905-14 he lived in Germany. He began teaching at
the Klindworth-Scharwenka Conservatory in Berlin, but resigned

after a year because of the demands of his large private classes. An excellent teacher, he attracted students from many countries and had such a large number that he required six assistants. When the outbreak of World War I forced him to leave Berlin, twelve of his pupils moved to New York City with him. He taught private classes in New York, a weekly class in Philadelphia and six hours a week at the Von Ende School of Music, New York. For several summers he held classes in Salt Lake City, UT. Despite his heavy teaching schedule, he continued to give recitals. Jonas's impressive piano repertoire includes both transcriptions and original works, some with a genuine Spanish flavor. [I]

JOSEFFY, RAFAEL (b. Hunfalu, Hungary, 3 July 1852; d. New York, NY, 25 June 1915). Pianist, teacher, composer. He was raised in the Hungarian city of Miskolc, where he began piano lessons at the age of eight; later studied with Brauer (Stephen Heller's first piano teacher) in Budapest, and then continued his musical education in Germany. He enrolled at the Leipzig Conservatory (1866–68), where he studied mostly with Ernst F. Wenzel but also had a few lessons with the elderly Ignaz Moscheles; spent two years in Berlin working under Carl Tausig, who proved to be his most influential teacher (1868–70); and also had lessons with Liszt during two summers at Weimar (1870, 1871). After making his début in Berlin (1872), he toured Europe with spectacular success, winning acclaim especially for his formidable technique. Although the Austrian critic Eduard Hanslick admired his technique he found his playing cold, yet when Liszt heard him play in Vienna, he called his playing "delicious," and in a letter addressed him as "my successor and heir." From 1879 he made his home in New York City, arriving in America already considered by many to be the greatest pianist alive. He made his American début in October, 1879 with an orchestra under Leopold Damrosch, and soon captured America, audiences and critics alike, just as he had won Europe. As he matured he gained in musicianship, losing none of his virtuosity but adding a warmth and poetic feeling to his interpretations. He gave recitals, toured with the Theodore Thomas Orchestra and was invited to play at least once yearly with the New York Philharmonic Society (12 appearances during 1880–90). Still in great demand and at the peak of his talent, he gradually withdrew from the concert stage, possibly because of the strain on his highly nervous nature. In his self-imposed retirement he taught privately and also at the National Conservatory in New York (1888–1906), and would sometimes make public appearances. He was one of the first to perform Brahms's works regularly in the United States. He published the **School of Advanced Piano Playing** (1902) and **First Studies for the Piano** (1913) and edited the **Complete Works of Chopin** (1915). His library of piano music is now largely at the Music Library of the University of Illinois, Urbana. A superb pianist, Joseffy wrote refined keyboard music and made transcriptions and paraphrases that are of consistently high quality. His concepts of melodic phrasing, rhythmic drive and harmonic design were often original. [I,II,V]

KAUN, HUGO (b. Berlin, Germany, 21 March 1863; d. Berlin, 2 April 1932). Teacher, conductor, composer. A precocious and prolific composer, he composed more than 100 works before he was 16. Trained wholly in Berlin, he spent a year at the Hochschule für Musik (1879-80), then studied piano with Oscar Raif and attended Friedrich Kiel's composition classes at the Berlin Academy of Arts. He taught piano, composed and conducted a chorus, and in 1887 went to the United States and settled in Milwaukee, WI, a city with a large German community. During his 15-year residence there he composed, taught many pupils, founded the Wisconsin Conservatory of Music and directed the Milwaukee Liederkranz. Between 1898 and 1903 five of his works (two symphonic poems, a symphony, an overture and a festival march and hymn) were performed by the Chicago Symphony under Theodore Thomas, who was an admirer and supporter of Kaun's music. In 1902 he returned to his native Berlin, and won recognition as both composer and teacher. In 1922 he was appointed to teach composition at the Klindworth-Scharwenka Conservatory. He was elected a member of the Royal Academy of Arts (1912), and published **Harmonie und Modulationslehre** (1915) and **Aus meinem Leben** (1932). Kaun wrote much piano music. In general it is solidly constructed, pianistic and reflects his Germanic background. **[I,IV,V]**

KELLER, WALTER (b. Chicago, IL, 23 February 1873; d. Chicago, 8 July 1940). Teacher, organist, composer. He attended Baldwin-Wallace College in Berea, OH, and in Chicago studied at the American Conservatory (1891-94) and privately with Frederick Grant Gleason (1892-93). After additional studies with Carl Piutti and Paul Homeyer at the Leipzig Conservatory (1894-96), he returned to Chicago and resumed his studies with Gleason (1896-98). He taught at the School of Music, Northwestern University, Evanston, IL (1898-1904); at the Sherwood Music School in Chicago (1906-40), where he was also director from 1911; and was dean of the School of Music at DePaul University, Chicago (1912-20). He was also organist at St. Vincent de Paul Church (1903-18) and later at the Fifth Church of Christ, Scientist. He gave many organ recitals in the East and Midwest. DePaul University awarded him an honorary Mus.D. in 1916. Keller was primarily an organist. His piano music shows prominent contrapuntal texture. **[I,IV]**

KELLEY, EDGAR STILLMAN (b. Sparta, WI, 14 April 1857; d. New York, NY, 12 November 1944). Teacher, organist, writer, composer. He began piano lessons with his mother at the age of eight, also studied with a local teacher named F. W. Merriam (1870-74) and with Clarence Eddy and Napoleon Ledochowski in Chicago (1874-76). After advanced studies with Wilhelm Speidel, Friedrich Finck and Max Seifriz in Stuttgart (1876-80), he returned to the United States and for 22 years divided his time between San Francisco and New York, maintaining a diverse career as composer, teacher, lecturer and writer. He went first to San Francisco (1880-86), where he taught piano, organ and theory and was organist at several churches. He composed as well, and already some of his works were being performed: the "Overture" to his music to Macbeth was played by the Theodore Thomas Orchestra in Chicago in 1883, and the complete score for orchestra and chorus was used in a long run of the play in San Francisco in 1885. San Francisco's large, cultural Chinese community gave him a perfect opportunity to absorb the sounds and tone colors of the Chinese music he later imitated in his orchestral suite **Aladdin.** While living in New York City (1886-92), he toured the eastern United States as director of a comic operetta company and supervised the production of his operetta **Puritania,** which had 100 performances in Boston, MA (1892). He returned to San Francisco in November, 1892 and was for a time music critic for the **San Francisco Examiner** (1893-95), then spent another four years in New York, where he taught composition at the New York College of Music and lectured in New York University's extension division. He was acting professor of music and conductor of the orchestra at Yale University while Horatio Parker was on leave during the academic year 1901-02, an appointment that greatly enhanced his reputation as a scholarly teacher and conductor. From 1902 to 1910 he lived in Berlin as teacher and composer, and when he returned to the United States he settled in Oxford, OH, having been awarded a lifetime composer fellowship by the Western College for Women (now part of Miami University), an award that provided him with a home on the campus and ample time for composing. At the same time he was for 23 years a part-time lecturer and teacher at the Cincinnati Conservatory in Ohio. During his lifetime his works received many performances, and after he retired from active teaching (1934) he continued to travel to supervise performances of his works. He was awarded a Litt.D. from Miami University (1916) and an LL.D from the University of Cincinnati (1917). He was a member of the National Institute of Arts and Letters; he published **Chopin the Composer** (1913) and **The History of Musical Instruments** (1925) and contributed articles to several music journals. Many of Kelley's piano works--both dance-derived compositions and descriptive pieces--seem fresh and spontaneous today. [I]

KLEIN, BRUNO OSCAR (b. Osnabrück, Germany, 6 June 1858; d. New York, NY, 22 June 1911). Pianist, organist, teacher, composer. He had his first musical instruction from his father Carl Klein, organist at the Osnabrück Cathedral, and later studied with Carl Baermann, Joseph Rheinberger and Franz Wüllner at the Munich Conservatory. In 1877 he visited a brother in Philadelphia, PA, and the following year emigrated to the United States. For five years he toured the country with various concert companies, making a name as an exceptional accompanist and sight-reader, then settled in New York. He was organist at St. Francis Xavier's Church (1884-94) and at St. Ignatius's church (1904-11). He taught at the Sacred Heart Convent (1884-1911) and at the National Conservatory of Music (1887-92). Klein composed many piano works, but his best writing appears in his fine, romantic character pieces. [I,III]

KOELLING, ADOLPH (b. Hamburg, Germany, 9 February 1840; d.?). Pianist, teacher, composer. He had his first music lessons with his brother Carl, a noted salon-music composer; at the age of ten began studying with Degenhardt, the organist at St. Catherine's Church in Hamburg; and in 1856 became a pupil of Eduard Marxsen, Brahms's teacher. The following year he began composing and performing his own piano variations. He studied further with Carl Graedener, taught for a time in London, then returned to Hamburg and worked under August Riccius. In 1872 he emigrated to America, where he was for many years head of the composition department at the Chicago Musical College. He was a brother of Carl Koelling. Adolph Koelling was a forward-looking composer whose keyboard works sometimes show an early use of dissonance. [I]

KOELLING, CARL W. P. (b. Hamburg, Germany, 28 February 1831; d. Chicago, IL, ca. 3 May 1914). Teacher, composer. A composer and music teacher in Hamburg, he emigrated to the United States and for many years was on the faculty of the Chicago Musical College in Chicago, IL. He was a brother of Adolph Koelling. Carl Koelling was a successful composer of salon music, and many of his virtuosic, flamboyant pieces are great fun to play. [I,III]

KREIDER, NOBLE [WICKHAM] (b. Goshen, IN, 20 September 1874; d. Goshen, 20 December 1959). Teacher, composer. Although he often traveled, he lived and worked in Goshen all his life. His principal teacher was Clarence Forsythe of Indianapolis, and he may have lived with the Forsythe family for some time. He went abroad with the Forsythes, and when he returned to Goshen became a teacher of piano and theory. During his early career he gave piano recitals, but he was more interested in teaching and composing than performing. He composed mood music for silent movies, but in his later years ceased composing though he continued to teach. In 1960 Professor Charles Burkhart of Queen's College, one of Kreider's former piano students, compiled a Catalog of Kreider's works and delivered the music manuscripts to the New York Public Library (Americana Collection, Music Division). Professor Burkhart has also furnished the above biographical information. Kreider was an important contributor to the Wa-Wan Press. Some of his works are neatly laced with dissonance. [I]

KROEGER, ERNEST RICHARD (b. St. Louis, MO, 10 August 1862; d. St. Louis, 7 April 1934). Organist, pianist, teacher, composer. His life centered in St. Louis, where he was born, received all his musical education and lived throughout his career. He began music studies with his father, an amateur musician, and at the age of five started violin lessons with Ernst Spiering. He later studied piano with Egmont Froelich and Waldemar Malmene and theory with P. G. Anton. He was a choirboy at Trinity Episcopal Church until his voice changed, and at 15 began his career as organist: six months at Grace Episcopal Church, eight years at Trinity Episcopal Church,

26 years at the Church of the Messiah (Unitarian) and finally at the Delmar Baptist Church. It was also when he was 15 that his father became ill and he went to work as a clerk in a mercantile firm to help support his family (1877-85), yet he continued to practice and study. In the meanwhile he met Charles Kunkel, the St. Louis pianist-composer known for performing duo-piano concerts with his brother Jacob. Kunkel coached Kroeger for about two years, and for more than 20 years they played successful two-piano concerts. As a solo recitalist he gave a series of concerts each year for 25 years (1893-1918). At the age of 23 he left his clerk's job and began giving music lessons, the start of his 48-year career as a music teacher. In 1887 he became head of music at the Kirkwood Seminary, later Forest Park College; in 1904 he founded the Kroeger School of Music, which he directed until his death and his daughter maintained until 1975. He conducted the women's Morning Choral Club (1893-1903) and the men's Amphion Club (1910-12). He was master of programs at the Louisiana Purchase Centennial Exposition (St. Louis, 1904), in charge of all programs for orchestral, organ and choral concerts, and he also played organ recitals at the Panama-Pacific International Exposition (San Francisco, 1915). He was elected a member of the Académie Française (1904) and a member of the National Institute of Arts and Letters (1915). Kroeger was a prolific composer. His stylish, stimulating piano repertoire shows consistently fine workmanship. [I]

KÜRSTEINER, JEAN PAUL (b. Catskill, NY, 8 July 1864; d. Los Angeles, CA, 19 March 1943). Pianist, teacher, composer. At the Leipzig Conservatory (1887-92) he studied with Salomon Jadassohn, Johannes Weidenbach, Richard Hofmann and Robert Teichmüller, and from 1888 was Teichmüller's assistant. Upon returning to the United States, he taught at the Ogontz School, Philadelphia, PA (1893-1930) and also at The Baldwin School, Bryn Mawr, PA (1896-1906). From 1906 he also held classes in New York City. In 1938 he moved to Los Angeles. He wrote **Essays on Expert Aid to Artistic Piano-Playing** and was a contributor to music journals. His small piano collection derives noticeably from Chopin. [I]

KUNKEL, CHARLES (b. Sippersfeld, Rhineland-Palatinate, Germany, 22 July 1840; d. St. Louis, MO, 3 December 1923). Music publisher, pianist, teacher, composer. He learned music from his father, a professor of music at a school in Sippersfeld, and continued his studies after the family emigrated to America and settled in Cincinnati, OH (1848). A concert pianist from about the age of ten, he became a very well-known performer and on several occasions, particularly during the 1862-63 seasons, was invited to perform two-piano compositions with the famous Louis Moreau Gottschalk. In 1868 he and his brother Jacob moved to St. Louis, where they quickly opened a music store dealing in pianos, organs and sheet music. Within a year they were also publishing sheet music, and their firm (Kunkel Bros. Music Co.) eventually expanded to become one of the most successful music publishers west of the

Mississippi. The brothers, much admired for their two-piano recitals, injected a new spirit into the city's concert life and became influential members of the musical community. The enterprising pair also founded the St. Louis Conservatory of Music (1872), a school which they operated for several years in classrooms above the store. Perhaps their most important venture was **Kunkel's Musical Review,** a monthly journal "devoted to music, art, literature and the drama" (issued Sept. 1878-April 1909, possibly longer) with an increasing emphasis on music. It included concert reviews, a calendar of musical events, lists of new publications, biographical sketches with portraits, short essays, European and domestic news, letters, printed music (vocal and instrumental) and lessons on that music. After Jacob's death in 1882 Charles carried on the business and gave two-piano recitals with Louis Conrath. Around 1884 he organized the St. Louis Handel and Haydn Society to give concerts but, wisely in tune with the public tastes, he soon changed the title to "Kunkel's Popular Concerts." Although he was criticized by some for including popular music in his concerts, the series lasted until after the turn of the century and was both successful and profitable. He was also for many years manager of the Temple Building, an important theater of the time, and in his role of impresario brought important musical events and celebrities to St. Louis. For more than half a century Charles Kunkel was a vital force and major contributor to St. Louis's musical and cultural life, acquiring wealth and fame not so much because he was an excellent teacher and performer but because he knew exactly what kind of music the contemporary public wanted. As a composer he sometimes used one of several pseudonyms, especially Claude Melnotte, Jean Paul and Carl Sidus. Kunkel wrote basically salon music, and within its own framework it is elegant and musicianly. [I,II,III,IV]

KUNKEL, JACOB (b. Sippersfeld, Rhineland-Palatinate, Germany, 22 October 1846; d. St. Louis, MO, 16 October 1882). Pianist, music publisher, composer. Until his untimely death at the age of 36 he was a partner in most of his older brother Charles's musical activities. He had music lessons with both his father and Charles, and after the family emigrated to the United States in 1848 had some coaching from Louis Moreau Gottschalk. He was said to be an exceptionally gifted pianist and a better musician than Charles. Much of Jacob's keyboard salon music is virtuosic and sparkling. [I]

LA FORGE, FRANK (b. Rockford, IL, 22 October 1879; d. New York, NY, 5 May 1953). Accompanist, voice teacher, composer. He studied with his sister Ruth La Forge Hall until he was about 17, continued with Harrison M. Wild in Chicago (1896-1900) and completed his musical training in Vienna (1900-04), where he studied with Theodore Leschetizky, Joseph Labor and Karel Navrátil. Gifted with a remarkable memory--he had an enormous repertoire of songs he could play at any time--he was considered by many critics to be the finest accompanist of his day. He toured with Mme. Joanna Gadski for several seasons, for six years accompanied Mme. Marcella Sembrich on tours in the United States and Europe and also accompanied Frances Alda, Margarete Matzenauer and Ernestine Schumann-Heink. When not touring he lived in New York City, where in 1920 he and Ernesto Berúmen founded the La Forge-Berúmen Studios. He taught accompanying and piano and coached vocalists, counting Marian Anderson, Lawrence Tibbett and Richard Crooks among his most famous pupils. Still active, he died unexpectedly while playing the piano at an annual dinner and concert at The Musicians Club in New York. La Forge lived well into the 20th century, but his piano compositions prove that he was an avowed romantic. [I]

LA HACHE, THEODORE VON (b. Dresden, Saxony [now East Germany], ca.March, 1822; d. New Orleans, LA, 21 November 1869). Organist, teacher, music publisher, composer. It is believed that he studied music in Dresden, mostly with Carl Gottlieb Reissiger. How he supported himself after arriving in New Orleans in 1842 is not known, but it seems likely that he gave music lessons and played the organ at some church. His first known published work appeared in 1846, and by 1852 he had established a reputation as a music teacher, organist and composer. He was organist and choirmaster at St. Theresa of Avila Church (1850-66), and was also a co-founder of both the New Orleans Philharmonic Society (1852) and the New Orleans Harmonic Society (1866). A prolific and versatile composer (piano works, songs, and from 1851, Masses and other sacred music), most of his works were greatly admired, performed and published in his lifetime; however, only the sacred works survived after his death (his **Mass of St. Theresa** was published by McLaughlin and Reilly of Boston as late as 1926). In 1866 a serious illness, thought to be lead poisoning caused from drinking water from contaminated pipes, forced him to give up his pupils and delegate most of his duties at St. Theresa's to his son Theodore, Jr. Unable to support himself by teaching or playing, that same year he went into business with George W. Doll. Their firm (La Hache and Doll) sold pianos and other musical merchandise, and the next year began to publish music. The partners separated (April, 1867) but with the help of his son Emile he continued in business, expanding his publishing activities and also selling sheet music. A 27-year resident of New Orleans, he was remembered as a generous and talented contributor to the city's musical life. In 1949 his grandson Theodore Vincent Martinez initiated--and later endowed--the La Hache Music Library at the New Orleans Public Library. La Hache's piano music is, for the most part, very attractive and idiomatic. His repertoire consistly largely of improvisations, variations and vivacious dance settings like the polka. [I]

LAMBERT, ALEXANDER (b. Warsaw, Poland, 1 November 1862; d. New York, NY, 31 December 1929). Pianist, teacher, composer. He began music lessons with his father at about the age of nine, and from 12 to 16 studied at the Vienna Conservatory, where his teachers included Julius Epstein (piano) and Anton Bruckner (composition). After two years of practicing and studying on his own, he visited the United States in 1880. Although unknown, his recitals were well received by American audiences and critics and he was invited to play a concert with Eduard Reményi, the eminent Hungarian violinist. After three years of concertizing and teaching, he went to Germany with the desire to polish his performance technique. He was coached by Moritz Moszkowski in Berlin; made a tour of Germany with Joseph Joachim and a tour of Russia with Pablo de Sarasate; gave many solo recitals and also appeared with the Berlin Philharmonic Orchestra. After a final three months with Liszt at Weimar, he returned to the United States (1884) and, concertizing widely, confirmed his reputation as a concert pianist. In 1892 he retired from the concert field to give all his time to teaching. He was director of the New York College of Music (1887-1905) and on the faculty of Curtis Institute of Music in Philadelphia, PA (1928-29); he also taught many private piano pupils. His textbooks **A Systematic Course of Studies** (1907) and **Piano Method for Beginners** were widely used in his lifetime. Lambert's few well-written piano pieces make excellent study pieces in rhythm and keyboard technique. [I]

LANE, [SIDNEY] EASTWOOD (b. Brewerton, NY, 22 November 1879; d. Central Square, NY, 22 January 1951). Writer, composer. Not long after he was born his family moved to the neighboring village of Central Square, where his father owned a hardware business. A ruggedly individual talent, he had no formal musical education, and all his life proudly described himself as a musical amateur. He regarded music as an enjoyable diversion, and believed that too much formal education would spoil his spontaneity. During his childhood his only contact with music came from his father, who sang regularly in a local church choir, and from an aunt who owned both a phonograph and a square piano upon which he loved to strum and experiment. At the College of Fine Arts at Syracuse University, Syracuse, NY (the 1898-99, 1900-01, 1901-02 catalogs list his name but not the 1899-1900 catalog) he had a weekly class in music but apparently no advanced music courses; however, according to his diary (1900) he practiced many hours a day while at college, having learned the keyboard by playing the Ampico (an elaborate grand-piano version of the player piano) very slowly and fitting his fingers into the automatically depressed keys. An indifferent student, he left college after three and a half years and spent the next eight years, thanks to a small legacy from his grandfather, reading voraciously, practicing the piano, listening to music and making his first attempts at composition. As assistant director of the Wanamaker Auditorium in New York (1910-34), he arranged programs by famous contemporary musical and literary personalities, and many of his works were composed during this stimulating period. A man of broad culture, he had a wide circle of artistic friends—musicians, authors, artists—and was a member of the famous Algonquin Hotel "Round Table." He married in

1933, retired from his Wanamaker position in 1934 and thereafter devoted his time to composing, reading and enjoying his New York life.   His works were especially popular during the 1920s; **Persimmon Pucker** and **Sea Burial** were among those arranged by Ferde Grofé for performance with the Paul Whiteman concert orchestra. Lane's eclectic keyboard repertoire ranges from romantic pieces through more contemporary works to compositions inspired by jazz. [I]

LANG, MARGARET RUTHVEN (b. Boston, MA, 27 November 1867; d. Boston, 29 May 1972). Composer. She had a fine musical background. Her father was Benjamin Johnson Lang, one of Boston's most distinguished musicians, and her mother was a talented amateur singer.   She had early music lessons with one of her father's pupils, then studied piano and harmony with her father and violin with Louis Schmidt. She had further training in Munich (1886-87), where she studied with Ludwig Abel and Victor Gluth, among others, and when she returned to Boston she studied composition with Edward MacDowell and orchestration with George Chadwick. Although she never performed on the concert stage, she made many nonprofessional appearances with clubs in programs of her own music. She was the first woman composer to have an orchestral work performed by the Boston Symphony Orchestra (**Dramatic Overture, Op.12**, performed under Arthur Nikisch, April 8, 1893); and other major orchestras also performed some of her large-scale orchestral and choral works.   Three days before her 100th birthday—she lived to be 104!—she attended the Friday afternoon performance of the Boston Symphony, just as she had done since the founding of the orchestra in 1881. With Eric Leinsdorf conducting, the orchestra played the psalm tune **Old Hundredth** in her honor and the seat she had held in Symphony Hall throughout the century was dedicated to her. Margaret Lang's piano music is openly and attractively romantic. [I]

LAVALEE, CALIXA (b. Ste. Théodosie de Verchères [now Calixa-Lavallée], Quebec, Canada, 28 December 1842; d. Boston, MA, 21 January 1891). Pianist, teacher, composer. He studied with his father, an amateur musician and instrument maker, and had further training in Montreal. He learned to play three instruments (piano, violin, cornet) and from about 1857 worked as a traveling musician in Canada and the United States. Since the "concerts" were likely to be vaudeville entertainments featuring instrumental stunts and vocal acrobatics, he often performed on all three instruments at one event. After winning a musical competition in New Orleans, LA in the late 1850s, he was engaged by the Spanish violinist Olivera for a concert tour of Brazil, the West Indies and parts of the United States. In 1861 he enlisted in the northern army in the American Civil War and became bandmaster of a Rhode Island regimental band.   Mustered out about a year later, he resumed his career as a teacher and traveling musician in Montreal, California, New Orleans and Lowell, MA, where he married in 1867. About 1870 he became conductor and artistic director of the New York Grand Opera House, where minstrel shows were usually performed, but two years later the owner was assassinated and the Opera House closed. Friends in Montreal underwrote further musical training for him at the Paris Conservatory (1873-75), where his teachers included Emmanuel Bazin, Adrien Louis Boieldieu and Antoine Marmontel, and he returned to Canada imbued with the idea of promoting Canadian national music. He opened a studio and put enormous efforts into trying to convince the Canadian government to subsidize a national conservatory and permanent opera company. Although the public applauded his productions (Gounod's **Jeanne d'Arc** and Boieldieu's **La Dame Blanche**) the state failed to supply financial support. In 1880 the music committee for the Fête Nationale des Canadiens-français asked him to compose music for **O Canada** (text by Judge Adolphe B. Routheir), the song that later became the Canadian national anthem. At the age of 38, frustrated by lack of support for national music in Canada, he returned to the United States, settled in Boston and found the recognition that had evaded him at home. At first he supported his family by playing the piano on a Fall River-New York steamer, then later became director of music at the Roman Catholic cathedral and a teacher at the Petersilea Academy in Boston, MA. As a member of the Music Teachers' National Association he actively promoted American music, and helped to organize some of the first concerts of all-American music at the MTNA meetings in Cleveland (1884) and New York (1886). He was president of MTNA (1887) and was the United States representative at the London conference of the National Society of Professional Musicians (1888). In 1933 his remains were reburied in Montreal with a ceremony witnessed by thousands. He is remembered for his unusual role as advocate for the national music of two different countries. As a composer Lavallée wrote a few descriptive--and difficult--salon pieces which were very popular in their own day. [I]

LEVY, HENIOT (b. Warsaw, Poland, 19 July 1879; d. Chicago, IL, 16 June 1946). Pianist, teacher, composer. He received all his musical education in Berlin, where he studied piano with Oscar Raif and Carl Barth at the Hochschule für Musik (graduated 1897) and composition with Max Bruch and Heinrich von Herzogenberg at the Meisterschule für Komposition. After making his début with the Berlin Philharmonic Orchestra (1898), he made concert tours in southern Europe, Germany and Scandinavia (1899-1904). From 1904 he lived in Chicago, having been appointed, on the recommendation of Leopold Godowsky, to the faculty of the American Conservatory of Music. He taught piano there and from 1919 was associate director. Most of Lévy's piano works are serious, intense and technically demanding concert pieces. [I,IV]

LEWING, ADELE (b. Hanover, Germany, 6 August 1866; d. New York, NY, 16 February 1943). Pianist, teacher, composer. She studied with her grandfather August Prell, first cellist in the Hanover court orchestra, and with Carl Reinecke and Salomon Jadassohn at the Leipzig Conservatory. After graduating in 1885, she began a career as teacher and performer. She emigrated to America, formed a class of piano students in Chicago, IL and gave her first American concert there in December, 1888. She taught privately, gave solo recitals and appeared with leading orchestras until 1893, when she went to Vienna to complete her musical training under Theodore Leschetizky (piano) and Robert Fuchs (composition). She returned to the United States in 1896, from 1897 lived in New York as teacher, performer and composer. In 1899 she married Dr. Benjamin Stiefel. She won many prizes for her works, including a gold medal at the World's Columbian Exposition (1893). Her few piano compositions are pleasant and unpretentious. [I]

LIEBLING, EMIL (b. Plessa, Germany, 12 April 1851; d. Chicago, IL, 20 January 1914). Pianist, teacher, writer, composer. He studied music with his father and with Alfred Ehrlich in Berlin (1866), and emigrated to the United States in 1867. He earned his living as a music teacher, first in the area around Covington, KY and later in Cincinnati, OH, often acquiring pupils by riding horseback through the countryside and playing for any family with a piano. In 1872 he began teaching in Chicago, but soon decided to return to Europe to complete his musical training. He studied with Theodore Kullak, Heinrich Dorn and Eduard Rohde in Berlin and with Joseph Dachs in Vienna, meanwhile supporting himself by teaching private pupils and sometimes teaching at the Kullak Academy. After spending some time with Liszt at Weimar in the spring of 1876, he returned to America and made his permanent home in Chicago. He won distinction as a writer, composer and, according to music critic Harold Schonberg, "the best teacher and pianist in Chicago." He compiled, with W. S. B. Mathews, the **Pronouncing and Defining Dictionary of Music** (1896); edited **The Essentials of Music**, the final volume of **The American History and Encyclopedia of Music** (1908-10); and wrote numerous articles for music periodicals. He was a brother of Georg Liebling. Emil Liebling was a superb musician, completely at ease writing taut, dramatic serious works or sparkling salon pieces. [I]

LIEBLING, GEORG (b. Berlin, Germany, 22 January 1865; d. New York, NY, 7 February 1946). Pianist, teacher, composer. He was educated at Heidelberg University, studied music with Theodore and Franz Kullak, Heinrich Urban and Heinrich Dorn in Berlin and, like his brother Emil, had some coaching from the elderly Liszt. During 1881-94 he made frequent tours, sometimes as soloist and sometimes as accompanist for other artists, such as the soprano Marcella Sembrich and violinist Maurice Dengremont. He toured not only in Europe but as far away as South Africa and China, acquiring a reputation for his enormous repertoire and phenomenal technique. When not touring he taught at the Kullak Academy, Berlin (1880-85); served as court pianist to the Duke of Saxe-Coburg (1890); directed his own piano school in Berlin (1894-97); was a professor at the

Guildhall School of Music, London (1898-1908); and directed his own conservatory in Munich (1908-23). In 1923 he went to the United States, made his début in New York the following year and remained as a teacher, concert pianist and composer. Liebling wrote some very fine, difficult concert pieces for the mature pianist. [I,V]

LINLEY, FRANCIS (b. Doncaster, England, ca.1770; d. Doncaster, 1800). Organist, composer, music editor. During a brief visit to the United States (1796-99) he published his **New Assistant for the Piano-forte or Harpsichord** (see Bibliography) which contains six sonatas by Benjamin Carr.

LOEFFLER, CHARLES MARTIN [TORNOW] (b. Mulhouse, Alsace, 30 January 1861; d. Medfield, MA, 19 May 1935). Violinist, teacher, composer. At the age of eight he began violin lessons with a German musician in Smjela, a small town near Kiev, where his father worked for the Russian government. By the time he reached 14 he had made his first attempts at composition and determined to become a musician. In 1875 he went to Berlin, where he studied violin with Eduard Rappoldi (who prepared pupils for Joseph Joachim), theory with Friedrich Kiel and Bach motets with Woldemar Bargiel; then had further training in Paris with Joseph Massart (violin) and Ernest Guiraud (composition). After playing one season with the Pasdeloup Orchestra, in 1879 he was engaged as violinist in the private orchestra of Paul von Derwies, a Russian baron with residences in Italy and France. In 1881 he emigrated to America with letters from Joachim to Leopold Damrosch and Theodore Thomas in New York. During the 1881-82 season he played in several concerts under Damrosch, and the following spring found a permanent position with the newly organized Boston Symphony Orchestra. He was a violinist with that orchestra for 21 years (1882-1903), and from 1885 shared the first desk with Franz Kneisel. He became a distinguished figure in Boston musical and social circles, recognized not only as a brilliant violinist but as a composer, and his works were frequently performed by the BSO and other major orchestras. He continued to teach and compose after retiring from the orchestra. He was an officer of the French Academy (1906), a Chevalier of the Legion of Honor (1919), a member of the American Academy of Arts and Letters and was awarded a Mus.D. from Yale University (1926). His father sometimes used the nom de plume "Tornow," and Loeffler later added it to his name. A meticulous craftsman who frequently revised his works, Loeffler is known by only one piano composition, the masterful **Pagan Poem**. [V]

LOOMIS, HARVEY WORTHINGTON (b. Brooklyn, NY, 5 February 1865; d. Roxbury, MA, 25 December 1930). Composer. His father was a tenor and his mother a soprano of some note and also one of the founders of the Brooklyn Philharmonic Society. He was educated at the Polytechnic Institute of Brooklyn and at the National Conservatory of Music in New York City, having won a three-year scholarship

(1891-93) with his setting of Joseph von Eichendorff's "Frühlingsnacht." He studied composition with Antonin Dvořák, then director of the Conservatory, and in addition had piano lessons with Madeleine Schiller. He spent most of his life in Boston composing, writing and lecturing, especially on Indian music, and he achieved an outstanding reputation in his day. As late as 1940 (**Musical Quarterly**, Jan.) Carl Engel wrote that he "bore the authentic marks of originality and genius"; however, of his more than 500 works, only a few were published, chiefly by the Wa-Wan Press, and even those are rarely heard today. He was an editor for C. C. Birchard and Co. publications in Boston, and also contributed numerous articles to musical journals. Many of his manuscripts can be found at the Library of Congress. Loomis's **Lyrics of the Red Man**, two volumes of piano pieces based on American Indian melodies, contain some of his most convincing writing and are remarkable for their authentic Indian mood and atmosphere. [I]

LYNES, FRANK (b. Cambridge, MA, 16 May 1858; d. Bristol, NH, 24 June 1913). Organist, teacher, composer. He studied music for a long period of time. At the age of ten he began lessons with a local teacher, later attended the New England Conservatory in Boston and also studied with Benjamin J. Lang and John Knowles Paine. He had further training at the Leipzig Conservatory (1883-85), where he studied with Carl Reinecke, Bruno Zwintscher, Salomon Jadassohn and Alfred Richter. From 1885 he made his home in Boston, and for more than 25 years was active there as organist, teacher and composer. He was organist at St. Paul's Church, the Church of the Disciples and the First Parish Unitarian Church in Brookline; for many years he was also conductor of the Cantabrigia Chorus. Lynes's many short attractive compositions make excellent teaching pieces. [I]

MAAS, LOUIS [PHILIPP OTTO] (b. Wiesbaden, Germany, 21 June 1852; d. Jamaica Plain, MA, 17 September 1889). Pianist, teacher, composer. He was raised in London, his family having moved there when he was about two, and began piano studies at an early age with his father, a music teacher. After graduating from King's College (1867) he took advanced musical training at the Leipzig Conservatory (1867-71), working principally with Carl Reinecke and Benjamin Papperitz. Meanwhile he had already begun to compose, and several of his works were performed at Gewandhaus concerts: first overture (1868), second overture (1869) and first symphony, which he conducted (1872). After graduating from the Conservatory, he taught at the Kullak Academy in Berlin (1873-74), and for three summers worked under Liszt at Weimar. During 1875-80 he taught piano at the Leipzig Conservatory, concertized and composed. In 1880 he emigrated to the United States, and from that time made his home in Boston, MA. He taught at the New England Conservatory and also had many private pupils, made concert tours and composed. His **On the Prairies, Op.15**, an American symphony, was inspired by a tour he made through the West. Maas's **Concerto, Op.12**, a sturdy, serious work, is one of the very finest piano concertos from the 19th century. His solo compositions, particularly the short character pieces, are also worth studying. [I,V]

MACDOWELL, EDWARD [EDGAR THORN] (b. New York, NY, 18 December 1860; d. New York, 23 January 1908). Pianist, teacher, composer. He began piano lessons at the age of eight with Juan Buitrago, a Colombian violinist, later studied with Buitrago's Cuban friend Pablo Desvernine and also had informal--and beneficial--instruction from the well-known Venezuelan pianist Teresa Carreño, who became his lifelong friend and champion and was one of the first in America to include his works on concert programs. In April, 1876 his mother took him to Paris, where he studied piano privately with Antoine Marmontel for about a year, attended Marie Gabriel Savard's theory class at the Paris Conservatory and spent a significant amount of his time composing. Officially enrolled at the Conservatory in February, 1877, he won a scholarship that October but withdrew about a year later, having heard Nicholas Rubinstein perform a Tchaikovsky piano concerto and been convinced that if he wanted to play like Rubinstein he would have to study in Germany. After a few unsatisfactory weeks of study with Siegmund Lebert at the Stuttgart Conservatory, he went to Wiesbaden on the recommendation of the violinist Emile Sauret (a family friend and also Carreño's first husband), and spent the winter and spring (1878-79) studying theory and composition with Louis Ehlert and piano with Carl Heymann. In May, 1879 he enrolled at the Hoch Conservatory at Frankfort, where he continued his piano training under Heymann, studied counterpoint and fugue with Franz Böhme and studied composition with director Joachim Raff, who became his good friend and advisor. At the Conservatory he concentrated on the piano and performed often, on three occasions heard by Liszt. Still undecided between composing and performing, he left the Conservatory at the end of July (1880) and began private piano teaching, at the same time continuing his studies with Heymann and Raff through the winter. He derived additional income from accompanying singers, appearing with orchestras and teaching at the Darmstadt Conservatory (1881-82), a position he resigned because he had too little time for composition. On Liszt's recommendation he was invited to perform his **First Modern Suite, Op.10** at a meeting of the General Society of German Musicians in Zurich (July, 1882), and the success of the **Suite** may have been a turning point for him, the time when he realized that he really wanted to be a composer, not a performer. He found encouragement in that direction when he wrote to his friend Teresa Carreño seeking advice (1883). She responded warmly, urging him to continue as a composer and supporting him with performances of his music, playing the Andantino from the **First Modern Suite** at Saratoga, NY (August 4, 1883) and giving the first American performance of his **Second Modern Suite, Op.14** in Chicago (March 8, 1884). Meanwhile on Liszt's recommendation both suites were published in 1883 by Breitkopf and Härtel, and by 1885 ten of his works had been published in Germany. MacDowell married Marian Nevins, a former pupil, in New York (July, 1884). They lived first in Frankfort, where he composed and taught privately, but after moving to Wiesbaden in the Fall of 1885 he concentrated all his creative energies on composition. Within three years he produced more than 25 works (including 8 solo piano pieces, two piano duets and the **Piano Concerto No.2**), and his music was being heard in frequent performances in both Europe and America. It was in Wiesbaden early in 1886 that he met the American expatriate George Templeton Strong, and the two young composers formed a spontaneous and lasting friendship. In the Fall of 1888 he returned to the United States and settled in Boston, MA, and that November reluctantly made his American début as a pianist. As composer, performer and teacher, his eight years in Boston were creatively and financially rewarding. He composed more than ever and there was an increasing demand for his music; he acquired a great many piano students, including Henry F. B. Gilbert; and he performed often, playing his own works. Now recognized as one of America's most eminent musical personalities, he was invited (1896) to become the first professor of music at Columbia University in New York City, where he would be in charge of establishing a new department of music. He managed alone until Leonard McWhood, a former pupil, became his assistant in 1898, then in 1899 Gustav Hinrichs was appointed as conductor of the student orchestra and chorus. Besides his duties at Columbia, he conducted the Mendelssohn Glee Club (a New York male chorus), taught private piano pupils, gave recitals when possible and was also president of the newly founded Society of American Musicians and Composers (1899–1900). Although during the Columbia years he had only the summers wholly free for composition, he produced a great many works, including some of his finest piano compositions: **Sea Pieces, Op.55; Third (Norse) Sonata, Op.57; Fourth (Keltic) Sonata, Op.59; Fireside Tales, Op.61;** and **New England Idyls, Op.62.** Within this same period he also published several works (Op.1–7) under the pseudonym Edgar Thorn (Thorne), with the royalties designated for his wife's old nurse. In 1904 he resigned from Columbia because of a public conflict with Nicholas Murray Butler, the new (1902) president of Columbia, over music-department policies and the establishment of a new division of fine arts. After leaving Columbia, he continued to teach privately. However, about this same time he began to show signs of mental weakness, a condition most likely aggravated when he was struck and injured by a horse carriage in the winter of 1904–05. Within a year he had deteriorated completely, and for the rest of his life had to be cared for like a child. After his death friends organized the MacDowell Memorial Association, to which his wife deeded their property at Peterborough, NH, to form the MacDowell Colony, an artistic center where musicians, artists, sculptors and writers can be accommodated to have time and freedom to create. MacDowell was awarded honorary doctorates in music from Princeton University (1896) and the University of Pennsylvania (1902). He looms large among nineteenth-century American composers. Like Louis Moreau Gottschalk (q.v.), he was one of the first Americans to achieve an international reputation, and he is one of the few whose music is still occasionally performed. MacDowell's superb piano music is surely worthy of study by all pianists. It shows the composer as a tone poet, creating his moods through rich harmony, modulation, dissonance, thick texture and an onrushing flow of rhythms and dynamics. [I,III,V]

MACFADYEN, ALEXANDER (b. Milwaukee, WI, 12 July 1879; d. Chicago, IL, 6 June 1936). Pianist, teacher, composer. He studied with Julius Klauser and William Borchert in Milwaukee, and spent several years at the Chicago Musical College, where he was a pupil of Rudolph Ganz, Arthur Friedheim, Felix Borowski, Herman Devries and Louis Falk. After graduating in 1905 he made his début at the Chicago Auditorium in June, performing as a soloist with an orchestra conducted by Hans von Schiller. He subsequently appeared as soloist with the Chicago Symphony Orchestra under Frederick Stock, went on tour with the Leonora Jackson Concert Co. and toured through the United States and Canada as a piano soloist on the Orpheum circuit. He taught at the International Conservatory in New York City and at the Wisconsin College of Music in Milwaukee. MacFadyen's conservative piano music provides a variety of styles and types—structured études and scherzi, a sturdy sonata, paraphrases, improvisations—usually conceived in a romantic setting. [I,IV,V]

MANNEY, CHARLES FONTEYN (b. Brooklyn, NY, 8 February 1872; d.   New York, NY, 31 October 1951). Editor, conductor, composer. As a boy he sang solo soprano in a church choir. He was educated at the Polytechnic Institute of Brooklyn, and studied music with William Arms Fisher in New York and with J. Wallace Goodrich and Percy Goetschius in Boston, MA. In 1898 he moved to Boston, where he was an associate editor of the Oliver Ditson Co. (1898-1930) and also conductor of the Footlight Orchestra and several choruses. After retiring from Ditson, he lived in New York. Manney's piano pieces, some of them quite sentimental, are predominantly salon music. [I]

MARETZEK, MAX (b. Brünn, Moravia [now Brno, Czechoslovakia], 28 June 1821; d. Pleasant Plains, Staten Island, NY, 14 May 1897). Impresario, conductor, violinist, composer. He was preparing for a career as a surgeon until faced with the fact that he was not suited to the realities of surgery. Having studied music with Ignaz von Seyfried (pupil and friend of Mozart), he decided on a career in music. His first opera **Hamlet** was produced in Brünn in 1843, and for several years thereafter he traveled in Germany, France and England as either theater conductor, violinist or composer. In September, 1848 he emigrated to America, having been engaged as conductor of the Italian Opera Company at the Astor Place Opera House, New York, then under the management of Edward P. Fry. When Fry's company failed in early 1849, he took over as manager-conductor and reopened that same year with most of Fry's artists. For three decades he was a ubiquitous, aggressive impresario-conductor, the first five years as impresario at the

Astor Place Opera House and then at various times and seasons at the Academy of Music, Niblo's, the Winter Garden and Castle Garden, meanwhile often taking his company on tour in the United States and Mexico and to Havana. In 1860 he resumed his conducting career and began conducting with other companies as well as his own. Although his productions were usually successful with the public, he often lost money. He had difficulty handling people--his orchestra and chorus sometimes went on strike--yet he was regarded as an honest, intelligent and enterprising manager. He was one of the first to give the American public fairly regular seasons of opera, mostly historical Italian operas but also modern French and Italian stage works. Some of the operas he presented, often in their first New York performance, have become standard in the modern repertoire: **Don Giovanni, Rigoletto, Il Trovatore, La Traviata, Romeo and Juliet.** After retiring as an impresario, he devoted his time to teaching voice, coaching would-be opera singers and writing articles for American, French and German journals and periodicals. In honor of the 50th anniversary of his career as a conductor a golden jubilee concert was held at the Metropolitan Opera House (1889), a gesture of affection and respect tendered him by some of the most famous musical celebrities of the day. He was a colorful, theatrical personage, a bon vivant known as "Maretzek the magnificent," and he described himself, his times and other musicians in **Crotchets and Quavers; or Revelations of an Opera Manager in America** (1855, DaCapo reprint 1966) and in its sequel **Sharps and Flats** (1890). Maretzek wrote only a few piano works and most of them are light polkas. [I]

MARSTON, GEORGE W. (b. Sandwich, MA, 23 May 1840; d. Sandwich, 2 February 1901). Organist, teacher, composer. As a boy he sang in a church choir, from the age of 12 to 18 he studied music with local teachers and at 16 was organist at the First Congregational Church. After graduating from the Sandwich Academy, he spent about a year at Waterville, ME, where he gave piano lessons and was organist at the First Baptist Church. Around 1860 he moved to Portland, ME, where he studied piano and harmony with John W. Tufts and made a career as organist-choirmaster and music teacher. During his more than 30 years there he was successively organist at St. Luke's Episcopal Church, Congress Square Universalist Church and State Street Congregational Church. He made two trips to Germany for further training, studying the Beethoven sonatas with Giuseppe Buonamici in Munich in 1870 and composition with Joachim Raff in Wiesbaden in 1874-75. About six years before his death he moved to Boston, MA but frequently returned to Portland to see pupils and attend concerts. Marston's piano music is pleasant to hear and to play. His style can be exquisitely joyful, profoundly somber, or quaintly simple. [I]

MASON, DANIEL GREGORY (b. Brookline, MA, 20 November 1873; d. Greenwich, CT, 4 December 1953). Teacher, writer, lecturer, composer. He came from an exceptionally musical family.

Grandfather Lowell Mason was a hymn-tune composer and a pioneer in establishing music education in American public schools; uncle William Mason was a composer and also one of the finest music teachers of his generation; and his father Henry Mason was one of the founders of Mason and Hamlin, piano manufacturers. After his first music lessons with Nellie Coolidge, a local teacher, he studied with Clayton Johns in Boston, MA. At Harvard (1891-95) he took John Knowles Paine's music courses, and later studied with George Chadwick and Percy Goetschius in Boston. After graduation he moved to New York City, where he met many famous musical personalities (Paderewski, MacDowell, Dohnányi, Brockway) at his uncle William Mason's home, studied piano with Arthur Whiting and prepared for a career in music. However, financial problems (after his father's death in 1890 the family business declined) and a lame arm (he suffered from a general neurasthenic weakness) forced him to give up music for a time. He returned to Boston, and earned his living as an assistant in the English department at Harvard; unable to practice, he read a great deal and began to write. Various magazines published his essays and articles, especially his series on composers (Brahms, Grieg, Dvořák, Saint-Saëns, Franck, Tchaikovsky), published first in **Outlook** and later the basis for his first book **From Grieg to Brahms.** He spent the academic year 1902-03 teaching at Princeton University (on a subsidy provided by Princeton alumnus Rudolph E. Schirmer, who hoped to get the undergraduates interested in music), then moved to New York, where he had been engaged as editor of the new magazine **Masters in Music.** In 1905 he was appointed lecturer in music at Columbia University, and taught there for 37 years: assistant professor (1910); MacDowell Professor (1929); head of the music department (1929-40); professor emeritus (1942). From about 1904, when he began what he described as an endless (more than 250) series of lectures for the New York Board of Education, he was much in demand as a lecturer at major universities and other institutions. On one of his frequent trips to Europe he had several sessions with Vincent d'Indy, who criticized his compositions (Paris, 1913). In retirement he continued to write and compose. During his lifetime his compositions were frequently performed by leading American orchestras, but since his death his books (author of 17 and coauthor of 2) have endured better than his music. He received honorary doctorates from Tufts University, Medford, MA (1929), Oberlin Conservatory, Oberlin, OH (1931) and the Eastman School of Music, Rochester, NY (1932). He was also a member of the National Institute of Arts and Letters. In many of his piano compositions Mason attempted, with varying success, to combine a fading romanticism with the then emerging contemporary style. [I,IV,V]

MASON, WILLIAM (b. Boston, MA, 24 January 1829; d. New York, NY, 14 July 1908). Teacher, pianist, composer. His father Lowell Mason, a prominent hymnist and a pioneer in establishing music in American public schools, wanted him to be a minister and not a professional musician, so as a boy he studied only with his mother but practiced a great deal on his own. In 1843 he was sent to

Newport, RI as apprentice to the Rev. T. T. Thayer, but he kept up his music and played the organ in Thayer's church. When he returned to Boston about two years later, he became the organist at the Winter Street Congregational Church, where his father was music director, and was allowed to take piano lessons with Henry Schmidt. After making his professional début as a pianist at the Boston Academy of Music (March, 1846), he gave piano recitals in Boston and nearby cities, then in 1849 went to Europe for advanced training.   At the Leipzig Conservatory he studied with Ignaz Moscheles, Moritz Hauptmann and Ernst F. Richter, then had about nine months of intensive study with Alexander Dreyschock in Prague, Czechoslovakia. He polished his piano technique, gaining experience with appearances in Prague, Frankfort, Weimar and London, where he appeared with the Harmonic Union Orchestra in January, 1853. He finally spent time at Weimar with Liszt, having irregular lessons and reaping all the benefits of membership in Liszt's inner circle (April, 1853-July, 1854). He returned to Boston and that autumn made a two-month tour, giving solo recitals in New England, New York, Ohio and Chicago, and he may have been the first pianist in the United States to tour alone, without assisting singers or instrumentalists.   Although his concerts were reasonably successful, he loathed touring and in 1855 settled in New York City as a teacher and composer; for about ten years he also gave solo recitals and appeared with orchestras.   With Theodore Thomas and others he founded the Mason and Thomas Chamber Music Soirées (1855-68), an ensemble that specialized in bringing Romantic works to New York audiences.   A lifelong organist, he played at the Fifth Avenue Presbyterian Church (1855-60), briefly at the New Jerusalem Church and for many years at the Orange Valley Congregational Church, Orange, NJ. After 1880 he accepted fewer pupils but continued to teach until a year before his death. Known for his high standards, he reputedly was the best piano teacher in the country.   He wrote several piano teaching manuals, notably **Touch and Technic, Op.44,** and developed a finger-pulling exercise known in the United States as "the Mason touch." He was awarded a Mus.D from Yale University (1872). Mason's large piano catalog consists primarily of very fine compositions written in a lushly romantic style. [I,III]

MAYLATH, HEINRICH [HENRY] (b. Vienna, Austria, 4 December 1827; d. New York, NY, 31 December 1883). Pianist, teacher, composer. Apart from the brief entries in Baker and Grove, little is known about his life and career. He had piano instruction from his father and made concert tours in Europe, including Russia, until 1867 when he emigrated to the United States and settled in New York as a teacher and pianist. He published some useful piano teaching pieces, several virtuosic concert pieces and numerous transcriptions. [I]

MEINEKE [MEINECKE], CHRISTOPHER [CHARLES, CARL] (b. Germany, ca. 1782; d. Baltimore, MD, 6 November 1850). Pianist, organist, composer. He was the son of Carl Meineke, organist to the Duke of

Oldenburg in Germany, and consequently had a thorough musical education. He emigrated to the United States (1800) and settled in Baltimore, where he attained a reputation as an excellent pianist--a brilliant concerto player, quick reader and sympathetic accompanist. According to Wolfe, he returned to Germany for a visit in 1817 and was introduced to Beethoven, to whom he submitted a "concerto" and "won the master's praise." He returned to Baltimore in 1819 and for the rest of his life was organist at St. Paul's Episcopal Church. He wrote **A New Instruction for the Piano Forte** (1823) and **Music for the Church** (62 psalms and hymn tunes composed for the use of the choirs at St. Paul's Church). He composed vocal and instrumental works, and made many piano transcriptions. In **Shadows on the Wall** (1877) John Hewitt wrote that "his piano music, generally variations, was quite popular." Some of the variations are still enjoyable for both playing and listening. [I]

MELNOTTE, CLAUDE [See **CHARLES KUNKEL**]

MERZ, CARL (b. Bensheim, Germany, 10 September 1836; d. Wooster, OH, 30 January 1890). Teacher, organist, writer, composer. He had early organ and violin lessons with his father, organist of the parish church, and further studies with Franz Joseph Kunkel at the Bensheim Teachers' Seminary. After graduating from the Seminary (1853), he spent a year teaching in a small town near Bingen, then emigrated to America and settled in Philadelphia, PA (1854). With help from Johann Heinrich Bonawitz, a young German pianist who had come to America two years earlier, he found work as a violinist in theater orchestras and also earned money playing the organ at the Sixth Presbyterian Church. He taught music at Eden Hall Seminary, a girls' school at Lancaster, PA (1856-59) and at other girls' schools in Virginia (1859-61). Vacationing in the North when the Civil War erupted (1861), he could not return to Virginia, but that September he was appointed a professor of music at the Oxford Female College (later Oxford College for Women) at Oxford, OH. From 1865 he gave an annual series of concerts at Oxford and before each concert gave a preview to help the audience understand and appreciate the music. In 1882 he became director of the newly established conservatory at the University of Wooster (now The College of Wooster) in Wooster, OH, and was still teaching there at the time of his death. Recognized as an outstanding teacher, lecturer and writer, he was affiliated with **Brainard's Musical World** (1868-90), first as a regular contributor, from 1871 as associate editor, from 1873 as editor. He published **Musical Hints for the Million** (1875), **The Modern Method for the Reed Organ** (1876), **The Elements of Harmony and Musical Composition** (1881) and **Carl Merz's Piano Method** (1885); **Music and Culture** (1890), a volume of his essays and lectures, was published posthumously. The University of Wooster awarded him an honorary Mus.D. in 1882. His impressive library (ca.1450 vols.) was purchased and presented to the Carnegie Library, Pittsburgh, PA. Although Merz wrote some serious compositions for the piano, he was at his best with the sentimental salon piece. [I,III]

METZ, JULIUS (fl.New York, NY, 1819-57). Pianist, singer, composer. He is listed as a professor of music in the New York city directories (1819-57). According to Wolverton, he first appeared in New York as a singer (December, 1819) and later was also active as a pianist and composer. His name appears as a pianist on the roster of the New York Philharmonic Society during its second season (1842). Metz wrote mostly dance-inspired pieces plus several variation sets for the piano. [I]

MILDENBERG, ALBERT (b. Brooklyn, NY, 13 January 1878; d. Brooklyn, 3 July 1918). Pianist, teacher, composer. He had piano lessons with his mother until he was 15, then studied with Rafael Joseffy and Bruno Oscar Klein in New York (ca.1900-04). He studied with Giovanni Sgambati at the Liceo Musicale of the St. Cecilia Academy in Rome (1905-06) and with Jules Massenet in Paris (1906-08), where he also conducted the Société Symphonique for one season (1907-08). He was appointed a professor of piano and organ at Meredith College, Raleigh, NC in 1913, became director of the school of music in 1915 but resigned because of ill health (1917). He received an honorary Mus.D. from Wake Forest College, Winston-Salem, NC (1916). Mildenberg wrote mostly salon music. [I]

MILLER, W. B. (fl.1860s). An unidentified composer. He is known as the composer of attractive variations on the popular song "The Girl I Left behind Me." [I]

MILLS, SEBASTIAN BACH (b. Cirencester, England, 13 March 1838; d. Wiesbaden, Germany, 21 December 1898). Pianist, teacher, composer. He studied first with his father, an organist, and P. Cipriani Potter in London. Considered a prodigy, at the age of seven he played a command performance for Queen Victoria, and at 17 became organist of the Roman Catholic cathedral at Sheffield. He completed his musical education at the Leipzig Conservatory, where he was a pupil of Ignaz Moscheles, Louis Plaidy, Julius Rietz and Moritz Hauptmann, and immediately after graduation (1859) he went to the United States. He made his first American appearance with the New York Philharmonic Society (March 26, 1859) under Carl Bergmann, playing Schumann's **Concerto in A Minor,** and the response was so enthusiastic he decided to remain in America. Thereafter a frequent guest with the Philharmonic Society, he played every season until his last appearance (November 24, 1877), and became especially noted for introducing piano works not previously heard in New York. In 1860 he gave the first New York performance of Moscheles' **Concerto in G Minor,** in 1861 Chopin's **Concerto in F Minor,** in 1863 Hiller's **Concerto in F-sharp Minor,** in 1864 the Weber-Liszt **Polonaise,** in 1865 Mozart's **Concerto in C, K.503,** in 1867 Liszt's

Concerto in E Flat, in 1872 Reinecke's **Concerto in F-sharp Minor** and in 1877 von Bronsart's **Concerto** and Raff's **Suite, Op.200.** With his innovative programs, skillful playing and fine teaching, he exerted an important and beneficial influence on New York's musical life for nearly four decades. A year before his death he moved to Wiesbaden. Mills excelled in the concert paraphrase and difficult pianistic showpieces. [I]

MOKREJS, JOHN (b. Cedar Rapids, IA, 10 February 1875; d. Cedar Rapids, 11 November 1968). Teacher, pianist, composer. His mother's vast repertoire of Bohemian folk songs and tales made him aware of his Czech heritage, of which he was always immensely proud. He had his first music lessons with Margaret Skillman West, a local teacher, and practiced on a piano in Slapnicka's Music Store, where he worked in exchange for practice time. By the time he was 14 he had composed several songs and piano pieces. After spending two years at Coe College in Cedar Rapids, which had no music department, he studied with Gertrude Murdough at the American Conservatory in Chicago, IL. To help finance his Chicago expenses he organized a benefit concert (Sept., 1896), the first of a series of annual concerts he presented in Cedar Rapids over the next decade, and received additional help when he was engaged as an assistant teacher at the Conservatory. In September, 1903 he began further training with A. K. Virgil at the Virgil School of Music in New York City, where he was also engaged to teach, and in 1905 studied with Percy Goetschius at the newly established Institute of Musical Art (later part of Juilliard). Around 1905 he opened a studio in Carnegie Hall, and for 40 years lived an active, productive life in New York, mostly teaching and composing. A trip to Bohemia in 1911 renewed his pride in the heritage that inspired many of his works. At the age of 70 he moved to Brentwood, CA (1945) with the intention of teaching less and composing more; however, he not only continued to teach but also conducted seminars for other piano teachers and traveled throughout the West judging piano competitions for the National Guild of Piano Teachers. He returned to Cedar Rapids in 1966. Many of his works were published by the Odowan Press, a company that he founded around 1906 because he was dissatisfied with his then publishers. Since he often revised a work previously published, then reissued it--with a different opus number--in an Odowan edition, his opus numbers are confusing. He wrote many articles for **Piano Guild Notes** and several instruction books on harmony, rhythm, sight-reading, counterpoint and fingering. Mokrejs's piano works are generally charming because of their Bohemian authenticity. [I]

MOLLER, JOHN CHRISTOPHER [JOHANN CHRISTOPH] (b. Germany, 1755; d. New York, NY, 21 September 1803). Organist, concert manager, music publisher, composer. Before emigrating to America he lived in London, where many of his important works were published. His first known appearance in America--he played a sonata on the harpsichord--was at a concert given at the City Tavern in New York

on Sept. 10, 1790. He soon moved to Philadelphia, where he became
organist of the Zion Lutheran Church (October), and for the next
five years was an active and outstanding figure in the city's
musical life. In an attempt to revive the City Concerts that had
been discontinued since 1788, he joined Alexander Reinagle and
Henri Capron in presenting eight concerts between December 1, 1792
and March 31, 1793. An active performer, he appeared as pianist or
violist in some of these concerts and in many later Philadelphia
concerts; he also played the glass harmonica, a favorite instrument
which he tried to reintroduce to the American public. In March,
1793 he and Capron established Moller and Capron, a music
publishing firm that may have been the first in the United States
for printing only music. As advertised in the **Federal Gazette**
(March, 1793), they planned to issue the "Moller and Capron Monthly
Numbers," each a six-page number containing "the newest vocal and
instrumental music." The publishing firm, which was combined with
a music store and music school, was a short-lived venture, but at
least three and possibly more monthly numbers were issued. Whether
because he lost a good source of income when the Zion Church burned
in December, 1794 or for other reasons, he moved to New York City
in 1795, and in November of that year joined the Van Hagens in
organizing the New York City Conceerts. They presented three
concerts during January–February, 1796, then later that year the
Van Hagens moved to Boston and Moller attempted to continue the
series. He was an active performer in New York at least through
1800, appearing as a soloist or in duets with his wife, daughter or
other musicians. In 1799 he played organ concertos at the Columbia
Garden concerts; in March, 1800 he played a duet for two performers
on the piano with a Mr. Weldon. Although he lived in America for
perhaps less than 15 years, he had a noteworthy impact on music in
early New York and Philadelphia. Moller's piano compositions are
written in a pleasant Classic style. [I]

MORAN, PETER K. (d. New York, NY, 10 February 1831). Organist,
teacher, cellist, composer. Wolfe's **Secular Music in America
1800–1825: A Bibliography** provides the information about this
composer. On December 26, 1817 Moran placed a notice in the **New
York Evening Post** announcing that he and his wife, a singer, had
arrived from Dublin. A New Yorker for the rest of his life, he is
listed in the city directories (1818-30) as "musician," "professor
of music" or "teacher." Not only a teacher but obviously a
versatile performer, he appeared in New York musical events as
pianist, organist and cellist. He performed as a pianist from
about 1818 and as organist at sacred-music concerts from about
1821. He was organist at Grace Church (1823); organist at the first
concert of the New York Choral Society (April 20, 1824); and
according to his obituary (**NYEP** February 11, 1831), he was finally
organist at St. John's Church. Since he was hired as a cellist in
the orchestra engaged by the Garcia Opera Co. for its performance
of **The Barber of Seville** (November 29, 1825)--the first of 11
operas (79 performances) presented by Garcia in New York that
season (1825-26)--it seems likely that he played the cello

frequently during Garcia's engagement. Besides teaching and performing, he owned a piano and music store (1822-23), from which he issued some music publications. He arranged concert appearances for his daughter, a prodigy who appeared as pianist and singer from the age of five, and sometimes performed piano duets with her. Moran was a prolific and a popular composer. His piano variations and rondos are indeed appealing, and are worth hearing today. [I,III]

MURDEN, ELIZA [née **CRAWLEY**] (b. Baltimore, MD, ca.1783; d. Charleston, SC, 1 January 1847). Poet, teacher, composer. From her last will and testament (April 14, 1845) we learn that she was (1) a widow, (2) born in Baltimore but a resident of Charleston from childhood, and (3) the mother of a son (Edgar) and four daughters (Malvina, Octavia, Victoria, Rosaline). Her marriage to Jeremiah Murden, a Charleston merchant, on December 25, 1808 was reported in the **Charleston Courier,** December 28, 1808. In 1828 she and her eldest daughter Malvina founded Mrs. Murden and Daughter's Seminary for Young Ladies, a school that existed without a break until just before World War I. She was head of the school, located on Society Street, until her death; Malvina was director until 1890, maintaining it throughout the Civil War by removing it to Greenville, SC, then reinstating it in Charleston at a new location on Legare Street (1865); and Eliza's granddaughters (the Misses Sass, daughters of Octavia, who married Jacob K. Sass) operated the school until it closed. At the 85th anniversary celebration in 1913 J. P. Kennedy Bryan noted that the school had been a vital force in the community, with as many as five generations of some families attending. A comparison of the title pages of the two editions of Eliza's poems indicates that she was the "young lady of Charleston." The title page of the first volume, published before her marriage, reads: "**Poems** by a Young Lady of Charleston, Miss Eliza Murden (handwritten on a signature line), Charleston, S.C., Printed by J. Hoff, No.6 Broad Street, 1801." The cover page of the second edition, published after her marriage, reads: "**Miscellaneous Poems** by Mrs. Eliza Murden, Second Edition, New York, published by the Author, Samuel Wood and Sons, Printers, 1827." However, the title page reads: "**Miscellaneous Poems** by a Lady of Charleston, S.C., Second edition." This second edition includes several poems written to Eliza by various friends and possibly pupils. One such poem, titled "Extempore," is headed "On sending a mutilated copy of Miss Crawley's, now Mrs. Murden's Poems, to the author." Like the **Poems,** the **March** included in the Bibliography is signed "by a young lady of Charleston." [I]

NEVIN, ARTHUR FINLEY (b. Edgeworth, PA, 27 April 1871; d. Sewickley, PA, 10 July 1943). Teacher, choral conductor, composer. A younger brother of the composer Ethelbert Nevin, he was educated at the Sewickley Academy and at Park University in Allegheny, PA. He studied music at the New England Conservatory, Boston, MA (1891-93), where his teachers included Percy Goetschius and Otto

Bendix, and in Berlin (1893-97), where he studied piano with Carl Klindworth and composition with Otis B. Boise. He taught and composed in Sewickley (1897-1910) except during the summers of 1903 and 1904, when he lived with the Blackfeet Indians in the northwestern corner of Montana (now part of Glacier National Park) and studied their history, legends and music. His research provided subject matter for lectures, an article ("Two Summers with the Blackfeet Indians of Montana," published in **The Musical Quarterly**, 1916, ii, p.257) and his opera **Poia**. By invitation of President Roosevelt he gave an illustrated lecture on **Poia** at the White House (April, 1907), and the opera was first performed at the Royal Opera of Berlin (April, 1910). He lived at Charlottesville, VA, concentrating his creative energy on composition (1911-14), and also conducted the MacDowell Chorus at Peterborough, NH during the 1914 and 1915 seasons. In 1915 he was appointed professor of music at the University of Kansas at Lawrence, where he taught classes in orchestration, ensemble, conducting and music appreciation; gave lectures throughout the state; and organized community choruses. In 1917 he had 20 choral groups prepared for a massed concert when the United States entered World War I. He took leave from the University, served as music director at Camp Grant, IL, then returned to Lawrence and taught until 1920. In 1920-22 he was director of municipal music and dramatic art at Memphis, TN, the first city in the United States, so he claimed, to create such a department. He was a music editor for The John Church Company (1923-25), and then lived for many years in New Canaan, CT, where he devoted his time to composing and teaching. Nevin wrote mostly collections of short, descriptive genre pieces for the piano. [I]

NEVIN, ETHELBERT [WOODBRIDGE] (b. Edgeworth, PA, 25 November 1862; d. New Haven, CT, 17 February 1901). Pianist, teacher, composer; brother of Arthur Finley Nevin. Having displayed musical talent from the age of five, he had early music lessons with local teachers in nearby Pittsburgh, and later his parents took him to Europe for a year of study and travel (1877-78). He visited art museums and attended concerts in Dresden, Leipzig, Berlin and Vienna, and while in Dresden also studied music with Franz Böhme. He spent a year at the University of Pittsburgh (1878-79), usually neglecting his academic studies in order to compose and play in the college orchestra, then to satisfy his father, who deplored the idea of his becoming a professional musician, he worked for several months in a printing shop. He lived at home for about a year, composing and studying on his own, and in the Fall of 1881 moved to Boston, MA, where he studied piano with Benjamin J. Lang and theory with Stephen Emery. In the Fall of 1883 he opened a teaching studio in Pittsburgh but within a year left for Europe for further training. He studied in Berlin with Carl Klindworth, Otto Tiersch and Carl Bial, and completed the three-year course at Klindworth's school in only two years (1884-86). He made his professional début as a pianist in Pittsburgh (December, 1886), then settled in Boston. While living there (1887-91), he composed, taught privately, was organist at Christ Church, Quincy (1888-89) and gave numerous piano recitals in the East and Midwest. After leaving Boston in May, 1891, he moved restlessly about, always maintaining a demanding schedule--composing, teaching and concertizing--that overburdened his already frail health and nerves. He went to Paris first; in April, 1892 he moved to Berlin; and returned to Boston in December, 1892. A year later he had a nervous breakdown but by March, 1894, having recuperated on a six-week trip through Algiers, France and England, he had begun another year of concerts. He lived in Florence (1895-96) and Paris (1896-97), then opened a studio in New York in September, 1897. By the end of the season he had to withdraw to his father's home at Edgeworth, where despite increasingly poor health, aggravated by alcoholism, he composed a great deal and occasionally gave recitals. In October, 1900 he moved to New Haven, CT, where he continued to compose almost until the time of his death. He is remembered largely because of the astonishing success of his most popular song **The Rosary** and most popular piano piece **Narcissus**. Many of his other piano works, equal in quality, deserve recognition. [I,III]

NEWMAN, MR (fl.early 1800s). Nothing is known about his life, and to date only his three sonatas have been discovered. These Hadynesque miniatures are quite charming. [I]

NICHOLL, HORACE WADHAM (b. Tipton, near Birmingham, England, 17 March 1848; d. New York, NY, 10 March 1922). Organist, composer. A descendant of the founder of Wadham College, Oxford, he studied music with his father and the organist Samuel Prince. He later became organist at Dudley, near Birmingham (ca.1867-69) and at Stoke-on-Trent (ca.1869-70). In 1870 he emigrated to the United States and settled in Pittsburgh, PA, where he taught at a women's college, gave many recitals and was organist at St. Paul's Cathedral and later at the Third Presbyterian Church. After 1878 he lived in New York. He was organist at St. Mark's Church (1879-80). From 1883 he was for many years a reader for Schirmer's and was also editor of the organ department of Freund's **Music Trades' Review**. From 1888 to 1895 he was an associate of Bernardus Boekelman at Miss Porter's and Mrs. Dow's School at Farmington, CT, where he taught harmony and ensemble playing. Nicholl's most convincing piano compositions are the preludes and fugues, an obvious result of his preoccupation with organ repertoire. [I]

OLDBERG, ARNE (b. Youngstown, OH, 12 July 1874; d. Evanston, IL, 17 February 1962). Teacher, pianist, composer. He began piano lessons with his father, an amateur musician, and after his family moved to Chicago, IL, took private lessons with August Hyllested (1886-90). He was graduated from the Gottschalk Lyric School, Chicago (1892), then studied the piano with Theodore Leschetizky in Vienna (1893-95). When he returned to Chicago, he taught privately and at the Chicago Conservatory, where he was an assistant to Leopold Godowsky, and also gave many piano recitals. Already beginning to compose, he studied composition with Wilhelm Middelschulte, Adolph Koelling and Frederick Grant Gleason. He taught piano at Northwestern University in Evanston for one year (1897-98), the next year studied composition with Joseph Rheinberger in Munich, and in 1899 was appointed professor of music at Northwestern. He was at Northwestern for 42 years--as professor of piano, later head of the piano department, then director of the Graduate School of the School of Music--and during that time did most of his composing while on summer vacation in Colorado. From 1930 he frequently taught summer sessions at the University of California and Mount St. Mary's College in Los Angeles. He retired from Northwestern in 1941 but continued to compose. He was a member of the National Institute of Arts and Letters (1915) and received an honorary A.M. from Northwestern (1916). Oldberg was an excellent composer whose stylish piano compositions, with their shimmering beauty, rhapsodic sweep and often improvisatory character, are most worthy of performance today. [I,V]

OREM, PRESTON WARE (b. Philadelphia, PA, 17 October 1865; d. Philadelphia, 26 May 1938). Organist, editor, composer. He spent most of his life in his native city, where he studied organ with Hugh A. Clarke and piano with Charles H. Jarvis, and earned a bachelor's degree in music at the University of Pennsylvania (1887). He taught piano and theory at the Philadelphia Conservatory (1887-89), then was appointed organist at St. Paul's Cathedral (Episcopal) in Los Angeles, CA (1889-95). Returning to Philadelphia, he taught again at the Philadelphia Conservatory (1895-96), later at the Combs Conservatory (1896-1905), and was also organist at the Walnut Street Presbyterian Church (1901-10). He was editor and critic for the Theodore Presser Co. for 31 years and simultaneously conductor of the Presser Choral Society (1900-31). After retiring from Presser, he was an editor for Clayton F. Summy Co. in Chicago, IL for about three years, then returned to Philadelphia. He was awarded a Mus.D. from Ohio Northern University in 1930. His **Harmony Book for Beginners** was widely used at one time. The impressive, flamboyant **American Indian Rhapsody** is the best of Orem's few piano compositions. [I]

ORTH, JOHN (b. Annweiler, Germany, 2 December 1850; d. Boston, MA, 3 May 1932). Pianist, teacher, composer. He was about a year old when his family moved to America and settled in Taunton, MA, where his father found employment as organist at St. Mary's Church. At the age of eight he began music lessons with his father, and by the time he was 12 was able to assist at St. Mary's by playing the organ for some of the services. Inspired by his father's stories about Liszt, he worked even as a boy to save money so that he might one day go to Germany and study with Liszt. He studied and worked in Boston (1866-70), earning money by giving lessons and playing the organ at various churches, then spent five years in Germany (1870-75). He studied in Berlin with Theodore Kullak, Friedrich Kiel, Philipp Scharwenka, Ludwig Deppe and Carl F. Weitzmann and in

Stuttgart with Dionys Pruckner, Siegmund Lebert and Immanuel Faiszt. Having been accepted as a Liszt pupil (July, 1883), he spent two years at Weimar in Liszt's inner circle, where his fellow students included Vincent d'Indy, Amy Fay, William H. Sherwood and Rafael Joseffy. He then returned to the United States, and for the rest of his life lived in Boston as a pianist and teacher, becoming especially known for his lecture-recitals entitled "With Liszt in Weimar, with personal reminiscences by his pupil John Orth." In his later years he often appeared on radio broadcasts. Orth was a thorough musician whose piano compositions make effective teaching pieces as well as recital works. [I]

O'SULLIVAN, PATRICK (b. Louisville, KY, 23 August 1871; d. Los Angeles, CA, 18 March 1947). Pianist, organist, teacher, composer. He was one of nine children, all musical because their father filled the house with instruments--flute, violin, cello, melodeon, piano, cabinet organ. After several years of music lessons with his brother Hugh, he studied with William Frese, a local teacher, and made his professional début as a pianist in Louisville in 1891. He taught privately and gave recitals in the area until 1898 when he went abroad to complete his musical education. He lived in Europe for ten years, studying in Paris with Harold Bauer and Camille Chevillard and in Berlin with Phillip Scharwenka and Wilhelm Berger. He played in concerts in various European cities, often including his own works on the program, and also composed and had some of his works published. When he returned to America (1908) he opened a teaching studio in Chicago, IL, and became director of the Chicago School of Opera and the Irish Choral Society. In 1912 he returned to his native Louisville, where he taught privately, served as organist at the Sacred Heart Church and later at the Temple Adath Israel and St. Mary Magdalene Church, and was a member of the original faculty of the Louisville Conservatory of Music (1915-21). From 1921 until he retired in 1942 he taught at the St. Agnes Conservatory of Music (later the Memphis Conservatory) in Memphis, Tennessee. O'Sullivan's piano works are conservative and he obviously admired Chopin. [I]

OTTERSTROM, THORWALD (b. Copenhagen, Denmark, 17 July 1868; d. Chicago, IL, 16 August 1942). Teacher, composer. He studied music in Copenhagen and with Sophie Menter at the St. Petersburg Conservatory in Russia. In 1892 he emigrated to the United States and settled permanently in Chicago, where he was for many years a professor of composition and theory at the Chicago Musical College. During his lifetime his piano works were often played by pianists such as Rudolph Ganz and Fanny Bloomfield Zeisler, and two of his orchestral works--**Elegy, Chorale and Fugue** and **American Negro Suite**--were performed (a total of seven times) by the Chicago Symphony Orchestra. Otterström's fine piano compositions are for the mature, advanced pianist. [I]

PAINE, JOHN KNOWLES (b. Portland, ME, 9 January 1839; d. Cambridge, MA, 25 April 1906). Teacher, organist, composer. His early music studies with Hermann Kotzschmar, a German musician living in Portland, prepared him well for further training in Berlin (1858-61), where he studied organ with Carl August Haupt and orchestration and composition with Wilhelm Friedrich Wieprecht. He was a serious student, and the three years of intensive study with German teachers and broad exposure to German musical culture exerted a strong influence on his entire career. He gave highly successful organ recitals in Berlin and London, and when he returned to the United States (June, 1861) gave equally successful recitals in his native Portland. In October he settled permanently in Boston, where he quickly attained a reputation as a leading recitalist, and in November was engaged as organist at the historic West Church (1861-64). When Levi Parsons Homer, musical instructor and organist at Harvard University, died on March 10, 1862, the college faculty voted to engage Paine as "teacher of Sacred Music" through July. He began teaching the classes in vocal music at once, and on March 25 assumed the additional duties of playing the organ daily at the Chapel, training the choir, and providing a substitute for Sunday services (he was still organist at West church and did not resign until April, 1864). He taught at Harvard for 43 years (1862-1905). Promoted to assistant professor in 1873 and professor in 1875, he was the first professor of music in any American university. Highly regarded by his fellow composers and much admired by the public, he had the rare satisfaction of having his music performed regularly during his lifetime, especially his large-scale works (by 1899 the Boston Symphony Orchestra had given more than 18 performances of his works). It is an indication of his standing as a composer that he was commissioned to write the commemorative work for each of the major expositions held in America during his lifetime: **Centennial Hymn** for the Centennial Exposition in Philadelphia, PA, 1876; **Columbus March and Hymn** for the World's Columbian Exposition in Chicago, IL, 1893; **Hymn of the West** for the Louisiana Purchase Centennial Exposition in St. Louis, MO, 1904. Paine's music is now seldom heard but he remains a historical figure in American musical history. He developed a music department at Harvard--for 33 years he was the only faculty member--that has served as a model for music departments in many other American colleges and universities. He was a pioneer in bringing music into the college curriculum and establishing it as an integral part of higher education, a subject on equal standing with the sciences, philosophy and literature. As the teacher of many pupils who later became distinguished composers--Foote, Converse, Carpenter and D. G. Mason, among others--he exerted an enormous influence on American music. After retiring from Harvard in May, 1905, he remained active and continued to compose. He was awarded an honorary A.M. at Harvard (1869) and a Mus.D. at Yale (1890). He was co-editor, with Carl Klauser and Theodore Thomas, of **Famous Composers and Their Works** (1891), and wrote **The History of Music to the Death of Schubert,** published posthumously in 1909. Paine was a romantic with a flair for tone color, and his piano music exploits this talent with rare expertise. [I,III]

PALMER, COURTLANDT (1872-1951). He is mentioned briefly in John Tasker Howard's **Our American Music**. Apparently born in New York City, he composed a considerable amount of orchestral and chamber music, including the **Concerto** for piano, a **Berceuse** for violin and piano, an **Elegie** for cello and many songs and piano pieces. The piano music, particularly the romantic three-movement sonata, is well structured but conservative. [I,V]

PALMER, WILLIAM HENRY [ROBERT HELLER] (b. Canterbury, England, ca. 1830; d. Philadelphia, PA, 28 November 1878). Magician, mime, pianist, composer. He studied music with his father, organist at the Canterbury Cathedral, and at the age of 14 earned a scholarship at the Royal Academy of Music, London. Watching the French magician (Jean Eugène Robert) Houdin perform on a London stage utterly fascinated him; and when he realized that practicing the piano had given him nimble fingers, he determined to become a professional magician. He studied music and magic and, having adopted the stage name "Robert Heller," made his début as a magician in London in 1851. The following year he emigrated to America, where he performed as a magician in Albany, NY, and made his début as a pianist, playing his own **Fantaisie de Piano**, at a farewell concert for Mlle. Camille Urso in New York City (November, 1852). He put on very successful magic shows in New York and Philadelphia for about a year, then for some reason retired as a magician and for several years earned his living as a pianist. During the 1853-54 season he played a series of ten subscription concerts with the Germania Musical Society in Boston, MA, performing his own compositions as well as works by Beethoven, Chopin, Thalberg and Mendelssohn, and in 1854 played with the Society in Philadelphia, Baltimore and Washington, DC. He then spent several years in Washington, DC, not as "Robert Heller" but as "William Henry Palmer, professor of music." He taught piano, played in concerts and may have been organist at one of the Washington churches. In 1861 he reverted to "Robert Heller, magician" and, after hiring a professional manager in 1864, became an extremely popular and successful magician-entertainer of worldwide fame. In April, 1864 he opened Heller's **Salle Diabolique** on Broadway, and for a year New Yorkers flocked to his performances. He made frequent tours in the United States, an extensive world tour (1869-73) and an extended tour of the British Isles (1873-76). He never gave up music, however, for on every program he appeared as solo pianist, usually playing his own compositions. Palmer excelled in writing flamboyant, old-fashioned--and utterly charming--salon pieces for the piano. [I]

PARKER, HORATIO WILLIAM (b. Auburndale, MA, 15 September 1863; d. Cedarhurst, Long Island, NY, 18 December 1919). Teacher, organist, conductor, composer. Not interested in music as a boy, he was 14 when he began piano and organ lessons with his mother, a gifted musician and literate who later assisted him with the texts for some of his important choral works. He progressed rapidly and at

the age of 16 became organist at St. Paul's Episcopal Church in Dedham, where he immediately began to compose hymn tunes, anthems and services for the choir (1880-82). At the same time he studied piano with John Orth, composition with George Chadwick and theory with Stephen Emery in Boston, then spent three years at the Munich Conservatory (1882-85) under the guidance of Joseph Rheinberger, who grounded him thoroughly in contrapuntal choral writing and organ technique. Several works composed during his stay in Munich were performed at Conservatory concerts, and at graduation his cantata **King Trojan** was performed under his direction. Immediately after graduation he returned to Boston, where he opened a studio with Arthur Whiting, but soon moved to New York, having been engaged to teach music at St. Paul's (boys) and St. Mary's (girls) cathedral schools at Garden City, Long Island (1886-90). He later taught at the General Theological Seminary (1892) and the National Conservatory (1892-93). A lifelong organist, he found organ positions at St. Luke's Church of Brooklyn (1885-87), St. Andrew's in Harlem (1887-88) and the Church of the Holy Trinity in Manhattan (1888-93). He also composed steadily while in New York (1886-93), mostly sacred music, some secular choral works and keyboard pieces. The cantata **Dream-King and his Love** won the National Conservatory prize in 1893; and the oratorio **Hora novissima** (his mother translated the Bernard de Morlaix hymn), performed by the Church Choral Society of New York (1893), ultimately achieved wide fame in both the United States and England. In 1893 he returned to Boston to become organist and choirmaster at historic Trinity Church. A year later Yale University awarded him an honorary A.M. and offered him the Battell Professorship of Music. He accepted the position and remained at Yale until his death; however, he continued as organist at Trinity Church until 1901, each week commuting between New Haven and Boston. From 1904 he was dean of the School of Music, and under his leadership Yale acquired a national reputation for training composers. He taught instrumentation, counterpoint and composition; lectured on the history of music; and conducted the New Haven Symphony Orchestra (1895-1918) and New Haven Oratorio Society (1903-14). Outside of New Haven he was organist of the collegiate church of St. Nicholas (Dutch Reformed) in New York (1902-10) and conductor of the Eurydice and Orpheus choral clubs in Philadelphia and the Derby Choral Club in Derby, CT. He composed steadily throughout his busy life and achieved a remarkable success in England as well as the United States, especially with his sacred choral works. He was awarded an honorary Mus.D. at Cambridge University in 1902; was elected to the American Academy of Arts and Letters in 1905, and after his death the Academy established a scholarship in his name in Rome, to benefit American students. He wrote **Music and Public Entertainment** (1911) and the **Progressive Music Series,** a basic course in music instruction for all grades through the first year of high school. Parker's romantic character pieces for piano are excellent. He often achieves a deep poetic feeling through harmonic richness, deft chromaticisms and skillful modulations.
[I]

PARKER, JAMES CUTLER DUNN (b. Boston, MA, 2 June 1828, d. Brookline, MA, 27 November 1916). Organist, teacher, composer. He had an interesting musical background. His father Samuel Hale Parker was a prominent Boston music publisher and dealer (in 1823 Samuel Parker hired 12-year-old Oliver Ditson as an apprentice; in 1836 they formed Parker and Ditson; in 1842 Ditson acquired Parker's interest) and was also one of the founders of the Boston Handel and Haydn Society. James C. D. Parker apparently knew and enjoyed music, but after graduating from the Boston Latin School and Harvard (1848) he studied law for three years before choosing music as a profession. In 1851 he went to Germany for advanced musical study, being one of the first of generations of Americans to do so, and spent three years at the Leipzig Conservatory, where his teachers included Ignaz Moscheles, Louis Plaidy, Moritz Hauptmann, Ernst F. Richter and Julius Rietz. When he returned to Boston in September, 1854, he gave music lessons and became the pianist for the Mendelssohn Quintet. He was an influential presence in Boston's musical community for more than 50 years: organist at Trinity Church for 27 years (1864-91), including the full term of Philipps Brooks's rectorate; organist of the Handel and Haydn Society for many years; director of the Parker Club, an amateur singing society (1862-72); member of the Harvard Musical Association; and for 41 years teacher and examiner at the New England Conservatory, teacher from 1871 to 1897 and examiner from 1897 to 1912, the year he retired from most of his musical activities. He earned an A.M. at Harvard (1856) and was granted an honorary Mus.D. from Alfred University, Alfred, NY (1887). He published a **Manual of Harmony** (1855) and the **Theoretical and Practical Harmony** (1870), and translated several works including Plaidy's **Technical Studies for the Pianoforte** (1855) and Richter's **Manual of Harmony** (1873). So far as is known Parker published only one serious piano composition—the early **Polonaise brillante** (1857)—but it is an elegant and meritorious example of this stylized dance. [I]

PARSONS, ALBERT ROSS (b. Sandusky, OH, 16 September 1847; d. Mt. Kisco, NY, 14 June 1933). Pianist, teacher, writer, composer. He had piano lessons with Robert Denton in Buffalo, NY, and gave his first public performance there when he was about nine. After his family moved to Indianapolis, IN, he left school to become the fulltime organist at a local church (1860-63). He studied for three years with Frédéric Louis Ritter in New York City (1863-66), then entered the Leipzig Conservatory (1867-69), where he was a pupil of Ignaz Moscheles, Carl Reinecke, Benjamin Papperitz, Ernst F. Wenzel and Ernst F. Richter. While in Berlin serving as secretary to George Bancroft, American minister to Germany, he continued his musical education with Carl Tausig, Theodore Kullak and Carl F. Weitzmann (1870-72). He then returned to the United States (1872) and spent the rest of his long life as a piano teacher in New York. He was organist at Holy Trinity Church (1872-76) and at the Fifth Avenue Presbyterian Church (1876-85), but thereafter devoted his time to teaching, writing, lecturing and composing. In 1886 he joined the piano faculty of the newly organized Metropolitan Conservatory of Music (from 1891 Metropolitan College of Music; from 1900 American Institute of Applied Music), and he taught there until about five years before his death. Although he had no formal schooling beyond the age of 12, he learned several languages and was exceptionally well read, with wide-ranging interests (philosophy, genealogy, astronomy) beyond music. He was an ardent supporter of Richard Wagner, and in 1872 published an English translation of Wagner's **Beethoven.** He also translated Lessmann's **Franz Liszt** and edited, in English, Kullak's edition of Chopin and the Holländer edition of Schumann. He published several books, including **The Science of Pianoforte Practice** (1886), **Parsifal, or the Finding of Christ through Art** (1893) and **The Virtuoso Handling of the Pianoforte** (1917). He lectured on Dante and the Shakespeare-Bacon controversy as well as on music, music education and music reforms, and he lived long enough to be acknowledged as the dean of New York piano teachers. Most of Parsons's keyboard repertoire consists of transcriptions and paraphrases. [I]

PARSONS, EDWARD A. (b. Hartford, CT, 2 November 1849; d. New Haven, CT, January 1929). Teacher, organist, composer. He studied music in New York City with William Mason, Sebastian Bach Mills and Theodore Thomas, then for more than 50 years taught piano, organ and theory in New Haven, and at times also in Middletown, CT and New York. He was organist at St. Paul's Church and Dwight Place Church in New Haven and at the Church of the Divine Paternity in New York. He wrote very few piano compositions, and most are salon paraphrases, often styled as caprices or fantasies. [I]

PATTISON, JOHN NELSON (b. Niagara Falls, NY, 22 October 1840; d. New York, NY, 27 July 1905). Pianist, teacher, composer. While attending school at Lockport, NY, he studied music surreptitiously because his family refused to support his musical ambitions. He began medical studies in Buffalo, NY, at his father's insistence, but left when he was about 15 to join a concert troupe on a tour of Canada. At the conclusion of the tour he settled in New York, where he earned his living by appearing in concerts, and on one occasion introduced himself to Sigismond Thalberg, then touring in the United States. Thalberg encouraged him to continue with music, advised him to go abroad for additional training, and gave him free admission to all the Thalberg concerts in the United States. Needing money for study abroad, he purchased a life insurance policy and used it as collateral for a loan from a friend, then spent about two years in Berlin studying with Moritz Hauptmann, Carl Reinecke and Hans von Bülow. He made concert appearances in Berlin and Paris and toured Italy with Thalberg, gaining a reputation as a fine pianist. In 1862 he settled in New York as a concert performer and teacher, and from about 1870 toured the United States with artists like Parepa-Rosa, Emma Albani, Louise Kellogg, Pauline Lucca and Ole Bull. Between May 10 and November 11, 1876 he played 183 recitals at the Philadelphia Centennial

Exhibition. Pattison's piano music is elegant, romantic and eminently idiomatic. [I]

PAUL, JEAN [see **CHARLES KUNKEL**]

PEASE, ALFRED HUMPHREYS (b. Cleveland, OH, 6 May 1838; d. St. Louis, MO, 12 July 1882). Pianist, composer. His talent in both music and art showed at an early age but his parents, fearing that he might become a professional musician, insisted on a strict classical training that prepared him to enter Kenyon College, Gambier, OH at the age of 16. At college (1855-57) his painting and drawing so impressed a young German artist that he persuaded the parents to send the boy to Germany. When he first arrived in Berlin, he studied only German and other languages, then inevitably began piano lessons with Theodore Kullak and eventually received parental approval to study music. He studied piano with Kullak, composition with Richard Wüerst and orchestration with Wilhelm F. Wieprecht for three years, made a quick visit home in 1860 and then spent another three years in Berlin studying with Hans von Bülow. Following his début as a pianist in New York (February 8, 1864), he made a career as a concert performer, touring the United States and Canada as both soloist and assisting artist and gaining recognition for his brilliant technique. He played his **Concerto in E Flat** (perhaps still in manuscript) in a concert of all-American music conducted by Theodore Thomas at the Centennial Exposition in Philadelphia (July 19, 1876). During the last 12 years of his life he lived in New York City. His early death was attributed to alcoholism; on a visit to St. Louis he wandered away, was missing for several weeks and finally found dead outside a St. Louis hotel. Pease's known piano music consists mainly of flamboyant fantasies, concert paraphrases and transcriptions. [I]

PENFIELD, SMITH NEWELL (b. Oberlin, OH, 4 April 1837; d. New York, NY, 7 January 1920). Organist, teacher, composer. He entered the preparatory department at Oberlin College in 1849, became a freshman in 1854, was graduated in 1858 and received his A.M. in 1861. In the meantime he also studied music with James Flint in New York City. After teaching music in Sandusky, OH for one year (1858-59) and in Rochester, NY for eight years (1859-67), he enrolled at the Leipzig Conservatory, where he was a pupil of Ignaz Moscheles, Carl Reinecke, Louis Plaidy, Benjamin Papperitz, Ernst F. Richter and Moritz Hauptmann. He was graduated in 1869, then studied with Charles Delioux in Paris. Upon returning to America, he taught in Savannah, GA (1870-75), then for more than 40 years lived in Brooklyn or New York City, achieving a reputation as a distinguished teacher, church organist and concert organist. He was for many years organist at the Broadway Tabernacle, where he frequently gave recitals, and for a number of years director of music at New York University, where he received an honorary Mus.D (1885). He also founded the Arion Conservatory in Brooklyn and conducted several choral societies. Judging from his extant piano compositions, Penfield enjoyed the unorthodox piece (a canon disguised as a gavotte) and provocative titles (mystical names for sonata movements). [I]

PERABO [JOHANN] ERNST (b. Wiesbaden, Germany, 14 November 1845; d. West Roxbury, MA, 29 October 1920). Pianist, teacher, composer. The youngest and most talented in a large musical family, he began piano lessons at the age of five with his father, a school teacher and musician, and at the age of 12 could play Bach's **Well-Tempered Clavier** from memory. In 1852 the family emigrated to the United States, settling wherever his father found employment. The first two years they lived in New York City, where he had violin and piano lessons and performed at Professor Heinrich's grand valedictory concert on April 21, 1853, an appearance described as "the first appearance of a talented little pianist, Master Perabeau (sic), only seven years of age." The family spent two years in Dover, NH; a year in Boston, where he had violin lessons with Wilhelm Schultze of the Mendelssohn Quintet; and then settled in Chicago, IL. At about this time his mother took him to Washington, DC, where they had an interview with President Buchanan and requested financial support for the boy's education. President Buchanan declined but William Scharfenberg, a prominent New York musician, found patrons (Henry C. Timm, Robert Goldbeck, Jan Pychowski and others) willing to sponsor him. From September, 1858 to November, 1865 he lived in Germany, first at Eimsbüttel, near Hamburg, where he had general studies with a Professor Andersen, then from October, 1862 at Leipzig, where his teachers included Ignaz Moscheles, Ernst F. Wenzel, Benjamin Papperitz, Moritz Hauptmann, Ernst F. Richter and Carl Reinecke. When he returned to America in 1865 he gave several concerts in Sandusky, OH, where his parents were then living, and in other midwestern cities, then for a few months taught and performed in New York, notably a series of concerts in which he played all the Schubert piano sonatas. He finally settled in Boston, making his first appearance there at a Harvard Musical Association concert on April 19, 1866, the first of many annual concerts with that organization. Active in Boston for more than 50 years, he was greatly respected as teacher, pianist and composer. Perabo made many piano transcriptions and composed a few effective, often difficult concert pieces. [I]

PERRY, EDWARD BAXTER (b. Haverhill, MA, 14 February 1855; d. Camden ME, 13 June 1924). Pianist, lecture-recitalist, writer, composer. He was educated at public schools in Medford and in 1871 entered the Perkins Institute for the Blind (an early childhood accident caused his blindness) at South Boston, MA, where he specialized in English literature, and at the same time studied piano with Junius W. Hill of Boston (1871-75). He continued his education in Berlin (1875-78), studying music with Theodore Kullak and Carl August Haupt and taking academic courses (German, history, literature, philosophy) at the University of Berlin. He spent the last summer with Liszt at Weimar (1878). Upon returning to Boston, he appeared as a pianist and taught privately, then in 1881 joined the piano faculty at Oberlin College, Oberlin, OH, but left in 1883 in order to pursue further studies abroad. Going first to Stuttgart (1883-84), he worked with Dionys Pruckner and Max Seifriz and also took general courses at the Polytechnic Institute, then studied with Clara Schumann at Frankfort (1884-85). Returning again to Boston, he taught at the Tremont School of Music (1886-89) and began to make lecture-recital tours, gradually increasing the number of tours and extending them throughout the United States and Canada. Between 1886 and 1917 he gave more than 3000 lecture-recitals covering almost all of the piano literature then available, and he may have been the first American musician to make a special career as a lecture-recitalist. Despite his staggering recital schedule, he wrote numerous articles for musical journals--more than 300 for **Etude**--and in later years accepted short-term teaching positions at the National Conservatory, Dallas, TX (1905); Woman's College of Alabama (now Huntingdon College) in Montgomery (1918-21); Hood College, Frederick, MD (1921-22); and Lebanon Valley College in Annville, PA (1922-24). While in Paris during a successful tour of Europe (1897-98), he was made a Chevalier de Mélusine by Prince Guy de Lusignan, grand master of the Order of Mélusine (the name comes from a medieval legend about Mélusine, guardian fairy of the Lusignan family) in recognition of the artistic merits of his suite **Mélusine.** He wrote **Descriptive Analyses of Piano Works** (1902) and **Stories of Standard Teaching Pieces** (1910). An inspired romantic, Perry wrote some splendid character pieces for the piano. [I]

PIRANI, EUGENIO (b. Bologna, Italy, 8 September 1852; d. Berlin, Germany, 12 January 1939). Pianist, teacher, composer. He was a pupil of Stefano Golinelli at the Bologna Liceo Musicale (graduated 1869), and later studied piano with Theodore Kullak and composition with Friedrich Kiel in Berlin. He taught at the Kullak Academy in Berlin (1873-83), meanwhile making extensive tours as a pianist in Italy, Germany, France, Russia and England. In his native Italy he was elected to several Academies and received many decorations, and in 1888 he was head of the German committee for the International Music Exhibition at Bologna. In 1895 he moved to Berlin, where he was critic for the **Kleines Journal** (1898-1901). During 1901-06 he toured in Europe and America with the soprano Alma Webster Powell, a former pupil with whom he founded the Powell and Pirani Musical Institute in Brooklyn, NY (1904). He was still actively directing the Institute in the 1920s and maintained a Brooklyn address as late as 1931. He wrote **High School of Piano Playing** (1908) and **Secrets of the Success of Great Musicians** (1922). Pirani was an excellent craftsman. His descriptive piano études are particularly useful for the development of technique. [I,IV,V]

PLATT, RICHARD BARNES (b. St. Louis, MO, 9 January 1877; d. ?). Pianist, teacher, composer. He had early music lessons with Nellie

Strong Stevenson, a well-known St. Louis teacher, and later studied
with Carl Heinrich Barth and Heinrich Urban in Berlin. In 1905 he
settled in Boston, MA, and from that year through 1945 he is listed
in the city directories as a music teacher. In 1922 he remodeled
the old Toy Theater on Lime Street into a residence, teaching
studio and music and drama salon where he and other Boston artists
gave informal musicales. Platt's few piano pieces show his obvious
admiration for the French impressionist school. [I,IV]

PRATT, SILAS GAMALIEL (b. Addison, VT, 4 August 1846; d.
Pittsburgh, PA, 30 October 1916). Pianist, teacher, composer.
Raised in Chicago IL, he was mostly self-educated since he had to
leave school at the age of 12 and find employment. He worked first
at Higgins Music Store, then at Root and Cady and finally became a
clerk with Lyon and Healy. When he could afford music lessons he
studied with Paul Becker and Louis Staab in Chicago, and later with
Franz Bendel, Theodore Kullak, Richard Wüerst and Friedrich Kiel in
Berlin (1868-71). He hoped to be a concert pianist but abandoned
the idea after injuring his wrist, possibly from overzealous
practicing. Upon returning to Chicago (1871), he was rehired by
Lyon and Healy and engaged as organist at the Church of the
Messiah. He also composed and gave private lessons, and in
September, 1872 joined George P. Upton in organizing the Apollo
Club. During a second visit to Germany (1875-77) he studied with
Heinrich Dorn in Berlin and with Liszt at Weimar, and in 1876
conducted his **Centennial Overture** with great success in both Berlin
and London. He returned once more to Chicago (1877-88), where he
was especially successful as an opera composer. His second opera
Zenobia, Queen of Palmyra was presented in concert form at Central
Music Hall (June, 1882) and produced at McVicker's Theater (March,
1883); his first opera **Lucille** (formerly titled **Antonio**) was
produced at the Columbia Theater (March, 1887). In 1888 he moved to
New York City. From 1888 until 1902 he taught at the Metropolitan
Conservatory (from 1891 Metropolitan College of Music; from 1900
American Institute of Applied Music), and from 1895 was also
director of the West End School of Music. In 1906 he founded the
Pratt Institute of Music and Art in Pittsburgh, and was its
president until the time of his death. Pratt's piano music, some
of it quite attractive, is mostly salon music. [I]

PREYER, CARL ADOLPH (b. Pforzheim, Germany, 28 July 1863; d.
Kansas City, MO, 10 November 1947). Teacher, pianist, composer. He
had early music lessons with a Professor Schmidt at Pforzheim and
later attended the Stuttgart Conservatory. In 1881 he emigrated to
the United States, where he lived with an uncle in Newark, NJ and
began his teaching career. He taught for a brief time in New York
City and then headed west, making stops at Belleville, IL, St.
Louis, MO and Jefferson City, MO, where he tried unsuccessfully to
establish the Jefferson City Conservatory. By 1886 he had settled
at Leavenworth, KS with his father, who had emigrated to America
some years earlier. He became organist at the First Methodist

Church, opened a teaching studio and also taught at Park College in Parkville, MO, traveling there on horseback over the Missouri River. From 1888 to 1890 he was head of the piano department at Baker University, Baldwin, KS, then took a year's leave to study piano with Theodore Leschetizky (only a few lessons because Leschetizky was ill) and composition with Karel Navrátil in Vienna. When he returned to the United States (1891) he was appointed head of the piano department at the University of Kansas at Lawrence, an affiliation that lasted for more than 50 years. On a semester leave in 1895 he studied piano with Carl Heinrich Barth and composition with Heinrich Urban in Berlin. Although he lived mostly at Lawrence he often commuted to Kansas City, MO to teach large classes of students. From 1915 until his retirement in 1939 he was associate dean of the School of Fine Arts. He continued to teach privately and advise advanced students right up to the time of his death.   Preyer's piano compositions, whether short rhythmical studies, lyrical sketches, or serious variation sets and sonatas, are remarkable in their attention to detail and use of basic musical materials. [I,IV,V]

RALSTON, FRANCES [FANNY] MARION (b. St. Louis, MO, 8 January 1875; d. Los Angeles, CA, 5 February 1952). Teacher, pianist, composer. Until she was 17 she studied in St. Louis with her mother Lucy B. Ralston, a well-known teacher, and with Ernest R. Kroeger. She then spent a year at the New England Conservatory in Boston, MA, where she was a pupil of Benjamin Cutter, Arthur Foote, Louis Elson, Percy Goetschius and Carl Faelten. A teacher of piano, theory and composition all her life, she taught private classes in St. Louis for about ten years (1895-1900, 1902-06), and for about 14 years taught at various colleges: Sullins College, Bristol, VA (1901-02); Central College, Lexington, MO (1906-08); Rockford College, Rockford, IL (1908-18); and Wellesley College, Wellesley, MA (1918-19). She resigned from Wellesley and settled permanently in Pasadena, CA, where she composed, taught privately and occasionally gave recitals.   She wrote **Reflections of a Musician** (1920) and **Melodic Design: Practical Applications of Intervals to Melody Writing** (1930). Ralston's music suggests a pervasive seriousness. Both her large-scale and short piano compositions show her adept handling of melodic and harmonic elements. [I,V]

REINAGLE, ALEXANDER (b. Portsmouth, England, baptized 23 April 1756; d. Baltimore, MD, 21 September 1809). Pianist, conductor, teacher, composer. He studied with his father Joseph Reinagle, an Austrian musician removed to England, and after the family moved to Edinburgh, Scotland (ca.1763), where his father had been appointed trumpeter to the king, he studied with Rayner Taylor, then employed as a singer at the New Theater Royal. On April 9, 1770 he made his first known public appearance at that theater, playing a harpsichord sonata, and by the early 1780s he was teaching the harpsichord and composing keyboard works: two sets of "short and easy" instructional pieces written around 1780-81; a collection of

the most favorite Scots tunes with variations for the harpsichord
(ca.1782); and six sonatas for piano or harpsichord with violin
accompaniment (1783). On a visit to Hamburg, Germany sometime
around 1784 he met C. P. E. Bach, and the two composers
subsequently carried on a brief correspondence. In October, 1784
he accompanied his brother Hugh, a victim of tuberculosis, to
Lisbon, Portugal, where he appeared in a public concert on January
8, 1785 and the following week performed for the royal family.
After Hugh's death in March, he returned to England (May 17, 1785)
but stayed only a year before emigrating to America. He arrived in
New York in the late Spring of 1786, and on June 9 advertised
himself as a member of the Society of Royal Musicians in London now
prepared to give lessons on the piano, harpsichord and violin and
to supply the public with instruments and printed music "on the
same terms sold in the shops, only allowing for freight and
package." On July 20 he gave a "grand concert" in New York,
performing as singer, violinist and pianist, most likely playing
one of his own sonatas. By September he had moved to Philadelphia,
where he immediately assumed an important role in every type of
concert, either as musician (singer, pianist, violinist, composer)
or organizer, and often as both. For example, as early as
September 21 he participated in a benefit concert for the cellist
Henri Capron; on October 12 he "took" a benefit for himself; and he
appeared regularly in benefit concerts during 1787. When he took
another benefit for himself on June 12, 1787, George Washington was
in the audience, perhaps because Washington's adopted daughter
Nellie Custis may have been Reinagle's pupil. Besides appearing as
a performer, he joined Capron, William Brown and Alexander Juhan in
reviving the Philadelphia City Concerts. They presented 12 during
the 1786-87 season; he and Brown organized nine during the 1787-88
season; then the concerts were discontinued until he, Capron and
John Christopher Moller made a second attempt to revive the series,
presenting eight programs between December 1, 1792 and March 31,
1793. Meanwhile he had extended his activities to New York, where
he is known to have organized three Subscription Concerts in
September-October, 1788, appeared in a benefit for Capron on
October 23, 1788, and with Capron organized another three concerts
in 1789. Having quickly established a distinguished reputation, he
was in great demand as a teacher, especially for Philadelphia's
prominent families. Although he continued to perform in concerts,
from about 1793 until his death he was mostly involved with
theatrical productions, having formed a partnership with the
English actor Thomas Wignell (d. 1803) and Wignell's successors.
The New Company (so-called to distinguish it from the Old American
Company) built theaters in both Philadelphia and Baltimore. The
Philadelphia season ran from December to July, the Baltimore season
the following September through November, and the repertory was
divided equally between musical dramas (usually English ballad
operas) and spoken dramas. During his 15 years with the New
Company, Reinagle was in charge of the music for hundreds of
productions. He directed the orchestra, often from the piano or
harpsichord, and provided whatever music was required, either
arranging an existing score to suit a drama or composing original

music: songs, overtures, incidental music, choruses and at times
complete scores. Most of this music was lost when the Philadelphia
New Theater burned on April 2, 1820. From 1803 he made his home in
Baltimore. His unquestionable talent, discriminating tastes and
high standards won him the respect and admiration of his
contemporaries; those same qualities have earned him a place in
history as one of early America's most influential musicians.
Reinagle's keyboard compositions, pre-Classic in style, are
musicianly and idiomatic. His Philadelphia sonatas are the finest
American piano compositions of this early period. [I]

RITTER, FREDERIC LOUIS (b. Strasbourg, Alsace, 22 June 1834; d.
Antwerp, Belgium, 6 July 1891). Conductor, teacher, music
historian, composer. He studied with Hans Schletterer and Franz
Hauser in Strasbourg, and at the age of 16 went to Paris to study
with his cousin Jean Georges Kastner. From 1852 to 1856 he taught
music at the Protestant seminary at Fénétrange, Lorraine, then
emigrated to the United States. Settling first in Cincinnati, OH
(1856-61), he organized the Cecilia Society and the Philharmonic
Society, and as director of these organizations introduced many
important classical works to Cincinnati. In 1861 he moved to New
York City, where he became conductor of the Harmonic Society and
the Arion Society, and in 1867 organized the city's first music
festival. That same year he was appointed professor of music at
Vassar College in Poughkeepsie, NY, where he taught until his
death, and from 1878 was also director of the School of Music. He
was awarded an honorary Mus.D from the University of the City of
New York in 1878. A prominent writer, his works include the **History
of Music** (2 vols., 1870-74), **Music in England** (1883), **Music in
America** (1883), **Music in Its Relation to Intellectual Life** (1891),
and **Musical Dictation, a Practical Method for Instruction of Choral
Classes** (1891). Ritter composed serious, impressive, multitextured
piano works. [I]

RIVE-KING, JULIE (b. Cincinnati, OH, 30 October 1854; d.
Indianapolis, IN, 24 July 1937). Pianist, teacher, composer. She
was the daughter of Caroline Rivé, a well-known music teacher who
trained her until she was about nine and then took her to New York
(1866-72) to study with William Mason and Sebastian Bach Mills.
From 1872 to 1875 she was in Europe studying with Carl Reinecke in
Leipzig, Wilhelm Rischbieter in Dresden and briefly with Liszt at
Weimar. At the age of 17 she played Beethoven's **C Minor Concerto**
and a Liszt Rhapsody at a Leipzig concert conducted by Reinecke.
After returning to the United States, she appeared with the New
York Philharmonic Society on April 24, 1875, playing Liszt's
Concerto in E Flat and Schumann's **Faschungsschwank aus Wien.** Over
the next 18 years she made a remarkable record as a concert
pianist, touring the United States and Canada and playing more than
4000 recitals and concerts, 500 of them with orchestra. Her large
and brilliant repertoire (including works by Beethoven, Liszt,
Chopin, Mendelssohn, Schumann, Schubert, Weber) and her masterly

technique elevated the standards for repertoire and performance in
the concert world.   Around 1876 she married Frank H. King, her
manager for many years, and after his death in 1900 she moved to
Chicago, IL, and began a teaching career in addition to her concert
career.   In 1905 she joined the faculty of the Bush Conservatory,
later taught at the Chicago Musical College and continued to teach
until a few months before her death.   Although she wrote both
serious works and salon pieces, Mme. Rivé-King is best known for
her scintillating and difficult salon keyboard compositions.   [I]

ROBJOHN, WILLIAM JAMES [CARYL FLORIO] (b. Tavistock, Devon,
England, 2 November 1843; d. Morganton, NC, 21 November 1920).
Organist, conductor, actor, teacher, composer.   Although he had
only a few lessons as a child and was largely self-taught in music,
he developed into an extremely versatile musician, not as William
Robjohn but as Caryl Florio, a pseudonym adopted in 1870 because
his parents objected to his profession.   Around 1858 his family
emigrated to the United States and settled in New York City, where
he became the first boy soloist at Trinity Church.   In 1862 he
turned actor and made a tour of the northern states, an engagement
that led to other similar jobs.   During 1865-66 he was secretary to
George Root in Chicago, IL, then was appointed director of music at
the Baptist Female Institute in Indianapolis, IN. He returned to
New York in 1868, and for about 22 years managed a diverse career
as conductor, organist, pianist, teacher and critic.   He was
organist at the Zion Church in New York, Trinity Church in Newport,
RI and Calvary Church in Baltimore, MD. He conducted the Amicitia
Orchestra and the Palestrina Choir and was accompanist for the
Vocal Society, all in New York, and sometimes conducted opera
orchestras in New York, Philadelphia, and Havana. In 1890-92 he was
director of music at Wells College in Aurora, NY, then returned to
the City for another four years.   From March, 1896 until October
1901 he was director of music at "Biltmore," the George Vanderbilt
estate near Asheville, NC, and also organist-choirmaster at All
Souls' Church.   He spent a final two years in New York before
returning permanently to Asheville, where he resumed his post as
organist-choirmaster at All Souls' Church, conducted the Choral
Society, the Orpheus Society and the St. Cecilia Society and also
taught privately.   Robjohn's best, most characteristic piano works
are his sparkling, elegant salon pieces.   [I]

ROBYN, ALFRED GEORGE (b. St. Louis, MO, 29 April 1860; d. New
York, NY, 18 October 1935).   Organist, conductor, pianist,
composer.   He studied music with his father William Robyn, and when
he was 11 succeeded his father as organist of St. John's Church. At
the age of 17 he toured the country as solo pianist with the Emma
Abbott Concert Company, then for several years gave piano recitals
throughout the United States. In 1884 he opened a piano studio in
St. Louis, and devoted himself to teaching.   He was the pianist for
the Beethoven Trio Club (1891-93), conductor of the Apollo Club
(1894-1902) and organist at the Grand Avenue Presbyterian Church,

the Temple Israel and the Episcopal Church of the Holy Communion. While visiting Europe in 1891, he performed in a large number of concerts. In 1910 he moved to New York, having been appointed to succeed Clarence Eddy as organist at the Tompkins Place Congregational Church in Brooklyn, but two years later resigned to become organist at St. Andrew's Methodist Church. Remaining in New York until his death, he gained public attention as chief organist at the Rialto and Capitol theaters. In 1909 St. Louis University awarded him an honorary Mus.D. Robyn's choicest piano works are those which emphasize lyricism and compact design. [I,II]

ROGERS, CLARA KATHLEEN [née **BARNETT**, stage name **CLARA DORIA**] (b. Cheltenham, England, 14 January 1844; d. Boston, MA, 8 March 1931). Singer, teacher, composer. With well-known musicians on both sides of her family--her father John Barnett was a composer, her maternal grandfather Robert Lindley a cellist--it was a foregone gone conclusion that she and her sister Rosamond would have musical careers. Her parents trained her until she was 12, then decided that for the sake of the girls' careers the mother should take them to live in Leipzig while the father continued to teach in Cheltenham, visiting the family whenever possible. Despite her youth, she was accepted as a pupil at the Leipzig Conservatory (1857-60), where she studied piano with Ignaz Moscheles and Louis Plaidy, theory with Ernst F. Richter and Benjamin Papperitz and singing with Franz Götze. She then studied piano with Hans von Bülow in Berlin for about six months and voice training with Antonio Sangiovanni in Milan, Italy for about a year and a half. Taking the stage name "Clara Doria," she made her début at Turin, Italy in 1863, singing the role of Isabella in **Robert le Diable**. Other roles followed, and she remained in Italy until 1867, when she returned to England and began concertizing. In 1871 she went to the United States with the Parepa-Rosa Opera Co., and made her American début at the New York Academy of Music in **The Bohemian Girl**. The following season (1872-73) she sang with Max Maretzek's company, and during 1874-75 she made an eight-month tour through New England, New York, the Midwest and Canada with Camilla Urso. From about 1873 she made her home in Boston, where she sang in the Trinity Church choir and began to teach voice and to give serious attention to composition. She also appeared in recitals and concerts, but gradually gave up concertizing in favor of teaching. In 1878 she married Henry M. Rogers, a Boston lawyer. Her books include **The Philosophy of Singing** (1893), **My Voice and I** (1910), **Memories of a Musical Career** (1919) and **The Story of Two Lives** (1932). Rogers's few piano pieces show a keen sensitivity to melodic contour and rhythmic drive. [I]

ROGERS, JAMES HOTCHKISS (b. Fair Haven, CT, 7 February 1857; d. Pasadena, CA, 28 November 1940). Organist, teacher, critic, composer. After his family moved to Chicago, IL (1869), he studied music with Clarence Eddy, and on Eddy's advice continued his training in Europe. He studied in Berlin (1875-78) with Albert

Loeschhorn, Eduard Rohde, Alfred Ehrlich and Carl August Haupt and
in Paris (1878-80) with Alexandre Guilmant, Charles M. Widor and
Alexis Fissot. Upon returning to the United States, he was for a
brief time organist in Burlington, IA, then from 1881 made his
career in Cleveland, OH as organist, teacher, composer and critic.
He was organist and music director for the Anshe Chesed
Congregation (later known as the Euclid Avenue Temple, then the
Fairmont Temple) for 50 years (1881-1931), meanwhile also serving
as organist at the Euclid Avenue Baptist Church for 20 years and at
the First Unitarian Church for 25 years. He taught organ and
composition privately, was conductor of the Rubinstein Club and for
17 years was music editor for the Cleveland **Plain Dealer** (1915-32).
Eight years before his death he retired to Pasadena, CA. In a **Plain
Dealer** article (January 27, 1957) written on the 100th anniversary
of his birth, he is described as "the grand old man of Cleveland
music." A practical composer, Rogers wrote many light piano pieces
which, with their sparkling melodies and artful technical planning,
can still be used for teaching purposes. [I]

RUBNER, CORNELIUS [see **PETER MARTIN CORNELIUS RYBNER**]

RUGGLES, CARL [CHARLES SPRAGUE] (b. East Marion, MA, 11 March 1876;
d. Bennington, VT, 24 October 1971): Teacher, composer. After
fashioning a toy violin from a cigar box when he was about six, he
was given violin lessons with George Hill, a New Bedford
bandmaster. During his late teens he worked in theater orchestras,
attended Boston Symphony Orchestra concerts and began to play in
chamber ensembles with members of that orchestra. He also
continued his musical education in Boston, taking violin lessons
with Felix Winternitz, theory with Josef Claus and composition with
John Knowles Paine. (It may have been Paine's pervasive Germanism
that prompted him to change his name from Charles to Carl). Around
1900 he worked as an engraver for the Boston music publisher F. H.
Gilson and as music critic for a Cambridge paper. In 1903 he took
a course in English literature at Harvard, and in 1906 began to
give lectures at music clubs, speaking on modern music and the
worthiness of Wagner, d'Indy, Franck and Debussy. From 1907 to 1917
he lived in Winona, MN, where he taught at the Mar d'Mar School and
founded the Winona Symphony Orchestra, with which he presented
concert versions of several operas. Having begun work on his own
opera **The Sunken Bell** and hoping to interest the Metropolitan Opera
in the work, he moved to New York (1917). He gave composition
lessons but also received some support from private patronage, and
he organized an orchestra at the Rand School. Never a prolific
composer--he worked slowly and carefully and constantly revised--he
composed more during this New York period than at any other time,
and many of his compositions were performed under the sponsorship
of the International Composers' Guild. A talented painter, in 1932
he designed the cover for Charles Ives's **Lincoln the Great
Commoner**. As fellow promoters of modern art, the two composers
developed a respectful and sympathetic friendship. Around 1920 he

began to spend most of his summers at Arlington, VT, where he ultimately settled. During 1938-43 he supervised a composition class at the University of Miami at Coral Gables, FL, but thereafter devoted himself mostly to painting and to revising some of his compositions. He was elected to the National Institute of Arts and Letters (1954), awarded a Mus.D. from the University of Vermont (1960) and given the Brandeis University Creative Arts Award (1964). Ruggles's piano compositions are late works, written in an uncompromising contemporary idiom. [I]

RYBNER [RUBNER], PETER MARTIN CORNELIUS (b. Copenhagen, Denmark, 26 October 1853; d. New York, NY, 21 January 1929). Pianist, violinist, conductor, teacher, composer. He was educated at the University of Copenhagen and studied music at the Copenhagen Conservatory, where he was a pupil of Niels Gade, Johann P. Hartmann and Lars Tofte. He continued his studies at Leipzig with Ferdinand David and Carl Reinecke, then had further training with Hans von Bülow and Anton Rubinstein. He made his début as a concert violinist in Copenhagen and as a concert pianist in Leipzig, then made successful tours as a pianist in Scandinavia, Germany, France, Italy and England. In 1875 he became director of the choral society at Baden-Baden, Germany. Between 1886 and 1904 he lived at Karlsruhe, Germany, where he was director of the conservatory and assistant to Felix Mottl, conductor of both the Karlsruhe opera and the Philharmonic Society. In 1892 he succeeded Mottl as conductor of the Philharmonic and held that position until 1900. From 1904 he lived in New York City, having been appointed to succeed Edward MacDowell as head of the music department at Columbia University. He resigned from Columbia in 1919 to devote more time to performing and composing; however, from 1924 until his death he taught composition at the New York College of Music. Rybner wrote engaging character pieces for the piano as well as at least one terrific Wagnerian operatic paraphrase. [I]

RYDER, THOMAS PHILANDER (b. Cohasset, MA, 29 June 1836; d. Somerville, MA, 2 December 1887). Organist, teacher, composer. He spent his entire life in Massachusetts. Although he showed musical talent as a child, he had no training until he was 14 when, his father having died, he was sent to a school for indigent boys in Boston. Here an assistant teacher noticed his talent and began to give him music lessons. He made rapid progress, and later had additional lessons with Gustav Satter. About 1852 his mother sent him to Hyannis to learn a trade, but he became organist at one of the local churches and subsequently abandoned his apprenticeship. He was organist and teacher in Hingham and Stoughton, then from 1865 lived in Boston, where the city directories (1865-85) list him as a music teacher. For about six months he played the organ at "Church Green" on Summer Street; when that church was torn down, he became organist at the Tremont Temple, a position he held for about ten years. He became a popular teacher and choir director, and over the years attracted many pupils. As a composer he produced

mostly church music, and his hymns were at one time widely used.
He compiled the **Golden Treasure,** a collection of hymn tunes,
anthems, chants and other music for public worship, together with
part-songs and glees (for mixed and male voices) for music
conventions. Ryder composed sentimental, sometimes flamboyant
salon music for the piano. [I]

SAAR, LOUIS VICTOR FRANZ (b. Rotterdam, Holland, 10 December 1868;
d. St. Louis, MO, 23 November 1937). Teacher, pianist, composer.
He was graduated (1884) from the Gymnasium at Strasbourg, Alsace,
then attended the University there for about two years. He studied
music at the Munich Conservatory (1886-89), where he was a pupil of
Josef Rheinberger and Ludwig Abel, and later spent one winter
working under Brahms in Vienna. In 1894-1906 he lived in New York
City, where he was an accompanist at the Metropolitan Opera House
(1894-96) and a teacher of harmony and composition at the New York
College of Music (1898-1906). From 1906 to 1917 he was in charge of
theory and composition at the Cincinnati College of Music in Ohio;
from 1917 to 1933 he was head of the theory department at the
Chicago Musical College in Illinois. From 1934 until his death he
taught at the St. Louis Institute of Music, St. Louis, MO. Saar
wrote durable, musicianly piano music, some of it showing a
definite Brahms influence. [I,II,IV]

SALMON, ALVAH GLOVER (b. Southold, Long Island, NY, 23 September
1868; d. Boston, MA, 17 September 1917). Pianist, teacher,
lecturer, composer. He studied music in Boston with Otto Bendix at
the New England Conservatory (graduated 1888) and privately with
Benjamin J. Lang. After further training with Sebastian Bach Mills,
Percy Goetschius and Edward MacDowell in New York City, he went to
St. Petersburg, Russia to work under Alexander Glazunoff.
Fascinated with Russian music, he became an authority on the
subject. When he returned to the United States he gave
lecture-recitals at colleges, universities and musical
organizations, speaking on Russian music and introducing his
audiences to works by Russian composers. From 1895 he lived in
Boston, where he taught privately, actively promoted Russian music
and wrote articles about it for musical journals. He acquired an
important library of Russian music (3000 vols.) and an extensive
collection of autographs, musical excerpts and photographs,
memorabilia given to him by eminent Russian composers. Salmon's
piano music has many admirable lyrical and rhythmic qualities to
recommend it. [I]

SCHEHLMANN, LOUIS (b. Mechstersheim, near Speyer, now in West
Germany, 22 October 1854; d. Lynchburg, VA, 8 April 1903).
Teacher, conductor, pianist, composer. He was educated in
Stuttgart, Germany, and at the age of 18 emigrated to the United
States (1872). After spending about ten years as a music teacher
and choral conductor in Cleveland, OH, around the mid 1880s he

settled permanently in Lynchburg, VA, where he had been appointed, on the recommendation of Dr. Leopold Damrosch, as conductor of both the Mozart Musical Association and the Concordia Glee Club. He taught privately and was a member of the music faculty at Randolph-Macon Woman's College from 1891, the year the college was founded, until his death. Schehlmann's German background supplies the basic influence for all of his graceful, romantic piano compositions. [I]

SCHELLING, ERNEST HENRY (b. Belvidere, NJ, 26 July 1876; d. New York, NY, 8 December 1939). Pianist, conductor, composer. From the age of two, when he began his first piano lessons, until the age of 16 he was sternly trained and aggressively promoted by a father obsessed with a desire to develop one of his children into a celebrated musician. He was only four when he made his first public appearance as a pianist, playing the boy Mozart in a "living tableau" at the Philadelphia Academy of Music, and when he reached six his father took him abroad for nearly ten years of intensive musical study under eight different teachers. Despite his young age, he was accepted as a student at the Paris Conservatory, where he was a pupil of George Mathias and Isidor Philipp, and subsequently studied with Dionys Pruckner and Percy Goetschius at Stuttgart, Theodore Leschetizky in Vienna, Hans Huber at Basel and finally with Moritz Moskowski and Carl Heinrich Barth in Berlin. Whenever possible, his father arranged for him to play in public concerts and at social musicales before wealthy Europeans and royalty. He was 16 when he returned to the United States, bothered with neuritis in his hands and exhausted from studying, practicing and performing. Withdrawing from the concert stage, for a few years (1892-96) he earned just enough money to live on by giving piano lessons and playing the organ, then when his health was fully restored he began to think again of a concert career. In 1896 he went on tour with Mme. Emma Albani, and in that same year had an opportunity to play for Paderewski, who agreed to take him as a pupil at his home in Morges, Switzerland. However, he had to save money for two years before he was able to get to Switzerland to study with Paderewski (1898-1900). The two developed a close friendship, and when Paderewski was unable to perform at the Chopin Centennial Festival at Lemburg, Poland (1910), he recommended Schelling as his substitute, writing that "Though I cannot play myself, I send you instead the man who is best fitted to take my place, my friend and colleague, Ernest Schelling." He was court pianist to the Princess of Saxe-Weimar-Eisenach, sister of Kaiser Wilhelm II (1900-01), then began his career as an adult concert pianist. He toured extensively in France, Germany, Spain, Russia, England, South America and, after making his American début with the Boston Symphony Orchestra (1904), performed widely in the United States. Meanwhile he developed as a composer, and his works received frequent performances with leading orchestras. He made his home in New York City and spent the long May-to-October break between concert seasons at his summer home on Mt. Desert Island, ME or at his home in Switzerland, where he was near Paderewski. During

World War I he served overseas (1917-20) with U. S. Army Intelligence, then returned to New York. From 1924 until his death he was best known as the conductor of the young people's concerts of the New York Philharmonic Orchestra, recognized not so much for his conducting as for his technique of combining an orchestral concert with an illustrated lecture. As he discussed the music and the orchestral instruments, he illustrated his talk with slides of places and events connected with music and musicians, usually slides from his own large collection gathered during his many travels. The young people's concerts became extremely popular with adults as well as children, and he was often invited to present similar concerts with other orchestras. He conducted the Baltimore Symphony Orchestra during the 1935-36 season. He was awarded the French Legion of Honor (1918) for his war work and an honorary Mus.D. from the University of Pennsylvania (1928). Schelling's piano music is usually difficult. It presents the performer with generous use of different stylistic approaches such as glissando and emphasis on the lower register. [I,V]

SCHLESINGER, SEBASTIAN BENSON (b. Hamburg, Germany, 24 September 1837; d. Nice, France, 8 January 1917). Amateur composer. He was 13 when his family emigrated to America and settled in Boston, MA. Although his parents allowed him to study music with Otto Dresel, they opposed his becoming a professional musician and prepared him instead for a career in business. While amassing a fortune as a partner in Naylor and Co., iron and steel merchants, he became one of Boston's most distinguished amateur composers and performers. He was for 17 years the German consul in Boston. After retiring from business to devote his whole time to music, he lived awhile in London, then spent his last 25 years in Paris. Most of Schlesinger's piano pieces are old-fashioned and thoroughly charming "songs without words." [I]

SCHOENEFELD, HENRY (b. Milwaukee, WI, 4 October 1857; d. Los Angeles, CA, 4 August 1936). Conductor, teacher, composer. He was educated in the Milwaukee public schools and had music lessons with his father Frederick, a cellist, and his brother Theodore, a violinist. At the age of 16 he was engaged to play violin in the Milwaukee Symphony Orchestra. He attended the Leipzig Conservatory (1875-78), where he was a pupil of Carl Reinecke, Ernst Richter, Benjamin Papperitz and Leo Grill, then spent one season at Weimar working under Eduard Lassen. After returning to the United States, he lived for 25 years in Chicago, IL (1879-1904) as composer, teacher and conductor. He taught at the Chicago Musical College and the Columbia College of Music, and conducted the Germania Männerchor (1891-1902) and other choral groups. From 1904 he lived in Los Angeles, where he was conductor of the Germania Turnverein and the Women's Symphony Orchestra. In 1915 he was director of the first German Sängerfest held on the West Coast. One of the first composers to recognize the artistic possibilities in native American music, he devoted the last years of his life to the study of Indian lore and Indian musical themes, a study which inspired such works as **Atala, or The Love of Two Savages,** an opera based on a tragedy of Indian life in Florida; **Suite caractéristique,** for string orchestra; **Wachicanta,** an Indian pantomime; and **Two Indian Legends,** for small orchestra. Schoenefeld's few piano pieces, most of them early works, are useful for teaching purposes. [I]

SEEBOECK, WILLIAM CHARLES ERNEST (b. Vienna, Austria, 21 August 1859; d. Chicago, IL, 1907). Teacher, pianist, composer. He had his first music lessons with his mother, a singer who had been a pupil of Mathilde Marchesi, and at the age of 10 began piano lessons with Hermann Grädener. He later studied with Julius Epstein and Martin Nottebohm, and at the same time attended the Theresianum, the state gymnasium in Vienna. In 1875 he studied with Brahms and finally worked for 16 months in St. Petersburg, Russia under the tutelage of Anton Rubinstein (1877-79). After traveling extensively in Turkey, Egypt and India, around 1880 he emigrated to America, settled in Chicago as pianist, teacher and composer, and lived there for the rest of his life. He taught at the Chicago Musical College and the College of Vocal and Instrumental Art, was organist at the Jefferson Park Presbyterian Church and for about 12 years was the pianist for the Apollo Club. Seeboeck's ingratiating piano pieces include elements of both serious and salon-music styles. [I,IV]

SEVEN OCTAVES [see **LOUIS MOREAU GOTTSCHALK**]

SHAW, OLIVER (b. Middleboro, MA, 13 March 1779; d; Providence, RI, 31 December 1848). Organist, teacher, singer, composer. His family having moved to Taunton, MA, he was educated at the Bristol Academy there and then left with his father, a sea captain, on a voyage to the West Indies. Already blind in his right eye from a childhood accident, at 21 he became totally blind when he injured his left eye while taking nautical sightings. After two years of music study with John L. Berkenhead, a blind organist and teacher living in Newport, RI, he spent another two years in Boston studying piano and organ with Gottlieb Graupner and wind instruments with Thomas Granger. He began his teaching career in Dedham, MA, where he may have had Lowell Mason, who lived in nearby Medfield, as one of his pupils. (Mason later acknowledged that he was "indebted to him [Oliver Shaw] for his start in life and owed all to him.") From 1807 he lived in Providence. He became an extremely successful teacher, often giving as many as 40 lessons weekly, and as his reputation spread he attracted pupils from beyond Providence, even from other New England states, and would board as many as ten students at a time at his home. He was also for many years organist at the First Congregational Church. In 1809 he was one of a small group, including Moses Noyes and Thomas S. Webb, that began to meet informally to discuss ways of improving psalmody. In 1816 they incorporated the Psallonian Society for the purpose of "improving their knowledge and performance of sacred music, and inculcating a more correct taste in the choice and performance of it." Shaw was the first and only president of the incorporated Society, which lasted 16 years, the final meeting being held in October, 1832. Under his leadership the Society presented works by Handel, Haydn, Mozart, Beethoven and Mendelssohn as well as works by native composers, and he deserves recognition for his role in giving the early American public a better selection of music and higher standards of performance, not only in Providence but throughout Rhode Island. In 1815 he assisted Thomas Webb, who had moved to Boston, in organizing the Handel and Haydn Society, which later played many of his compositions. In 1817 he started a music repository where he sold music and published many of his works. He had a most distinguished reputation in his lifetime, and his hymns and sacred songs and secular songs and ballads were immensely popular. His **For the Gentlemen** (1807), a collection of instrumental compositions written chiefly in four parts, is one of the earliest American collections of chamber music in score. Shaw wrote mostly vocal music. Apart from **Welcome the Nation's Guest,** his piano pieces are primarily light, sprightly dances and marches, probably designed for practical purposes. [I]

SHEPHERD, ARTHUR (b. Paris, ID, 19 February 1880; d. Cleveland, OH, 12 January 1958). Teacher, pianist, conductor, composer. From earliest childhood he remembered his family making music on their reed organ and his uncles singing English glees. Having a natural gift for sight-reading, as a very small boy he played in the Paris fife and drum band, and later played cornet in the city's brass band. He had formal music lessons with two local teachers, George Haessel and Otto Haenisch, and at the latter's suggestion was sent at the age of 12 to the New England Conservatory in Boston, MA (1892-97), where he studied piano with Charles Dennée and Carl Faelten, theory with Louis Elson, harmony with Benjamin Cutter and Percy Goetschius and composition with George Chadwick. During his five years in Boston his quick sight-reading skill helped him to find jobs playing in small ensembles and in a hotel orchestra. After graduation he lived in Salt Lake City, UT, where he was appointed director of music at the Salt Lake Theater (1897-1908). He also opened a private studio there, reactivated and for several years conducted the Salt Lake Symphony Orchestra and, because of his acquaintance with Arthur Farwell and the Wa-Wan movement, organized a Wa-Wan center. Despite his many duties, he carried on a correspondence course in scoring and counterpoint with Goetschius and composed whenever possible, and his works began to receive recognition: **Overture joyeuse,** for orchestra, won the Paderewski prize in 1902. In 1908 he returned to Boston to study further with Goetschius, and the next year he joined the faculty of the New England Conservatory (1909-1917). He taught harmony and piano, played chamber music and sometimes conducted the school orchestra, and he also continued to compose. In World War I he served as a bandmaster in France for about eight months (1917-18), then returned briefly to the New England Conservatory. In 1920 he moved to Cleveland to become associate conductor of the Cleveland Symphony Orchestra under Nikolai Sokoloff. He played the piano, conducted the chorus, rehearsed the orchestra and conducted it when necessary, wrote program notes (1920-30), gave preconcert lectures for the children's concerts and, from 1924 to 1927, was conductor of those children's concerts. Since his many duties left him little time for composing, he resigned from the orchestra in 1927 to become an instructor in music at Cleveland College of Western Reserve University, where he had more time for composition. In 1930 he became a professor of music at the university graduate school, was head of the music department (1933-48), and retired in 1950. Although he was 70, he spent the year following his retirement teaching at the Longy School in Cambridge, MA, then returned to Cleveland. He was music editor of the Cleveland **Press** (1928-31). He received an honorary Mus.D. from Western Reserve University (1937) and was elected to the National Institute of Arts and Letters (1941). He wrote **The Cadence in the Music of J. S. Bach** (1934), **The String Quartets of Ludwig van Beethoven** (1935) and "'Papa' Goetschius in Retrospect," (**MQ**, xxx, 1944, 307). Shepherd's musicianly piano works progress from a late romantic through a mildly dissonant to a severely contemporary style. [I]

SHERWOOD, EDGAR HARMON (b. Lyons, NY, 29 January 1845; d. Rochester, NY, 2 June 1919). Pianist, teacher, composer, publisher. His musical talent appeared at an early age but it was not nurtured by his father, a prominent lawyer who wanted him to become a physician, not a musician. However, while serving as an apprentice in the office of a local doctor (1861), he studied music on his own. During the Civil War he served in the Union Army (1862-65), then returned home and, having determined to make a career in music, began intensive training. He taught music in Dansville, NY and in Chicago and New York City before settling permanently in Rochester, where city directories list him as a music teacher in 1874-79 and 1882-1919, so he may have left Rochester for about two years. He was a music teacher associated with the Henry S. Mackie music store at 82 State Street (1874-79 and 1882-83), then became an independent teacher. Around 1906 he also began to publish music, including his own works, at his Central Music Store located at 49 Franklin Street. Around 1895 he was appointed national music director of the Union Veterans Union, with the rank of colonel. He was the uncle of William H. Sherwood, a well-known pianist. Edgar Sherwood wrote polished, elegant salon pieces for the piano. [I]

SHERWOOD, WILLIAM HALL (b. Lyons, NY, 31 January 1854; d. Chicago, IL, 7 January 1911). Pianist, teacher, composer. He began music lessons with an aunt who taught at the Lyons Musical Academy (founded by his father in 1854) and from age 7 to 17 studied with his father, meanwhile appearing in concerts in New York, Pennsylvania and Canada. He later studied with Edward Heimburger in Rochester, NY, with Jan Pychowski in New York City and in 1871 with

William Mason, who was conducting a normal institute at Binghamton, NY. He then spent five years in Germany (1871-76) studying and performing. He was a pupil of Theodore Kullak and Carl Weitzmann in Berlin, Ludwig Deppe in Hamburg, Arpad Doppler in Stuttgart and spent one season with Liszt at Weimar (1875). He was organist at the English Chapel in Berlin and at the English Church in Stuttgart, and he made concert appearances in Berlin and Hamburg. When he returned to the United States in 1876, he began his career as teacher and concert pianist, performing in major cities throughout the East and Midwest and establishing a reputation as a virtuoso pianist, known for his dazzling technique and sensitive interpretation. He taught a few years at the New England Conservatory in Boston, MA, then in New York and finally in Chicago (1889-1911). After eight years as director of the piano department at the Chicago Conservatory (1889-97), he founded the Sherwood Music School, and was director until his death. He was an exceptionally successful teacher, not only in Chicago but at the Chautauqua Institution in New York, where he was head of the music department for 22 summers (1889-1911). In 1912 a Music Studio was erected at Chautauqua in his memory. He was one of the first successful American pianists to attempt to include at least one American work on each of his concert programs. He was the nephew of Edgar Harmon Sherwood. William Sherwood's piano works, consistently intriguing to the listener and satisfying for the performer, effectively highlight lyricism and dramatic expression.
[I]

SIEVEKING, MARTINUS (b. Amsterdam, Holland, 24 March 1867; d. Pasadena, CA, 26 November 1950). Pianist, teacher, composer. After early piano lessons with his father, he became a private pupil of Julius Röntgen and Franz Coenen. He made his piano début in Amsterdam in 1890, and in 1891-92 accompanied Adelina Patti on an extensive tour of England. When he visited the United States (ca. 1893) to see the World's Columbian Exposition, he made his American début with the Boston Symphony Orchestra, and subsequently played 14 concerts on tour with that orchestra. During 1895-96 he taught piano and composition at the University of Nebraska at Lincoln, then returned to the concert stage, performing numerous solo recitals and appearing with leading orchestras under Anton Seidl, Walter Damrosch and Theodore Thomas. A physical giant with hands that could span a fourteeenth, his powerful, brilliant and uninhibited playing (he was known as "The Flying Dutchman") fascinated American audiences. An immensely successful pianist, he was personally dissatisfied with his playing and withdrew from the stage for two years of study with Theodore Leschetizky in Vienna. He concertized in Europe for several years, meanwhile developing a method using relaxed weight, which he claimed led to absolute virtuosity within two years. When he returned to the United States around 1915--his obituary states that he was a resident for 34 years--he settled in New York City as a teacher, performer and composer. He founded a school to teach his playing method but it apparently was not successful. Thereafter he taught both privately and at the Institute of Musical Art in the Bronx. Two years before his death he moved to Pasadena, where he continued to take private pupils. Sieveking wrote some worthwhile salon pieces and at least one difficult variation set (**Variations et Fugue**). [I]

SMITH, GERRIT (b. Hagerstown, MD, 11 December 1859; d. Darien, CT, 21 July 1912). Organist, teacher, composer. While attending Hobart College in Geneva, NY, he studied music with Mme. Towler, a pupil of Ignaz Moscheles, and the last two years was organist of the college chapel. After graduation he spent some months in Stuttgart studying music and architecture, then lived in New York City, where he studied organ with Samuel P. Warren, organist of Grace Church. He also studied organ with Eugene Thayer and piano with William Sherwood, most likely at Chautauqua, then for a brief time was organist at St. Paul's Church in Buffalo, NY. He spent a year in Berlin studying organ with Carl August Haupt and composition with Eduard Rohde, and when he returned to the United States he was organist at St. Peter's Church in Albany, NY. From 1885 until his death he was organist and choirmaster at the South Church (Dutch Reformed) in New York City, where he played numerous free organ recitals and attained fame as a concert organist. Over the years he gave more than 300 recitals in the United States, England and Europe. He was director of music at the Union Theological Seminary (1890-1904) and also taught theory at the Master School in Brooklyn. He was one of the founders of both the Manuscript Society and the American Guild of Organists. He was awarded a Mus.D. from Hobart College in 1891. Smith wrote mostly light, descriptive character pieces for the piano. [I]

SMITH, WILSON GEORGE (b. Elyria, OH, 19 August 1855; d. Cleveland, OH, 26 February 1929). Teacher, editor, composer. He graduated from West High School in Cleveland and worked for several years in a mercantile house before starting music lessons with Otto Singer in Cincinnati, OH (1876-80). He spent two years in Berlin (1880-82) studying with Moritz Moskowski, Friedrich Kiel, Theodore Kullak, Oscar Raif and the Scharwenka brothers, then from 1882 until his death lived in Cleveland. He composed, taught privately and was music editor of the Cleveland **Plain Dealer** (1902-28). In the 1920s he founded the Cleveland Musical Association for the purpose of providing performance opportunities for local artists, and he was editor of the Association's official organ, the Cleveland **Musical Review**. Smith's piano compositions, eminently idiomatic, are imaginative and frequently quite original. [I]

SONNECK, OSCAR GEORGE THEODORE (b. Lafayette [now part of Jersey City], NJ, 6 October 1873; d. New York, NY, 30 October 1928). Musicologist, librarian, editor, composer. He was raised and educated in Germany, at the Gelehrtenschule at Kiel (1883-89), the Kaiser Friedrich Gymnasium at Frankfort (1889-93) and the University of Munich (1893-97), where he pursued his interest in psychology and philosophy, studied musicology with Adolph Sandberger and composition with Melchior Ernst Sachs. He studied piano with James Kwast and instrumentation with Iwan Knorr in Frankfort, and conducting with Carl Schröder at Sondershausen, then spent part of the year 1899 working in libraries in Padua, Bologna and Venice. He returned to the United States late that year and began a three-year investigation of American musical life prior to 1800, checking old newspaper files and other sources in libraries in the North and as far south as South Carolina, a project which resulted in his **Bibliography of Early Secular American Music**. As chief of the Music Division of the Library of Congress (1902-17), he developed one of the most comprehensive, well-organized music libraries in the world, and his system for classifying music and music literature remains the basis of organization of the music collections (music, manuscripts and books) at the Library of Congress. In 1911 he represented the United States at the Rome and London international music congresses. In 1917 he resigned from the Library of Congress to become director of the publication department of G. Schirmer, having been editor of Schirmer's **Musical Quarterly** since its first issue in 1915, and in 1921 became vice president at Schirmer's. As one of the organizers of the Society for the Publication of American Music (New York, 1919), he strongly supported serious music by American composers like Ernest Bloch, John Alden Carpenter, Henry F. Gilbert, Charles T. Griffes and Charles M. Loeffler. He was secretary and librarian of the Beethoven Association, founded in New York in 1919. Among his many writings the **Classification: Class M, Music; Class ML, Literature of Music; Class MT, Musical Instruction** (adopted 1902, published 1904), **Bibliography of Early Secular American Music** (1905) and **Early Concert-Life in America: 1731-1800** (1907) are landmarks in the history of American music scholarship. Sonneck's few piano pieces are musically stimulating and technically quite demanding. [I]

SPANUTH, AUGUST (b. Brinkum, near Hanover, Germany, 15 March 1857; d. Berlin, Germany, 9 January 1920). Pianist, teacher, editor, composer. He studied piano with Carl Heymann and composition with Joseph Raff at the Hoch Conservatory in Frankfort, then lived as a concert pianist and teacher in Koblenz and Bremen. He made his home in the United States for 20 years (1886-1906), touring the country the first year. He taught at the Chicago Musical College in Illinois (1887-93), and from 1893 lived in New York City, where he taught privately and was music critic for the **Staatszeitung** (1893-1906). In 1906 he returned to Berlin to teach at the Stern Conservatory; in 1907 he became editor of the famous Leipzig **Signale für die Musikalische Welt**. He published several piano instruction books, edited Liszt's piano compositions (Ditson's Musicians Library, 3 vols.) and translated Caruso's **How To Sing** (1914) into German. Spanuth's few piano compositions are appealingly romantic. [I]

SPROSS, CHARLES GILBERT (b. Poughkeepsie, NY, 6 January 1874; d. Poughkeepsie, 23 December 1961). Organist, pianist, composer. He studied with Adolph Kuehn and Helen Andrus in Poughkeepsie and, after moving to New York City in 1900, studied piano with Xaver Scharwenka and composition with Carl Lachmund. Playing in the Hotel Majestic orchestra for five years gave him opportunity to meet and play for famous singers, and he became much in demand as an accompanist for many of them, including Mary Garden, Mme. Schumann-Heink, Alma Gluck, Pasquale Amato, Louise Homer, Lillian Nordica and Nellie Melba. An organist throughout his adult life, he served at St. Paul's Church in Poughkeepsie (1892-1900), Second Presbyterian Church in Paterson, NJ (1900-04 and 1909-12), Rutgers Presbyterian Church in New York (1905-09), First Presbyterian Church in Poughkeepsie (1913-30) and finally the First Congregational Church, Poughkeepsie (1930-56). Spross composed some structured, serious works (polonaise, scherzo) which, although markedly conservative, are impressive. [I,II,IV]

STERNBERG, CONSTANTIN IVANOVITCH, Edler von (b. St. Petersburg, now Leningrad, Russia, 9 July 1852; d. Philadelphia, PA, 31 March 1924). Pianist, teacher, writer, composer. He began music lessons at the age of six, was 11 when his family moved to Weimar, Germany, and was only just past 12 when Liszt heard him play and gave him a letter of recommendation to Ignaz Moscheles at the Leipzig Conservatory. Accepted as a pupil, the Conservatory having waived its age-14 requirement, he began studies with Moscheles, Ernst F. Richter and Moritz Hauptmann. When cholera struck Leipzig in 1866 he was removed temporarily to Dresden, where he had piano lessons with Friedrich Wieck, then returned to Leipzig and completed his studies. Dissatisfied with himself as a pianist, he turned to conducting. Despite his youth--he was not quite 15--he was employed for five years as a conductor of minor operas and assistant chorus master for larger operas in various German opera centers. In 1872 he returned to the piano. Working under the guidance of Theodore Kullak in Berlin (1872-74), he modernized and improved his technique and made a successful début--Rubinstein attended and applauded vigorously--in Berlin (February, 1875). He toured Germany that summer and later that year was appointed court pianist to the Duke of Mecklenburg at Schwerin (1875-78). Meanwhile in 1877 he spent six weeks with Liszt in Rome. In 1879 he joined the singer Désirée Artot on an arduous tour which he later described as taking them "over most of Europe, also to Egypt, and finally through the entire empire of Russia, into Asia Minor down to the border of Persia, and up through Siberia almost to the Arctic regions." The tour ended in March, 1880, the following year he made his first tour of the United States, then for the next five years toured the country regularly, usually as a soloist but once with the violinist August Wilhelmj and once with the singer Minnie Hauk. He taught in Atlanta, GA (1886-89), and in 1890 settled permanently in Philadelphia, where he established the Sternberg School of Music (ca.1914) and was its director until the time of his death. He published **Ethics and Esthetics of Piano-Playing**

(1917); **Tempo Rubato and Other Essays** (1920), and many articles for musical journals, including "The Making of A Musician As Shown in Reminiscences of Constantin von Sternberg" (**The Musician,** Dec. 1913, Jan. 1914, Feb. 1914). Sternberg was a superb composer. His piano compositions, geared to the mature performer, have distinguished, enduring musical qualities that make them worthwhile today. [I]

STOCKHOFF, WALTER WILLIAM (b. St. Louis, MO, 12 November 1876; d. St. Louis, 1 April 1968). Pianist, teacher, composer. He had some musical instruction from Ernest Kroeger but otherwise was a self-taught musician. At the age of 17 he began teaching piano, harmony and composition in St. Louis and, except for a few months spent in New York City (1915) and several years in Europe (1922-27), he lived his entire life there as a teacher. While abroad, he stayed three years in Germany, where he composed and performed, and also visited Poland, Austria, France and England. As a composer he received greater recognition in Germany—many of his works were performed there—than in his native St. Louis. Stockhoff's severe, uncompromising piano compositions (canon, sonata, fantasia) are the product of a disciplined, intellectual mind. [I]

STOJOWSKI, SIGISMOND (b. Strzelce, Poland, 8 April 1876; d. New York, NY, 5 November 1946). Pianist, teacher, composer. He was educated at the Cracow Lyceum and studied composition with Wladislaw Zelenski, founder of the Cracow Conservatory. From 1890 to 1906 he lived in Paris. He received a degree at the Sorbonne and studied music at the Paris Conservatory, where he was a pupil of Louis Diémer (piano) and Léo Delibes (composition). He studied briefly with Paderewski, who sometimes included Stojowski compositions on his programs; for example, Paderewski gave the first performance in the United States of Stojowski's second concerto, playing with the New York Symphony Orchestra under Walter Damrosch. Stojowski composed and gave successful concerts in London, Paris and other European capitals until he emigrated to the United States in 1906, settled in New York and lived there for the rest of his life. A renowned teacher, from 1906 to 1912 he was head of the piano department at the newly opened New York Institute of Musical Art (later merged with Juilliard), taught at the Von Ende School (1912-17) and continued to teach privately up to the time of his death. Stojowski wrote a great quantity of piano compositions. The best of them mirror his romantic sensitivity and complete command of pianistic resources. [I,V]

STRAKOSCH, MAURICE (b. Gross-Seelowitz, near Brünn, Moravia [now Brno, Czechoslovakia], ca.1825; d. Paris, France, 9 October 1887). Impresario, pianist, teacher, composer. He studied music with Simon Sechter in Vienna, Austria, and later toured as a pianist in Denmark and Russia. Preferring to be an opera singer (tenor) rather than a concert pianist, he studied voice with Mme. Giuditta Pasta at her villa near Lake Como in Italy but, after three years of training, she persuaded him to remain a pianist. He toured extensively in France, Spain and Italy, then from 1848 to 1860 lived in the United States. He settled in New York City as a music teacher and concert pianist, and in the early years was apparently a very active touring performer. He is known to have appeared in concerts in Richmond, VA almost every year from 1849 to 1857 and known to have performed in New Orleans, LA at least four times in 1849 and three times in 1850. Meanwhile he had also embarked on his career as manager. His first year in New York he organized a music festival (October 2, 1848) with the Italian Opera Co. of the United States, a troupe including members of the Salvatore Patti family. A close associate of that family, he married Amalia (1852) and managed the young Adelina as a concert singer from 1851 until 1855 and as an adult opera star from her début in 1859 until her first marriage (1868). After 1856 he seems to have given up his career as a concert pianist in order to devote his efforts to his career as opera and concert manager. He was manager of the New York Academy of Music from January 21, 1857 until 1860, in 1859 taking his opera troupe as far west as Chicago and Cincinnati. In 1858 he also appeared in Richmond with a troupe called Strakosch's Grand Combined Italian Opera Company. After he returned to Europe in 1860, his American enterprises were carried on by his younger brother Max. He was manager of the Paris Opera (1873-74) and co-manager with Max of the Apollo Theater in Rome (1884-85). He wrote **Souvenirs d'un Impresario** (1887) and **Ten Commandments of Music for the Perfection of the Voice** (posthumous, 1896). As a composer he wrote mostly piano pieces plus two operas **Giovanna di Napoli** (performed New York 1851) and **Sardanapalus**. Strakosch was one of the very best salon-music composers of the period. He used classic techniques with skill and sensitivity. [I,II]

STRONG, [GEORGE]   TEMPLETON (b. New York, NY, 26 May 1856; d. Geneva, Switzerland, 27 June 1948). Composer. His musical interests were encouraged by both parents, his mother being an amateur pianist and his father an amateur organist as well as president of the New York Philharmonic Society (1870-74) and founder of the New York Church Music Association. As a youth he studied the oboe, and he had already begun to compose before he went abroad for further training. From 1879 to 1886 he lived mostly in Leipzig, where he studied counterpoint with Salomon Jadassohn, orchestration with Richard Hofmann and horn with Friedrich Gumpert. While visiting Frankfort in 1881 he became friends with Joachim Raff, who persuaded him to return to Leipzig for further study. He also became a familiar of the Liszt circle at Weimar (1881-86), a group that included Emil Sauer, Alexander Siloti and Arthur Friedheim. In 1886 he settled in Wiesbaden and there formed an enduring friendship with Edward MacDowell, who encouraged him to return to the United States and helped him to obtain a faculty appointment at the New England Conservatory in Boston, MA. He taught theory at the Conservatory just one year (1891-92), then returned to Vevey,

Switzerland, where he had established a home in 1889. Discouraged because he felt American composers were ignored in their own country, he gave up composition for a few years and turned his attention to watercolor painting (he founded the Société Vaudoise des Aquarellistes). One of America's earliest musical expatriates, he spent the rest of his life--more than 50 years--in Switzerland, making only occasional visits to the United States. Strong was a skilled craftsman. His moderately chromatic descriptive piano pieces are striking, particularly those written for two pianos. [I,IV]

TAYLOR, RAYNER (b. ca.1747; d. Philadelphia, PA, 17 August 1825). Organist, singer, teacher, composer. As a chorister of the Chapel Royal in London (ca.1756-64), he received a sound musical training and valuable performance experience singing at sacred and secular events: church services, royal ceremonies, festivals, state funerals (he sang at Handel's funeral in 1759). By mid-1764 he had left the Chapel Royal and was employed as a singer at Marylebone (Marybone) Gardens, where he later also appeared as organist and composer. At the close of the 1768-69 season, he moved to Edinburgh, Scotland, where he earned his living as a singer at the New Theater Royal and as a music teacher, one of his pupils being Alexander Reinagle. By the middle of 1772 he was back in London, then for more than a decade was organist of St. Mary the Virgin, the parish church at Chelmsford, Essex (ca.1773-84). He must have followed a busy schedule at Chelmsford. Besides playing the organ and composing sacred music for the services at St. Mary's, he taught private students at their homes and other students at local schools and academies; gave organ concerts, which earned him a reputation as a skilled improviser; managed the concerts presented during the yearly race meetings at Chelmsford; and composed burlettas for the London stage. He left Chelmsford to become musical director of the Sadler's Wells Theater in London, and during what must have been eight busy years there he composed the music for at least 20 new theatricals, wrote songs and incidental music and appeared onstage in singing roles. In the Fall of 1792 he went to the United States, where he quickly resumed musical activities. On September 12 he presented a musical evening in Richmond, VA at which he sang, recited and played the piano. The next month he was in Baltimore, MD, where he put on at least two musical extravaganzas (olios), then by November he was in Annapolis, MD. He was organist at St. Anne's Church in Annapolis for about six months (ca. November, 1792-May 1793), and also gave music lessons and produced two olios (January and February). He left St. Anne's in May because of salary problems and moved to Philadelphia, which would be his home for the rest of his life. From the time of his arrival until about 1819 he was active as organist, teacher, singer and music dealer. From around 1797 until 1813 he was a regular organist at St. Peter's Church, resigning to accept a better paying organ position at St. Paul's Church. He was one of the founders and directors of the Musical Fund Society (1820). From about 1803 to 1815 he was director of music for commencements at the University of Pennsylvania. As a composer he combined unique skills, being equally gifted in writing sacred music for the church and secular settings for theatrical entertainments. Taylor's early piano (or harpsichord) pieces, mostly variations, use Handel as a basic model. His later works—rondos, variations, divertimentos—are written in a compelling Classic style. [I]

THIBAULT, CHARLES (d. ca.1853). Pianist, teacher, composer. Little is known about him. According to Wolfe he is listed as a professor of music or music master in the New York city directories from 1818 to 1852. He appeared in concerts in New York City from 1818 until the 1830s. In an advertisement for a concert he gave in Boston, MA in September, 1818 he claimed that he had received the "Grand Premium of the Royal Conservatory of France," which suggests that he was born or educated, perhaps both, in France. No record of his death has been found but letters of administration in his case were recorded May 20, 1853. Thibault was a progressive composer. His excellent piano compositions show a timely blend of Classicism and Romanticism. [I]

THORN, EDGAR [see **EDWARD MACDOWELL**]

TROYER, CARLOS (b. Mainz, Germany, 12 January 1837; d. Berkeley, CA, 26 July 1920). Researcher, compiler, composer. His **Indian Music Lecture** (Presser, 1913) is prefaced by a "biographical appreciation" written by the composer Charles Wakefield Cadman; however, the undocumented facts presented obviously came from Troyer himself. He claimed to have known both Jenny Lind and Liszt and to have often played for the great composer. He studied violin and piano and, after arriving in the United States at an early age, gave music lessons in New York until he tired of the teaching routine and joined an opera company on tour through the West Indies and South America. When the troupe disbanded he went alone to Brazil to study the songs of tropical birds and the music and customs of the Orinoco Indians. He later traveled into the Inca territory of Bolivia and Peru, where he was captured and spent nine months studying and recording more than 400 tribal songs. He apparently settled in San Francisco in 1871. His name appears in San Francisco directories (1871-1917) listed variously as musician (1871); pianist (1875); teacher of music (1880-90); pianist and composer, specialist in artistic voice culture, new system of lung development (1898); and pianist and composer (after 1900). As a life member of the California Academy of Sciences in San Francisco, he is registered twice, as Charles Troyer joining in 1874 and as Carlos Troyer joining in 1876. He was librarian at the Academy from 1876 until 1895. After meeting Frank Hamilton Cushing, the ethnologist who made a five-year study of the Zuñi Indians of New Mexico, he undertook a prolonged study of Zuñi music and later often lectured on the subject. Troyer fashioned his few piano settings of American Indian music with care and skill. [I]

TURNER, ALFRED DUDLEY (b. St. Albans, ME, 24 August 1854; d. St. Albans, 7 May 1888). Pianist, teacher, composer. At the age of nine he began piano studies with James Cutler Dunn Parker in Boston, and later studied there with Mme. Madeleine Schiller. He graduated from the New England Conservatory, immediately joined the faculty as a piano instructor and taught there until his death. He wrote a series of octave studies that were at one time widely used. Turner was a progressive, imaginative composer for his day. His unusual piano pieces, particularly those in quintuple meter and those with fugue subjects structured in octaves, are worth exploring. [I]

VENTH, CARL (b. Cologne, Germany, 16 February 1860; d. San Antonio, TX, 29 January 1938). Teacher, violinist, conductor, composer. He was a choirboy at the Cologne Cathedral, where his father was the organist, and until the age of ten had violin lessons with his father. He later studied with Georg Japha, Otto Klauwell, Gustav Jensen and Ferdinand Hiller at the Cologne Conservatory and with Henri Wieniawski and Auguste Dupont at the Brussels Conservatory (1875-77). He was concertmaster at the **Opéra Bouffe** in Brussels (1876-77), concertmaster of the symphony orchestra in Utrecht, Holland for a brief time, and concertmaster of Jacques Offenbach's **Opéra Comique** in Paris. At the end of the 1879-80 season, he emigrated to the United States and settled in New York. He worked for eight years as a violinist, the first four with different orchestras and another four with the Metropolitan Opera orchestra (1884-88). From 1888 to 1906 he was director of the Venth College of Music in Brooklyn, where he also conducted the Brooklyn Symphony Orchestra (1889-1902) and various local choruses. After 27 years in Brooklyn and New York, he was for one year concertmaster and assistant conductor of the St. Paul Symphony Orchestra in Minnesota (1907), then from 1908 lived in Texas. He was head of the violin department at the Kidd-Key Conservatory in Sherman, TX (1908-11); he organized and conducted the Dallas Symphony Orchestra (1911-13) and the Fort Worth Symphony (1914-17); he was dean of fine arts at Texas Woman's College in Fort Worth (1914-31) and dean of fine arts at Westmoorland College in San Antonio (1931-38). He received an honorary Mus.D. from the New York College of Music in 1931. Venth exerted greater influence as a teacher--he taught for more than 50 years--than as either performer or composer. Being a professional violinist, he wrote very little piano music. Some of his descriptive tone portraits are strikingly effective. [I]

VOGRICH, MAX [WILHELM CARL] (b. Hermannstadt, Transylvania [now Sibiu, Romania], 24 January 1852; d. New York, NY, 10 June 1916). Pianist, editor, composer. He studied at the Leipzig Conservatory (1866-69) with Ignaz Moscheles, Ernst Wenzel, Carl Reinecke, Moritz

Hauptmann and Ernst Richter, and the following year embarked on a peripatetic career as a concert pianist. From 1870 to 1878 he toured in Europe--Germany, Austria, Russia, France, Italy, Spain--and later Mexico and South America. Between 1878 and 1882 he lived in the United States, where he gave several recitals in New York City and made a tour with the violinist August Wilhelmj. After living in Australia (1882-86), he settled in New York for 16 years (1886-1902), a period in which he devoted most of his time to composing and to editing music. He lived in Weimar (1902-08), in London (1908-14) and finally again in New York, where he was a consultant with G. Schirmer. He edited Schumann's complete piano works, Clementi's **Gradus ad Parnassum**, works by modern Russian composers and other collections. Vogrich wrote many substantial piano works, the most impressive being the difficult and demanding pieces designed for concert performance. [I,V]

WARREN, GEORGE WILLIAM (b. Albany, NY, 17 August 1828; d. New York, NY, 17 March 1902). Organist, composer. He attended Racine College but was a self-taught musician. A lifelong organist, he served at St. Peter's (1846-58) and St. Paul's (1858-60) churches in Albany, at Holy Trinity in Brooklyn (1860-70) and finally at St. Thomas's Church in New York City (1870-1902). He composed many hymn tunes, including the "National Hymn" to which "God of Our Fathers" is sung, and many piano pieces. **The Andes, Marche di Bravura,** most likely his most famous piano composition, was a great favorite of the early 1860s, especially in the two-piano version arranged by Louis Moreau Gottschalk. He edited **Warren's Hymns and Tunes, as Sung at St. Thomas Church** (1888). Apart from **The Andes,** Warren wrote many other striking piano pieces, mostly flamboyant salon music. [I]

WARREN, SAMUEL PROWSE (b. Montreal, Canada, 18 February 1841; d. New York, NY, 7 October 1915). Organist, teacher, composer. His father, an American from Rhode Island, owned an organ factory in Montreal, so even as a small child he was familiar with that instrument. After early piano lessons, he began organ training at the age of 11, and when he was 12 he gave an organ recital at St. Stephen's Chapel. A church organist from his early teens, he began his career at the American Presbyterian Church in Montreal, where he played for eight years. He studied in Berlin (1861-64) with Carl August Haupt, Gustav Schumann and Paul Wieprecht, returned to Montreal for two years, then settled in New York City. He was organist at All Souls Unitarian Church (1866-68) and at Grace Church (1868-74, 1876-94), his 24 years there being interrupted by two years of service at Holy Trinity Episcopal Church (1874-76). From 1895 until his death he played the organ at the First Presbyterian Church in East Orange, NJ. Possessed of an extensive repertoire and a masterful technique, during his New York years he presented a striking series of organ recitals--more than 230--which brought him national prominence. He conducted the chorus choir at Grace Church and the New York Vocal Union (1880-88). He was a founding member of the American Guild of Organists (1896). He edited the organ works of Mendelssohn, Guilmant and Lemmens and made excellent organ transcriptions of works by Weber, Beethoven, Schumann and Wagner. Predominantly an organist, Warren wrote little piano music. The **Prelude and Fugue** (1901) is a genuinely fine example of his best writing for piano. [I]

WEBER, HENRY [HEINRICH FREDERICK] (b. Marburg, Germany, 15 April 1812; d. Nashville, TN, 17 May 1878). Teacher, composer. He was a professor of music and art in Marburg but left Germany because of the Revolution of 1848, and ultimately settled in North Carolina. In 1852 he married Margaret Walker in Pittsboro, NC, and for three years they both taught at the Columbia Institute in Columbia, TN. They opened a school in East Nashville, TN in 1856, but with the outbreak of the Civil War he, being a Union sympathizer, went North while his wife returned to her family in North Carolina. After the War they reopened their school in East Nashville, and he taught there until his death. His two "storm" pieces were apparently very popular in their day, and he is known to have also written a Te Deum and the music for "Hail Tennessee." [I]

WELS, CHARLES (b. Prague, Czechoslovakia, 24 August 1825; d. New York, NY, 12 May 1906). Teacher, organist, pianist, composer. He was a pupil of Jan Tomaschek in Prague. After serving as court pianist at Warsaw (1847-49), he emigrated to America and settled in New York. Although he gave occasional piano recitals, he became better known as a successful teacher. He was organist at St. Stephen's Church from 1852 to 1859 and again from 1896 to 1901; in the meantime he had been organist at St. Cecilia's Church, the Church of the Disciples and at All Saints' Church. Wels wrote attractive and useful nocturnes and preludes for the piano. On the lighter side his numerous transcriptions, paraphrases, and sentimental salon pieces have a charm of their own. [I,III]

WHELPLEY, BENJAMIN LINCOLN (b. Eastport, ME, 23 October 1864; d. Boston, MA, 15 February 1946). Organist, pianist, teacher composer. He had piano and organ lessons, and from the age of 12 to 15 was organist of the Unitarian Church in Eastport. From the age of 16 until his death he lived in Boston--city directories list him regularly from 1880 through 1945--and spent his holidays at Eastport. He enrolled at the New England Conservatory, studying with Alfred Dudley Turner and Stephen Emery, among others, and was also a private pupil of Charles Capen, Benjamin Lang, Sidney Homer and George Summer. About two years after his arrival in Boston, he began his extended career as a church organist, during which he served at the First Reformed Episcopal Church, the Meeting House Hill Church (Unitarian), Temple Adath Israel, South Congregational Church and the Arlington Street Church. In 1890 he studied with Elie Delaborde in Paris. More than 60 years in Boston, he achieved distinction as church musician, teacher and composer. Whelpley wrote short, pleasant character pieces for the piano. [I]

WHITING, ARTHUR BATELLE (b. Cambridge, MA, 20 June 1861; d. Beverly, MA, 20 July 1936). Pianist, teacher, composer. He studied at the New England Conservatory with William H. Sherwood, Louis Maas, James C. D. Parker and George Chadwick, then attended the Munich Conservatory (1883-85), where he was a pupil of Joseph Rheinberger, Hans Bussmeyer and Ludwig Abel. He worked in Boston for about ten years, and in 1895 moved permanently to New York City, where he became a well-known teacher, composer, concert pianist and chamber-music advocate. He gave solo recitals and appeared with orchestras, often playing his **Concerto in D Minor** and **Fantasy, Op.11**. From 1907 to 1930 he presented an annual series (usually five) of free chamber-music concerts for students at various colleges and universities (Princeton, Yale, Harvard, Columbia, Wesleyan, Union, Bryn Mawr and others) with the hope of acquainting the students with the standard works of the repertory and stimulating their interest in a better kind of music. At these "expositions of chamber music," as he called them, he made comments on the structure of each composition and discussed its significance in the development of music. An authority on music for old instruments, from 1911 he played the harpsichord (Constance Edson, violin; Georges Barrère, flute; Paul Kéfer, viola da gamba) in concerts of early music. He was a nephew of the Boston organist George Elbridge Whiting. He wrote articles on music for the **Yale Review** (1919), **The Outlook** (1908, 1915) and the **New Musical Review** (1909). Arthur Whiting was a serious, musicianly composer whose piano pieces are eminently idiomatic and expertly designed. [I,V]

WHITING, GEORGE ELBRIDGE (b. Holliston, MA, 14 September 1840; d. Cambridge, MA, 14 October 1923). Organist, teacher, composer. He was five when he began music lessons with his brother Amos, a church organist, and about 18 when he became organist at the North Congregational Church in Hartford, CT, the beginning of his long, successful career as a church musician. While in Hartford he was also organist for the Beethoven Society concerts. By 1862 he was living in Boston as organist of the Mount Vernon Church. That same year he studied with George W. Morgan, organist of Grace Church in New York City, and the following year went to England to study with William Thomas Best in Liverpool. When he returned to the United States, he went to Albany, NY as organist at St. Joseph's Church (1865-68), then back to Boston, where he was organist and choir director at King's Chapel (1868-73) and also organist at the Boston Music Hall for about a year. He went to Berlin in 1874 to study with Carl August Haupt and Rudolph Radecke, returned once again to Boston and, except for a term as head of the College of Music in Cincinnati, OH (1879-82), he lived there for the rest of his life. He was organist of the Church of the Immaculate Conception for more than 30 years (1876-79, 1882-1910) and a faculty member at the New England Conservatory for 18 years (1876-79, 1882-97). One of the foremost organists of his time, he helped to create an organ repertory and to develop the art of organ performance in America. The pianist Arthur Batelle Whiting was his nephew. George Whiting wrote a few short romantic piano pieces showing some interesting rhythmic and lyrical features. [I]

WHITNEY, SAMUEL BRENTON (b. Woodstock, VT, 4 June 1842; d. Woodstock, 3 August 1914). Organist, choirmaster, composer. Unlike most musicians of his time, he studied only in the United States, first with local teachers and later with Charles Wels in New York. He was organist at Christ Church in Montpelier, VT (four years), at St. Peter's in Albany, NY and at St. Paul's in Burlington, VT before going to Boston to continue his studies with John Knowles Paine. He assisted Paine as organist of the Appleton Chapel in Cambridge, and during his early years in Boston gave many organ recitals. Although noted for his masterful playing of Bach and splendid organ improvisations, he was better known for his work as organist and choirmaster of the Church of the Advent (1871-1908), where he introduced the sung English liturgical service and established one of America's earliest boy choirs. He composed a **Communion Service in G** for his 25th anniversary at the church (1896) and a **Magnificat and Nunc Dimmitis in E-Flat** for his 35th anniversary (1906). He promoted--and frequently directed--parish choir festivals throughout New England; he was one of the founders--and for many years director--of the Massachusetts Diocesan Choir Guild (1876). A teacher at the New England Conservatory, he introduced a class in church music in which he instructed both voice students and organ students in the proper performance of sacred music. Most of Whitney's extant piano pieces are charming, old-fashioned salon-music compositions. [I]

WILSON, GRENVILLE DEAN (b. Plymouth, CT, 26 January 1833; d. South Nyack, NY, 20 September 1897). Teacher, conductor, composer. He was raised in Lenox, MA, where he studied piano with his mother and a German musician named Donheim, and later studied harmony and composition with A. W. Johnson in Boston. He began his teaching career at the age of 18 in Lenox, and also taught at the Temple Grove Seminary in Saratoga Springs, NY and the Lasell Seminary in Auburndale, MA. From 1872 he lived in Nyack, where he taught at the Mansfield Seminary and in 1876 became director of music at the Rockland Institute. He organized the Nyack Philharmonic Society (1876) and the Nyack Choral Society (1880), which he conducted up to the time of his death. Wilson composed a large quantity of salon pieces for the piano, some of them quite expressive. [I]

WOLFSOHN, CARL (b. Alzey, Germany, 14 December 1834; d. Deal, NJ, 30 July 1907). Pianist, conductor, teacher, composer. He started piano lessons at the age of seven, and from the age of 12 to 14 was a pupil of Aloys Schmitt in Frankfort, where he made his début playing the piano part of the Beethoven **Quintet, Op.16** (December, 1848). He studied with Vincenz Lachner in Mannheim for about two

years, in 1851 toured Rhenish Bavaria with the violinist Teresa
Milanollo, then spent two years in London. In 1854 he emigrated to
the United States and settled in Philadelphia, PA as pianist,
teacher, and composer (1854-73). From 1856 he played in an annual
series of chamber-music concerts; in 1863 he gave an impressive
series of recitals in which he played all the Beethoven piano
sonatas, first in Philadelphia and then in New York; the following
year he repeated the series with great success in both cities, and
later gave recitals covering all the Schumann piano works and all
the Chopin piano works. An ardent student of Beethoven, he founded
the Beethoven Society in Philadelphia in 1869, and in 1873 moved to
Illinois in order to conduct the Beethoven Society of Chicago
(1873-84). He played the Beethoven piano series in Chicago in 1874,
the Schumann in 1875 and the Chopin in 1876, and in addition
performed in monthly chamber-music concerts. He had wide musical
interests. Although a devotee of Beethoven, he was one of the
early supporters of Wagner in America, and when he was 60 began a
study of Brahms, then being introduced into America, and played all
the Brahms piano works in a series of recitals. Surprisingly, this
eminent pianist composed a good deal of salon music, albeit
impressive salon music--polkas and other dances, operatic
paraphrases, etc. He also wrote more sturdy concert works calling
for mature technique. [I]

WOLLENHAUPT, HERMANN ADOLPH (b. Schkeuditz, Germany, 27 September
1827; d. New York, NY, 18 September 1863). Pianist, teacher,
composer. He studied piano with Julius Knorr and composition with
Moritz Hauptmann at the Leipzig Conservatory. In 1845 he emigrated
to America and settled in New York, where he attained an excellent
reputation as concert pianist and teacher. He made a concert tour
in Germany in 1855. Although he died at the age of 36, Wollenhaupt
composed about 100 piano pieces, many of them becoming extremely
popular during the late 19th century. In general, they have many
attractive features--scintillating scale fioriture, fascinating
rhythmic patterns and colorful harmonic progressions. They are
still worth playing and worth reviving. [I,III]

Appendix A
Music Publishers
and Abbreviations

American	American Music Edition, New York, NY
André	André and Co., New York, NY
André-G	G. André, Philadelphia, PA
André-J	J. André, Offenbach am Main, Germany
Appel	John Appel, New York, NY
Arrow	Arrow Music Press, New York, NY
ArtPS	Art Publication Society, St. Louis, MO
Ascherberg	E. Ascherberg and Co., London, England
Ashdown	Edwin Ashdown, London, England
Ashmall	Wm. E. Ashmall, New York, NY
Associated	Associated Music Publishers, New York, NY
Atwill	J. F. Atwill, New York, NY
Augener	Augener and Co.(Limited), London, England
Author	The Author (i.e. Composer)
Bach	Bach Music Co., Boston, MA
Bacher	T. A. Bacher, Philadelphia, PA
Bacon	A. Bacon, Philadelphia, PA
BaconH	Bacon and Hart, Philadelphia, PA
Badger	The Badger Music Publishing Co., Milwaukee, WI
Balmer	Balmer and Weber, St. Louis, MO
Bech	Bech and Lawton, Philadelphia, PA
Beer	Beer and Schirmer, New York, NY
Benson	G. D. Benson, Nashville, TN
Benteen	F. D. Benteen, Baltimore, MD
Bethune	J. G. Bethune, New York, NY
Birchard	C. C. Birchard, Boston, MA
Blackmar	A. E. Blackmar and Bros., New Orleans, LA; Augusta, GA
Blake	G. E. Blake, Philadelphia, PA
Boardman	Boardman and Gray, Albany, NY

Bollinger	Bollinger Alumni Association, St. Louis, MO
Boner	W. H. Boner and Co., Philadelphia, PA.
Boosey	Boosey and Co., New York, NY
BooseyH	Boosey and Hawkes, London, England; New York, NY
Boston	The Boston Music Co., Boston, MA
BostonC	Boston Conservatory Music Store, Boston, MA
Bote	Bote und Bock, Berlin, Germany
Bradlee	C. (Charles S.) Bradlee, Boston, MA
Brainard	S. Brainard and Co., Cleveland, OH
BrainardS	S. Brainard's Sons Co., Chicago, IL; Cleveland, OH
Breitkopf	Breitkopf und Härtel, Leipzig, Germany; New York, NY
Brentano	Brentano's Literary Emporium, New York, NY
Breusing	C. Breusing, New York, NY
Broude	Broude Brothers, New York, NY
Bryant	Bryant Music Co., New York, NY
Cady	C. M. Cady, New York, NY
Carisch	Carisch S. P. A., Milano, Italy
Carr	B. Carr, Philadelphia, PA
Carr-B	B. Carr's Musical Repository, New York, NY; Philadelphia, PA
Carr-J	J. Carr, Baltimore, MD
CarrMR	Carr's Musical Repository, Philadelphia, PA
CarrMS	Carr's Music Store, Baltimore, MD
CarrS	Carr and Schetky, Philadelphia, PA
Carr-T	T. Carr, Baltimore, MD
Century	Century Music Co., New York, NY
Challier	C. A. Challier and Co., Berlin, Germany
Chandler	Chandler-Ebel Music Co., Brooklyn, NY
Chandler-FS	F. S. Chandler, Chicago, IL
Chappell	Chappell, London, England
Chicago	The Chicago Music Co., Chicago, IL
Chickering	C. F. Chickering, Boston, MA
Christman	C. G. Christman, New York, NY
Church	The John Church Co., Cincinnati, OH; Boston, MA
Clapham	H. L. Clapham, Washington, D. C.
Clarke	Clarke, Nichols and Co., Pittsfield, MA
Cluett	Wm. Cluett and Son, Albany, NY
Cocks	Robert Cocks and Co., London, England
Cole	John Cole, Baltimore, MD
Combs	Combs' Conservatory Publishing Co., Philadelphia, PA
Composer	The Composer
ComposerMC	Composers' Music Corporation, New York, NY
ComposerP	The Composers' Press, Inc., New York, NY
Consolidated	Consolidated Music Co., Milwaukee, WI
Cook	Cook and Brother, New York, NY
Cory	John A. Cory, Providence, RI
Cottier	Cottier and Denton, Buffalo, NY
Cranz	A.(August) Cranz, Leipzig and Hamburg, Germany
Curwen	J. Curwen and Sons, Ltd., London, England
Ditson	Oliver Ditson, Boston, MA; New York, NY
Ditson-CH	C. H. Ditson and Co., New York, NY
Dobmeyer	J. J. Dobmeyer and Co., Cincinnati, OH
Dodworth	H. B. Dodworth, New York, NY

Dubois	Wm. Dubois, New York, NY
DuboisB	Dubois and Bacon, New York, NY
DuboisS	Dubois and Stodart, New York, NY
Durand	Durand et Cie (fils), Paris, France
Durdilly	E. Durdilly, Ch. Hayet, Paris, France
Ebner	Edouard Ebner, Stuttgart, Germany
Ellis	John F. Ellis and Co., Washington, DC
Escudier	Léon Escudier, Paris, France
Everson	John Everson, Pittsburg, PA
Feist	Leo Feist, New York, NY
Fiot	A. Fiot, Philadelphia, PA
FiotM	Fiot, Meignen and Co., Philadelphia, PA
Firnberg	Firnberg, Frankfort, Germany
FirthH	Firth and Hall, New York, NY
FirthP	Firth, Pond and Co., New York, NY
FirthS	Firth, Son and Co., New York, NY
Firth-T	Thaddeus Firth, New York, NY
Fischer	Carl Fischer, New York, NY
Fischer-J	J. Fischer and Bro., New York, NY
Flaxland	G. Flaxland, Paris, France
Fontana	Fontana-Roux, Baltimore, MD
Forberg	R. Forberg, Leipzig, Germany
Fourwinds	The "Fourwinds" Press, Westwood, MA
Fox	Sam Fox Publishing Co., New York, NY; Cleveland, OH
Franklin	John Franklin Music Co., New York, NY
Fries	Fries und Holzmann, Zurich, Switzerland
Friis	P. Friis, Copenhagen, Denmark
Fritzsch	E. W. Fritzsch, Leipzig, Germany
Gamble	Gamble Hinged Music Co., Chicago, IL
Geib	J. A. and W. Geib, New York, NY
Gibbons	Gibbons and Stone, Rochester, NY
Gilbert	The Gilbert Music Co., Chicago, IL
Gilfert	Charles Gilfert and Co., Charleston, SC
Gordon	S. T. Gordon, New York, NY
GordonS	S. T. Gordon and Son, New York, NY
Gould	J. E. Gould, Philadelphia, PA
Grand	Grand Conservatory Publishing Co., New York, NY
Graupner	G. Graupner, Boston, MA
Gray	M. Gray, San Francisco, CA
Gray-HW	H. W. Gray, New York, NY
Grude	Emil Grude, Leipzig, Germany
Hagen	Theo. Hagen, New York, NY
Hainauer	Julius Hainauer, Breslau, Germany
Hall	C. Hall, Jr., New York, NY
HallS	Wm. Hall and Son, New York, NY
Hall-W	Wm. Hall, New York, NY
Hansen	W. Hansen, Copenhagen, Denmark
Harms	T. B. Harms and Co., New York, NY
Harris	Charles W. Harris, New York, NY
Hartmann	G. Hartmann, Paris, France
Harvard	Harvard Musical Revue, Cambridge, MA
Hasey	W. B. Hasey, Boston, MA
Hatch	Hatch Music Co., Philadelphia, PA

Heinrichs	Heinrichshofen's Verlag, Magdeburg, Germany
Henn	Edition A. Henn, Genève, Switzerland
Heugel	Heugel et Cie., Paris, France
Hewitt	J. Hewitt, New York, NY; Boston, MA
HewittMR	James Hewitt's Musical Repository and Library, New York, NY
Hidley	J. H. Hidley, Albany, NY
Higgins	H. M. Higgins, Chicago, IL
Himan	A.(Alberto) Himan, New York, NY
Hinds	Hinds, Noble and Eldridge, New York, NY
Hinshaw	Hinshaw Music, Chapel Hill, NC
Hofmeister	Friedrich Hofmeister, Leipzig, Germany
Holt	C. Holt, Jr., New York, NY
Hug	Komissionsverlag von Gebrüder Hug und Co., Leipzig, Germany; Zurich, Switzerland
International	International Music Co., New York, NY
Jackson	C. and E. W. Jackson, Boston, MA
Jackson-E	E. W. Jackson, Boston, MA
Johanning	Johanning and Co., London, England
Jones	E. P. Jones, Troy, NY
Jost	Jost und Sander, Leipzig, Germany
Jung	P. L. Jung, New York, NY
Kahnt	C. F. Kahnt Nachfolger, Leipzig, Germany
Kaun	W. A. Kaun Music Co., Milwaukee, WI; New York, NY
Kerksieg	Kerksieg and Breusing, New York, NY
Kistner	Fr. Kistner, Leipzig, Germany
Kleber	H. Kleber and Bros. Pittsburgh, PA
Koppitz	Koppitz, Prüfer and Co., Boston, MA
Kranich	Kranich and Bach, New York, NY
Kunkel	Kunkel Bros., St. Louis, MO
Kürsteiner	Kürsteiner and Rice, New York, NY
Lafont	A. Lafont, Paris, France
Laudy	Laudy and Co., London, England; Paris, France
Lee	Lee and Walker, Philadelphia, PA
Leuckart	F. E. C. Leuckart, Leipzig, Germany
Longman	Longman, Lukey and Broderip, London, England
Lucas	Stanley Lucas, Weber, Pitt and Hartzfeld, Ltd., London, England
Luckhardt	Friedrich Luckhardt, Berlin, Germany
LuckhardtB	Luckhardt and Belder, New York, NY
Lyon	Lyon and Healy, Chicago, IL
McClure	James A. McClure, Nashville, TN
MacDowell	Edward MacDowell Association, Inc., New York, NY
Mackie	H. S. Mackie, Rochester, NY
Manuscript	Manuscript Music Society, Philadelphia, PA
Marks	Edward B. Marks Music Corp., New York, NY
Martens	Martens Brothers, New York, NY
Maxwell	Wm. Maxwell Music Co., New York, NY
Mayo	W. T. Mayo, New Orleans, LA
Mercury	Mercury Music Corp., Bryn Mawr, PA; New York, NY
Merion	Merion Music, Bryn Mawr, PA
Mesier	E. S. Mesier, New York, NY
Metropolitan	Metropolitan Music Co., Minneapolis, MN

Meyer	Frederick Meyer, New York, NY
Meyer-L	Louis Meyer, Philadelphia, PA
MeyerT	Meyer and Tretbar, Buffalo, NY
Miles	Miles and Thompson, Boston, MA
Miller	Miller and Beacham, Baltimore, MD
Millet	J. B. Millet and Co., Boston, MA
Mills	Mills Music Co., New York, NY
Mills-FA	F. A. Mills, New York, NY
Modern	Modern Music Publishing Co., New York, NY
Mollenhauer	Mollenhauer and Elss, Jersey City, NJ
Moller	Moller and Capron, Philadelphia, PA
Morrison	Morrison Music, Los Angeles, CA
Musical	Musical Americana, Philadelphia, PA
MusicL	Music Library of Chicago, Chicago, IL
MusicP	Music Press, New York, NY
New England	New England Conservatory Music Store, Boston, MA
Newhall	George D. Newhall and Co., Cincinnati, OH
NewM	New Music, New York, NY
New YorkW	New York World, New York, NY
Nolting	J. B. Nolting, Amsterdam, The Netherlands
Nordheimer	A. and S. Nordheimer, Montreal, Canada
North	F. A. North and Co., Philadelphia, PA
Novello	Novello and Co., Ltd., London, England
Oakes	Wm. H. Oakes, Boston, MA
Oates	George Oates, Charleston, SC
Odowan	Odowan Publishing Co., Cedar Rapids, IA; New York, NY
Oppenheimer	H. Oppenheimer, Leipzig and London
Oxford	Oxford University Press, New York, NY
Pantheon	Pantheon Verlag, Berlin, Germany
Paull	E. T. Paull Music Co., New York, NY
Pearson	S. Pearson, New York, NY
Peer	Peer, New York, NY
Peters-AC	A. C. Peters, Cincinnati, OH
Peters-CF	C. F. Peters, Leipzig, Germany; New York, NY
Peters-JL	J. L. Peters, New York, NY
Peters-WC	W. C. Peters, Cincinnati, OH; Baltimore, MD; Louisville, KY
Petersilea	Petersilea Academy, Boston, MA
Pleyel	I. Pleyel et Cie., Paris, France
Pond	Wm. A. Pond and Co., New York, NY
Presser	Theo. Presser, Philadelphia, PA; Bryn Mawr, PA
Prochàzka	J. O. von Prochàzka, New York, NY
Prüfer	Carl Prüfer, Boston, MA
Rahter	D. Rahter, Hamburg and Leipzig, Germany
Reed	G. P. Reed and Co., Boston, MA
Remick	Remick Music Corp., New York, NY
Remick-J	Jerome H. Remick and Co., Detroit, MI; New York, NY
Richardson	Nathan Richardson, Boston, MA
Ricordi	G. Ricordi, New York, NY; Buenos Aires, Argentina
Ries	Ries und Erler, Berlin, Germany
Riley	E. Riley, Buffalo, NY
Robyn	Alfred G. Robyn, St. Louis, MO

Rockar	F. A. Rockar, New York, NY
Roeder	C. G. Roeder, Leipzig, Germany
Rohlfing	Wm. Rohlfing and Sons Music Co., Milwaukee, WI
Root	The Root and Sons Music Co., Chicago, IL
RootC	Root and Cady, Chicago, IL
Ross	Louis H. Ross and Co., Boston, MA
Rottenbach	August Rottenbach, Buffalo, NY
Rozsavölgyi	Rozsavölgyi and Co., Budapest, Hungary; Leipzig, Germany
Russell	G. D. Russell and Co., Boston, MA
RussellT	Russell and Tolman, Boston, MA
Saalfield	R. A. Saalfield, New York, NY
Sarles	Sarles and Adey, Springfield, MA
Sawyer	C. C. Sawyer, Brooklyn, NY
Scharfenberg	Scharfenberg and Luis, New York, NY
Schirmer	G. Schirmer, New York, NY
Schirmer-EC	E. C. Schirmer, Boston, MA
SchirmerJr	G. Schirmer, Jr., New York, NY; Boston, MA
Schlesinger	Schlesinger'sche Buch-und Musik-handlung (Rob. Lienau), Berlin, Germany
Schmidt	Arthur P. Schmidt, Boston, MA; New York, NY; Leipzig, Germany
Schmitt	Paul A. Schmitt, Minneapolis, MN
Schott	B. Schott's Söhne (Les fils de B. Schott), Mainz, Germany
Schroeder	J. H. Schroeder, New York, NY
SchroederN	H. S. Schroeder's Nachfolger, Berlin, Germany
Schuberth	Schuberth and Co., New York, NY; Hamburg, Germany
Schuberth-E	Edward Schuberth and Co., New York, NY
Schuberth-F	F.(Fritz) Schuberth, Leipzig, Germany; New York, NY
Schuberth-J	J. Schuberth and Co., Leipzig, Germany; New York, NY
SchuberthJr	Fritz Schuberth, Jr., Leipzig, Germany
Shattinger	Shattinger Piano and Music Co., St. Louis, MO
Shaw	W. F. Shaw, Philadelphia, PA
Shaw-JP	Joseph P. Shaw, Rochester, NY
Sheard	Chas. Sheard and Co., London, England
Siegel	C. F. W. Siegel's Musicalienhandlung (R. Linnemann), Leipzig, Germany
Siegling	J. Siegling, Charleston, SC
Simrock	N. Simrock, Berlin, Germany
Snow	J. H. Snow, Mobile, AL
Spear	Spear and Dehnhoff, New York, NY
Spina	C. A. Spina, Vienna, Austria
Stahl	Albert Stahl, Berlin, Germany
Stech	G. Stech and Co., New York, NY
Steffan	Steffan Music Co., Milwaukee, WI
Stevens	H. B. Stevens, Boston, MA
Summy	C. F. Summy, Chicago, IL
SummyB	Summy-Birchard Co., Evanston, IL
Thiebes	Thiebes-Stierlin Music Co., St. Louis, MO
Thompson	Chas. W. Thompson and Co., Boston, MA
Tolman	Henry Tolman and Co., Boston, MA
Tremaine	C. M. Tremaine, New York, NY

Truette	Everette E. Truette and Co., Boston, MA
Vanderbeek	Wm. Vanderbeek, New York, NY
Vieweg	C. F. Vieweg, Berlin, Germany
Walker	Edward L. Walker, Philadelphia, PA
Waters	Horace Waters, New York, NY
Wa-Wan	The Wa-Wan Press, Newton Center, MA
Werlein	P. P. Werlein, New Orleans, LA
Wetherbee	S. Wetherbee, Boston, MA
Weygand	F. J. Weygand, The Hague, The Netherlands
White	White and Goullaud, Boston, MA
WhiteS	White, Smith and Co., Boston, MA
White-S	White-Smith Publishing Co., Boston, MA
WhiteSP	White, Smith and Perry, Boston, MA
Whitney	C. J. Whitney, Detroit, MI
Whittemore	J. Henry Whittemore, Detroit, MI
WhittemoreSS	Whittemore, Swan and Stephens, Detroit, MI
Well	Well and Co., London, England
Willig	George Willig, Baltimore, MD
Willig-G	G. Willig, Philadelphia, PA
WilligJr	George Willig, Jr., Baltimore, MD
Willis	W. H. Willis and Co., Cincinnati, OH
WillisM	Willis Music Co., Cincinnati, OH
WillisW	Willis Woodward and Co., New York, NY
Witmark	M. Witmark and Sons, New York, NY
Wood	The B. F. Wood Music Co., Boston, MA
Zimmermann	J. H. Zimmermann, Leipzig, Germany; St. Petersburg, Russia
Zumsteeg	G. A. Zumsteeg, Stuttgart, Germany

Appendix B
Library Sources
and Abbreviations

California
CU   Music Library, University of California, Berkeley, CA
        94720
Connecticut
CtHT-W Special Collections, Watkinson Library, Trinity College,
        Hartford, CT 06106
CtNLC   Greer Music Library, Connecticut College, New London, CT
        06320
CtY   Music Library, Yale University, 98 Wall St., New Haven,
        CT 06520
District of Columbia
DLC   Music Division, Library of Congress, Washington, D. C.
        20540
Delaware
DeWHi   Historical Society of Delaware, 505 Market Street Mall,
        Wilmington, DE 19801
Illinois
ICN   The Newberry Library, 60 W. Walton St., Chicago IL 60610
ICRo   Music Library, Roosevelt University, 430 S. Michigan
        Ave., Chicago, IL 60605
IE   Dept. of Art, Music and Film, Evanston Public Library,
        1703 Orrington Ave., Evanston, IL 60201
IEN   Music Library, Northwestern University, Evanston, IL
        60201
IU   Music Library, The University of Illinois, 1114 West Ne-
        vada, Urbana, IL 61801. All music is at the Music Li-
        brary, except that marked x or MaL (i.e. Main Library).
        Joseffy signifies the Joseffy Collection of piano
        music in the music library.

Iowa
  IaCrC   Fisher Music Library, Coe College, 1220 First Ave, NE,
           Cedar Rapids, IA 52402
Indiana
  InU   Starr Sheet Music Collection, The Lilly Library, Indiana
           University, Bloomington, IN 47405
Kansas
  KU   Music Library and University Archives, The University of
           Kansas, Lawrence, KS 66045
Kentucky
  KyLoU   Dwight Anderson Memorial Music Library, University of
           Louisville, 2302 South Third Street, Louisville, KY
           40292
Louisiana
  LN   Dept. of Art, Music and Recreation, New Orleans Public
           Library, 219 Loyola Ave., New Orleans, LA 70140
  LNH   The Historic New Orleans Collection, 533 Royal St.,
           New Orleans, LA 70130
  LNT   Maxwell Music Library (except where indicated), Tulane
           University, New Orleans, LA 70118
Massachusetts
  MBH   Harvard Music Association, 57A Chestnut St., Boston,
           MA 02108
  MB-N   Spaulding Library, New England Conservatory, 33 Gains-
           borough St., Boston, MA 02115
  MNS   Werner Josten Library, Smith College, Northhampton, MA
           01063
  MTO   Old Colony Historical Society, 66 Church Green, Taunton,
           MA 02780-3463
  MU   Music Library, University of Massachusetts, Amherst,
           MA 01003
Maryland
  MdBP   Music Library, Peabody Conservatory of Music, 21 E.
           Mount Vernon Place, Baltimore, MD 21202
Maine
  MeB   Music Library, Baudoin College, Brunswick, ME 04011
  MeP   Special Collections, Portland Public Library, Portland,
           ME 04101
Michigan
  MiU-C   William L. Clements Library, University of Michigan,
           909 South University, Ann Arbor, MI 48109
Missouri
  MoS   Music Room, Saint Louis Public Library, 1303 Olive St.,
           St. Louis, MO 63103
  MoSHi   Missouri Historical Society, Jefferson Memorial Bldg.,
           St. Louis, MO 63112
  MoSW   Gaylord Music Library, Washington University, St. Louis,
           MO 53105
New York
  NBu   Buffalo and Erie County Public Library, Lafayette Square,
           Buffalo, NY 14203. The uncatalogued music is in two
           collections, works published before 1866 and those
           published after 1865.

NNLc   Music Division, Performing Arts Research Center, The New
        York Public Library, Lincoln Center, 111 Amsterdam
        Ave., New York, NY 10023
NPA   The Adriance Memorial Library, 93 Market, St., Pough-
        keepsie, NY 12601
NRU-E   Sibley Music Library, Eastman School of Music, Rochester,
        NY 14604

North Carolina
NcA   N.C. Collection, Asheville-Buncome Library System, 67
        Haywood St., Asheville, NC 28801
NcD   Music Library, Duke University, Durham, NC 27706. Some
        music, marked RBR, is located in the Rare Book Room.
NcU   Music Library, The University of North Carolina, Hill
        Hall 020A, Chapel Hill, NC 27514

New Hampshire
Nh   New Hampshire State Library, 20 Park Street, Concord,
        NH 03302

New Jersey
NjP   Music Library, Princeton University, Princeton, NJ 08544

Ohio
OC   Dept. of Art and Music, Public Library of Cincinnati and
        Hamilton County, 800 Vine St., Cincinnati, OH 45202
OCl   Dept. of Art and Music, Cleveland Public Library, 325
        Superior Ave., Cleveland, OH 44114
ODa   Dept. of Art and Music, Dayton and Montgomery County Pub-
        lic Library, 215 E. Third St., Dayton, OH 45402
OO   Music Library, Conservatory of Music, Oberlin College,
        Oberlin, OH 44074
OU   Music Library, The Ohio State University, 1813 N. High
        St., Columbus, OH 43210

Pennsylvania
PP   Music Dept., Free Library of Philadelphia, Logan Square,
        Philadelphia, PA 19103. The letter K refers to the
        Keffer Collection, filed in numbered boxes. The
        letters Fl. refer to the Fleisher Collection.
PPi   Dept. of Music and Art, Carnegie Library of Pittsburgh,
        4400 Forbes Ave., Pittsburgh, PA 15213
PWm   James V. Brown Library of Williamsport and Lycoming Co.,
        19 E. 4th St., Williamsport, PA 17701

Rhode Island
RPB   John Hay Library, Brown University, Providence, RI 02912

South Carolina
ScCC   Museum Library, Charleston Museum, 360 Meeting St.,
        Charleston, SC 29403

Virginia
ViRV   Valentine Museum, 1015 E. Clay St., Richmond, Va.
        23219-1590
ViU   The University of Virginia, Charlottesville, VA 22903.
        All music is located in the Alderman Library except
        where marked Music, i.e. Music Library. McR. indicates
        the **Computer Catalog of Nineteenth-Century American-
        Imprint Sheet Music,** compiled by Lynn T. McRae (Univer-
        sity of Virginia, Charlottesville, VA, 1979).

Vermont
  VtU   Special Collections, Guy W. Bailey Memorial Library,
             University of Vermont, Burlington, VT 05401
Wisconsin
  WM   Dept. of Art and Music, Milwaukee Public Library, 814
             West Wisconsin Ave., Milwaukee, WI 53233

Appendix C
Anthologies and Reprint
Editions with Abbreviations

AB-D   **The American Book for Piano,** ed. Wm. Deguire.
      New York: Galaxy Music Corporation, 1975.

AC   **American Composers.** Album of Ten Pieces for the Piano.
      Boston: The Boston Music Co., 1905.

A-C   **Anthology of Early American Keyboard Music,** ed. J. Bunker
      Clark.
      Madison: A-R Editions, 1977. 2 vols.

BC-G   **The Bicentennial Collection of American Keyboard Music
      1790-1900,** ed. Edward Gold.
      Dayton: McAfee Music Corporation, 1975.

C-MH   **A Collection of Early American Keyboard Music,** ed.
      McClenny and Hinson.
      Cincinnati: Willis Music Co., 1971.

CMJ   **Benjamin Carr: Musical Journal**
      Wilmington: Scholarly Resources, Inc., 1972. 2 vols.

CMM-M   **Benjamin Carr: Musical Miscellany in Occasional Numbers,**
      ed. Eve. R. Meyer.
      New York: DaCapo Press, 1982.

EA-I   **Easy American Piano Classics,** ed. Stuart Isacoff.
      New York: Consolidated Music Publishers, 1978.

FA-H   **Arthur Farwell: American Indian Melodies,** ed. Maurice
      Hinson.
      Chapel Hill: Hinshaw Music, 1977.

FH-M   **Francis Hopkinson's Lessons,** ed. David P. McKay.
      Washington, DC: C. T. Wagner, 1979. Facsimile ed.

FHR   **Foster Hall Reproductions.** Songs, compositions and
      arrangements by Stephen Collins Foster.
      Indianapolis: privately printed by Josiah Kirby Lilly, 1933.

FPP   **Fifty-One Piano Pieces from the Modern Repertoire.**
      New York: G. Schirmer, 1940.

GP-B   **Piano Music by Louis Moreau Gottschalk,** ed. Jeanne Behrend.
        Bryn Mawr: Theodore Presser Co., 1956.
GP-J   **Piano Music of Louis Moreau Gottschalk,** ed. Richard
        Jackson.
        New York: Dover Publications, Inc., 1973.
GP-L   **The Piano Music of Louis Moreau Gottschalk,** ed. Vera
        Brodsky Lawrence.
        New York: Arno Press and the New York Times, 1969. 5 vols.
HC-W   **James Hewitt: Selected Compositions,** ed. John W. Wagner.
        Madison: A-R Editions, Inc., 1980.
HDM   **Anthony Philip Heinrich: The Dawning of Music in Kentucky
        or The Pleasures of Harmony in the Solitudes of Nature.**
        New York: DaCapo Press, 1972.
HH-K   **Half Hours with the Best Composers,** ed. Karl Klauser.
        Boston: J. B. Millet, 1894-95. 5 vols.
MA-MG   **Music in America,** ed. Marrocco and Gleason.
        New York: W. W. Norton and Co., Inc., 1964.
M-E   **Music from the Days of Washington,** ed. Carl Engel.
        Washington, DC: George Washington Bicentennial Com-
        mission, 1931.
        Reprint by AMS Press (New York, 1970).
MP-H   **Edward MacDowell: Piano Pieces Op.51, 55, 61, 62,** ed.
        H. Wiley Hitchcock.
        New York: DaCapo Press, 1972.
NC-G   **Nineteenth Century American Piano Music,** ed. John Gillespie.
        New York: Dover Publications, Inc., 1978.
P-A   **Pianorama of American Classics,** ed. Denes Agay.
        Bryn Mawr: Theodore Presser Co., 1955.
P-H   **A Program of Early American Piano Music,** ed. John Tasker
        Howard.
        New York: J. Fischer and Bro., 1931.
PM-H   **Piano Music in Nineteenth Century America,** ed. Maurice
        Hinson.
        Chapel Hill: Hinshaw Music, Inc., 1975. 2 vols.
PP-S   **John Knowles Paine: Complete Piano Music,** ed. John C. Schmidt.
        New York: DaCapo Press, 1983.
P-S   **Prestige Piano Solos,** ed. John W. Schaum.
        Milwaukee: Schaum Publications, Inc., 1962.
PW-ICR **Piano Works by Charles Ives, Henry Cowell, Carl Ruggles.**
        20th anniversary ed.
        New York: New Music, October, 1947.
RP-H   **Alexander Reinagle: The Philadelphia Sonatas,** ed. Robert
        Hopkins.
        Madison: A-R Editions, Inc., 1978.
RS-HM   **Alexander Reinagle: A Selection of the most favorite Scots
        Tunes, with Variations for the Pianoforte or Harpsichord,**
        ed. Hinson and McClenny Krauss.
        Chapel Hill: Hinshaw Music, Inc., 1975.
WW-L   **The Wa-Wan Press 1901-1911,** ed. Vera Brodsky Lawrence.
        New York: Arno Press, 1970. 5 vols.

Appendix D
Select Reference Sources

Aldrich, Richard. **Concert Life in New York (1902-1923).** Edited by
    Harold Johnson. Freeport, NY: Books for Libraries Press, 1971.
Alexander, J. Heywood. **It Must Be Heard.** Cleveland: Western Re-
    serve Historical Society, 1981.
The American History and Encyclopedia of Music: Musical Biographies.
    2 vols. Edited by W. L. Hubbard, compiled by Janet M. Green.
    Toledo: Irving Squire, 1908.
Annals of Music in Philadelphia and History of the Musical Fund So-
    ciety. Compiled by Louis C. Madeira. 1896. Reprint. New York:
    Da Capo Press, 1973.
Anthology of Early American Keyboard Music 1787-1830. 2 vols. Ed-
    ited by J. Bunker Clark. Madison, WI: A-R Editions, 1977.
Axsom, Ronald B. "The Orchestral Music of Charles Hommann." Mas-
    ter's thesis, West Chester State College, 1982.
Baker's Biographical Dictionary of Musicians. 3rd ed., ed. A. Remy.
    New York: G. Schirmer, 1919. 6th ed., ed. N. Slonimsky. New
    York: Schirmer Books, 1978.
Baron, John H. "Paul Emile Johns of New Orleans: Tycoon, Musician,
    and Friend of Chopin." In **Report of the Eleventh Congress of**
    the International Musicological Society, Copenhagen, 1972,
    vol. I, 246.
Bio-Bibliographical Index of Musicians in the United States of Amer-
    ica since Colonial Times. 2nd ed. Washington, DC: Pan-
    American Union, Music Section, 1956.
Bruce, Frank N. **The Piano Pieces of Anthony Philip Heinrich con-**
    tained in "The Dawning of Music in Kentucky" and "The Western
    Minstrel". Ann Arbor, MI: University Microfilms, 1981.
Caldwell, James L. "The Life and Works of James Cutler Dunn Par-
    ker." Ph.D. diss., Florida State University, 1968.

Campbell, Douglas G. "George W. Chadwick: His Life and Works."
    Ph.D. diss., University of Rochester, Eastman School of Music,
    1957.
Canfield, John C. "Henry Kimball Hadley: His Life and Works (1871-
    1937." Ph.D. diss., Florida State University, 1960.
Caswell, Mina H. **Ministry of Music: The Life of William Rogers
    Chapman.** Portland, ME.: Southworth-Anthoensen Press, 1938.
Chadwick, George W. **Horatio Parker.** New Haven: Yale University
    Press, 1921.
Chase, Gilbert. **America's Music: From the Pilgrims to the Present.**
    2nd ed., rev. New York: McGraw-Hill, 1966.
Cuthbert, John A. **Rayner Taylor and Anglo-American Musical Life.**
    Ann Arbor, MI: University Microfilms, 1983.
De Koven, Anna (Mrs. Reginald De Koven). **A Musician and his Wife.**
    New York: Harper and Bros., 1926.
Denison, Frederic, A. A. Stanley and E. K. Glezen. **A Memorial of
    Oliver Shaw.** Providence: Rhode Island Veteran Citizens' His-
    torical Association, 1884.
Dictionary of American Biography. Edited by Allen Johnson and
    Dumas Malone. New York: Charles Scribner's Sons, 1927.
Downes, Olin. **Frank Lynes.** Boston: Woodberry Press, 1941.
Edwards, George T. **Music and Musicians of Maine.** Portland:
    Southworth Press, 1928.
Ehrlich, A. [Albert Payne]. **Celebrated Pianists Past and Present:
    A Collection of 116 Biographies of Great Pianoforte Players.**
    London: Harold Reeves, 1894.
Elson, Louis C., and Arthur Elson. **The History of American Music.**
    New York: Macmillan, 1925.
Fields, Warren C. **The Life and Works of Theodore von La Hache.**
    2 vols. Ann Arbor, MI: University Microfilms, 1983.
Fish, Joan T. **John Mokrejs: Iowa Pedagogue, Composer, and Pianist:
    An Essay together with a Comprehensive Performance Project in
    Piano Literature.** Ann Arbor, MI: University Microfilms,
    1983.
Fisher, William A. **Notes on Music in Old Boston.** Boston: Oliver
    Ditson, 1918.
_____. **One Hundred and Fifty Years of Music Publishing in The
    United States (1783-1933).** Boston: Oliver Ditson, 1933.
Foote, Arthur William. **Arthur Foote (1853-1937): An Autobiography.**
    1946. Reprint, with new Introduction and Notes by Wilma R.
    Cipolla. New York: Da Capo Press, 1979.
Foster, Agness G. **Eleanor Everest Freer—Patriot—and her Col-
    leagues.** Chicago: Musical Art Publishing Co., 1927.
Garofalo, Robert J. "The Life and Works of Frederick Shepherd
    Converse (1871-1940)." Ph.D. diss., Catholic University, 1969.
Gerson, Robert A. **Music in Philadelphia.** 1940. Reprint.
    Westport, CT: Greenwood Press, 1970.
Gilman, Lawrence. **Edward MacDowell: A Study.** 1908. Reprint,
    with new Introduction by Margery L. Morgan. New York: Da Capo
    Press, 1969.
Gloyne, Howard F. **Carl A. Preyer: The Life of a Kansas Musician.**
    Lawrence: University of Kansas, Preyer Memorial Committee, 1949.

Gottschalk, Louis Moreau. **Notes of a Pianist.** 1964. Reprint,
    edited, with a prelude, postlude and explanatory notes, by
    Jeanne Behrend. New York: Da Capo Press, 1979.
Graber, Kenneth G. **The Life and Works of William Mason (1829–
    1908).** Ann Arbor, MI: University Microfilms, 1983.
Graydon, Nell S., and Margaret D. Sizemore. **The Amazing Marriage
    of Marie Eustis and Josef Hofmann.** Columbia, SC: University
    of South Carolina Press, 1965.
Grossman, F. Karl. **A History of Music in Cleveland.** Cleveland:
    Case Western Reserve University, 1972.
Grove's Dictionary of Music and Musicians. Edited by Stanley
    Sadie. London: Macmillan, 1980.
Grove's Dictionary of Music and Musicians: American Supplement.
    Edited by W. S. Pratt and C. N. Boyd. Philadelphia: Theodore
    Presser, 1923.
Half Hours with the Best Composers. 6 vols. Edited by Karl
    Klauser, with an Introduction by Theodore Thomas. Boston:
    J. B. Millet, 1894.
Hall, Constance H., and Helen I. Tetlow. **Helen Hopekirk.** Cam-
    bridge, MA: Printed for the authors, 1954.
A Handbook of American Music and Musicians. 1886. Edited by
    F. O. Jones. Reprint. New York: Da Capo Press, 1971.
Hewitt, John H. **Shadows on the Wall, or Glimpses of the Past:
    A Retrospect of the Past Fifty Years.** 1877. Reprint. New
    York: AMS Press, 1971.
Hill, Thomas H. **Ernest Schelling (1876–1939): His Life and Con-
    tributions to Music Education through Educational Concerts.**
    Ann Arbor, MI: University Microfilms, 1970.
Hipsher, Edward. **American Opera and its Composers.** Phila-
    delphia: Theodore Presser, 1927.
Hitchcock, H. Wiley. **Music in the United States: A Historical
    Introduction.** Englewood Cliffs, NJ: Prentice-Hall, 1969.
Hoffman, Richard. **Some Musical Recollections of Fifty Years.**
    With a Biographical Sketch by his wife. London: William Reeves,
    1910.
Horton, Charles A. "Serious Art and Concert Music for Piano in
    America in the 100 Years from Alexander Reinagle to Edward
    MacDowell." Ph.D. diss., University of North Carolina, 1965.
Howard, John T. **Ethelbert Nevin.** New York: Thomas Y. Crowell,
    1935.
_____. **Our American Music: A Comprehensive History from 1620 to
    the Present.** 4th ed. New York: Thomas Y. Crowell, 1965.
_____. **Studies of American Composers: Eastwood Lane.** New York:
    J. Fischer and Bro., 1925.
Hughes, Rupert, and Arthur Elson. **American Composers.** 2nd ed.
    Boston: Page, 1914.
A Hundred Years of Music in America. 1889. Edited by W. S. B.
    Mathews. Reprint. New York: AMS Press, 1970.
Huneker, James G. **The Philharmonic Society of New York and its
    Seventy–Fifth Anniversary: A Retrospect.** New York: Philharmonic
    Society, 1917.
The International Cyclopedia of Music and Musicians. 4th ed., ed.
    B. Bohle. New York: Dodd, Mead, 1975.

International Who's Who in Music and Musical Gazeteer. Edited by
    César Saerchinger. New York: Current Literature Publishing Co.,
    1918.
Jablonski, Edward. **The Encyclopedia of American Music.** Garden
    City, NY: Doubleday, 1981.
Johns, Clayton. **Reminiscences of a Musician.** Cambridge, MA:
    Washburn and Thomas, 1929.
Johnson, Frances Hall. **Musical Memories of Hartford.** Hartford:
    Witkower's, 1931.
Johnson, H. Earle. **Musical Interludes in Boston: 1795–1830.** 1943.
    Reprint. New York: AMS Press, 1967.
Kallmann, Helmut. **A History of Music in Canada 1534–1914.**
    Toronto: University of Toronto Press, 1960.
King, Maurice R. "Edgar Stillman Kelley: American Composer, Teacher,
    and Author." Ph.D. diss., Florida State University, 1970.
Knauss, David E. "William Clifford Heilman." Master's thesis,
    Mansfield (PA) State College, 1981.
Kopp, Frederick E. "Arthur Foote: American Composer and Theorist."
    Ph.D. diss., University of Rochester, Eastman School of Music,
    1957.
Krehbiel, Henry E. **The Philharmonic Society of New York: A
    Memorial.** New York and London: Novello, Ewer, 1892.
Krohn, Ernst C. **Missouri Music.** New York: Da Capo Press, 1971.
Lahee, Henry C. **Annals of Music in America: A Chronological
    Record of Significant Musical Events, from 1640 to the Present
    Day, with Comments on the Various Periods into which the Work
    is Divided.** 1922. Reprint. New York: AMS Press, 1969.
_____. **Famous Pianists of Today and Yesterday.** Boston: Page,
    1900.
Laurel Winners: Portraits and Silhouettes of Modern Composers.
    Cincinnati: John Church, 1900.
Loucks, Richard. **Arthur Shepherd: American Composer.** Provo,
    UT: Brigham Young University Press, n.d.
Lowens, Irving. **Benjamin Carr's Federal Overture (1794).** Phila-
    delphia: Musical Americana, 1957.
_____. **Music and Musicians in Early America.** New York: Norton,
    1964.
Maretzek, Max. **Crotchets and Quavers, or Revelations of an Opera
    Manager in America.** 1855. Reprint. New York: Da Capo Press,
    1966.
**The Marvelous Musical Prodigy, Blind Tom, the Negro Boy Pianist:
    Anecdotes, Songs, Sketches of the Life.** New York: French and
    Wheat, 1866.
Mason, Daniel Gregory. **Music in My Time.** New York: Macmillan,
    1938.
**Memoir of J. N. Pattison, the Great Pianist and Composer, with
    Notices of his Performances.** Edited and compiled by G. R.
    Cromwell. New York: Torrey Bros., 1868.
Merrill, E. Lindsey. "Mrs. H. H. A. Beach: Her Life and Music."
    Ph.D. diss., University of Rochester, Eastman School of Music,
    1963.
Metcalf, Frank J. **American Writers and Compilers of Sacred
    Music.** New York: Russell and Russell, 1967.

Milinowski, Marta. **Teresa Carreño "by the grace of God".** 1940.
    Reprint. New York: Da Capo Press, 1977.
Miller, Francesca Falk. **Across the Little Space: The Life Story
    of Dr. Louis Falk.** Chicago: W. D. Bauman, 1933.
Music in America (The Art of Music: Volume Four). Edited by Arthur
    Farwell and W. Dermot Darby, with Introduction by Farwell.
    New York: National Society of Music, 1915.
The New Encyclopedia of Music and Musicians. 2nd ed., ed. Waldo
    S. Pratt. New York: Macmillan, 1929.
Palmer, William H. **Melody Magic.** Compiled by Harry L. Clapham.
    Biographical Sketch by Henry Ridgely Evans. Washington, DC:
    Clapham, 1932.
Panzeri, Louis. **Louisiana Composers.** New Orleans: Louisiana
    Federation of Music Clubs, 1972.
Portraits of the World's Best-Known Musicians. Compiled and
    edited by Guy McCoy. Philadelphia: Theodore Presser, 1946.
Ritter, Frédéric L. **Music in America.** 2nd ed. New York:
    Charles Scribner's Sons, 1895.
Rogers, Clara Kathleen [Clara Doria, pseud.]. **Memories of a
    Musical Career.** Boston: Little, Brown and Co., 1919.
Rohrer, Gertrude M. **Music and Musicians of Pennsylvania.**
    Port Washington, NY: Kennikat Press, 1970.
Schonberg, Harold C. **The Great Pianists from Mozart to the
    Present.** New York: Simon and Schuster, 1963.
Semler, Isabel Parker, and Pierson Underwood. **Horatio Parker.**
    New York: G. P. Putnam's Sons, 1942.
Sonneck, Oscar G. **Early Concert-Life in America (1731-1800).**
    1907. Reprint. Wiesbaden: Dr. Martin Sändig oHG, 1969.
_____. **Francis Hopkinson, the First American Poet-Composer
    (1737-1791) and James Lyon, Patriot, Preacher, Psalmodist (1735-
    1794).** 1905. Reprint, with new Introduction by Richard A.
    Crawford. New York: Da Capo Press, 1967.
Sonneck, Oscar G., and William Treat Upton. **A Bibliography of
    Early Secular American Music (18th Century).** 1945. Reprint,
    with a Preface by Irving Lowens. New York: Da Capo Press, 1964.
Southall, Geneva H. **Blind Tom: The Post-Civil War Enslavement
    of a Black Musical Genius.** Minneapolis: Challenge Productions,
    1979 (Book I), 1983 (Book II).
Spaulding, Walter R. **Music at Harvard: A Historical Review of
    Men and Events.** New York: Coward-McCann, 1935.
Sprenkle, Charles A. "The Life and Works of Benjamin Carr (1768-
    1831)." Ph.D. diss., Johns Hopkins University, Peabody Conser-
    vatory, 1970.
Stoutamire, Albert. **Music of the Old South: Colony to Confederacy.**
    Rutherford, NJ: Fairleigh Dickinson University Press, 1972.
Strakosch, Maurice. **Souvenirs d'un Impresario.** Paris: Paul
    Ollendorff, 1887.
Strassburg, Robert. **Ernest Bloch: Voice in the Wilderness (A Bio-
    graphical Study).** Los Angeles: California State University,
    1977.
Tipton, Patricia G. **The Contributions of Charles Kunkel to Musi-
    cal Life in St. Louis.** Ann Arbor, MI: University Microfilms,
    1982.

Troyer, Carlos. **The Zuñi Indians and their Music.** With a bio-
    graphical appreciation by Charles W. Cadman. Philadelphia:
    Theodore Presser, 1913.
Upton, William Treat. **Anthony Philip Heinrich: A Nineteenth-
    Century Composer in America.** 1939. Reprint. New York: AMS
    Press, 1967.
_____. **Art-Song in America: A Study in the Development of
    American Music.** Boston: Oliver Ditson, 1930.
Venth, Carl. **My Memories.** San Antonio: Alamo Printing Co.,
    1939.
Wiggin, Frances T. **Maine Composers and their Music: A Biographi-
    cal Dictionary.** Rockland, ME: Bald Mountain Printing Co.
    for Maine Federation of Music Clubs, 1959.
Wolfe, Richard J. **Secular Music in America 1801-1825: A Biblio-
    graphy.** 3 vols. New York: New York Public Library, 1964.
Wolverton, Byron A. "Keyboard Music and Musicians in the Colonies
    and United States of America before 1830." Ph.D. diss.,
    Indiana University, 1966.

About the Authors

JOHN GILLESPIE is Professor of Music at the University of California, Santa Barbara. He is the author of *Nineteenth-Century European Piano Music, Nineteenth-Century American Piano Music, Five Centuries of Keyboard Music, The Musical Experience*, and articles appearing in *Essays on Eighteenth-Century Music, Essays in Honor of Pauline Alderman,* and the *Journal* of the Historical Society of Delaware.

ANNA GILLESPIE has collaborated with her husband on his earlier projects.